UNDERSTANDING FINANCIAL ACCOUNTING

UNDERSTANDING FINANCIAL ACCOUNTING

A GUIDE FOR NON-SPECIALISTS

JIMMY WINFIELD, MARK GRAHAM, & TARYN MILLER

OXFORD
UNIVERSITY PRESS

Great Clarendon Street, Oxford, OX2 6DP,
United Kingdom

Oxford University Press is a department of the University of Oxford.
It furthers the University's objective of excellence in research, scholarship,
and education by publishing worldwide. Oxford is a registered trade mark of
Oxford University Press in the UK and in certain other countries

Published in the United States of America by Oxford University Press
198 Madison Avenue, New York, NY 10016, United States of America

British Library Cataloguing in Publication Data

Data available

Library of Congress Control Number: 2020946565

ISBN 978-0-19-884727-4

Printed in Great Britain by
Bell & Bain Ltd., Glasgow

We are proud of this book, and so would like to
dedicate it to our children, of whom we are infinitely prouder:
Tommy, Sarah, Luciana, Jack, Micah, Asher, and Liana.

PREFACE

This book is not so much about accounting as it is about financial statements. This may seem a subtle distinction to make, but in fact the difference is very important: accounting is the name given to the process of recording and reporting the financial information of a business, whereas financial statements are the end product of this process. There are, in truth, many types of financial statements that can be produced, but in this book, we shall limit ourselves to the financial statements produced by businesses that report according to International Financial Reporting Standards, or IFRS. These include the statement of financial position, the statement of comprehensive income (which may include an income statement), the statement of changes in equity, and the statement of cash flows.

Why write a book that focuses on the financial statements, rather than the process by which they are produced? We think there is a very good reason: the vast majority of people doing business studies—degree, diploma, professional qualification, or self-study—are not accountants, and are not planning on becoming accountants. They need to learn neither the complex process by which financial statements are produced nor all the other functions that accountants are paid to perform. They do, however, all aim to play a valuable role in business, and as such, like it or not, they need to understand the financial statements themselves.

This is because the financial statements are a business's scorecard. You wouldn't play a sport without knowing how to tell the score, so if you want to be in business, you need to understand the key measures of its success. Thus, our main objective is to help students of business to unlock the true value of financial accounting. By the end of reading this book, you will be able to pick up the financial statements of your own business, the business you work for, a competitor's business, or even a business you are interested in buying some shares in, and use the incredibly rich and powerful information contained in them to make better business decisions. This is why, throughout the book, we emphasise not how the statements are *prepared*, but how the information that they contain *can be used* to understand the business.

If financial statements are the scorecard, then accounting is the language of business. In reaching our main objective, it will be necessary along the way to cover just enough of the recording and preparation processes to give readers a big-picture understanding of accounting. This will vastly improve their fluency with terms like 'assets', 'profit', 'goodwill', and all the other technical accounting terms often discussed in business without people really knowing what they mean. But our mission is not to give you a grammar lesson: it is to help you read the poetry. The virtue of focusing on the financial statements is that we do not have to get bogged down in the laborious, technical procedures and calculations that have earned accounting, and accounting books, their infamous reputation.

In this preface, we shall explain some of the features of the book, and recommend how you can get the most out of them.

Focus on IFRS

As you will learn in Chapter 3, the accounting standards known as IFRS now govern how the largest businesses in over 140 countries prepare their financial statements. If you are reading this book, the chances are that every company listed on the stock exchange nearest you uses IFRS, and most other sizeable businesses in your region use either IFRS itself or a reporting framework which has a great deal in common with IFRS. Thus, by learning about IFRS, you will be empowered to understand the reporting of all of the major businesses around you.

Practical approach

Obtaining insights from reading financial statements is a practical skill, and so our approach is ruthlessly practical too. We have tried as far as possible to supplement the theory you are learning with regular examples, often drawn from real-world companies. We encourage you to take this one step further: as you read, it would be an excellent idea to apply what you are learning by looking at the financial statements of a business you are interested in. It is probably easier to obtain them than you think: listed companies' financial statements are usually accessed in seconds by typing 'financial statements' and the company name into a search engine.

Global perspective

The examples in this book are drawn from all over the world. You will learn about major companies in other countries that perhaps you have never heard of, and you will see examples in currencies that you might not recognise. This is not just because the book is written for a global market; it is also because business itself is globalised. We therefore believe that giving you the broadest possible exposure is a key part of our job as authors.

Recurring case studies

We all learn one step at a time, and so each chapter is designed to uncover the meaning behind just a few features of the financial statements. Ultimately, however, we want you to be able to understand the *whole set* of statements, including the notes which accompany them, which often run to more than 100 pages. Thus, to help you build up a clear picture of what financial statements in their entirety mean about a business, we make regular use of a particular multinational case study, Burberry. In most chapters, therefore, you shall be making sense of financial accounting using Burberry's financial statements, which are displayed in Appendix I. Similarly, the questions at the end of most chapters ask you to apply and discuss what you have learned using the financial statements of Daimler, contained in Appendix II.

Debits and credits

In Chapter 2, you will read about debits and credits, which are used to increase and decrease accounts using the standard double-entry accounting system. Debits and credits are absolutely fundamental to the accounting process, but they do not appear at all in the financial statements. It is our experience that some non-specialists wish to know about them and others do not. We have thus written the book so that it can be read either way: we always refer non-technically to increases and decreases in accounts, and then insert the term 'debit' or 'credit' in brackets, for those who value the technical terms.

Glossary and index

Debits and credits are hardly the only technical terms in accounting. In fact, the discipline is full of its own jargon, and has even borrowed a lot of words from ordinary language and repurposed them with specialised meanings. Of course, it would be disruptive for us to explain these terms every time they come up, so we have taken pains to include the words that occur frequently in the glossary. You may also find the index very helpful for quickly finding all of the sections that deal with a particular term or concept.

Online material

We have spent several months creating the online material which accompanies this book. It includes all kinds of supplementary material, including multiple-choice questions based on each chapter; more case studies; additional worked examples; and some advanced material that goes a little beyond the book itself. There is also a list of all the real-world financial statements that we refer to in the book, with links to their financial statements. We hope this convinces you that the online material is not a mere afterthought: rather, it has great potential to help you get even more out of your purchase of this book!

Structure

If you are the sort of reader who appreciates a map of the road ahead, the following information may be helpful before you begin. For each chapter, you can see how it fits into the overall flow of the book and a brief list of the highlights you will discover within it.

Background to financial accounting	Chapter 1	*Financial Accounting in Context.* The landscape of accounting; key characteristics of businesses; how businesses create value; the purpose of the financial statements.
	Chapter 2	*Accounting Basics.* A simplified overview of the mechanics of the accounting system and how it produces the financial statements, using fourteen typical transactions.
	Chapter 3	*Financial Reporting Standards.* A brief history of accounting standards; an overview of IFRS, including critiques and responses; and IFRS for SMEs.

	Chapter 4	*Income and Expenses.* All the key items that appear on a statement of comprehensive income, including revenue, operating and finance expenses, profit, and EPS.
	Chapter 5	*Cash Flows.* The differences between profit and cash flows; quality of earnings; direct and indirect statements of cash flows; working capital management.
	Chapter 6	*Assets.* The asset definition and recognition criteria; depreciation, amortisation, and impairment; PPE, investment properties, intangibles, inventory, and financial assets.
The content of financial statements	Chapter 7	*Liabilities.* The liability definition and recognition criteria; commitments; contingent liabilities; deferred income, accruals, grants, provisions, and financial liabilities.
	Chapter 8	*Leases, Foreign Exchange, and Deferred Tax.* Lease accounting by a lessee; lease accounting by a lessor; foreign transactions; foreign operations; deferred tax.
	Chapter 9	*Group Financial Statements.* Groups of companies; consolidation of subsidiaries; non-controlling interests; goodwill; equity accounting of associates and joint ventures.
	Chapter 10	*Equity.* The statement of changes in equity; transactions between businesses and their owners; reserves; changes in accounting policy and material errors.
Using financial statements	Chapter 11	*Financial Analysis.* Risk–return profiles; benchmarks; understanding the story of the financial statements; Du Pont and other ratio analysis; financial analysis challenges.
	Chapter 12	*Business Valuations.* Book value, market value, and intrinsic value; discounted cash flow valuation models; valuation multiples methods.
Broader issues	Chapter 13	*Creative Accounting.* Reasons businesses prepare misleading information; common ways in which financial statements have been manipulated; countermeasures.
	Chapter 14	*Trends in Corporate Reporting.* Developments in IFRS; XBRL and iXBRL; blockchain; environmental, social, and governance reporting; integrated reporting.

The following pages will walk you through the many learning features included and how to use them. We recommend that you spend a few minutes looking them over in order to make sure you obtain maximum value from every page!

GETTING THE MOST OUT OF *UNDERSTANDING FINANCIAL ACCOUNTING*

Understanding Financial Accounting is enhanced with a range of features designed to help support and reinforce your learning. This guided tour shows you how to fully utilise the content and get the most out of the book. Throughout the text you will find prompts to continue your development via the online resources which you can find at www.oup.com /he/winfield-graham-miller1e.

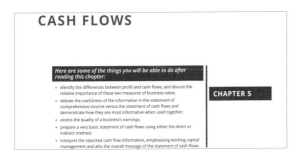

Start each chapter on a sure foothold

Each chapter begins with a bulleted outline of the main ideas you will encounter, providing a helpful signpost to what you can expect to learn. Where appropriate, important concepts from previous chapters are reviewed to ensure that these are fresh in your mind.

EXAMPLE 4.3

Extract from Carrefour's 2019 Consolidated Income Statement		
€m	2019	2018
Net income from continuing operations	219	36
Net income (loss) from discontinued operations	1 092	(380)
Net income (loss) for the year	1 311	(344)

See financial accounting in action through case studies and examples

Multiple examples from real, multinational businesses are woven into the text to help you appreciate the relevance of accounting. The authors present frequent, manageable illustrations of financial statements and contextual examples to help you connect with the content and encourage you to perform financial statement analysis yourself. Case study material is indicated in the margins. Further examples with accompanying questions and answers are available online.

Reinforce your understanding through chapter summaries, 'key concepts', and 'misconception' boxes

The authors anticipate your questions, carefully explaining areas that often cause confusion in 'misconception' boxes. Central points and concepts are emphasised in the margins of the chapters and are distilled into summaries at the end of each chapter, providing checkpoints for you to strengthen your learning.

Develop your skills by attempting the questions provided

Concept questions, applied questions, discussion questions, and investigation questions are presented at the ends of chapters, enabling you to evaluate your understanding, put what you have learned into practice, and improve your independent thinking and critical skills. Answer guidance for all questions can be found in Appendix III. In addition, multiple-choice questions with instant feedback are also hosted online, giving you more opportunities to quickly check your recall.

Revise glossary terms

Key terms are highlighted throughout the content and are clearly defined in the glossary. You can test your understanding by looking at the interactive flashcard glossary presented online.

Push your learning further

Do the additional worked examples and read the bonus advanced material accompanying Chapters 6, 7, and 11 online to help you foster a more robust understanding.

MISCONCEPTION

Lessees recognise the total of all future lease payments as a liability.

No; because the lease liability is measured at the present value of future lease payments, it represents only the capital amount outstanding. The discount is unwound as interest expense over the remaining lease period.

Let's now consider how the lease asset is measured. Its initial measurement is basically the same amount as the liability, and then this amount is depreciated over the lease period. If, as is usual, the depreciation is spread evenly, the annual charge in our example will be €8 590.32 (€25 770.97 ÷ 3). In Example 8.2, you can see the asset's carrying amount decreasing by this amount each year, as well as the lease liability and the effect of the lease on the statement of comprehensive income.

The lessee recognises a right-of-use asset and a liability to pay for it. Over the lease period, the lessee reports two expenses: depreciation of the asset and interest expense.

CONCEPT QUESTIONS

CQ 14.1 Explain the trade-off between using fair value or cost as the basis for measuring assets to be reported in the statement of financial position.

CQ 14.2 Briefly outline the aims of the IASB's Primary Financial Statements project.

CQ 14.3 Explain what 'XBRL' refers to, and identify two of its advantages.

CQ 14.4 What is the key difference between an ESG report and an integrated report?

CQ 14.5 Broadly speaking, what sort of information is communicated in the management commentary section of an annual report?

INVESTIGATION QUESTIONS

IQ 14.6 Inspect the IASB's workplan (available at https://www.ifrs.org/projects/work-plan). To what extent do you think that the IASB's current initiatives will improve the degree to which financial statements will provide users with relevant informa-

For lecturers

Further materials are available to lecturers. Registering is easy: visit the **online resources** www.oup.com/he/winfield-graham-miller1e, click on 'Lecturer Resources' and complete a simple registration form that allows you to choose your own username and password. The online resource material includes:

- Instructors' guide to using the book and setting assessments
- Fully customisable PowerPoint slides.

ACKNOWLEDGEMENTS

We are deeply grateful, firstly and most especially, to Laura, Michele, and Jonathan, for their endless support, and, um, near-endless patience, during the long days, nights, weeks, weekends, and months of writing.

We also would like to thank all of our colleagues, who have been a provocative and vital source of inspiration throughout our careers. Special praise goes to Geoff Everingham and Alex Watson for being intellectual giants for us: your voices have guided us sagely and silently as we have sought the simple essence of the trickiest accounting concepts.

No less influential are our students, past and present, who continually help us to return to our subject with fresh eyes and renewed energy. Thank you for teaching us to be teachers.

Thanks too to two people with whom we consulted: Shaun Parsons, for sharing his valuable insights about blockchain; and the Chairman, Justin Bothner, for indulging us with his deep expertise in matters of finance.

Finally, thank you to Felicity Boughton and the excellent team at OUP, with whom it has been a constant pleasure to work.

BRIEF TABLE OF CONTENTS

FULL TABLE OF CONTENTS

FINANCIAL ACCOUNTING IN CONTEXT

- comfortably use terms like 'accounting', 'management accounting', 'financial accounting', 'financial reporting', 'financial statements', 'reporting periods', and 'International Financial Reporting Standards (IFRS)';
- contrast the key accounting functions of recording and reporting;
- explain the distinguishing objective of business and the basic forms of business;
- recognise the advantages of incorporating a business with limited liability, and describe the differences between types of companies, including between listed and unlisted companies;
- discuss the financing, investing, and operating activities of a business and the dividend decision, and describe how financial accounting achieves its objective to report the effects of these activities and decisions;
- list the financial statements using the names favoured by IFRS.

When you begin to explore a technical subject, it helps to know at the outset what that subject is all about. So in this chapter we will be answering the question, 'What is financial accounting?' We will zoom out and have a look at the broad landscape in which financial accounting is just one feature: the **accounting** discipline as a whole. As this book is primarily about the financial accounting done by business enterprises, we will also explore businesses: their various forms, their basic characteristics, and the means by which they create value. The chapter concludes with some basic but essential information about the purpose and practice of financial accounting for businesses.

1

1.1 **THE ACCOUNTING LANDSCAPE**

Accounting is the recording and reporting of financial information about an entity. The entity could be a business, a government institution, a club, a society, or even an individual or a family. The principles and practices of accounting are similar no matter what entity it is serving, although there are some small differences. We will not concern ourselves with these differences in this book, which focuses on accounting for businesses.

That is not the only way we will be reducing our field of view. As you have already learned, accounting consists of two processes: recording and reporting. *Recording* involves entering financial information into an accounting system, which is usually a software package. Before computerised systems became commonplace, recording was done in books called journals and ledgers, which is why the people employed to enter the information were, and still are, called bookkeepers. If you studied accounting at school level, you would have learned a lot about recording, or **bookkeeping**, because the modern economy still requires a lot of bookkeepers, and school curricula are designed to develop skills needed by large numbers of people. However, you will encounter very little about the recording function of accounting in this book, which is not designed for would-be bookkeepers, but rather for a wide range of business professionals who wish to understand the reporting generated by accountants.

However, our scope is even narrower than that, for there are two main types of *reporting*, each aligned with one of the two accounting subdisciplines: financial accounting and management accounting. Reports generated by a **management accounting** system are—you guessed it!—for management's purposes. They help the **directors** of companies and other executives understand the financial affairs of their businesses, and to make decisions based on this understanding. For example, management accountants might prepare reports to help a manager know the weekly volumes of **sales** per branch, or the total **cost** of each unit produced in a factory, or how much profit could be earned in a new market. In fact, if a business decision is impacted by financial considerations, then a management accountant should be able to design a report to reveal those considerations. This means that there are as many management accounting reports as there are decisions for managers to make. In designing each report, management accountants must apply their minds analytically to the particular needs of the moment, aided by some general principles taught in management accounting courses, but unconstrained by rules or regulations, because the report will only be for internal use, and may even be unique.

Financial accounting, also called **financial reporting**, is very different. It is intended to inform the decisions made by people external to the business, such as investors considering whether to buy shares in the company, or bankers determining whether to recall a loan. Because the users of financial accountants' reports do not know and understand the business as well as insiders, these reports are extremely comprehensive, and this means they need to be highly standardised. Each business prepares the same four or five reports, packed with dense information and supplementary notes, using the same set of tightly regulated guidelines as other businesses. These reports—the output of the financial reporting process—are called **financial statements**, and they are the main subject of this book.

FIGURE 1.1 The landscape of accounting, showing the focus area of this book

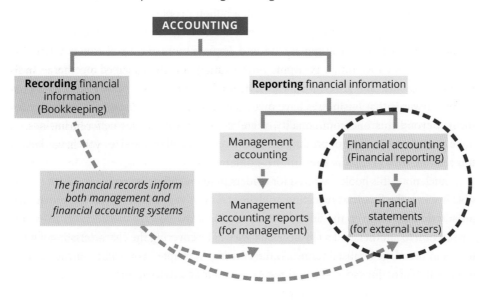

Figure 1.1 may help you consolidate your understanding of how financial statements fit into the landscape of accounting.

Section 1.4 will describe the four or five financial statements. People who aspire to become financial accountants must learn to prepare all of them for every type of business, which requires knowing every aspect of the recording process, and also how any possible business event should be represented in the financial statements. Moreover, in order to be able to perform a wide range of accounting functions, financial accounting students will also study management accounting, tax, and several other subjects. As you can imagine, acquiring this knowledge requires many years of training and experience.

This book is not for those accounting specialists who aspire to *prepare* financial statements. Instead, it is written for people who wish to *use* financial statements effectively in business. As we explained in the preface, financial statements are the scorecard, and accounting is the language of business. Anyone who occupies, or seeks to occupy, a key role in business—whether as an investor, director, manager, founder, entrepreneur, or frankly just an effective and impressive member of any business team—must understand the scorecard and be able to speak the language.

Every businessperson should be familiar with accounting, which is the language of business, and should be able to read financial statements, which are the scorecard.

1.2 **CHARACTERISTICS OF BUSINESSES**

As we've mentioned, the financial statements you will be learning to understand are those of businesses. Of course, everyone has some sense of what a business is, but it is important, before we start, to make sure that the essential features of businesses are clear.

Let us start with a simple question: what is it that makes a business different from other organisations? After all, there is a huge diversity of businesses, from the independent

1

hairdresser down the road, hoping for fifty clients a week, to a company like Apple Inc, which has sold its products to well over half a billion people, and whose market extends to virtually every patch of the planet.[1] One could be forgiven for thinking that the hairdresser is more like the local sports club, and Apple is more like a powerful government, than they are like each other. Yet Apple and the hairdresser are grouped together as businesses, while clubs and governments are not. Why is this?

The answer is that businesses have owners who want the business to create value for them. Beyond this one commonality, there are many differences between businesses, quite apart from the type of products and services they sell or the size of their market. In this section, we will explore some of these differences.

A quick note: this book is written for readers in many different countries, which is possible because the financial reporting guidelines do not vary much between countries (or **jurisdictions**). However, the finer details of business law do vary considerably from one jurisdiction to another, and so by necessity we will be covering the characteristics of businesses in broad, generalised terms. At the end of this chapter, you will be encouraged to investigate the major aspects of business law in your country specifically.

1.2.1 **Unincorporated businesses**

The least complicated form of business is often called a **sole trader** or **sole proprietor**. As the name implies, a sole trader has just one owner. It is one example of an unincorporated business, which simply means the business has not been established by law to be a separate entity from the owner. In other words, legally speaking, it is the owner who owns the assets used by the business, and who owes the debts of the business. In law, the business assets and debts are treated no differently from the owner's house and the bank loan they used to buy that house. Indeed, even the term 'sole trader' has this same characteristic: it refers both to the business itself (as in 'that phone repair shop is a sole trader'), and also the owner of the business (as in 'Michelle is a sole trader').

One consequence of not being incorporated is that the tax authority will generally tax any **income** made by the business as if it were the owner's own income (that is, at the owner's individual tax rate). As individual tax rates are often—though not always—higher than the tax rate that applies to incorporated businesses, this is often a disadvantage of operating as a sole trader. However, a clear advantage of operating as a sole trader is simplicity, insofar as the owner does not have to comply with the extensive administrative requirements—the so-called 'red tape'—involved in starting and running a company. This advantage erodes as a business grows, so that over a certain size the benefits of incorporation justify having to deal with the red tape. Thus, sole traders tend to be small businesses.

The two most common forms of unincorporated businesses are sole traders and partnerships (though some partnerships may be incorporated, depending on the jurisdiction).

Not all small businesses are owned by only one person, of course. An unincorporated business with more than one owner is called a '**partnership**', and the individuals who own it are called 'partners'. A partnership agreement typically outlines several key features of the business, such as: the responsibilities of each partner; the way in which profits and **losses** will be allocated; and the way in which the partnership will be dissolved. Unincorporated partnerships are legally much like sole traders, except that ownership of the business assets and responsibility for the business debts are held jointly by the partners.

Because the business and owners are not legally distinct, the owners of unincorporated businesses need to be involved in any substantial transactions, such as taking loans, buying insurance, and acquiring productive capacity, which means that sole traders and partners are typically closely involved in managing their businesses.

It is worth briefly considering how the accounting works for unincorporated businesses. Whilst the businesses themselves are not *legally* separate from the owner, the business's *accounting* is kept apart from the financial affairs of the owners. Even in a tiny sole trader, decisions should be informed by a clear understanding of the financial position and performance of the business itself, and this requires a set of financial records and reports that ignores personal transactions such as the owner's spending on housing, food, and recreation. The need for separate accounting is even stronger in partnerships, where partners need to know precisely how the business is performing in order to know how the gains (or losses) should be divided. Also, some partners may not be as involved as others in the daily financial administration of the business, which means that stricter financial controls and record-keeping are desirable. This principle—that for accounting purposes businesses are treated as distinct from their owners, even if they are not in fact legally separate entities—is known as the **entity concept**.

1.2.2 **Incorporation**

In Latin, the word 'corpus' means 'body', and so '**incorporation**' means to give something a body, metaphorically speaking. Thus, to incorporate a business is to register it with the legal authorities as an entity separate from its owners.

Although commonplace, this is a bizarre idea, which needs some explanation. The law uses the term 'natural persons' to describe real, flesh-and-blood people, but it also recognises a separate, artificial category of legal person: a 'juristic' person. Juristic persons do not have all of the same legal rights and responsibilities as natural persons (eg they cannot marry, and since they cannot drive, they do not have to obey speed limits), but many laws apply equally to both types of legal person. So an incorporated entity can own assets, borrow money, sue other legal persons (or be sued by them), and be punished by the law in appropriate ways.

> By establishing a business as a separate legal person entitled to own assets, owe debts, sue, and be sued, incorporation allows the business to transact in its own capacity.

Not all incorporated entities are businesses. For example, in most parts of the world, charities, universities, and clubs may be incorporated. Conversely, especially in developed countries, most businesses are incorporated. When a business incorporates, legal ownership of its assets and the legal obligation for its debts transfer to the new entity. Thus, sole traders or partners effectively sell their direct stakes in their businesses for an indirect stake: the right to benefit from the value generated by the business's operations.

Depending on the country, there may be a variety of incorporated business forms. For example, in the UK, the limited liability partnership, or 'LLP', is one such form. (Note that this is an exception to the general convention that partnerships are unincorporated.) But in every jurisdiction, by far the most common form of incorporated business is the **company**. On incorporation as a company, a business's owners become **shareholders**, which is to say that they become owners (or holders) of shares that represent their stake in the business. These shares can be traded between existing shareholders, or sold by existing shareholders to new shareholders. The buying and selling of these shares are transactions between parties that are separate from the business, and so this trading does not affect the business as such. For example, if existing Shareholder A sells shares to new Shareholder B, then Shareholder B will pay a sum of money to Shareholder A and take ownership of these shares. The transaction affects Shareholders A and B financially, but not the business, which merely has a new owner.

This characteristic of incorporated entities confers a major practical benefit: it is a mechanism by which small portions of the ownership stake in a business can be sold (or, say, be bestowed by a will), which is usually a lot more challenging for unincorporated businesses.

> Incorporation makes it easier for business owners to sell portions of their ownership, and makes it easier for accountants to record these transfers of ownership.

There is also a substantial accounting benefit. When any portion of the ownership in a sole trader or unincorporated partnership is sold or inherited, elaborate accounting is required to recognise the legal end of one business and the beginning of another. However, because incorporated businesses are legally distinct from their owners, none of this is necessary, since the accounting for the business can continue regardless of the change in ownership. This feature of incorporation is known as perpetual succession.

1.2.3 Limited liability

Because there is no legal distinction between unincorporated businesses and their owners, these owners are personally responsible, or liable, for the businesses' debts. In other words, if somehow it became impossible to pay the businesses' debts using the businesses' assets, the owners' personal possessions will be expropriated to pay off the debts.

Suppose that a sole trader puts in €1 000 to start a business, which is then used to pay the 20% deposit required to purchase €5 000 of high-end sunscreen. The business takes delivery of the sunscreen, expecting to be able to sell the sunscreen for €7 000, pay back the supplier the debt of €4 000, and end up with €3 000 in the bank. However, it turns out that there is a flaw in the business model: it is winter, and no one wants sunscreen. Instead, the best the sole trader can do is flog the sunscreen for €500, leaving only one business asset: a bank account containing €500. This is not nearly enough to pay back the supplier, who is still owed €4 000. The supplier can therefore make a claim against the sole trader's personal assets. Perhaps, for example, they will have to sell their car to pay the additional €3 500 owing to the supplier.

We thus say that unincorporated businesses have 'unlimited liability': there is no limit to the amount of money that owners stand to lose. When there is more than one owner, this is especially risky, because one partner may be held personally responsible for debts arising from poor business decisions made by other partners.

This introduces a major potential advantage of incorporation written into the law: **limited liability**. Typically, the shareholders of a company do not risk losing their personal possessions if the business goes bankrupt; instead, the most they can lose is the investment they have already made.

If the sunscreen business was incorporated as a company with limited liability, the supplier would not be able to make a legal claim against the shareholder's personal assets: they would receive only the €500 from the business's bank account. The owner—now called a shareholder of course—loses their initial €1 000 investment, but that is all.

If this seems too good to be true, it is worth knowing that in practice, banks and other major lenders are keenly aware of the dangers of giving credit to a client protected by limited liability, and will typically ask the shareholders or executives to personally secure business loans (that is, sign an agreement to allow their personal assets to be taken if the business cannot pay). Thus, especially in smaller businesses funded with bank loans, limited liability is unlikely to offer full protection for the owners. However, it certainly does protect them from being forced to pay *unsecured* debts, like the amount owed to the sunscreen supplier. And it fully protects the personal assets of investors who buy the shares of much bigger companies on a **stock exchange**: the most they can lose is what they pay for their shares.

Not all incorporated businesses have limited liability. For example, in some countries, professional practices like those of lawyers, doctors, or accountants are entitled to incorporate, but are nevertheless prevented from obtaining limited liability. This is in order to increase the level of accountability with which such professionals operate. There are even some notable businesses, for example Irish **subsidiaries** of Apple Inc, which have chosen to register as unlimited liability companies, in order to avoid the obligation to publicly disclose key financial information each year.[2] However, the shareholders of the vast majority of companies are protected by limited liability.

Table 1.1 summarises the chief differences between incorporated and unincorporated businesses, focusing on the benefits enjoyed by each. Note how, generally speaking, the advantages of incorporation kick in as soon as a business grows beyond being very small.

TABLE 1.1 Summary of the benefits enjoyed by unincorporated and incorporated businesses

	Unincorporated businesses (eg sole traders and partnerships)	Incorporated businesses (eg companies)
Less 'red tape'	Yes	No
Owners can avoid management responsibility	No	Yes
Easy transfer of portions of ownership	No	Yes (though may be restricted)
Perpetual succession	No	Yes
Limited liability	No	Yes (though not for all types)
Tax savings	Usually better for incorporated businesses, though this depends on business size, tax rates, and other features of tax legislation	

1.2.4 **Types of companies**

Business law in your country almost certainly establishes a few different types of companies. For example, non-profit organisations like charities are often able to register as companies, even though they are not businesses, as they do not aim to make their shareholders wealthier. In the UK and Australia, charities are often incorporated as Companies Limited by Guarantee; in Germany, the equivalent type of company is a *gemeinnützige Gesellschaft mit beschränkter Haftung*, or gGmbH; and so on.

When it comes to limited liability companies that are for-profit, there is generally a distinction between **private companies** and **public companies**. The primary difference is that the shares of a private company, as the name suggests, may not be publicly traded, whereas a public company's shares are not subject to any trading restrictions. This, of course, limits the extent to which a private company can raise financing, but at the same time protects its shareholders from any undesirable changes in shareholding. For example, if the shareholders in a private company agree that, before any of them can sell their shares, they must first offer them to the other shareholders, they are then all protected from the risk of having to share their ownership of the business with someone they do not approve of.

On the whole, private companies are smaller, and their shareholders often play a role in managing the business. The shareholders of public companies are generally not involved in the business operations; instead, they appoint a **board of directors** to manage the business on their behalf, and the board in turn selects a managing director (known by a variety of titles, including 'chief executive officer' or 'CEO') who takes overall responsibility for running the business. If the shareholders are unhappy with the way in which the company is being run, they can appoint a new board of directors who will (hopefully) run the company according to their wishes.

The official name of a company usually includes a designation at the end of its name, such as 'LLC', 'SA', 'Inc', or 'Ltd' and so on, to indicate what type of company it is. If you like, a quick internet search will help you decode the various companies' designations in your country.

1.2.5 **Listed companies**

A public company may choose to **list** its shares on a stock exchange (that is, a market where shares are bought and sold) as a means to boost the marketability of its shares. Marketability may be important for many shareholders, as it allows them to sell their shares more easily when they require cash, or when they decide the company is no longer a good investment. If the shares are not listed on a stock exchange (usually we simply say that the shares are 'unlisted'), then the shareholders may have difficulty in finding a buyer for their shares when they wish to disinvest. Similarly, a prospective investor will find it much easier to acquire shares in a listed company than in an unlisted company.

Because of the restrictions on the sale of their shares, private companies cannot be listed. Not all public companies are listed: those which are not will typically have far fewer shareholders, who have each acquired relatively large investments directly from the company or from a previous shareholder.

FIGURE 1.2 The locations of the world's largest stock exchanges

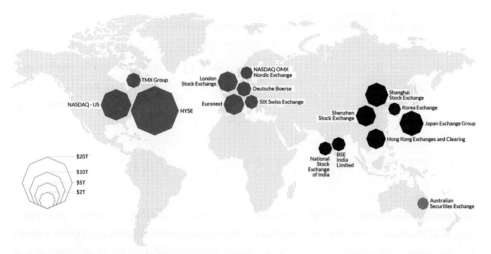

Source: Desjardins, J 2016. *All of the World's Stock Exchanges by Size.* The Money Project. 16 February 2016. Available at: http://money.visualcapitalist.com/all-of-the-worlds-stock-exchanges-by-size.

Figure 1.2 shows the world's largest stock exchanges, as measured by the total market price of the listed shares.

1.2.6 **Public interest entities**

You may hear that a certain company is a '**public interest entity**', or '**PIE**' (yes, it is pronounced like the food product!). This is a term used in the business law of several jurisdictions to indicate a high level of public accountability and transparency demanded of that entity. In general, PIEs are defined to include all listed companies and other very large companies, and they are held to the strictest accounting requirements.

For example, virtually all companies are required to keep detailed accounting records and to produce annual financial statements. However, PIEs (or, in jurisdictions which do not use this term, listed companies) must do so in accordance with the rigorous and demanding standards set by the **International Accounting Standards Board (IASB)**, called '**International Financial Reporting Standards**' (or '**IFRS**'). Other companies are generally able to choose to report using less onerous guidelines. We shall discuss financial reporting requirements in detail in Chapter 3.

> Public interest entities and similar companies are generally required to produce financial statements in accordance with IFRS.

The financial statements of PIEs and similar companies must also be subjected to an annual **audit**. This means that external auditors—a team of independent experts in financial reporting—must verify the validity, accuracy, and completeness of the company's financial statements each year, via a thorough investigation of the company's accounting system and records. Other companies may be permitted to undergo a less onerous review of their financial statements.

The financial statements we will be considering in this book are prepared according to IFRS and are audited, because they belong to listed, public companies, like Burberry, which by dint of being a listed, UK-based company is also a PIE.

Figure 1.3 illustrates the context of the various business forms that we have looked at in this chapter, showing the application of the terms we have been using.

FIGURE 1.3 Overview of the most common business forms

UNINCORPORATED BUSINESSES	INCORPORATED BUSINESSES	
Sole traders	Listed public companies	▬ Public interest entities (PIEs)
	Unlisted public companies	
Unincorporated partnerships	Private companies	May be PIEs, depending on the extent of their influence on the public interest
	Other incorporated types of business	

1.3 CREATING BUSINESS VALUE

We have already established that businesses are distinct from other organisations because they aim to create value for their owners. This distinguishing objective applies equally to companies, partnerships, sole traders, and all other business forms. Any enterprise to whom it does not apply is, by definition, not a business.

Many people believe that businesses also ought to achieve other objectives, for example taking care of employees, protecting the environment, and operating responsibly within the wider social context. These are noble and important goals, and businesses can certainly achieve them. The huge advances in human living standards, affluence, and well-being that have been achieved over the past few hundred years have come from many different sources: science, technology, political progress, and so on. But it is no exaggeration to say that much of this development has been driven forward by businesses. On the whole, agricultural production has been expanded, life-saving medicines have been developed, modern conveniences have been supplied, communication has been facilitated, and retirement savings have been grown, all by businesses. No matter what goods or services a business sells, it is essentially a **value creation** machine, and—in the best-case scenario—the value it creates can be spread far and wide.

In Chapter 14, we shall discuss forms of corporate reporting which explicitly report how well a business has created value for a wide variety of **stakeholders**. However, as you will see, the principles and practices underlying these reports are substantially different from those which you will learn about in the first thirteen chapters.

This is because financial accounting—our main subject—is unashamedly designed to focus on the creation of value from a very specific point of view: those who have a financial stake in the business.

1.3.1 Introduction to the value creation cycle

It can be very difficult to create value in practice—just ask any business manager!—so let's begin with a simple illustration. There are many ways to depict the **value creation cycle**, but given our focus on the creation of value from the perspective of those who have contributed funding to the business, we shall use Figure 1.4.

FIGURE 1.4 Overview of the value creation cycle

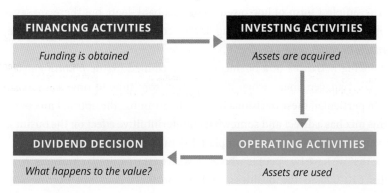

Put simply, business managers must obtain funding, acquire assets with this funding, and then use the assets to generate additional value. They then from time to time make a decision about whether to distribute some of this value directly to the owners in the form of a **dividend**, which is usually in the form of cash, although other items of value are sometimes transferred. They may instead decide to keep the value in the business and use it as funding for further value creation.

Over the next few sections, we shall build up your understanding of each phase of the value creation cycle, so that in section 1.3.6 we will be able to present a much more comprehensive picture of the process.

1.3.2 **Financing activities**

There are two main sources from which a business may be financed, which we call **debt** and **equity**. Equity is the funding that can be attributed to the owners, and it consists of two basic components. The first, called '**capital**', is what the owners contribute to the business when it starts, or later when it needs more funds to grow. The other component of equity is the value that the business has created but not yet paid out to the owners as a dividend. This value is often known as '**retained earnings**'. We will return to this concept in section 1.3.5 on the dividend decision.

Figure 1.5 summarises the sources of funding.

FIGURE 1.5 The basic sources of business funding

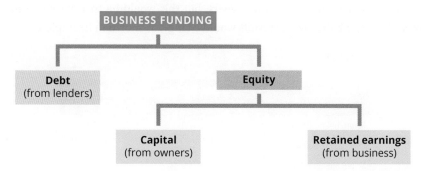

To the extent that a business is financed with debt, it is using funds borrowed from lenders. The simplest form of borrowed funds is a bank loan, but there are several other ways to obtain debt financing, including **bonds**, corporate **debentures**, and simply buying **inventory** or other goods on credit.

The **financing activities** of a business are determined by the *financing decisions* that the business's managers make when it starts, and from time to time as more funding is required. In particular, these decisions involve determining the optimal mix of equity and debt, as this mix has a direct and somewhat counterintuitive effect on the business's ability to create value for the owners, as Example 1.1 demonstrates.

Suppose that we have two people who each wish to start a similar business. Mr Cautious contributes £10 000 to the business, and his business does not borrow any money. Ms Risky also contributes £10 000 to her business, but this business borrows a further £10 000 from the bank at an interest rate of 8% pa. Each of their businesses uses the funds raised to invest in assets which earn a 10% return (before interest) each year, resulting in the following outcomes for the year.

EXAMPLE 1.1

	Mr Cautious £	Ms Risky £
Return before interest (£10 000 × 10%, £20 000 × 10%)	1 000	2 000
Interest (£10 000 × 8%)	——	− 800
Return after interest	1 000	1 200

It is clear that, although Mr Cautious and Ms Risky both contributed £10 000 to their respective businesses, Ms Risky's business made a return after interest of £1 200, compared to Mr Cautious's result of £1 000. Borrowing £10 000 from the bank has boosted the amount of value Ms Risky was able to create. This wonderful effect is known as **leverage** or **gearing**.

Leverage allows businesses to create more value for owners by borrowing, so long as the rate of return before interest is higher than the interest rate itself. In Ms Risky's case, she was able to borrow money from the bank at 8% and use it to produce a return of 10%, thus effectively making 2% for herself on the borrowed money (it is no coincidence that her additional £200 return is equal to 2% of her £10 000 borrowings).

On learning about the positive effect of debt, one may feel tempted to borrow as much as possible to lever up the returns to owners, but this would be treacherous. If interest rates were to rise to 25%, say, the results would change, as shown in Example 1.2:

EXAMPLE 1.2

	Mr Cautious £	Ms Risky £
Return before interest	1 000	2 000
Interest (£10 000 × 25%)	——	− 2 500
Return after interest	1 000	− 500

Assuming that business activity remains the same after the increase in interest rates, both businesses would still make a return before interest of 10%. And Mr Cautious would still make a return after interest of £1 000, but now Ms Risky would make a negative return—a loss—of £500. In fact, in reality this scenario is likely to be even worse for Ms Risky: when interest rates rise in an economy, customers tend to spend less (because more of their salary goes towards the higher interest payments on their mortgages), causing most businesses' sales to fall. Thus, value creation in Ms Risky's business would probably be squeezed by both a lower return before interest and also rising interest payments, resulting in an even greater loss than £500.

We can see from this example one of the great trade-offs in business, if not in life: on the whole, you cannot get greater returns without taking on more risk. When interest rates are low, Ms Risky is able to make returns superior to those of Mr Cautious, but these higher returns are more risky, as we see when interest rates rise.

In our example, who made the better financing decision? If interest rates remain low, Ms Risky's decision to borrow appears correct, but if interest rates rise, then the decision of the risk-averse Mr Cautious appears better, since he at least earns a positive return overall. Ultimately, there is no correct level of borrowings: it depends on the business and the economic conditions. If interest rates are low, and if the business can consistently use its assets to generate high rates of return, then additional borrowings are probably worth the risk; but when economic changes lead to higher interest rates, and/or when the business's assets are likely to be less productive, it would be well advised to borrow less.

So financing decisions are important, but not easy. A vast amount of research has been done over the years on the optimal **capital structure** (ie the mix of debt and equity) and, although some of the findings may be useful to those who have to make the financing decisions, the quick answer is that there is no simple rule for them to follow.

> A business is financed through a mix of debt and equity called the capital structure. Debt can leverage up returns to owners powerfully, but also increases the risk of a business making a loss.

1.3.3 **Investing activities**

Once the business has raised funding, it must do something with this money. The resulting **investing activities** might include procuring an office building, constructing a factory, acquiring another business, investing in a brand, developing a new consultancy service, or indeed purchasing a million other things. You probably already know that the items a business acquires for use in the value creation process are called 'assets' by accountants. This book will have a great deal more to say about assets, and in time we'll give you a much more formal definition, but for now let's move on, confident that it is easy to appreciate the importance of the managers' investing decisions. After all, the business's assets are the only means by which it ultimately creates any value at all.

1.3.4 **Operating activities**

The assets acquired by the business's investing activities are now used in a wide-ranging multitude of **operating activities**: manufacturing, maintenance, software development, marketing, administration, and everything else that happens in a business each day to achieve the sale of its goods or services. For the creation of value, not only do these processes need to run efficiently and effectively, but key operating decisions need to be made well. These include, for example, decisions about the price at which goods or services are sold, the way in which costs are controlled, the extent to which advertising is used to promote goods and services, whether or not key functions are outsourced, and a myriad other decisions made on a day-to-day basis.

In overseeing a business's operating activities, managers need to pay close attention to three different indicators of value creation. Because of their importance, these items are each given great prominence in the financial statements. The first is **revenue**, the total amount for which a business's goods and/or services are sold. Of course, a business cannot create value unless it generates revenue. However, success in business is not actually about maximising revenue, because of a business's costs, known by accountants as '**expenses**'. For example, if a business had to spend €1.2 million in order to generate revenue of €1 million, then its expenses exceed its revenue, and the business would not be creating value, but instead destroying it. It would be better, say, to earn only €800 000 of revenue, if that could be achieved by spending only €500 000 on expenses. This is because value is only created to the extent that revenue exceeds expenses; that is, if **profit** is earned. Thus, profit is the second vital indicator of value creation.

The third is **cash flow**. The difference between profit and cash flow will be explained fully in Chapter 2. For now, it is enough for you to know that when accountants work out revenue, they include the full value of the sales that have been made on credit, even before the cash has been received. Similarly, they report the cost of using assets as an expense when the assets are actually used, not when they are paid for. For example, a machine costing €1 million that will be used for ten years will likely cause an expense of €100 000 for each of its ten years of use, even if it is paid for in full in the first year.

This means that it is perfectly possible for a business to be reporting profit and yet for these profits not to be producing net cash inflows. This may be remedied in the short term by obtaining more debt funding, but this comes at the cost of interest. And borrowing may not even be an option if, for example, the business has already reached its borrowing limit. Running out of cash is a major problem for a business because it means its debts cannot be

> To create value, a business's operating activities must use its assets to generate revenue, from this revenue earn profit, and then convert the profit into net operating cash inflows.

settled, new products cannot be acquired, employees cannot be paid, and so on, threatening near-term sustainability. Indeed, many businesses have collapsed soon after reporting healthy profits because they were not generating the cash they needed to operate.

On the other hand, if a business's operations generate sizeable net cash inflows, this money can be used to sustain the business in the short term and also to engage in more investing activities to expand the business's market and ultimately create more value. Although revenue and profits are two key indicators of financial performance, it is a business's ability to turn profits into net operating cash inflows which is the ultimate test of value creation.

1.3.5 **The dividend decision**

> Value can either be kept in the business as retained earnings, or paid out as dividends.

Once the business has made financing decisions to obtain funding, investing decisions to acquire assets, and then through its operations has generated revenue, profit, and cash, its managers will be in a position to decide what it should do with the value that has been created. As we have already observed, this decision is a choice between paying out dividends to owners, or instead increasing the value of the owners' stake in the business by retaining the **earnings** and using them to finance further growth.

This brings us to a dilemma experienced by listed companies in particular. From the business's perspective, if there are lucrative opportunities to create more value using more assets, then it would be better if the business spent its earnings on acquiring these assets instead of paying the earnings out as a dividend. And in theory, rational investors should also prefer for value to be retained by a business. Unless they need the cash, they would have to spend time and energy deciding how to invest the dividends they receive. During that time, the money will sit in their bank accounts, where it will earn a relatively low return. If the business has good growth prospects, it would be better instead to quickly reinvest the dividends by using them to purchase more shares in the same business. However, this is inefficient: not only are taxes often **payable** on receipt of a dividend, but also stockbrokers and banks charge fees on these transactions. It would be better to skip the cycle of distribution and reinvestment and just leave the value in the business. After all, should investors need the money, or prefer to purchase a different investment, they could always 'monetise' their stake in the business by selling some of their shares.

However, in practice other factors influence the dividend decision. These are largely psychological in nature (in financial theory, such factors are called 'behavioural'), resulting from a deep-rooted cynicism about the trustworthiness of big corporations, whose investors generally have no involvement in day-to-day operations. Investing in a business is risky, and shareholders are continually looking for signals that there is a problem with their investment. You will see, as you work through this book, that a business's financial performance is difficult to understand: investors can never be sure that a business's success is sustainable.

> The dividend decision has a signalling effect in financial markets: a deviation from expectations is understood to be an important indicator of the business's prospects.

Thus, when businesses do not pay a dividend, or when they cut the number of dividends that they pay, this is perceived by investors as a sign that there may be a problem in the business. Investors immediately fear either that the business has no cash or that something ominous is going to happen in the future. The dividend is thus seen as a powerful signalling mechanism, one which investors and consequently businesses take very seriously.

As with other business decisions, there is no simple rule for making dividend decisions: business managers have to balance the benefits of retaining earnings in the business against the signalling effects of a reduced or zero dividend.

1.3.6 Detailed illustration of the value creation cycle

Now that you have learned more about the value creation cycle, we can present a fuller picture as follows in Figure 1.6.

Bear in mind that paying a dividend is not the only way that a business can transfer value to its owners. By retaining some value, and putting it to work in the value creation cycle, businesses themselves become more valuable. This additional value raises the price for which the owners can sell their stakes in the business. This happens for any thriving business, but it is particularly noticeable in listed companies, whose success reveals itself

1

FIGURE 1.6 A detailed illustration of the value creation cycle

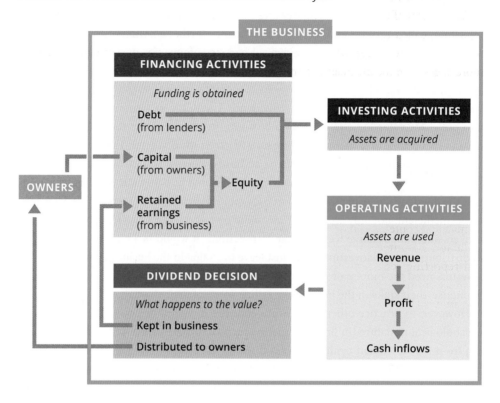

in higher published share prices over the long term, which in many cases in fact enrich their shareholders by substantially more than the dividends they pay.

This conception of how business value is created, from the perspective of someone with a financial stake in the business, is critical to your learning about business in general. It is also vitally important for your understanding of financial accounting, which is designed to report the business's financial position and performance in terms of this cycle. If you do not yet feel comfortable with any aspect of Figure 1.6, it would be advisable to revisit the relevant sections before moving on.

Financial statements comprise the statement of financial position, the statement of comprehensive income, the statement of cash flows, and the statement of changes in equity, accompanied by detailed notes.

1.4 FINANCIAL STATEMENTS

The financial statements officially consist of the **statement of financial position**, the **statement of comprehensive income**, the **statement of cash flows**, and the **statement of changes in equity**. Note, however, that this list suggests that there are four financial statements, but you should not expect always to see only four financial statements. The statement of comprehensive income is often split into two **separate financial statements** (the larger of which is often called the **income statement**, or **statement of profit or loss**), making a total of five. Indeed, there is yet one more component to a company's financial reporting, called the **notes to the financial statements**, sometimes more casually referred to as 'disclosures', which contain supporting information that usually covers far more pages than the financial statements themselves.

1.4.1 Twenty-first-century changes to the financial statements

If you learned some accounting in the late twentieth century, you would be forgiven for thinking that the financial statements are the **balance sheet**, income statement, and cash flow statement. Things have changed since then, with many resulting changes to the name, format, and contents of most companies' financial statements.

Table 1.2 is intended as a guide for those readers more familiar with earlier financial reporting requirements. In the first column, the financial statements that may be most familiar to such readers are listed, and the second column lists the financial statements that are currently required, indicating their relationship with the old financial statements.

TABLE 1.2 Summary of the twenty-first-century changes to financial statements

Earlier financial statement	Newer financial statement	Comments
Balance sheet	Statement of financial position	The new name is not compulsory. The new statement is not substantially different from the old statement. The chief contents of this statement are assets (see Chapter 6), liabilities (see Chapter 7), and equity (see Chapter 10).
Cash flow statement	Statement of cash flows	The new name is not compulsory. The format of the new statement is no different from the format of the old statement. The contents of this statement are cash inflows and outflows (see Chapter 5).
Income statement	Statement of comprehensive income (or statement of profit or loss and other comprehensive income)	The new name is not compulsory. The format has changed substantially, especially because of a new section reporting other comprehensive income. This statement can be presented in either a one-statement or two-statement format. The contents of this statement are items of income and expense (see Chapter 4).
	Statement of changes in equity	There was no twentieth-century equivalent of this statement, though much, if not all, of its content could be found in the *notes* to older financial statements. Particular attention is paid to this statement in Chapter 10.

1.4.2 Financial reporting periods

A set of financial statements is prepared for a particular period, known as the **reporting period**. In theory, this period could be any length of time—reporting the effects of the business events that occurred in a particular day, week, month, decade, and so on—but the standard financial reporting period is a year, known as a **financial year** or **fiscal year**.

That said, companies may have to prepare financial statements quarterly (every three months) or semi-annually (every six months), depending on whether they are public interest entities, whether they are listed, and the laws of the country in which they are based. These financial statements are called **interim financial statements**, but they typically attract less attention than annual financial statements, which are required of practically every company.

In most jurisdictions, the twelve months of a company's financial year do not have to align with the twelve months of the calendar: generally, companies are able to choose a year-end to suit them, which often is not 31 December. For example, H&M's year-end is 30 November. Some companies prefer their financial years to be composed of an exact number of weeks, usually because they measure performance during the year on a weekly basis. This is how, for example, Wm Morrison Supermarkets plc, which aims for a year-end near 31 January, had a fifty-three-week financial year ending on 4 February 2018, followed by a fifty-two-week year ending on 3 February 2019. Interestingly, Burberry recently adopted this policy, following its reporting period of a full year ended 31 March 2018 with a fifty-two-week period ended 30 March 2019.

When financial years do not end on 31 December, they are usually named according to the calendar year in which they do actually end. For example, even though the vast majority of the fifty-two weeks in Burberry's financial year that ended on 30 March 2019 were in the 2018 calendar year, it is nonetheless known as the '2019 financial year'. Even more trickily, quite often the words 'financial year' are dropped, and so when financial folks talk about '2019' at Burberry, they are talking about a period that ended only three months into the 2019 calendar year.

1.4.3 What the financial statements report

The objective of the financial statements is, in formal terms, 'to provide financial information about the reporting entity that is useful to existing and potential investors, lenders and other **creditors** in making decisions about providing resources to the entity'.[3]

In other words, the financial statements should enable these primary users of the financial statements—actual and potential providers of funding—to assess the business's financing, investing, and operating activities, and the quality of the dividend decision.

1

In particular, the outcomes of the financing and investing activities are reported on the statement of financial position, which shows the sources of funding, and to what use the funding has been put. The latter is shown by a list of the assets that the business has acquired (eg property, equipment, **financial instruments**, inventory, and so on). The sources of funding are shown as a list of the types of debt and equity that have been used to finance the business. The statement of financial position is often referred to as a 'snapshot' of the business: in other words, a view of the business at a distinct point in time, which is the end of the business's reporting period. This snapshot feature makes the statement of financial position unique: it is the only financial statement which is not in fact reporting for a period of time.

> The statement of financial position shows the business's situation at a point in time, like a snapshot.

The statement of comprehensive income primarily reports the results of the business's operating activities; in other words, it shows how well the business has used its assets to create value, focusing on revenue, expenses, and profit. It also shows the interest costs of any debt arising from financing decisions. Whilst the statement of financial position is seen as a snapshot, the statement of comprehensive income is more like a movie, as it is a summary of events that influenced the business's performance during the reporting period.

The statement of cash flows also presents a summary of events that influenced the business's performance; but it does this by looking purely at the cash flows into and out of the business. These cash flows are carefully categorised according to whether they relate to the operating, investing, or financing activities of the business.

> The statements of comprehensive income and of cash flows show financial performance over time, like a movie.

The statement of changes in equity explains how the amounts reported in each category of equity on the statement of financial position at the end of the reporting period changed since the beginning of the period. The effects of the dividend decision are also reported on this statement.

Whilst most of the information contained in the financial statements is historic, the insights they provide into the business should enable users to take a view of its ability to create value in the future. In particular, the ability to generate future cash flows is fundamental to any decisions that the users of the financial statements may wish to make, and therefore much of the information in the financial statements and accompanying notes is intended to help users understand the timing and certainty of these future cash flows. We will discuss this in much greater detail in Chapter 11 on financial analysis and Chapter 12 on business valuations.

CONCLUSION

Now that you understand the context of financial reporting, you are ready for a shallow dive into the mechanics of the accounting system. In Chapter 2, we shall explore the basic elements of recording a business's transactions, and in so doing, show how the system generates financial statements that achieve their objective and embody the characteristics we have described so far.

SUMMARY OF KEY POINTS

- Accounting consists of recording and reporting.
- Management accounting and financial accounting both make use of the recording function, but the reporting produced by these two subdisciplines is very different because the former is intended to inform the decisions of management, while the latter is intended to inform the decisions of existing and potential investors, lenders, and other creditors.
- The reports generated by financial accounting are called the financial statements. They consist of the statement of financial position, the statement of comprehensive income, the statement of cash flows, and the statement of changes in equity.
- In many respects, accounting is the language of business, and financial statements are the scorecard. This is why it is so important for anyone in business to understand them.
- Once a business has grown beyond being very small, there are many benefits of incorporating it, usually by registering it as a company. (See Table 1.1 for a list of the benefits of incorporation.)
- There are many business forms, including several different types of companies, the most influential of which are typically designated as 'public interest entities'. These must prepare their annual financial statements according to IFRS. (See Figure 1.3 for an overview of the most common business forms.)
- 'IFRS' stands for 'International Financial Reporting Standards' and consists of a rigorous and demanding set of international guidelines about how to prepare financial statements.
- Businesses are different from other organisations because they aim to create value for their owners, although they can—and often do—create value for other stakeholders too.
- The value creation cycle involves financing, investing, and operating activities, and ultimately a dividend decision. (See Figure 1.6 for a detailed illustration of the value creation cycle.)
- Businesses are financed by a capital structure, which is a combination of debt and equity. Equity usually consists of capital contributions from owners and also retained earnings.
- Through an effect known as 'leverage', financing a business with debt (as opposed to equity) can increase returns to owners, but also increases the risk of losses.
- In overseeing a business's operating activities, managers must pay close attention to three important figures: revenue, profit, and operating cash flows. To create value, a business must earn revenue, earn as much profit as possible from this revenue, and ensure that this profit produces as much net operating cash inflow as possible.
- Although in theory it is better for a successful listed company to retain earnings instead of paying out dividends, in practice this risks triggering a signal to financial markets that the company is in some kind of distress.
- The names and formats of the financial statements have changed since the beginning of the twenty-first century. (See Table 1.2 for a summary of these changes.)
- Reporting periods are usually a year long, but may be, for example, fifty-two weeks. A reporting period that ends in March 2019 is called the '2019 financial year'.
- The statement of financial position reports the business's situation on the reporting date in respect of its financing and investing activities.

- The statement of comprehensive income shows the business's financial performance during the reporting period. It reports the effects of operating activities, focusing on revenue, expenses, and profit.
- The statement of cash flows also shows financial performance, but from a different perspective. It reports exclusively cash flows for the reporting period, categorised according to financing, investing, and operating activities.
- The statement of changes in equity reports movements in the categories of equity reported on the statement of financial position, including the effects of the dividend decision.

CHAPTER QUESTIONS

The suggested solutions to the concept questions (marked 'CQ') can be found in Appendix III. Also, don't forget the **online resources** available at www.oup.com/he/winfield-graham-miller1e, which contain multiple-choice questions based on the material in this chapter, in addition to many other helpful resources.

CONCEPT QUESTIONS

CQ 1.1   Briefly explain the difference between management accounting and financial accounting.

CQ 1.2   Identify three typical benefits of incorporating a business.

CQ 1.3   Explain what it means to say that a company is 'listed'.

CQ 1.4   Describe what it means to 'leverage' a business's capital structure. Explain the purpose of leverage, and also the circumstances under which it will achieve its purpose.

CQ 1.5   Identify the four main financial statements and briefly describe what each tells us about the business.

CQ 1.6   List the four phases in the value creation cycle viewed from the perspective of the providers of funding.

INVESTIGATION QUESTIONS

IQ 1.7   Investigate the different business forms in your country. Determine whether business law in your country establishes all of the forms mentioned in this chapter: sole trader, unincorporated partnership, incorporated partnership, private company, unlisted public company, and listed public company. What terms are used to describe these entities in your country and what designation appears at the end of the businesses' names in each case? Are there any other business forms available in your country?

IQ 1.8   Identify the prominent stock exchange in your country and obtain a list of the companies that are listed on this stock exchange. (They can usually be found on the stock exchange's website or in the financial press.) How many companies are listed on this stock exchange? List those companies with which you are familiar.

1

IQ 1.9   Identify a listed retail company based in your country and obtain its latest financial statements. (They can usually be found quickly via an internet search using the term 'financial statements' and the company's name.) Identify its financial year-end and locate each of the individual financial statements. Look through these statements for items that interest you and then find out more about those items in the notes to the financial statements.

REFERENCES

[1]   Leswing, K 2016. 'Investors are Overlooking Apple's Next $50 Billion Business'. *Business Insider*. 4 April.

[2]   Daly, G 2016. 'Apple Firm Re-Registers as Unlimited Company'. *The Business Post*. 15 July.

[3]   IASB 2018. *Conceptual Framework for Financial Reporting*. Section 1.2.

ACCOUNTING BASICS

> **Here are some of the things you will be able to do after reading this chapter:**
>
> - comfortably use accounting terms like 'equity', 'asset', 'liability', 'income', 'expense', 'depreciation', 'impairment', 'current', and 'non-current';
> - describe the principles of double-entry and recognise the role of debits and credits;
> - analyse the fourteen main types of business events in terms of the accounting equation and prepare very basic financial statements to report them;
> - contrast the information reported using accrual accounting with the cash basis of accounting;
> - distinguish between items of other comprehensive income and items reported in profit or loss.

This chapter describes the basics of the financial accounting system. The main objective is to give you a clear understanding of the principles underlying the three most important outputs of the system: the **statement of financial position**, the **statement of comprehensive income**, and the **statement of cash flows**. (The statement of changes in equity will be covered in Chapter 10 on Equity.) You will also learn just enough information about the internal dynamics of the accounting system—double-entry **bookkeeping** and year-end procedures—to facilitate your understanding of these financial statements.

Often, the best way to understand fundamental concepts is by considering simple examples. In this chapter, we will introduce you to an imaginary business, the Pizza Business, which makes and sells pizza slices. We will account for fourteen basic transactions and other events in the financial statements of the Pizza Business using the accounting equation, the terminology of debits and credits, and numerous explanations of key principles. These transactions have been carefully chosen to represent the main types of business event, such that the vast majority of events that occur in practice are merely variations of these basic ones.

2.1 THE FINANCIAL ACCOUNTING SYSTEM

Any system takes inputs, submits them to a process, and then produces outputs. The inputs into a canning process, for example, are unpackaged food items and sheet metal, which are then submitted to a mechanised process whose outputs are canned food products. A schooling system submits children of school-going age to a multifaceted process simply called 'education', and thus produces educated school leavers. The financial accounting system is represented in Figure 2.1.

FIGURE 2.1 Overview of the financial accounting system

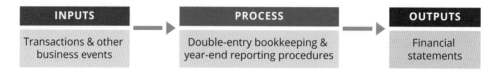

2.1.1 Assets, liabilities, equity, and the accounting equation

An accounting system contains just five elements. Three of these elements are assets, liabilities, and equity. **Assets** are items that we **control**, such as inventory, motor vehicles, buildings, patents, accounts **receivable**, etc. They include both tangible items (physical things, like machines) and intangible items like brands or copyrights. **Liabilities** are amounts that we owe to others, such as bank loans and accounts payable. 'Liability' is really just the accounting term for what people usually call simply '**debt**'. **Equity** is a combination of the capital contributed by owners and the value created and retained by the business.

These three elements are linked to each other by the **accounting equation** that underpins the system. One formulation of this equation is as follows.

$$\text{Assets} = \text{Equity} + \text{Liabilities}$$

The discussion of the **value creation cycle** in section 1.3 explained that a business is funded by a combination of debt and equity, and that this funding is then used to acquire assets. The above formulation of the accounting equation follows logically from this. The total amount of a business's assets must be equal to the total sum of the funding used to acquire them.

We can rearrange the accounting equation so that it tells us something else, as follows.

$$\text{Assets} - \text{Liabilities} = \text{Equity}$$

Equity can be understood as the accounting value of the owners' claim on the business. (It is therefore often referred to as the '**book value**' of the business.) In this second formulation of the equation, we see that equity can be calculated by subtracting the amount of liabilities from the amount of assets. Indeed, the formal definition of equity is 'the residual interest in the assets of the entity after deducting all its liabilities'.[1] This also makes logical sense. After all, what you have minus what you owe is what you are worth. For example, if the business were to liquidate, the owners would receive the difference between what is received from the sale of assets and what is paid to settle the liabilities. It is this relationship which leads to equity also being called '**net asset value**', or simply 'net assets'.

In sections 6.1.1 and 7.1.1 respectively, we will look at more formal definitions of assets and liabilities; and in section 10.1, we'll ask whether net asset value really does present a reliable valuation of a business. For now, though, there are more basic matters to which we must turn our attention.

2.1.2 Income and expenses

The remaining two elements of accounting are **income** and **expenses**. These do not appear in the accounting equation because they are different in nature from the other three elements, for they represent changes in equity. *Income is defined as any increase in equity that is not caused by a contribution by owners. An expense is any decrease in equity not caused by a distribution to owners.* These definitions mean that income and expense are measures of the extent to which the business's **operating activities** have created value for the owners. This is easiest to explain using examples, which we will soon encounter in Events 5–13 of the Pizza Business.

For now, you know the complete list of the five **elements of accounting**: everything that is recorded or reported in a financial accounting system belongs to one of these five broad classifications.

The five elements of accounting are assets, liabilities, equity, income, and expenses.

2.1.3 Debits, credits, and accounts

In accounting, the information relating to each type of asset, liability, equity, income, and expense is stored in a single place, called an account. Every transaction has two distinct effects on the accounts, which is why accounting systems are described as using 'double-entry'. One effect is called a **debit** and the other is a **credit**. A debit or credit is really just an addition to, or subtraction from, the figures stored in an account. We could simply say that the accounts are increased or decreased, but it is more common to say that they are debited or credited.

A debit increases an asset account, whilst a credit decreases an asset account. Consider for the moment one of the simplest transactions: a cash purchase of some equipment. Can you guess what the two effects are? One is a reduction in the business's cash asset, which will be recorded in the business's accounting system as a credit to the account usually called 'bank', which stores the information relating to the cash asset. (Sometimes this is instead simply referred to as the 'cash' account.) The other effect is an increase in the equipment asset, and so that will be recorded as a debit to the equipment account, which of course stores the information relating to the business's equipment.

2

> **MISCONCEPTION**
>
> You need to understand debits and credits to understand accounting.
>
> No, you do not. Accounting can be understood by thinking and talking in terms of specific accounts increasing or decreasing. Nevertheless, it is true that accountants talk in terms of debits and credits, so if you plan to speak to accountants about business, it would be useful to understand how these terms are used.

Here is a nuance of the accounting system which will seem counterintuitive, until we later show that it is in fact a bit of genius: the debits and credits for liability and equity accounts work the opposite way to assets. So, when equity and liability accounts increase, we call this a credit; when they decrease, it's a debit. Because income and expense are changes in equity, they follow the same pattern as equity. Income is an increase in equity and thus causes a credit to the related income account, whilst expenses are decreases in equity and so this would result in a debit to the expense account.

TABLE 2.1 The debit and credit conventions of double-entry

Assets	–	Liabilities	=	Equity
Increases are debits		Increases are credits		Increases are credits
Decreases are credits		Decreases are debits		Decreases are debits

All of this may well seem confusing to begin with, but it is worth knowing the rules before we consider an example, which will no doubt make everything a lot clearer.

> **MISCONCEPTION**
>
> When one's bank balance goes up, the increase is a credit on one's bank statement. Thus an increase in an asset is a credit.
>
> No. It is true that increases on a business's bank statement appear as credits, but these increases are in fact recorded as debits in the business's own accounting records. The debits and credits on the bank statement are from the bank's point of view. The bank's credit represents an increase in the bank's liability to pay it back to the depositor on request. In the business's own records, however, it is an increase in their bank asset (a debit). Thus, debits and credits on a bank statement are exactly opposite to the movements in the business's own records. If banks would only talk to their customers from the customers' point of view, most problems that people have with understanding debits and credits would vanish!

> **MISCONCEPTION**
>
> Debits are good, or debits are bad.
>
> A debit (or credit for that matter) is neither good nor bad. If you buy a car (an asset), the resulting debit would presumably be a good thing, whilst if you got a speeding fine (an expense), the resulting debit would definitely be a bad thing. Try not to think of debits as being good or bad.

2.2 **THE PIZZA BUSINESS**

Suppose that two friends start a small business that will make and sell pizza slices during the summer at a popular European holiday spot. They decide to call it the Pizza Business, or 'PB'. In the first year, fourteen distinct business events occur.

THE EVENTS

1. The two owners each contribute €300 to the business's bank account.
2. In order to raise additional funding, PB borrows €100 from the bank. The capital amount will be repaid in four years' time.
3. PB buys a very small plot of land for €450 and a portable pizza oven for €120. These amounts are paid in cash.
4. PB buys ingredients for €80 (half with cash and half on credit).
5. PB makes and sells 100 pizza slices at €3 each (half with cash and half on credit).
6. At the year-end, ingredients with a **cost** of €20 are still on hand.
7. PB pays salaries of €50.
8. At the year-end, PB owes the power utility a total of €40 for electricity consumed during the year.
9. The pizza oven is expected to last for a total of three years, after which it will be scrapped.
10. At the year-end, PB receives €2 of interest on its bank account balance for the year.
11. At the year-end, PB pays interest for the year on the loan (see Event 2). The loan was granted on the first day of the year. The interest rate is 7% pa ('pa' stands for 'per annum' or 'per year').
12. At the year-end, corporate income tax is due at a rate of 20%.
13. At the year-end, the land has a market value of €500.
14. At the year-end, dividends for the year of €20 (that is, €10 to each of the owners) are declared. These dividends will only be paid in the next financial year.

For each event, we will now:

- identify how assets and/or liabilities are affected by the event;
- establish whether there is a change in equity, and if so, whether this change represents an item of income or expense;
- identify the accounts affected by the event;
- identify whether these accounts increase or decrease (in brackets, we will show whether this is recorded as a debit or a credit, for those readers who aim to use the language of double-entry);
- identify how the event affects the statement of financial position and/or statement of comprehensive income.

2.2.1 **Event 1: capital contribution**

We start with the kind of financing activity with which most businesses begin: a capital contribution by the owners, which in this case totals €600.

Recall that each transaction has two effects, causing a change in two accounts. As the contributions are made in cash, PB's cash asset grows, and to record this, the bank account is increased (debit). No other assets or liabilities of the business change due to this contribution.

> **MISCONCEPTION**
>
> Money contributed to the business by the owners in the form of capital Is a liability of the business.
>
> No, a capital contribution is not a liability, it is equity. It is not owed to the owners, as the business has no legal obligation to repay it to them. If they want their money back, they would have to either liquidate (wind up) the business and hope that in fact there is still money left over after the business has paid off its liabilities, or sell their stake in the business to another potential investor. (Another way for owners of a company to get their money back would be through **a share buyback**, which we will cover in Chapter 10.)

When we consider this increase in a solitary asset account in the light of the formulation of the accounting equation which states that $A - L = E$, we see that the left-hand side of the equation, $A - L$, has increased. This means that the right-hand side, E, must also have increased. Thus, an equity account representing the combined contributions of owners over time is increased (credit). (This increase in equity does not count as income, as it is the result of a contribution by owners. You can check the definition of income in section 2.1.2.)

Recall that the **entity concept** requires that the business is accounted for as a separate entity, whether or not it is legally distinct from the two owners. The only difference between accounting for an incorporated versus an unincorporated entity might be the names of the accounts. If this were a **partnership**, the equity account might simply be called 'capital'. However, as this book focuses on the financial statements prepared by companies, we'll assume PB is a company. As a company's shares are issued in exchange for owners' contributions, the equity account to record such contributions is called 'share capital'.

On the left side of the Summary of Event 1, you can see the increase in assets of €600 and no change in liabilities, inevitably leading, according to the accounting equation, to an increase in equity of €600. On the right, you can see that the asset account to be increased is bank, and the equity account to be increased is share capital. Those readers who wish to use the language of debits and credits can refer to the column headings on the right, which reveal that double-entry conventions would thus record this transaction by debiting the bank account, and crediting the share capital account, with €600. (Refer to Table 2.1 for a reminder of how increases and decreases in each element translate into debits and credits.)

SUMMARY OF EVENT 1 The two owners each contribute €300 to the business.

Assets	−	Liabilities	=	Equity
+ €600				
				+ €600

Debit	Credit
Bank	
	Share capital

Note that the debits equal the credits. This is not a coincidence; it is true because of that counterintuitive recording convention shown in Table 2.1: asset accounts work in the opposite direction to equity and liabilities. This, combined with the dynamics of the accounting equation, means that for every event entered into the accounting system, the debits always equal the credits. The only exception is when an event has been recorded incorrectly, which reveals the genius of the double-entry process: many recording errors are quickly detected and eliminated simply because the debits do not equal the credits.

The statement of financial position

You can see the effects of this transaction in the following Statement of Financial Position 1.

The statement of financial position reports assets, equity, and liabilities.

PB: STATEMENT OF FINANCIAL POSITION 1

	Before Event 1	Event 1	€ After Event 1
Assets			
Current assets:			
Bank	0	+ 600	600
Total assets	0	+ 600	600
Equity and liabilities			
Equity:			
Share capital	0	+ 600	600
Total equity and liabilities	0	+ 600	600

In Statement of Financial Position 1, the first column shows the starting point: unsurprisingly, all of the amounts, including the bank and share capital accounts, started at zero. The second column shows the movement in the accounts as a result of the transaction: a €600 increase in the bank asset and the share capital equity account. The third column shows the figures in these accounts once the transaction is complete. This column contains the information that would be presented in the statement of financial position if it were drawn up immediately after the transaction. The first two columns are shown here only so that we can follow each individual transaction.

Like the statement of financial position of many real-world companies, PB's statement is laid out according to the formulation of the accounting equation which states that A = E + L, to demonstrate how the assets have been financed. For example, at this stage, PB has total assets of €600, made up entirely of cash, which have been financed entirely by equity, specifically **shareholders**' capital contributions. You can see why a statement of financial position used to be (and often still is) called a '**balance sheet**': it is constructed so that the top half always equals (or balances with) the bottom half.

It is relevant here to mention a different use of the term 'balance': the running total of the figures in each account on the statement of financial position is also known as a balance. For example, when in Event 2 the loan of €100 is received, we might say that the balance on the asset account known as bank increases to €700, and when €570 is spent on **investing activities** in Event 3, the balance will change again to €130.

This is not the only common layout of the statement of financial position. In fact, many real-world companies, like Burberry in Appendix I, lay theirs out according to the other formulation of the accounting equation, A – L = E. Businesses may use whichever layout they wish.

Assets on the statement of financial position are grouped according to whether they are current or non-current. The term '**current assets**' refers to the business's cash resources, items that are traded, and all other assets whose benefits are generally expected to be obtained within twelve months of the **reporting date**. All other assets are **non-current assets**. As the €600 in the bank account is a cash resource, it is classified as a current asset.

At this stage, the business has not yet earned any income or incurred any expenses, so there is no need for a statement of comprehensive income.

In section 10.3, in the chapter on equity, we will return to capital contributions and discuss several other transactions between the owners and the business.

2.2.2 Event 2: raising borrowings

Event 1 dealt with financing activities that employ equity funding, while Event 2 introduces debt financing. In this case, the debt is a €100 loan, which financial statements generally refer to as 'interest-bearing borrowings'.

As expected, when the lender gives the €100 to PB, the cash asset we have been calling 'bank' increases by €100 (debit). The business also now owes the lender €100 and thus liabilities (specifically interest-bearing borrowings) are increased by €100 (credit). On the left side of the Summary of Event 2, you can see that since assets and liabilities increase by the same amount 'A – L' has not changed overall, so there is no change in the right-hand side of the equation; that is, no change in equity. This transaction also does not generate either income or expense because income and expenses are both changes in equity (again, you may wish to check the definitions in section 2.1.2).

SUMMARY OF EVENT 2 PB borrows €100 from the bank.

Assets	–	Liabilities	=	Equity
+€100				
		+€100		

Debit	Credit
Bank	
	Borrowings

This event gives rise to the statement of financial position represented in the column furthest to the right in Statement of Financial Position 2. Note that the column headed 'Before Event 2' represents the state of affairs after the previous event; that is, Event 1.

PB: STATEMENT OF FINANCIAL POSITION 2

	Before Event 2	Event 2	€ After Event 2
Assets			
Current assets:			
Bank	600	+ 100	700
Total assets	600	+ 100	700
Equity and liabilities			
Equity:			
Share capital	600		600
Non-current liabilities:			
Interest-bearing borrowings		+ 100	100
Total equity and liabilities	600	+ 100	700

Both assets and liabilities have increased by €100, and thus, as always, the statement of financial position balances. In total, assets are now €700, financed by €600 from the shareholders, and by €100 from the lender.

Liabilities are, like assets, grouped on the statement of financial position into those that are current and those that are non-current. **Current liabilities** are those that the business intends to settle (that is, repay) within twelve months of the reporting date, whilst all longer-term debts are **non-current liabilities**. PB's borrowings appear under non-current liabilities, as they will be repaid after more than twelve months. If a portion of these borrowings were due to be repaid in the next financial year, it would be shown under current liabilities.

In Chapter 7, we will explain more about liabilities like borrowings, and also cover a wide variety of other types of liabilities.

2.2.3 Event 3: acquisition of non-current assets

The business has obtained total funding of €700. The next phase in the value creation cycle is to engage in investing activities, and so PB now uses some of this funding to purchase a plot of land for €450 and a pizza oven for €120.

Both of these new assets would be classified under the collective term 'property plant and equipment' (PPE) on the statement of financial position. We thus increase **PPE** with €570 (debit). Items of PPE appear on the statement of financial position as non-current assets, as it will take more than twelve months for their benefits to be consumed.

As this PPE has been purchased with cash, the bank balance will decrease by €570 (credit). Thus, one category of assets has increased (PPE), and one has decreased (bank). In effect, part of the bank asset has simply been replaced with two PPE assets. There are no changes to liabilities or (since again, the overall change to 'A − L' is zero) to equity, as shown in Summary of Event 3 below.

SUMMARY OF EVENT 3 PB buys land for €450 and a pizza oven for €120.

Assets	− Liabilities =	Equity		Debit	Credit
+ €570				PPE	
− €570					Bank

Statement of Financial Position 3 informs us that the business now has two categories of assets: bank of €130, and PPE of €570. The financing of the business (that is, the combination of equity and liabilities) has not changed. In particular, the fact that equity has not been affected indicates that this transaction has not yet created value for the owners.

PB: STATEMENT OF FINANCIAL POSITION 3

			€
	Before Event 3	Event 3	After Event 3
Assets			
Non-current assets:			
Property, plant and equipment		+ 570	570
Current assets:			
Bank	700	− 570	130
Total assets	700	0	700
Equity and liabilities			
Equity:			
Share capital	600		600
Non-current liabilities:			
Interest-bearing borrowings	100		100
Total equity and liabilities	700	0	700

MISCONCEPTION

When a business buys an asset, there is an effect on profit.

No, simply buying an asset has no effect on profit. One asset has merely been exchanged for another asset of equivalent value. The new asset is reported on the statement of financial position, and the asset given up in exchange (bank) is removed. (When assets are acquired on credit, it is a liability which increases instead, as in Event 4.) An asset will affect profit only when the business uses it in its operating activities, as in Events 5 and 6.

We will cover PPE in much more detail in Chapter 6 on assets, specifically in section 6.2.

2.2.4 **Event 4: purchase of inventory**

When PB purchases ingredients for €80, another type of asset account will increase. These ingredients (such as flour, tomatoes, cheese, and so on) are the raw materials that will be used to make what the business sells (in this case, pizza slices), and are therefore called 'inventory'. As inventory is traded by the business, we list it in the current assets section of the statement of financial position.

The business acquired this inventory by using a combination of cash and credit. The bank balance therefore decreases by €40 (credit). The other €40 of this purchase was 'on credit' (or 'on account'), which means that—although PB has acquired the inventory and should regard it as its own asset—the business has not yet paid for it: it owes €40 to the supplier of the ingredients. Thus a liability, which we call 'accounts payable', has increased by €40 (credit).

> **MISCONCEPTION**
>
> When items are purchased on credit, they do not belong to the buyer until they are paid for, and so they shouldn't be recorded until the date of payment.
>
> This claim is in fact doubly mistaken. First, in most **credit sales** transactions, legal ownership of the goods transfers on the date of sale, with the seller giving up ownership of the goods in exchange for a right to receive payment.
>
> Second, to record a sale, accountants do not require legal ownership to pass: all that is required to pass is control over the goods. On the date that the purchaser acquires control, the asset is introduced into the purchaser's books, along with a corresponding liability representing the obligation to pay for it. If this accounting treatment surprises you, look out for our later discussions of accrual accounting (section 2.2.7) and the asset definition (section 6.1.1).

SUMMARY OF EVENT 4 PB buys ingredients for €80 (half with cash and half on credit).

Assets	−	Liabilities	=	Equity		Debit	Credit
+ €80						Inventory	
− €40							Bank
		+ €40					Accounts payable

Once again, in Summary of Event 4 the overall change in 'A − L' means that this purchase has no effect on equity.

It may strike you as odd that the purchase appears to have had three effects, indicated by the three lines in the summary of the event. Perhaps this appears to contradict the idea of double-entry, that every transaction has two effects. However, one could say that really, there are two transactions here: a cash purchase, with two effects of €40 each (an increase in inventory and a decrease in bank) and a credit purchase, also with two effects of €40 each (an increase in inventory and an increase in accounts payable). An accounting system can legitimately record the transaction either way, provided that the total amount of the debits equals the total amount of the credits, so that the accounting equation is observed, and the statement of financial position will balance.

> **MISCONCEPTION**
>
> There is a standard set of terminology in accounting. For example, the correct account name to use for amounts owed to suppliers is not 'accounts payable', but rather 'creditors control', or 'trade payables'.

Whilst there is a loose trend towards some standardisation of the language of accounting, many variations exist. The terms businesses use to record transactions are entirely up to them, and even when preparing financial statements, terms are rarely prescribed. For example, the following terms generally have the same meaning: 'profit' and 'earnings'; 'inventory' and 'stock'; 'accounts receivable', 'trade receivables', and 'debtors'; 'accounts payable', 'trade payables', and 'creditors'; 'bank' and 'cash'; 'retained earnings', 'retained income', and 'accumulated profit'.

PB: STATEMENT OF FINANCIAL POSITION 4

			€
	Before Event 4	Event 4	After Event 4
Assets			
Non-current assets:			
Property, plant and equipment	570		570
Current assets:			
Inventories		+ 80	80
Bank	130	− 40	90
Total assets	700	+ 40	740
Equity and liabilities			
Equity:			
Share capital	600		600
Non-current liabilities:			
Interest-bearing borrowings	100		100
Current liabilities:			
Accounts payable		+ 40	40
Total equity and liabilities	700	+ 40	740

The statement of financial position reports the results of the business's financing activities (equity and liabilities) and the results of its investing activities (assets).

The accounts payable account is reported in the current liabilities section of Statement of Financial Position 4, as it will have to be paid within the next year. There are still no items of income or expense, so there is still no need for a statement of comprehensive income.

Note that the statement of financial position reveals that PB has employed another source of funding, albeit short-term funding: now, accounts payable has funded €40 of the total assets of €740.

We will revisit inventory and accounts payable in detail in sections 6.5 and Chapter 7, respectively.

> **MISCONCEPTION**
>
> Borrowings are the only kind of liability.
>
> No, there are many different kinds of liabilities in addition to straightforward borrowings: accounts payable, warranty obligations, debts owed to the employees' pension fund, and so on. In fact, if you take a peek at Burberry's group balance sheet in Appendix I, you'll notice that the business lists as many categories of liabilities as it does assets, and of these, only one—the bank overdrafts—would count as borrowings. We'll cover the full variety of liabilities in Chapter 7.

2.2.5 **Event 5: revenue**

PB has been financed, and investing activities have led to the acquisition of land, a pizza oven, and some inventory. Now, for the first time, the business embarks on operating activities by using these assets to create some value. Specifically, it makes and sells pizza slices for a total of €300 (100 slices × €3 each).

Half of the sales are for cash, and therefore increase the bank account by €150 (debit). The other half are sold on credit. People who owe the business are called '**debtors**', and the business's right to receive payment from them—an asset—is called 'accounts receivable'. Thus, a new account called accounts receivable is introduced into the records for €150 (also a debit). Accounts receivable is reported in the statement of financial position as a current asset, since debtors would no doubt be expected to settle the amount they owe for credit sales within less than twelve months.

> **MISCONCEPTION**
>
> A sale is only recorded when the cash from the sale is received.
>
> No. The accounting system processes economic events, including sales, when the event occurs, regardless of whether cash has changed hands. Besides, a receivable is quite clearly something of value—you would prefer to be owed €150 than to be owed nothing!—and, like any asset, it should be recognised by the accounting system when it arises.

Recording the other effect of this sale transaction (the credit) is a bit more complicated and you may not understand it the first time you read it. It will help if—for the moment—you overlook the fact that the business has incurred costs to make these pizza slices. In Event 6, we will consider these costs.

There has been an increase of €300 in two asset accounts, yet (unlike in Event 4) the increase is not balanced by a decrease in another asset and (unlike in Event 5) it is not balanced by an increase in a liability. Thus, 'A − L' has increased, and so the right-hand side of the equation—equity—must also have increased. What is more, this is exactly the sort of increase in equity that creates value, because (unlike in Event 1) it has not resulted directly from a capital contribution by the owners; rather, it is thanks to operating activities.

Because this sort of change in equity is a measure of value creation—because it is so essential to achieving the business objective—it is recognised as a new accounting element. Recall the definition of income from section 2.1.2: an increase in equity that is not the direct result of owners' contributions. So we have our first item of income.

The opposite of income—a decrease in equity that is not the result of a dividend distribution—is an expense. With a few rare exceptions, which we will cover when we get to Event 13, profit (also known as 'earnings' or 'net income') is equal to income minus expenses.

In the statement of financial position, the income created by PB's sale of pizza slices will thus lead to an increase in the account 'retained earnings' (also known as 'accumulated profits' or 'retained income'). This equity account reports all of the profits earned by the business, less any dividends distributed, since the business began. Note, in Statement of Financial Position 5, how the increases in bank and accounts receivable are balanced by the increase in retained earnings.

PB: STATEMENT OF FINANCIAL POSITION 5

			€
	Before Event 5	Event 5	After Event 5
Assets			
Non-current assets:			
Property, plant and equipment	570		570
Current assets:			
Inventories	80		80
Accounts receivable		+ 150	150
Bank	90	+ 150	240
Total assets	740	+ 300	1 040
Equity and liabilities			
Equity:			
Share capital	600		600
Retained earnings		+ 300	300
Non-current liabilities:			
Interest-bearing borrowings	100		100
Current liabilities:			
Accounts payable	40		40
Total equity and liabilities	740	+ 300	1 040

The equity of the business is now made up of the capital contributed by the owners (that is, the €600 share capital) together with the €300 made from the sale of pizza slices (reported as retained earnings).

We now come to a limitation of the statement of financial position, for this is far from the only event that will be reported in retained earnings. Like any other business, PB will engage in multiple transactions that affect earnings. For example, Event 10 will also generate income, and Events 6, 7, 8, 9, 11, and 12 all lead to expenses. Each of these will also be added to (in the case of the income) or subtracted from (in the case of the expenses) the retained earnings account. Thus, the details relating to these extremely important events—the operating activities actually creating business value—will be lost within this one line on the statement of financial position.

The solution is first to record these changes in equity in their own special income and expense accounts, to be reported on a different financial statement—the statement of comprehensive income—before their effects are aggregated in retained earnings on the statement of financial position.

The statement of comprehensive income

The general term used by accountants for income earned from a business's ordinary activities is '**revenue**' and so we shall use an account with this name to record the sale of pizza slices (businesses may instead use an account called '**turnover**', 'sales income', or just 'sales').

As income is an increase in equity, the double-entry conventions require income to be recorded by crediting the relevant account, in this case revenue, as in Summary of Event 5.

SUMMARY OF EVENT 5 PB sells 100 pizza slices at €3 each (half with cash and half on credit).

Assets	–	Liabilities	=	Equity		Debit	Credit
+ €150						Bank	
+ €150						Accounts receivable	
				+ €300 (income)			Revenue

The revenue account is reported not on the statement of financial position, but rather on the statement of comprehensive income, as follows.

PB: STATEMENT OF COMPREHENSIVE INCOME 1

	€
Revenue	300
Cost of sales	—
Gross profit	300
Operating expenses:	
Electricity	
Salaries	
Operating profit	300
Interest income	
Interest expense	
Profit before tax	300
Tax	—
Profit	300

We have shown in Statement of Comprehensive Income 1 all of the items of income and expense that will ultimately affect the profit of PB, to demonstrate how the statement paints a detailed picture of financial performance. So far, however, we have encountered only one item: the revenue of €300. We will complete the other items as we work through the remaining events in PB's financial year.

Note how the revenue has increased several other 'summation' lines in the statement of comprehensive income. As we have not yet recorded any expenses, the 'gross profit', 'operating profit', 'profit before tax', and 'profit' subtotals in the statement of comprehensive income all reflect the €300 increase in income that appears above them. Note too that only revenue and cost of sales affect gross profit, whereas progressively more line-items affect the subtotals further down the statement.

The profit figure, and all of the line-items above it, provide expanded detail about the increase in the retained earnings figure on the statement of financial position. Thus, the sales of €300 have not been recorded twice; rather, they have been recorded initially as a credit to revenue, to appear on the statement of comprehensive income, and then will flow, along with the other items of income and expense, into the retained earnings figure on the statement of financial position. (This is achieved using an accounting technique known as the 'closing entry', but we needn't go into that level of detail here.)

2

The statement of comprehensive income shows all items of income and expense and nothing else.

> **MISCONCEPTION**
>
> The statement of comprehensive income reports how much cash a business has received.
>
> This is clearly not the case, as can be seen here. The statement of comprehensive income shows revenue of €300, whilst only €150 cash has been received to date, with the other €150 still due. The statement of comprehensive income does not report cash flows. Rather, that is the purpose of the statement of cash flows, discussed in section 2.2.14.

You will learn much more about revenue in section 4.3, and about accounts receivable in section 6.6.

2.2.6 Event 6: cost of sales

If you have been thinking that we were too hasty in treating the entire €300 as profit, you would be quite right. We now turn to the cost of making the pizza slices, and begin with how to calculate that cost, before explaining how it will be reported in the financial statements.

Now, if the business manufactured aeroplanes like Airbus, or sold luxury cars like a Ferrari dealership, it could—and probably would—calculate and record the cost of each product it sells. There are few enough of them, and they are so expensive, that it would be worth the effort. But imagine doing this for pizza slices: trying to calculate and record the exact cost of the flour, tomatoes, cheese, and other toppings in each slice would be practically impossible. Not only would it be extremely time-consuming to attempt to record how much of each ingredient is used on each slice, but also it would be very difficult to keep track of the cost of the ingredients. After all, just one ingredient of the pizzas made on a particular day (say, the cheese) may have been acquired from multiple purchases made on different occasions for varying prices!

There is a shortcut to get around this difficulty: instead of calculating the cost of each individual slice, it is far easier to calculate the total cost of all the slices sold during the year. The business does this by keeping a record of its total spending on inventory for the year, and then at year-end performing a stock take (or inventory count) of the ingredients on hand, and thus deriving the cost of the ingredients consumed throughout the year.

For example, PB's year-end inventory count revealed ingredients on hand with a cost of €20. This is called 'closing inventory'. As the business started with no inventory, and then purchased ingredients for €80, it must have used inventory costing €60 (€80 − €20). This is therefore the cost of the pizza slices sold, and so we call it, quite literally, **cost of sales**.

Calculating cost of sales is a little more complicated when a business starts the year with some inventory already on hand. Suppose that in PB's second financial year, the business were to spend €100 on ingredients, and have €15 of ingredients left over at year-end. How would cost of sales for this second year be calculated, given the €20 of opening inventory (that is, Year 1's closing inventory)?

Well, we know that PB had ingredients costing a total of €120 available to use (opening inventory of €20 + purchases of €100). Given that €15 were not consumed, the cost of sales in Year 2 would be €105 (€120 − €15). Cost of sales can thus be calculated using the following formula.

$$\text{Cost of sales} = \text{opening inventory} + \text{purchases} - \text{closing inventory}$$

Note that calculating the cost of sales in this way means that PB's cost of sales includes not only the cost of ingredients that actually went into the pizza, but also the cost of goods that perished and had to be thrown away (mouldy cheese, say), and even any ingredients that were lost or stolen. Although this makes the term 'cost of sales' appear a little misleading, it is standard accounting procedure: wasted, damaged, lost, and stolen ingredients are treated as an inherent part of the cost of making the slices sold during the year.

The truth is that many businesses which sell high volumes do not have to resort to such an indirect method of calculating cost of sales. Thanks to computerised inventory systems and point-of-sale scanners, most retailers can determine the cost of each item sold. However, such businesses still need to do an inventory count in order to determine the amount of wasted, damaged, lost, or stolen goods.

For example, if PB knew, thanks to technology like this, that the cost of all the pizza slices sold was €50, then it would expect closing inventory in theory to be €30 (purchases of €80 − sales costing €50). When the inventory count revealed actual closing inventory of €20, this would imply inventory of €10 had perished or been lost or stolen. The total cost of sales would again be €60 (€50 actually sold + €10).

Although both methods of calculating cost of sales produce the same cost of sales figure, the second method has the advantage of revealing the amount of shrinkage.

This information, however, comes at a high price: the costs of the technology required to record the cost of each item sold.

> **MISCONCEPTION**
>
> When retailers discuss stock shrinkage, they mean that items of inventory got smaller.
>
> No, shrinkage really means that inventory was lost, wasted, damaged, or stolen.

Now that we know how to calculate the cost of the business's sales, how is this cost processed in the accounting system? In Event 5, focusing on the money received (and to be received) as a result of the sale, we identified an increase in equity, which, since it was caused by operating activities rather than a contribution by the owners, we called 'income'. Now, if we instead focus on the €60 decrease in the inventory asset, we see that there is a corresponding decrease in equity, which is caused by operating activities rather than by a distribution of dividends. So the €60 decrease in equity meets the definition of an expense (see section 2.1.2).

As an expense is a decrease in equity, the double-entry conventions require expenses to be recorded by debiting the relevant account, in this case cost of sales, as shown in Summary of Event 6.

SUMMARY OF EVENT 6 At the year-end, ingredients with a cost of €20 are on hand.

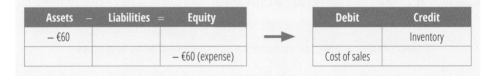

Assets	−	Liabilities	=	Equity		Debit	Credit
− €60							Inventory
				− €60 (expense)		Cost of sales	

Like revenue, cost of sales expense is reported on Statement of Comprehensive Income 2, except that its effects are negative, and so it *reduces* profit.

PB: STATEMENT OF COMPREHENSIVE INCOME 2

	€
Revenue	300
Cost of sales	− 60
Gross profit	240
Operating expenses:	
Electricity	
Salaries	
Operating profit	240
Interest income	
Interest expense	
Profit before tax	240
Tax	
Profit	240

We now have a more accurate reflection of the profit earned from selling pizza slices (that is, €240). This difference between revenue and cost of sales is called '**gross profit**'. This is still not the final (or 'net') profit, though, as there are other items of income and expense that still need to be taken into account.

Note that cost of sales in the statement of comprehensive income is not the amount of inventories that were *purchased* during the year, but the amount of inventories that *have been used* to make the pizza slices that have been sold.

MISCONCEPTION

If a business purchases a large amount of inventory during the year, its profit for the year will decrease.

No, inventory is reported as an expense only when it is sold, not when it is purchased. The cost of inventory still on hand at year-end does not affect profit.

For example, if the business starts the year with no inventory, purchases inventory for £5m, and uses only £1m, it will have closing inventory of £4m. Cost of sales would be £1m (opening inventory of £0 + purchases of £5m − closing inventory of £4m) and the effect on profit would therefore be a reduction of only the £1m cost of sales.

Like revenue, cost of sales expense affects retained earnings on the statement of financial position, although of course its effect on the figure is negative.

PB: STATEMENT OF FINANCIAL POSITION 6

	Before Event 6	Event 6	After Event 6
			€
Assets			
Non-current assets:			
Property, plant and equipment	570		570
Current assets:			
Inventories	80	− 60	20
Accounts receivable	150		1 500
Bank	240		240
Total assets	1040	− 60	980
Equity and liabilities			
Equity:			
Share capital	600		600
Retained earnings	300	− 60	240
Non-current liabilities:			
Interest-bearing borrowings	100		100
Current liabilities:			
Accounts payable	40		40
Total equity and liabilities	1040	− 60	980

Statement of Financial Position 6 now shows that PB's assets of €980 have been funded by €100 of bank loan, €40 of accounts payable, direct contributions from owners of €600, and €240 of earnings that have been generated by the business's operating activities and (so far) not distributed to owners.

You will have an opportunity to further your understanding of cost of sales in section 4.4.1.

2.2.7 Events 7 and 8: operating expenses

Now that we have encountered our first expense, we shall consider a few more. Of course, businesses have all sorts of expenses. Even in little old PB, you may be wondering how the heat in the pizza oven is generated. You may also be pondering what other assets the business has, like a cash register perhaps. If so, we are asking you to make some heroic assumptions for the sake of keeping the example simple: the pizza oven is fired by wood from free local alien vegetation and the cash register and other unmentioned assets were obtained free of charge!

Whereas in reality we would have all sorts of operating expenses, to keep the example as concise and unrepetitive as possible, we'll consider only salaries and electricity.

The salaries of €50 are paid out of the bank account, and so the bank asset decreases by this amount (credit). Unlike in Event 3, when the oven was purchased, there is no other asset for which this cash is being exchanged. Rather, the payment was made for something that has already been used up: the past year's labour. Thus, the decrease in the bank asset causes a decrease in equity, which, since it is brought about by operating activities and not a dividend, is an expense. The other effect of the event is therefore recorded as 'salaries expense' of €50 (debit) in Summary of Event 7.

SUMMARY OF EVENT 7 PB pays salaries of €50.

Assets	−	Liabilities	=	Equity		Debit	Credit
− €50							Bank
				− €50 (expense)		Salaries expense	

The electricity is a little different, because it has not yet been paid for. However, this does not mean that we record nothing, for the business has a liability to pay for the electricity. Thus, we record an increase in a liability account, accounts payable (credit). (A business may also call this kind of liability account an 'accrual' or an '**accrued expense**'.) When we record this liability, again the left-hand side of A − L = E decreases, after which the same logic applies as for the salaries. The only difference is in this case, of course, the expense is called 'electricity expense' in Summary of Event 8.

SUMMARY OF EVENT 8 PB owes €40 for electricity consumed during the year.

Assets	−	Liabilities	=	Equity		Debit	Credit
		+ €40					Accounts payable
				− €40 (expense)		Electricity expense	

Like all expenses, electricity and salaries expense must be reported on the statement of comprehensive income, where they are often categorised as **operating expenses**, to differentiate them from cost of sales expense and from financial expenses like interest. The effect of operating expenses filters down the statement, ultimately decreasing profit.

PB: STATEMENT OF COMPREHENSIVE INCOME 3

	€
Revenue	300
Cost of sales	− 60
Gross profit	240
Operating expenses:	
Electricity	− 40
Salaries	− 50
Operating profit	150
Interest income	
Interest expense	
Profit before tax	150
Tax	
Profit	150

Note that on Statement of Comprehensive Income 3, expenses that have been incurred but not yet paid for (like the electricity, in this case) are reported no differently from those that have been paid for (like the salaries).

Similarly, on Statement of Financial Position 7 these expenses both have the effect of reducing retained earnings in the equity section. However, one can see the difference between these two kinds of events in the other two sections: one increases liabilities, whereas the other reduces assets.

PB: STATEMENT OF FINANCIAL POSITION 7

	Before Events 7 and 8	Events 7 and 8	€ After Events 7 and 8
Assets			
Non-current assets:			
Property, plant and equipment	570		570
Current assets:			
Inventories	20		20
Accounts receivable	150		150
Bank	240	− 50	190
Total assets	980	− 50	930
Equity and liabilities			
Equity:			
Share capital	600		600
Retained earnings	240	− 90	150
Non-current liabilities:			
Interest-bearing borrowings	100		100
Current liabilities:			
Accounts payable	40	+ 40	80
Total equity and liabilities	980	− 50	930

In section 4.4.2, we will return to the topic of operating expenses. Although they are always subtracted from profit or loss in the statement of comprehensive income, and flow through to retained earnings in the statement of financial position, you will learn about some variations in the ways that operating expenses are presented in real-world financial statements.

2.2.8 **Accrual accounting**

Let's revisit a few of the accounting treatments you have learned about so far:

- The ingredients purchased in Event 4 were not treated as an expense, but rather as an asset.
- The credit sales in Event 5 were treated as income, although the cash had not yet been received.
- In Event 6, only the cost of the ingredients consumed was treated as an expense, not what was still on hand at year-end. And this expense was reported even though some of the ingredients had not yet been paid for.
- In Event 8, the cost of electricity consumed during the year was treated as an expense, even though none of it had yet been paid for.

If you are learning about accounting for the first time, you may be surprised by at least some of the treatments listed above, but in fact they are all consistent with a fundamental concept known as '**accrual accounting**', which officially 'depicts the effects of transactions and other events . . . in the periods in which those effects occur, even if the resulting cash receipts and payments occur in a different period'.[2]

What this means in practice is that the income from a sale is recorded and reported in the period when the sale happens, regardless of when the cash is received. Likewise, other items of income (interest income, say) appear in the statement of comprehensive income for the period in which they were earned, even if they haven't yet been received. For expenses, when a business consumes resources, the cost of doing so is recorded and reported in the period when the consumption occurs, not when it is paid for. Thus, cost of sales is reported in the period when the sale occurs; electricity, telephone, and water expense when the service is received; rent expense when the property is occupied by the tenant; interest expense in the period for which it is charged; and so on.

Accrual accounting reports the effects of transactions when the transactions themselves occur, not necessarily when cash changes hands.

Accrual accounting may be counterintuitive at first, but it is vital that you understand it, as it is the basis on which all but one of the financial statements are prepared. (The exception is the statement of cash flows.)

In case you are struggling to wrap your mind around the concept of accrual accounting, you can rest assured that it causes more headaches for accountants. This is because at the end of each financial period they must process an assortment of **accrual adjustments**: entries into the financial records to make sure that every transaction will be reported using the accrual concept, rather than simply based on when it causes cash to change hands. For example, without a payment by year-end, the electricity in Event 8 is very unlikely to have been captured by the accounting system, and so it is the accountant's task to identify it and process an adjustment so that it is correctly reported in the correct period.

2.2.9 **Event 9: depreciation**

We now come to another surprising consequence of accrual accounting. Recall that when the pizza oven was acquired for €120 in Event 3, it was not expensed in the statement of comprehensive income, but instead was recognised as an asset on the statement of financial position. This made sense at that stage, as the oven had not yet been used and so—unlike consumed ingredients, salaries for work already done, and electricity used—the full amount of economic benefits associated with the oven was still unutilised.

However, as the oven begins to be used to make pizza, these economic benefits begin to be consumed. By the end of the oven's useful life, they will be entirely used up. As this happens, the value of the asset decreases, and there is a corresponding reduction in equity, according to A − L = E. To report this decrease in equity through operating activities, an expense called 'depreciation' is processed, to match the gradual writing-off (that is, reduction) of the asset over its estimated useful life.

In the first of the oven's three years, one-third of the benefits are consumed, and so the decrease in the PPE asset and consequent depreciation expense amount to €40 (€120 ÷ 3 years), as shown in Summary of Event 9 below.

SUMMARY OF EVENT 9 The pizza oven has been used for one year of its expected three years.

Assets −	Liabilities =	Equity		Debit	Credit
− €40					PPE
		− €40 (expense)		Depreciation expense	

Depreciation is another example of accrual accounting because it involves reporting the effects of a business event—in this case, using the oven to make pizzas—when the event itself occurs, not when the cash changed hands.

The land purchased in Event 3 is not depreciated, as it has an unlimited useful life. That is, the economic benefits of the land will not be consumed, and so it would be unnecessary and inappropriate to reduce the amount at which it has been recorded.

The reduction in PPE means that the amount at which the oven is reported, or 'carried' in the accounting records, known as its **carrying amount**, decreases to its **depreciated cost** of €80. This reflects the fact that one-third of its benefits (for which €120 was paid) have been consumed. PPE on the statement of financial position will now be reported at €530, as it still includes €450 for the land.

As usual, the expense causes a decrease in retained earnings in Statement of Financial Position 8, which balances the €40 decrease of the same amount in the PPE asset.

Depreciation is the gradual reduction in the carrying amount of an asset to reflect the cost of using up the economic benefits it produces.

PB: STATEMENT OF FINANCIAL POSITION 8

			€
	Before Event 9	Event 9	After Event 9
Assets			
Non-current assets:			
Property, plant and equipment	570	− 40	530
Current assets:			
Inventories	20		20
Accounts receivable	150		150
Bank	190		190
Total assets	930	− 40	890
Equity and liabilities			
Equity:			
Share capital	600		600
Retained earnings	150	− 40	110
Non-current liabilities:			
Interest-bearing borrowings	100		100
Current liabilities:			
Accounts payable	80		80
Total equity and liabilities	930	− 40	890

One might expect that depreciation expense is included in the statement of comprehensive income as an operating expense. This would indeed be the case if, for example, the depreciated asset was a pizza delivery vehicle: then, we would see depreciation of €40 listed along with salaries and electricity. However, in this case, the depreciation is in fact included in cost of sales, as in Statement of Comprehensive Income 4.

PB: STATEMENT OF COMPREHENSIVE INCOME 4

	€
Revenue	300
Cost of sales (€60 + €40)	− 100
Gross profit	200
Operating expenses:	
Electricity	− 40
Salaries	− 50
Operating profit	110
Interest income	
Interest expense	
Profit before tax	110
Tax	
Profit	110

The pizza oven is required to make the inventory (that is, the pizza slices), and so the depreciation of the oven, just like the ingredients, is expensed as cost of sales to reflect the cost of making the pizza slices that have been sold.

The same logic applies to the salaries in Event 7: if they had been paid to people who rolled the pizza dough, added the toppings, or moved the pizzas in and out of the oven, those salaries would also have been expensed as cost of sales. For the sake of keeping things simple, our treatment of the salaries as an operating expense in section 2.2.7 assumed that they were paid to staff who were not involved with the making of pizza, like the people who take orders or work the cash register.

The use of estimates in accounting

Have you been wondering how it was determined that the pizza oven would last three years? We have now come to our first clear case of the exercise of judgement in accounting. To calculate depreciation, accountants are required to use their best estimate of the useful life of the asset, and in this case, the pizza oven was judged to be good for three years. But what if someone else thought that it would last two years, or four years, or perhaps even fifty years? All of these useful-life estimates might be valid, depending on the assumptions that are made, but they would produce wildly differing depreciation expense. A useful life of two years would give a yearly depreciation charge of €60 (€120 ÷ 2 years); four years would result in €30 depreciation per year (€120 ÷ 4 years); and so on. Of course, varying depreciation charges mean varying profit figures: had PB expensed €60 on depreciation this year, its profit would have been €90, whilst a depreciation charge of €30 would have meant profit of €120!

So which of these is the correct profit? Well, they all are! This is one of the most important things to realise about the profit figure in accounting; that it is dependent on the estimates and assumptions made by the preparers of the financial statements. And don't make the mistake of thinking that estimates are rare: in a real business, there are many items and issues that require estimates like this to be made.

Profit depends on estimates and assumptions—it is an opinion!

There is a good deal more to learn about depreciation, which we'll return to in section 6.2.2.

Depreciation vs impairment

At year-end, thanks to depreciation of €40, the carrying amount of the oven is €80. But what if it had been damaged in some way, and its value was only €20? In this case, we would 'write down' the oven by reducing PPE by a further €60 (credit), and report a revised carrying amount of €20 in the statement of financial position. This sort of write-down of an asset is called an '**impairment**' and its other effect is a €60 expense in the statement of comprehensive income (debit). In section 6.1.8 you will learn how this principle is common to all assets: accountants impair any asset whose actual value to the business is considered to be less than the amount at which it would otherwise be reported.

> **MISCONCEPTION**
>
> Depreciation and impairment are the same thing.
>
> Although they are very similar insofar as they both result in a decrease in the value of an asset (credit) and an expense in the statement of comprehensive income (debit), depreciation and impairment result from very different circumstances.
>
> Depreciation is the gradual and consistent writing-off of the asset over its useful life, whilst impairment is an unanticipated, usually one-off, event. Depreciation is caused by the routine consumption of the economic benefits inherent in the asset, whereas impairment is usually caused by an unexpected event that accelerates the decline in value of an asset. For example, if a tree falls on the pizza oven, or if a surge of low-carb dieters means that fewer pizza slices will be sold, then the resultant decline in the value of the oven would require an impairment.

2.2.10 Event 10: interest income

PB now receives €2 of interest, thanks to having a positive balance at the bank. The receipt of cash of course increases the bank asset, and so—in the absence of any other asset or any liabilities changing—equity also increases by €2. As this is not a capital contribution by the owner, it is income.

SUMMARY OF EVENT 10 PB earns interest of €2.

Assets	–	Liabilities	=	Equity		Debit	Credit
+ €2						Bank	
				+ €2 (income)			Interest income

This sort of interest income is unlikely to be treated as revenue by businesses, and so is part of what is sometimes called 'other income'. (Revenue is officially defined as 'income arising in the course of an entity's ordinary activities',[3] which is usually interpreted to imply that revenue is the income arising from the main ways in which a business seeks to create value. This, of course, excludes the interest earned on a business's bank account, although a bank, for example, may treat as revenue the interest it earns on the loans it grants. Also, a retailer whose business model involves large inflows of interest from credit customers may also categorise this interest income as revenue.)

On the statement of comprehensive income, it is typical to find interest income between the 'operating profit' and 'profit before tax' subtotals, as in Statement of Comprehensive Income 5.

PB: STATEMENT OF COMPREHENSIVE INCOME 5

	€
Revenue	300
Cost of sales	− 100
Gross profit	200
Operating expenses:	
Electricity	− 40
Salaries	− 50
Operating profit	110
Interest income	2
Interest expense	—
Profit before tax	112
Tax	—
Profit	112

2.2.11 Event 11: interest expense

One of the primary ways in which banks create value is by charging interest on the loans they grant to borrowers at a higher rate than they pay to their depositors (that is, the people and entities who deposit money with them). At year-end, PB has to pay a total of €7 of interest (€100 × 7%), which is the annual cost of the €100 loan raised in Event 2. By applying the same logic to this decrease in the bank asset (credit) as we did to the receipt of interest in Event 10, we know that the other effect of this transaction is an expense (debit), as shown in Summary of Event 11 below.

SUMMARY OF EVENT 11 PB pays interest of €7.

Assets	−	Liabilities	=	Equity		Debit	Credit
− €7							Bank
				− €7 (expense)		Interest expense	

Interest expense is also typically reported just above profit before tax, where it is often called 'finance costs'. Sometimes, the interest income (or 'finance income') and the interest expense are netted off (that is, one is subtracted from the other) in a single line-item with a name like 'net finance costs'. However, we have kept the reporting of interest in Statement of Comprehensive Income 6 as straightforward as we can.

2

PB: STATEMENT OF COMPREHENSIVE INCOME 6

	€
Revenue	300
Cost of sales	− 100
Gross profit	200
Operating expenses:	
Electricity	− 40
Salaries	− 50
Operating profit	110
Interest income	2
Interest expense	− 7
Profit before tax	105
Tax	
Profit	105

Statement of Financial Position 9 reveals the combined effects of Events 10 and 11: a net €5 decrease in the bank asset, and, thanks to the income and expense reported in profit or loss, an equivalent reduction in retained earnings.

PB: STATEMENT OF FINANCIAL POSITION 9

			R
	Before Events 10 and 11	Events 10 and 11	After Events 10 and 11
Assets			
Non-current assets:			
Property, plant and equipment	530		530
Current assets:			
Inventories	20		20
Accounts receivable	150		150
Bank	190	+ 2, − 7	185
Total assets	890	− 5	885
Equity and liabilities			
Equity:			
Share capital	600		600
Retained earnings	110	+ 2, − 7	105
Non-current liabilities:			
Interest-bearing borrowings	100		100
Current liabilities:			
Accounts payable	80		80
Total equity and liabilities	890	− 5	885

2.2.12 **Event 12: taxation**

We have reached the reporting date, and the statement of comprehensive income shows that the business has made a profit of €105. However, this is not the end of the story, as the tax authority will want its own slice of this profit, called '**income tax**'. The amount of tax that will have to be paid is not calculated simply as **accounting** profit multiplied by the applicable tax rate. On the contrary, the calculation of tax is extremely complicated. Tax is calculated by applying the tax rate to a business's taxable income, which is determined in accordance with the tax legislation in effect in the **jurisdiction(s)** in which the business operates.

> A business's income tax is not based on accounting profit. Rather, it is based on the rules for determining taxable income established by the country's tax legislation.

MISCONCEPTION

> If a company depreciates assets over a shorter period than their true useful life, this will reduce profit, and thereby reduce income tax.

This thinking results from two misconceptions. First, tax is not calculated using the profit-before-tax figure on a statement of comprehensive income. Rather, tax authorities have their own rules for determining taxable income. Second, they are not stupid: they do not allow these calculations to be influenced by companies' self-interested judgement. Instead, included in their rules are specific depreciation rates that must be used for each type of depreciable asset. This is one of the reasons that profit before tax and taxable income are seldom the same.

You will learn more about the complexities of accounting for taxation elsewhere in this book, particularly in sections 4.4.4 and 8.3. For the moment, we will make the simplifying assumptions that PB's profit before tax does in fact equal taxable income, and that the applicable corporate tax rate is 20%. Thus the amount of tax on the current year's profits would be €21 (€105 × 20%).

The tax calculation normally takes place after the year-end, as we first need to have a record of all the year's events before we can calculate tax. To make sure that tax is collected on time, tax authorities generally require businesses to make tax payments during the year based on estimates of what their final tax will be. In our example, though, we assume that PB has not done this, and so owes the full amount of tax at year-end. We record the tax due by increasing the current liability named tax payable (credit), and the consequent decrease in equity (debit) is named 'tax expense'.

SUMMARY OF EVENT 12 PB owes corporate income tax at a rate of 20%.

Assets	−	Liabilities	=	Equity		Debit	Credit
		+ €21					Tax payable
				− €21 (expense)		Tax expense	

Tax expense is shown near the bottom of Statement of Comprehensive Income 7, usually between 'Profit before tax' and the final profit figure. This shows clearly how the tax has reduced the business's profit to €84.

PB: STATEMENT OF COMPREHENSIVE INCOME 7

	€
Revenue	300
Cost of sales	− 100
Gross profit	200
Operating expenses:	
Electricity	− 40
Salaries	− 50
Operating profit	110
Interest income	2
Interest expense	− 7
Profit before tax	105
Tax	− 21
Profit	84

Just as it has decreased profit in the statement of comprehensive income, the tax expense will also reduce retained earnings in Statement of Financial Position 10 by €21.

PB: STATEMENT OF FINANCIAL POSITION 10

	Before Event 12	Event 12	€ After Event 12
Assets			
Non-current assets:			
Property, plant and equipment	530		530
Current assets:			
Inventories	20		20
Accounts receivable	150		150
Bank	185		185
Total assets	885	0	885
Equity and liabilities			
Equity:			
Share capital	600		600
Retained earnings	105	− 21	84
Non-current liabilities:			
Interest-bearing borrowings	100		100
Current liabilities:			
Accounts payable	80		80
Tax payable		+ 21	21
Total equity and liabilities	885	0	885

2.2.13 Event 13: revaluation gain

We remarked in our discussion of depreciation that the land, as a result of its infinite useful life, is not depreciated. You may wonder: what if the value of the land does what usually happens over time, and goes up? In fact, this is Event 13, when an expert determines that the market value of the land, which was acquired in Event 3 for €450, has risen to €500 at year-end.

The fact is that in the vast majority of cases, this information would have no effect on the financial statements, as most businesses choose an accounting policy for land which—at least until the land is sold—ignores increases in its value above its original cost. The land would continue to be reported on the statements of financial position of such businesses at the cost of €450.

However, businesses are sometimes allowed to make a choice between alternative **accounting policies**. If they report according to **IFRS**, for example, they may, subject to provisos that you will learn about in section 6.2.1, elect to increase the carrying amount of land to its market value. Suppose that PB has chosen this accounting policy. It must now increase its PPE asset by €50 (€500 − €450). This increase in an asset (without an equivalent decrease in an asset or increase in a liability) causes an increase in equity. Recall from section 2.1.2 that the only type of increase in equity not treated as income is an increase caused by a contribution made by the owner, and so the increase of €50 is quite clearly income.

> **MISCONCEPTION**
>
> The increase in the carrying amount of PPE should not be reported as income because it is **unrealised** (that is, it has not yet been obtained in cash).
>
> Incorrect. Recall that we report other unrealised increases in equity, such as credit sales, as income. Whether an item should be treated as income does not depend on whether cash is received; it depends purely on whether the definition of income is met. As long as some change in assets and/or liabilities causes an increase in equity, and this change is not caused by a capital contribution, then income has been earned, and must be reported.

The term often used to refer to the sort of income that arises as a result of an increase in the value of an asset is '**gain**', and so this particular item of income is usually called a '**revaluation** gain' as in Summary of Event 13.

SUMMARY OF EVENT 13 The land has a market value of €500 at the end of Year 1.

Assets	−	Liabilities	=	Equity		Debit	Credit
+ €50						PPE	
				+ €50 (income)			Revaluation gain

On the statement of comprehensive income, one might expect the revaluation gain to be inserted at some point above the profit figure, so that it increases profit. For reasons that we will explore in section 4.2, this is not what happens. Instead, it is treated as an item of 'other comprehensive income' or 'OCI', which appears below the profit figure in an extra section of the statement of comprehensive income known as the 'Other comprehensive income' or 'OCI' section, as in Statement of Comprehensive Income 8.

PB: STATEMENT OF COMPREHENSIVE INCOME 8

	€	
Revenue	300	
Cost of sales	− 100	
Gross profit	200	
Operating expenses:		
Electricity	− 40	
Salaries	− 50	Items of income and expense which appear
Operating profit	110	here are described as being reported 'in
Interest income	2	profit or loss'.
Interest expense	−7	
Profit before tax	105	
Tax	− 21	
Profit	84	
Other comprehensive income:		Items which appear here are described as
Revaluation gain	50	being reported 'in other comprehensive
Total comprehensive income	134	income', or 'in OCI'.

A gain on the revaluation of PPE is the first item of income or expense we have come across which should be reported in OCI rather than in profit or loss. Of the multitude of events that affect the financial statements, only a handful of items of income and expense are reported in OCI. We will introduce the others in section 4.8, and cover each in detail as they arise from the material in Chapters 6–10.

Note that the line-item 'Total comprehensive income' is the sum of the profit for the period and all the items of other comprehensive income (although in this case, of course, there is only one: the revaluation gain). Thus, total income less total expenses equals total comprehensive income, which therefore reflects the net amount by which equity—the book value of the business—has changed during the reporting period, not counting contributions by, and distributions to, owners. Technically, therefore, total comprehensive income might be superior to profit as a measure of the value created by a business.

However, the fact is that the notion of comprehensive income is quite new, and many professional accountants, financial analysts, and business leaders are unconvinced by the informational value of the items of OCI. We expect that it will be some time before this rather awkward term replaces the universally familiar phrase 'profit' as a popular shorthand to describe the creation of business value.

Just as items of OCI have a substantially different effect on the statement of comprehensive income than items of profit or loss, the same is true on the statement of financial position. Whereas all items of profit or loss ultimately affect retained earnings, the items of OCI generally affect different equity accounts in the statement of financial position. In the case of revaluation gains (and losses), their effects are captured in the 'revaluation surplus' account, as can be seen in Statement of Financial Position 11.

PB: STATEMENT OF FINANCIAL POSITION 11

		€	
	Before Event 13	Event 13	After Event 13
Assets			
Non-current assets:			
Property, plant and equipment	530	+ 50	580
Current assets:			
Inventories	20		20
Accounts receivable	150		150
Bank	185		185
Total assets	885	+ 50	935
Equity and liabilities			
Equity:			
Share capital	600		600
Retained earnings	84		84
Revaluation surplus		+ 50	50
Non-current liabilities:			
Interest-bearing borrowings	100		100
Current liabilities:			
Accounts payable	80		80
Tax payable	21		21
Total equity and liabilities	885	+ 50	935

2.2.14 Event 14: dividends

Whether you choose profit or total comprehensive income as the measure of value creation, the fact that both are positive implies that value has been created. The business must decide how much of this value should be distributed to the owners and how much should be retained, or re-invested, in the business. In other words, a dividend decision needs to be made.

The dividend decision should be made after a clear-headed analysis of the growth prospects of the business, the expectations of the owners, and contextual factors, including, for example, that the revaluation gain has not increased the amount of available cash and should therefore not be considered a good source for a distribution. In this case, hopefully after a thorough analysis, PB declares a €20 dividend, to be paid in the next financial year.

Once the dividends have been declared, they are owed to the shareholders. As they have not been paid by the year-end, a current liability must be created (credit) to recognise this obligation. The standard name for this liability account is called 'shareholders for dividend'.

As no other assets or liabilities have changed, this is a decrease in equity. At this point, you may be expecting that these dividends will be treated as an expense, but recall that the definition of an expense specifically excludes distributions to owners (see section 2.1.2). The definitions of income and expense exclude transfers of value between the owners and the business so that they measure only increases and decreases in the amount of value created by the business. Dividends, for example, simply transfer the value generated by the business from the business's bank account to the owners' personal bank accounts. They thus do not reflect the financial performance of the business and they are not an expense.

As only income and expenses appear in the statement of comprehensive income, the dividend is not reported there. Instead, the dividend simply bypasses the statement of comprehensive income and directly reduces the retained earnings figure in the statement of financial position (debit), as depicted in Summary of Event 14 below. In Chapter 10, you will learn more about the **financial reporting** of dividends, including how the dividend amount can be seen on the statement of changes in equity.

> Dividends are not an expense and are not shown in the statement of comprehensive income.

SUMMARY OF EVENT 14 Dividends of €20 are declared, to be paid next year.

Assets	– Liabilities	= Equity		Debit	Credit
	+ €20				Shareholders for dividend
		– €20		Retained earnings	

We can now draft the statement of financial position at the end of Year 1, which shows the liability to shareholders as well as the final retained earnings figure for the year.

PB: STATEMENT OF FINANCIAL POSITION

			€
as at the end of Year 1	Before Event 14	Event 14	After Event 14
Assets			
Non-current assets:			
Property, plant and equipment	580		580
Current assets:			
Inventories	20		20
Accounts receivable	150		150
Bank	185		185
Total assets	935	0	935
Equity and liabilities			
Equity:			
Share capital	600		600
Retained earnings	84	– 20	64
Revaluation surplus	50		50
Non-current liabilities:			
Interest-bearing borrowings	100		100
Current liabilities:			
Accounts payable	80		80
Tax payable	21		21
Shareholders for dividend		+ 20	20
Total equity and liabilities	935	0	935

As dividends are not reported on the statement of comprehensive income, the final Statement of Comprehensive Income for Year 1 is unchanged by the dividend declaration, but we nevertheless present it here for completeness.

PB: STATEMENT OF COMPREHENSIVE INCOME

for Year 1	€
Revenue	300
Cost of sales	− 100
Gross profit	200
Operating expenses:	
Electricity	− 40
Salaries	− 50
Operating profit	110
Interest income	2
Interest expense	− 7
Profit before tax	105
Tax	− 21
Profit	84
Other comprehensive income:	
Revaluation gain	50
Total comprehensive income	134

It is worth noting that in reality, a dividend is often declared after the year-end, once the profits for that year have been finalised. In this case, no dividend would be reported in the current year (that is, *this* year), and instead the dividend would be mentioned in the **notes** to the financial statements. The transaction would only be recorded and reported in the following year, when the dividend is declared. The logic behind this is that there is no obligation to pay the dividend at the current year-end, so no liability—and no corresponding decrease in retained earnings—should be recognised.

2.2.15 **The statement of cash flows**

PB's statement of comprehensive income for Year 1 reports that the business made a profit of €84, but because of accrual accounting (see section 2.2.8), this will not be the amount of cash generated during the year. The alternative to accrual accounting is the **cash basis of accounting**, which accounts purely for cash inflows and outflows. Table 2.2 shows how each of the items affecting PB's financial statements affect profit, determined using accrual accounting, and cash flow, using the cash basis. Those items which lead to differences between profit and cash flow have been shaded.

The overall effect in the middle column is the €84 profit for the year shown in the statement of comprehensive income. The aggregate effect in the third column is the €185 net increase in cash for the period, shown on the statement of cash flows that we will prepare next.

The statement of cash flows reports only the actual cash that came into, and went out of, the business during the year.

TABLE 2.2 The effects on profit and cash flow of each of PB's events; items treated differently are shaded

Item	Effect on profit (accrual accounting)	Effect on cash flow (cash basis of accounting)
Capital contribution (Event 1)	No effect; no income or expense	Increase of €600; cash received from owners
Loan (Event 2)	No effect; no income or expense	Increase of €100; cash received from lender
Land (Events 3 and 13)	No effect; as an item of OCI, the revaluation gain does not affect profit	Decrease of €450; cash paid to acquire
Pizza oven (Events 3 and 9)	Decrease of €40; depreciation included in cost of sales expense	Decrease of €120; cash paid to acquire
Cost of inventory (Events 4 and 6)	Decrease of €60; inventory consumed included in cost of sales expense	Decrease of €40; amount paid for cash purchases
Sale of inventory (Event 5)	Increase of €300; revenue	Increase of €150; amount received for cash sales
Salaries (Event 7)	Decrease of €50; salaries expense	Decrease of €50; amount paid to employees
Electricity (Event 8)	Decrease of €40; electricity expense	No effect; no cash yet paid
Interest (Events 10 and 11)	Net decrease of €5; interest expense of €7 less interest income of €2	Net decrease of €5; interest paid of €7 less interest received of €2
Tax (Event 12)	Decrease of €21; tax expense	No effect; no cash yet paid
Dividends (Event 14)	No effect; dividends are not expenses	No effect; no cash yet paid
Total effect	**€84 profit**	**€185 net cash inflow**

Fortunately, the statement of cash flows is simple to understand: because it is prepared on the cash basis, it reports no more and no less than the cash flows that came into, and went out of, the business during the year. These cash flows are then listed in a structured fashion to distinguish between those cash flows that relate to operating, investing and financing activities, as in Statement of Cash Flows for Year 1.

PB: STATEMENT OF CASH FLOWS

for Year 1	€
Operating activities:	
Cash received from customers	150
Cash paid to suppliers and employees	− 90
Cash generated from operations	60
Interest received	2
Interest paid	− 7
Tax paid	
Net cash from operating activities	55
Investing activities:	
Acquisition of property and equipment	− 570
Net cash from investing activities	− 570
Financing activities:	
Issue of shares	600
Dividends paid	
Borrowings raised	100
Net cash from financing activities	700
Net increase in cash	185
Cash at beginning of period	0
Cash at end of period	185

Cash flows from operating activities are listed first. They describe the cash inflows and outflows directly relating to the making and selling of pizza slices.

The first line shows the amount of cash received from customers; that is, the €150 received for the fifty pizza slices sold for cash in Event 5. The other fifty pizza slices were sold on credit and so do not appear on the statement of cash flows. When those receivables are collected (presumably in Year 2), the cash inflow will be recorded in the statement of cash flows for that period. Alternatively, if a debtor **defaults** and the business never actually receives the cash for that sale, then the amount would never appear in the statement of cash flows.

The second line shows the amount of cash paid to suppliers and employees of the business. In PB, this €90 consists of the €40 paid for ingredients in Event 4 (as the other €40 was on credit) and the €50 of salaries paid to employees in Event 7. Had any of these amounts not been paid, they would not appear in the statement of cash flows, just as the unpaid electricity bill of €40 is not included here, despite the fact that it was reported as an expense in the statement of comprehensive income. The electricity payment would only appear in the statement of cash flows in the year that it is actually paid.

The next few lines of the statement of cash flows relate to interest received, interest paid, and tax paid, except that no amount is shown for tax paid because the tax due has not yet been settled. We would expect to see tax paid of (at least) €21 appearing in Year 2's statement of cash flows.

Thus, the total cash received from operating activities (the making and selling of pizza slices) was €55. The depreciation expense of €40 (Event 9) and the revaluation gain of €50 (Event 13) are not shown in the statement of cash flows as they are not cash flow items.

The only cash flow that has occurred with respect to these non-current assets occurred when €570 was paid to acquire them (Event 3). This event is disclosed in the statement of cash flows, but in the investing activities section in the line 'Acquisition of property and equipment'.

As its name suggests, the financing activities section reports those cash flows related to the funding provided from owners and lenders. In PB, the issue of shares in Event 1 for €600 and the borrowings of €100 from the bank in Event 2 are cash flows that fall under financing activities. If some of the borrowings during the year had been repaid, the cash outflow would also appear in the financing activities section. No dividends paid amount appears in PB's statement of cash flows, as the dividend declared this year will only be paid next year.

Finally, the statement of cash flows aggregates the net cash flows from each section, and reports the net increase (or decrease) in cash for the year. In PB, operating and financing cash inflows of €55 and €700 respectively more than funded the outflow consumed by investing activities of €570, producing a net cash inflow of €185. Adding this amount to the cash balance at the beginning of the year (which was nil, as this is the first year of business) gives a closing cash balance of €185. It is no accident that this is the amount reported as the bank balance in the statement of financial position at year-end.

As discussed in section 1.3.4, to assess a business's creation of value, it is immensely important to consider not only profit, but also cash flows, and so the statement of cash flows is a vital component of the financial statements. Because the statement is organised according to the phases of the value creation cycle, it straightforwardly maps onto Figure 1.4 (see section 1.3.1), allowing us to quickly illustrate the business's overall value creation from a cash perspective, as follows in Figure 2.2.

FIGURE 2.2 Overview of PB's Year 1 value creation cycle, from a cash perspective

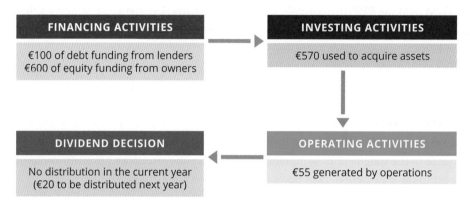

It is worth noting that the investing activities section of the statement of cash flows does not include every cash outflow to acquire assets; instead, it mainly includes only payments for non-current assets. Payments for inventory and most other current assets are reported under operating activities. This is because the operating activities section shows all day-to-day cash inflows and outflows involved in the making and selling of goods and services. Section 5.4 will demonstrate why this is the most useful way to present these payments.

The information in the statement of financial position and statement of comprehensive income is also essential to a full evaluation of the business's value creation cycle, but they do not map so easily onto Figure 1.4. Now that you have seen them in action, we encourage you to go back to section 1.4.3 to consolidate your high-level, contextual understanding of what the financial statements report.

We shall return to this topic in section 11.2.1 on financial analysis, where we will demonstrate how to understand that the entire story of the business is told by the financial statements working together.

2.2.16 **Year 2's financial statements**

We have now accounted for all the events that occurred in PB's first year of business. What would you need to know to prepare financial statements for the second year?

The most important thing to realise is that the statement of comprehensive income and statement of cash flows show only what happened in each financial year (as mentioned in section 1.4.3, they are analogous to a movie of the year's activities), and, as such, Year 2's statement of comprehensive income should report only Year 2's income and expenses, and the statement of cash flows should report only Year 2's cash flows.

However, the statement of financial position, the 'snapshot' at the reporting date, includes the effects of all of the business's transactions from its very first transaction. To prepare the statement of financial position at the end of Year 2, the accountant would start with the previous year's closing balances, use them as Year 2's opening balances, and then add the effects of Year 2's events to these opening balances. For example, if the business purchased another item of PPE in Year 2, say a vehicle for €60, this amount would be added onto the PPE opening balance of €580, resulting in a new PPE balance of €640. The pizza oven and the vehicle would then be depreciated in Year 2, resulting in a closing balance in the statement of financial position for PPE of something less than €640, unless the fair value of the land increases again. This process continues throughout the life of the business, with amounts in the statement of financial position continually being adjusted as events occur.

To put it another way, the statement of financial position shows the balances on the various asset, liability, and equity accounts and, like your own personal bank balance, which does not start at zero each year, these balances continue to increase or decrease as events occur.

This principle is no less true for the retained earnings account. At the end of Year 1, the retained earnings balance of €64 amounted to the profit made during the year minus the dividend declared. The opening balance for Year 2 would be this closing balance of €64, increased by Year 2's profit and decreased by Year 2's dividend. This ultimately means that at the end of any reporting period, the retained earnings account represents all the profits that the business has ever made since it started, less all the dividends that it has ever declared. This explains fully why the account is usually called either 'Retained earnings' or 'Accumulated profits'.

> Whereas the statement of comprehensive income and the statement of cash flows start from zero each year, the balances on the statement of financial position are carried forward to the next year.

MISCONCEPTION

When retained earnings are very high, the business should return these profits, or some of them, to the owners.

No, a business cannot really return profits to the owners: only assets, usually cash, can be given to the owners. And it is very unlikely that the retained earnings are matched by a similar cash balance. After all, these earnings have been retained by the business in order to fund assets. To return retained earnings to the owners, the business would need to transfer to them the assets funded by retained earnings, or sell these assets and return the cash thus obtained; but that would deprive the business of the assets it needs to operate.

CONCLUSION

Hopefully this chapter has given you a basic understanding of accounting, if only so that you can tell the difference between assets, liabilities, equity, income, and expense; know what simple financial statements look like; and feel that you are beginning to understand how figures make their way onto these financial statements.

2

If you would like to go over some fresh examples of transactions like we have seen in this chapter, you will find an exercise with the **online resources** (www.oup.com/he/winfield-graham-miller1e) which sets out PB's hypothetical Year 2, with worked examples of how each transaction would be reported in the financial statements.

In Chapters 4–10, we will go into much more detail about far more complex business events and how they are required to be reported in the financial statements. First, though, in Chapter 3 we will explore the origin, evolution, and current status of all of these reporting requirements.

SUMMARY OF KEY POINTS

- The inputs into a financial accounting system are transactions and other business events; the outputs are the financial statements.
- Assets, liabilities, equity, income, and expense are the five elements of an accounting system.
- One formulation of the accounting equation states that A = E + L. The statement of financial position is laid out according to this formulation. Another formulation states that A – L = E, which is helpful for identifying the effect of assets and liabilities on equity.
- Income and expenses are increases and decreases in equity that are not the result of transactions directly with owners.
- Accounting information relating to each item of assets, liabilities, equity, income, and expense is stored in an account for that item. Accounts change by being debited or credited according to the convention shown in Table 2.1.
- The double-entry system involves recording a transaction by debiting one account and crediting another account. Unless an error has been made, the debits always equal the credits.
- The statement of financial position reports assets, liabilities, and equity at the reporting date.
- Current assets are expected to be consumed during the next twelve months; non-current assets are expected to take longer to be consumed.
- Current liabilities are expected to be settled within the next twelve months; non-current liabilities are expected to be settled over a longer period.
- The statement of comprehensive income reports income and expenses for the reporting period.
- Revenue is income earned in the ordinary course of a business's activities. It appears at the top of the statement of comprehensive income.
- Broadly speaking, profit is the result of subtracting cost of sales, net operating costs, net interest expense, and tax expense from revenue. These items are all referred to as items of profit or loss.
- Depreciation is a process of gradually writing off an item of PPE as it is used, resulting in an expense charged over the useful life of the asset. It is different from impairment, which is an unexpected reduction in the value of the asset (eg because of damage), also resulting in an expense.
- Income tax is not charged on a business's accounting profit, but is instead calculated using the complex rules contained in tax legislation. It is, however, an expense of the business.

2

- All items of profit or loss flow through to retained earnings in the equity section of the statement of financial position. Dividends, which are not an expense, are subtracted directly from retained earnings without first appearing in the statement of comprehensive income.
- Some items of income and expense (eg revaluation gains on PPE) are designated as other comprehensive income and appear in their own section below profit on a statement of comprehensive income, followed by total comprehensive income. They also flow to their own equity account on the statement of financial position (eg revaluation surplus).
- The statement of financial position and statement of comprehensive income are prepared using the concept of accrual accounting, according to which the effects of transactions are reported when the transactions themselves occur, not necessarily when cash changes hands. Thus, a credit sale's revenue and cost of sales are reported when it occurs, even though there is no cash flow.
- The statement of cash flows is prepared on the cash basis of accounting, which means that it reports only cash inflows and outflows for the reporting period. It separately groups those cash flows that relate to operating, investing, and financing activities.
- Whereas the statement of comprehensive income and the statement of cash flows start from zero each year, the balances on the statement of financial position are carried forward to the next year.

CHAPTER QUESTIONS

The suggested solutions to the concept questions (marked 'CQ') can be found in Appendix III. Also, don't forget the **online resources** available at www.oup.com/he/winfield-graham-miller1e, which contain multiple-choice questions based on the material in this chapter, and a worked example of Year 2 of the Pizza Business, in addition to many other helpful resources.

CONCEPT QUESTIONS

CQ 2.1   Identify and briefly describe the five accounting elements which make up financial statements prepared according to accrual accounting.

CQ 2.2   The 'E' in the accounting equation stands for 'equity'. Explain how the term 'equity' is best understood in each of the following formulations of the accounting equation: $A = E + L$ and $A - L = E$. Write a short paragraph for each explanation.

CQ 2.3   Briefly explain the term 'accrual accounting' and use an example to support your explanation.

CQ 2.4   Do items that appear on the statement of comprehensive income also affect the statement of financial position? Explain your answer.

CQ 2.5   Describe how the statement of comprehensive income differs from the statement of cash flows.

INVESTIGATION QUESTIONS

IQ 2.6   Identify a **listed** retail company that is based in your country and obtain its financial statements. (They can usually be found quickly via an internet search using

2

the term 'financial statements' and the company's name.) Examine this company's financial statements and identify as many items on the statement of financial position, statement of comprehensive income, and statement of cash flows as you can understand after reading this chapter. (There will be many items with which you are still unfamiliar. Don't panic: most, if not all, of them will be covered in the remaining chapters of this book!)

IQ 2.7   You may be surprised to discover that accounting has had a major influence on the course of history. For example, the most ancient form of writing—cuneiform—was in fact a system of accounting.[4] Also, the development of double-entry bookkeeping is widely regarded as being one of the catalysts that helped to enable the rise of global capitalism. Do some research to find out how and where double-entry bookkeeping arose and to explain how it had such a profound impact on the world.

IQ 2.8   The calculation of profit depends on a wide range of estimates and assumptions made by the preparer. For example, the best estimate of the useful life of an asset determines how much depreciation expense is charged to the statement of comprehensive income each year. Do you think that this flexibility is appropriate, or should there be a clear set of rules in determining profit, to negate the need for estimates and assumptions?

REFERENCES

[1]   IASB 2018. *Conceptual Framework for Financial Reporting.* Section 4.2.

[2]   IASB 2018. *Conceptual Framework for Financial Reporting.* Section 1.17.

[3]   IASB 2015. *IFRS 15: Revenue from Contracts with Customers.* Definitions section.

[4]   Harford, T 2017. 'The Earliest Accountants Were the True Authors of Writing'. *Accounting and Business.* October. Available at: https://www.accaglobal.com/my/en/member/member/accounting-business/2017/10/insights/cuneiform-writing.html.

FINANCIAL REPORTING STANDARDS

Here are some of the things you will be able to do after reading this chapter:

- explain the reasons for, and nature of, the regulation of financial reporting;
- describe a brief history of the harmonisation of accounting standards;
- discuss the development of IFRS and its current state of adoption by listed companies and other public interest entities around the world;
- distinguish from IFRS the sorts of reporting requirements that apply to smaller businesses, including IFRS for SMEs and examples of standards released by national standard-setters;
- present some common critiques of IFRS and the IASB's response to some of these critiques.

Chapter 1 identified the users of **financial statements** as existing and potential investors, and lenders and other creditors. In other words, financial reporting is for people external to the reporting **entity**, who may very well be looking at the financial statements of many different companies in order to identify those which are suitable investment opportunities.

Chapter 2 mentioned that, even in the simplest of hypothetical businesses, financial accounting requires judgement (eg in calculating depreciation estimates) and also that there is not always consensus about reporting methods (eg the designation of some items of income and expense as other comprehensive income). The scope for differences of opinion is only compounded in real-world businesses, which often enter into complicated transactions involving sophisticated assets and liabilities in complex scenarios. Accounting is not nearly as cut-and-dried as most people imagine!

There is thus a tension inherent in financial reporting. On one hand, to best inform users' decisions they should be as accurate a report of the business's activities as possible. This suggests that each business's accountants should be given wide discretion to

3

prepare their financial statements in whatever way they think most effectively achieves this goal. On the other hand, the users of financial statements need them to be similar enough from one business to another to be comparable, and familiar enough that they can be understood relatively quickly. If financial reporting were left up to each business's accountants, their subjectivity would result in financial statements that are too dissimilar to meet this need. (Note that this is true even assuming that every accountant makes their financial reporting decisions in good faith. This is not always the case, as we shall discuss in Chapter 13.)

To resolve this tension, financial reporting has been regulated. In any economy—no matter where it falls on the spectrum between capitalism and socialism—there is regulation. Regulation conveys many benefits. For example, it is the reason that you can take medication knowing that it has been thoroughly tested; that you are not overcharged for basic utilities; and that there are not more plane crashes. It is also the source of many (sometimes frustrating) responsibilities: working people have to pay tax; we all fill out more forms than we would like; and, if you were to start a business, you would need to interact with a long and probably exhausting list of government departments.

Regulation of financial reporting ensures that businesses prepare financial statements that are comparable, using principles and practices with which users of the financial statements are familiar.

Regulation involves both the setting and enforcement of accounting standards.

Perhaps depending on your political persuasions, you may believe that the benefits of certain regulation are outweighed by the frustrations, but there are some forms of regulation whose overall value ought to be uncontested. One of these is aeroplane safety standards. Another is standardised financial reporting. Even the most die-hard capitalists want to be able to travel safely and make well-informed choices about how and where to invest their wealth. We can all agree, therefore, that all businesses should report financial information according to a well-devised set of accounting practices.

Financial reporting regulation has to achieve two major tasks: first, establish the standards according to which businesses should report; and second, enforce these standards. The methods of enforcement vary from one **jurisdiction** to another, but they generally rely on a mix of company law, stock exchange oversight bodies, and governmental and non-governmental regulatory agencies. Chapter 13 discusses various breaches of the accounting rules and the regulatory response.

In this chapter, we will examine the first task of regulation, briefly exploring the origin of **international financial reporting standards (IFRS)**, and the current state of standardisation across the world.

3.1 FINANCIAL REPORTING STANDARDS IN THE TWENTIETH CENTURY

Because the benefits of standardisation are so obvious, regulation about how to prepare financial statements has been around for many decades. Historically, company law and stock exchange rules have dictated broad financial reporting requirements, but the detail has been left to a designated standard-setting body that specialises in developing comprehensive guidance about how to report. This guidance has become known as 'generally accepted accounting practice', or 'GAAP'.

GAAP really consists of a set of documents known as accounting standards, or—more correctly—financial reporting standards. Each standard tends to deal with a single area of accounting, though the areas can and do overlap. For example, standards might prescribe: how to report items of property, plant and equipment; when to report income from the sale of a business's products; what format the financial statements ought to use; and how to account for payments and receipts in foreign currencies.

During the twentieth century, these financial reporting standards were developed within each country by national standard-setters. This should not be surprising, for most regulation is implemented at the state level. However, the requirements of these various national accounting standards were often quite different from one jurisdiction to another, and so an event that would lead to a certain accounting treatment in one country could lead to quite different treatments elsewhere.

The extent to which the figures produced under different reporting regimes differed only really became clear in the early 1990s as the globalisation of business began to intensify. At this time, Daimler-Benz, the German automobile manufacturer, wanted to list its shares on the New York Stock Exchange in order to gain access to the US capital market. The company's financial statements, prepared in accordance with German GAAP, would not have made much sense to US investors, who were familiar with financial statements prepared according to US accounting standards. Consequently, the US authorities required Daimler-Benz to prepare another set of financial statements in accordance with US GAAP. This was one of the first times that a large business had had to prepare financial statements for exactly the same period but using two separate sets of accounting standards, and the results of the exercise were surprising, to say the least.

Using German GAAP, Daimler-Benz made a respectable profit for the 1993 financial year, which, translated into dollars, amounted to $360.3 million. However, when US GAAP was used to calculate Daimler-Benz's profits *for exactly the same events in exactly the same period*, the result morphed into a loss of $1.08 billion![1]

You may be wondering: which of these two amounts was correct? The answer is that, according to the principles and rules of accounting in the respective countries, both were correct. Of course, it is possible for one set of guidelines to be better than another, but the grey areas of accounting are so wide that it is quite possible to argue that neither German nor US GAAP was superior to the other.

Accelerating globalisation meant that, like Daimler-Benz, businesses were increasingly needing to report and raise capital in jurisdictions other than their own. Not only was preparing multiple sets of financial reports extremely expensive, but also, after the Daimler-Benz fiasco, it became clear that the convention of using national accounting standards—with their wildly differing effects—could not continue. All of the disparate and incongruent GAAP from around the world sorely needed to be harmonised.

Standard-setting has historically been the task of national standard-setters, who have produced 'generally accepted accounting practice', or 'GAAP', for their own jurisdictions.

3.2 **INTERNATIONAL HARMONISATION**

In 1995, the then International Accounting Standards Committee (IASC) began the process of producing a core set of accounting standards that could form the basis for financial reporting by multinational companies with cross-border listings. When in 2001 the **International Accounting Standards Board**, or **IASB**, replaced the IASC, significant strides were made in this endeavour.

The IASB's objective is to develop a single set of high-quality, understandable, enforceable, and globally accepted financial reporting standards based on clearly articulated principles. These standards are known as '**International Financial Reporting Standards**', or '**IFRS**'. The IASB comprises fourteen members, representing every habitable continent, who are selected and overseen by the trustees of the IFRS Foundation. The Foundation is an independent, not-for-profit, private-sector organisation working in the public interest, comprising a geographically diverse body of twenty trustees. It is funded by major accounting firms, private financial institutions, industrial companies, and other international and professional organisations. The IASB is supported in its work by various bodies and committees to try to achieve its goal of global acceptance of the standards it produces.

The IASB's website (www.ifrs.org) provides an interactive map, a version of which is shown here as Figure 3.1, to check the status of IFRS adoption in every country.[2] In 2018, the IFRS Foundation reported that 144 of the world's accounting jurisdictions now require that IFRS is used by all **public interest entities** (**PIEs**) in countries which designate PIEs, and by all listed companies in other countries.[3] An additional twelve jurisdictions (notably including Switzerland) permit—but do not require—such companies to use IFRS. Only a handful of jurisdictions neither require nor permit IFRS for their public companies and instead use their own national standards. These include Bolivia, Egypt, Indonesia, Macao, the United States, and Vietnam. (One of these should stand out because of its immense economic size. We will return to it in section 3.3.) Technically, China and India have also not adopted IFRS, but since 2007 their national standards have been almost identical to IFRS. A large portion of the Chinese market reports using IFRS anyway, due to dual listings in Hong Kong and other IFRS-compliant markets.

The extraordinary success of the IASB in meeting its objective of worldwide adoption—with that one important exception we are about to discuss—has not been easy to achieve. The international community consists of a broad array of cultures, business forms, languages, and opinions on the right way to do accounting. For example, Christopher Nobes, in the fascinating little book *Accounting: A Very Short Introduction*, explains how 'the EU had always been opposed to the IASC, as a Trojan horse of Anglo-American accounting, but eventually it accepted IFRS as the only practical way of getting harmonised standards for EU capital markets'. Nobes also observes that 'the inability of governments in Roman law countries (e.g. France) to give up control of accounting has led to constant attempts at political interference from the EU in the operations of the IASB. For example, under political pressure, the IASB changed IAS 39 [the previous accounting standard for financial instruments]'.[4]

The IASB's objective is to develop a single set of high-quality, understandable, enforceable, and globally accepted financial reporting standards based on clearly articulated principles.

More than 140 countries require listed companies and other public interest entities to use IFRS.

FIGURE 3.1 The countries (in blue) that require domestic public companies to use IFRS

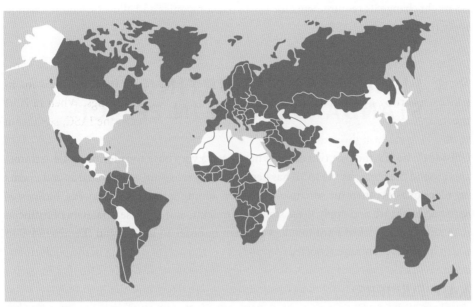

Source: Copyright © 2019 of the IFRS Foundation.

3.3 US GAAP

One of the major challenges to the IASB's objective has been gaining the support of the US standard-setters, who have strongly resisted giving up their own national standards. These are known as 'FASBs' (pronounced 'faz-bees') after the **Financial Accounting Standards Board (FASB)**, the US standard-setting body. However, in 2002, shortly after the collapse of several major businesses amidst high-profile accounting scandals (such as Enron's, covered in Chapter 13), they agreed to work together with the IASB to remove differences between IFRS and their own standards.

This process, commonly referred to as 'convergence', has not happened quickly. Perhaps the largest obstacle is that the two regimes have approached standard-setting in two fundamentally different ways: IFRS takes a 'principles-based' approach, giving companies some degree of latitude to make judgements about how best to present and quantify their financial information. On the whole, the US standards are 'rules-based' and tend to give fewer options. The nature of rules is that they leave far less to discretion than principles, and attempt to cover every eventuality.[5] You might think IFRS is long at nearly 2 000 pages, but perhaps not when you hear that US GAAP consists of 2 000 separate documents, many of which are hundreds of pages long![6]

US GAAP is rules-based, whereas IFRS is principles-based.

Until 2007, US authorities insisted that non-US companies which were listed in the US and which reported in terms of IFRS should reconcile various amounts in their financial statements to the amounts that would be obtained under US GAAP. This reconciliation process had long been a major deterrent for non-US companies wanting to list in the US. A major milestone was achieved in 2007, when this requirement was scrapped. However, despite mixed messaging from US authorities, it is unclear whether, when, or how the US might change its requirements for US-based companies and allow or require them to apply IFRS instead of FASBs.

3.4 FINANCIAL REPORTING STANDARDS NOW IN EFFECT

Outside of the US, the past two decades have been a very busy time for financial accountants around the globe, as the IASB has been regularly releasing new standards and updating older ones. As their jurisdictions have been adopting the IFRS standards, businesses have had to absorb and apply these standards quickly, and likewise, the users of financial statements have worked hard to adapt to them in order to understand the new ways in which business events are reported.

3.4.1 Full IFRS

The IFRS standards required to be applied by the largest companies are more precisely known as 'full IFRS'. They currently comprise over forty standards and more than twenty interpretations of these standards. In addition, at any point in time a number of draft standards (known as exposure drafts) are in issue which, once approved, will be issued as standards. The IASB is also working on a number of other issues which have not yet resulted in draft standards (more on this in Chapter 14).

Table 3.1 shows a list of all the IFRS standards issued up to the end of March 2020.

The first item in the list, the 'Conceptual Framework for Financial Reporting', or 'Conceptual Framework' for short, is not technically an accounting standard, but we have included it because it is the cornerstone of IFRS. The Conceptual Framework deals with a host of foundational issues, which impact all the accounting standards below it in the list. For example, it contains the definitions of income and expense that were covered in section 2.1.2. Similarly, Sections 6.1 and 7.1 will describe several general principles used to account for assets and liabilities, most of which come from the Conceptual Framework.

The role of the other forty-five or so documents in the list is—for the topics they cover—to provide specific guidance that is not provided in the Conceptual Framework.

3.4.2 IFRS for SMEs

As you might have guessed after seeing such a long list of IFRS standards, it is burdensome to prepare financial statements in accordance with full IFRS. For very large businesses, the burden is justified, given the enormous influence they have on the public interest.

TABLE 3.1 The accounting standards which make up 'full IFRS'

Conceptual Framework for Financial Reporting	IAS 16 Property, Plant and Equipment
IFRS 1 First-Time Adoption of International Financial Reporting Standards	IAS 17 Leases
	IAS 18 Revenue
IFRS 2 Share-Based Payment	IAS 19 Employee Benefits
IFRS 3 Business Combinations	IAS 20 Accounting for Government Grants and Disclosure of Government Assistance
IFRS 4 Insurance Contracts	
IFRS 5 Non-Current Assets Held for Sale and Discontinued Operations	IAS 21 The Effects of Changes in Foreign Exchange Rates
	IAS 23 Borrowing Costs
IFRS 6 Exploration for and Evaluation of Mineral Resources	IAS 24 Related Party Disclosures
IFRS 7 Financial Instruments: Disclosures	IAS 26 Accounting and Reporting by Retirement Benefit Plans
IFRS 8 Operating Segments	
IFRS 9 Financial Instruments	IAS 27 Separate Financial Statements
IFRS 10 Consolidated Financial Statements	IAS 28 Investments in Associates and Joint Ventures
IFRS 11 Joint Arrangements	IAS 29 Financial Reporting in Hyperinflationary Economies
IFRS 12 Disclosure of Interests in Other Entities	IAS 32 Financial Instruments: Presentation
IFRS 13 Fair Value Measurement	IAS 33 Earnings per Share
IFRS 14 Regulatory Deferral Accounts	IAS 34 Interim Financial Reporting
IFRS 15 Revenue from Contracts with Customers	IAS 36 Impairment of Assets
IFRS 16 Leases	IAS 37 Provisions, Contingent Liabilities and Contingent Assets
IFRS 17 Insurance Contracts	
IAS 1 Presentation of Financial Statements	IAS 38 Intangible Assets
IAS 2 Inventories	IAS 39 Financial Instruments: Recognition and Measurement
IAS 7 Statement of Cash Flows	
IAS 8 Accounting Policies, Changes in Accounting Estimates and Errors	IAS 40 Investment Property
	IAS 41 Agriculture
IAS 10 Events after the Reporting Period	
IAS 11 Construction Contracts	
IAS 12 Income Taxes	

However, for users of smaller business's financial statements, the time and cost required to comply with full IFRS tend to outweigh the benefits. The IASB has consequently developed a separate standard, 'IFRS for Small and Medium-Sized Entities', commonly known as '**IFRS for SMEs**'. In many accounting jurisdictions, especially in less developed nations, this standard has been adopted outright for businesses which are not PIEs or listed companies.[7]

IFRS for SMEs is stand-alone, in the sense that a smaller business ought to be able to prepare a full set of financial statements by referring to this standard only. For a business looking to avoid the complexities of preparing financial statements in accordance with full IFRS, its main advantages over IFRS are:

- it is written using less technical language;

- it is relatively short: whereas full IFRS runs to a total of more than 2 000 pages, IFRS for SMEs covers fewer than 200 pages;

- it requires the use of simpler accounting techniques, for example allowing certain assets simply to be reported at their cost, where full IFRS would require that their carrying amounts are frequently changed, based on complicated calculations;

- it requires far fewer items to be disclosed: approximately 400 items are required by IFRS for SMEs, in comparison with a maximum of about 3 000 items in full IFRS;

- it omits topics not generally relevant to SMEs (if a business has to account for an event that is not covered by IFRS for SMEs, then it should use the relevant standard in full IFRS);

- it eliminates some accounting options allowed by full IFRS; for example, the option to revalue PPE to its market value (like in section 2.2.12) is absent from IFRS for SMEs.

At the end of the chapter, we have included Table 3.2, which summarises the main differences between the accounting treatments required by full IFRS and by IFRS for SMEs. As this table refers to material that we have not yet covered, we recommend that you consult it after reading the later sections describing the accounting treatments required by full IFRS.

3.4.3 Standards released by national standard-setters

National standard-setting bodies still exist in most accounting jurisdictions. Their responsibilities often include: sending relevant feedback to the IASB about its exposure drafts; supporting the implementation of a new IFRS by, for example, giving technical advice about it to local accountants; and continuing to set national accounting standards when company law, regulatory conventions, or economic conditions peculiar to their jurisdiction mean that neither full IFRS nor IFRS for SMEs applies. For example, in some countries public-sector accounting (that is, financial reporting for governmental bodies) is done in accordance with standards set locally.

Where IFRS for SMEs has not been adopted for smaller businesses, such as in the UK, the European Union (EU), Australia, and Canada, the national standard-setters have released accounting standards for smaller businesses that are less onerous in the same way as IFRS for SMEs. Indeed, in many cases, these standards are basically local adaptations of IFRS for SMEs. In the UK, for example, most unlisted companies report in accordance with the local UK standard FRS102. This is based on IFRS for SMEs, but includes various adaptations to the UK context. For example, it preserves the option to revalue PPE, because that option had long been available to smaller businesses in the UK.

3

IFRS for SMEs is a stand-alone accounting standard which is intended for small and medium-sized businesses. It is much simpler to apply than full IFRS.

FRS102 is not the only standard in UK GAAP. For example, in 2019 Burberry took advantage of the option to prepare its **company financial statements** according to FRS101, which requires that businesses use the same accounting techniques as full IFRS, but with fewer items needing to be disclosed. (Note: these are not the Burberry **group financial statements** which appear in Appendix I, and which we shall be using as a recurring case study in this book. Those financial statements are prepared according to full IFRS, as required by law. Not until you have read Chapter 9 should you expect to understand the difference between 'company' and 'group' financial statements.) In several other jurisdictions, it is common for companies to do something similar to Burberry, for example in Germany, where there is an unusually close correspondence between German GAAP and the rules for determining German tax, making it much more efficient to prepare 'company' financial statements according to German GAAP.

3

3.5 CRITIQUES OF IFRS

The development of IFRS means that practically every listed company except US companies prepares its financial statements according to the same standards. Furthermore, because the IASB represents a collaboration of worldwide experts, with a diversity of opinions and perspectives, it is generally acknowledged that it has produced excellent standards. IFRS has generally improved the volume and quality of disclosure, prohibited questionable reporting practices, and introduced consistency into the way in which many events are treated across the entire set of financial statements.

Yet any complex, impactful activity is never immune to criticism. The most commonly voiced complaints include:

- IFRS standards are complicated, even though they are principles-based, and the guidance on applying them is often lengthy and complex.

- They are not always consistent in their treatment of similar items. For example, in Chapter 6 you will learn that when investment properties are revalued, the **gain** is reported in profit or loss in the statement of comprehensive income, but when other properties are revalued, the gain is treated as other comprehensive income.

- There is too much choice, especially in respect of how to measure assets. For example, according to IFRS, a building could be reported at depreciated cost, at a revalued amount (if used in the business's operations), at market value (if it is an investment), at cost (if the owner is a property developer), or at its market value less selling costs (if it will soon be sold). All of these options seem to undermine the key objective of enhancing comparability.

Critiques of IFRS include that it is too long and complex, that some of the accounting treatments it prescribes are inconsistent, and that it offers too many different options.

The IASB is aware of these and other criticisms of the current set of IFRSs and has responded by professing its objective to make the standards understandable and comparable, whilst maintaining the fundamental characteristics of relevance and faithful representation. This is not just talk, though: many of the standards that the IASB has released have later been substantially revised in response to feedback. For example, a few years ago a new standard on **leases** (IFRS 16) was released to improve the consistency of the reporting requirements, a feature which its predecessor had lacked.

CONCLUSION

The next several chapters are devoted to a detailed examination of the accounting treatments of specific items and business events. In them, we present the requirements of full IFRS, as it governs the financial statements produced by large companies around the world, which are the companies that most of our readers seek to understand. However, as we focus on the *principles* of financial reporting, the majority of what you will learn also applies to the financial statements prepared according to the various other reporting requirements in most countries.

As you work through these next few chapters, bear in mind that current accounting requirements are not always perfect. You should appreciate that—in a sense—the development of high-quality global accounting standards really only began in 1995. Accounting is still in its early days.

The consequence of this is that not only is accounting getting more complicated, but it is also changing at an ever-increasing pace, as the standard-setters continually hone the vocabulary and grammar of the language of business. We will do our best to simplify as much as possible, in an effort to make this language as accessible for you as possible. We ask that *you* do your best to follow along!

Table 3.2 summarises some of the major differences in accounting treatments prescribed by IFRS for SMEs and full IFRS. The final column indicates the chapter of this book which explains the accounting treatment required by full IFRS. As mentioned in section 3.4.2, this table will make more sense to you if you consult it after reading the related chapter.

TABLE 3.2 Some of the major differences in accounting treatments prescribed by IFRS for SMEs and full IFRS

Topic	IFRS for SMEs	Full IFRS	Chapter
Statement of comprehensive income	Layout may be slightly different		4
Assets held for sale	Need not be separately disclosed on statement of financial position	Must be separately disclosed on statement of financial position	6
Investment properties	Must be measured using fair value if it can be reliably measured; otherwise depreciated cost	Businesses may choose to measure investment properties using either fair value or depreciated cost	6
Property, plant and equipment	Must be measured using cost model only (from 2017 an option to revalue property, plant and equipment is allowed)	Businesses may choose to measure using either revaluation or cost model	6

TABLE 3.2 (*Continued*)

Topic	IFRS for SMEs	Full IFRS	Chapter
Intangible assets	Must be measured using cost model only; development costs always expensed	Businesses may choose to measure using either revaluation or cost model; development costs may be capitalised if certain criteria are met	6
Agricultural assets	Only required to be measured using fair value if it can be determined without undue cost or effort; otherwise cost	Must be measured using fair value	6
Costs of acquiring a business	Included in purchase consideration and therefore included in goodwill	Expensed on acquisition	9
Goodwill	Amortised over useful life, or over ten years if useful life cannot be reliably measured; tested for impairment only if signs of impairment	No amortisation; tested annually for impairment	9
Non-controlling interests	May not be measured at fair value on acquisition; must be reported at share of reported net assets	May be measured either at fair value on acquisition, or at share of reported net assets	9
Associates	May be included in group financial statements either at cost, fair value, or using equity accounting	Must be included in group financial statements using equity accounting only	9
Joint ventures	May be included in group financial statements either at cost, fair value, or using equity accounting	Must be included in group financial statements using equity accounting only	9

SUMMARY OF KEY POINTS

- Regulation of financial reporting ensures that businesses prepare financial statements that are comparable, using principles and practices with which users of the financial statements are familiar.
- Regulation involves both the setting and enforcement of accounting standards.
- Enforcement is generally the task of a combination of company law, stock exchange oversight bodies, and governmental and non-governmental regulatory agencies.
- Standard-setting has historically been the task of national standard-setters, who have produced 'generally accepted accounting practice', or 'GAAP', for their own accounting jurisdictions.
- With the notable exception of the US, in the twenty-first century, through the process of international harmonisation, the IASB has increasingly taken on the standard-setting task by releasing International Financial Reporting Standards, or 'IFRS'.

- Now, more than 140 countries require listed companies and other public interest entities to use full IFRS, which consists of more than forty accounting standards that specify principles and practices for virtually every event that could affect the financial statements.
- The accounting standards begin with the Conceptual Framework for Financial Reporting, which sets out the foundational principles on which the other standards are based.
- It is too onerous for most smaller businesses to apply full IFRS. In many accounting jurisdictions, these businesses are permitted to report instead according to a much simplified, stand-alone accounting standard called 'IFRS for SMEs'.
- In other jurisdictions, such as the UK, the EU, Australia, and Canada, the national standard-setters have instead set financial reporting standards for smaller businesses. These are typically quite closely based on IFRS for SMEs.
- IFRS is not without its critics. Common critiques include that it is too long and complex, that some of the accounting treatments it prescribes are inconsistent, and that it offers too many different accounting options. The IASB has responded to at least some of this criticism, often by revising the standards which have been most heavily criticised.

CHAPTER QUESTIONS

The suggested solutions to the concept questions (marked 'CQ') can be found in Appendix III. Also, don't forget the **online resources** available at www.oup.com/he/winfield-graham-miller1e, which contain multiple-choice questions based on the material in this chapter, in addition to many other helpful resources.

CONCEPT QUESTIONS

CQ 3.1   Explain what you understand by the terms 'GAAP', 'IFRS', and 'FASBs'.

CQ 3.2   What is the fundamental difference between IFRS and the FASBs?

CQ 3.3   Some companies are listed on more than one stock exchange, in different countries. Do non-US companies that have a listing in the US have to comply with the FASBs or provide a reconciliation between the FASBs and IFRS?

CQ 3.4   What is the objective of the IASB?

CQ 3.5   What are the three main criticisms of IFRS?

INVESTIGATION QUESTIONS

IQ 3.6   Do some research of your own into the variety of GAAP standards used by businesses in your country. Determine whether or not listed companies in your jurisdiction use IFRS for their 'group' financial statements and if the 'company' financial statements use IFRS or a local GAAP standard. Also, establish whether there is an option for some businesses to use 'IFRS for Small and Medium-Sized Entities'.

IQ 3.7   Describe three issues that the IASB is currently grappling with in terms of IFRS and its implementation. (A useful place to start would be to read the speeches made by trustees, board members, and staff of the IASB. They can be found on the IASB's website at www.ifrs.org/media/#speeches.)

IQ 3.8   Why have the US standard-setters not embraced IFRS, and do you think that there will ever be a complete convergence between the US standards and IFRS?

REFERENCES

1   Reuters 1994. 'Daimler-Benz Reports Losses'. *The New York Times*. 14 April. Available at: https://www.nytimes.com/1994/04/14/business/daimler-benz-reports-loss.html.

2   The IASB's website is available at www.ifrs.org. The interactive map is available at: https://www.ifrs.org/use-around-the-world/use-of-ifrs-standards-by-jurisdiction.

3   IFRS Foundation 2018. *Use of IFRS Standards around The World*. Available at: https://www.ifrs.org/-/media/feature/around-the-world/adoption/use-of-ifrs-around-the-world-overview-sept-2018.pdf.

4   Nobes, C 2014. *Accounting: A Very Short Introduction*. Oxford University Press, pp 75–6.

5   The major technical differences between IFRS and US GAAP can be found at: https://www.pwc.com/us/en/cfodirect/assets/pdf/accounting-guides/pwc-ifrs-us-gaap-similarities-and-differences.pdf.

6   Gill, L 2007. 'IFRS: Coming to America'. *Journal of Accountancy*. 1 June. Available at: https://www.journalofaccountancy.com/issues/2007/jun/ifrscomingtoamerica.html.

7   Kaya, D and Kock, M 2015. 'Countries' Adoption of the International Financial Reporting Standard for Small and Medium-Sized Entities (IFRS for SMEs)—Early Empirical Evidence'. *Accounting and Business Research*, Vol 45, Issue 1, pp 93–120.

3

INCOME AND EXPENSES

CHAPTER 4

Here are some of the things you will be able to do after reading this chapter:

- recognise the two alternative formats of the statement of comprehensive income;
- list the items of income and expense that are designated as other comprehensive income, and explain in broad terms the reasons for the creation of this designation;
- apply the basic principles for when revenue is reported, and how it is measured;
- explain the significance of the other items often found on a statement of comprehensive income;
- describe the nature and purpose of alternative performance measures, and justify their use;
- discuss the significance and value of the basic and diluted earnings per share figures.

This chapter builds on material covered in earlier chapters. If you don't feel comfortable with any of the following items, we recommend that you briefly go back now to the sections referenced.

- **Income** is defined as an increase in **equity** that is not the result of a **capital** contribution by owners (the definition is in section 2.1.2, and it was applied in sections 2.2.5, 2.2.10, and 2.2.12).
- **Expenses** are defined as decreases in equity that are not the result of distributions to owners (the definition is in section 2.1.2, and it was applied in several sections, including 2.2.6, 2.2.7, and 2.2.9).

- All of a business's items of income and expense for a period, and only the items of income and expense, are reported in the **statement of comprehensive income** (the most complete example thus far appeared in section 2.2.14).

- Using **accrual accounting** (described in section 2.2.8), the statement of comprehensive income tells a story of the business's financial performance; that is, the extent to which its **operating activities** created value for the business's owners (see sections 1.3.6 and 1.4.3).

- Many accounting principles and practices of relevance to this chapter were demonstrated at a simple level in Chapter 2, using the hypothetical example of a very small business that sells pizza slices, called the Pizza Business, or 'PB'. We shall refer to PB in this chapter too.

4

We will be examining income and expenses in detail in this chapter. To do so, we will be working through Burberry's 2019 statement of comprehensive income, which is presented on two pages in Appendix I, with the titles 'Group income statement' and 'Group statement of comprehensive income'. While you read this chapter, you should plan to look at them often, as we shall be referring to them frequently, to ensure that you consolidate your learning in the context of a real example.

We should begin with a warning. If the statement of comprehensive income tells a story, you should bear in mind that, as the old saying goes, no two stories are the same. If you compare any of Burberry's financial statements with the financial statements of another business, you will find that they are laid out in different ways, provide varying amounts of detail, and use alternative terms to describe the same events.

Some of these variations exist because different stories need to be told in different ways. A bank's financial statements, for example, necessarily look different from those of a gold mine. Other variations are more superficial, resulting from the fact that the accounting standard-setters are wary of being too dogmatic, and have intentionally left room for businesses to decide for themselves how their financial statements ought to look.

However, the standard-setters have ensured that all financial statements have a similar underlying structure and follow the same principles. Although the stories are not told in exactly the same way, it is as if each storyteller studied oratory with the same grand master! With a little patience and understanding, it is possible to unlock their secrets and unravel their complexities.

The **notes** to Burberry's 2019 **financial statements** are forty-five pages long and therefore not included in the book, but they are accessible by a very quick internet search. Indeed, you will rapidly find practically any listed company's financial statements by searching for the company's name followed by 'financial statements' and the financial year in which you are interested. We encourage you to download Burberry's entire annual report so that you can follow along when we mention the notes to the financial statements, which we will do often in the next several chapters.

4.1 FORMAT OF THE STATEMENT OF COMPREHENSIVE INCOME

A complication we should deal with right away is that, like the majority of businesses, Burberry has used two statements, rather than one, to present the information we cover in this chapter. Businesses are indeed allowed to opt for one of two alternative presentation formats. The format presented in section 2.2.14 consists of a single statement, called the statement of comprehensive income, which reports items of income and expense in two sections: 'profit or loss' and 'other comprehensive income' (OCI).

The format Burberry has chosen consists of two financial statements. The first Burberry has called its 'income statement', though this sort of statement goes by other names too, such as 'statement of comprehensive income' (see Daimler's financial statements in Appendix II, for instance) or 'statement of profit or loss'. The second statement Burberry has called the 'statement of comprehensive income', which is typical, despite the unfortunate overlap with the name of the single statement on the other format. (If you are curious as to why Burberry has added the word 'group' in front of the names of its financial statements, rest assured that this will be explained in Chapter 9.)

The two presentation options are illustrated in Figure 4.1.

FIGURE 4.1 The two alternative formats of the statement of comprehensive income

ONE-STATEMENT FORMAT		TWO-STATEMENT FORMAT	
Statement of comprehensive income		**Income statement**	
Profit or loss:			
Item 1	x	Item 1	x
Item 2	(x)	Item 2	(x)
Item 3	(x)	Item 3	(x)
Profit/loss	xx	Profit/loss	xx
		Statement of comprehensive income	
		Profit/loss	xx
Other comprehensive income:		*Other comprehensive income:*	
Item 4	y	Item 4	y
Item 5	(y)	Item 5	(y)
	yy		yy
Total comprehensive income	xxyy	Total comprehensive income	xxyy

The profit or loss section of the one-statement format contains exactly the same items as the income statement on the two-statement format. These items of income and expense are often described as 'reported in profit or loss' or 'taken to profit or loss'. Naturally, if an item of income is reported in profit or loss on the one-statement format, or in the income statement on the two-statement format, it increases the business's **profit** (or decreases the **loss**); similarly, if an expense is taken to profit or loss, it decreases the business's profit (or increases the loss).

The enigmatic **OCI section** of the one-statement format contains the same items of income and expense as the second statement on the two-statement format, although the latter starts with 'profit or loss for the period' so as to be able to end with the same figure as the one-statement format: '**total comprehensive income**', or '**TCI**'. A good example of a statement of comprehensive income prepared using the one-statement format belongs to the Norwegian seafood company, Mowi.[1]

Perhaps it will now be clear why the more formal name for the statement of comprehensive income is an even larger mouthful: the '**statement of profit or loss and other comprehensive income**'.

4.2 THE HISTORICAL EXPLANATION FOR THE OCI SECTION

Why are items of income and expense divided between those that are included in profit or loss and items of OCI? The answer lies in history: some items have been used to measure financial performance for so long that *not* doing so is unthinkable, whereas there is discomfort about the idea of letting the profit figure be impacted by other items.

For example, no one would question that sales and cost of sales should impact profit, but the gain resulting from an upwards **revaluation** of PPE is much more controversial. Before the harmonisation of accounting standards, most jurisdictions did not even allow the accounting record for PPE to be adjusted for increases in its value, let alone permit these increases to affect profit, which (as explained in section 1.3.4) is a critical indicator of value creation.

Yet, if the carrying amount of an item of PPE is to be adjusted upwards, the accounting equation means that this will cause a change in equity. And the only changes in equity which do not appear on the statement of comprehensive income are the transactions that represent neither an increase nor a decrease in the amount of value created by the business: transfers of value between the business and its owners. A revaluation gain is not a mere transfer: it represents an actual change in business value. Thus, if it is going to be recognised at all, it results in an item of income which must be reported on the statement of comprehensive income.

Faced with a dilemma between wreaking potential havoc with the influential profit figure and not recognising a genuine change in business value, the standard-setters reached an ingenious compromise. They invented the OCI section, so that items like these revaluation gains can be reported on the statement of comprehensive income, but not affect the business's profit.

MISCONCEPTION

The revaluation gain on PPE is reported in OCI and not in profit or loss because it is **unrealised** (that is, it has not yet been obtained in cash).

Incorrect. In section 2.2.13 we debunked a similar misconception: that the revaluation gain should not even be income because it is unrealised. We pointed out that credit sales, for example, are unrealised, yet they are reported as income. Here, we can point out that credit sales are reported in profit or loss, so being unrealised cannot be what condemns a revaluation gain to the OCI section.

The uncomfortable truth is that there is no underlying principle that distinguishes reliably between items of OCI and income and expense reported in profit or loss. The best explanation for the standard-setters' introducing this odd treatment is not one of principle, but rather one of history: because they had never previously been recognised as items of income or expense at all, it would have been too bold to demand that not only would they now be recognised, but also that they would affect the profit figure.

A full list of items that may appear in OCI will be provided in section 4.8. For now, having dispensed with the issue of format, we can embark on our examination of income and expenses, starting at the top of Burberry's group income statement, and working our way down to the bottom of its group statement of comprehensive income. Here and there, we will introduce some items which Burberry does not report, but which you may well come across in other businesses' reporting.

No such detour is necessary to begin with, however, as Burberry, like virtually every other company, lists '**revenue**' as its first item of income or expense.

4.3 REVENUE

Revenue is one of the most significant figures in the entire set of financial statements. Almost all businesses aim for growth, and revenue is the ultimate measure of the business's size in the market. After all, the more you sell, the bigger you are. Because of its importance, an entire accounting standard (IFRS 15) is dedicated to the recognition and measurement of revenue. This is especially remarkable when one considers that most standards focus on assets or liabilities, not on items that appear in the statement of comprehensive income.

Revenue is 'income arising in the course of an entity's ordinary activities'.[2] When PB sold pizza slices in Chapter 2, we of course reported (or 'recognised') revenue. But there are many ways of generating revenue other than simply selling inventory. Courier businesses charge for the service of moving things from one location to another; many online businesses receive income for every 'click' on the adverts they host on their site; music production businesses receive royalties from the sale of their songs; and so on. Broadly speaking, 'revenue' is thus the collective term for income from the sale of goods and from the rendering of services. That is, it is the income arising from the main ways in which a business seeks to create value. This is often described less formally as 'sales' or 'turnover'.

It follows that, although all revenue is income, *not* all income is revenue. When, in section 2.2.10, PB earned interest, we did not add it to revenue, but instead reported it in a separate line further down the statement of comprehensive income. Similarly, if PB were to make a **gain** when one day it sells the pizza oven, this would be income, but—since it is not PB's ordinary business to sell ovens—it is not revenue.

Whenever a business sells goods or services, two key questions are: *when* should revenue be reported and *how much* revenue should be reported? Accountants refer to these as questions of 'timing' and '**measurement**', respectively. Let's begin with timing.

4.3.1 Timing of revenue recognition

In PB, we recognised the revenue for credit sales on the day the slices were sold, even though we still had not received the cash for those sales by the end of the financial year. This treatment arises from the concept of accrual accounting, which requires that income is reported when the sale occurs, and not necessarily when the cash is received. But perhaps you are wondering: if it is not the receipt of the money, what exactly *is* the event which indicates that a sale has occurred? IFRS 15 answers that question definitively: the sale happens (and therefore the revenue should be reported) when **control** over the goods passes to the customer. In the case of a sale of a pizza slice, that is the point in time when the slice is handed to the customer, beyond which PB has nothing more to do with it.

> Revenue from the sale of goods is reported only when the business has transferred control of the goods to the customer.

It is not always so easy to identify the point when control passes from a business to its customer. Consider the case of a construction business, which builds homes. Naturally, the building process takes a long time. If, say, two years are required to build a home, when does control over the building pass from the business to the new owner? The answer will determine whether revenue should be reported in the financial periods during which construction is ongoing (that is, in financial years 1, 2, and 3 in Figure 4.2), or only when the build is complete (that is, in financial year 3).

FIGURE 4.2 A two-year construction contract that spans three financial years

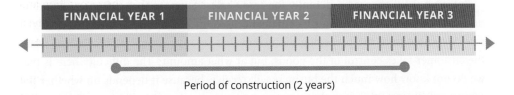

Period of construction (2 years)

You will observe throughout the rest of this book how the correct accounting treatment often depends on the circumstances, and this is true here. For example, if the construction business developed the property by buying the land, and retains ownership of the land and buildings throughout the period of the build, then control over the home would only pass to the customer once the home is completed. Thus, all the revenue from the contract would only be reported at the end of the contract term; that is, in financial year 3.

Sometimes, however, control does not pass at a single point in time, in which case revenue is recognised over time, as control passes. For example, if the customer owns the land, and the contract between the construction business and the customer allows for control over the partially completed building to pass to the customer as building progresses, then revenue will be reported over the period that the work is performed, so the revenue from the contract will be spread across financial years 1, 2, and 3.

When a business sells services, IFRS 15 requires that revenue is recognised once the business has performed *and* the customer has acquired the benefits of the business's performance. For example, a twelve-month contract to provide monthly payroll administration would result in revenue being recognised each month. Thus, if the contract spanned two financial years, as in Figure 4.2, revenue would be reported in both financial years.

On the other hand, consider a twelve-month contract in which a management consulting business must answer a key strategic question (about, say, entering a new market overseas). Presumably their work will only deliver benefits when they finally present their answer to the client's question. Thus, revenue would only be recognised at the end of the contract. In a scenario such as Figure 4.3, all of the revenue would be reported in financial year 2.

> Revenue from providing a service is reported only when the business has provided the service and the customer has acquired the benefits of that service.

FIGURE 4.3 A twelve-month contract that spans two financial years

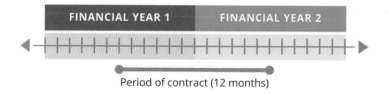

4.3.2 Measurement of revenue: variable considerations

The second major question about revenue is the measurement issue: *at what amount* should it be reported? Once again, this is often easy: in section 2.2.5, when PB sold a pizza slice for €3, we measured the revenue at the selling price of €3 irrespective of whether the sale was for cash or on credit.

But what if PB charged differently for credit sales? Suppose that customers who buy on credit owe €4, but receive a €1 'settlement discount' if they pay within a week of the sale. We know from the preceding discussion that revenue should be recognised when the customer takes control of the goods, but at what amount? The difficulty here is that we do not know how much the business will receive, because it depends on whether the customer will pay within a week. Common business practices like discounts, rebates, and other price concessions often introduce this kind of uncertainty: the business will receive what is known as a 'variable consideration'.

However, lack of certainty does not give accountants the option to wait until the ambiguity resolves. As we already know from our discussion of the IFRS 15 timing requirements, the revenue must be recognised when control passes, at which point the amount that will ultimately be received is still unknown. So instead, an estimate must be made.

The key principle used for an estimate like this is that revenue should be measured at *the amount the business expects* to receive. In PB's settlement discount example, the accountant would have to make a judgement call about the likelihood of customers taking the discount. If they are expected to pay €3 within a week, €3 of revenue should be recognised. If not, then the full €4 of revenue should be recognised.

In the latter case, if the customer defies expectations and pays early, €1 of the $4 that was originally recognised for revenue would have to be subtracted. This would not be done lightly, however: users of financial statements do not like to see accountants appearing to manipulate revenue figures, as it reduces their confidence in the accountants' figures more generally. (Section 13.2 will detail the rich variety of ways in which unscrupulous accountants have been caught manipulating revenue for illicit purposes.)

Businesses therefore put a lot of effort into estimating revenue for variable considerations. In practice, the most accurate estimate is likely to be somewhere between the two possible outcomes, implying that PB should recognise as revenue some portion of the €1 discount based on what fraction of customers it expects will take advantage of the credit terms. In other words, if historical analysis of customers' settlements suggests that 20% will pay within a week, revenue for each sale ought to be measured at €3.80 (80% × €4 + 20% × €3). Although, of course, no single customer will pay that amount, this approach will lead to the aggregate estimate of revenue being as accurate as possible.

The amount of revenue recognised on the date of sale is summarised in Example 4.1. Note how the measurement is dependent on the business's expectations in each scenario.

> Revenue is measured at the amount that the business ultimately expects to receive for the goods or service.

EXAMPLE 4.1

Scenarios, in which a settlement discount of €1 is offered on a sales price of €4	Revenue
If the business *does not* expect the customer to pay within the discount period	€4.00
If the business *does* expect the customer to pay within the discount period	€3.00
If the business expects 20% of customers to pay within the discount period	€3.80

4.3.3 Measurement of revenue: recognition over time

Recall from section 4.3.1 that certain contracts (like a building, where control passes to the buyer during construction, and monthly payroll administration) result in revenue being recognised over the contract period. We haven't yet discussed *how much* revenue is reported for each reporting period. In the case of the payroll services, if each month's service involves roughly the same scope of work, of course one-twelfth of the total revenue would be recognised each month.

In more complicated cases, a reasonable measure of progress is used. Suppose, for example, that a construction contract allows for control to pass as building progresses, and that the two-year construction period spans three financial years, as in Figure 4.2. The construction business needs to report revenue for financial year 1, to which the information in Example 4.2 applies.

4

EXAMPLE 4.2

Information at end of financial year 1 (costs in €)	
Costs to date:	2 million
Costs to complete:	6 million
Total price of the contract:	10 million
Estimated measure of progress:	25%

As construction is 25% complete, in financial year 1, the business would recognise 25% of the contract price as revenue; that is, €2.5 million (€10 million × 25%). The year's costs of €2 million would also be reported, so that the contract reports a net effect of €500 000 of profit for financial year 1. A similar calculation would be performed in financial years 2 and 3.

You might wonder: on what basis is the measure of progress estimated? IFRS 15 requires the business to choose the measurement basis that best depicts the transfer of goods or services to the customer. Potential bases include *inputs* such as costs incurred, labour hours, and time lapsed; or *outputs* such as units produced or delivered and surveys or appraisals of work completed.

4.3.4 Multiple performance obligations

We have addressed the two key questions which apply to every instance of revenue recognition: timing and measurement. In this section, we will consider the subset of instances in which a sale contract obliges the business to do more than one kind of thing for its customer.

Revenue from a contract imposing multiple performance obligations on the business is recognised separately, as the business meets the recognition requirements for each obligation.

You may be aware that motor dealers often sell cars together with a service plan to maintain the vehicle for the next few years. In such cases, control of the car passes to the buyer straight away, and yet the buyer does not acquire the benefits of the service plan until some time has passed. When should revenue be recognised, and for how much? The answer is quite intuitive once you know the trick: essentially, the dealer is committing to two things, which are known in IFRS 15 as **performance obligations**. One is the sale of the car itself; the other is its servicing. Having teased these two performance obligations out of the single contract, the dealer's accountant must separately report the revenue arising from each of them. In terms of timing, the portion of revenue that relates to the sale of the car will be recognised on the date of sale (that is, when control of the car passes to the customer), and the portion relating to the annual services is only recognised as revenue when they are performed, because that is when the customer acquires the benefits of each service.

In terms of measurement, revenue is recognised in proportion to what the performance obligations would be sold for separately. Suppose that the motor dealer usually sells this type of car without a service plan for €20 000, and usually sells service plans (say, for cars purchased elsewhere) for €5 000. Then, when a vehicle is sold with a service plan, four-fifths (€20 000 ÷ €25 000) of the revenue from the sale is deemed to be the portion of revenue arising from the sale of the car; and one-fifth (€5 000 ÷ €25 000) is deemed to be the revenue arising from the services.

Thus, if the buyer pays €23 000 on the day that control of the car transfers, then four-fifths of £23 000 would immediately be recognised as revenue, as shown in the following summary of the accounting that would happen on that day.

SUMMARY OF EVENT 1 A car dealer sells a car with a service plan deemed to be worth one-fifth of the price.

Assets	– Liabilities	= Equity		Debit	Credit
+ £23 000				Bank	
	+ £4 600				Deferred income
		+ £18 400 (income)			Revenue

Because it has not yet been earned, the one-fifth which relates to the annual services is treated as a liability when it is received. This liability goes by various names, including 'income received in advance', 'unearned income', or simply 'contract liability'. We shall use the most common term, '**deferred income**', which alludes to how the money has been received, but the income has been deferred until later. As the services are performed over the next few years, the deferred income liability will be decreased (debit), and revenue will be reported (credit), using a reasonable measure of progress.

4.3.5 **Deferred payments**

Suppose that today you buy a couch, and accept delivery (that is, acquire control of the couch). Instead of paying for it today, you arrange with the retailer that you will only pay for it in twelve months' time. This is an example of what is known as a deferred payment. Would the retailer sell it to you for the same price as they would charge to a customer who pays cash today? No, because they are providing you with more than just the piece of furniture: they are also giving you a twelve-month loan. If you pay $500 for a couch which normally goes for $420 cash, then the cost of the couch is $420, and you are paying $80 ($500 – $420) for the loan. You could call the $80 'interest', as that is the term used for the cost of a loan.

The same logic applies from the seller's point of view. The furniture retailer should report $420 of revenue on the date of sale, and then report $80 interest income over time, until payment is received from the customer, as depicted in Summary of Event 2 below.

SUMMARY OF EVENT 2 A retailer sells furniture worth $420 for a $500 payment in twelve months' time.

On the date of sale (that is, when control of the furniture passes to the customer):

Assets	– Liabilities	= Equity		Debit	Credit
+ $420				Accounts receivable	
		+ $420 (income)			Revenue

(Continued)

Over the period between the date of sale and the receipt of cash:

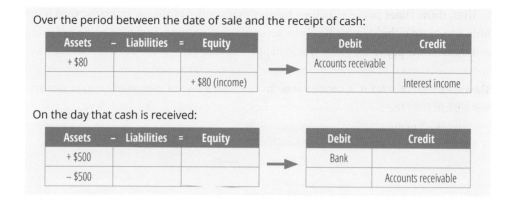

Assets	–	Liabilities	=	Equity
+ $80				
				+ $80 (income)

Debit	Credit
Accounts receivable	
	Interest income

On the day that cash is received:

Assets	–	Liabilities	=	Equity
+ $500				
– $500				

Debit	Credit
Bank	
	Accounts receivable

This treatment is consistent with the fundamental principle of finance known as the 'time value of money', which maintains that an amount of money in the future has less value than the same amount of money today. If you are not convinced by this, suppose that some kindly soul—an aunt, perhaps—decides to give you $500. She asks you if you would prefer it today or a year from now. If your economic outlook conforms with most people's, you would unhesitatingly choose to receive it today. This is not just because of price inflation (which means that $500 will buy you less a year from now), but also for other reasons, like the fact that receiving it today means that you have the option to invest the money and potentially increase its value in the next year. In fact, you should rationally be willing to accept less than $500 today, instead of $500 in the future. How much less will vary from person to person, because it depends on the circumstances.

Because we know what the retailer would sell the item for today, we know that, as far as this transaction is concerned, the value of $500 in a year's time is $420 today. The difference between these two figures—the portion we have treated as interest income—is referred to as the 'discount' (not to be confused with other sorts of discounts, such as sales and settlement discounts, for example).

The process of recognising interest income over the period of credit is thus called, rather poetically, 'unwinding the discount'. This alludes to the way in which the discount is reported over time in the statement of comprehensive income, a little like unwinding a spool of thread.

Here, we can work out the 'discount rate' of 19.0% by dividing the $80 by the present value of $420. In cases where it is unclear what the couch would be sold for a cash payment today (perhaps because the retailer doesn't offer sales for cash), the present value can be estimated by determining what the market interest rate is for a transaction of this sort, and then using this as the discount rate to calculate the present value of the future payment.

Of course, this process of discounting and unwinding is far more complex than simply recording and reporting as revenue the amount received. Generally speaking, IFRS therefore only requires businesses to engage in this process when the time value of money is material. 'Materiality' is a word used frequently by accountants, and is defined in the Conceptual Framework as follows: 'Information is material if omitting it or misstating it could influence decisions that the primary users of [the financial statements] make on the

Information is 'material' if omitting it or misstating it could influence the decisions that users make on the basis of the financial statements.

basis of those [financial statements]'. Thus, the process of discounting and unwinding is only necessary if the length of the period might make an impactful difference.

For deferred payments, IFRS 15 explicitly stipulates the materiality threshold: businesses are allowed to ignore the time value of money if the period between the sale and the collection of cash is a year or less. In our example, the period was exactly twelve months, and so the business could have taken this option. If so, it would have recognised no interest, and simply reported revenue of $500. Had the credit period been any longer, it would have been required to use the sort of treatment we have described here.

4.3.6 Advance payments

The logic behind the treatment of deferred payments works in the opposite direction for an advance payment. If a manufacturer accepts payment of $320 from a customer, say, eighteen months before control of the goods passes, it will subtract this amount paid from the price it would charge to a customer who only pays on the date of sale (again, let's say this is $420). The difference of $100 is the amount of interest expense to be reported by the business over the period between receiving the cash and delivering the product.

The accounting analysis of this transaction (Summary of Event 3) shows how the revenue will ultimately be measured as the amount of cash which would ordinarily be paid on the date of sale, just as for a deferred payment.

SUMMARY OF EVENT 3 A manufacturer accepts $320 in advance for an item worth $420.

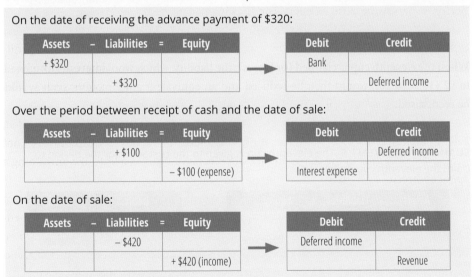

On the date of receiving the advance payment of $320:

Assets	–	Liabilities	=	Equity
+ $320				
		+ $320		

Debit	Credit
Bank	
	Deferred income

Over the period between receipt of cash and the date of sale:

Assets	–	Liabilities	=	Equity
		+ $100		
				– $100 (expense)

Debit	Credit
	Deferred income
Interest expense	

On the date of sale:

Assets	–	Liabilities	=	Equity
		– $420		
				+ $420 (income)

Debit	Credit
Deferred income	
	Revenue

4.3.7 Customer loyalty programmes

Businesses looking to increase their revenue are typically happy to give away some of their products for free to customers who purchase in large volumes. This is often formalised as a customer loyalty programme. For example, a coffee shop might offer a free cup of coffee

4

to anyone who purchases ten cups. However, just as there are 'no free lunches', coffee shops don't really give away their coffee for free. In truth, the customer is paying a little bit towards that eleventh cup each time the first ten cups are purchased.

Having read section 4.3.4, perhaps you can anticipate how IFRS 15 requires accountants to think about this sort of arrangement. With each sale, the coffee shop is taking on two performance obligations: one cup provided immediately, and also a fraction of a right to receive a cup in future. The revenue from the different performance obligations must be recognised separately, so the money received for each of the first ten coffees will be split between the two obligations. The portion that relates to the eleventh coffee is recognised as a liability until that performance obligation is met; that is, when the customer collects the eleventh cup.

Ultimately, one round of the loyalty programme involves selling eleven cups of coffee, so the appropriate portion in this case is one-eleventh. For example, if these coffees were priced at £2.20 each, every time the customer pays for a cup, revenue of £2 (£2.20 × 10/11) is reported, and the deferred income liability would increase by £0.20 (£2.20 × 1/11), as shown here in Summary of Event 4.

SUMMARY OF EVENT 4 A coffee shop sells one cup of coffee as part of an eleven-for-ten loyalty programme.

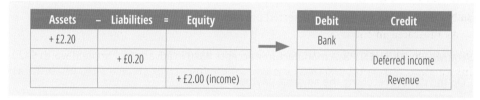

Assets	–	Liabilities	=	Equity		Debit	Credit
+ £2.20						Bank	
		+ £0.20					Deferred income
				+ £2.00 (income)			Revenue

When the eleventh cup is claimed (or lapses), the liability, which would have accumulated to £2 (10 × £0.20), would then be reduced and an equivalent amount of revenue would be recognised.

SUMMARY OF EVENT 5 The eleventh cup is given to the customer (or the period to claim the eleventh cup ends).

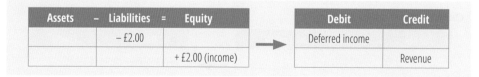

Assets	–	Liabilities	=	Equity		Debit	Credit
		– £2.00				Deferred income	
				+ £2.00 (income)			Revenue

4.3.8 Revenue at Burberry

Burberry makes revenue from the sale of its merchandise, and reports the total amount of revenue as the first line-item on its group income statement: £2 720.2 million in its 2019 financial year. That was a very slight decline of 0.5% relative to the previous year, whose revenue is shown in the column to the right.

MISCONCEPTION

There is more than one way to calculate a percentage change, and so there is more than one correct result if you are asked about a percentage change.

Incorrect. It is true that there are different ways to do the maths, but they should all give the same result. Mastery of the mathematical technique for calculating percentage increases or decreases is vital for working with financial statements, so make sure you know how to get the correct answer. The calculation here is (£2 720.2m – £2 732.8m) ÷ £2 732.8m, which is then converted to a percentage by dividing by 100. It may help to remember the mantra, popular among school maths teachers, 'new minus old, all over old'.

For the sake of flow, the rest of this book will not show calculations of percentage changes.

Incidentally, it may strike you as odd that the columns are arranged as they are, with the most recent year appearing to the left of the prior year, as if time has been reversed. This is in fact the usual convention in presenting financial statements, but rest assured that the space–time continuum is still firmly in place: the intention is merely to give prominence to the most recent information!

We shall return to the 0.5% decline in revenue, and the reason for it, in section 11.2.3 of the chapter on financial analysis. In this chapter, we shall instead aim for you to understand where to find the relevant information, how it is determined, and what it basically means.

As indicated in the column to the left of the revenue figure, note 3 contains more detail about this revenue. However, before turning to the notes containing numerical information, it is good practice for a user of the financial statements to search the accounting policies note for the item in which they are interested. The accounting policies are usually set out in one lengthy note near the beginning of the notes to the financial statements. Burberry's accounting policies, for example, are all described in Note 2, with the policies for revenue appearing first, in note 2a, starting on p 168 of the 2019 annual report.

This information suggests that Burberry's revenue recognition is (a) entirely consistent with the requirements of IFRS 15; and (b) not as varied and complex as many of the issues we have discussed in this chapter. However, a careful reading does reveal a few answers to questions you may have been wondering about:

- Royalties are part of revenue. In Burberry's case, they are essentially the fee for the service of allowing other businesses to use its trademarks.

- Revenue is measured net of (that is, after subtracting) any payments to customers for services directly related to making the sale. For example, if Burberry pays a rebate to a wholesale customer who buys a lot of its products, this will be deducted from the revenue reported for sales to that customer, according to the principles outlined in section 4.3.2. (Incidentally, Value Added Tax (VAT), and any other sales taxes which form part of the selling price, are also not included in revenue, as these amounts have not been earned by the seller, which is simply acting as an agent on behalf of the tax authorities to facilitate their collection.)

- The value of sales returns and other allowances (eg trade discounts) are also deducted from the reported revenue figure, likewise following the principle that requires revenue to be measured at the amount which the business ultimately expects to receive for the related sale.

In providing more information about revenue, note 3 on pp 177 and 178 of the annual report reveals useful details about the relative success of the business's strategic initiatives. For example, it shows how much revenue Burberry earned in each channel (retail, wholesale, or licence); region (Asia Pacific; the Americas; or Europe, Middle East, India, and Africa); and product category (accessories, women's, men's, beauty, or children and other).

4.4 EXPENSES AND OTHER ITEMS OF INCOME

Revenue is a major storyline in the tale of the business's performance told by the statement of comprehensive income, but it is never the dramatic climax. That honour is usually reserved for profit (though, as we discussed in section 2.2.13, some might say TCI). Thus, the story of the statement of comprehensive income now turns to the sequence of events by which revenue becomes profit.

4.4.1 Cost of sales

When goods or services have been sold, the cost of these goods or services is included in the statement of comprehensive income as cost of sales. Other terms for this line-item are 'Cost of inventories', 'Cost of inventories expensed', and 'Production costs'. For retailers and manufacturers, this is almost always their largest single expense.

As explained in section 2.2.6, one component of the cost of sales figure is the cost of the inventory actually sold. This means that if a particular item of inventory is sold, all of the costs incurred to bring it to its location, and get it into a condition for sale, must appear in cost of sales. In the case of a retail item, this may just be the cost of purchase; but for a manufactured item, it will include the costs of the raw materials and all the costs of converting them into finished goods. Hence why, in section 2.2.9, the depreciation of PB's pizza oven was included in cost of sales. See section 6.5 for more detail about the cost of inventory.

Cost of sales does not include advertising or other costs related to selling the inventory. However, in addition to the cost of inventory actually sold during a period, the cost of sales figure does include:

- the cost of any inventory lost, perished, or stolen during the period;
- the amount of any normal expenditure on waste in the manufacturing process;

- any amounts by which inventory has been written down below its cost during the period. The reasons for such **write-downs** may be damage, obsolescence, use as a display item, or any other circumstances which lead to an expectation that the item will be sold for an amount below its cost.

To understand the effect of write-downs on cost of sales, suppose, for example, that in Year 1 Burberry purchased a batch of luxury accessories at a cost of £50 each, but sales volumes are very low, and by the end of Year 1, it seems that their selling price will have to be marked down below cost, to £40 each. This requires a write-down of £10 per item at the year-end, as in Summary of Event 6.

SUMMARY OF EVENT 6 An item of Burberry's inventory with a cost of £50 is written down to £40 in Year 1.

Assets	–	Liabilities	=	Equity		Debit	Credit
– £10							Inventory
				– £10 (expense)		Cost of sales	

This has the effect of reporting the expenses related to inventory in the period in which the events that give rise to the expense—in this case, the decline in the accessory's marketability—occurred.

Occasionally, a write-down turns out in a later financial period to have been too large. Suppose that in Year 2 a major online influencer discovers and promotes Burberry's product, dramatically increasing its marketability so that it can, after all, be sold for more than its cost of £50. Thus, it has turned out that the Year 1 write-down was not necessary. Rather than restate the Year 1 financial statements, however, the write-down is simply 'reversed' in Year 2. A **reversal** is an entry in the accounting system that increases what was previously decreased, or decreases what was previously increased, as in Summary of Event 7.

SUMMARY OF EVENT 7 An item of Burberry's inventory with a cost of £50 was written down to £40 in Year 1. Then, in Year 2, conditions indicate that it can be sold above cost.

Assets	–	Liabilities	=	Equity		Debit	Credit
+ £10						Inventory	
				+ £10 (income)			Cost of sales

Note that the reversal is the exact opposite of the entry it reverses. Thus, although technically this increase in equity meets the definition of income, in practice it is rather recorded, and ultimately reported, as a decrease in an expense. The effect is to correct the previous year's expense that has turned out—through no fault of the business—to have been charged in error. After the reversal, the inventory is now again carried in the accounting records at its cost of £50, and so this is the amount that will be expensed when the product is finally sold.

In a service environment, the cost of sales figure represents the costs of providing the services. For example, in a business that provides IT services, cost of sales would include the wages of the business's technicians and also consumables, such as the cabling that they use.

Usually, cost of sales appears as the second line of the statement of comprehensive income, just below revenue or sales income, and the difference between these two figures is shown on the next line as **gross profit**. This figure is very important for understanding the operating activities of a business, especially a retailer or manufacturer. Take, for example, Burberry's 2019 gross profit of £1 860.8 million, obtained after cost of sales of £859.4 million was deducted from revenue. This is a decline of 1.9% from £1 897.4 million in 2018, which is larger than the 0.5% decline in revenue we identified in section 4.3.8.

Now, it is possible for gross profit to improve while revenue remains flat; for example, if a 25% increase in a business's selling prices causes a 20% decline in volumes, revenue will be unchanged (because 125% × 80% =100%), yet cost of sales should decrease because of the decline in volumes. The fact that gross profit decreased by more than revenue indicates clearly that this is not what happened at Burberry in 2019. Rather, the gap between their selling prices and the direct costs of making their products has shrunk, so either selling prices have declined or the cost of producing the goods has increased, or both. In sections 11.2.3 and 11.5.1, we will examine the changes in revenue and gross profit in greater detail.

Interestingly, the accounting standards do not require that cost of sales is reported on the **face** of the statement of comprehensive income (that is, on the statement itself), instead allowing it to be disclosed in the notes to the financial statements. When this happens, if you want to know gross profit you have to calculate it yourself by subtracting cost of sales from revenue.

4.4.2 Net operating expenses

In section 2.2.7, PB presented its two operating expenses—salaries and electricity expense—on the statement of comprehensive income. This is similar to the way Daimler chose to present its 2019 Consolidated Statement of Income, which you can see in Appendix II. Of course, Daimler has far more such expenses, which it has summarised into categories—selling expenses, general administrative expenses, and research and non-capitalised development costs—to avoid using up many pages just for one statement. As with Daimler, when businesses present their operating expenses this way, there is usually a line-item 'Other operating expenses', into which all the expenses that do not fit into the established categories are collapsed.

When businesses show the list that makes up net operating expenses, it is typical to see the line-item 'Other operating income'. This summarises the income that is neither revenue nor income from financial assets (like interest income), which are both typically disclosed separately. Other operating income therefore includes items such as government

---

Gross profit is an important indicator of the performance of a business's operating activities, especially for a retailer or manufacturer.

4

grants and subsidies, and profits made on the sale of assets other than inventory (equipment that is being replaced, for example). Also, if some operating expenses that had been estimated and reported in previous years turn out in reality to have been lower than expected, then other operating income may include reversals. This is similar to the reversal of inventory write-downs discussed in section 4.4.1, though they had the effect of decreasing cost of sales.

Other businesses, like Burberry, include far less detail on the face of their income statements, simply reporting the single line-item 'Net operating expenses'. This figure will be made up of all the same sorts of operating expenses as for businesses who provide more detail like Daimler, minus the operating income (hence the word 'net'). If you have taken our advice to download Burberry's annual report, you can see that note 4 on p 178 breaks net operating expenses down into just two major categories: selling and distribution costs; and administrative expenses. Evidently, Burberry decided that users of the financial statements would not be interested to know more than this level of detail.

4

However, several types of costs must be disclosed according to the accounting standards and/or local legislation. These 'disclosable' expenses are usually found in a note to the financial statements, sometimes along with other cost figures which the business voluntarily discloses, in case they would be of value to users of the financial statements. This sort of information is to be found in Burberry's note 5 on p 179, which lists items such as depreciation, impairment, and employee costs. We will cover all of these expenses in later chapters when we consider the related assets and liabilities.

Although they often do not appear individually on the face of the financial statements, several operating expenses are required by IFRS to be disclosed, such as depreciation and employee costs.

Gross profit less net operating expenses is generally referred to as '**operating profit**' or 'profit before interest and tax'. Not all businesses show this subtotal (for instance, Daimler doesn't), but then users ought to calculate it for themselves since it is another important number in the profit story, revealing what is left of the business's revenue after subtracting both cost of sales and net operating expenses.

Burberry's operating profit increased 6.6% from £410.3 million in 2018 to £437.2 million in 2019. When viewed alongside the 1.9% decline in gross profit, this highlights the impact of the 4.3% decrease in net operating expenses: these cost savings are in fact the best explanation of how the business managed to improve overall profit for the year. We shall return to this key aspect of Burberry's 2019 performance in section.11.5.2.

4.4.3 Finance income and expense

In sections 2.2.10 and 2.2.11, we explained that it is typical for interest income and interest expense to be shown in a section below the operating profit subtotal and above the 'profit before tax' subtotal. However, the names of these items vary considerably. Some businesses label their interest expense 'finance costs' or 'finance expense', as Burberry has done. And interest income is likewise given a different name, like Burberry's 'finance income'.

Finance expenses, or finance costs, may include interest on borrowings and overdrafts, bank charges on borrowings, and interest expense arising from the unwinding of discounts.

4

And, of course, in the real world these terms describe more complex items than the interest PB earned on its bank account and incurred on its loan. Finance income can include the interest a business charges on the loans it makes to others; and also the interest income arising from the unwinding of discounts, for example on deferred payments from customers (see section 4.3.5). Sometimes, if the business owns shares in other companies, and earns dividends from these investments, this dividend income is grouped along with interest income in a line-item named 'Investment income'.

Finance expense may include bank charges on borrowings and also interest expense arising from the unwinding of discounts, for example on purchases the business makes using deferred payments. We will deal with all of these sorts of items in much more detail in section 6.6 about loans and receivables, and in Chapter 7 on liabilities.

Burberry's note 9 provides some detail about the income and expenses summarised by the three financial line-items on its income statement. For example, the bulk of finance income is bank interest, and finance expense includes interest on bank loans and overdrafts, as well as bank charges. It is important to note that Burberry's finance income being larger than its finance expense is unusual: most businesses take on far more debt than Burberry, and therefore their interest expense far exceeds their interest income. In section 11.3.5 in the chapter on financial analysis, we discuss Burberry's decision not to take advantage of the effects of leverage that we discussed in section 1.3.2.

4.4.4 Taxation

A quick look at note 10 to Burberry's financial statements reveals that for a real, sizeable business, there is quite a lot more to the taxation expense figure than we admitted when we briefly discussed PB's tax in section 2.2.12. Burberry's tax bill is levied not only by the UK, the country in which it is based, but also by foreign countries in which it operates. By summarising the effect of double-taxation agreements and adjustments in respect of prior years, the note acknowledges just a few of the complexities involved in the estimation of tax expense each year.

Although understanding the intricacies of the tax charged in any country is a lifelong challenge, even for tax professionals, it is reasonably easy to understand for our purposes. There is an old saying that 'Nothing in life is certain, except death and taxes', which is a reminder not to look for too much meaning in the tax figure, and just to accept that it is a cost of doing business. In the absence of any financial scandal to the contrary, it is reasonable to assume that Burberry—like just about any other business—has kept its tax expense to the minimum required by law and ethics. Anyone with a stake in the business would expect nothing less, given that, in 2019 for example, tax consumed 23.0% of Burberry's profit before tax (£101.5 m ÷ £440.6 m × 100).

A third component of the taxation expense is a notional tax called deferred tax. This concept—one of the trickiest in all of accounting—will be covered in section 8.3.

4.5 **PROFIT**

The 'additive' portion of the income statement (or of the profit or loss section, if the business uses the single-statement format of the statement of comprehensive income) ends with the profit figure. In years gone by, before several innovations in the presentation of this statement, profit was in fact the very last line of the statement, which is why it is still popularly referred to as the 'bottom line'. The profit figure is often also called '**earnings**', '**net income**', or 'profit or loss' (because a negative profit is called a 'loss').

Burberry's profit increased by 15.5% from £293.6 million in 2018 to £339.1 million in 2019. This is a very favourable overall change in one of the primary measures of the value created by a business, especially given that the business's revenue plateaued. You may also naturally be impressed by the absolute size of this figure—let's be honest, £340 million sounds like an awfully large amount of profit—but there's a danger when judgements about corporations' nine-digit numbers are made by people who in their personal lives deal in numbers with far fewer digits. In analysing the content of the financial statements, it is always best to use *relative* measures, of which there are many. (For instance, a relative measure that we shall cover in detail in section 11.3.4 is return on assets. This financial ratio calculates profit as a percentage of the business's average assets. At 14.9%, it confirms that Burberry indeed earned an impressive amount of profit in 2019.)

Below the profit figure, Burberry includes a breakdown of its profit into amounts attributable to the owners of the company versus amounts attributable to '**non-controlling interests**'.

This sort of split occurs whenever there are subsidiary companies that are only partially owned by the group of companies that make up the business. This requires an understanding of group financial statements, and so we'll be wise to leave it for now, and return to it in Chapter 9.

When people talk about the 'bottom line', they are usually referring to profit, which used to be the last line on a business's income statement.

4.6 **ALTERNATIVE PERFORMANCE MEASURES**

Accounting standards have been set with the intention of ensuring that profit is a key measure of financial performance. Total comprehensive income is another. But many businesses believe that there are other, perhaps superior ways to measure their performance, which they are permitted to disclose in their financial statements, despite not being prescribed by the standards. They are referred to as '**alternative performance measures**' or '**APMs**'.

Some APMs are well known and have been around for many decades, such as **EBITDA** (pronounced 'E-bit-dah'), which is an acronym for 'earnings before interest, tax, depreciation, and amortisation'. This is often seen as a proxy for operating cash flows because interest and tax are not operating costs, and depreciation and amortisation are not cash costs.

In some cases, the use of an APM is in fact mandated by an authority. For example, companies listed on the Johannesburg Stock Exchange in South Africa are required to disclose a 'headline earnings' figure, the determination of which is prescribed by a local regulatory body.

In most cases, however, the method used to determine an APM is decided by the business disclosing it. Because most users of the financial statements aim to predict future cash flows, one common way for a business to construct an APM is to remove from profit the items that are unlikely to recur. This is what Burberry has done, in an effort to report the most reliable indicator of the business's potential to generate sustainable earnings from its core business. Burberry gives its APM the title 'Adjusted profit before taxation—non-GAAP measure', for some reason deciding not to use the more common title '**Underlying profit**'.

A summarised reconciliation of this APM with profit before taxation appears towards the bottom of the income statement. Note 5 provides the full list of items that have been treated differently, and notes 6 and 7 offer rather full descriptions of each of these items. We will consider the implications of Burberry's APM when we analyse the business in section 11.2.4.

In most jurisdictions, businesses cannot disclose any APMs they like. For example, the European Securities and Markets Authority (ESMA) has released guidelines setting out basic requirements for APMs, such as that they should be fully explained, consistently calculated from year to year, and explicitly reconciled to the most directly reconcilable line-item in the statement of comprehensive income.[3]

4.7 DISCONTINUED OPERATIONS

Although Burberry's income statement includes no such line-item, you may well come across another business which reports an item such as 'profit from continuing operations', 'loss on discontinued operations', or 'loss on discontinuance'.

A **discontinued operation** is a major business unit that the business as a whole has disposed of, or is going to dispose of in the near future. On the statement of financial position, the assets and liabilities of a discontinued operation are required to be shown separately from those of continuing operations, as are the related cash flows on the statement of cash flows. In section 6.8, we shall explain the reporting of non-current assets held for sale.

The statement of comprehensive income is similar: the profit or loss relating to the discontinued operation must appear separately from the items of income and expense relating to continuing operations. Furthermore, the notes to the financial statements disclose the revenue, expenses, pre-tax profit or loss, and tax relating to

---

Alternative performance measures, or APMs, are typically disclosed at each business's discretion, although in most jurisdictions any APM a business chooses must comply with some basic requirements.

4

A discontinued operation is a business unit that the business has disposed of or is going to dispose of in the near future.

the discontinued operation. The reason for this echoes the thinking behind the calculation of APMs: when the information about the discontinued operation is disclosed separately, users are more easily able to assess the business's potential for future profits and cash flows, given that the discontinued operation will not contribute to either.

For example, in its 2019 consolidated income statement the European retail giant Carrefour reported a net income of €1 311 million (yes, that's €1.3 billion!), a massive improvement on its 2018 performance, a loss of €344 million.[4] However, during 2019, it sold 80% of its operation in China to a local retail business, and also disposed of a property business called Cargo. The income statement contains a line-item just above the net income figure called 'net income from discontinued operations' (see Example 4.3), which contributed €1 092 million, making up a very large portion of the net income for the year.

EXAMPLE 4.3

Extract from Carrefour's 2019 Consolidated Income Statement		
€m	2019	2018
Net income from continuing operations	219	36
Net income (loss) from discontinued operations	1 092	(380)
Net income (loss) for the year	1 311	(344)

The profit or loss from a discontinued operation has two components: the profit or loss it earned during the portion of the year while it was still part of the group; and the profit or loss that the group made when it disposed of the operation. It is not uncommon for discontinued operations to contribute a profit overall, like Carrefour's in 2019, but they often instead cause a loss. After all, the business usually disposes of them because they are underperforming. This is what happened in 2018, when Carrefour disposed of 273 struggling integrated convenience stores within its Dia network. These stores were doing so poorly that only twenty-seven of them were in fact sold, and the rest were simply closed.[5]

No one should overlook the huge creation of value in 2019, and the destruction of value in 2018, brought by the discontinued operations: they had a real and profound influence on the business's performance in those years. However, any user of the financial statements ought to have at least one eye on the future, and this is why the separate disclosure of the results from discontinued operations is so helpful. Instead of letting ourselves imagine that the business can sustain profits in excess of €1 billion, we ought to pay close attention to the profitability of the operations the business has retained, which followed a much more modest—though impressively upward—path, from profit of €36 million in 2018 to €219 million in 2019.

4.8 ITEMS OF OTHER COMPREHENSIVE INCOME

We now move to the second section on the one-statement format, or the second statement on the two-statement format. The following list contains the main items of income and expense currently reported in OCI. As you will no doubt notice on reading this list, they all are the result of complex business events, which we will therefore explain when we have a chance to deal with them in detail, in the sections indicated:

- gains and losses on revaluation of property, plant and equipment, or intangible assets (section 6.2.1);
- gains and losses on financial instruments that are either required or allowed to be recognised in OCI (section 6.7.2);
- gains and losses on cash flow hedges (section 6.7.3);
- gains and losses arising on the actuarial valuation of employers' post-retirement obligations to employees (section 7.2.7);
- gains and losses arising from the effect of changes in 'own credit risk' on the valuation of financial liabilities (section 7.3.1);
- gains and losses that arise when translating the results of foreign operations from the foreign currency (section 8.2.3);
- gains and losses for net investment hedges relating to foreign operations (section 8.2.3);
- gains and losses on revaluation of *available-for-sale* financial instruments (these were the result of an accounting standard that has been replaced, but we have left them in for completeness).

It may seem surprising that 'losses' can appear in OCI, which is, after all, the section of the statement of comprehensive income which does not affect profit or 'loss'. The explanation for this paradox is that there are two meanings of the term 'loss'. When it is used in expressions such as 'revaluation loss' or 'loss on sale of non-current asset', it refers to a specific, relatively uncommon transaction or event which has decreased the value of the business. In this sense, a loss is an expense, and the negative of a 'gain'. These sorts of losses (and gains) may appear either in the profit or loss section or in the OCI section, depending on the requirements of the accounting standards.

The other meaning of the word 'loss' is the one we encountered in section 4.5: the overall performance of a business if a negative result is obtained when subtracting items of expense from items of income in the profit or loss section. In this sense, a loss is the negative of a 'profit'.

A glance at Burberry's group statement of comprehensive income reveals three of the items in the list—cash flow hedges, net investment hedges, and foreign currency translation differences—with their tax effects shown separately. It is worth noting that the net effect of all of these items is a mere £13.0 million contribution to TCI, which is therefore

In accounting, the word 'loss' has two meanings: (1) the opposite of a gain, arising from a single event; and (2) the opposite of a profit, which is the combined result of the effects of many events.

4

that much higher than the profit of £339.1 million. At the bottom of the statement, TCI is split between owners of the company and non-controlling interests, like profit was in the income statement. (Again, this will be explained in Chapter 9.)

In both 2018 and 2019, the item of OCI that had by far the largest effect on TCI was the foreign currency translation differences, which—even without having read Chapter 8—you can correctly guess are subject to the whims of international rates of exchange. Therefore, like Carrefour's discontinued operations, this item is unlikely to be very helpful in predicting future performance, despite its genuine effect on performance in these years.

4.9 EARNINGS PER SHARE

We have covered almost every item that appears on Burberry's income statement and statement of comprehensive income, but you may have noticed that we skipped over the measures of earnings per share (EPS) disclosed near the bottom of the income statement. In fact, it is an IFRS requirement that listed companies present EPS figures on the face of the statement of comprehensive income, but we have left them until last, as they often appear at the end. (In fact, the final items shown on the face of Burberry's income statement are dividends per share figures. It is a little odd that the business's accountants chose to put this figure here, as the dividends themselves are disclosed on the statement of changes in equity. For this reason, we will defer our discussion of dividends per share until section 10.3.3.)

4.9.1 Purpose of EPS

The purpose of EPS is to facilitate two types of comparisons of business performance: first, from one business to another, in the same reporting period; and second, from one reporting period to the next, for the same business.

To understand the first notion of comparability, suppose that Business A and Business B made profits of €1 000 and €2 000, respectively. From the profit figures alone, it appears that B is the business with better performance, with double the profits of A. But let's develop the scenario, by supposing that Business A has had 500 shares in issue all year, whilst Business B has had 2 000 shares in issue. Thus, we could say that each share in Business A earned €2 profit (€1 000 ÷ 500 shares), whilst Business B earned only €1 profit per share (€2 000 ÷ 2 000 shares).

It is tempting to reverse our previous claim, and suggest instead that Business B was the better performer, since we would be better off with one share in Business A rather than one share in Business B. However, to *correctly* identify the better investment, we also need to consider the price of each share. If a share in Business A costs twice the amount of a share in Business B, then—since its shares each earned twice as much—the return from each share will be roughly equivalent from the investors' perspective. However, if Business B's shares

The disclosure of EPS figures achieves two main purposes: (1) comparability between different companies of varying sizes; and (2) comparability from one period to another for the same company.

4

cost less than half of Business A's, then Business B would be the more lucrative investment, and vice-versa. In this way, the EPS figure, when viewed in light of the share prices, allows us to make sensible comparisons between businesses that are of different sizes. We shall return to this point when we consider the price–earnings ratio in section 11.8.2.

To understand the second type of comparability facilitated by EPS, suppose that during Years 1 and 2, Business C makes profits of £2 000 and £3 000, respectively. At first glance, it would appear that Year 2 was the more successful year, with a 50% increase in profits. However, if Business C had 1 000 shares in issue during Year 1, but then issued another 1 000 shares at the beginning of Year 2, the increase in profitability is not so impressive, for the EPS in Year 1 was 200 pence per share (£2 000 ÷ 1 000 shares), whilst the Year 2 EPS dropped to 150 p (£3 000 ÷ 2 000 shares). Thus, on a share-by-share basis, Year 1 was a more profitable year. And so EPS figures, because they are a function of the number of shares in issue, also help with performance comparisons over time for the same business.

4.9.2 Basic earnings per share

Without defining it precisely, we have so far been considering the measure of EPS referred to as '**basic EPS**'. In practice, the calculation of this figure can be complicated, as there are often complexities in the share structure or share issues during the year which require a company to adjust the calculation to find the most meaningful measure of each share's earnings. These details are so intricate that there is an entire accounting standard, IAS 33, dedicated to calculating EPS. We shall happily avoid that level of detail here, as it is sufficient for our purposes to think that in essence basic EPS is calculated by dividing the profit for the year by the average number of shares in issue.

In simplest terms, basic EPS is the profit for the year divided by the average number of shares in issue.

The word 'basic' to describe this measure of EPS is not a reference to the ease of calculating it, but rather to differentiate it from the other measure of EPS that listed companies are required to report: **diluted EPS**.

4.9.3 The impact of new share issues on existing shareholders

Before we explain diluted EPS, we must first dispense with a popular misconception about the effect that share issues to new shareholders have on the value of the existing shareholders' shares.

MISCONCEPTION

If shares are issued to new shareholders, then existing shareholders lose out because the value of their shares is decreased, or 'diluted'.

This is not necessarily true. It all depends on whether the new shares are issued in exchange for resources that increase the business's value in proportion to the drop in the existing shareholders' fraction of the business.

Suppose that the only two shareholders of Business D each owns 500 shares, and that the value of the business is $2 000. They then bring in another shareholder, who receives 500 new shares and in return contributes $1 000 of capital. Each existing shareholder now owns a smaller fraction (one-third) of the business, which is why some people think that the value of their shares is diluted. But remember, the business is now worth $3 000 (the pre-issue value of $2 000, plus the capital contribution of $1 000). The existing shareholders have therefore not lost out: the value of their shareholding is still $1 000 each ($3 000 × ⅓). They have a smaller slice, but of a bigger pie.

In fact, if the additional capital can be invested in profitable opportunities, it is quite possible that, in time, bringing in the new shareholder will actually *create value* for the existing shareholders. Figure 4.4 illustrates the three scenarios we have considered pertaining to Business D. D1 represents the situation before the share issue. In D2, you see how—even after the share issue—the existing shareholders still own $2 000 of value. And D3 shows how the $1 000 of new capital may well lead to the growth of value for everyone, including the existing shareholders.

FIGURE 4.4 Four scenarios showing the varying possible impacts of new share issues

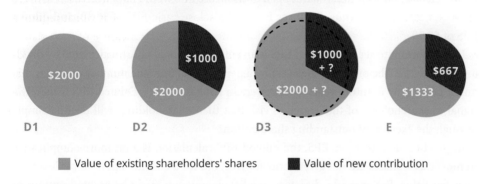

Scenario E represents a case in which existing shareholders do in fact experience a dilution. Suppose that Business E, with 1 000 shares in issue at the end of Year 1, has promised directors that at the beginning of Year 2, they will be given the option to acquire 500 new shares in Business E for free. This sort of promise is known as a **share option**. We will discuss the financial accounting for share options themselves in section 10.3.4. Here, we will discuss only the implications of share options for the reporting of EPS.

Presumably the directors will exercise their free option to acquire the shares. Then there would be 1 500 shares in issue, and—as is always the case when shares are issued to new shareholders—existing shareholders would own a smaller proportion of the business. Unlike scenarios D2 and D3, though, Business E is not worth any more after the share issue than it was before the issue, because the new shares are issued for free. If the business is worth $2 000, then the value of their shares would drop overnight from $2 each to $1.333 ($2 000 ÷ 1 500), so that the total value of the existing shareholders' shares would 'dilute' to $1 333 (1 000 × 1.333).

Of course, at the end of Year 1, the shareholders ought to be informed about an impending **dilution** like this. But how could the financial statements warn them about it? If financial statements provided an accurate valuation of the business, then they could point out how, say, the value attributable to the existing shareholders might drop from $2 000 to $1 333. But financial statements do not give business valuations. Indeed, Chapter 12 describes how any business valuation requires so many estimates and assumptions that it will inevitably be wrong. Financial accountants do not dare produce figures with such a high likelihood of error! (Section 10.1 will explain three reasons why equity—the so-called 'book value' of the business—is not a reliable business valuation.)

4.9.4 Diluted earnings per share

The solution to this dilemma is that the potentially dilutive effects of outstanding share options (and other similar arrangements) are shown, quite ingeniously, using EPS. The trick is to show how different the EPS for the year would have been had the share options already been exercised. If Business E made a profit of, say, $300 during Year 1, when it had 1 000 shares in issue, its basic EPS would be $0.30 ($300 ÷ 1 000 shares). However, had 500 additional shares been in issue, the EPS would have decreased to $0.20 ($300 ÷ 1 500 shares). Thus, Business E would disclose basic EPS of $0.30, and diluted EPS of $0.20.

It is important to see that diluted EPS is an entirely notional figure, calculated by dividing a real figure (the profit for the year) by a hypothetical one (the number of shares that might be in issue in future years, as if it were in issue this year). Diluted EPS is merely a signal to shareholders of the degree of risk that their shareholdings will decline simply through the exercise of outstanding share options.

In practice, as with basic EPS, the diluted EPS calculation is a bit more complicated. In most cases, shares are not given away for free, but for a consideration that is less than their fair value. For example, directors in a listed company might be granted options to acquire shares in the future for the current market price of $2. If in the future the shares are trading for, say, $3, then the dilutive effect of shares being issued at a discount of $1 is much smaller than the dilution that would be caused by an issue for free. The calculation of diluted EPS takes this into account.

It is also worth noting that usually there are conditions attached to share options. For example, directors may only be granted the share options if profitability improves substantially. In cases where the share price stipulated by the option is not overly generous, and where the conditions are sufficiently demanding, the notional effect indicated by diluted EPS may never come to pass, as the increased future profitability might more than compensate for the notional dilution. In such cases, existing shareholders should, of course, be happy with the growth in the value of their shares, and be willing to allow directors to share in these gains, to the extent that they were generated by the directors' excellent performance.

Diluted EPS is intended to indicate outstanding share options' potentially dilutive effect for existing shareholders.

4.9.5 EPS information on Burberry's income statement

Near the middle of Burberry's income statement, the 2019 'basic' EPS figure is reported to be 82.3 p per share. Just below that, diluted EPS of 81.7 p is shown. This indicates a relatively small potential dilution of 0.7% for the shareholders of Burberry. Note 11 explains that this potential dilution is caused by the existence of share options and awards made under the employee share incentive scheme, which at some time in the future might have a dilutive effect equivalent to issuing 2.8 million shares for free.

In a box below basic and diluted EPS, Burberry discloses 'Adjusted EPS' measures which align with its APM, 'Adjusted profit before taxation—non-GAAP measure'. The figures of 82.7 p and 82.1 p are meant to show what the business would have achieved had the non-recurring items not in fact occurred this year. Although this is not an EPS measure prescribed by IFRS, there's nothing wrong with Burberry disclosing it. In fact, there is no limit to the number of EPS figures a company may disclose, or to the number of names that might be given to them. For example, when you look at other businesses' financial statements, you should expect to see 'normalised EPS', 'underlying EPS', 'core EPS', 'pro forma EPS', 'recurring EPS', and several other interesting terms.

> There is no limit to the number of EPS figures a business may disclose.

As you will discover in Chapter 11 on financial analysis, EPS is regarded as a key figure by analysts, and is also an input into the formulas used to calculate a few critical financial ratios. Given that EPS has such a profound influence on investment decisions, it is little wonder that businesses typically take the opportunity to provide as many EPS figures as they think will be useful.

MISCONCEPTION

There is one earnings figure that captures the success of the business.

No single figure can capture the performance of a business. The more measures that you look at, the greater will be your understanding of that business. This is why a measure such as Burberry's adjusted EPS is valuable.

An EPS figure that Burberry did not present in 2019 was EPS from continuing operations, as it had no discontinued operations that year. Like all businesses with discontinued operations, Carrefour was required by IFRS to disclose, either on the face of the statement of comprehensive income, or in the notes to the financial statements, both basic and diluted EPS from continuing operations. Carrefour elected to put the figures on the face: they were both €0.04, indicating that any dilutive effect was too small to have an impact when rounded to the nearest cent. By contrast, the effect of the discontinued operations was remarkable: basic EPS from the discontinued operations was €1.39, with its diluted equivalent similarly revealing a huge impact.

Finally, you may have noticed that we have varied the way we have presented the EPS figures in this section. We have done so to match reality. In the UK, businesses traditionally report their earnings per share figures in pence, as Burberry has done. A few other countries also follow this convention, though Eurozone countries and the US do not, quoting EPS in euros and dollars, respectively.

4

MISCONCEPTION

The dividends that a company pays to its shareholders are reported in the statement of comprehensive income.

As we discussed in section 2.2.14, dividends are not an expense, and as such do not appear in the statement of comprehensive income. They are in fact a return to the shareholders and are shown as a subtraction from retained earnings in the statement of changes in equity (see section 10.2). Don't be thrown off by the fact that Burberry made the unusual choice to disclose dividends per share on its income statement. Presumably, this is intended to show how much of the EPS was distributed to shareholders as a dividend; it is not because dividends themselves appear on the income statement.

CONCLUSION

The story of a business's income and expenses is told by the statement of comprehensive income. From it, we can learn how well the business managed to use its assets to generate revenue, what costs were incurred to sell its goods and services, and consequently how these sales translated into profits. There is also an epilogue about the gains and losses reported in OCI. The story is told in instalments, using several subtotals which show the aggregate effects of related items of income and expense, such as gross profit, operating profit, profit, total comprehensive income, and so on. These help us to understand the various layers of activity within the business.

On their statements of comprehensive income, businesses also disclose a number of earnings per share figures that contextualise the profit relative to the number of shares that have been issued, along with the potential dilutive effects of outstanding share options and similar arrangements.

To see a further illustration of how statements of comprehensive income are presented, take a look at an example on the **online resources** (www.oup.com/he/winfield-graham-miller1e).

One of the most important things to remember about items of income and expense is that they arise from accrual accounting, which means they are reported regardless of whether cash has changed hands. Another is that the measurement of many items of income (such as revenue when the amount to be received is uncertain) and expense (such as depreciation) requires estimates based on judgement and opinion.

These two features of income and expense mean that they are contestable. Cash flows, on the other hand, are a much less theoretical measure of performance. The disclosure of cash inflows and outflows is covered in Chapter 5.

SUMMARY OF KEY POINTS

- The layout, level of detail, and terminology on different businesses' statements of comprehensive income vary a lot, but they conform to the same underlying structure and accounting principles.

- Income and expenses are reported using either a one-statement format (when the statement is often called the statement of comprehensive income) or a two-statement format (when the two statements are often called the income statement and the statement of comprehensive income, respectively).

- There are just a few items of OCI. The best explanation for the existence of OCI is the standard-setters' aversion to breaking with history and allowing these items to affect profit.

- Revenue from the sale of goods is recognised when control of the goods passes to the customer.

- Revenue from the sale of services is recognised when the service has been performed and the customer has acquired the benefits of the service.

- When a business will receive consideration from its customer that is variable because the final amount depends on what happens in the future, revenue is measured at the amount that the business ultimately expects to receive.

- When revenue is recognised over time, a reasonable measure of progress may be used to determine how much of the revenue to recognise in each financial period.

- Revenue from a contract that imposes multiple performance obligations on the business (such as the sale of a vehicle along with a service plan) is split between each obligation and recognised separately, as the business meets the revenue recognition requirements for each obligation.

- In a process known as 'unwinding the discount', deferred and advance payments received from customers result, respectively, in interest income and expense being recognised for the difference between the amount received and the selling price that would be charged for a cash sale.

- The financial accounting for customer loyalty programmes involves the deferring of some revenue as a deferred income liability until such time as the customers' loyalty is rewarded.

- Cost of sales includes the cost of inventory actually sold, and also the cost of inventory lost, perished, and stolen, as well as normal waste and write-downs for damage and obsolescence.

- When write-down estimates turn out in a later financial period to have been larger than required, they can be reversed, which produces the opposite effect in the later financial period.

- Although they often do not appear individually on the face of the financial statements, several operating expenses are required by IFRS to be disclosed, such as depreciation and employee costs.

- The finance expenses or finance costs line-item on a statement of comprehensive income may include interest on borrowings and overdrafts, bank charges on borrowings, and unwound discounts on advance payments for sales or deferred payments for purchases.

- Alternative performance measures, or APMs, are measures of performance that a business believes will be useful for users of the financial statements, as an alternative to the measures (such as profit) required to be reported by IFRS. They are reported at each business's discretion.

4

- The profits or losses from a business's discontinued operations are disclosed separately in order that users can assess the profitability of the operations that the business will retain in the future.
- Earnings per share, or EPS, figures are required to be disclosed by companies, to enhance comparability between different companies, and between financial periods for the same company.
- 'Basic' EPS is essentially calculated by dividing the profit for the year by the number of shares in issue during the year.
- 'Diluted' EPS is a notional figure intended to give an indication of the potential dilutive effects of outstanding share options and similar arrangements.
- Issues of new shares, provided they are issued for their fair value, do not have a dilutive effect on the value of the existing shareholders' shares, and may even add value.

CHAPTER QUESTIONS

The applied questions (marked 'AQ') and the discussion questions (marked 'DQ') relate to the financial statements of Daimler, contained in Appendix II. The suggested solutions to these questions, and also to the concept questions (marked 'CQ'), can be found in Appendix III.

Also, don't forget the **online resources** available at www.oup.com/he/winfield-graham-miller1e, which contain multiple-choice questions based on the material in this chapter, in addition to many other helpful resources, including two mini case studies, and accompanying questions and answers.

CONCEPT QUESTIONS

CQ 4.1 Briefly describe the two alternative formats that a business may use to present its statement of comprehensive income.

CQ 4.2 Explain the difference between the terms 'income' and 'revenue'.

CQ 4.3 If, on its statement of financial position, a business were to revalue its land from an amount of €10 million to €15 million, would the increase of €5 million be reported as income? Would it be added to profit for the period?

CQ 4.4 Explain why the taxation expense figure reported on a business's statement of comprehensive income (or income statement) according to IFRS is unlikely to equal the figure you would get if you multiply the profit before tax figure by the rate of taxation in the business's jurisdiction.

CQ 4.5 Describe briefly how an earnings per share figure is calculated, and explain why this is an important measure for the shareholders of a company.

APPLIED QUESTIONS

AQ 4.6 During what time period did the events whose effects are reported on Daimler's 2019 consolidated statement of income take place?

AQ 4.7 Identify which format option Daimler has chosen to report its items of income and expense. Name the related components and briefly describe the logical flow of this reporting.

AQ 4.8   Does Daimler's 2019 revenue amount of €172 745 million, reported in its statement of income, comprise sales made for cash, or on credit, or both? Justify your answer.

AQ 4.9   Daimler's 2019 statement of income reports other operating income of €2 837 million. Interrogate Daimler's notes to the financial statements to discover three items that are included in this amount. List these three items and explain where you found them.

AQ 4.10   Daimler's statement of income reports cost of sales of €143 580 million and selling expenses of €12 801 million. Briefly explain how the content of these two items differs.

AQ 4.11   The basic earnings per share amount of €2.22 reported on Daimler's statement of income is the same as the diluted earnings per share amount. What does this tell you?

AQ 4.12   Using the 2019 figures, show mathematically how Daimler's net profit, other comprehensive income/loss, and total comprehensive income are related.

DISCUSSION QUESTIONS

DQ 4.13   Comment on how Daimler's revenue changed between 2018 and 2019.

DQ 4.14   To help users of the financial statements understand its revenue, what useful disaggregated information does Daimler provide in the notes to the consolidated financial statements?

DQ 4.15   If, during 2019, Daimler had acquired a large amount of inventory that remained unsold at the year-end (31 December 2019), what effect would this have on the cost of sales figure of €143 580 million reported on its statement of income?

DQ 4.16   Discuss the extent to which Daimler's finance costs affected its profits in 2019.

DQ 4.17   How did Daimler's profitability change between 2018 and 2019? Indicate at least two reasons for this change, using evidence you find in the notes to the financial statements.

DQ 4.18   Between 2018 and 2019, Daimler's revenue increased by 3.2% and yet its gross profit declined by 11.7%. What does this tell you about Daimler's operations in 2019? Your answer should include some possible reasons for any inference that you draw.

DQ 4.19   Daimler's net profit for the year was €2 709 million and its total comprehensive income was €551 million. Which of these amounts—net profit or total comprehensive income—is a more meaningful measure of Daimler's core business performance for the year?

DQ 4.20   Is there any evidence to suggest that Daimler has more than one performance obligation with respect to the items that it sells? If so, explain the nature of these performance obligations and their accounting treatment.

INVESTIGATION QUESTIONS

IQ 4.21   Identify a listed retail company that is based in your country and obtain its financial statements. Examine this company's statement of comprehensive income, and establish the major factors that influence the company's profitability.

IQ 4.22   Imagine that you are consulting to the International Accounting Standards Board (IASB). Explain whether you think that the structure of the statement of comprehensive income is an effective way in which to report a business's performance. If not, suggest ways in which you think the current layout could be improved. (Hint: think about trading versus non-trading income, realised versus non-realised income, and the other comprehensive income section.)

IQ 4.23   When did Daimler adopt *IFRS 15: Revenue from Contracts with Customers*, and what were the main financial effects of adopting this new standard?

REFERENCES

1   Mowi ASA 2019. *Integrated Annual Report 2019*. Available at: https://corpsite.azureedge.net/corpsite/wp-content/uploads/2020/03/Mowi_Annual_Report_2019.pdf.

2   IASB 2015. *IFRS 15: Revenue from Contracts with Customers*. Definitions section.

3   European Securities and Markets Authority 2015. *ESMA Guidelines on Alternative Performance Measures*. Available at: https://www.esma.europa.eu/sites/default/files/library/2015/10/2015-esma-1415en.pdf.

4   Carrefour Group 2019. Consolidated financial statements as of 31 December 2019, pp 3, 12, and 13. Available at: https://www.carrefour.com/sites/default/files/2020-07/Comptes%20consolide%CC%81s%202019%20ANGLAIS.pdf.

5   Carrefour Group 2018. Consolidated financial statements as of 31 December 2018, p 13. Available at: https://www.carrefour.com/sites/default/files/2020-07/comptes_consolides_2018_-_version_anglaise_0.pdf.

CASH FLOWS

> ### Here are some of the things you will be able to do after reading this chapter:
>
> - identify the differences between profit and cash flows, and discuss the relative importance of these two measures of business value;
> - debate the usefulness of the information in the statement of comprehensive income versus the statement of cash flows and demonstrate how they are most informative when used together;
> - assess the quality of a business's earnings;
> - prepare a very basic statement of cash flows using either the direct or indirect method;
> - interpret the reported cash flow information, emphasising working capital management and also the overall message of the statement of cash flows.

This chapter builds on material covered in earlier chapters. If you don't feel comfortable with any of the following items, we recommend that you briefly go back now to the sections referenced.

- The **statement of cash flows** and the **statement of comprehensive income** both report a business's financial performance. The latter does this using **accrual accounting** (see section 2.2.8), whereas the statement of cash flows uses the **cash basis** (see section 2.2.15).

- This means that all of a business's **cash flows** for a period are reported in the statement of cash flows. The only items in the statement that are not cash flows are the opening and closing cash balances for the period, which appear at the bottom of the statement (there is a basic example of a statement of cash flows in section 2.2.15).

- The statement of cash flows categorises cash flows according to whether they relate to the **operating**, **investing,** or **financing activities** of the business (these were explained in section 1.3). The sections thus contain very different information for interpreting the business's activities.

- Many accounting principles and practices of relevance to this chapter were demonstrated at a simple level in Chapter 2, using the hypothetical example of a very small business that sells pizza slices, called the Pizza Business or 'PB'. We shall refer to PB in this chapter too.

The figures in the statement of cash flows do not require any estimates, judgements, or opinions.

If cash has been received or paid during the year, it will be reported on the statement of cash flows. If a transaction does not involve a cash flow, it will have no effect on the statement. The preparation of a statement of cash flows therefore requires no estimates, judgements, or opinions; so it is the only financial statement that is unambiguously a statement of fact.

This should not imply, however, that understanding a business's cash flows is a trivial matter. On the contrary, all of the following is true of the statement of cash flows: it presents information that has rich significance; it is prepared using some complex principles; and it demands a nuanced understanding of the role that cash plays in a business's daily operating activities. In this chapter, we will explore all of these topics, using Burberry as an example. Again, we encourage you to keep referring to the Burberry statement of cash flows presented in Appendix I, and also to have the downloaded notes to the financial statements at hand.

5.1 CASH AND CASH EQUIVALENTS

So far in this book, we have mentioned cash as if it is clear what we're talking about, but in fact the definition of cash is—for good reason—broader than you might imagine. For example, you may have coins and paper money in your wallet right now, but perhaps you also have a bank account from which you can draw when you need to. You may even have a savings facility which you cannot draw from without giving the bank a few days' warning. Do all of these count as cash in the sense that the term is used in the statement of cash flows? Yes, they do. IAS 7, the International Financial Reporting Standards (IFRS) accounting standard dedicated to the statement of cash flows, states that it is in fact a report of flows of '**cash** and **cash equivalents**'. These comprise notes, coins, demand deposits (also known as cheque or current accounts), and also all other 'short-term . . . investments that are readily convertible into known amounts of cash, and which are subject to an insignificant risk of changes in value'.[1]

The cash flows reported on a statement of cash flows are receipts or payments of 'cash and cash equivalents'.

Thus, if you make a transfer from your bank account to purchase shares in Burberry, your asset has ceased to be cash, just as if you had paid for groceries with a bank card or bought a book online. Although listed shares are easy to convert back into cash by selling them, they are subject to changes in value (that is, share price movements) in a way that cash and cash equivalents are not. The statement of cash flows would report such a transaction as an outflow of cash to purchase an investment. On the other hand, there is no cash flow when you deposit paper money into your bank account: in that case, your cash and cash equivalents are just changing from one form to another.

Thus, broadly speaking, the statement of cash flows reports as a cash outflow any payment made using cash, cheque, or electronic transfers to purchase assets other than cash or cash equivalents. Similarly, so long as they don't come from another source of the business's cash and cash equivalents, the receipt of coins, notes, or funds into a bank account would be reported as a cash inflow on the statement of cash flows.

5.2 PROFIT VERSUS CASH FLOWS

Section 1.3.4 described how, to create value, a business's operating activities must achieve three objectives: use assets to generate revenue; from this revenue earn profit; and then convert this profit into net operating cash inflows, as shown in Figure 5.1.

In Chapter 4, we investigated revenue and profit in detail; now we will focus on the third objective. Let's start by asking, 'Why is generating cash ultimately more important than earning profit?'

The short answer is that cash is real, whereas profit is a notional construct of the accounting equation. If you're not convinced by this, try the following experiment. Next time you're at the shops, tell the cashier that you don't have any money to pay for your shopping, and ask if instead you could pay with some profit. When they inevitably ask you what you mean, tell them, 'Well, I'd like to pay you with the positive difference between increases and decreases in my business's equity that have not been caused by transfers of value between me and my business.' Then see what they tell you!

Businesses must generate cash because cash is what pays the bills. In the short term (that is, in the next few days and weeks), businesses have to meet payment deadlines in order to ensure business continuity. And in the longer term (that is, several months or years from now), only by generating cash flow will businesses create the sort of value that can be transferred to owners.

Does it follow, then, that a **financial analyst**, whose job it is to assess the performance of businesses, should regard the statement of cash flows as more important than the statement of comprehensive income? Perhaps the short answer will surprise you: 'no'. The two

FIGURE 5.1 Extract of Figure 1.6

statements each perform vital, though different, functions for understanding a business and its financial performance. Asking a financial analyst which is more important is like asking them whether hearts or lungs are more important. Both are quite necessary.

A simple example can illustrate this. Consider the following statement of comprehensive income shown in Example 5.1.

EXAMPLE 5.1

Statement of comprehensive income	€
Revenue	100
Cost of sales	(50)
Gross profit	50
Operating expenses	(10)
Operating profit	40

Whether or not any cash had been exchanged, this information would be reported by a business which had purchased goods for €50 and then sold them for €100, incurring a €10 sales commission.

Supposing the business had not yet paid its sales staff or the supplier of inventory, or collected the money from the customer, the statement of cash flows would appear as in Example 5.2.

EXAMPLE 5.2

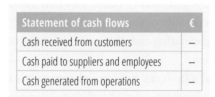

Statement of cash flows	€
Cash received from customers	–
Cash paid to suppliers and employees	–
Cash generated from operations	–

There is clearly a big difference between the informational content of the two financial statements. If we were to look only at the statement of comprehensive income in Example 5.1, we would see that the business has made an operating profit of €40, which reflects well on its performance. We would, however, miss a major point of concern, perhaps even a sign of an impending bankruptcy: it has generated no cash to pay its employees, suppliers, and lenders, or the tax authority. We can only know this by looking at the statement of cash flows.

But what if we were to look only at the statement of cash flows? It would seem that the business has achieved nothing at all, yet this is not the case. It has in fact made some profitable sales, which is a lot better than nothing. The statement of cash flows gives no indication of this, or of the likelihood that, thanks to its activities this year, the business will soon be netting a cash inflow of €40.

Thus, although the statement of cash flows is always the authoritative source for critical information about the short-term sustainability of the business, it is ironically the statement of comprehensive income which is the better indicator of future cash flows. Indeed, this idea—that the statement of comprehensive income more reliably predicts a business's ability to achieve its ultimate value creation goal of long-term net cash inflows—is conventional wisdom among financial analysts. Though at first counterintuitive, it makes sense when you think about it: accrual accounting should smooth out the short-term distortions in the statement of cash flows caused by the sporadic (or 'lumpy') inflows and outflows of cash.

As an aside, for those readers who aspire one day to become financial analysts themselves, we should point out that this is a contested notion. Although there is quite a lot of research which seems to support it,[2] there is other research which suggests that the information reported on the statement of cash flows may actually predict future cash flows more reliably.[3]

At the end of the day, no one who uses financial statements to make important decisions about a business would ignore either statement. They both tell us important—yet very different—things about the business's financial performance.

> The statement of comprehensive income and statement of cash flows tell us important—yet very different—things about the business's financial performance.

5.3 QUALITY OF EARNINGS

The way to get the most insight out of these two financial statements is to consult them together, and even to compare them. After all, the third objective of the business's operating activities involves converting the kind of value reported on the statement of comprehensive income—profit—into the kind of value reported on the statement of cash flows.

When financial analysts do a direct comparison of accrual figures with cash flows, we say that they are measuring the **quality of earnings**.

For the business whose financial statements are in Examples 5.1 and 5.2, the quality of earnings is very low because the operating profit has not been converted into even one euro of cash inflow. This sends three kinds of warnings to analysts, as follows.

> A business's quality of earnings is a measure of the extent to which its profits are converted into net cash inflows.

- The third value creation objective of operating activities is not currently being achieved. If the business is going to create any value at all in the long term, its ability to produce net cash inflows must improve dramatically.

- In the short term, there is a severe danger of the business going bankrupt because it is not generating the cash it needs to meet its payment obligations to creditors, employees, and so on.

- The positive returns reported by accrual accounting now seem a little suspect. Remember, the figures in the statement of comprehensive income are partly a function of financial accountants' subjective estimates, whereas the information on the statement of cash inflows is purely factual. Perhaps there is even some illicit manipulation of the accounting figures (see Chapter 13 for a plethora of real-world examples of this).

Of course, just having high profits and low net cash inflows does not mean that a business will ultimately fail to create value, go bankrupt in the near term, or be bust for accounting fraud. Perhaps the business has just started, or launched a new product, and the cash inflows are just around the corner. However, bear in mind that users of financial statements are mostly external to an organisation, and therefore working with limited information. They need to make decisions based on the balance of probability. And whether the low quality of earnings is just the result of an immature **value creation cycle** or outright accounting trickery, analysts would be sensible to view instances of low earnings quality with less confidence than cases where profits are being successfully converted into cash inflows.

Different kinds of quality of earnings can be assessed using different figures on the statement of comprehensive income. When we compared Examples 5.1 and 5.2, we were assessing the quality of operating profit by comparing it with cash generated from operations. In section 5.4.1, we will also assess the **quality of revenue** by contrasting the revenue figure with cash received from customers. You may come across other comparisons of figures from the two statements; these would also essentially be assessing earnings quality in some form.

When contrasting these figures, it is important that apples are compared with apples. That is, the two figures under comparison should be composed of amounts that broadly report the same events: one using accrual accounting, and the other on the cash basis. Accordingly, the quality of revenue is assessed by comparing how the two statements report sales of goods and services; and the quality of operating profit is assessed by comparing how they report the net effects of these sales and transactions with suppliers and employees.

For the rest of this chapter, we will cover in detail how cash flows are reported, beginning with the first section, which is packed with the richest information about the business's cash performance: operating activities.

5.4 OPERATING ACTIVITIES SECTION

The operating activities section consists of two subsections: one to report cash generated from operations; the other to report interest, dividend, and/or tax cash flows.

IAS 7 defines operating activities as the principal revenue-producing activities of the business, which means that any cash flow involved in the making or selling of a business's goods or services is likely to be reported in this section. Even tax cash flows, for example, fall into it. Basically, unless a payment or receipt clearly belongs in the investing or financing activities sections, then it will be found under operating activities.

There are two subsections in most businesses' operating activities sections. The second subsection reports the cash flows relating to interest, dividends, and/or tax cash flows. We will deal with that subsection later, in section 5.4.5.

The first subsection varies in length, but you can identify it because it ends with a subtotal named something like 'Cash generated from operations' (CGFO). Burberry has called this subtotal 'Cash generated from operating activities'. Slight variations in wording are common, but to understand a business, it is worth taking some time to locate this subtotal, because it reports the net cash generated from core business activities. That is, it is the difference between the cash received from customers and the cash paid to suppliers and employees during the year. This number is vitally important because, in the end, the value creation cycle is about generating cash for goods or services in excess of the amounts that are paid to buy or produce them, sell them, and administer the business.

Whilst this may seem simple enough, a complication arises as to how a business presents the calculation of the CGFO subtotal. Two methods are available to derive this number, namely the 'direct' and 'indirect' methods. Becoming familiar with each of these two methods will improve your understanding of the important relationship between profit and cash, and so we shall now spend some time explaining them.

> The first subsection of the operating activities section is prepared on either the direct method or the indirect method.

5.4.1 The direct method statement of cash flows

The direct method of presenting cash flows from operations is the simpler method to understand, and it is the one which IFRS encourages businesses to use. However, as it requires complex recording practices, relatively few businesses do actually use it. If you would like to see an example from the real world, we recommend that you download the 2019 financial statements of the Spanish telecoms giant Telefónica: the statement of cash flows presents a highly abbreviated direct method, which is fleshed out in note 28.[4]

You are already familiar with the direct method: we used it to present the first subsection of the operating activities section of PB's statement of cash flows in section 2.2.15. We have reproduced it here in Example 5.3 for easy reference, but we encourage you to go back and review where the numbers came from.

> The direct method calculates CGFO directly by subtracting the cash paid to suppliers and employees from the cash received from customers.

EXAMPLE 5.3

PB: STATEMENT OF CASH FLOWS (direct method)	
for Year 1	€
Operating activities:	
Cash received from customers	150
Cash paid to suppliers and employees	− 90
Cash generated from operations	60

The 'Cash received from customers' line-item reported on the direct method is very useful, as it allows analysts to assess the quality of revenue by comparing it to revenue in the statement of comprehensive income, which we have also reproduced here in Example 5.4.

EXAMPLE 5.4

PB: STATEMENT OF COMPREHENSIVE INCOME	
for Year 1	€
Revenue	300
Cost of sales	− 100
Gross profit	200
Operating expenses:	
Electricity	− 40
Salaries	− 50
Operating profit	110

PB's revenue of €300 is only half-matched by the cash received from customers, indicating a relatively weak quality of revenue. Ideally, there would be a closer match, but a mitigating factor here is that this was PB's first year. Indeed, if in any year a business experiences a significant increase in credit sales, a portion of which will only be collected next year, it is to be expected that revenue will be higher than the amount of cash received from customers. In such a case, we would expect to see an increase in accounts receivables in the statement of financial position, and would need to be satisfied as to the collectability of these receivables. (More on this in sections 6.6.2 and 6.6.3.)

In section 5.2, we explained how the CGFO figure can be contrasted with operating profit to assess the quality of operating earnings. In PB's case, the comparison of €60 with €110 indicates that its quality of operating earnings is not much stronger than its quality of revenue.

5.4.2 The differences between operating profit and CGFO

It will be very helpful at this point to reflect on *why* there is this difference between the €110 operating profit and the €60 CGFO. Of course, we know the high-level answer: one figure has been calculated using accrual accounting and the other is a result of the cash basis of accounting. But what are the *precise* reasons for this €50 difference? We know it's not simply one reason; that, say, €50 of credit sales haven't yet been collected. Rather, there are a number of items that have caused this difference, each of them treated differently by accrual accounting and the cash basis.

Table 2.2 in section 2.2.15 showed how each of PB's events was reported on these two bases of accounting, focusing on how they affected profit and net cash flow for the year. Table 5.1 presents a similar analysis, except that it summarises each item's effect on operating profit and CGFO. Those items that lead to differences between operating profit and CGFO are shaded.

TABLE 5.1 The effects on operating profit and CGFO of each of PB's events

Item	Effect on operating profit (accrual accounting)	Effect on CGFO (cash basis of accounting)
Capital contribution (Event 1)	No effect; no income or expense	No effect; cash inflow on receipt of capital is not an operating cash flow
Loan (Event 2)	No effect; no income or expense	No effect; cash inflow on receipt of loan is not an operating cash flow
Land (Events 3 and 13)	No effect; revaluation gain reported in OCI, so does not affect operating profit	No effect; cash outflow on acquisition is not an operating cash flow
Pizza oven (Events 3 and 9)	Decrease of €40; depreciation included in cost of sales expense	No effect; cash outflow on acquisition is not an operating cash flow
Cost of inventory (Events 4 and 6)	Decrease of €60; inventory consumed included in cost of sales expense	Decrease of €40; amount paid for cash purchases
Sale of inventory (Event 5)	Increase of €300; revenue	Increase of €150; amount received for cash sales
Salaries (Event 7)	Decrease of €50; salaries expense	Decrease of €50; amount paid to employees
Electricity (Event 8)	Decrease of €40; electricity expense	No effect; no cash yet paid
Interest (Events 10 and 11)	No effect; reported below operating profit, so does not affect it	No effect; these cash flows not reported in first subsection of operating activities
Tax (Event 12)	No effect; reported below operating profit, so does not affect it	No effect; no cash yet paid
Dividends (Event 14)	No effect; dividends are not expenses	No effect; no cash yet paid
Total effect	**€110 operating profit**	**€60 cash generated from operations**

We can immediately see how different the effects of accrual accounting and the cash basis are: of the five items that affected operating profit and/or CGFO, there was only one item which had the same effect on both figures: the salaries. The other four items, all shaded in the table, led to differences between operating profit and CGFO, as follows:

- pizza oven: depreciation caused operating profit to be *lower* by €40 than CGFO;
- cost of inventory: the difference between cost of sales and the cash paid for inventory caused operating profit to be *lower* by €20 than CGFO (€60 – €40);
- sale of inventory: the difference between revenue and the cash actually received from customers caused operating profit to be *higher* by €150 than CGFO;
- electricity: the difference between the expense and what was paid (in this case, zero) caused operating profit to be *lower* by €40 than CGFO.

So *these* are the precise reasons that operating profit was higher than CGFO. The overall difference of €50 was the net effect of these four differences (that is, − €40 − €20 + €150 − €40 = + €50).

Now that we have identified these specific explanations for PB, let's try to identify in general terms *why* they each caused a difference, so that we can understand what sorts of items will cause a difference between the operating profit and CGFO of *any* business.

- Pizza oven: depreciation reduced operating profit, but it did not affect CGFO. The reason for this is that it is not associated with an operating cash flow: as section 2.2.9 explained, depreciation is an invention of financial accountants to expense, over the useful life of a non-current asset, the cost of acquiring it. So if there's a cash flow associated with depreciation, it is an investing cash flow, not an operating cash flow. Other items that affect operating profit but which are not associated with an operating cash flow include: amortisation (see section 6.4.4); impairment (see section 6.1.10); and gains and losses on the sale of non-current assets (see section 6.1.9). Note that most of these are expenses, but not all of them, like a gain on the sale of a non-current asset.

- Cost of inventory: there are two reasons that cost of sales is different from the cash paid for inventory. One is that a business rarely sells the same amount of inventory as it purchases. PB, for example, expensed €60 of inventory sold, but it purchased €80, so that €20 was left in inventory at year-end. Thus, if (like with PB) a business's inventory balance is larger at the end of the year than at the beginning, then it must have purchased more than it sold, and vice-versa. The other reason is that the business rarely pays during a year for the same amount as it has purchased during the year. For example, PB purchased €80 of inventory, but paid for only €40, leaving another €40 of accounts payable. Thus, if (as with PB) the accounts payable balance for inventory is larger at the end of the year than at the beginning, then the business must have paid for less than it purchased, and vice-versa.

- Sale of inventory: PB's revenue was larger than cash received from customers because of the credit sales still owing at year-end. Revenue is not always the bigger figure, however. Imagine a business with high accounts receivable at the beginning of a year: the collection of these debts might cause cash received from customers to be *higher* than revenue for that year. Thus, if (as with PB) a business's accounts receivable balance is larger at the end of the year than at the beginning, then its revenue must be higher than the amount of cash it received, and vice-versa.

- Electricity: the expense was higher than the cash paid because of how much was still due at year-end (in PB's case, all of it). Sometimes, expenses are instead *lower* than the cash payments because large amounts owing at the beginning of the year are paid during the year. Thus, if (as with PB) a business's accounts payable balance for operating expenses is larger at the end of the year than at the beginning, then its expense must be higher than the cash outflow, and vice-versa.

From the above analysis, with careful thought we can draw some very important general conclusions about the precise reasons that, taken together, cause the overall difference between a business's operating profit and its CGFO:

1. Operating expenses not associated with an operating cash flow (like depreciation, amortisation, and impairment) cause operating profit to be lower than CGFO.

2. Operating income not associated with an operating cash flow (like a gain on the sale of a non-current asset) cause operating profit to be higher than CGFO.

3. An increase in inventory causes operating profit to be higher than CGFO, and vice-versa.

4. An increase in accounts payable (whether for inventory or operating expenses) causes operating profit to be lower than CGFO, and vice-versa.

5. An increase in accounts receivable causes operating profit to be higher than CGFO, and vice-versa.

5.4.3 Preparing the indirect method statement of cash flows

On Burberry's statement of cash flows, you will not see the two line-items 'Cash received from customers' and 'Cash paid to suppliers and employees', as the retailer has not used the direct method to calculate CGFO. Instead, it has used the indirect method, which, as the name suggests, arrives at the CGFO figure *indirectly*. This involves starting with the operating profit figure from the statement of comprehensive income and making a series of changes to that figure in order to remove the effects of any differences between it and CGFO. (Daimler's statement of cash flows in Appendix II is also prepared using the indirect method, but Daimler has started with 'Profit before income taxes' because it did not include an operating profit subtotal in its statement of income. This is a trivial matter: the principles described here apply just the same.)

The indirect method calculates CGFO indirectly by starting with operating profit and then removing the effects of any differences between that figure and CGFO.

We can deduce what changes are necessary to remove the effect of each difference between operating profit and CGFO in our numbered list in section 5.4.2, as follows:

1. Operating expenses not associated with an operating cash flow (like depreciation, amortisation, and impairment) should be *added back* to operating profit.

2. Operating income not associated with an operating cash flow (like a gain on the sale of a non-current asset) should be *subtracted from* operating profit.

3. An increase in inventory should be *subtracted from* operating profit, and vice-versa.

4. An increase in accounts payable should be *added to* operating profit, and vice-versa.

5. An increase in accounts receivable should be *subtracted from* operating profit, and vice-versa.

Let us return to PB and see if we can arrive at the same CGFO figure that we had on the direct method, but this time using the indirect method. We start with the operating profit of €110, and then proceed through the steps outlined above.

1. Add back to operating profit depreciation of €40.

2. As PB did not report any operating income that was not associated with an operating cash flow, this step is unnecessary.

3. Subtract from operating profit the increase in inventory of €20.

4. Add to operating profit the increase in accounts payable of €80.

5. Subtract from operating profit the increase in accounts receivable of €150.

In Example 5.5, we have taken these steps to prepare the first subsection of PB's operating activities section on the 'indirect method'. Steps 3–5 are often presented under the heading 'Working capital changes', as shown here.

EXAMPLE 5.5

PB: STATEMENT OF CASH FLOWS (indirect method)	
for Year 1	€
Operating activities:	
Operating profit	110
Non-cash flow item:	
Depreciation	+ 40
Working capital changes:	
Increase in inventory	− 20
Increase in accounts payable	+ 80
Increase in accounts receivable	− 150
Cash generated from operations	60

Note that the CGFO amount is the same in both the indirect and the direct statement of cash flows; only the way we arrive at it is different. From that point on (that is, below the CGFO line-item), there are no differences between the statements of cash flows prepared using the two methods.

At this point, a few words of reassurance may be necessary. The indirect method's reconciling of operating profit and CGFO is conceptually very challenging, and gives sleepless nights to many aspiring accountants. If you have followed the basic logic of this section, that is more than enough for a non-specialist. At minimum, you should have a rough sense of the reasons that a business's operating profit and its CGFO almost always differ; and you should understand that the indirect method calculates CGFO by beginning with operating profit (or some similar profit figure from the statement of comprehensive income) and then reversing the effects of every item that makes it different from CGFO.

Test your understanding by attempting to prepare a simple statement of cash flows using the indirect method yourself: the **online resources** include a worked example for doing this.

5.4.4 Interpreting the indirect method statement of cash flows

In section 5.4.3, we allowed ourselves to focus on the preparation of a financial statement, despite the fact that we do not wish to turn our readers into accountants. The reason we are asking you to make this effort to understand at a basic level how the indirect method works is because then you will understand what it really means about the business, which *is* what we are aiming for. So now let's turn explicitly to the question of what useful information the indirect method contains for a user of the financial statements.

Recall that the third—and arguably most important—value creation objective of a business's operating activities is to convert profit into operating cash inflow. Recall too that the term 'quality of earnings' describes whether this has been achieved. Well, the indirect method is essentially a report to explain a business's quality of earnings, as it shows the precise reasons for the differences between operating profit and operating cash flow.

Now, at the end of section 5.4.2 you saw the list of all possible such reasons. There are five of them, falling into two types. The reasons numbered 1 and 2 are of one type: operating profit may have been affected by items of income and expense that are not associated with operating cash flows, like depreciation. Reasons 3–5 are of the second type: the reasons whose effects were removed under the heading 'Working capital changes' in the indirect method statement of cash flows.

The first type of reason should almost always cause operating profit to be *lower* than CGFO. This is because it is almost always the case that there are more items of expense not associated with operating cash flows than there are items of income not associated with operating cash flows. For PB, there was one such expense—depreciation—and no such items of income. You will see when, in section 5.4.6, we look at Burberry's statement of cash flows that in 2019 Burberry had six such expenses and just two such items of income, with the amounts of the expenses dwarfing the amounts of income.

This means that it is the other type of reasons—the working capital changes—which determine whether a business has managed to convert operating profit into operating cash flows. So let's focus on them, and let's start by asking what exactly working capital is.

Working capital management

Put simply, **working capital** consists of the business's **current assets** and **current liabilities**. Generally, therefore, working capital is made up of accounts receivable, inventory, cash, and accounts payable, along with a few smaller items in some businesses. The components of working capital are connected in a complex system, such that any single operating activity affects them in multiple ways.

Careful management of this system—namely, working capital management—is absolutely essential for any business, or it risks running out of cash. It is therefore appropriate

A business's working capital consists of its current assets and current liabilities.

for you to invest some effort to understand Figure 5.2. A quick warning: as the system is complex, any representation of it needs to be fairly complex too, so getting to grips with it may require a little more time and energy than usual.

FIGURE 5.2 The complex system of working capital, illustrating how value flows between the components

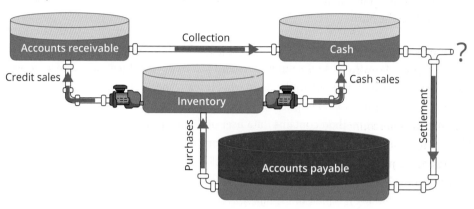

5

Working capital must be carefully managed in order to ensure that debts can be paid when they fall due.

Because inventory, accounts receivable, and cash are assets, they are stores of value, and so in the illustration we have depicted them as water (or some other precious liquid) stored in tanks.

As accounts payable is a liability, it works differently. Here, the whole tank represents the maximum credit that suppliers are willing to grant the business. The empty red space represents accounts payable: the amount they currently owe suppliers. The liquid in the tank represents the suppliers' value (their goods and services) still available to be transferred to the business on credit.

The business's operating activities cause value to flow between these tanks, as depicted by the arrows.

- *Purchases of inventory* move value from the suppliers to the business, while creating an obligation to transfer value back to the supplier later (in the form of cash). The more that is transferred from suppliers, the larger the red area representing the obligation. When it arrives in the business, it is recognised as inventory. (Note that all these purchases are on credit: we have not depicted cash purchases in the illustration, as they are rare in real-world businesses.)

- The next event, the *sale of inventory*, involves not just a flow of value, but also—assuming that it is sold for more than its cost—the potential creation of additional value (depicted by the pumps).

- *Cash sales* cause value to flow directly from inventory to cash.

- *Credit sales* cause value to flow from inventory to the accounts receivable asset, from where it flows to the cash asset when the debt is collected.

- Cash is used for a wide variety of purposes, such as the repayment of long-term loans, acquisition of non-current assets, payment of dividends, settling the tax bill, and so on. As there are too many such payments to list, we have depicted them with a simple question mark.

- From a working capital perspective, the key payment is the cash flow to accounts payable; that is, the *settlement* of the business's obligation to pay for inventory whose purchase began the working capital cycle. This reduces accounts payable, the red space in that tank, and replenishes the liquid, the amount that suppliers are willing to sell to the business on credit.

There are several very important lessons to be learned from the illustration. First, there's the big picture. We already know that the ultimate value creation goal of a business is net operating cash inflows, so the business can only claim to have succeeded in creating value when it receives cash. In that sense, the tank representing cash is by far the most important. But the interconnected nature of the system means that any of the events depicted is likely to have an effect on cash, so all of the other components of working capital need to be considered just as seriously as cash.

For the next lesson, since it is most important, let's focus on the tank representing cash. At any point in time it is vital that the business has enough cash on hand to be able to settle its payment obligations. This means that it is not sufficient simply to know that *right now* there is enough cash on hand, for that level could change very quickly. Even more important are the future *flows* of cash—in from inventory and accounts receivable; out to accounts payable—which must be carefully anticipated and managed so that for the foreseeable future there will be enough cash to pay debts as they fall due.

> **MISCONCEPTION**
>
> A business should keep as much money in its bank account as possible.
>
> No. Whilst it is important that a business has some cash in its bank account, it is inefficient for a business to hold large cash balances because the interest it earns is much lower than the return the business should be able to earn through its operations. A business should instead focus on forecasting future cash flows so that it holds no more cash than the amount required to cover the necessary outflows before the next inflows.

The third important lesson is about inventory. You might think that the higher the level of a business's assets, the better, but of course this is only true if the assets are being used to generate revenue. Look at the tank representing inventory. What does it mean if inventory levels are increasing? Only one thing: purchases are higher than sales. Since sales are the way in which inventory generates revenue, increasing inventory balances do not indicate value creation. In fact, they may indicate a danger of the business running out of cash: debts to suppliers are expanding, but the flow of value that will ultimately pay for these debts is not keeping up. If a business's working capital management increases the risk of running out of cash like this, it is called 'inefficient'. It is best to make inventory as efficient as possible, by keeping only as much of it as is required to maintain the product range and avoid **stock-outs**. Thus, decreases in inventory down to this level should not be interpreted as a disappointing sign of a contracting asset base; rather, they represent more efficient working capital management.

Fourth, there is a similar lesson about accounts receivable. While a good sign of impending cash inflows, accounts receivable only actually produces value for the business once the debts are collected. As is plain from Figure 5.2, increases in accounts receivable simply mean that collections are not keeping up with sales, which is inefficient working capital management, because the due date to pay suppliers for this inventory is approaching, if not already past, and meanwhile, the cash has not been collected. It is best to keep receivables balances no higher than is required to discourage potential customers from patronising competitors who are offering better credit terms. Decreases in accounts receivable, provided they are not caused by a tightening of credit terms that chases customers away, represent more efficient working capital management.

Fifth, there is a very different lesson to be learned about accounts payable, which is typically a cheap source of business funding. Efficient working capital management involves reducing the flow out of the cash tank to the suppliers' tank, and thus allowing accounts payable—the red space in that tank—to grow as large as possible. *Increases* in accounts payable are efficient. However, the tank must not run completely dry: if value keeps flowing out of the tank, and not back in, accounts payable will become so large that suppliers will no longer be willing to sell to the business, at least not on favourable terms. In other words, it is best to let accounts payable grow as big as possible, provided this doesn't damage relationships with suppliers or incur high interest costs. Decreases in accounts payable, on the other hand, are inefficient because of their negative effect on cash flow, so good working capital management requires businesses to avoid paying creditors any sooner than necessary.

Finally, as in most complex systems, there are some trade-offs available to managers of working capital. For example, suppose that a business's marketing team implements a new strategy to increase the product range in order to grow market share. This requires an increased flow of purchases to ensure that the business carries a viable stock of the new product lines, forcing the level in the inventory tank to rise. It may be possible to trade away this inefficiency by making one of the other components of the system more efficient. For example, if the business could negotiate longer credit terms with suppliers, then the delay in settlements would avoid an immediate demand for additional cash outflow. In Figure 5.2, this would be like enlarging the suppliers' tank and the liquid in it, so that the extra purchases do not cause the tank to run dry. The rising inventory levels would thus be balanced by increased accounts payable, and the rest of the system can function much as it did before. Ideally, when sales of the new product lines begin to add to the flows out of the inventory tank, they will lead over time to a larger inflow of cash, to match the increased outflow required to settle the larger accounts payable balance by the time the extended credit period expires.

If suppliers refuse to offer more generous credit terms, the cash outflow required to settle accounts payable will have to increase sooner. But there may be other trade-offs available. For example, perhaps the new product range could be sold for cash only. In terms of Figure 5.2, this would divert more of the outflow from the rising levels in the inventory tank directly to cash, rather than to the longer route via accounts receivable. This would boost the inflow to the cash tank in a way that compensates for the increased outflow to accounts payable.

Because of its importance and complexity, working capital management is a topic that would fill many more pages of a book on financial management. If you want the businesses

---

5

Efficient working capital management involves keeping inventory and receivables balances as low as possible and payables balances as high as possible.

When, for some reason, a component of working capital becomes less efficient, trade-offs are often available to reduce or eliminate the overall inefficiency in the system.

that you are involved in to be successful, we recommend that you learn much more about it. Our task here is just to introduce you to the topic, and to show you how a statement of cash flows prepared using the indirect method plays a helpful role in reporting how changes in working capital have impacted the cash flows of the business.

Working capital on the indirect method statement of cash flows

Let's now return to the indirect method statement of cash flows in Example 5.5, focusing on the working capital changes. The statement shows quite plainly how the increase in inventory has had a negative effect on PB's cash flows. That additional inventory has either had to be paid for already, or will have to be paid for soon, but it hasn't yet delivered any cash to the business.

The increase in accounts payable, on the other hand, has—at least so far—had a positive cash flow effect: it has saved the business's precious cash. Yes, these bills will have to be paid for one day, but the further in the future that day is, the better for working capital management.

Like the increase in inventory, the increase in accounts receivable has had a negative cash effect. Of course, it's great to make profitable sales, but until that profit is converted into cash, the business has not achieved the ultimate value creation objective.

Had these changes in working capital not occurred, CGFO would have been *higher* than operating profit by the €40 depreciation charge: the working capital changes in sum conspired to delay the conversion of €80 of operating profit into cash.

We will revisit working capital management in section 11.4, in the chapter on financial analysis. In the meantime, Table 5.2 summarises the cash flow effects of increases in inventory, accounts receivable, and accounts payable. Decreases in these accounts would, of course, have the opposite effects.

TABLE 5.2 Effect on cash flow of increases in working capital components

Account increased	Effect on cash flow
Inventory	Decrease
Accounts receivable	Decrease
Accounts payable	Increase

Although it is a component of working capital, cash itself is not in this list because it is just the cash *balance*, and has no effect on *cash flow*, just as the level of water in a tank today does not influence how much the level will change in the coming week. Rather, it is the other components of working capital that determine operating cash flow.

One last thing about working capital: some business analysts like to talk about working capital (or 'net working capital') as the result of the following formula.

$$(Net) \text{ working capital} = \text{Current assets} - \text{Current liabilities}$$

You may therefore hear about working capital itself increasing or decreasing. For all the reasons we have discussed in this section, increases in working capital are inefficient, unless the component of working capital that is increasing is cash itself; and vice-versa.

5.4.5 **The second subsection of the operating activities section**

We have now dealt with the first subsection of the operating activities section, the one that ends with CGFO. The second subsection usually reports the receipt and payment of interest, the receipt of dividends (if the business owns the shares of other companies), and the payment of tax. You may be surprised to see some of these items in the operating activities section at all, as interest and dividends received are really returns from investing activities, and interest paid is a cost of a business's financing activities. Indeed, some businesses do disclose them in those other sections of the statement. However, many businesses take the option granted by IAS 7 to list them under operating cash flows. There is some sense in this, as these events are reported (albeit using accrual accounting) in the determination of profit in the statement of comprehensive income. Therefore, along with the other items included in the operating activities section of the statement of cash flows, they can aid users in assessing the quality of earnings and in understanding the differences between profit and cash.

We have chosen this option for PB, and for the sake of comparison, have presented the entire operating activities section on the direct and indirect methods, side by side in Example 5.6. The second subsection is highlighted, revealing how it is exactly the same on both methods.

EXAMPLE 5.6

PB: STATEMENT OF CASH FLOWS (direct method)		PB: STATEMENT OF CASH FLOWS (indirect method)	
for Year 1	€	for Year 1	€
Operating activities:		Operating activities:	
Cash received from customers	150	Operating profit	110
Cash paid to suppliers and employees	− 90	Non-cash flow item:	
Cash generated from operations	60	Depreciation	+ 40
Dividends received	0	Working capital changes:	
Interest received	2	Increase in inventory	− 20
Interest paid	− 7	Increase in accounts payable	+ 80
Tax paid	0	Increase in accounts receivable	− 150
Net cash from operating activities	55	Cash generated from operations	60
		Dividends received	0
		Interest received	2
		Interest paid	− 7
		Tax paid	0
		Net cash from operating activities	55

5.4.6 **Burberry's operating activities**

We now turn to the operating activities section of Burberry's statement of cash flows, which—you should now be able to tell—uses the indirect method. (Clues include the operating profit figure in the first line and then line-items like depreciation: such items have no place on a statement prepared using the direct method, in which every line-item strictly reports an operating cash flow.)

At first glance, you may think that this section of Burberry's statement looks substantially different from PB's, but in fact the only major difference is the one we have already mentioned: it lists not one, but eight, items of income or expense which are not associated with an operating cash flow. (The list begins with 'Depreciation' and ends with 'Charge in respect of employee share incentive schemes'.) Although you will have to read the rest of this book to understand what many of these items represent, it is clear that they are accrual-based items not associated with an operating cash flow, for the expenses (or losses) are added back to operating profit, and the items of income (or gains) are subtracted.

The next line-item, 'Receipt from settlement of equity swap contracts', is interesting because it is in fact a cash flow. As you know, at this point the indirect method usually removes the effects of items that were included in operating profit, but which should not be included in CGFO. However, accrual accounting required this event to affect operating profit in previous years, not in 2019. Since the cash flow did occur in 2019, it now needs to be added in order to calculate CGFO correctly.

The rest of the section should look very familiar, as it is virtually a carbon copy of PB's: even the direction of the 2019 working capital changes is the same, although of course the amounts are vastly different. Also, the word 'provisions' has been added to the payables line-item. Provisions are dealt with thoroughly in Chapter 7 on liabilities, but for now it will be enough for you to know that they are just a type of payable. In fact, PB's unpaid electricity is an example of a provision.

Because Burberry has not used the direct method to prepare its statement of cash flows, we cannot see how much cash the business received from its customers, and so we cannot assess its quality of revenue. Overall, though, the quality of Burberry's operating earnings appears to be high: in 2019, CGFO was £515.9 million, compared with operating profit of £437.2 million; and in 2018 the positive difference was even more pronounced. This motivates for confidence in Burberry's long-term value creation capabilities, its short-term sustainability, and also the authenticity of the accrual-based figures on Burberry's income statement.

If you wonder how cash flows can be so much higher than profits, especially in 2018, then you have an opportunity to employ your newfound ability to scrutinise the indirect method for the reasons. The first kind of reason is contained in those eight items of income or expense that are not associated with an operating cash flow, by far the largest of which is depreciation.

The other kind of reason is relatively efficient management of working capital. In 2019, the positive effect of the increase in payables cancelled out the negative effect of the

High quality of earnings motivates for confidence in a business's long-term value creation capability, its short-term sustainability, and the authenticity of its statement of comprehensive income.

increase in receivables, and the negative effect of the increase in inventories was much smaller than the positive differences explained by depreciation and the other items in the list of eight.

Even more impressive was the giant leap forward that Burberry's working capital management took in 2018, with each one of the three components of working capital, especially payables and provisions, generating a positive difference between profit and cash. These efficiencies are the root explanation for the excellent quality of earnings in 2018, delivering a total of £220.8 million (£37.2 m + £68.1 m + £115.5 m) more cash than profit. By comparison, in 2019, the 6.6% year-on-year improvement in operating profit was easily wiped out by the working capital changes, which dropped the cash flow £59.0 million below operating profit (− £59.3 m − £54.6 m + £54.9 m).

MISCONCEPTION

This year's working capital changes can be compared straightforwardly to the previous year's working capital changes in a meaningful way.

This thinking betrays a misunderstanding. Suppose, for example, that this year accounts receivable decreased by €10 million and last year it also decreased, but by €25 million. It might be tempting to conclude, because this year's figure is smaller than last year's, that the management of accounts receivable has become less efficient. But remember what a decrease in accounts receivable means: the business received more cash than revenue because the amount owed by debtors declined between last year and this year. Clearly, any decrease in accounts receivable is an improvement on last year, no matter what change in accounts receivable was reported on last year's statement of cash flows.

All working capital changes work this way: it is not possible to compare them straightforwardly from year to year. Although you may obtain great insight into a business by contrasting most figures in the financial statements with their equivalents for the previous year, we recommend that you do not do this with working capital changes.

In case you have tried to reconcile the working capital changes reported in the statement of cash flows with the changes in the relevant balances in Burberry's 2018 and 2019 balance sheets, we should mention that this will not usually work for a large business. There are a few quite complicated reasons for this, including that when a business unit is acquired or sold, the changes to the balances on the working capital accounts are disclosed under investing activities, and not in the working capital changes reported in the operating activities section. The figures which best reflect a business's working capital management are those in the statement of cash flows.

5.5 INVESTING ACTIVITIES SECTION

The investing activities section of the statement of cash flows typically reports the outflows and inflows that arise from the acquisition and disposal of non-current assets.

According to IAS 7, for the purposes of categorising items on the statement of cash flows, investing activities involve the acquisition and disposal of non-current assets and other investments. Thus, in the investing activities section, you will find cash outflows resulting from the purchase of property, plant and equipment, intangible assets, and even entire business units, along with cash inflows relating to the sale of these items. Cash inflows and outflows resulting from providing loans and investing in debt instruments (such as government or corporate bonds) would also be reported here.

As we noted in section 2.2.15, transactions relating to *current* assets like inventory are categorised on the statement of cash flows as operating activities rather than investing activities. After reading section 5.4, it should be clear to you why this is the more useful arrangement for understanding the business's cash performance.

The extent of a business's investment in non-current assets generally determines its operating capacity; that is, the scale of operations that it is capable of producing. The larger its factory, the greater a manufacturer's potential output. The more branches a physical retailer has, the bigger the market it can reach. The higher its spend on hardware and software, the more users a tech business can serve, and so on. Thus, disclosure of a business's investing cash flows during the year will help users of the financial statements to forecast the scale of potential future revenues.

Often the investing activities section simply lists all the relevant cash inflows and outflows. Sometimes businesses also split these cash flows between those that will *maintain* operating capacity and those that will *expand* it. This split has some additional predictive value, because acquisitions which expand operating capacity have the potential ultimately to increase operating cash flows, whilst spending on maintenance is likely (unless there are significant cost-saving opportunities) merely to preserve existing returns.

Burberry provides relatively little detail about its cash flows relating to investing activities, and does not distinguish between purchases which maintain, and those which expand, operating capacity. To get a rough idea, though, we can compare the cash outflows to acquire new **property, plant and equipment** (PPE) to the depreciation charge shown higher up the statement. When we do this, we can see that in both years, Burberry spent significantly less on new PPE than the average cost of using the assets it already has. Ordinarily, this would suggest that the business may not be investing enough in its infrastructure in order to be able to operate sustainably at current levels into the future.

In fact, in the **management commentary** section of Burberry's 2019 annual report, the business explains that this is part of a strategy to prioritise 'investment in capabilities such as digital and brand experience over physical infrastructure'.[5] Thus, the apparent underinvestment in PPE is in fact an intentional move to hold back physical expansion and instead focus on expanding the **intangible asset** base, such as trademarks, licences, and computer software. For these sorts of assets, the equivalent of depreciation is called '**amortisation**', which is also shown higher up the statement. The figures confirm that Burberry is indeed employing its strategy: while spending on new PPE is well below the depreciation charge, spending on intangible assets is almost double the amortisation charge in both 2018 and 2019. (See section 6.4 for more detail about financial accounting for intangible assets.)

Burberry's investing activities section also reports the cash flows from the sale and acquisition of business operations. In 2018, Burberry sold the licensing rights to sell its line of fragrance and beauty products to the global cosmetics company, Coty, and also transferred the related business operations to Coty. Thanks to the information in the statement of cash flows, we can see that this transaction brought in cash of £61.1 million that year, and another £600 000 in 2019. (Note 5 to the financial statements explains that the sale price constituted a £5.2 million gain for Burberry.)

A smaller business acquisition, this one involving Burberry as the buyer, took place in 2019, requiring a payment that year of £14.5 million. Note 28 identifies the acquired business as Burberry Manifattura, a Florence-based manufacturer of leather handbags and accessories; and informs us that a further £6.7 million is expected to be paid for the acquisition in 2021.

The German theologian Martin Luther is said to have claimed, 'Show me where a man spends his time and money, and I'll show you his God.' Like the other information in the investing activities section, the cash flow information about the purchase and sale of business units is very helpful for assessing a business's growth prospects and strategic priorities.

5.6 FINANCING ACTIVITIES SECTION

The financing activities section of the statement of cash flows typically reports the cash flows arising from transactions with owners and long-term lenders.

Financing activities are those activities which affect the capital structure (the mix of long-term debt and equity) of the business. Listed in this section, you can expect to find the amounts of cash received from the issue of shares and how much was paid if shares were bought back by the business (see section 10.3.2 about share buybacks). Cash flows from raising and repaying borrowings would also be reported in the financing activities section.

In section 4.4.3, we referred to Note 9 to Burberry's financial statements, which revealed that the business's only interest-bearing liabilities are short-term bank loans and overdrafts. Due to their short-term nature, these are part of the working capital, not the capital structure, of the business, and therefore no cash flows relating to debt are reported in Burberry's financing activities section.

There are, however, several noteworthy cash flows relating to equity. The first is a result of the dividend decision (see section 1.3.5): dividend payments to shareholders of £171.1 million. By looking at Note 12, we see that this was the sum of two dividends: the previous year's final dividend, as well as this year's **interim dividend**, which is usually declared approximately midway through the financial year.

Incidentally, though most businesses disclose dividends paid in the financing activities section, some take the option to include them under operating activities, presumably to show the extent to which the business can afford to pay dividends out of the cash generated by basic business operations. We can do this by simply glancing up the statement, and seeing that the £411.4 million net cash generated from operating activities is amply sufficient to cover the £171.1 million dividend payments.

Most of the other equity cash flows are, at a high level, fairly self-explanatory (though you may appreciate being told that 'ESOP' stands for 'Employee Share Ownership Plan'). The context of the transactions, however, is quite complex, and best left to the chapters dedicated to groups of companies, Chapter 9, and to equity, Chapter 10. It is worth drawing attention, though, to the size of the outflow relating to the share buyback in 2018: a cool £355 million! This is by far the biggest single outflow of cash on the statement of cash flows, and appears to be Burberry's preferred way to use the cash it has generated from operating activities. It is a reasonable guess that, had the business generated as much cash in 2019, it would have spent as much again on share buybacks. In section 10.3.2, we will explain why share buybacks are considered by many companies to be such a worthwhile use of cash.

5.7 THE BOTTOM OF THE STATEMENT OF CASH FLOWS

The bottom of the statement of cash flows includes a reconciliation of the net cash flow for the period to the opening and closing balances of cash and cash equivalents found in the statement of financial position. In real-world financial statements, this reconciliation often contains two more steps than the statement of cash flows that we presented for PB in section 2.2.15.

First, most businesses have multiple bank accounts, some of which are in overdraft (that is, they have negative balances) and therefore appear on the statement of financial position as current liabilities. In such cases, this bottom of the statement of cash flows shows, as Burberry's does, how the closing cash and cash equivalents is really a 'net cash' figure obtained by subtracting the bank overdrafts balance from the cash and cash equivalents balance reported in the current assets section.

Second, businesses with bank accounts in foreign currencies need to include a line to deal with what Burberry calls the 'effect of exchange rate changes'. We will deal with other accounting challenges caused by foreign exchange rates in section 8.2, but we can explain this item briefly now, by means of the following example.

Suppose that a business has ₹10 million (ten million rupees) in a bank account in India. If the exchange rate at the beginning of the year was €1 = ₹80, then in euro terms this cash would be worth €125 000 (₹10 m ÷ ₹80). However, if the business still had ₹10 million in the bank account at the end of the year, but the exchange rate had changed to €1 = ₹85, this ₹10 million would now be worth only €117 647 (₹10 m ÷ ₹85). In this case, in its euro-based financial statements, the business would appear to have €7 353 less cash (€125 000 − €117 647).

This is not a cash flow, as the business has neither paid nor received cash in respect of this bank account. Yet the business does need to include a line on its statement of cash flows to explain how it has less cash in euro terms. This line appears in the reconciliation at the bottom of the statement. Of course, a line like this is necessary even when the closing balance on the foreign account is different from the opening balance, though the calculation will be trickier in ways that need not concern us. In Burberry's case, these sorts of exchange rate fluctuations meant an increase in cash holdings of £1.7 million in 2019 and a £14.5 million decrease in 2018.

5.8 THE OVERALL MESSAGE

The structure of the statement of cash flows gives us a good view of the big picture from a cash flow perspective. For example, Burberry's 2019 statement reveals that the business generated £515.9 million from its operations, of which it had to pay £110.8 million in tax, but virtually nothing in interest because of its equity-based capital structure. Of the net £411.4 million, it spent €124.5 million on non-current assets, through what appears to be maintenance of PPE, expansion of intangible assets, and an acquisition of an Italian manufacturing business. The remaining cash was used primarily to pay for two important financing activities: a dividend distribution and a share buyback. After all the receipts and payments were tabulated, the business had £56.5 million less cash than at the previous year-end. This did not appear to be a cause for worry, however, as after this outflow for the year was subtracted from last year's net cash balance, and adjusted for the small effect of foreign exchange rate changes, the business was still left with a very large net cash balance of £837.3 million.

> **MISCONCEPTION**
>
> A net cash outflow for the year indicates a poor cash flow situation.
>
> Not really. The CGFO and cash flow from operating activities figures are more effective indicators of a business's success in generating cash flows in pursuit of value creation. To understand why, consider an example from the personal life of an individual. If you were earning €200 000 a year and you purchase a new house for €600 000, paid for out of past savings, you would presumably not consider yourself to have had a bad year, despite the overall negative net cash flow.

In section 11.2.6, we shall generalise this discussion of the overall message of the statement of cash flows, by considering a few important ways that the message delivered by other businesses' statements might differ from the contents of Burberry's 2019 statement.

CONCLUSION

The most important thing to remember about the statement of cash flows is that—apart from in the reconciliation at the bottom—it shows cash payments and receipts, and only cash payments and receipts. If an event does not involve a payment or receipt, it will not appear in the statement.

Cash flows tell us a lot of valuable information about a business. After all, at least from the perspective of the providers of funding, the generation of net operating cash flows is the ultimate means of creating long-term business value. And in the short term, the harsh reality is that many otherwise successful businesses fail because of cash flow problems. Sometimes, the statement of comprehensive income does not alert anyone to an impending disaster—the restaurant is full every night, the goods are flying off the shelves—how could there be a problem? In such cases, only a proper understanding and analysis of the statement of cash flows has the power to inform users about the business's potentially ruinous cash flow situation.

You may have come across the cliché 'Cash is king', but now you know that it is not quite accurate. Rather, cash *flow* is king!

We shall now turn our attention away from the two statements of financial performance to the one and only statement of financial position. We shall begin in Chapter 6 with a thorough investigation of assets.

5

SUMMARY OF KEY POINTS

- The statement of cash flows gives a detailed breakdown of cash inflows and outflows during the year, split between the three main activities of the business: operating, investing, and financing. The totals of these are added together to get a net cash flow figure for the year, which is finally added to the opening cash balance to obtain the closing cash balance.
- As accountants are required to make no estimates, judgements, or opinions when determining the figures to report in a statement of cash flows, it is a statement of fact.
- Technically, the statement of cash flows reports flows of cash and cash equivalents, which include investments that are easily convertible into cash and not subject to risks of changes in value.
- Cash flow, not profit, is the ultimate measure of business value, because cash is real, whereas profit is a notional construct of the accounting equation.
- Poor cash flow in the short term can make a business unsustainable. Poor cash flow in the long term means that the business is not creating value.
- The statement of cash flows gives the best indication of short-term cash performance. However, the statement of comprehensive income is widely regarded as a more reliable predictor of future cash flows.
- In comparing figures from the statement of comprehensive income and the statement of cash flows, financial analysts can assess a business's quality of earnings.
- Quality of earnings indicates the extent to which a business is converting profits into cash, its exposure to short-term sustainability risks, and the likely authenticity of the accrual-based figures.
- The operating activities section consists of two subsections. The first reports cash generated from operations (CGFO); the other reports interest, dividend, and/or tax cash flows.
- The first subsection is prepared using either the direct or indirect method. The direct method presents CGFO as the difference between cash received from customers and cash paid to suppliers and employees. The indirect method starts with operating profit (or a similar profit figure) and calculates CGFO by removing the effects of differences between the starting point and CGFO.

■ The differences between operating profit and CGFO are of two types: those caused by items of income and expense that are not associated with operating cash flows; and those caused by working capital changes.

■ Working capital consists of current assets and current liabilities, primarily inventory, receivables, cash, and payables, which are connected together in a complex system. It is important to manage working capital efficiently in order to ensure that debts can be paid when they fall due.

■ Efficient working capital management involves keeping inventory and receivables balances as low as possible, and payables balances as high as possible.

■ The investing activities section of the statement of cash flows reports the cash flows arising from the acquisition and disposal of non-current assets, including entire business units. It indicates the operating capacity of the business, and also signals its growth prospects and strategic priorities.

■ The financing activities section of the statement of cash flows reports the cash inflows and outflows arising from transactions with owners and long-term lenders.

■ Businesses which have bank accounts denominated in a foreign currency include a line at the bottom of the statement of cash flows to explain the changes caused by exchange rate changes.

CHAPTER QUESTIONS

The applied questions (marked 'AQ') and the discussion questions (marked 'DQ') relate to the financial statements of Daimler, contained in Appendix II. The suggested solutions to these questions, and also to the concept questions (marked 'CQ'), can be found in Appendix III.

Also, don't forget the **online resources** available at www.oup.com/he/winfield-graham-miller1e, which contain multiple-choice questions based on the material in this chapter, in addition to many other helpful resources, including two mini case studies, and accompanying questions and answers, and a worked example of Year 2 of the Pizza Business.

CONCEPT QUESTIONS

CQ 5.1   Explain what can be found within the three major sections that are commonly found in the statement of cash flows.

CQ 5.2   Which is the more important statement: the statement of cash flows or the statement of comprehensive income?

CQ 5.3   Explain the key difference between a statement of cash flows that is prepared using the 'direct' method and one that is prepared using the 'indirect' method.

CQ 5.4   What are the four main components of working capital, and what is their significance for a statement of cash flows prepared using the indirect method?

CQ 5.5   Describe how the information in a statement of cash flows connects directly to the information in the statement of financial position.

APPLIED QUESTIONS

AQ 5.6   Describe how it is that Daimler's cash flows from operating, financing, and investing activities, plus the effect of foreign exchange rate changes, resulted in the 2019 net increase in cash and cash equivalents of €3 030 million.

AQ 5.7   Why is the amount of €2 107 million paid for income taxes reported on Daimler's 2019 statement of cash flows different to the expense figure of €1 121 million for income taxes reported on its 2019 statement of income?

AQ 5.8   Explain carefully why the 'depreciation and amortization/impairments' amount of €7 751 million has been added to the 'Profit before income taxes' line-item in the 2019 statement of cash flows.

AQ 5.9   The statement of cash flows reports a change in inventories of €99 million in 2019. Does this represent an increase or decrease in the amount of inventories on hand? Justify your answer.

AQ 5.10   The statement of cash flows reports a change in trade payables (or accounts payable) of €1 625 million in 2019. Does this represent an increase or decrease in the amount of trade payables? Justify your answer.

AQ 5.11   Daimler's statement of cash flows includes dividends paid in the financing activities section. Where else in the statement could Daimler have chosen to present this cash outflow?

AQ 5.12   Explain why the 2019 statement of cash flows includes the line-item 'Effect of foreign exchange rate changes on cash and cash equivalents', amounting to €121 million.

AQ 5.13   Where in the statement of financial position are the cash and cash equivalents of €18 833 million reported on the last line of the 2019 statement of cash flows shown?

DISCUSSION QUESTIONS

DQ 5.14   Does Daimler present its statement of cash flows using the direct or indirect method? Justify your answer.

DQ 5.15   Did Daimler's change in working capital (that is, operating assets and liabilities) during 2019 have a positive or negative effect on the cash flows of the group?

DQ 5.16   What is the main reason that Daimler's cash flow from operations increased from a net inflow of €343 million in 2018 to a net inflow of €7 888 million in 2019, even though the profit before income and taxes in 2019 showed a significant decline from 2018?

DQ 5.17   What major investing activities with respect to PPE and intangible assets did Daimler undertake during the 2019 financial year?

DQ 5.18   Does the statement of cash flows indicate any significant changes to the group's capital structure during 2019? If so, what?

DQ 5.19   Comment on Daimler's overall ability during 2019 to generate cash flows from its operations. What line-item interests you most?

DQ 5.20   The working capital item 'Other operating assets and liabilities' increased by €5 641 million during 2019. What is the major component of this item? Explain why it is included as a working capital adjustment.

DQ 5.21   Is the entire amount of cash and cash equivalents of €18 883 million available to be used by Daimler as it wishes? If not, explain why.

INVESTIGATION QUESTIONS

IQ 5.22   Identify a listed retail company that is based in your country and obtain its financial statements. Examine this company's statement of cash flows, and identify the major issues that influence the company's ability to generate operating cash flows. Pay particular attention to any changes in working capital.

IQ 5.23   Imagine that you are consulting to the International Accounting Standards Board. Explain whether you think that there might be a more useful way to present the statement of cash flows, or perhaps even the statement of comprehensive income, in order to better help users understand the difference between a business's profit and its cash flows.

IQ 5.24   Even though in IAS 7 the standard-setters encourage businesses to report cash flows from operating activities using the direct method, most do not. Identify and explain at least one reason for this.

REFERENCES

[1]   IASB 2016. *IAS 7: Statements of Cash Flows*. Section 6.

[2]   See, for example, Dechowa, P, Kotharib, S, and Watts, R 1998. 'The Relation between Earnings and Cash Flows'. *Journal of Accounting and Economics*, Vol 25, Issue 2. 27 May, pp 133–68.

[3]   See, for example, Nallareddy, S, Sethuraman, M, and Venkatachalam, M 2018. 'Earnings or Cash Flows: Which is a Better Predictor of Future Cash Flows?' 10 August. Available at SSRN: https://ssrn.com/abstract=3054644 or http://dx.doi.org/10.2139/ssrn.3054644.

[4]   Telefónica, SA 2019. *Auditor's Report, Consolidated Annual Accounts, and Consolidated Management Report at 31 December 2019*. Available at: https://www.telefonica.com/documents/162467/141705152/Consolidated-Annual-Accounts-2019.pdf/2532d380-3cfd-5d90-d0d8-a475f7a4251f. See p 8 for the statement of cash flows and p 115 for note 28.

[5]   From p 19 of the Burberry 2018/19 *Annual Report*.

ASSETS

CHAPTER 6

Here are some of the things you will be able to do after reading this chapter:

- apply the definition of an asset, and the criteria that assets must satisfy to be recognised;
- describe the measurement principles that generally apply to assets;
- contrast depreciation, amortisation, and impairment; and demonstrate the effects of each on the financial statements;
- explain the treatment of changes in estimates and events after the reporting date;
- discuss the recognition and measurement principles specific to the most common asset categories, including: property, plant and equipment; investment properties; intangible assets; inventory; loans and receivables; and other financial assets.

This chapter builds on material covered in earlier chapters. If you don't feel comfortable with any of the following items, we recommend that you briefly go back now to the sections referenced.

- The financial statements are designed to enable providers of funding to understand the results of the business's **value creation cycle**. The ultimate goal of this cycle is to produce net operating cash inflows (see sections 1.3.1 and 1.3.4).
- A key phase of this cycle is **investing activities**, which involves acquiring **assets** (see Figure 1.6 in section 1.3.6 for an illustration of the value creation cycle).
- The next key phase of the value creation cycle is **operating activities**, which involve these assets being used to generate revenue (a full discussion of revenue is in section 4.3).
- A business's assets themselves are reported on its **statement of financial position**, or **balance sheet** (see section 2.2.14 for a basic example).
- **Current assets** are cash, items purchased for trading, and those whose benefits are expected to be obtained by the business's operating activities within twelve

months of the reporting date. They are part of the business's **working capital** (see section 5.4.4). All other assets are **non-current assets**, which make up the business's operating capacity (see section 5.5).

- The results of using assets—that is, the financial performance of the business—are reported as items of income and expense on the **statement of comprehensive income**, using **accrual accounting**, in either the **profit or loss** or **other comprehensive income (OCI) section** (see Chapter 4).

- Many accounting principles and practices of relevance to this chapter were demonstrated at a simple level in Chapter 2, using the example of a very small business that sells pizza slices, called 'PB'. We shall refer to PB in this chapter too.

Businesses have all sorts of assets: buildings, shop fittings, trademarks, shares in other businesses, inventory, receivables, cash, and so on and so forth. In this chapter, we will cover the vast majority of them. We shall emphasise the crucial role they play in generating revenue, and how that revenue can produce the ultimate value creation goal: net operating cash inflow. Table 6.2 at the end of the chapter summarises the financial accounting treatments of all the types of assets we cover here.

For reasons that will become clear, we shall leave the discussion of a few kinds of assets—such as deferred tax, leased assets, goodwill, and investments in associates or joint ventures—to later chapters.

6.1 GENERAL PRINCIPLES OF ACCOUNTING FOR ASSETS

The accounting treatment of different types of assets conforms to the same basic set of principles.

Even very different assets are reported in ways that conform to the same basic principles, most of which are contained in the **Conceptual Framework for Financial Reporting** that we introduced you to in section 3.4.1. So we will begin this chapter by running through the story of the life of a typical asset, and discuss in general terms how the major events are reported in the financial statements. Section 6.2 and beyond will then deal with each category of assets in turn, so that you can understand the accounting treatments peculiar to each category.

6.1.1 The asset definition

In Chapter 2, PB, like any business, spent money. Some of its money was spent on salaries and electricity, which were reported as expenses in the statement of comprehensive income. The business also spent money on land, a pizza oven, and inventory, all of which were recognised as assets in the statement of financial position. In both cases, money was spent, but sometimes the **expenditure** resulted in an asset and, at other times, in an expense. When it is treated as an asset, we say that it has been '**capitalised**', and call it '**capital expenditure**'. When it is treated as an expense, we say that it has been 'expensed' and call it 'operating expenditure' or 'revenue expenditure'. But why is there this difference between the treatment of these items of expenditure? In other words, what makes an asset an asset?

> **MISCONCEPTION**
>
> An expenditure of the business is an expense of the business.
>
> The word 'expenditure' simply refers to spending. A business spends on assets as well as expenses—it is the accountants' job to decide whether this decrease in the bank asset (the credit) should be balanced by an increase in another asset, or by an expense (the debit).

The Conceptual Framework answers this question by providing a formal asset definition: 'a present economic resource controlled by the entity as a result of past events'.[1] It also helpfully defines the term '**economic resource**': a 'right that has the potential to produce economic benefits'.[2] There are thus three key requirements for any expenditure to meet the asset definition:

- it must give rise to a right, such as a right to use a physical object; use intellectual property; or receive cash, goods, services, or other economic resources;

- the right must have the potential to produce economic benefits in the future;

- the business must control this economic resource (that is, the event that causes the business to control the resource must have happened).

The expenditure on the pizza oven, for example, meets this definition, as in Application of Definition 1.

The three key requirements for any expenditure to meet the asset definition are: a right, the potential to produce economic benefits, and control.

6

APPLICATION OF DEFINITION 1 Application of the asset definition: PB spends €120 on a pizza oven.

Definition	Met?	Reason
Gives rise to a right	Yes	The expenditure gave rise to a physical object—the oven—and the right to use it
Potential to produce economic benefits in future	Yes	The oven has the potential to produce economic benefits (by baking pizzas for sale)
Business controls the economic resource	Yes	PB controls the right to use the oven as a result of the past event of purchasing it

Since each requirement is met, the pizza oven is PB's asset. You may have noticed that there is no mention of ownership in the asset definition. In fact, some assets that a business does not own nevertheless qualify as the business's assets. For example, suppose that PB enters into a hire purchase agreement (also known as an instalment plan) to acquire the pizza oven, according to which it will pay instalments for a period of three years before becoming the legal owner. In this case, the definition would still be met because it requires merely that PB controls the resource, *not* that it owns it. Items purchased using instalment plans are examples of leased assets, which are dealt with in greater detail in section 8.1.

Let's now see if the salaries paid to staff who take orders or work the cash register meet the asset definition in Application of Definition 2.

APPLICATION OF DEFINITION 2 Application of the asset definition: PB spends €50 on the cashier's salary.

Definition	Met?	Reason
Gives rise to a right	Yes	Salaries do not give rise to a right to use the person paid, but rather the right to use the product of their work
Potential to produce economic benefits in future	No	The benefits produced by the work of these staff are in the past, not the future
Business controls the economic resource	–	Both of the first two requirements must be met for there to be an economic resource to control

Since every requirement must be met for the entire definition to be met, the salaries do not give rise to an asset. Thus, the decrease in cash when the salaries are paid causes a decrease in equity. Since this decrease is not caused by a distribution to owners, the salaries, instead of meeting the asset definition, in fact meet the expense definition described in section 2.1.2.

In the analysis in Summary of Event 1, you can see the accounting consequences of these two definitions for the €170 paid for the pizza oven and salaries.

SUMMARY OF EVENT 1 PB spends €120 on a pizza oven and €50 on salaries.

Assets	–	Liabilities	=	Equity		Debit	Credit
– €170							Bank
+ €120						PPE	
				– €50 (expense)		Salaries expense	

A business does not always have to spend money to have an asset. A business's cash is quite obviously an asset, despite the fact that money may not have been spent to obtain it (eg it may have been received as a result of a bank loan or a contribution from owners). Similarly, when inventory is sold on credit, the business is not paying anything: instead, it is giving up inventory in exchange for a promise that the customer will pay. Let's apply the definition in Application of Definition 3 to see why this promise, accounts receivable, is an asset.

APPLICATION OF DEFINITION 3 Application of the asset definition: PB's accounts receivable.

Definition	Met?	Reason
Gives rise to a right	Yes	Accounts receivable is a right to collect payment
Potential to produce economic benefits in future	Yes	The collection of payment will produce economic benefits in the form of the cash received
Business controls the economic resource	Yes	The right to collect payment belongs to PB (businesses can even sell their right to collect payment from debtors)

It is relatively easy to decide whether a pizza oven or a salary payment or a receivable should be treated as an asset or an expense, but for many other items in the contemporary world of business it is trickier to apply the definitions in the Conceptual Framework. In such cases, accountants refer to a more detailed accounting standard that deals specifically with the item under consideration. Sometimes even that does not entirely settle the matter, and then they have to exercise their professional judgement. This is just one more area of accounting that is not quite as precise as many non-accountants might expect it to be.

6.1.2 **The recognition criteria**

You would think that meeting the definition of an asset would automatically mean that a resource would be recognised and reported on the statement of financial position, but in fact meeting the definition is not quite enough. The Conceptual Framework also requires that recognising the resource as an asset would result in relevant information which achieves a faithful representation of the economic reality of the business.[3]

In practice, these **recognition criteria** mean that an asset is not recognised if any of the following is true:

- there is uncertainty about whether the asset exists;[4]
- there is a low probability of an inflow of economic benefits from the asset;[5]
- there is a high level of uncertainty about the measurement of the asset.[6]

None of these is true of PB's pizza oven: it is a physical resource, so there is no doubt about its existence; it will almost certainly be used to make pizzas that will result in economic benefits for PB; and it is easily measurable, initially at its cost, and then on subsequent reporting dates, at its depreciated cost.

Despite not being physical in nature, accounts receivable also exists, as evidenced by a contract, and it has a reasonable probability of delivering benefits in the form of cash, the amount of which is relatively certain.

You may be thinking that perhaps some of PB's debtors would end up not paying, and therefore that it cannot be measured with certainty, but it is perfectly acceptable in

Only if the recognition criteria are satisfied is the asset reported on the statement of financial position.

6

accounting to use estimates. For example, if PB expects that debtors will default for about 5% of the total amount owed, the appropriate measurement of the receivable would be 95% of the amount owed. (See section 6.6.3 for more on how this works exactly.) So long as they are not wild guesses, and could instead be said to faithfully represent economic reality, measurements that are estimates satisfy the recognition criteria.

With items that meet the definition of an asset but which fail to meet the recognition criteria, any amounts spent on these assets are expensed. We shall encounter several examples, such as advertising and internally generated brands, later in this chapter.

You may wonder how an asset might fail the first test for recognition: how could it be true that there is uncertainty about an asset's *existence*? Well, an example would be an insurance claim where it is not clear whether the loss is covered by the insurance contract. Perhaps the business is insured against theft by employees, but the wording in the contract is ambiguous about whether part-time staff would count as employees. Thus, if a part-time staff member steals something, and the business submits a claim to recover the loss from the insurance company, there is uncertainty about whether the right (that is, the asset) exists. Assets like this which fail the first test for recognition are classed as **contingent assets**, and are disclosed in the notes instead of being recognised in the statement of financial position.

However, the contingent asset definition does not include assets that fail the second and third tests,[7] which therefore appear in neither the statement of financial position nor the notes to the financial statements.

6.1.3 Initial measurement

An asset's '**initial measurement**' is the amount at which it is first recognised as an asset by the business. When PB acquired the pizza oven, for example, the initial measurement was the €120 paid to the seller.

Many asset acquisitions are more complicated than that, though. For one thing, they might involve several different costs. Suppose, for example, that the pizza oven was not portable, and PB had to pay not only the purchase price of €120 but also €8 for installation. Would these installation costs be included in the initial measurement of the asset, or simply expensed? The answer is that all transaction costs are included in the initial measurement of the asset, which would thus be €128. Furthermore, if the pizza oven had to be shipped from Italy, off-loaded at the harbour, transported to the restaurant, and installed, then all of these costs would be included too.

And what if PB didn't pay for the oven immediately, but instead was allowed to pay €120 in twelve months' time? If the seller charges PB interest at an appropriate rate, then the purchase price would continue to be measured at €120, and the interest would be expensed in profit or loss. But if no interest was charged, the initial measurement would be discounted to the **present value** of the future payment. Just as the revenue from deferred payments was discounted in section 4.3.5, this is another reflection of the **time value of money**: €120 in twelve months' time is worth less than €120 now. The **discount rate** is the market interest rate for this sort of transaction. If it is 20% in this case, the purchase price would be discounted to €100, being the present value of €120 discounted at 20%

(calculated as €120 ÷ 1.20), and the discount of €20 would be unwound over the next twelve months.

Summary of Event 2 shows the accounting treatment of the purchase of the oven on the scenario just described, including the installation, for which €8 is paid on the date of purchase.

SUMMARY OF EVENT 2 PB purchases a pizza oven for €120, to be paid in twelve months' time; installation costs €8.

On the date of purchase (that is, when control of the pizza oven passes to PB):

Assets	–	Liabilities	=	Equity		Debit	Credit
+ €108						PPE	
– €8							Bank
		+ €100					Accounts payable

Over the period between the date of purchase and the payment of the purchase price:

Assets	–	Liabilities	=	Equity		Debit	Credit
		+ €20					Accounts payable
				– €20 (expense)		Interest expense	

On the day that the purchase price is paid:

Assets	–	Liabilities	=	Equity		Debit	Credit
– €120							Bank
		– €120				Accounts payable	

The basic principle behind the accounting for the deferred payment is that, just as there are no free lunches, there is really no such thing as an interest-free loan. With this in mind, the financial statements report the *substance* of the transaction, which is that the payment of €120 consists of two parts: a loan to buy a pizza oven costing €100 and finance charges of €20.

As for deferred receipts of revenue, this discounting and unwinding is only necessary when the time value of money is **material**; that is, if it might make a difference to the decisions of users of the financial statements.

6.1.4 **Subsequent measurement**

While an item's initial measurement is the amount at which it is first recognised in the business's accounting records, the term '**subsequent measurement**' refers to how an item's **carrying amount** is determined on each reporting date after acquisition. These requirements vary widely, depending on the different category of assets being measured.

In PB, for example, the inventory on the statement of financial position at the end of Year 1 was measured at its historic cost, the pizza oven was measured at depreciated cost, and the land was measured at its market value.

We shall cover the peculiarities of subsequent measurement when we later narrow the focus to each asset category in sections 6.2–6.9, but first, in sections 6.1.5–6.1.9, we will deal with a few general issues relating to subsequent measurement.

If, along the way, you struggle a little to keep track of the different approaches, Table 6.2 at the end of this chapter may prove useful, as it summarises the various approaches to subsequent measurement for different asset categories.

6.1.5 Fair value

Up until now, when we have referred to the amount at which PB's land is recognised at the end of Year 1, we have called it the 'market value', but in technical accounting-speak it is in fact the **fair value**. Only a few categories of assets are routinely measured at fair value, but the term is useful in other instances which apply more generally (eg impairment), and so it will be useful to explain it briefly now.

The Conceptual Framework defines fair value as 'the price that would be received to sell an asset . . . in an orderly transaction between market participants at the measurement date'.[8] For assets, therefore, fair value is an exit price: the amount that the business would receive if it were to sell the asset, rather than the amount that it would need to pay to buy or build a similar item. Thus, the difficulty of determining fair value varies. Assuming an active market exists for parcels of land like the one owned by PB, then fair value would indeed be the market value as determined by property experts. If PB owned shares in a listed company, their fair value would be the share price. However, the fair value of a one-year-old pizza oven would require a great deal more guesswork and some fairly complex calculations.

6.1.6 Subsequent costs

If at any point after acquisition, the business spends more on an asset, the amounts spent are called '**subsequent costs**'. For example, subsequent costs might be incurred to fix some minor damage to the pizza oven or to coat the outside of the oven so that the oven retains heat better. The question then arises: should the subsequent costs be expensed or capitalised? The answer lies in the thought process depicted in Figure 6.1.

FIGURE 6.1 Decision tree for the accounting treatment of subsequent costs

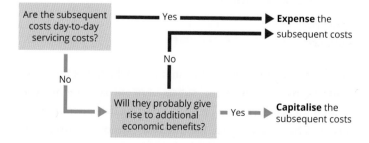

Thus, the amount PB spends on repairing damage to the pizza oven should not be capitalised, as it is part of day-to-day servicing costs. The thinking here is that this sort of expenditure will not give rise to any extra economic benefits: it will merely enable the oven to continue providing the benefits expected of it before it was damaged. These costs are thus expensed.

On the other hand, coating the oven is not day-to-day servicing, and it will result in fuel savings that will translate into greater economic benefits, so it will be capitalised. When subsequent costs are capitalised like this, they are not treated as an asset in themselves, but rather added to the carrying amount of the asset on which they have been spent.

6.1.7 **Expensing assets**

Although some expenditure is initially capitalised on the statement of financial position, it will eventually end up being expensed in the statement of comprehensive income. For example, in PB's Year 1, the cost of the ingredients that were consumed, after being recognised as inventory, was reported as cost of sales (see section 2.2.6); and part of the cost of the pizza oven, after being included in the initial measurement of **property, plant and equipment** (PPE), was also expensed, as a result of depreciation (see section 2.2.9).

Like items of PPE, most **intangible assets** are also written off over their useful lives, though we refer to this as '**amortisation**'. On the other hand, some intangible assets like **goodwill** (see section 9.3) are not amortised at all, but are instead subject to annual impairment tests.

To interpret the carrying amount of each asset, and to make sense of the reported profit, it is vital that you understand the process whereby the amount at which an asset is initially measured moves over time from the statement of financial position to the statement of comprehensive income. We will thus deal thoroughly with all these variations when we get to each asset category. However, there is one way that any asset might be expensed which we should deal with now.

6.1.8 **Impairment**

In section 2.2.8, we introduced the notion of **impairment**, which arises from the principle that no asset may be measured at an amount *greater* than its actual value to the business. When an asset is impaired, this is another way that its cost moves from the statement of financial position to the statement of comprehensive income, but bear in mind the major difference between depreciation (or amortisation) and impairment: depreciation is a regular, expected decrease in the carrying amount of the asset, caused by time and usage, whereas impairment is caused by an external shock that reduces the asset's value.

> Depreciation is a regular decrease in the carrying amount of the asset, caused by time and usage, whereas impairment is caused by some sort of shock that reduces the asset's value.

Impairment steps

In practice, identifying and calculating the amount of an impairment involves three discrete steps, as follows:

1. Review assets for signs of impairment.
2. If an asset shows signs of impairment, calculate its recoverable amount.
3. If the recoverable amount is below the current carrying amount, impair the asset down to the recoverable amount.

Signs of impairment may be as obvious as oil leaking from a machine, or a crack in the pizza oven, but there are also some less obvious signs that an asset may be impaired. For example, rising interest rates are potentially a sign that with less disposable income, people may buy fewer pizza slices from PB, causing a decrease in the cash-generating potential—and therefore value—of its pizza oven.

If there are no signs of impairment, no further action is required. But the second step must be taken if there are such signs: the **recoverable amount** of the asset needs to be calculated. This is the *higher* of its **value in use** and its fair value less costs to sell.

Fair value less costs to sell is just what it sounds like: the amount that the asset could reasonably be sold for, minus any costs that would be incurred to sell it. For example, if, at the end of the first year, the pizza oven showed signs of impairment, PB would have to determine the market price of a one-year-old pizza oven in a similar condition. Let's say that—because of a large crack—this was only €50. PB would then estimate how much it would cost to dismantle and transport the oven to a second-hand oven dealer. If that amount was €10, then the fair value less costs to sell would be €40 (€50 – €10).

An asset's value in use is the net amount of cash that it will generate as it is used over its life. To calculate this amount, PB would have to forecast the net future cash flows that the pizza oven would generate from the sale of pizza slices and also the inflow when the oven itself is ultimately sold, and then discount those cash flows at a rate that takes into account both the time value of money and also the risk that the cash flows may not be as expected. Let's suppose that amount turned out to be €60. Since the recoverable amount is the higher of this €60 and the fair value less costs to sell of €40, the recoverable amount of the cracked oven would be €60.

The third step is to impair the asset, if necessary, by writing it down to the recoverable amount. In our example, PB's oven at the end of Year 1 had a carrying amount of €80 (that is, the cost of €120 minus depreciation of €40), which on this scenario would have to be impaired by €20 (the current carrying amount of €80 minus the recoverable amount of €60; as shown in Summary of Event 3).

SUMMARY OF EVENT 3 Pizza oven has a carrying amount of €80 but a recoverable amount of €60.

Assets	–	Liabilities	=	Equity		Debit	Credit
– €20							PPE
				– €20 (expense)		Impairment loss	

Impaired assets are thus not necessarily measured at the amount by which the business will benefit if they are sold, but rather at their maximum future economic potential within the business. Of course, had the value in use been €50, and the fair value less costs to sell been €60, the oven would still have been impaired to €60, but in this case, the measurement would in fact be the amount by which the business will benefit through sale.

If you have been thinking that calculating the value in use must be a very challenging exercise, you are correct. In practice, if there are signs of impairment, businesses will

The general principle behind impairment is that no asset may be measured on the statement of financial position at an amount greater than its actual value to the business.

The recoverable amount is the higher of value in use and fair value less costs to sell. The asset must be impaired down to the recoverable amount if that is lower than its current carrying amount.

first calculate the fair value less costs to sell. If this is higher than the current carrying amount, then it is clear that no impairment will be necessary, because, since the recoverable amount is the higher of the value in use and the fair value less costs to sell, the recoverable amount must be higher than the current carrying amount. Thus, the need to calculate the value in use is avoided.

It is also worth noting that the three-step impairment exercise is unnecessary for assets whose subsequent measurement model involves them being carried at fair value. This is because write-downs in the carrying amount as a result of decreases in fair value are akin to an impairment anyway.

Subsequent measurement after an impairment

Suppose that the pizza oven had been impaired to €60. You may wonder what happens to the depreciation charge after that. After all, a depreciation charge of €40 was scheduled for Years 2 and 3, but it is not possible to charge more depreciation than the carrying amount. The solution is that the depreciation (or amortisation) charged to impaired assets is adjusted to reflect their new carrying amounts. In PB's case, the oven's annual depreciation would be changed to €30 (€60 ÷ 2 years).

If, after being impaired in a previous year, the value of the asset subsequently recovers, then a **reversal** is processed for the impairment loss, provided that the carrying amount is not raised to a higher figure than it would have been had it not been impaired. For example, suppose that at the end of Year 2, it turns out that the impairment was not necessary. (Perhaps the oven was impaired because of high interest rates making pizza slices less marketable, but now interest rates drop back to pre-impairment levels.) Now, the asset is currently carried at €30 (the Year 1 impaired carrying amount of €60 minus the adjusted depreciation charge of €30). It may be tempting to reverse the full Year 1 impairment loss of €20, raising the carrying amount to €50. Yet, had the impairment never occurred, the carrying amount would have been €40 (the Year 1 unimpaired carrying amount of €80 less depreciation charge of €40). Thus, only €10 of the impairment loss would be reversed, as follows in Summary of Event 4.

SUMMARY OF EVENT 4 Reversal of impairment for the pizza oven with an impaired carrying amount of €30. Had no impairment occurred, the carrying amount would now have been €40.

Assets	−	Liabilities	=	Equity		Debit	Credit
+ €10						PPE	
				+ €10 (income)			Reversal of impairment loss

A reversal of a prior year impairment loss is often not reported as a separate item of income, but instead it is netted off against any impairment losses for the asset category that year. This is consistent with section 4.4.1, in where we showed how prior year inventory write-downs may be reversed to cost of sales in the year of the reversal.

Note that the amounts used to calculate impairments are estimates. Thus, all significant impairments and their reversals are required to be described in the notes in sufficient detail for users of the financial statements to establish who made the estimates (management or external independent valuation experts) and how they were made.

6.1.9 Disposal

When assets are disposed of, they are removed from the business's accounting records, in a process known as '**derecognition**', and thus no longer appear on the statement of financial position. Chapters 2 and 4 explained in detail how the derecognition of inventory results in both revenue and cost of sales expense. However, for all other assets, only the net gain or loss resulting from their sale is included as an item of 'Other operating income' in the statement of comprehensive income.

For example, suppose that PB had sold the (unimpaired) pizza oven at the end of Year 1 for €100. As the carrying amount was €80, the transaction would be accounted for as shown in Summary of Event 5.

SUMMARY OF EVENT 5 PB sells the pizza oven (with a carrying amount of €80) for €100 cash.

Assets	–	Liabilities	=	Equity		Debit	Credit
+ €100						Bank	
– €80							PPE
				+ €20 (income)			Gain on sale of PPE

Some non-current assets are worthless when they are disposed of, in which case they are described as 'scrapped'. Unless they have already been written down to zero, scrapping will result in a loss on disposal equal to their carrying amount on the date of disposal.

6.1.10 Events after the reporting period

At the end of the financial year, it takes a while (usually between several weeks and a few months) to finalise the financial statements. For example, the last day of Burberry's 2019 financial year was 30 March, but the results were only approved for issue on 16 May 2019.

You may wonder: what if one of the major events in the life of an asset were to happen just after the year-end; would the financial statements currently being prepared report this **event after the reporting period**? For example, if serious damage to PB's pizza oven was discovered during the compilation of the financial statements, would the oven have to be impaired in the financial statements being compiled, even though they are dated *before* the discovery of the damage? The answer is as follows:

- If the event which occurred after the year-end provides evidence of conditions that existed at the year-end, it should be taken into account in the financial statements being prepared. This is known as an 'adjusting' event after the reporting period.

Thus, even if the discovery of damage to the oven happened after the year-end, if it could be established that the damage itself occurred *before* the year-end, then the statement of financial position would be adjusted to report the impaired measurement, and an impairment loss would appear in the statement of comprehensive income.

- If the event which occurred after the year-end does *not* provide evidence of conditions that existed at the year-end, then no adjustment is made to the financial statements currently being prepared. Thus, if the damage occurred after the year-end, then the impairment will instead affect the following year's financial statements, as it was in that year that the impairment event happened. For the time being, these 'non-adjusting' events after the reporting period are simply mentioned in the notes.

> If a major event after the year-end provides evidence of conditions that existed at year-end, then it impacts the financial statements being compiled. If not, it is merely reported in the notes.

This treatment may make logical sense, but from the perspective of a user with a financial stake in the business, an impairment event may be very significant regardless of whether it happened before or after the financial year ended. Therefore, it is important to look out for non-adjusting events reported in the notes. In addition to the destruction or impairment of physical assets, other such events include: a decrease in the quality of accounts receivable (caused, for example, by market interest rates increasing); a substantial liability that arises after the year-end; and a significant business acquisition.

Burberry reported no significant events between 30 March 2019 and the release of the 2019 financial statements, but note 32 to its 2018 financial statements did report an event belonging to the last type in this list. According to the note, on 9 May 2018, less than a week before the company's Board approved the financial statements for issue, Burberry committed to the acquisition of a leather goods manufacturing business. As this was a non-adjusting event, there was no effect on the 2018 financial statements themselves, but the note disclosed several pertinent details about the price and timing of the transaction. It kept the identity of the business confidential, however. Only later did we learn that the business in question was the Italian company Burberry Manifattura, whose acquisition was reported in the investing activities section of the 2019 statement of cash flows (see section 5.5).

6.1.11 Summary of general principles applying to events in the life of an asset

Table 6.1 summarises the key accounting questions that pertain to the main events in the life of an asset, and the general principles that the International Financial Reporting Standards (IFRS) expects businesses to employ when responding to these questions.

Given that most businesses have many assets of varying types, it should be clear that in any single year, these accounting requirements lead to a multitude of effects. The statements of financial position and comprehensive income present only the final outcome of all of these effects, but thankfully IFRS requires that the notes disclose the details relating to the key events in each asset category. As we work through the remaining sections in this

TABLE 6.1 Summary of the general accounting principles pertaining to events in the life of an asset

Event	Key questions	General accounting principles
Acquisition	Does it meet the asset definition?	Only if it meets the definition is it an asset.
	Does it satisfy the recognition criteria?	If so, then it is recognised as an asset on the statement of financial position.
	At what amount should it be initially measured?	All costs incurred to bring it to its location and condition for use are included. If the time value of money is material, deferred payments are discounted to present value.
Use	What subsequent measurement model is appropriate?	This determines the carrying amount of the asset in the statement of financial position. The principles vary, depending on the category of asset.
	Have subsequent costs been incurred?	If so, these costs should only be capitalised to the asset if they are not part of day-to-day servicing, and will probably produce additional economic benefits.
	Have economic benefits associated with the asset been consumed as expected this year?	If so, then part of the carrying amount of the asset is expensed in the statement of comprehensive income. If PPE, this is known as depreciation. If an intangible asset, it is called amortisation.
	Are there signs of impairment?	If so, then the asset is impaired down to recoverable amount if necessary. Impairments may be reversed in later years.
Disposal	Has the asset been disposed of this year?	If so, then the asset is derecognised, and the gain or loss on sale is reported as an operating item in the statement of comprehensive income. For inventory, however, revenue and cost of sales are reported.

chapter, each dedicated to a particular asset category, we will point out the information disclosed in the notes to Burberry's financial statements, and you will see how they can be a goldmine of information, vastly expanding our understanding of what is reported in the financial statements themselves.

We therefore recommend that you keep open your downloaded copy of the full Burberry financial statements, and refer to the notes often. For an even richer reading experience, why not also obtain the latest financial statements of another business in which you are interested? Then, as we discuss each asset category, you can have a look at the notes about it in that business's financial statements, and observe more applications of what you are learning.

6.2 PROPERTY, PLANT AND EQUIPMENT

The asset category property, plant and equipment (PPE) includes assets such as land, buildings, machinery, computers, motor vehicles, and so on. The accounting records will include separate accounts for each of these 'classes', but they are usually presented in aggregate in the financial statements themselves because they are dealt with by a single accounting standard. This standard, IAS 16, contains the following formal definition for the asset category: 'tangible items that (a) are held for use in the production or supply of goods and services, for rental to others, or for administrative purposes; and (b) are expected to be used for more than one period'.[9] Since PPE is defined as tangible, non-physical assets such as brands are not PPE.

> A business's PPE includes all the tangible, non-current assets that it uses to produce or supply goods and services, for rental to others, or for administration.

Note how the intended use of the asset determines what category it falls into, and therefore what accounting standard will govern the business's financial reporting in respect of it. This may be a surprise to you: perhaps you thought that a property, say, would be accounted for the same way by all businesses. Not so: you can tell from the definition that it will only be categorised as PPE if it is used by the business itself. However, if the business owns it purely for investment purposes, then instead it would be categorised as an investment property, and the accounting requirements of IAS 40 would apply to it. If the business is planning to sell the property, it would be treated as a non-current asset held for sale in terms of IFRS 5. That is, unless the business regularly buys and sells properties, in which case it would be categorised as inventory, and IAS 2 would determine how it is reported.

We will deal with investment properties, inventory, and non-current assets held for sale later in this chapter. In this section, we are focusing on those assets which meet the definition of PPE.

> How an asset is categorised and accounted for is determined by the business and its intentions regarding it.

There is nothing special about the recognition, initial measurement, impairment, and derecognition of PPE: they just follow the general principles described in section 6.1. But there is more to know about subsequent measurement and depreciation, so we shall focus on those two items here. (We will stick to this policy: in each section about a specific asset category, we will focus on the items where there is more to say. You can therefore trust that if we say nothing extra, then the accounting for those items simply conforms to the general principles.)

6.2.1 **Two subsequent measurement models**

For its items of PPE, a business has a choice between two subsequent measurement models: it can use either the **cost model** or the **revaluation model**.

> Businesses may generally choose between two subsequent measurement models for PPE: the cost model and the revaluation model.

The cost model is relatively straightforward, and is the model that we used to account for the pizza oven in Chapter 2. The asset is recorded at cost, depreciated over its useful life, and impaired where necessary. At no stage may the asset be carried at an amount greater than its depreciated cost. Thus, even if pizza ovens are in short supply and PB's comes to be worth €200 at the end of the first year, it would still be measured at its depreciated cost of €80. This has an important consequence for users of the financial statements: the amounts at which most items of PPE are carried on the statement of financial position often do not reflect their real value.

To overcome this problem, a business may choose to revalue any class of its PPE to fair value. PB chose this option for measuring its land in section 2.2.13: the carrying amount was raised from the initial measurement—its cost of €450—to its year-end fair value of

R€500. The €50 income bypassed profit or loss and appeared instead in **other comprehensive income** (**OCI**). This is the required treatment for all items of PPE measured using the revaluation model.

IAS 16 imposes a few conditions on a business's use of this model, including the following:

- If a business wishes to adopt a revaluation policy for a single asset (say, a piece of equipment, like a pizza oven), then all assets within that class (all items of equipment) need to be revalued.

- Revaluations need to be done with sufficient regularity to ensure that the carrying amount of the asset is never significantly different from its fair value.

- If depreciation is charged to the asset, then the depreciation calculation is based on the revalued amount. Thus, when fair value is higher than cost, the depreciation charge increases.

Although revaluation gains appear in OCI, the last of these conditions creates an indirect effect in the profit or loss section: the increased depreciation expense lowers profit. This, and also the time and effort required to comply with the other two conditions, are likely reasons that many businesses choose not to revalue their PPE. The few which do usually do so only for high-value, long-lived assets, such as land and buildings, whose market values can deviate substantially from a carrying amount based on cost. The incentive is highest for non-depreciable land, to which the third constraint does not apply, of course.

> **MISCONCEPTION**
>
> An impairment is a revaluation, because an impairment changes the value of an asset.
>
> In a general sense this is correct, but this is not how accountants use these terms. Impairment refers to an unanticipated decline in the value of an asset, which results in its being written down to an amount lower than its depreciated cost. A revaluation is usually the expected result of a policy to write assets up to amounts higher than their depreciated cost or, alternatively, a reversal of such an upward revaluation. At the risk of oversimplifying: if an item of PPE whose depreciated cost would be £100 has been revalued to £130, but then its fair value drops to £60, this would result in a revaluation loss of £30 in OCI, and an impairment loss of £40 in profit or loss.

6.2.2 Depreciation

The reason land is non-depreciable is that it has an indefinite useful life. On the other hand, just about every other item of PPE has a limited useful life and must be depreciated. (In fact, even some land, like that used for landfills, will be depreciated.)

In section 2.2.9, based on its initial measurement of €120, and its estimated useful life of three years, we calculated an annual depreciation charge for the pizza oven of €40. However, as with most things in accounting, it is not always this simple.

First, PB in fact had a choice between a few different depreciation methods. The chosen method should match the pattern of consumption of the benefits produced by the asset, and so there are methods which allow for the pattern to change from year to year. For example, IFRS allows the use of the diminishing balance depreciation method, where larger amounts are depreciated in the earlier years of an asset's life. Another method, called the units of production method, allows the depreciation charge to vary strictly with production: on this method, a machine that will produce a total of a million units will be depreciated in any given year based on whatever proportion of that total was produced in the year. In practice, however, these alternatives are largely ignored by most businesses, which depreciate all their depreciable assets using the so-called **straight-line depreciation method** that we used for PB.

The most commonly used depreciation method is straight-line depreciation, in which the annual charge is consistent.

Second, in Chapter 2 we ignored the amount which PB could earn from the sale of the oven at the end of its useful life. This is known as the '**residual value**', formally defined as 'the estimated amount that an entity would currently obtain from disposal of the asset, after deducting the estimated costs of disposal, if the asset were already of the age and in the condition expected at the end of its useful life'.[10] When PB acquired the oven, the business really should have estimated the oven's residual value and included it in the depreciation calculations, using the following formula for depreciation on the straight-line method:

$$\text{Annual depreciation} = \frac{\text{Cost} - \text{residual value}}{\text{Estimated useful life (in years)}}$$

If PB expects to sell the oven for €45 at the end of its useful life, the resulting depreciation charge would be €25 per year for three years ((€120 – €45) ÷ 3). The depreciation schedule shown in Example 6.1 demonstrates the effects on the financial statements for each year that the oven is used.

EXAMPLE 6.1

	€
Original cost	120
Depreciation expense in Year 1's statement of comprehensive income	– 25
Carrying amount in statement of financial position at end of Year 1	95
Depreciation expense in Year 2's statement of comprehensive income	– 25
Carrying amount in statement of financial position at end of Year 2	70
Depreciation expense in Year 3's statement of comprehensive income	– 25
Carrying amount in statement of financial position at end of Year 3	45

Note how, because we depreciate the €75 difference between the asset's cost and its residual value, the carrying amount at the end of the asset's useful life is its residual value. If the business then sells the asset for the expected amount, there would be no profit or loss on disposal, and the net amount that the asset cost the business would have been expensed smoothly over the period the asset was used.

Changes in depreciation estimates

There is another complexity to depreciation in practice: as time goes by, circumstances change, and as a result the depreciation estimates should change accordingly. By the second year, for example, PB might realise that the oven will last more or less than the three years originally anticipated, or that the residual value is not what was previously predicted.

Suppose that at the end of Year 2, although the residual value is still accurate, the estimate of the oven's estimated useful life changes to a total of five—not three—years. If this is not taken into account, the oven would be measured at its residual value on the statement of financial position at the end of Year 3, as in Example 6.1. However, that would be two years too early, with the effect that no depreciation would be charged for Years 4 and 5. Profits in those years would be substantially higher than in the first three years simply because of poor estimation, and not because the business actually performed any better.

To avoid this distortion, as soon as the previous estimate is discovered to be wrong, the new estimate must be used to recalculate the remaining depreciation. As the estimate changes before the financial statements are finalised for Year 2, the change can be taken into account for Years 2, 3, 4, and 5. Thus, in these years, we would depreciate the oven by €12.50 (the carrying amount at the end of the first year of €95, minus the residual value of €45, divided by the four years' remaining useful life), resulting in the depreciation schedule shown in Example 6.2.

EXAMPLE 6.2

	€
Original cost	120.00
Depreciation in Year 1, based on a three-year estimated useful life	− 25.00
Carrying amount in statement of financial position at end of Year 1	95.00
Depreciation in Year 2, based on a five-year estimated useful life	− 12.50
Carrying amount in statement of financial position at end of Year 2	82.50
Depreciation in Year 3, based on a five-year estimated useful life	− 12.50
Carrying amount in statement of financial position at end of Year 3	70.00
Depreciation in Year 4, based on a five-year estimated useful life	− 12.50
Carrying amount in statement of financial position at end of Year 4	57.50
Depreciation in Year 5, based on a five-year estimated useful life	− 12.50
Carrying amount in statement of financial position at end of Year 5	45.00

A similar exercise would be performed if the estimate of the residual value changed.

Changes in estimates result in prospective adjustments to the financial statements.

This example illustrates an important principle in IFRS: changes in estimates do not result in retrospective changes to prior years' financial statements, but are merely corrected prospectively, when the change is identified. IFRS also requires some details about these changes to be disclosed in the notes to the financial statements.

6.2.3 **Burberry's PPE**

Burberry's 2019 balance sheet reported PPE of £306.9 million, which made it by some distance the company's largest category of non-current asset. Note 14 to the financial statements shows a breakdown of the PPE balance. Horizontally, it divides PPE into four classes: freehold land and buildings; leasehold improvements (which are improvements that Burberry has made to properties that it leases from other businesses); fixtures, fittings and equipment; and assets in the course of construction. Vertically, it shows how the carrying amount disclosed in the balance sheet was calculated: it was the difference between the total cost of these items on 30 March 2019 of £971.5 million, and the total accumulated depreciation and impairment of £664.6 million.

Note 5 reveals that the 2019 income statement was impacted by several expenses related to PPE: depreciation totalling £87.2 million; a loss on disposal of £1.2 million; and 'net impairment' (that is, impairment losses for the year, minus reversals of impairment losses for previous years) of £7.5 million. A small amount of the depreciation was included in cost of sales, like the depreciation on the pizza oven in Chapter 2. The rest was split between the categories 'Selling and distribution costs' and 'Administrative expenses', depending on the functions served by the PPE being depreciated. Note 2, which describes the accounting policies used by Burberry, confirms that the company uses straight-line depreciation (by explaining that the cost less residual value is written off in 'equal annual instalments'), and indicates the estimated useful lives used for each subcategory of PPE.

All of the company's PPE is measured using the cost model, and so we see no revaluation gains or losses in the statement of comprehensive income, and no revaluation surplus in the balance sheet.

There is a lot of detail in note 14. Spend some time reading it, and seeing what you can make of it, for this is the most effective way to begin to learn how to unlock the meaning in the financial statements. At the same time, be patient with yourself: some of the items in this note, like the effects of foreign exchange rate changes, require you to progress further through this book before you can really hope to understand them.

MISCONCEPTION

Terminology is standardised in the financial statements.

Whilst there is a move towards some standardisation, there are still many variations in terminology. For example, Burberry's balance sheet refers to 'property, plant and equipment', echoing the term used by the relevant accounting standard, but other businesses call this line-item 'properties, fixtures, equipment, and vehicles', or '**fixed assets**', or some other variation on the theme. There is nothing wrong with this, as long as the chosen label is a meaningful description of the company's tangible, non-current assets.

6.3 **INVESTMENT PROPERTY**

IAS 40 defines an investment property as a property held 'to earn rentals or for capital appreciation or both'.[11] As with PPE, a business has a choice as to the subsequent measurement model that it uses to account for investment properties. These are the cost model and the **fair value model**.

Businesses may generally choose between two subsequent measurement models for investment properties: the cost model and the fair value model.

The cost model that is applicable to investment properties is exactly the same as the cost model used to account for PPE. The property is initially measured at cost, depreciated over its useful life (unless it is land), and impaired when necessary.

The fair value model for investment property, however, differs from the revaluation model for PPE in three ways, as follows:

- Increases and decreases in fair value are reported as gains and losses in profit or loss, not in OCI.
- The adjustment to fair value must be done every year, so the business has no discretion as to what constitutes 'sufficient regularity'.
- Investment properties carried at fair value are not depreciated.

Burberry has a small number of investment properties, which it measures using the cost model. In its 2019 balance sheet, the amount reported for investment properties was just £2.5 million. Note 2 mentions that these properties are depreciated over periods of up to fifty years, which explains how the depreciation charge was so small that, given no acquisitions or disposals, the figure had decreased by just one decimal point since 2018.

On the other hand, Lloyds Banking Group uses the fair value model. The company included a £108 million fair value loss on investment properties as part of net trading income reported in profit or loss for the year ended 31 December 2019. Note 27 revealed how the valuation of investment properties changed during the year, as follows.[12] (The first sort of item, 'Exchange and other adjustments', will be explained in section 8.2.)

EXTRACT FROM LLOYDS BANKING GROUP'S 2019 ANNUAL REPORT

	£ m
Valuation as at 1 January 2019	3 770
Exchange and other adjustments	16
Expenditure on investment properties	73
Change in fair value of investment properties	(108)
Disposals	(198)
Valuation as at 31 December 2019	3 553

Lloyds' accounting policy note (note I) gives a sense of the complexities involved in determining fair value: 'investment property is carried at fair value based on current prices for similar properties, adjusted for the specific characteristics of the property (such as location or condition). If this information is not available, the Group uses alternative valuation methods, such as discounted cash flow projections or recent prices in less active markets. These valuations are reviewed at least annually by independent, professionally qualified valuers'.

6.4 INTANGIBLE ASSETS

We now turn our attention to a class of assets that is becoming increasingly important in our era of rapid technological progress. In the contemporary economy, many businesses' largest assets are intangibles such as software, brands, customer lists, patents, and the like. Accounting for these assets is generally trickier than for tangible assets, as they are often difficult to identify and measure. Furthermore, their values are often subject to greater volatility than tangible assets: the value of a fashion label, for example, is much less stable, and more difficult to measure, than the value of a machine. Similarly, software can become outdated almost without warning.

Intangible assets are assets that you cannot touch. IAS 38, which prescribes the financial reporting for most intangible assets, defines an intangible as 'an identifiable, non-monetary asset without physical substance'.[13] A brand is thus an example of an intangible asset because it is identifiable (that is, it can be identified as a separate component of the value in the business), it has no physical substance, and it is non-monetary.

A monetary asset, by the way, is an asset to be received as a fixed or determinable amount of money, such as accounts receivable, and is excluded from the definition of intangible assets because it is very different in several ways. For one, the amount of money a business might receive from its intangible assets tends to vary greatly, depending on their success, whereas future cash flows from monetary assets are much more predictable.

6

An Intangible asset is 'an identifiable, non-monetary asset without physical substance'.

6.4.1 Meeting the recognition criteria

Whilst many assets in a business may meet the definition of an intangible asset, not many will satisfy the criteria for recognition on the statement of financial position. As explained in section 6.1.2, in practice these criteria require the asset to meet the following three conditions: its existence should not be in doubt, the probability of economic benefits should not be low, and measuring it should not involve high levels of uncertainty.

Take the Burberry brand, for example. There is little doubt that this is a leading fashion brand, known and respected the world over. No informed person would question its ability to generate future economic benefits, and so the first two conditions are met. However, the third condition is a problem: it would be very challenging to determine how much the Burberry brand has cost to develop, and just as challenging to establish a reliably measurable value for the brand. When accountants cannot measure the value of an asset reliably, they resort to a principle of **prudence**, which involves avoiding overstating assets, and so they don't even try to put a value to it. So brands which are generated internally are not shown on the statement of financial position. This is not because accountants do not think that they are assets, but because measuring them is fraught with uncertainty.

> **MISCONCEPTION**
>
> **It cannot be *that* difficult to value a brand.**
>
> Wrong. For example, in 2019 the highest-ranked global brand on the website www.brandirectory.com was Amazon, which was valued at $188 billion.[14] At www.interbrand.com, another reputable brand valuation enterprise, Amazon's 2019 brand was valued at $125 billion and ranked third.[15] Interbrand's top spot that year went to Apple, which was listed at $234 billion, though back at www.brandirectory.com, it was only thought to be worth $154 billion!
>
> These huge differences indicate a high degree of measurement uncertainty. Brand valuation is still in its early days, and, until a suitable model emerges (if ever), internally generated brands will not be making appearances on any statements of financial position.

However, if Burberry buys a brand from another business and agrees to pay, say, £5 million, measurability would not be an issue, and this brand would qualify for recognition on the business's statement of financial position. We are therefore in a strange position when accounting for brands: those that are generated internally are not recognised on the statement of financial position, but brands acquired from other parties are recognised.

In the case of some other intangible assets, it is not measurability that is the problem, but the probability of economic benefits. For example, consider research, which is work undertaken with the prospect of gaining new scientific or technical knowledge or understanding. It ranges from the traditional activities undertaken by a pharmaceutical company to a business researching the layout of its website. During the phase in which research expenditure has not yet delivered usable findings, it is expensed, because there is no probability of future economic benefits.

Sometimes, however, research results in new knowledge, ideas, plans, or formulas which can be used to generate income. Accountants consider this to be the point at which the research phase comes to an end and the development phase begins, when the research findings are applied with a higher likelihood of economic benefits. As soon as the business can demonstrate that development expenditure will probably produce benefits, the recognition criteria are met, and any expenditure incurred thereafter is recognised on the statement of financial position as an intangible asset.

6.4.2 Intangible assets that are always expensed

Because of the difficulty in determining whether or not the recognition criteria are met for some intangible assets, and to prevent the inconsistency that would result from different businesses' using their own subjective interpretations of the criteria, the accounting standard-setters have applied their minds to many of the more complex intangible items. Thus, IAS 38 stipulates that internally generated brands and research costs, as we have seen, are always expensed, as are the costs of advertising, opening a business, training,

Many intangible assets are not recognised on the statement of financial position, because either they cannot be measured reliably, or the probability of their producing economic benefits is in doubt.

6

publishing titles, and customer lists. However, if items like brands, research, publishing titles, and customer lists are purchased, rather than generated internally, they would be shown on the statement of financial position, as the recognition criteria would be met.

The requirement that advertising is always expensed means that the cost of developing websites which is used solely or primarily for promoting the business's products must be expensed. Expenditure to develop other websites—provided that the business can demonstrate probable future benefits—can be capitalised.[16]

6.4.3 Two subsequent measurement models

As with PPE, there are two subsequent measurement models that a business may apply to its intangible assets: the cost model or the revaluation model. However, it is extremely rare for a business to adopt the revaluation model for its intangible assets, as a condition for its use is that there is an active market for them, and yet the vast majority of intangible assets are unique.

6.4.4 Amortisation and impairment

Intangible assets are written off over their estimated useful lives in much the same way as tangible assets such as PPE. However, with intangible assets, the process is known as 'amortisation', rather than 'depreciation'.

Intangible assets are subject to impairment in the same way as other assets: the business must look for signs of impairment (like the brand is not selling, or there are few hits on the website), and if these signs exist, it must calculate the recoverable amount.

Some businesses claim that they have intangible assets whose useful life is unlimited. These indefinite-life intangibles are not amortised, but they must undergo an impairment test each year, regardless of whether there are signs of impairment. This prevents these assets appearing forever on the businesses' statements of financial position without good reason.

> Depreciation of intangible assets is called 'amortisation'.

6.4.5 Burberry's intangible assets

Because of the uncertainty inherent in measuring it, Burberry's brand is not recognised on its balance sheet. This may seem like a substantial omission from the financial statements. After all, Burberry is consistently ranked as one of the top 20 global fashion brands, and, for example, Interbrand, a leading brand valuation firm, has in recent years consistently ranked its value at $5 billion or more.[17] Bear in mind that the sum of the carrying amounts of all the assets recognised on Burberry's balance sheet as at 30 March 2019 was £2.332 billion, which on that date was equivalent to $3.042 billion. Even if Interbrand's valuation is quite wrong, it is still likely that Burberry's brand is worth more than the total recognised asset value! We shall return to this point from the perspective of a financial analyst in section 11.2.2.

Burberry does, however, report some intangible assets, which in 2019 were measured at £221.0 million. Leaving aside goodwill, which we shall discuss in section 9.3, note 13 to the financial statements shows that the company's intangible assets consist of: computer software; intangible assets in the course of construction; and trademarks, licences, and other intangible assets. As expected, they are measured using the cost model, not fair value. Note 5 reports that the amortisation of intangibles increased selling and distribution costs by £1.5 million and administrative expenses by £27.1 million. This follows from the fact that the biggest intangible recognised by Burberry is computer software used for administrative purposes.

Many other companies recognise substantially more intangible assets on their statements of financial position than Burberry does. Pharmaceutical companies, for example, typically report sizeable intellectual property assets, comprising expenditure on acquired patents, trademarks, dossiers, licences, rights to co-market or manufacture certain third-party products, drug master files, and other know-how. Though they are not physical in nature, there is certainty about the existence of these items, a high probability of their producing economic benefits, and low levels of measurement uncertainty. They are thus permitted by IFRS to appear on the statement of financial position. Similarly, such companies often recognise considerable assets relating to product development, while their research costs cause large expenses in their statements of comprehensive income.

6.4.6 **A modern accounting challenge**

The largest companies in today's economy are tech companies like Apple, Microsoft, Google, and Amazon. A huge amount of the value inherent in these companies is in their intellectual property. And this applies equally to many other businesses, which are increasingly investing in intangibles. *Capitalism without Capital: The Rise of the Intangible Economy* is one of many recent books which describe the rising importance of investment in software, research and development, design, branding, training, and business process engineering, which all represent extremely powerful business opportunities.[18] Yet, despite these huge investments underpinning the success of most modern businesses, they rarely meet the strict conditions necessary for them to be recognised on the statement of financial position.

Thus, the uncomfortable case of Burberry's unrecognised brand being worth more than all of the assets actually recognised on its balance sheet is not in fact unusual: a vast number of businesses do not report their most valuable investments in their financial statements. This is a large part of the reason that the stock market valuations of businesses which have invested heavily in intangibles are typically many multiples of the net asset value on their balance sheets, making the financial statements look wildly out of touch. This is a real challenge for the discipline of financial accounting, which has evolved over 500 years to report the financial position and performance of bricks-and-mortar businesses. In the digital age, the standard-setters will have to find ways to inform users of the financial statements about these huge reservoirs of potential value.

One way in which this reporting gap is now being partially filled is with a different kind of report: the **integrated report**. Released annually, and often accompanying the financial statements, the integrated report aims to give a broader, more holistic view of the value inherent in a business. Along with the sort of financial capital reported in the financial statements, the integrated report identifies several other 'capitals', one of which is intellectual capital. It is through its reporting about this category of value that a business can communicate the vast potential for future cash flows stored in the intangible assets that it does not report on its statement of financial position. We shall cover the integrated report in more detail in section 14.2.2.

6.5 **INVENTORY**

When PB acquired ingredients, they were shown as an asset called 'inventory' on the statement of financial position (see section 2.2.4) until such time as they were sold as pizza slices (see section 2.2.6).

Inventories are formally defined as 'assets: (a) held for sale in the ordinary course of business; or (b) in the process of production for sale; or (c) in the form of materials or supplies to be consumed in the production process or in the rendering of services'.[19] In a manufacturing environment (say, a shoe factory), inventory would therefore comprise the raw materials (such as leather, rubber, and shoelaces), and work in-progress (shoes in the process of being manufactured), in addition to the finished goods (shoes whose manufacture is complete).

In a service environment, inventory is usually classified as work-in-progress, and refers to the costs of providing a service for which the entity has not yet recognised the related revenue. For example, a law firm may have spent a significant amount of time on a contracted piece of work, but not yet have recognised the revenue from the contract because the client has not yet acquired the benefits of the work (see section 4.3.1). The expenses incurred (salaries, stationery, and so on) will be recognised on the statement of financial position as inventory, until such time as the contract revenue can be recognised. At that point, the inventory will be derecognised (credit), and reported as cost of sales (debit) in the statement of comprehensive income, in exactly the same way as the pizza ingredients were shown as cost of sales when the pizza slices were sold.

> **MISCONCEPTION**
>
> Inventories and stock are different things.
>
> 'Stock' is a word used in many retail environments to describe inventory. For example, the process of counting inventory is often referred to as a 'stock take'. Be careful using this term in the US, however, as the term 'stock' usually describes companies' shares, as in the 'stock market'.

6.5.1 **Initial measurement**

In accordance with the general principle described in section 6.1.3, inventory is initially measured at cost. The accounting standard on inventory, IAS 2, stipulates that its cost comprises all the costs of getting the inventory to its present location and condition for sale. Thus, included in raw materials would be not only the purchase price but also import duties, transport and handling costs, and any other costs that are directly attributable to their acquisition.

In section 2.2.8, when we expensed the salaries of €50, we supposed that they were paid to the staff who take orders or work the cash register, and not to the person who makes the pizzas. We were also assuming that the €40 electricity bill related to the power consumed by, say, the lights and the cash register. If the salaries were instead paid to the actual pizza chef and the electricity bill related to heating the pizza oven, this €90 would relate directly to the manufacture of the pizza slices, and would therefore be a cost incurred in the production of inventory. Like the depreciation of the oven, this amount would count as part of the cost of inventory, and so would be reported as cost of sales in the statement of comprehensive income.

Because pizza is made and sold so quickly, PB had no work-in-progress or finished goods on hand; its only inventory was raw materials. Thus, the depreciation costs were never reported as part of the inventory balance in PB's statement of financial position, and were instead expensed immediately as cost of sales. However, in businesses which take longer to manufacture and sell their inventory, the inventory balance will include as work-in-progress and/or finished goods all costs incurred directly in the production process: the depreciation of manufacturing assets, direct labour, and the cost of factory management and administration.

Expenditure on the following items is never capitalised by being included in the cost of inventory, and is instead expensed as soon as it is incurred:

- advertising or other costs related to selling inventory;
- administrative costs that do not contribute to bringing inventories to their present location and condition for sale, such as the salaries of office clerks;
- storage costs, unless these storage costs are necessary in the production process before a further production stage—for example, the storage of wine is a critical part of its production, and therefore the costs of its storage *are* included in the cost of inventory;
- the amount of any abnormal expenditure on waste (materials or labour) in the manufacturing process.

6.5.2 Cost formulas

In section 2.2.6, when calculating cost of sales, we observed a critical difference between PB's inventory and the inventory of an aircraft manufacturer or a luxury car dealership: it doesn't make sense for PB to keep a record of the cost of each item of inventory. PB sells too many pizza slices too quickly and at such low costs that it is easier simply to count what is left over at the end of the period, and thus work out how much inventory must have been sold. Businesses with fewer items of higher-value inventory which are sold less frequently find it much easier to attribute costs to items, and so their accounting systems can tell them the cost of each item sold.

6

We also acknowledged that in practice even many businesses that sell high volumes of cheaper goods more quickly use computerised inventory systems and point-of-sale scanners to record in real-time the cost of each item of inventory bought and sold. But these businesses face a different problem that we did not discuss in Chapter 2: their products are not unique. For example, a retailer might be receiving consignments of dog food each week, where each consignment is priced slightly differently. Once the bags of dog food are unpacked and put on the shelf, the retailer cannot possibly keep track of the specific cost of any individual bag, because they are identical all the way down to their bar codes.

Imagine that this morning, three bags were on the shelf, one acquired by the retailer for €20, the second for €33, and the third for €40. When a customer shows up at the cash register with a bag they wish to purchase for the retailer's selling price of €100, how could the system know which bag it is? Is the cost of sales €20, €33, or €40? And is the cost of the remaining inventory therefore €73, €60, or €53? The answer is that no one can possibly know which bag was actually sold, and which bags are left in inventory. IAS 2 therefore instructs businesses whose products cannot be specifically identified to use a cost formula as a way to approximate the correct cost of inventory.

One kind of cost formula makes an assumption about which item was sold. For example, the business could assume that the item most recently purchased is the first item sold. This is known as the 'last-in, first-out' (LIFO) method, and in our example would result in closing inventory of €53 (€20 + €33) in the statement of financial position, and a profit of €60 (sales of €100 less cost of sales of €40) in the statement of comprehensive income.

Alternatively, the retailer could assume that the first item purchased is the first item sold. This is known as the 'first-in, first-out' (FIFO) method. In this case, FIFO would result in closing inventory of €73 (€33 + €40) in the statement of financial position, and a profit of €80 (€100 – €20) in the statement of comprehensive income. IFRS allows businesses to use the FIFO cost formula, but not LIFO, as the latter can result in inventory balances based on severely outdated costs.

Instead of making an assumption about which one was sold, a different type of cost formula uses an average price to record inventory. Like FIFO, this is permissible in terms of IFRS, which refers to it as the 'weighted average' cost formula. The unit sold would be assumed to have been sold for the average cost of €31 (€20 + €33 + €40, divided by 3), resulting in closing inventory of €62 (€31 × 2), and a profit of €69 (€100 – €31).

The accounting effects of the two permissible methods are summarised in Example 6.3.

EXAMPLE 6.3

	FIFO €	Weighted average €
Statement of financial position		
Inventory	73	62
Statement of comprehensive income		
Sales	100	100
Cost of sales	(20)	(31)
Profit	80	69

The example shows that vastly different profit figures can result from different cost formulas. Which of these is correct? Well, they are both permissible, and therefore they are both correct. Once again, we see that profit is dependent on the choices made by accountants: in this case, the choice is not what estimate to make, but what accounting policy to use.

If you are thinking that this example is unrealistic because the costs are not likely to be so far apart, that is a fair point. But bear in mind that variations in costs of even a few pence or cents can add up to a very large difference in cost of sales for businesses selling high volumes.

You may sometimes see reference to the 'retail' or the 'standard cost' method of measuring inventories. Both are also accepted by IFRS, so long as they result in a cost figure similar to that assigned by the FIFO or weighted average methods.

6.5.3 Subsequent measurement

With one relatively obscure exception which applies to commodity-brokers, inventory is an unusual type of asset in that it is never permitted or required to be revalued upwards above its original cost. On one hand, this makes some sense: if a business were to revalue an item of inventory upwards, it would in effect be recognising a profit before it had sold the item! On the other hand, it does mean that inventory is usually carried at substantially less than its fair value on the statement of financial position.

Whilst inventories are not revalued upwards, they are certainly written down when their value decreases. This is consistent with what you have learned about impairing assets when the amount expected to be obtained from them is lower than their carrying amount. One difference, however, is that there is no need to calculate a recoverable amount for inventory by identifying the higher of the value in use and the fair value less costs to sell. This is because inventory is not *used* by the business; it is sold. Inventories are thus written down to their **net realisable value** if this is below cost. Net realisable value is the estimated selling price of the inventory less the estimated costs to (complete and) sell the inventory, which is really just another way of saying 'fair value less costs to sell'. As with other impairments, these expenses may be reversed in future years, though of course the inventory can never be written up to an amount higher than its original cost.

The accounting for inventory write-downs was covered comprehensively in section 4.4.1.

6.5.4 Recognition of inventories as an expense

The expense usually called 'cost of sales' sometimes goes by other names, such as 'cost of inventories expensed'. In fact, the latter term is more precise, because, as explained in section 4.4.1, this figure contains more than just the cost of inventories sold, but also write-downs to net realisable value, any reversals of these amounts, and also all losses of inventory through theft, loss, perishing, and wastage.

Unless the business is a commodity broker-trader, inventory is never revalued upwards above its original cost. It is instead always measured at the lower of cost and net realisable value.

6.5.5 **Burberry's inventory**

As is true for many retail businesses, the largest non-cash asset on Burberry's 2019 balance sheet is inventories, measured at £465.1 million. Note 17 provides more detail, for example showing the break-down of the year-end inventory balance into raw materials, work-in-progress, and finished goods (the latter is by far the biggest, at £448.8 million). It also discloses the cost of all this inventory—£557.3 million—and shows how this figure has been reduced by 'provisions' of £92.2 million (16.5% of the cost) so that items expected to be sold below cost are carried at net realisable value. (The term 'provisions' is technically incorrect here because a **provision** is a type of liability, as you will learn in section 7.3. This sort of reduction in an asset is more correctly called an 'allowance'.)

The paragraph below the tables in note 17 is also interesting: Burberry's management changed this write-down proportion to 16.5% from 18.1% in 2018. They rightly acknowledge the large impact that apparently small revisions can have, pointing out that 'a 200 basis point [that is, 2%] increase in provisions would result in a reduction in inventory of £11.1 million and a corresponding reduction in profit before tax'. The reason for the more optimistic write-down estimate is suggested a little further down the page: in 2019, £30.0 million of inventory provisions from the previous year were reversed, most likely because the goods were sold for more than the net realisable value that had been estimated for them.

Of course, much of Burberry's inventory cannot be specifically identified, and so the accounting policy note 2(m) tells us that the company uses a cost formula: the FIFO method.

Finally, note 17 declares that Burberry physically destroyed £2.2 million of inventory in 2019, and £28.6 million in 2018. Apparently, the business burns surplus inventory to prevent them from being stolen, and to stop cheap imitations being made![20]

6.6 **LOANS AND RECEIVABLES**

Most statements of financial position will include at least one line-item for loans or receivables, or some combination of these two. Burberry uses a very common description: 'Trade and other receivables'. No matter what they are called, these assets are all debts owed to the business by customers, employees, and sometimes other third parties. They are examples of the 'monetary assets' that you know from section 6.4 are excluded from the definition of intangible assets.

The accounting standard that governs the reporting of loans and receivables is IFRS 9, which also applies to the other financial assets that we will discuss in section 6.7.

6.6.1 **Measurement**

Section 4.3.5, in explaining how *revenue* is measured for deferred payments, also explained how *receivables* are measured. If you are reading the chapters out of order, or if you just need a reminder, please go back and read that section now.

Let's consider another example, this time focusing on the initial and subsequent measurement of the receivable. Suppose that a business makes a credit sale on the first day of Year 1, and charges no interest over a two-year credit period, such that the only cash it receives from the customer is a single payment of €10 000 on the first day of Year 3. Example 6.4 shows in the last column how the receivable would be measured at the present value of the expected cash inflow. The discount rate used for the present value calculation is the market interest rate for a transaction of this sort, which we'll assume to be 10%. Thus, the initial measurement of the receivable on the first day of Year 1 (just like the amount of revenue recognised on that date) would be €8 264.46 (€10 000 ÷ 1.10^2).

The interest income each year is calculated by multiplying the carrying amount at the beginning of the year by the discount rate, and then this is added to the carrying amount of the receivable. This is the process known as **unwinding the discount**. The total interest of €1 734.54 equals the discount: the difference between the initial measurement of the receivable and the cash inflow.

EXAMPLE 6.4

	Cash inflow *Debit bank* *Credit receivable* €	Interest income *Reported in P/L* *Debit receivable* *Credit income* €	Receivable *Carrying amount in* *statement of* *financial position* €
Day 1 of Year 1 (date of sale)	–	–	8 264.46
End of Year 1	–	826.45	9 090.91
End of Year 2	–	909.09	10 000.00
Day 1 of Year 3 (date of collection)	10 000	–	0.00
Totals	10 000	1 735.54	

A two-year interest-free loan would be treated in much the same way as the receivable in this example.

IFRS 9 calls its subsequent measurement policy for loans and receivables '**amortised cost**'. The word 'amortisation' can be understood to mean 'reduction over time'. You already know that the reduction in the carrying amount of an intangible asset over time is recognised as an expense called amortisation. In Example 6.4, you can see that amortisation of a loan or receivable asset often works in the opposite direction: earlier in its life it is measured at a reduced figure, after which the gradual increases in its carrying amount are recognised as income.

However, the amortised cost measurement policy does not always result in reduced carrying amounts early on. For example, discounting is unnecessary if the time value of money is **immaterial**, which would be generally true if the credit periods are twelve months or shorter, or if the business charges interest at market-related rates. In such cases, the measurement of loans and receivables is straightforward. Basically, receivables are measured at the sales amount and loans are measured at the amount the business lends the debtor.

To see this, let's now suppose that after the goods are sold on the first day of Year 1, monthly interest is charged at the market rate of 10% for the full two years of credit, before the €10 000 is collected from the customer on the first day of Year 3. Example 6.5 shows that the receivable would consistently be measured at €10 000 (which is also the amount at which the revenue would be recognised on day 1 of Year 1).

EXAMPLE 6.5

	Cash inflows *Debit bank* *Credit interest* *income/receivable* €	Interest income *Reported in profit* *or loss* €	Receivable *Carrying amount in* *statement of* *financial position* €
Day 1 of Year 1 (date of sale)	–	–	10 000.00
End of Year 1	1 000	1 000	10 000.00
End of Year 2	1 000	1 000	10 000.00
Day 1 of Year 3 (date of collection)	10 000	–	0.00
Totals	12 000	2 000	

In this section, we have given a very basic overview of amortised cost, which should be sufficient for most of our readers. However, if you would like to know about some trickier aspects of the subsequent measurement of loans and receivables, including the effective interest rate method, you will find these details in the advanced material for this chapter in the **online resources** available at www.oup.com/he/ winfield-graham-miller1e.

6.6.2 Impairment of loans and receivables

We now have an opportunity to clear up an issue that may have been bothering you ever since Chapter 2. When PB made sales on credit, we immediately reported the amount as both a receivable asset and as revenue, despite the fact that PB hadn't yet received payment. IFRS does prevent a business from recognising the asset and the revenue if, at the time of the sale, the customer already seemed unlikely to pay, though most businesses wouldn't make the sale if this were the case. However, perhaps you are still left wondering: what if it turns out that a debtor who initially seemed financially stable in fact cannot pay?

The risk of not receiving all or some of what is owed is known as '**default risk**' or '**credit risk**'. Financial accounting deals with this risk by impairing loans and receivables in accordance with the general principles of asset impairment covered in section 6.1.8. They are scrutinised for signs of impairment, and then written down if their recoverable amount is lower than their carrying amount.

The recoverable amount of loans and receivables is the amount of expected cash flows, discounted to present value if necessary. Thus, in circumstances where the expected future cash flows decrease, the asset will be impaired.

If one of PB's debtors was to go bankrupt, this would represent a substantial default risk, and would therefore be a sign of impairment. Assuming the future expected cash flows are now zero, the accounts receivable asset would be derecognised (credit), and reported as an expense (debit) of that amount in profit or loss, as in Summary of Event 6. This is usually called '**bad debts expense**'.

When a business identifies debtors who will not pay amounts they owe, the receivable is derecognised or impaired, and the resulting expense is reported as bad debts expense.

SUMMARY OF EVENT 6 A debtor who owes PB €30 for credit sales goes bankrupt. On the date of sale:

Assets	−	Liabilities	=	Equity		Debit	Credit
+ €30						Accounts receivable	
				+ €30 (income)			Revenue

When PB discovers that the debtor has gone bankrupt and will pay none of the amount owing:

Assets	−	Liabilities	=	Equity		Debit	Credit
− €30							Accounts receivable
				− €30 (expense)		Bad debts expense	

You may wonder why the business doesn't just reduce income by the amount of the write-down, rather than reporting a separate expense, but think about the informational value of being able to see the quantity of bad debts on the statement of comprehensive income versus this information being 'hidden' by being netted off against the revenue figure.

Sometimes defaulting debtors are able to pay some, but not all of the amounts they owe. In that case, the receivable is merely written down, not entirely written off. This is a small distinction: for example, had PB discovered that a debtor who owed €50 would pay only €20 in future, the entry would be just the same as in the second entry in the previous example.

As usual, impairment losses can be reversed, with the recovered amount reported in profit or loss as an item of income usually called 'bad debts recovered'.

6.6.3 **Allowance for doubtful debts**

It is not enough just to impair loans and receivables for those debtors who have been identified as having 'gone bad'. Of course, it is likely that some of the other debtors will default too, even if the situation has not yet reached the point where there is no reasonable expectation of recovering their debts (which would require the treatment described in section 6.6.2).

IFRS 9 therefore requires PB to categorise its remaining receivables into groups with similar credit risks, for example by socioeconomic segments, geographic locations, and/or 'age' (that is, for how long the debts have been due). Each category is impaired to the extent that the default risk of that group has increased since the debtors within that group were initially recognised. An economic downturn or an increase in borrowing rates would, for example, indicate an increased risk for that category, as would debtors' payments' being more than thirty days overdue. The impairment loss calculated is essentially an estimate of 'expected credit losses'; that is, the amount the business no longer expects to receive in future.

When a business impairs a category of debtors like this, it cannot remove or reduce any specific debts in the accounting records, as it does not know precisely which debtors will default. So the business leaves the amount owing in accounts receivable (a debit balance), and creates (credits) an account with the amount by which the receivable should be impaired. It is most correct to call this account an '**allowance for doubtful debts**', though it is often called a 'provision' in some accounting jurisdictions. The decrease in equity (debit) is once again known as bad debts expense.

When a debtor from the category that was impaired in fact defaults, then the amount owing is removed from accounts receivable (credit) and the allowance account (debit), with no further effect on profit. This is shown in Summary of Event 7.

> Even when a business cannot identify the debtors who will default, it must impair accounts receivable for the debts it expects not to collect. It does so using an allowance for doubtful debts.

SUMMARY OF EVENT 7 At the end of Year 1, a category of debtors is expected to default by €30 during Year 2.

At the end of Year 1:

Assets	−	Liabilities	=	Equity		Debit	Credit
− €30							Allowance for doubtful debts
				− €30 (expense)		Bad debts expense	

During Year 2, assuming the debtors default as expected:

Assets	−	Liabilities	=	Equity		Debit	Credit
− €30							Accounts receivable
+ €30						Allowance for doubtful debts	

On its statement of financial position, the business reports the net amount of accounts receivable (that is, the balance on accounts receivable in its accounting records minus the balance on the allowance).

IFRS requires the notes to the financial statements to disclose the movements on the allowance account each year. This allows users to understand the level of bad debts within a business and to evaluate the quality of the business's credit policies. This is essential information because it indicates the general creditworthiness of a business's customers, which directly impacts future cash flows.

6.6.4 **Burberry's loans and receivables**

Burberry's note 16 to its 2019 financial statements reveals the components of the current and non-current trade and other receivables. These include 'Other non-financial receivables' (typically, non-cash items owed to the business) and 'Prepayments'. Prepaying rent, for example, gives the business a right to occupy premises in the future, which meets the definition of an asset: it is an economic resource controlled by the business as a result of the payment.

If Burberry has made loans, these would be disclosed as 'Other financial receivables', split into non-current and current portions, depending on the repayment terms.

By far the largest component of Burberry's trade and other receivables is 'Trade receivables' itself, which describes the amounts owed by customers for credit sales. On 30 March 2019, these totalled £124.5 million. Of course, not all of these debts are expected to be settled in full, because when any business sells that quantity of merchandise on credit, some of its customers will default. Accordingly, Burberry recognises a 'provision for doubtful debts' of £4.8 million against the gross figure, leaving net trade receivables of £119.7 million.

6

MISCONCEPTION

The 'provision for doubtful debts' is truly a provision.

No; although the term 'provision' is used widely in some jurisdictions, an allowance is not a provision as defined in terms of the accounting standards. Provisions are a type of liability, and liabilities result in an outflow of economic resources (usually cash). When a business writes down its accounts receivable by creating a 'provision', it is not expecting to pay anything, and so there is no liability, and therefore no provision.

The correct label for this sort of asset impairment account is 'allowance', so technically its name ought to be 'allowance for doubtful debts'. Similarly, Burberry's 'provision' for obsolete inventory would more correctly be called an allowance.

On p 200 of the Burberry 2019 annual report, note 26 summarises how the business has analysed the recoverability of the amounts owed. The business's debtors have been segmented into different categories, and within these, expected loss rates have been shown for each age category of receivable. In the total column, it is possible to see how the loss allowances in each of these categories have been compiled to create the total 'provision' of €4.8 million shown in note 16. Over the page, the movements on Burberry's 'provision' since 31 March 2018 are shown. Most notably, it was reduced by a £3.1 million write-off of receivables, and, interestingly, a £5.3 million 'unused amount'. It seems that the business decided that its previous expectations about debtors defaulting had been too pessimistic.

6.7 **OTHER FINANCIAL ASSETS**

A **financial instrument** is any contract which gives rise to a **financial asset** for one party, and either a financial liability or an equity instrument for another party. Thus, shares, **bonds,** and derivatives are all examples of financial instruments. The accounting implications for a business which has a financial liability as a result of a financial instrument will be covered in section 7.3. Equity instruments will be covered in section 10.3. As this chapter is about assets, we will deal with the financial assets that arise from financial instruments here. These often appear on statements of financial position as 'investments', or 'other investments', or with words that describe them more precisely, such as Burberry's 'derivative financial assets'.

In section 6.6, we dealt with one variety of financial assets—loans and receivables—which you now know are measured using amortised cost. IFRS 9 identifies other financial assets that should be measured in the same way, while requiring that others are measured at fair value.

> IFRS 9 requires financial assets to be measured in one of two broad ways: amortised cost or fair value.

6.7.1 Subsequent measurement at amortised cost

Financial assets measured at amortised cost meet both of the following conditions:

- they are held in order to collect cash flows (rather than for the purposes of speculation or trading);
- the cash flows arising from them are solely payments of capital and interest.

Thus, if a business buys **debentures** or bonds for the sake of the cash flows associated with them, they will be accounted for using exactly the same principles as were explained in section 6.6.

6.7.2 Subsequent measurement at fair value

All other financial assets are measured at fair value. These include any financial instruments that a business is actively trading, and shares in other companies (which give rise to the receipt of dividends, but not interest or capital repayments).

The carrying amounts of these instruments are adjusted to fair value at each year-end, and the resulting gain or loss is reported as an item of income or expense. For example, if a business purchases 100 000 shares in Burberry for £20 each, it would have initially recorded the shares at the cost of £2 million on the statement of financial position. If at the business's year-end, the shares are worth £21 each, then the fair value of its financial asset would be £2.1 million. The carrying amount in the statement of financial position would be increased by £100 000 (debit), and £100 000 would be reported as an investment gain (credit) in the statement of comprehensive income. If, in the following year, the Burberry share price fell to £18, the asset's carrying amount would be reduced to £1.8 million, and a loss of €300 000 would be reported.

The shares continue to be written up or down to their market value each year until they are sold. This process is sometimes called '**marking to market**'. This renders unnecessary a separate impairment process like for assets measured at amortised cost: as these assets are always reported at fair value, any drop in the economic benefits to be obtained from the asset are automatically taken into account.

We have not yet mentioned whether the income or expense arising from marking to market is recognised in profit or loss or OCI. The answer is that they are generally presented in profit or loss. There is, however, an option available for the gains and losses on shares to be recognised in OCI instead, provided that they are not held for trading.

Whichever section they are reported in, these items of income and expense are recognised despite the fact that they only currently exist on paper and will only be realised—that is, received in cash—if the shares are sold.

There is a category of financial assets that requires an interesting hybrid of amortised cost and fair value measurement. These are debentures or bonds purchased for their contractual cash flows but expected to be sold before they mature. They are reported in the statement financial position at their fair value, but the statement of comprehensive income reports a combination of amortised cost adjustments in profit or loss and fair value adjustments in OCI. The details are too complicated for us to go into, but it may help you to know that not all bonds and similar investments are measured at amortised cost, and that this is a further instance of the use of the infamous OCI.

MISCONCEPTION

For financial instruments, only realised gains and losses appear in the statement of comprehensive income.

No; as with many other kinds of assets, both realised and unrealised gains are reported as income. For example, when shares that are held for trading are revalued, the gain or loss is reported in profit or loss, even though it is unrealised.

To distinguish between realised and unrealised gains and losses, the statement of cash flows will be more help than the statement of comprehensive income.

6.7.3 Derivatives

Derivative financial instruments also lead to businesses recognising financial assets. This section explains what derivatives are, and why this is the case. Although it is not our aim to explain all the complexities of derivatives, some basic understanding of these instruments would be advantageous to readers, as most sizeable businesses use derivatives of one form or another.

Derivatives are complex financial contracts which can be used to reduce a variety of risks in a business. They can also be entered into for purely speculative purposes, although this is not generally recommended for businesses, as it is essentially gambling. The main characteristic of a derivative is that its value is derived from something else, which is sometimes called 'the **underlying**'.

The most common type of derivative in business is a **forward exchange contract**, whose purpose is to **hedge** against losses that might arise from exchange rate movements. 'Hedging' involves entering into a transaction in order to reduce the risk associated with a different transaction, which is the one being hedged. It is a bit like betting on the opposing team to reduce your disappointment if your team were to lose.

For example, suppose that a UK-based importer orders goods for ¥10 million from a supplier in China when the exchange rate is £1 = ¥10 (that is, 10 yuan to the pound), and

To 'hedge' a transaction is to enter into another transaction that will reduce the risk associated with the hedged transaction.

that the payment will be made in three months' time. On ordering the goods, the importer is expecting to pay £1 million (¥10 million ÷ ¥10). However, if the exchange rate moves to £1 = ¥8 by the time the payment falls due, then the importer will have to pay £1.25 million (¥10 million ÷ ¥8).

To avoid this risk, the importer could enter into a forward exchange contract with a bank to buy ¥10 million in three months' time at a rate—called the 'forward rate'—of, say, £1 = ¥9.8. In three months' time—on the 'exercise date'—the importer will buy ¥10 million from the bank at a cost of £1 020 408 (¥10 million ÷ ¥9.8), irrespective of what has happened to exchange rates, and pay the supplier the ¥10 million. The importer has effectively locked in an exchange rate of £1 = ¥9.8, and in so doing has eliminated any risk that might be caused by adverse exchange rate movements. This is known as taking 'forward cover'.

The value of a derivative

The forward exchange contract has a value, and can be traded in the forward exchange market. If, for example, the importer no longer needs the forward exchange contract because the deal falls through, then it could be sold to another importer looking to take forward cover against a decline in the exchange rate. Its value will depend on the expected exchange rate on the exercise date. If, since the contract was entered into, the yuan strengthens against the pound so that the exchange rate becomes £1 = ¥8, then other UK-based importers should be willing to pay handsomely for a contract to buy yuan at £1 = ¥9.8. After all, the contract would entitle them to get 9.8 yuan for every pound, when others are likely to be getting only about 8 yuan. In this scenario, the contract is clearly an asset of the business.

If, however, the yuan were to weaken after the forward exchange contract was entered into, so that the exchange rate changes to say £1 = ¥11, other importers will not be willing to pay anything for the contract. No one will want to get only 9.8 yuan for a pound if it is likely that they could get something like 11 yuan on the open market. The only way for the holder of the forward exchange contract to escape the contract would be to *pay* another party to take over the contract. In this scenario, the derivative has become a financial liability of the business.

The forward exchange contract is a derivative because its value is determined, at least in part, by movements in the actual exchange rate (which is therefore the 'underlying' in this case).

Other types of derivatives include contracts that reduce the risk of losses caused by changes in interest rates (such as interest rate swaps), share prices (such as share options and warrants), commodity prices (such as gold futures), and credit ratings (known as credit derivatives).

In each case, for each party to a derivative financial instrument, the variations in the value of the underlying will affect whether the derivative is an asset or a liability, as well as its value.

Subsequent measurement of derivatives

If a business holds derivatives for a reason other than hedging, then those derivatives are measured like other financial assets which it intends to trade. In other words, they are marked to market by increasing or decreasing their carrying amounts to fair value, with the gains or losses recognised in profit or loss.

However, where the derivative is used as a hedge, it is measured using hedge accounting. Simply put, this aims to avoid the volatile effects on profit or loss that would be caused by the standard accounting treatment, when in fact the whole point of hedging is to reduce the effects of volatility in the hedged transaction.

Let us return to our example. Suppose that in Year 1 our UK-based importer entered into a forward exchange contract to buy ¥10 million at a rate of £1 = ¥9.8, and at the end of Year 1, the yuan had strengthened and the contract could be sold for £50 000. Instead of selling it for that amount, the importer continues to hold the derivative until the exercise date in Year 2, and then pays £1 020 408 for inventory delivered worth ¥10 million, having saved a substantial amount of money now that the exchange rate is, say, £1 = ¥8.

At the end of Year 1, the derivative instrument is a financial asset, and therefore is recognised in the statement of financial position. However, hedge accounting prevents the gain from affecting profit or loss before the hedged transaction has even taken place; that is, before the inventory has even been acquired. The gain is instead reported in OCI for the first year, rather than in profit or loss. Like other items of OCI, the gain will be recognised in the equity section of the statement of financial position in an account created just for this sort of gain. As forward exchange contracts are examples of '**cash flow hedges**', this special equity account is often called the 'cash flow hedging reserve'.

The inventory is recognised when it is received in the second year, and so the derivative financial asset is derecognised and the amount in the cash flow hedging reserve is removed. This allows the inventory to be recognised at its true, hedged cost to the business. The accounting effects are summarised in Example 6.6.

EXAMPLE 6.6

	Year 1 £	Year 2 £
Statement of financial position		
Derivative financial asset	50 000	–
Inventory	–	1 020 408
Bank	–	– 1 020 408
Cash flow hedging reserve	50 000	–
Statement of comprehensive income		
Effect on profit or loss	–	–
Effect on OCI	50 000	–

Sometimes the hedged transaction results in a gain or loss in the profit or loss section (an example of such a transaction is described in section 8.2.2). In that case, to the extent that the hedge has effectively cancelled this gain or loss, the fair value loss or gain on the derivative is also reported in profit or loss, thus ensuring that the net effect on profit or loss of the successful hedge is as close to zero as possible.

In practice, cash flow hedge accounting can be quite a bit more complicated than this, but what's important is only that you understand its key purpose: to prevent the usual accounting principles from leading to gains and losses in profit or loss when in fact the hedge has achieved its purpose of neutralising the risk of gains and losses on the hedged transaction.

MISCONCEPTION

Accounting for financial instruments is straightforward.

No, it's not. According to legend, Sir David Tweedie (then chairman of the IASB) was once heard saying, 'If you think you understand the standard on financial instruments, then you haven't read it properly.' Some financial instruments are measured at amortised cost; others at fair value. Furthermore, with those that are measured at fair value, in some cases, the fair value adjustment is taken to profit or loss, whilst in other cases, the adjustment is taken to OCI; not to mention the complex requirements of hedge accounting.

6.7.4 Burberry's other financial assets

Other than trade and other receivables, and cash, Burberry's balance sheet refers to only one type of financial asset. These are 'Derivative financial assets', which appear in both the non-current and current sections. On p 174, an accounting policy note explains that the business 'uses derivative financial instruments to hedge its exposure to fluctuations in foreign exchange rates arising on certain trading transactions. The principal derivative instruments used are forward foreign exchange contracts taken out to hedge highly probable cash flows in relation to future sales and product purchases.' In other words, Burberry mostly uses its derivatives in the same way as the importer in our example in section 6.7.3.

It should be no surprise, then, that 'cash flow hedges' appears as an item of OCI in the statement of comprehensive income, and that there is a 'hedging reserve' in the equity section of the balance sheet. These are the result of Burberry applying hedge accounting to its derivatives.

In note 26, Burberry includes a fair amount of detail about its exposure to foreign exchange risk that its hedging strategy seeks to reduce. Across five pages of the annual report, this note (entitled 'financial risk management') seeks to comply with the requirements of IFRS 7 to 'disclose information that enables users of its financial statements to evaluate the nature and extent of risks arising from financial instruments to which the entity is exposed at the end of the reporting period'.[21] As it is about risks arising from financial instruments generally, this note refers not only to financial assets, but also to financial liabilities and equity instruments, and contains sections on share price risk, interest rate risk, credit risk, **liquidity risk**, and capital risk. In accordance with the standard, the information provided is both quantitative (based on numbers) and qualitative (based on descriptions).

6.8 NON-CURRENT ASSETS HELD FOR SALE

Non-current assets such as PPE, investment properties, and intangibles are by definition expected to be used for a number of years to generate cash and profits. The way in which these assets are measured takes this into account: for example, depreciation or amortisation is typically charged to report the effects of using them, and when they are impaired, their value in use is taken into account.

Yet sometimes on a business's reporting date it has an item of PPE, an intangible asset, or an investment property that it plans to sell in the near future. If so, provided that the sale is highly probable and the asset is ready to be sold, it is no longer included in its usual category, but instead appears in a separate category called non-current assets held for sale, for which the relevant accounting standard is IFRS 5. As the cash flows that it will generate, unlike the other non-current assets, will be based solely on those that result from the sale, these assets are required to be measured differently. Depreciation or amortisation ceases, and they are written down to fair value less costs to sell, if this is lower than the amount at which they are currently carried.

Non-current assets held for sale do not appear on Burberry's 2019 balance sheet, but in that year the UK retailer Tesco did report this asset category on its group balance sheet.[22] As is quite common, Tesco included the line-item (which it called 'Non-current assets classified as held for sale') in neither the non-current assets section nor the current assets section, but instead put it in a little section all of its own at the end of the list of assets. Note 7 explained that these assets, measured at £98 million, consisted mainly of properties due to be sold within one year.

The energy company BP disclosed a far larger amount of 'assets classified as held for sale' in its 2019 group balance sheet: US$7 465 million.[23] In note 2, the company listed all of the asset categories that make up this figure: PPE, intangible assets, investments, inventories, and trade and other receivables. It also explained why even current assets were included in the list: all of these assets belonged to two whole business units which BP had agreed to sell within the next twelve months: its Alaska operations and its operations in the San Juan basin in Colorado. Because these business units would be sold along with the debts they owed, BP also separated out their total liabilities of US$1 393 million on the balance sheet, putting them in a line-item named 'Liabilities directly associated with assets classified as held for sale'.

Of course, when assets (and liabilities) are moved to a separate category because they are held for sale, they are removed from the category in which they were previously reported. Thus, BP's note 12 about PPE, for example, showed 'reclassification as assets held for sale' as one of the reasons that the business's PPE balance reduced, along with reasons like depreciation and disposals (which BP calls 'deletions').

If a business plans to sell a non-current asset soon after the reporting date, it is removed from its usual asset category and instead reported as 'held for sale'.

6

6.9 AGRICULTURAL ASSETS

Farming businesses transform or grow agricultural assets, which are disclosed in their financial statements as a separate type of asset. The accounting standard dedicated to agriculture, IAS 41, divides agricultural assets into two subcategories: biological assets (living animals and plants); and agricultural produce (the produce that is harvested from biological assets such as meat, milk, eggs, and nuts).

Both subcategories are measured at fair value less costs to sell. For example, the amount at which a herd of cattle is reported on the statement of financial position would be the animals' current market price, less the transport and other costs of getting them to that market, less any selling costs such as commissions or fees.

If the cattle produce milk, then this would be recognised as agricultural produce at fair value less costs to sell. If the milk is made into cheese, it would be inventory, not agricultural produce, because it is a processed product resulting from the agricultural produce. IAS 2, the accounting standard on inventory, thus applies to the cheese, and so it is measured at the lower of cost and net realisable value. Its cost is determined by adding the costs of processing the cheese to the milk's carrying amount.

Any changes in the measurement of agricultural assets (such as the increase in a beef cow's fair value as it grows), and gains that arise on initial recognition of these items (such as the birth of a calf), are reported as items of income or expense in profit or loss each year.

In addition to inventory, agricultural businesses, of course, have many assets that are not agricultural assets. These are accounted for according to the other sections of this chapter. For example, farm buildings and equipment would be reported as PPE in accordance with IAS 16.

A good example of an agricultural business's financial statements belongs to the Norwegian seafood company, Mowi. Its 2019 statement of financial position reported biological assets of €1 522.4 million. This figure, representing the fair value less costs to sell of the business's eggs, juveniles, smolt, and fish in the sea, was larger than any other asset category.[24]

> Agricultural assets consist of biological assets (living animals and plants) and agricultural produce (the produce that is harvested from biological assets such as meat, eggs, and nuts).

> Any changes in the fair value less costs to sell of agricultural assets are recognised as gains or losses in profit or loss each year.

CONCLUSION

In order to assess a business's ability to achieve its ultimate goal—producing net operating cash inflows—we must consider how its investing activities have put it in a position to do this. In other words, we must obtain a sound understanding of the business's assets by interrogating the vast amount of information about them in the statement of financial position and the related notes.

Although there is a good deal of commonality in the accounting for different asset categories, there are also some significant differences in their measurement and recognition.

Some assets are carried at cost; some at depreciated cost; some are revalued; some of these revalued assets are carried at fair value, whilst others are carried at fair value less costs to sell; and some impaired assets may be carried at their value in use. In some cases, the gains or losses arising on revaluation are reported in profit or loss in the statement of comprehensive income, whilst for other assets they appear in the OCI section. A few major assets—especially many internally generated intangibles—are not recognised at all.

In order to unravel these complexities, users of the financial statements have to be willing to pay special attention to a business's accounting policies and other notes. You are now well prepared to do this. This chapter has covered most, if not all, of the assets you will find on real-world statements of financial position. You may also come across a handful of other assets. Rest assured that most of these are covered in other chapters: **cash** and **cash equivalents** in section 5.1; pension fund assets in section 7.2.7; leased (or 'right-of-use') assets in section 8.1; **deferred tax** assets in section 8.3; goodwill in section 9.3; and investments in associates or joint ventures in section 9.4. Any assets not specifically mentioned in this book are likely to be self-explanatory. For example, Burberry's 2019 balance sheet included 'Income tax receivables' of £14.9 million. This is exactly what you would suppose: overpayments of income tax that are now owed to the business by the tax authorities.

While working through the summary of key points, look out for Table 6.2, which presents a brief synopsis of the accounting treatment of the asset categories that we have covered in this chapter.

SUMMARY OF KEY POINTS

- The Conceptual Framework for Financial Reporting contains several basic concepts and broad principles which apply to the financial reporting of all asset categories. See Table 6.1 for a summary.
- To qualify as an asset, a resource must meet the three key requirements of the asset definition: it must give rise to a right, the right should have the potential to produce economic benefits, and the business must control the resource.
- To be recognised as an asset on the business's statement of financial position, an asset must meet the recognition criteria of relevance and faithful representation, which effectively prohibit recognition if there is: uncertainty about whether the asset exists, a low probability of an inflow of economic benefits from the asset, or a high level of uncertainty about the asset's measurement.
- The initial measurement of an asset—that is, the amount at which it is first recorded in the accounting system—includes all costs incurred to get it to the point where it can help generate revenue. These costs are discounted to present value if payment is deferred to the point that the time value of money becomes material.
- If subsequent costs are incurred on an asset, they are capitalised to the asset's carrying amount only if they are not for day-to-day servicing and they will probably give rise to economic benefits.
- Expenditure initially recognised as an asset on the statement of financial position does eventually end up being expensed in the statement of comprehensive income, usually as cost of sales, depreciation, amortisation, or impairment.
- Asset impairment generally involves three steps: review assets for signs of impairment; if an asset shows signs of impairment, calculate its recoverable amount (which is the higher of value in use and fair value less costs to sell); if the recoverable amount is below the current carrying amount, impair the asset down to the recoverable amount.

■ Disposal of assets leads to derecognition of the asset, and the difference between its carrying amount and the proceeds being reported as a net gain or loss in the statement of comprehensive income (except in the case of inventory, whose disposal results in revenue and cost of sales).

■ Significant events that occur after the business's year-end but before the financial statements are compiled affect those financial statements only if they provide

TABLE 6.2 Summary of the accounting treatments of asset categories covered in Chapter 6

Category (and IFRS)	Definition/variety	Measurement model	Effect on statement of comprehensive income
PPE (IAS 16)	Tangible; held for use in business; benefits expected to last for more than one period	Cost model	Depreciation Possible impairment
		Revaluation model	Depreciation Possible impairment Revaluation gains and losses to OCI
Investment property (IAS 40)	Held to earn rentals and/or for capital appreciation, not owner-occupied	Cost model	Depreciation Possible impairment
		Fair value model	No depreciation Fair-value adjustments to profit or loss
Intangibles (IAS 38)	Identifiable non-monetary asset without physical substance	Cost model	Amortisation Possible impairment Indefinite life intangibles not amortised, but subject to annual impairment
		Revaluation model	Same as PPE on revaluation model
Inventory (IAS 2)	Held for sale; in process of production; materials or supplies	Lower of cost and net realisable value	Cost of sales Possible impairment
Financial instruments (IFRS 9)	Loans and receivables	Amortised cost	Impairments through profit or loss Interest income (if any) through profit or loss
Financial instruments (IFRS 9)	Bonds/debentures (not for trading and not planned to be sold)	Amortised cost	Impairments through profit or loss Interest income through profit or loss
Financial instruments (IFRS 9)	Other investments	Fair value	Fair value adjustments in profit or loss (but may be through OCI in some instances) Dividend income through profit or loss
Financial instruments (IFRS 9)	Derivative instruments (such as forward exchange contracts)	Fair value (whether asset or liability)	Fair value adjustments in profit or loss, except for some hedges, when in OCI
Non-current assets held for sale (IFRS 9)	Non-current, intended to be sold within the next reporting period	Lower of carrying amount or fair value less costs to sell	No depreciation Possible impairment
Agricultural assets (IAS 41)	Living animals and plants, and the products harvested from them via agricultural activity	Fair value less costs to sell	Fair value adjustments to profit or loss

6

evidence about conditions that existed at the year-end. Otherwise, they are disclosed in a note to the financial statements.

■ How an asset is categorised and accounted for depends on the business's intentions regarding it, so that a building could, for example, by categorised as PPE, investment property, non-current asset held for sale, or inventory.

■ Depreciation and amortisation reduce the carrying amount of an asset down to its residual value over its estimated useful life, thus expensing the net amount that the asset has cost the business.

■ There are various depreciation methods, such as straight-line, diminishing balance, and units of production. A business should use the method which best represents the pattern of consumption of the asset's benefits.

■ Many intangible assets are not recognised as assets because they do not satisfy the recognition criteria. Internally generated brands, research, advertising, training, and the costs of opening a business are examples of intangibles that are always expensed.

■ As a result of the previous point, the statements of financial position of businesses with large investments in intellectual property generally omit their biggest assets. This is a challenge for financial analysts and other users of the financial statements.

■ When the cost of a business's products cannot be individually identified, it must use a cost formula permitted by IFRS—such as FIFO or weighted average—to approximate the cost of its inventory.

■ When there is no reasonable expectation of recovering a debt, or part of a debt, owed to it, the business impairs the receivable down to what is recoverable, and reports bad debts expense. In less certain cases, when a business merely expects that some debtors will default, it raises an allowance for doubtful debts against its receivables balance and reports bad debts expense.

■ Table 6.2 on the previous page presents a summary of the definitions, subsequent measurement models, and impacts on the statement of comprehensive income of the asset categories covered in this chapter.

CHAPTER QUESTIONS

The applied questions (marked 'AQ') and the discussion questions (marked 'DQ') relate to the financial statements of Daimler, contained in Appendix II. The suggested solutions to these questions, and also to the concept questions (marked 'CQ'), can be found in Appendix III.

 Also, don't forget the **online resources** available at www.oup.com/he/winfield-graham-miller1e, which contain multiple-choice questions based on the material in this chapter. You will also find many other helpful resources, including two mini case studies with accompanying questions and answers, and advanced material on some aspects of assets.

CONCEPT QUESTIONS

CQ 6.1 Briefly outline the two ways in which a business's expenditure may be accounted for.

CQ 6.2 Can a business report an asset on its statement of financial position if it does not legally own that asset? Explain your answer.

CQ 6.3 Outline the difference between a current and a non-current asset.

CQ 6.4 Briefly explain, and distinguish between, the following two terms often applied to assets: 'subsequent costs' and 'subsequent measurement'.

CQ 6.5   Briefly outline how the accounting process known as impairment would be applied to an item of PPE measured on the cost model.

APPLIED QUESTIONS

AQ 6.6   What was the total carrying amount (or 'book value') of Daimler's assets on 31 December 2019, and what was the split between current and non-current assets?

AQ 6.7   What events might have caused a movement from 2018 to 2019 in the carrying amount of PPE reported on Daimler's statement of financial position? Distinguish between events which might increase the carrying amount and those which might decrease it.

AQ 6.8   By how much did Daimler depreciate its PPE (excluding right-of-use assets) during 2019?

AQ 6.9   By how much did Daimler amortise its intangible assets during 2019? In which line-item on the consolidated statement of income is most of this expense included?

AQ 6.10   Daimler's 2019 statement of financial position reports intangible assets of €15 978 million. Table F.25 (on p 255) lists the components of this figure: goodwill of €1 217 million, development costs of €12 525 million, and other intangible assets of €2 236 million. Explain how the development costs have arisen.

AQ 6.11   What are the components of the of €29 757 million reported as Daimler's inventories on its 2019 statement of financial position, and what will happen to these amounts in the following financial year?

AQ 6.12   Daimler's 2019 statement of financial position reports trade receivables of €12 332 million. Does this amount include the value of any receivables that Daimler is not expecting to collect? What is the value of the receivables that Daimler has estimated that it will not collect?

AQ 6.13   Has Daimler reported any significant events after the reporting period? If so, what are these events? Are they 'adjusting' or 'non-adjusting' events, and why?

DISCUSSION QUESTIONS

DQ 6.14   Where on its statement of financial position is the value of Daimler's staff reported?

DQ 6.15   According to www.brandirectory.com, Daimler's Mercedes-Benz brand was worth $60 355 million in 2019.[25] Why is it not reported on Daimler's statement of financial position?

DQ 6.16   Which assets currently reported on Daimler's statement of financial position might be carried at an amount significantly below their fair value?

DQ 6.17   In the section that outlines Daimler's accounting policies, Table F.08 on p 237 reveals that Daimler depreciates technical equipment and machinery over their useful lives of between five and twenty-five years. Discuss why there is such a wide range of useful lives for these assets.

DQ 6.18   Discuss the risk that Daimler's assets will not generate future cash flows, distinguishing examples of low-risk and high-risk assets.

DQ 6.19   The accounting policy note on p 237 explains the policy for measurement of PPE, implying that the revaluation model is not used. Suggest two further ways that the consolidated financial statements confirm that PPE is indeed not measured using the revaluation model.

DQ 6.20   If Daimler had chosen the revaluation model to measure items of PPE, and the fair value of PPE increases, what primary effects would this have on the financial statements?

DQ 6.21   Suggest at least three ways in which judgements and opinions exercised by Daimler's financial accountants could influence the carrying amount of PPE reported by Daimler on its consolidated statement of financial position.

INVESTIGATION QUESTIONS

IQ 6.22   Identify a listed retail company that is based in your country and obtain its financial statements. Identify the three largest asset categories reported on its statement of financial position. Consider whether the business might have other important assets that are not reported.

IQ 6.23   Identify three listed companies that are based in your country and obtain their financial statements. Establish the cause and extent of any asset impairments that have been reported in these financial statements.

IQ 6.24   Do you think that in the future there should be some attempt to include the value of a business's human capital on its statement of financial position? If so, how might this be done?

REFERENCES

[1]   IASB 2018. *Conceptual Framework for Financial Reporting*. Section 4.3.

[2]   IASB 2018. *Conceptual Framework for Financial Reporting*. Section 4.4.

[3]   IASB 2018. *Conceptual Framework for Financial Reporting*. Section 5.7.

[4]   IASB 2018. *Conceptual Framework for Financial Reporting*. Section 5.14.

[5]   IASB 2018. *Conceptual Framework for Financial Reporting*. Section 5.16.

[6]   IASB 2018. *Conceptual Framework for Financial Reporting*. Section 5.20.

[7]   IASB 2018. *IAS 37: Provisions, Contingent Liabilities and Contingent Assets*. Para 10.

[8]   IASB 2018. *Conceptual Framework for Financial Reporting*. Section 6.12.

[9]   IASB 2018. *IAS 16: Property, Plant and Equipment*. Section 6.

[10] IASB 2018. *IAS 16: Property, Plant and Equipment*. Section 6.

[11] IASB 2018. *IAS 40: Investment Properties*. Section 5.

[12] Lloyds Banking Group 2019. *Helping Britain Prosper: Annual Report and Accounts 2019*. Information extracted from notes 7 and 27. Available at: https://www.lloydsbankinggroup.com/globalassets/documents/investors/2019/2019_lbg_annual_report_v3.pdf.

[13] IASB 2018. *IAS 38: Intangible Assets*. Section 8.

[14] https://brandirectory.com/rankings/global-500-2019.

[15] https://www.interbrand.com/best-brands/best-global-brands/2019/ranking.

[16] IASB 2002. *SIC-32: Intangible Assets—Web Site Costs*.

[17] https://www.interbrand.com/best-brands/best-global-brands/2019/ranking/burberry.

[18] Haskell, J and Westlake, S 2017. *Capitalism without Capital: The Rise of the Intangible Economy*. Princeton University Press.

[19] IASB 2018. *IAS 2: Inventories*. Section 6.

[20] BBC News 2018. 'Burberry Burns Bags, Clothes and Perfume Worth Millions'. 19 July. Available at: https://www.bbc.com/news/business-44885983.

[21] IASB 2019. *IFRS 7: Financial Instruments: Disclosures*. Section 7.

[22] Tesco plc 2019. *Annual Report and Financial Statements 2019*. Available at: https://www.tescoplc.com/media/476422/tesco_ara2019_full_report_web.pdf.

[23] BP plc 2019. *Annual Report and Form 20-F 2019*. Available at: https://www.bp.com/content/dam/bp/business-sites/en/global/corporate/pdfs/investors/bp-annual-report-and-form-20f-financial-statements-2019.pdf.

[24] Mowi ASA 2019. *Integrated Annual Report 2019*. Available at: https://corpsite.azureedge.net/corpsite/wp-content/uploads/2020/03/Mowi_Annual_Report_2019.pdf.

[25] Brand Finance 2019. *Automotive Industry 2019*. March. Available at: https://brandirectory.com/download-report/brand-finance-automotive-industry-2019-preview.pdf.

LIABILITIES

Here are some of the things you will be able to do after reading this chapter:

- explain the significance of liabilities for users of the financial statements, and link this to the ways in which they are reported on the statement of financial position;
- apply the liability definition, and the criteria that a liability must satisfy to be recognised;
- identify certain items as contingent liabilities or commitments, and explain their inclusion in the notes to the financial statements;
- describe the measurement of liabilities in general, and distinguish this from financial liabilities measured at fair value;
- explain how some liabilities, such as deferred income and government grants, are not settled by paying a creditor;
- identify a variety of provisions, such as for warranty obligations, environmental rehabilitation, employee benefits, and onerous contracts; and discuss the accounting treatment of them.

CHAPTER 7

This chapter builds on material covered in earlier chapters. If you don't feel comfortable with any of the following items, we recommend that you briefly go back now to the sections referenced.

- The financial statements are designed to enable providers of funding to understand the results of the business's **value creation cycle**. The ultimate goal of this cycle is to produce net operating cash inflows (see sections 1.3.1 and 1.3.4).
- A key phase of this cycle is **financing activities**, which involves obtaining funding, sometimes in the form of debt (see Figure 1.6 in section 1.3.6 for an illustration of the value creation cycle).
- Debt funding and other obligations of the business are reported as **liabilities** on its **statement of financial position**, or **balance sheet** (see section 2.2.14 for a basic example).

- Borrowings are a type of liability. Lenders charge interest, which the borrower expenses using **accrual accounting** (described in section 2.2.8) in the **profit or loss section** of the **statement of comprehensive income**, often near the bottom in a line-item called 'Finance costs' or 'Finance expense' (see section 2.2.11).

- Some items of **income** and **expense** are reported on the statement of comprehensive income in the **'other comprehensive income' (OCI) section**, and so do not affect profit or loss (see section 4.1 for the statement format, section 4.2 for an explanation of the OCI section, and section 4.8 for a list of items of OCI).

- Many accounting principles and practices of relevance to this chapter were demonstrated at a simple level in Chapter 2, using the example of a very small business that sells pizza slices, called 'PB'. We shall refer to PB in this chapter too.

We have already encountered quite a few liabilities, including four on PB's statement of financial position at the end of Year 1 (interest-bearing borrowings, accounts payable, tax payable, and shareholders for dividend), as well as the obligation to provide goods or services to a customer who has paid in advance, called **deferred income** (see sections 4.3.4 and 4.3.6); and bank overdrafts (see section 5.7). Almost all liabilities lead to cash outflows. (This is true even for most liabilities that will not be settled directly with cash (eg deferred income), for the goods or services that settle them do ultimately cost the business money.) Thus, whereas **assets** indicate the potential for future cash inflows, liabilities reveal the prospects for future cash outflows, and so a thorough understanding of liabilities is as vital to an informed assessment of a business as is knowledge of its assets.

The accounting treatments of all the liabilities conform to a few general principles, which are presented in section 7.1. After that, we will discuss a special variety of liabilities—provisions—and then in section 7.3, we'll briefly cover complex financial liabilities. At the very end of the chapter you will find Table 7.1, which summarises the accounting treatment of the most common liabilities.

This chapter covers most liabilities, but we will leave two—lease liabilities and deferred tax liabilities—until Chapter 8, for reasons that will become clear in that chapter.

7.1 GENERAL PRINCIPLES OF ACCOUNTING FOR LIABILITIES

Like it does for assets, the Conceptual Framework for Financial Reporting lays down several basic concepts and general principles to account for liabilities. In this section, we will explain them, along with some of the content in other accounting standards that applies to most liabilities.

7.1.1 The liability definition

The Conceptual Framework contains the following formal definition of a liability: 'a present obligation of the entity to transfer an **economic resource** as a result of past events'.[1]

There are thus three key requirements that must be met before an item can be considered a liability:

- the business has an obligation which it cannot practically avoid;
- the obligation is expected to be settled by transferring an economic resource, such as cash or another asset, to another entity or person;
- the key event required to make the obligation 'present' must have happened. This is known as the '**obligating event**'.

A liability is 'a present obligation of the entity to transfer an economic resource as a result of past events'.

In Chapter 2, PB came to the end of Year 1 with several liabilities, one of which was accounts payable. Let's apply the liability definition in Application of Definition 1 to demonstrate why this is a liability.

APPLICATION OF DEFINITION 1 Application of the liability definition: PB owes €40 to suppliers for pizza ingredients that have been delivered.

Definition	Met?	Reason
The business has an obligation which it cannot practically avoid	Yes	PB's debt to its suppliers is a legal obligation. PB would likely be sued if it were to default on this debt
The obligation is expected to be settled by transferring an economic resource	Yes	The debt is expected to be settled by paying €40 cash to the suppliers
The key event which makes the obligation present is in the past	Yes	The obligating event was accepting delivery of the pizza ingredients, which occurred earlier in the year

PB also recognised a liability known as 'shareholders for dividend'. The definition can be applied to this amount owed to shareholders as in Application of Definition 2.

APPLICATION OF DEFINITION 2 Application of the liability definition: PB owes shareholders €20 of dividends that have been declared.

Definition	Met?	Reason
The business has an obligation which it cannot practically avoid	Yes	PB's debt to the shareholders is a legal obligation. Again, the business could be sued if it were to default
The obligation is expected to be settled by transferring an economic resource	Yes	The debt is expected to be settled by paying €20 cash to the shareholders
The key event which makes the obligation present is in the past	Yes	The obligating event was the declaration of dividends, which occurred during the year (albeit on the last day)

On the other hand, the €200 capital contribution by PB's owners does not meet the definition of a liability, as the business has no obligation to repay this sum to the owners. It is instead reported as equity on the statement of financial position. Similarly, there is no obligation by the business to pay out the amount reported as retained earnings. As shown in the analysis, an obligation to pay a dividend only becomes present once the dividend is declared. Thus, only on the date of declaration was the liability definition met, and so

7

only then was the amount of the dividend transferred from retained earnings to liabilities (see section 2.2.14).

The obligating event makes all the difference. When something you might have thought was a liability is not in fact a liability, it is usually this third requirement of the definition which is not met. Here is another example: the salaries that PB will have to pay at the end of the first month of Year 2. Why are they not a liability at the end of Year 1? Certainly, at that point an employer is obliged by employment contracts to pay its employees, and of course the payment of salaries in a month's time will be a transfer of an economic resource to settle this obligation. However, the obligation has not yet become present. This is because the obligating event that obliges PB to pay next month's salary is the work done by the employees next month, which is quite plainly not yet in the past.

Generally speaking, a party to a contract only has a liability if the other party performs first in terms of the contract. If payment happens at the end of the work, for example, the client of a construction company has a liability (to pay) once the construction has been done. If payment is made in advance, the construction company has a liability (to do the work) when payment is received.

You will notice that when one party has a liability, the other party usually has an asset.

> A party to a contract generally has a liability only if the other party performs first in terms of the contract.

7

7.1.2 **Commitments**

We now know that, had PB signed a contract to build a new pizza restaurant, this would not in itself constitute a liability: there is no 'present' obligation because the obligating event (the construction of the building) has not yet occurred.

> If the obligating event has not occurred, but the business has committed to significant future expenditure, this is a commitment, which is disclosed in the notes.

However, the business's plan to build a restaurant would still be very relevant to users of the financial statements, as it will no doubt involve very substantial future cash out-flows. Businesses typically therefore disclose these unrecognised contractual commitments in a note labelled '**Commitments**', 'Capital commitments', 'Future capital expenditure', or words to that effect. This note usually appears towards the end of the notes to the financial statements.

Indeed, note 25 on p 197 of Burberry's 2019 annual report contains a note about capital commitments amounting to £24.6 million. These relate to the construction of new property, plant and equipment (PPE) and intangible assets where the work has either already been contracted, or has in fact begun. Users ought to use this sort of information to carefully assess the business's ability to meet its commitments. In this case, as Burberry has net cash balances of close to £840 million, this is not in much doubt.

Note 24 contains information about a commitment relating to non-cancellable lease contracts, which Burberry calls 'financial commitments'. However, this is now outdated, as the very next year, Burberry adopted IFRS 16, a new standard for leases, which requires tenants to recognise these sorts of obligations as liabilities. In other words, IFRS 16, which became effective for all financial years ending in 2020, has transformed businesses' obligations in respect of lease contracts from mere commitments to full-blown liabilities. You will learn about IFRS 16 in Section 8.1.

7.1.3 **Constructive obligations**

Let's get back to items that *do* meet the liability definition. First and foremost, a liability is an obligation, but it doesn't have to be a legal obligation, which derives from a legal contract or legislation. The business may instead have a **constructive obligation** if it has created a valid expectation that it will transfer economic resources in future, either by making an announcement or by past practice or published policies.

For example, it would have a constructive obligation if it has issued a press release that next year it will donate 1% of its current year's profits to a community project, and if the reputational costs of breaking this pledge would be prohibitively high. Application of Definition 3 shows how the liability definition would be met, even though the business has no legal obligation.

> A constructive obligation arises when a business's announcement or past practice creates a valid expectation that it will transfer resources in future.

APPLICATION OF DEFINITION 3 An announcement has been made that the business will donate 1% of this year's profits to a community project.

Definition	Met?	Reason
The business has an obligation which it cannot practically avoid	Yes	The business's announcement has created a valid expectation, which amounts to a constructive obligation. High reputational costs make it impractical to breach
The obligation is expected to be settled by transferring an economic resource	Yes	The obligation is expected to be settled with the payment of cash
The key event which makes the obligation present is in the past	Yes	The obligating event was either the announcement or the earning of profit in the current year, whichever happened second. By the year-end, the obligation is thus present

7.1.4 **The recognition criteria**

Whilst an obligation might meet the definition of a liability, it can only be recognised on the statement of financial position if its recognition would result in relevant information which achieves a faithful representation of the economic reality of the business.[2] Much like with assets, in practice these two **recognition criteria** are not met if any of the following is true:

> A liability cannot be reported on the statement of financial position unless the recognition criteria are met.

- there is uncertainty about whether the liability exists;[3]
- there is a low probability of an outflow of economic benefits to settle the liability;[4]
- there is a high level of uncertainty about the measurement of the liability.[5]

None of these is true of any of the liabilities that we have discussed so far in this chapter, and so those liabilities would all be recognised. However, if a liability fails just one of these tests, then it will not be recognised on the statement of financial position, and instead will be regarded as a **contingent liability**.

7.1.5 **Contingent liabilities**

Contingent liabilities are liabilities which do not satisfy the recognition criteria.

Suppose that a customer of PB got food poisoning after eating a pizza slice, and sues PB for damages. If it is true that the slice caused the illness, PB has a liability: an obligation to transfer cash, which is present because the obligating event—serving her the bad food—is in the past. However, what if it was unclear whether in fact PB's food caused the customer's illness? In this case, the existence of the liability is uncertain, meaning the liability fails the first test for recognition listed in section 7.1.4.

Even if it is definitely PB's food that made her sick, the liability might fail one of the other two tests: if PB strongly expects to win the case (making the probability of settlement low); or if losing the case is likely, but the amount to be paid cannot be determined (making for high measurement uncertainty).

Contingent liabilities are not recognised on the statement of financial position, but (unless the probability of settlement is remote) they are disclosed in a note to the financial statements.

These sorts of liabilities that fail the recognition criteria are known as contingent liabilities, and, although they do not appear on the statement of financial position itself, they are disclosed in the notes, unless the possibility of settlement is remote, in which case they are generally ignored by the business's financial reporting.

The contingent liability note includes a brief description of the nature of the contingent liability and, where practicable, an estimate of its potential financial effect, as well as an indication of the uncertainties involved.

You may recall that section 6.1.2 explained how assets which fail the first test for recognition (existence uncertainty) are classed as contingent assets, and are disclosed in the notes. However, the contingent asset definition does not include assets which fail the second and third tests, which are therefore not mentioned at all in the financial statements. The result is that you will read much more often about contingent liabilities than about contingent assets. This is an example of accountants' prudence. The Conceptual Framework defines prudence as 'the exercise of caution when making judgements under conditions of uncertainty. The exercise of prudence means that assets and income are not overstated and liabilities and expenses are not understated.'[6]

Note 31 on p 210 of Burberry's 2019 financial statements is about contingent liabilities, explaining that the business is subject to 'claims against it' and 'tax audits', that 'these matters are inherently difficult to quantify', and that it 'does not currently expect the outcome . . . to have a material effect on the Group's financial condition'. The implication seems to be that the high level of measurement uncertainty means that the recognition criteria are not met, but nonetheless Burberry is letting us know that liabilities potentially exist, though they are probably not significant enough for us to worry about. This is one more reminder that the quality of the information in the financial statements is often a function of the quality of the judgement of the preparers of the information, and the directors who take responsibility for it.

Do not let Burberry's short and reassuring note convince you that contingent liabilities can be routinely ignored. In fact, they can be extremely significant. To take an example from the public sector, the Irish Government in 2019 released an analysis of contingent liabilities in its own financial reporting, arguing that they deserved to be paid substantially more attention.[7] One example from its report: like most governments, it guarantees bank deposits, and in 2017 the shortfall between guarantees and funds to meet the guarantees was €98 billion! Although the probability of this liability needing to be settled is low (thus its classification as a contingent liability), in the unlikely event of a run on the banks, it would be potentially catastrophic for the government and people of Ireland.

A business whose contingent liabilities are similarly worthy of attention is the cigarette manufacturer, British American Tobacco. In its 2019 Annual Report, note 27 on contingent liabilities runs over twenty-one pages, mainly describing pending legal cases against the business.[8]

MISCONCEPTION

The contingent liability note cannot be very important, since it often appears near the end of the notes to the financial statements.

Wrong. It is vitally important, as it informs us about potential liabilities which have not been recognised on the statement of financial position as an obligation or in the statement of comprehensive income as an expense, and which may result in decreased profits and cash outflows in future. The order in which items appear in the notes does not correlate with their importance.

So far, we have covered several items which are not recognised as liabilities, either because they are not liabilities (like commitments), or because they do not satisfy the recognition criteria (in the case of contingent liabilities). The rest of this chapter will be dedicated to items that are recognised as liabilities, but before we move on, you may wish to see the distinctions between these different possibilities a little more clearly. If so, we recommend that you spend a few minutes tracing the various branches of the decision tree on the next page (Figure 7.1), which a financial accountant might use to decide how to treat one of the items we have discussed in the chapter so far.

7.1.6 Current versus non-current liabilities

Section 2.2.2 explained that liabilities which are expected to be settled within twelve months of the end of the reporting period are reported as **current liabilities**. Thus, PB presented accounts payable as current and the long-term loan as a **non-current liability**. Applying these same principles, if a portion of the loan were due to be repaid in the next year, the loan would be split between that portion (shown as current) and the portion to be repaid after more than a year (shown as non-current).

The distinction between current and non-current is an important indicator of the differing risks inherent in the timing of cash outflows. Current liabilities are generally more risky than non-current liabilities, as the business will need to find the cash to settle them

> The distinction between current and non-current liabilities is important to help the user understand the risks inherent in a business's various liabilities.

FIGURE 7.1 Decision tree for items that might qualify as liabilities, contingent liabilities, or commitments

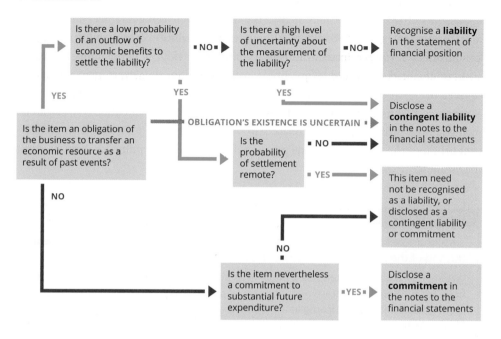

within the next year, whereas there is more time to come up with the cash to settle non-current liabilities.

The importance of this distinction was evident in an Australian court case several years ago. In what is commonly referred to as the 'Centro case', the court found that the Centro Group, one of Australia's largest listed real estate investment trusts, had classified current liabilities amounting to AUD1.5 billion as non-current liabilities, thus misleading investors about the riskiness of this debt. The court concluded that each director of the company should have identified this incorrect classification of debt and could be held liable for any losses suffered as a result.[9]

Furthermore, conventional business wisdom suggests that non-current assets like PPE should be funded with longer-term debt (that is, non-current liabilities), whereas it is appropriate to fund current assets like inventory and accounts receivable with current liabilities. The logic behind this is that assets should produce cash flows over the same sort of period as cash will be required to service the financing commitments related to them. Financing long-term assets with short-term debt would result in a timing mismatch between the cash flows generated from the asset and the cash flows required to pay interest and repay capital, which would put the business in a challenging, perhaps even impossible, situation.

The need for current assets and current liabilities to be managed in a coordinated way gives rise to the essential business activity called 'working capital management' that we covered in detail in section 5.4.4.

7.1.7 Interest-bearing versus non-interest-bearing liabilities

A further distinction that is often made in the liabilities section of the statement of financial position is between interest-bearing liabilities such as bank loans and non-interest-bearing liabilities like accounts payable. Once again, this distinction tells us about the inherent risks: interest-bearing debt is clearly riskier, as the interest payments are a regular drain on the business's cash flows.

7.1.8 Measurement

Most liabilities are measured at the amount that will be required to settle them. However, if the business is not charged interest, and the period between recognition and settlement is long enough to mean that the **time value of money** would make a significant difference to its initial measurement, then the initial measurement is determined by discounting future cash flows. We have covered this for deferred income in section 4.3.6, and for accounts payable in section 6.1.3. If you are reading the chapters out of order, or if you just need a reminder, please go back and read those sections now.

What those examples do not show is the subsequent measurement of the liabilities (that is, how to determine their carrying amounts on any statements of financial position prepared between recognition and settlement). The short answer is that both initial and subsequent measurement employ the same measurement principle: the liability should be carried at its present value.

A fuller answer requires an example. Suppose that on the first day of Year 1, a business acquires an asset in exchange for a single £10 000 payment in two years' time, on the first day of Year 3. Suppose too that the appropriate **discount rate** based on the market interest rate for similar transactions is 10%. The present value is thus £8 264.46 (£10 000 ÷ 1.10²). In other words, the time value of money means that £10 000 in two years' time is worth £8 264.46 today. Thus, the £10 000 is split so that £8 264.46 is allocated to measuring the asset, and the other £1 735.54 will be reported as a cost of financing it.

But what happens to the measurement of the liability, and what logic is behind *that*? Well, in the same way that the asset is not worth the same on the first day of Year 1 as the payment in two years' time, neither is the liability. Its present value also starts out at £8 264.46. After that, it gradually increases over time until eventually, on the day that the debt is due to be repaid, it is, of course, £10 000.

Thus, by the end of Year 1, the measurement of the liability will increase to its present value on that day of £9 090.91 (£10 000 ÷ 1.10), and by the end of Year 2, it will have risen to £10 000. This is achieved in the accounting system by **unwinding the discount**: that is, adding to the liability (credit) the amount that is expensed as interest (debit).

Example 7.1 shows the carrying amounts of the liability on each relevant date and the amount of interest that will be reported in profit or loss each year, as it is added to the liability. The total interest of €1 734.54 equals the discount: the difference between the initial measurement of the payable and the cash outflow.

EXAMPLE 7.1

	Cash outflow **Debit payable Credit bank** €	Interest expense **Reported in P/L Debit expense Credit payable** €	Payable **Carrying amount in statement of financial position** €
Day 1 of Year 1 (date of purchase)	–	–	8 264.46
End of Year 1	–	826.45	9 090.91
End of Year 2	–	909.09	10 000.00
Day 1 of Year 3 (date of settlement)	10 000	–	0.00
Totals	10 000	1 735.54	

If you have read section 6.6.1, these figures may look familiar: in fact, we have already considered the very same transaction from the point of view of the creditor. Take a look back there: the way the debtor measures its payable here is a mirror image of the creditor's measurement of its payable in Example 6.3. Indeed, this subsequent measurement policy for **financial liabilities** like borrowings and payables is also called 'amortised cost'.

This section offers a very basic overview of the measurement of liabilities. If you wish to learn more, including how the effective interest rate method applies to liabilities measured at amortised cost, please consult the advanced material for this chapter with the **online resources**.

7.1.9 **Settlement**

When a liability is settled, it is simply derecognised from the statement of financial position (debit) with a corresponding reduction in the asset—usually the bank account—used to settle it (credit).

If a liability is settled by paying an amount that is different from its carrying amount on the statement of financial position, then the difference would be recognised as a gain or loss in the profit or loss section of the statement of comprehensive income. This might happen, for example, if the amount of tax payable was overestimated last year, and so less tax has to be paid in the current year than the amount recognised as a liability at the end of last year.

Note that settling a liability does not always involve paying the entity or person to whom the liability is owed. One example is a warranty obligation which allows customers to return defective goods for a replacement. In that case, the liability is settled by transferring inventory, not cash, to the customer. Another example is an advance payment by a customer, which is similarly settled by transferring goods or services to the customer (see section 4.3.6).

Here is an example of a liability which is settled without transferring any resource to the entity to whom the obligation is owed: a **government grant**. This generally describes money received from the government that obliges the business to comply with whatever conditions are specified by the grant.

Suppose that at the end of Year 1, a biomedical business is granted £25 000 in cash by the government on condition that it conducts costly research into a new treatment during the following year. Accepting the grant means that the business has an obligation to conduct the research, and—so long as it is probable that the business will indeed do so—the correct treatment of the grant at the end of Year 1 is to recognise it as a deferred income liability. Yet this obligation is not settled by transferring assets to the government; rather, it is settled by spending money on research, as in Summary of Event 1.

SUMMARY OF EVENT 1 A biomedical firm accepts a £25 000 government grant, on condition that it conducts research into a certain treatment in Year 2.

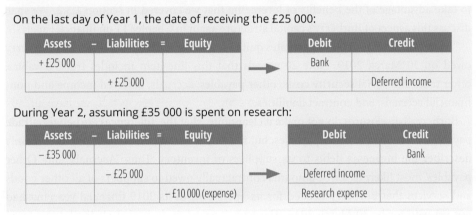

On the last day of Year 1, the date of receiving the £25 000:

Assets	−	Liabilities	=	Equity		Debit	Credit
+ £25 000						Bank	
		+ £25 000					Deferred income

During Year 2, assuming £35 000 is spent on research:

Assets	−	Liabilities	=	Equity		Debit	Credit
− £35 000							Bank
		− £25 000				Deferred income	
				− £10 000 (expense)		Research expense	

As explained in section 6.4.2, research costs are always expensed, but in this case, the research expense in the Year 1 statement of comprehensive income will be reported net of the release of £25 000 from the deferred income liability. By conducting the research, the business has settled its liability, which has in turn reduced the decrease in equity to £10 000.

IAS 20, the accounting standard on government grants, points out that grants can be received as compensation for expenses or losses already incurred (eg salaries and wages paid to employees during a national lockdown), or for the purpose of giving immediate financial support. In such cases, as the business has no obligation to meet any conditions in the future, no liability is recognised, and instead the amounts received are reported immediately as income.

Sometimes, when government grants are received to help a business purchase an asset, the grant is recognised not as a deferred income liability, but rather as a reduction in the measurement of the asset. It will still have the effect of reducing the business's expenses in future, as this reduced initial measurement of the asset moves over time to the statement of comprehensive income, for example as a result of depreciation (see section 6.1.7).

7.1.10 Burberry's straightforward liabilities

The accounting treatment of most liabilities on most business's financial statements conforms to the straightforward general principles that we have described thus far. For example, it is no surprise that Burberry discloses income tax liabilities on the face of its balance sheet. Higher up, 'Bank overdrafts' reports the total of the negative bank balances of the various businesses within the Burberry group. Whereas in an individual's personal life, a bank overdraft is a potentially negative sign, this figure is no cause for concern. As explained in section 5.4.4, good working capital involves avoiding keeping a lot of unused money in the bank. This means that sometimes a few of the business's bank accounts might go into overdraft. Anyway, by comparison with Burberry's cash and cash equivalents disclosed under current assets, its overdraft figure is unremarkable.

A liability that is noticeably absent from Burberry's balance sheet is any form of long-term borrowings, which on other businesses' statements of financial position is often the biggest liability. Indeed, it is unusual not to take on some long-term debt financing in order to take advantage of the benefits of leveraging that we covered in section 1.3.2. We shall discuss this aspect of Burberry's capital structure again in Chapter 11 on financial analysis.

'Trade and other payables' aggregates quite a few of the different liabilities that Burberry owed on 30 March 2019. Note 20 reveals that this line-item includes trade payables; other taxes and social security costs; other payables; accruals; deferred income and non-financial accruals; and contract liabilities.

Burberry's disclosures do not make it clear quite what the differences are between trade payables, accruals, and other payables, but it is safe to assume that 'trade' payables mainly describes the business's debts to its suppliers of inventory. Thus, 'Accruals' and 'Other payables' most likely describe amounts contractually owed to suppliers of all other goods and services that Burberry needed for its operations in its 2019 financial year, but had not yet paid for by 30 March 2019. The term 'accrual' is derived from the fundamental concept of **accrual accounting**, and is widely used by accountants to describe these sorts of liabilities, particularly for operating expenses, such as PB's electricity owing at year-end. Although in section 2.2.7 we just added it to accounts payable, we could have chosen instead to categorise this liability separately, as an 'accrued expense', or simply 'accrual'.

At the bottom of p 201, note 26 on financial risk management (which we explained briefly in section 6.7.4) states that 'all short-term trade and other payables, accruals, and bank overdrafts mature within one year or less. The carrying value of all financial liabilities due in less than one year is equal to their contractual undiscounted cash flows.' In other words, the business has taken the option to measure these current liabilities simply at the amount to be paid, instead of discounting them to present value in order to measure them at amortised cost. The financial liabilities included in the non-current portion of trade and other payables, on the other hand, would have been discounted to present value.

We will cover the rest of Burberry's liabilities—the less straightforward ones—in section 7.2 on provisions, section 7.3 on financial liabilities measured at fair value, and in section 8.3 on deferred tax.

7.2 **PROVISIONS**

A provision is a liability where there is some uncertainty about either the amount to be settled or the timing of the settlement, or both.

A **provision** is a liability where there is some uncertainty about either the amount to be settled or the timing of the settlement, or both. Thus accounts payable, although a liability, is not a provision, since the amount to be paid is certain and the date by which payment will be made is specified on the invoice.

On the other hand, recall our earlier example from section 7.1.5 about the food poisoning case against PB. Suppose that PB knows that it served the customer bad food, so the existence of the liability is not in doubt. Suppose too that the business's lawyers advise that it is probable that PB will be found culpable for the food poisoning, so the probability of payment is not low. And finally, suppose that the amount to be paid can be roughly estimated to be €100 000, so the level of measurement uncertainty is not high. Thus, the recognition criteria are met, and so the liability must be recognised. However, there is still no way that PB could be certain when the amount will fall due, or exactly how much it will have to pay, so this liability is a provision.

> **MISCONCEPTION**
>
> **Provisions and contingent liabilities are distinct kinds of liabilities.**
>
> This is only half right. It is true that all provisions and most contingent liabilities meet the liability definition, which makes them kinds of liabilities. However, they are not distinct categories. Some provisions are contingent liabilities, and others are not.
>
> To understand this, it will help if you recall the definitions of each: a provision is a liability of uncertain timing and/or amount; and a contingent liability is a liability which does not meet the liability recognition criteria. If a liability involves some uncertainty, but satisfies the recognition criteria, then it is a provision but not a contingent liability, and will be recognised as a provision on the statement of financial position. If a liability involves some uncertainty and also fails the recognition criteria, then it is both a provision and a contingent liability, and will merely be recognised in the notes.

7.2.1 Raising, utilising, reversing, and releasing a provision

Continuing the example, PB would *raise* a provision of €100 000 (credit), to be reported in the current liabilities section of the statement of financial position, and would report a €100 000 expense (debit) in profit or loss in the statement of comprehensive income. The expense essentially reflects a cost of doing business in the current year. Summary of Event 2 shows these effects, along with two alternative outcomes in Year 2.

SUMMARY OF EVENT 2 PB is the defendant in a legal case about food poisoning. In Year 1, the lawyers advise that in Year 2 the business is likely to be found guilty, and ordered to pay an estimated €100 000.

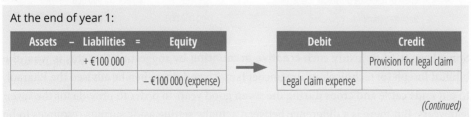

At the end of year 1:

Assets	– Liabilities	=	Equity		Debit	Credit
	+ €100 000					Provision for legal claim
			– €100 000 (expense)		Legal claim expense	

(Continued)

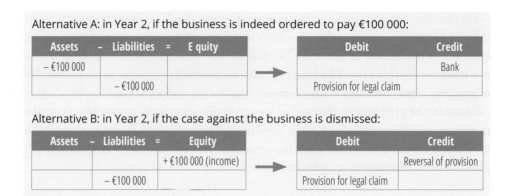

Alternative A: in Year 2, if the business is indeed ordered to pay €100 000:

Assets	– Liabilities	=	Equity		Debit	Credit
– €100 000						Bank
	– €100 000				Provision for legal claim	

Alternative B: in Year 2, if the case against the business is dismissed:

Assets	– Liabilities	=	Equity		Debit	Credit
			+ €100 000 (income)			Reversal of provision
	– €100 000				Provision for legal claim	

When a provision is settled, as in Alternative A, this is usually known as *utilising* the provision. When a provision is reversed, as in Alternative B, this is often called *releasing* the provision.

7.2.2 Provisions' history as profit-smoothing tools

In the past, provisions were often used as a tool to smooth profits. For example, if a business earned profits of £110 million when investors were only expecting profits of £100 million, then the business might strategically put £10 million of these profits aside for the future. It would do this by raising a spurious provision of £10 million (credit) on the statement of financial position for, say, future renovations to a building. This would in effect reduce profit (debit) by £10 million to £100 million. The investors would be happy enough, as they would see the profits that they expected.

If, in the following year, profits declined to £95 million, then the business could (again, strategically) decide that the renovations were not required after all. The provision would then be released (debit), causing an income (credit) of £10 million, thereby reporting improved profits of £105 million. This is despite the fact that profits were in truth on a downward trend from £110 million to £95 million. The manipulation of the business's earnings is shown in Example 7.2.

EXAMPLE 7.2

Statements of comprehensive income	Year 1 £	Year 2 £
'True' profit before effects of provision	110 000 000	95 000 000
Effect of raising provision	(10 000 000)	–
Effect of releasing provision	–	10 000 000
Reported profit	100 000 000	105 000 000

Some have tried to justify such **creative accounting** by suggesting that this is what the biblical Joseph (of technicolour dreamcoat fame) was doing when he advised the Pharaoh to put aside cattle and crops during the seven good years in order to provide for the seven lean years. But there is a difference between actually setting aside surplus resources to be used when they're needed and reporting misleading profits. The former is good business sense, the latter is accounting fraud. Thus, when the giant US home loan provider Freddie Mac was found to have understated earnings by almost $5 billion for the purposes of smoothing profits between 2000 and 2003, they were hit with a $125 million penalty.[10] We will uncover many more instances of creative accounting in Chapter 13.

The abuse of provisions to smooth profits has been acknowledged by the accounting standard-setters, and the specified accounting treatment of provisions now no longer allows this practice. A plan to do renovations in future cannot be recognised as a provision because there is no obligation to pay for the repair. The obligation (to pay for the renovations) will only arise if and when the obligating event—the renovation work—is in the past. Until then, there is no present obligation, no liability, and therefore no provision.

> **MISCONCEPTION**
>
> Provisions are sources of money that management has chosen to set aside in case the business falls upon leaner times.
>
> This idea that provisions are created to 'provide for a rainy day' is completely mistaken. First, a source of money would be recognised as an asset, not a liability. Second, businesses do not have discretion about whether to recognise provisions: if an obligation meets the liability definition and recognition criteria, and if there is uncertainty about the timing and/or amount of the cash flow to settle it, then it is a provision and must be recognised. If not, then the business cannot recognise a provision.

7.2.3 Measurement

The amount at which the provision should be recognised is the best estimate of the amount that a business would rationally pay to settle it at the end of the reporting period, or would pay to a third party for them to assume the obligation on that date.

Determining this amount requires estimates to be made based on experience from similar transactions, and in some cases, advice from independent experts. For example, in the food poisoning scenario, if PB's lawyer tells them that there is a 40% chance of having to pay €100 000 in compensation and a 60% chance of having to pay €200 000, then PB's provision could be measured at €160 000 (€100 000 × 40% + 200 000 × 60%). An estimated outflow calculated in this way is known as the 'expected value'.

When the effect of the time value of money is material, the business would discount the amount expected to settle the obligation. So if the lawyer advised PB at the end of Year 1 that the abovementioned amounts would be paid in a year's time, and if an appropriate discount rate was 10%, PB would measure its provision at €145 455 (€160 000 ÷ 1.10). During the course of the following year, to unwind the discount on this present-valued liability, the provision would be increased (credit) to €160 000 thanks to interest expense (debit) of €14 545 (€145 455 × 10%) being reported in profit or loss, in the way shown in Example 7.1.

The business restates the measurement of the provision whenever the estimate of the amount required to settle it changes. For example, suppose that at the end of Year 2, the

A provision is measured at the best estimate of the amount required to settle it or transfer it to a third party, discounted to present value if the time value of money is material.

food poisoning court case has been delayed, and now the lawyers predict that PB is likely to have to pay €210 000 in the first month of the next financial year. Since the provision is currently measured at €160 000, it is understated by €50 000. It must therefore by increased (credit) by €50 000, resulting in a legal claim expense of this amount in profit or loss for Year 2.

All of the effects discussed in this section are summarised in Example 7.3.

EXAMPLE 7.3

	Legal claim expense *Debit expense* *credit provision* €	Interest expense *Debit expense* *credit provision* €	Provision for legal claim (liability) *Carrying amount* €
End of Year 1	145 455	–	145 455
End of Year 2—before estimate change	–	14 545	160 000
End of Year 2—after estimate change	50 000	–	210 000

IAS 37, the accounting standard which deals with provisions, requires businesses to disclose in the notes to their financial statements quite a lot of detail relating to provisions. This includes a reconciliation of opening and closing balances for each class of provision (such as warranties, legal claims, and so on). These reconciliations show all movements during the year, including new charges to the provision, amounts utilised, amounts reversed (or released), the effects of unwinding the discount, and the effects of changes in estimates.

7.2.4 Provisions for warranty obligations

A provision usually raised by manufacturers and some retailers relates to the warranties they offer customers. Warranties are issued on sale, and usually allow customers to return defective goods, either for repair or replacement, within a specified period after the sale. We can apply the liability definition to this scenario in Application of Definition 4.

APPLICATION OF DEFINITION 4 Application of the liability definition: a six-month warranty for repair or replacement of defective goods.

Definition	Met?	Reason
The business has an obligation which it cannot practically avoid	Yes	The business has a legal obligation arising out of the sales contract to repair or replace defective goods. If it fails to do so, the businesses could be sued for breach of contract
The obligation is expected to be settled by transferring an economic resource	Yes	This obligation is expected to be settled by transferring new inventory to the customer, or by paying for the cost of repairs
The key event which makes the obligation present is in the past	Yes	The obligating event was the sale of goods; beyond that point, the business cannot influence whether the goods turn out to be defective

This application of the liability definition makes it clear that, although any transfer to settle the obligation would only occur later, it is the sale that gives rise to the obligation. Thus, at each year-end the business has a liability in respect of any goods it has sold which are still under warranty.

You may wonder whether this obligation satisfies the recognition criteria. For example, isn't there a low probability that the business will have to make the repair or provide a replacement? After all, any decent manufacturer will not sell any item of inventory which is itself likely to turn out to be defective. However, IAS 37 requires that 'the probability that an outflow will be required in settlement is determined by considering the class of obligations as a whole'.[11] This means that, so long as *some* of the business's goods under warranty will probably turn out to be defective, this requirement for recognition is met.

Perhaps instead you are thinking that the warranty obligation should not be recognised due to a high level of measurement uncertainty. Certainly, no business could predict very accurately how many of its products will be returned with defects, and quite how much it will cost to replace them over the next six months. But this raises an important point about liabilities: the level of measurement uncertainty required to prevent recognition is very high: IAS 37 itself says that such cases are 'extremely rare'.[12] Thus, the level of uncertainty inherent in predicting roughly how many items are likely to be returned, and the approximate cost of replacing them, falls easily within the zone that the standard-setters still consider measurable.

According to its annual report, the German automaker Bayerische Motoren Werke AG, better known as BMW, offers warranties prescribed by law, and other standard warranties and product guarantees, which resulted in its 2019 statement of financial position reporting a provision of €5 550 million for 'statutory and non-statutory warranty obligations, and product guarantees'. (Yes, that's €5.5 billion of costs that the business expected to incur on account of defects!) BMW clearly offers long warranty periods, as less than 30% of this figure was reported under current liabilities. Note 33 showed the movements on the provision for the year, as follows (we have added explanations in square brackets).

DATA FROM NOTE TO BMW GROUP'S 2019 FINANCIAL STATEMENTS

	€ m
33 PROVISION: STATUTORY AND NON-STATUTORY WARRANTY OBLIGATIONS, PRODUCT GUARANTEES	
Balance at 1 January 2019	5 147
Additions [new obligations due to new sales made under warranty this year]	2 831
Reversal of discounting [the unwinding of discount]	168
Utilised in year [the amount spent this year on honouring warranties]	(2 561)
Reversed [prior overestimates of the warranty obligation]	(104)
Translation differences [see Chapter 8]	69
Balance at 31 December 2019	5 550

Source: BMW Group. 2019. *Annual Report 2019.* Available at: https://www.bmwgroup.com/content/dam/grpw/websites/bmwgroup_com/ir/downloads/en/2020/gb/BMW-GB19_en_Finanzbericht.pdf

You may like to think about what the other effects of these movements were, in terms of the double-entry accounting system:

- Note 08 reports that €2 566 of the €2 831 additions (a credit to the provision) were charged to cost of sales for the year (debit), which was equivalent to about 5% of the business's 2019 manufacturing costs. The remaining additions would have been expensed in other line-items within profit or loss.

- The reversal of discounting (a credit to the provision) would have added to the year's interest expense or finance costs (debit).

- Utilisations (a debit to the provision) would, for example, have been caused by decreases (credit) in cash if repairs were paid for, or inventory if defective products were replaced.

- Reversals (debits) to the provision would have reduced the expense accounts to which the additions had been charged in prior years.

- Translation differences result from the inclusion of the results of BMW's foreign operations (see sections 8.2.3 and 8.2.4).

7.2.5 Provisions for environmental rehabilitation

Another classic provision is the obligation to rehabilitate natural resources damaged as a result of a business's activities. Of course, we should expect to find such a provision on the statement of financial position of Rio Tinto, one of the world's largest mining companies. Indeed, in 2019 the Anglo-Australian business had a provision for 'close-down and restoration/environmental' costs of over US$11 billion![13]

The company's related accounting policy note explains that the provision is 'based on all regulatory requirements and any other commitments made to stakeholders', so it appears that it arises out of both legal and constructive obligations. This very informative note goes on to explain that:

> the majority of close-down and restoration expenditure is incurred in the years following closure of the mine, refinery or smelter . . . Close-down and restoration costs are provided for in the accounting period when the obligation arising from the related disturbance occurs, based on the net present value of the estimated future costs of restoration.

In other words, despite the fact that the costs will only be paid in the future, since the obligation arises due to the key event of damaging land, the liability must be recognised as soon as land is damaged, using a present value calculation.

Note 26 states that the discount rate used for this calculation is 2%, and that the average period until its mines close is approximately eighteen years, and provides the required disclosure in a table, summarised as follows.

DATA FROM NOTES TO RIO TINTO'S 2019 FINANCIAL STATEMENTS

		US$ m
26	PROVISIONS: CLOSE-DOWN AND RESTORATION/ENVIRONMENTAL	
	Balance at 1 January 2019	9 975
	Changes in estimate [due to new information affecting the size of the provision]	840
	Increases to existing and new provisions [caused by further land damage this year]	171
	Amortisation [unwinding] of discount	383
	Utilised in year [the amount actually spent on restoration this year]	(330)
	Unused amounts reversed [prior overestimates of the obligation]	(19)
	Net effect of foreign exchange and group accounting [see Chapters 8 and 9]	70
	Balance at 31 December 2019	11 090

Source: Rio Tinto 2019. *Annual Report 2019.* Available at: https://www.riotinto.com/-/media/Content/Documents/Invest/Reports/Annual-reports/RT-Annual-report-2019.pdf. See accounting policy note 1(l) on p 160 and note 26 on p 189.

7.2.6 Provisions for employees' pay

There are several different types of liabilities relating to employees, ranging from a straightforward obligation to pay salaries and wages that are owed at month-end, to the more complex obligations that a business might have in terms of defined benefit pension schemes.

The general principle with all **employee benefits** is that if an employee has worked for the business during a particular year, then all the costs associated with employing that person for that year should be expensed in that year. This is nothing more than the now familiar concept of accrual accounting. Thus, if salaries had not been paid for the final month of the year, the business would accrue for these salaries by expensing them (debit) in the statement of comprehensive income and creating a liability (credit) on the statement of financial position. This would not be a provision, as the timing and amount of the payment is certain. If, however, at the year-end the business had not finalised the bonuses to be paid in the following year to staff for work done in the current year, then the liability for the expected value of the bonuses would be a provision.

Many businesses report another provision relating to employment contracts that is worth mentioning here because it is so common: the obligation they have for leave pay. If employees have an option to carry forward their leave entitlement to future years, then at year-end the business has an obligation to pay them in the future in respect of any days they have already worked when they were entitled to take leave. The resulting provision might be measured in two ways: either the estimated amount of cash the business would have to pay out if employees were to cash in their present leave entitlement or the estimated amount that will be paid to employees while they take leave in the future as a result of their present leave entitlements.

Interestingly, some businesses that allow employees to carry leave forward into future years do *not* report leave pay as a provision. This is because it is arguable whether leave pay is in fact a provision or a plain old liability. These businesses would no doubt admit that there is some uncertainty as to the timing or amount of the settlement of their leave

If an employee has worked for the business during a particular year, then all the costs associated with employing that person for that year should be expensed in that year.

pay obligation, but would also claim that there is not enough uncertainty to consider it to be a provision. After all, there is some uncertainty involved with most liabilities. Consider accounts payable: do you think most businesses are really completely certain about when in the future they will pay their suppliers?

The question of what degree of uncertainty distinguishes a provision from other liabilities is another example of the subjectivity inherent in financial accounting.

Businesses that do not report leave pay as a provision typically include it as one of the many components in the line-item on the statement of financial position called 'Trade and other payables'. So if you don't see leave pay in a business's list of provisions, don't assume it doesn't have any, as leave pay may be included elsewhere in the liabilities section. This looks to be the case at Burberry, whose leave pay obligation is probably contained within the 'Accruals' figure of £209.3 million in note 20 to the 2019 financial statements.

> Businesses have some discretion as to the level of uncertainty which distinguishes liabilities that are provisions from those that are not.

7.2.7 Provisions for post-employment benefits

> The two main types of retirement plans are defined contribution plans and defined benefit plans.

As employees work, they need to use this productive period of their lives to make sure not only that they have sufficient income to cover their current needs, but also that they will have enough income after they retire. For the vast majority of employees, the bulk of their post-employment income will come to them as a result of a retirement plan set up by their employer. This will be either a 'defined contribution' or a 'defined benefit' plan.

In a defined contribution plan, the employees, and perhaps also the employer, contribute a set amount of money each month to the retirement fund. When the employee retires, she receives the value of her portion of the fund. If the contributions are sufficient and the **asset manager** (whose job it is to invest the money, for example in shares, bonds, properties, or cash) has been successful, the employees will receive ample income in their retirement, but if the asset manager has not invested the contributions successfully or the employee did not make sufficient contributions, the employees will get less.

Note that in a defined contribution plan the risk of insufficient retirement income lies entirely with the employee: even if the business makes monthly contributions as the employee works, that is where its obligation ends. Thus, the accounting for defined contribution plans is relatively straightforward. Any employer contributions (credit to bank) are reported as a staff costs expense (debit) in the statement of comprehensive income in the year that they are paid.

> Defined benefit plans are more risky for the employer than defined contribution plans.

Defined benefit plans are much more risky for the employer, and more complicated for its accountants. Businesses with these plans effectively guarantee their employees a pension of a certain amount (usually calculated using a formula that takes into account final salary and years of service, for example). In other words, the business has an obligation to make sure that the stipulated benefit is in fact paid out to the employees in their retirement. This obligation is a liability because it is 'present'—the key event giving rise to the obligation is the employee's work for the business. It is a provision because the timing and amount of cash outflows are both dependent on uncertain factors, including how long the employee will live. Thus, although the transfer of economic resources will only happen after retirement, a provision is raised as soon as the employee begins work, and increases with each month of employment.

To measure the provision, an actuary is required to calculate the current value of the obligation to each employee, taking into account all the possible variables affecting it, such as future salary increases, final salary, the employee's anticipated number of years of service, their life expectancy, and so on.

Typically, the provision increases from one year to the next, and the resulting expense is split on the statement of comprehensive income between a portion that is recognised in profit or loss and a portion that is recognised in OCI. The precise manner of the split is especially complex and beyond the scope of this book, but simply put, the OCI component is the sum of certain actuarial and accounting adjustments. It thus usually appears on the statement of comprehensive income as a line-item with a name like 'Actuarial gains and losses arising from pension obligations'. Although items of OCI are often controversial, many commentators are in favour of this one, as it shields profit or loss from the volatility caused by the fickle movements of financial markets and changes in actuarial assumptions.

> The expenses arising on defined benefit plans are reported in both profit or loss and OCI.

Sensible employers set aside investments in order to fund this liability (in fact, in many jurisdictions, they are required by law to do so, often in a separate fund, managed by independent trustees), but of course these assets won't perfectly match the amount of the liability calculated by the actuary, resulting in either a deficit or a surplus. Depending on various factors that we needn't go into, statements of financial position differ as to how these defined benefit liabilities, and the investment assets set aside to settle them one day, are recognised: sometimes the liabilities and the assets both appear on the statement; sometimes just the net deficit or surplus is shown, as a liability or asset respectively.

Because of the increased risk inherent in defined benefit plans, amplified by stock market volatility, a lot of businesses around the world have ceased to offer defined benefit plans, and have switched their employees instead to defined contribution plans. However, especially in the US and the UK, many defined benefit funds still remain, and so in those jurisdictions, expect sometimes to come across significant retirement fund deficits which need to be made good by businesses. This is especially true when financial markets have provided poor investment returns.

Finally, note that provisions for post-employment benefits do not arise only as a result of obligations to provide *income* to employees after they retire. For example, a business may commit to funding employees' medical care when they retire. An actuary, taking account of factors like the life expectancy of retirees, medical cost inflation, and so on, can likewise estimate the value of this obligation. This would lead to the reporting of a post-employment medical benefits provision in the financial statements, in similar ways to defined benefit plans.

7.2.8 Onerous contracts

There is a rare exception to the general principle that a party to a contract has a liability only if the other party performs first in terms of the contract. This is a non-cancellable contract where the costs of completing the contract are higher than the benefits expected to be received from the contract. While ordinarily we would wait to recognise a liability,

Onerous contracts are non-cancellable contracts whose future costs will outweigh the benefits. They are recognised as liabilities immediately.

the loss-making nature of the contract, together with the prudent approach of the accounting standards, dictates that this sort of 'onerous contract' is recognised immediately as a liability.

An onerous contract would occur, for example, if PB were to sign a contract to supply 1 000 pizza slices in the next year to a school at a price of €3 a slice, and then, after the contract is signed, inflation in the price of cheese results in an estimated cost per slice of €4. The word 'estimated' implies that there is uncertainty as to the amounts relating to the onerous contract, and therefore the liability required to be recognised is a provision, measured at the amount that the business expects to lose. In this case, the amount would be €1 000 (1 000 × €1).

By recognising the liability immediately, the resulting decrease in equity causes an expense to be reported. This is a rare official departure from the principle of accrual accounting, since the effects of the transaction will be reported in an earlier period than the period in which the transaction takes place. It seems that in this case the standard-setters decided that the principle of prudence trumps accrual.

Businesses which agree to provide services well into the future, making their costs more difficult to predict, can sometimes have substantial onerous contracts. Shipping companies operate in such circumstances, sometimes committing to charters which unexpectedly require them to relocate vessels in ways that add enormously to fuel and ship running costs. An example is Pacific Basin Shipping, a global shipping company listed in Hong Kong. In 2014, the company reported a loss of US$280 million, much of which was caused by onerous contracts totalling US$101 million.[14]

7

Just because it expects to perform poorly, a business does not have a liability for future operating losses.

A word of warning: just because an onerous contract leads to the recognition of a liability for future losses, don't let this fool you into thinking that the prospect of any sort of future operating loss is a liability. It is not, because—unless there is a non-cancellable contract—a business has neither a legal nor a constructive obligation to make a loss in future: it could instead simply stop operating.

7.2.9 Burberry's provisions

Being a retailer, Burberry does not have any provisions for environmental restoration costs, but it has raised quite a few other provisions. For example, the notes to its 2018 and 2019 financial statements mention:

- provisions for expected sales returns, 'calculated based on historical return levels';
- provisions for future property reinstatement costs, 'where there is an obligation to return the leased property to its original condition at the end of [the lease period]';
- provisions for restructuring-related costs, which include 'employee termination payments, contract termination penalties and onerous contract payments';
- provisions for the termination of a distributor agreement.[15]

Note 21 to the financial statements is dedicated to provisions, and makes it clear that the abovementioned provisions are relatively small by comparison with the largest property obligations, which mostly consist of onerous lease obligations of £48.0 million. Indeed, leases of retail locations have often led to the recognition of onerous contracts liabilities, because they usually involve very long lease periods. If the merchandise in a retail location does not sell in high enough volumes, it may well be that the future rental payments will outweigh the income that the location will generate. And the longer the lease period, the larger the onerous contract. In an indication of how long Burberry's lease contracts are, note 21 explains that the onerous lease contract provision is 'expected to be utilised within 19 years'! (As it turned out, however, this onerous contract for leases disappeared from Burberry's 2020 financial statements because in that year it adopted IFRS 16, a new standard for leases, which requires tenants to report their leases very differently. You will learn about IFRS 16 in section 8.1.)

Burberry recognised another provision on the face of its 2019 balance sheet: a 'retirement benefit' obligation of £1.4 million. As a result of this figure being too small to make a difference to the decisions of any users of the financial statements—what accountants would call 'immaterial'—Burberry has provided no other information about this liability. Most likely, it relates to a defined benefit plan which has been long closed, with very few remaining members, given that accounting policy note (g) explains that 'eligible employees participate in defined contribution pension schemes', which, as you know from section 7.2.7, do not require the employer to recognise a liability, as it has no obligation to make future payments into the scheme in respect of past employment.

There is even a provision hiding inside the 'Trade and other payables' figure. This is the 'deferred consideration' liability of £2.7 million, which is explained in some detail by note 20 on p 194. In 2016, Burberry had purchased shares from some previous shareholders of its Middle East operation, whose compensation was in part deferred (or delayed) in terms of the share purchase agreement. This compensation has two components: a fixed fee paid annually until 2019 and a percentage of the operation's revenue paid annually until 2023. The note explains how Burberry has measured the liability at the present value of the estimated future cash outflows required to settle it. The note also describes how variations in some of the assumptions used would affect the financial statements, acknowledging that 'a 10% increase/decrease in the estimate of future revenues . . . would result in a £2.4 m increase/decrease in the carrying value of the deferred consideration . . . and a corresponding £2.4 m decrease/increase in the profit before taxation'.

It is particularly helpful when, like this, a business shows how changes in the assumptions underlying its measurement of its provisions—which are, by definition, uncertain—would affect the overall message of the financial statements.

7.3 FINANCIAL LIABILITIES MEASURED AT FAIR VALUE

If you have already read section 6.7 on **financial assets**, you know that if a **financial instrument** gives rise to a financial liability for one party, then it gives rise to a financial asset for another party. As you might therefore expect, financial liabilities are covered by

IFRS 9, the same accounting standard that applies to financial assets. The treatments are remarkably similar: for example, like financial assets, IFRS 9 splits financial liabilities into those measured at amortised cost, and those measured at fair value. We have already covered most of those which are typically carried at amortised cost, like bank borrowings, accounts payable, and bank overdrafts. In this section, we will briefly consider those financial liabilities which are measured at fair value.

The definition of the fair value of a liability is 'the price that would be . . . paid to transfer a liability . . . in an orderly transaction between market participants at the measurement date'.[16] Thus, just as the fair value of an asset is its exit price, the fair value of a liability is the amount a business would pay to get rid of it: to transfer it to someone else.

Liabilities that a business actively trades must be measured at fair value, and the business may also *choose* to measure some of its liabilities at fair value, in which case these liabilities are often described in the financial statements as 'financial liabilities designated at fair value through profit or loss'.

However, whereas businesses have an option to report in OCI the gains and losses on some financial assets carried at fair value, businesses have no choice about where in the statement of comprehensive income fair value adjustments for financial liabilities are reported. IFRS 9 requires that almost all of the gains and losses arising from financial liabilities carried at fair value are reported in profit or loss. The only exceptions are those discussed in section 7.3.1.

7.3.1 Own credit risk

The option to carry financial liabilities at fair value sometimes gives rise to a gain or loss in OCI. It occurs in a precise set of circumstances, where a business raises finance by issuing debt to the public, and then opts to measure this debt at fair value. Since the fair value of a financial instrument is the present value of its future cash flows, a gain or loss arises whenever either of the following change: the amounts of the expected cash flows or the discount rate used to determine fair value.

The treatment of the gain or loss depends on the reason for the change in fair value. It is reported in profit or loss if the amounts of the expected cash flows change, or if the discount rate changes *due to factors which are not about the business itself* (such as a change in national interest rates, which affects the way in which most investments are valued).

However, the discount rate can also change because of a change in the market's perceptions of the business's own credit risk. To understand this, suppose that a company's creditworthiness has deteriorated (that is, the business's own credit risk has increased because, say, the market has learned that it is experiencing cash-flow difficulties). In such circumstances, investors would require a higher return because the risk of not receiving their money back is higher, which means that the discount rate pertaining to this financial instrument increases and its fair value decreases.

Now suppose that this decrease in fair value was accounted for in the usual way: a decrease (debit) in the financial liability in the statement of financial position and a gain (credit) in profit or loss in the statement of comprehensive income. This would be a

7

perverse result: by virtue of becoming riskier, the company reports higher profits. (The alternative would also be true, of course: the debt instruments of a company whose performance improves become less risky, and as a result a *loss* is reported!)

Many people believe that this counterintuitive treatment amounts to misleading reporting, though accounting experts do defend it by pointing out that if the business ends up defaulting, then in fact it will have made a gain, based on the definition of income. Thus, recognising a gain as the creditworthiness declines spreads it across the period of financial instability, and therefore complies with the principle of accrual accounting.

IFRS 9 provides some level of comfort for those who are not convinced by this defence. It requires that, if gains or losses arising from changes in a financial liability's fair value are due to changes in the business's own credit risk, they should be reported in OCI. Thus, the gain will still be reported, but it will bypass profit or loss.

Be on the lookout for this infamous adjustment, as the impact can be very substantial. For example, in its results for 2008, during the financial crisis and prior to the IFRS 9 requirement that such items be reported in OCI, HSBC (in compliance with the preceding accounting standard on financial instruments) recognised a gain of US$6.5 billion in profit or loss from the change in fair value of its own debt. The pre-tax profit after recognising this amount was US$9.3 billion. Had it not recorded this gain in profit or loss (that is, had IFRS 9 applied at the time), its reported profit would have been a fraction of what was reported![17]

> For financial liabilities measured at fair value, gains and losses are reported in profit or loss, except those which arise from changes in the business's own credit risk, which are reported in OCI.

7.3.2 Derivatives

Section 6.7.3 explained what a **derivative financial instrument** is, and how in some circumstances (such as when the price of the **underlying** moves in a certain direction) a derivative can become valuable, in which case it is reported as a financial asset. Equally, in different circumstances (such as when the price of the underlying moves in the other direction), the derivative becomes a liability.

The accounting for derivatives that are financial liabilities is the same as the accounting for those that are financial assets: they are marked to market at each reporting date, with the gains or losses arising from these fair value adjustments appearing in the statement of comprehensive income. In which section they appear depends on whether they are hedges. If they are *not* hedges, the gains and losses always appear in profit or loss. If they *are* hedges, the gains and losses may appear in OCI, according to the principles of hedge accounting also described in section 6.7.3.

7.3.3 Burberry's financial liabilities measured at fair value

Burberry's only financial liabilities carried at fair value are its derivative financial liabilities, reported on the face of the balance sheet in both the non-current and current sections.

Note 18 reveals that Burberry's derivative financial liabilities arose in just the same ways as its derivative financial assets discussed in section 6.7.4: from **hedging** to mitigate against adverse movements in currencies affecting Burberry's many foreign cash flows.

The difference is that in this case the value of the forward exchange contracts moved in such a way as to mean that the business would in fact have been better off had they not hedged the underlying transaction.

Of course, Burberry could not have known this, and instead was employing good business practice by seeking to reduce its risk. While its hedging strategy happened to have resulted at the end of its 2019 year in a larger amount of derivative liabilities (£5.6 m) than assets (£3.0 m), it is utterly appropriate that a business whose main expertise is in retailing fashion apparel should not be playing games with foreign exchange rates!

CONCLUSION

The liabilities on a business's statement of financial position show its obligations that will most likely result in future cash outflows. The ways in which these liabilities are reported help to establish the size and timing of the cash flows, and also the degree of risk associated with each liability. The disclosure of contingent liabilities—and even of commitments, though they are not in fact liabilities—provides further important information to be able to predict future cash outflows.

After the summary of key points, Table 7.1 summarises the financial reporting principles usually applied to the most common types of liabilities.

SUMMARY OF KEY POINTS

- Liabilities are significant to users of financial statements because they indicate the prospects for future cash outflows from the business.
- To qualify as a liability, an item must meet the three key requirements of the liability definition: it must be an obligation which cannot practically be avoided; it must be expected to be settled by the transfer of an economic resource; and the obligating event—which makes the obligation 'present'—must be in the past.
- Generally speaking, a party to a contract only has a liability if the other party performs first in terms of the contract.
- If the obligating event has not yet occurred, but the business has nevertheless committed to significant future expenditure, this is a commitment, which is often disclosed in the notes to the financial statements.
- Liabilities are not restricted only to legal obligations; constructive obligations (created by announcements, or past practice, or published policies which generate valid expectations that the business will transfer resources in future) may also give rise to liabilities.
- To be recognised as a liability on the business's statement of financial position, a liability must meet the recognition criteria of relevance and faithful representation, which effectively prohibit recognition if there is: uncertainty about whether the liability exists; a low probability of an outflow of economic benefits to settle the liability; or a high level of uncertainty about the liability's measurement.
- If a liability does not satisfy the recognition criteria, it is called a contingent liability, and (unless the probability of an outflow is remote) is disclosed in the notes to the financial statements.

- Figure 7.1 is a decision tree which will help you distinguish between commitments, contingent liabilities, and items recognised as liabilities.
- The distinctions between current and non-current—and between interest-bearing and non-interest-bearing—liabilities are helpful for assessing the risks associated with future cash outflows.
- Most liabilities are measured at the amount of the outflow(s) required to settle them. However, when the time value of money is material, they are typically measured at the present value of the future cash outflows, which is known, in the case of financial liabilities, as 'amortised cost'. Some financial liabilities are measured at fair value.
- Not all liabilities are settled by paying cash to a creditor directly. For example, deferred income liabilities are settled by the delivery of goods or services, and a government grant liability is settled by the meeting of the conditions stipulated by the grant.
- A provision is a liability of uncertain timing and/or amount. In the past, provisions have been used to smooth (that is, manipulate) profits, but this is not permitted by IFRS.
- Common examples of provisions are warranty obligations, environmental rehabilitation provisions, provisions for employee pay, and provisions for employees' post-retirement benefits.
- The notes to the financial statements provide a reconciliation of the opening and closing balances of all significant provisions, which includes additions, utilisations, reversals, changes in estimates, and the effects of unwinding the discount.
- Onerous contracts are non-cancellable contracts whose future costs will outweigh the benefits. They are recognised as liabilities immediately, despite the fact that the transaction will only take place in the future.
- Table 7.1 presents a summary of the definitions, varieties, and accounting treatments of the types of liabilities covered in this chapter.

7

TABLE 7.1 Summary of the accounting treatments of the liability categories covered in Chapter 7

Type	Definition/variety	Usual accounting treatment
Financial liabilities	Bank borrowings, accounts payable, lease payables, bank overdrafts	Measured at amortised cost (or, where the time value of money is immaterial, simply measured at the amount due)
Financial liabilities	Actively traded financial liabilities, eg 'shorted' financial instruments (ie shares on loan to satisfy a contract of sale)	Measured at fair value, through profit or loss
Financial liabilities	Publicly traded debt instruments, eg corporate bonds that pay a fixed interest rate	Businesses have a choice between measurement at amortised cost or at fair value through profit or loss (though the effects of changes in own credit risk are recognised in OCI)
Financial liabilities	Derivative financial instruments with a credit balance	Measured at fair value, through profit or loss, except for some hedges, where the gains or losses are in OCI
Provisions	For legal proceedings, warranty obligations, restoration costs, leave pay, etc	Measured at the best estimate of the amount required to settle the provision, or to pay a third party to assume the obligation, at the end of the reporting period. Discounted to present value when the time value of money is material.

(Continued)

TABLE 7.1 (*Continued*)

Type	Definition/variety	Usual accounting treatment
Provisions	For post-employment benefits	If in a separately managed fund: deficits recognised as a liability, with specific gains and losses resulting from changes in measurement reported in OCI. If not in a separately managed fund: full obligation recognised as a liability, with specific gains and losses reported in OCI.
Provisions	Onerous contracts	Measured at the amount of the expected loss, discounted to present value when the time value of money is material
Contingent liabilities	Liabilities which do not satisfy the recognition criteria	Not recognised in the statement of financial position; instead, disclosed in the notes (unless probability of outflow is remote)
Commitments (not in fact liabilities)	Significant future expenditure committed to by the reporting date	Not recognised in the statement of financial position; instead, often disclosed in the notes

CHAPTER QUESTIONS

The applied questions (marked 'AQ') and the discussion questions (marked 'DQ') relate to the financial statements of Daimler, contained in Appendix II. The suggested solutions to these questions, and also to the concept questions (marked 'CQ'), can be found in Appendix III.

Also, don't forget the **online resources** available at www.oup.com/he/winfield-graham-miller1e, which contain multiple-choice questions based on the material in this chapter. You will also find many other helpful resources, including two mini case studies with accompanying questions and answers, and advanced material on some aspects of liabilities.

CONCEPT QUESTIONS

CQ 7.1   Why would a user of financial statements be interested in a business's liabilities?

CQ 7.2   What are the three key elements of the liability definition; that is, what three requirements must be met before a business can be said to have a liability?

CQ 7.3   How are significant future expenditures that do not meet the definition of a liability treated in the financial statements?

CQ 7.4   How are liabilities which do not satisfy the recognition criteria treated in the financial statements?

CQ 7.5   What is distinctive about liabilities called provisions?

CQ 7.6   How is a provision that is recognised on the statement of financial position measured?

APPLIED QUESTIONS

AQ 7.7   What was the value of Daimler's liabilities on 31 December 2019, and what was the split between current and non-current liabilities?

AQ 7.8   Daimler's 2019 statement of financial position reports 'Provisions for other risks' of €20 924 million (consisting of a non-current portion of €10 597 million, plus a current portion of €10 327 million). Locate the relevant note to the financial statements, and use it to identify the individual liabilities included in this line-item.

AQ 7.9   Table F.62 (on p 279) shows us that Daimler had a provision for product warranties of €7 043 million on 31 December 2018, which grew to €8 708 million by 31 December 2019. What caused this change?

AQ 7.10   For each change to the product warranties provision that you identified in AQ 7.9, indicate the other effect of the change, in terms of the double-entry accounting system. Your answer can ignore the final change listed by Daimler, relating to 'Currency translation and other changes'.

AQ 7.11   Explain how Daimler estimates the amount of its provision for product warranties when vehicles are sold, or when new warranty programmes are initiated.

AQ 7.12   What is the amount of Daimler's income tax liability on 31 December 2019, and where is it reported on the statement of financial position?

AQ 7.13   Daimler's statement of financial position reports 'Financing liabilities' of €161 780 million (split between a non-current portion of €99 179 million and a current portion of €62 601 million). Table F.63 (on p 279) reports that roughly half of this figure (€85 625 million) was made up of 'notes/bonds'. Do some research to identify what notes and bonds means in this context.

DISCUSSION QUESTIONS

DQ 7.14   Had current and non-current liabilities been incorrectly classified by Daimler, would there be any risk to a user of these financial statements?

DQ 7.15   Of all the liabilities on Daimler's 2019 statement of financial position, which one is measured at a figure that most accurately represents the amount that will in fact be paid to settle it? In other words, which liability has the lowest level of measurement uncertainty?

DQ 7.16   Does Daimler have any liabilities that are not reported on its statement of financial position? If so, where could one find out about them?

DQ 7.17   Using information in Daimler's 2019 financial statements, briefly discuss Daimler's obligation in terms of its employees' pensions.

DQ 7.18   Does Daimler have any financial liabilities that are measured at fair value through profit or loss? How do you know?

DQ 7.19   Page 246 reports that 'various legal proceedings, claims and governmental investigations are pending against Daimler AG and its subsidiaries on a wide range of topics'. How are the potential future cash outflows from these matters reflected in the 2019 consolidated financial statements?

DQ 7.20   Daimler does not appear to have a liability for dividends on 31 December 2019. Is this because Daimler did not declare dividends for the second half of its 2019 financial year?

DQ 7.21   Which of the current liabilities reported on Daimler's consolidated statement of financial position at 31 December 2019 will be settled in a manner other than by an outflow of cash? Indicate how these liabilities will be settled.

INVESTIGATION QUESTIONS

IQ 7.22   Identify a listed retail company that is based in your country and obtain its financial statements. Identify and discuss the three most significant liabilities reported on its statement of financial position.

IQ 7.23   Using the 'projects' feature of the International Accounting Standards Board web-site (https://www.ifrs.org/projects), research the current status of the accounting standard on provisions, and determine whether there might be any changes to the way in which provisions are reported in the future.

IQ 7.24   Establish whether businesses in your country have significant retirement fund deficits. If so, identify one or two such businesses, and determine the likely impact of their deficits on future cash flows.

REFERENCES

[1]   IASB 2018. *Conceptual Framework for Financial Reporting*. Section 4.26.

[2]   IASB 2018. *Conceptual Framework for Financial Reporting*. Section 5.7.

[3]   IASB 2018. *Conceptual Framework for Financial Reporting*. Section 5.14.

[4]   IASB 2018. *Conceptual Framework for Financial Reporting*. Section 5.16.

[5]   IASB 2018. *Conceptual Framework for Financial Reporting*. Section 5.20.

[6]   IASB 2018. *Conceptual Framework for Financial Reporting*. Section 2.16.

[7]   Parliamentary Budget Office (PBO), Republic of Ireland 2019. *An Overview and Analysis of Contingent Liabilities in Ireland*. PBO Publication 24. Available at: https://data.oireachtas.ie/ie/oireachtas/parliamentaryBudgetOffice/2019/2019-05-01_an-overview-and-analysis-of-contingent-liabilities-in-ireland_en.pdf. See p 5 for the discussion of the bank deposit guarantee.

[8]   British American Tobacco plc 2019. *Annual Report and Form 20-F 2019*. Available at: https://www.bat.com/group/sites/UK__9D9KCY.nsf/vwPagesWebLive/DOAWWGJT/$file/BAT_Annual_Report_and_Form_20-F_2019.pdf.

[9]   Department of Families, Housing, Community Services and Indigenous Affairs (FaHCSIA), Australian Government 2012. *Centro Case: Implications for FaHCSIA Portfolio Bodies*. Available at: https://www.dss.gov.au/sites/default/files/documents/05_2012/centro_case_fact_sheet_portfolio_bodies9feb12_0.pdf.

[10]   Weinberg, A 2003. 'Shaking Steady Freddie'. *Forbes*. 11 December. Available at: https://www.forbes.com/2003/12/11/cx_aw_1211freddie.html#1c5d6a6e3835.

[11]   IASB 2018. *IAS 37: Provisions, Contingent Liabilities and Contingent Assets*. Paragraph 24.

[12]   IASB. 2018. *IAS 37: Provisions, Contingent Liabilities and Contingent Assets*. Paragraph 26.

[13]   Rio Tinto 2019. *Annual Report 2019*. Available at: https://www.riotinto.com/-/media/Content/Documents/Invest/Reports/Annual-reports/RT-Annual-report-2019.pdf. See accounting policy note 1(l) on p 160 and note 26 on p 189.

[14]   Pacific Basin Shipping Limited 2014. *Annual Report 2014*. Available at: https://www.pacificbasin.com/upload/en/ir/financial_disclosure/report/2014/AR/e2343_AnnualReport2014.pdf. See the consolidated income statement on p 73 and note 22 on p 102.

[15]   These four provisions are respectively mentioned on: pp 169 and 172 of Burberry's *2018/19 Annual Report*; and on pp 147 and 154 of Burberry's *2017/18 Annual Report*.

[16]   IASB 2018. *Conceptual Framework for Financial Reporting*. Section 6.12.

[17]   HSBC Holdings plc 2008. *Annual Report and Accounts 2008*. Available at https://www.hsbc.com/-/files/hsbc/investors/investing-in-hsbc/all-reporting/group/2008/hsbc2008ara0.pdf. The income statement is on p 333, and the detail relating to the own credit risk gain (described as 'Changes in own credit spread on long-term debt') is in note 3, on p 360.

LEASES, FOREIGN EXCHANGE, AND DEFERRED TAX

Here are some of the things you will be able to do after reading this chapter:

- justify why, and explain how, a lessee usually recognises a right-of-use asset and a lease liability when a lease commences;
- describe how lessors distinguish between finance and operating leases, and explain the accounting treatment of each;
- discuss the implications of exchange rate changes on the reporting of foreign transactions and foreign operations;
- explain the basic principles underlying deferred tax, giving examples.

CHAPTER 8

Like all of the items discussed in Chapters 6 and 7, the three items we cover in this chapter can have substantial effects on a business's statement of financial position. The difference is that they often affect both the assets section *and* the liabilities section, and so we have given them their own chapter. Furthermore, they are quite complex accounting issues, best handled after you have absorbed the financial reporting principles for more straightforward assets and liabilities. We therefore recommend that you do not tackle this chapter until you have read Chapters 6 and 7.

8.1 LEASES

A lease is an arrangement whereby, for a certain period, the business which owns an **asset** gives the right to use it to another business, usually in exchange for a series of monthly or annual payments. Most businesses choose to lease, rather than purchase, some of the assets they need for their operations. There are a number of reasons for doing so, including the following:

- insufficient cash to purchase the asset (and an inability or unwillingness to borrow);
- the flexibility for the business of being able to return the asset when it is not required;
- needing the asset for less than its useful life;
- possible tax benefits.

Although any type of asset may be leased, the most common are properties, computer equipment, and vehicles. Rentals, hire purchase agreements, and instalment sale agreements are all treated as leases by accountants, who call the business that uses the asset the '**lessee**', and the business that legally owns the asset and receives payments the '**lessor**'. IFRS 16, the accounting standard on leases, requires lessees and lessors to think about leases quite differently. Let's first deal with the less complex approach: the 'lessees'.

8.1.1 How a lessee accounts for a lease

The asset definition in section 6.1.1 states that a business has an asset if it controls a right that has the potential to lead to future economic benefits. Accordingly, a lessee has an asset, for it controls a right to use the leased item for economic gain. IFRS 16 therefore requires a lessee to recognise this lease asset, often called a **right-of-use** asset, as soon as the lease commences. As it will be paid for by a series of lease payments, IFRS 16 also requires that, along with the asset, the business recognises a lease **liability** representing the lessee's obligation to make these payments. It will be best for us to consider the measurement of each of these items separately, beginning with the liability.

The lease liability is measured in much the same way as we described in section 7.1.8: the total amount to be paid is discounted to **present value**, and the discount is unwound as interest over the lease period. The **discount rate** to be used is essentially the lessee's cost of borrowing. A difference with the example shown in Example 7.1 is that, in the case of a lease, payment is not often made via one large cash flow at the end of the period, but instead the lease payments decrease the liability's carrying amount periodically.

To see this in action, suppose that a business leases a piece of equipment for three years, for which it is required to make lease payments of €10 000 at the end of each year. If the lessee's annual cost of borrowings is 8%, the initial measurement of the liability is the present value of three annual payments of €10 000, discounted at 8%, which a financial calculator will tell you is €25 770.97. Example 8.1 shows how this liability will be accounted for over the lease period.

EXAMPLE 8.1

	Cash outflow *Debit payable* *Credit bank* €	Interest expense *Reported in P/L* *Debit expense* *Credit payable* €	Payable *Carrying amount in* *statement of* *financial position* €
Day 1 of Year 1 (start of lease)	–	–	25 770.97
End of Year 1—before payment	–	2 061.68	27 832.65
End of Year 1—after payment	10 000.00	–	17 832.65
End of Year 2—before payments	–	1 426.61	19 259.26
End of Year 2—after payments	10 000.00	–	9 259.26
End of Year 3—before payments	–	740.74	10 000.00
End of Year 3—after payments	10 000.00	–	0
Totals	30 000.00	4 229.03	

Note how the total interest expense of €4 229.03 equals the discount: the difference between the €25 770.97 initial measurement of the lease and the total lease payments of €30 000.

8

> **MISCONCEPTION**
>
> Lessees recognise the total of all future lease payments as a liability.
>
> No; because the lease liability is measured at the present value of future lease payments, it represents only the capital amount outstanding. The discount is unwound as interest expense over the remaining lease period.

The lessee recognises a right-of-use asset and a liability to pay for it. Over the lease period, the lessee reports two expenses: depreciation of the asset and interest expense.

Let's now consider how the lease asset is measured. Its initial measurement is basically the same amount as the liability, and then this amount is depreciated over the lease period. If, as is usual, the depreciation is spread evenly, the annual charge in our example will be €8 590.32 (€25 770.97 ÷ 3). In Example 8.2, you can see the asset's carrying amount decreasing by this amount each year, as well as the lease liability and the effect of the lease on the statement of comprehensive income.

EXAMPLE 8.2

	Start of lease €	Year 1 €	Year 2 €	Year 3 €
Statement of financial position:				
Right-of-use asset	25 770.97	17 180.65	8 590.33	0.00
Lease liability	25 770.97	17 832.65	9 259.26	0.00
Statement of comprehensive income:				
Depreciation expense		8 590.32	8 590.32	8 590.33
Interest expense		2 061.68	1 426.61	740.74
Effect on profit/(loss) for year		− 10 652.00	− 10 016.93	− 9 331.07

Note how the total expense each year is not very different from the €10 000 cash outflow, and adds up over the lease period to the same €30 000 total.

If the lease period covers most of the physical asset's useful life, the carrying amount of the right-of-use asset is likely to be roughly equal to the value of the physical asset itself. This may initially strike you as odd: if the physical asset does not belong to the lessee, why is the lessee recognising an equivalent asset on its statement of financial position? Why not just expense the lease payments as they are made? In fact, when you really think about it, the required treatment does make sense. Leasing an asset is very much like buying it with borrowed money, and so the reporting should be similar: its cost is expensed over its useful life, that cost being less than the full amount paid because a portion of the payments is really a cost of financing.

In fact, from the perspective of a user of the financial statements, it is important that the treatment of leased assets is consistent with the treatment of assets that have been purchased using debt. After all, on its statement of comprehensive income the lessee reports all of the income from using leased assets, just the same as income from assets it owns. In Chapter 11 you will learn that a key part of evaluating a business's performance involves comparing its income with the assets it is using to produce that income. But it would be impossible to do this if some of those assets—the leased ones—are not represented on the statement of financial position simply because their acquisition has been financed via a different means to those which have been outright purchased.

Similarly, the debts owing for purchased assets are recognised on the **balance sheet**. Not recognising lease liabilities would amount to 'off-balance-sheet financing', a notorious accounting practice in which liabilities are hidden from users of the financial statements in order to make the business appear less indebted than it really is. (Section 13.2.6 will describe how Enron, in one of history's largest and messiest accounting scandals, engaged in off-balance-sheet financing via a different means.)

> **MISCONCEPTION**
>
> It is wrong for a business to recognise assets that it does not in fact own.
>
> The response to this is best summed up by Hans Hoogervorst, then IASB Chairman, who in 2016 commented on the newly introduced IFRS 16, saying:
>
> > these new accounting requirements bring lease accounting into the 21st century, ending the guesswork involved when calculating a company's often substantial lease obligations. The new standard will bring much-needed transparency on companies' leased assets and liabilities, meaning that off-balance-sheet financing is no longer lurking in the shadows. It will also improve comparability between companies that lease and those that borrow to buy.[1]

Don't be surprised if you don't see a 'right-of-use' asset on the statement of financial position of a business that leases some assets. There are at least three possible explanations:

- The financial statements may have been prepared before IFRS 16 was adopted. (The standard became effective for financial years ending in 2020.)

- The business may have chosen to present each leased asset in the same line-item as the equivalent owned assets. For example, both the buildings owned and the buildings leased by a business may be included in the asset category property, plant and equipment (PPE). In such cases, the notes to the financial statements disclose the split between owned and leased assets.

- IFRS 16 permits lease payments relating to assets of low value, or assets leased for less than twelve months, simply to be expensed as incurred, without recognising a leased asset or liability. This would be the case with a rental car hired by the business for a few days or weeks, for example.

One final point is that many lease contracts allow for the lease payments to vary. For example, they may be linked to inflation or to revenues earned from the asset, or may depend on a decision to be made later, such as an optional payment to acquire legal ownership of the asset after the lease term. In these cases, IFRS 16 provides detailed guidance to ensure that the asset and liability are recognised at amounts that best achieve the IFRS objectives of relevance and a faithful representation of economic reality.

8.1.2 How a lessor accounts for a finance lease

Accounting for a lease from the lessor's perspective depends greatly on whether it is a **finance lease**. This is a lease which effectively transfers to the lessee the risks and rewards of owning the asset, regardless of whether legal title is transferred.

IFRS 16 provides detailed guidance about how accountants can identify finance leases. Some examples of leases that are usually regarded as finance leases include those where:

- the asset is leased for a major portion of its economic life (such as a machine with an economic life of five years that is leased for four years);

A finance lease effectively transfers to the lessee the risks and rewards of owning the asset, regardless of whether legal title is transferred.

- the lessee will acquire ownership of the asset at the end of the lease term (often called a 'hire purchase' or 'instalment plan');

- the present value of the lease payments is virtually the same as the fair value of the asset;

- the asset is of a specialised nature and is thus unlikely to be used by anyone other than the lessee.

In each of these cases, you should be able to see that the asset's productivity largely affects the lessee, whereas the lessor shares in few, if any, of the risks and rewards normally associated with owning the leased asset. In fact, the lessor's risks and rewards are much more closely associated with a receivable asset representing the contractually agreed payments due to be paid over the lease term.

Let's reconsider the lease of equipment in our previous example, but this time from the lessor's point of view. Suppose that the contract stipulates that at the end of the lease term, the equipment will become the legal property of the lessee, making this a classic example of a finance lease. The accounting works very much like it did from the lessee's perspective. The lessor discounts the lease payments it will receive at an appropriate rate, which we can assume for the sake of the example also to be 8%, so the lessor would recognise a receivable asset equal to €25 770.97. As the lease period progresses, the receivable will increase by the amounts of interest income reported in the statement of comprehensive income and decrease by the amounts of each payment received.

> For a finance lease, the leased asset itself is not recognised on the statement of financial position of the lessor, even though the lessor legally owns it.

Of course, before the day the lease commences, the lessor would have had the item of equipment on its statement of financial position, at, say, a carrying amount of €20 000. When the receivable asset of €25 770.97 is recognised, the physical asset of €20 000 is derecognised, as if a sale has taken place. In effect, that is what has happened, of course, because the risks and rewards of owning the asset have been passed to the lessee. This results in a profit of €5 770.97 (€25 770.97 – €20 000) on the date of lease commencement, as shown in Example 8.3.

EXAMPLE 8.3

	Start of lease €	Year 1 €	Year 2 €	Year 3 €
Statement of financial position:				
Lease receivable asset	25 770.97	17 832.65	9 259.26	0.00
Statement of comprehensive income:				
Profit on commencement of lease		5 770.97		
Interest income		2 061.68	1 426.61	740.74
Effect on profit/(loss) for year		7 832.65	1 426.61	740.74

If the lessor is a manufacturer or a 'dealer lessor', for whom leasing is its primary business, the equipment would have been inventory, and so the €5 770.97 profit in Year 1 would be reported as revenue of €25 770.97 less cost of sales of €20 000. If, instead, the lessor's business is not mainly concerned with manufacturing or leasing equipment, then the €5 770.97 would simply appear as a gain on sale of PPE (see section 6.1.9).

Either way, note how the difference between the total €30 000 of lease payments received and the €20 000 carrying amount of the asset before the lease is equal to the total income of €10 000 over the lease period (€5 770.97 + €2 061.68 + €1 426.61 + €740.74), recognised partly as profit attributable to the effective sale, and partly as interest income earned for financing it.

8.1.3 How a lessor accounts for an operating lease

An **operating lease** is defined by IFRS 16 as any lease that is not a finance lease. In other words, it is a lease where the lessor does not effectively pass the risks and rewards of ownership to the lessee. A lessor accounts for operating leases accordingly: no effective sale is processed in the accounting records; no receivable asset is recognised up front; and no interest income is reported over the period of the lease. Instead, the lease payments are simply reported as income in profit or loss as they are received. The asset itself remains on the lessor's statement of financial position, and is depreciated as appropriate.

To adapt the example we have been discussing, suppose that in fact the equipment has a useful life of a decade, and is expected to be leased to several more lessees at the end of the three-year lease contract with the current lessee. In this case, the lessor retains the risks and rewards of ownership, so it will treat the lease as an operating lease. In the lessor's statement of comprehensive income, the lease payment of €10 000 would be reported as lease income, and depreciation based on an estimated useful life of ten years would be expensed. The equipment's cost of €20 000 would be used as the carrying amount at the start of the lease, and would later be gradually decreased by depreciation.

Example 8.4 shows how this operating lease would be reported in the financial statements of the lessor, assuming the equipment has no residual value so that straight-line depreciation is just €20 000 per year (€20 000 ÷ 10). Note how different this reporting is from that used for the finance lease in Example 8.3.

> For a finance lease, the lessor reports profit at the start of the lease as if the leased asset has been sold, and then interest income during the lease period.

> For the lessor, an important distinction is made between finance leases and operating leases.

> The lessor continues to recognise the asset leased under an operating lease, and reports lease payments as income when they are received.

EXAMPLE 8.4

	Start of lease €	Year 1 €	Year 2 €	Year 3 €
Statement of financial position:				
Equipment asset	20 000	18 000	16 000	14 000
Statement of comprehensive income:				
Lease income		10 000	10 000	10 000
Depreciation expense		(2 000)	(2 000)	(2 000)
Effect on profit/(loss) for year		8 000	8 000	8 000

It is not uncommon for lease payments to escalate. For example, when retailers begin renting space in a shopping complex, it usually takes time for them to become established, and so for the sake of managing their cash flows, they may arrange for the lease payments to be lower in earlier years than in later years. However, the lessor is providing the same property—and therefore the same basic service—from one year to the next. Thus, according to accrual accounting, the lessor should recognise income consistently over the lease term. Thus, operating leases are required to be 'straight-lined': each year the reported lease income is equal to the average annual cash inflow over the lease period.

This means that you may encounter some operating lease assets on a lessor's statement of financial position. However, these are not the same as the lease assets recognised for a finance lease: instead, they are simply **accrual adjustments** for the difference between the income reported and the cash flows received so far. For example, if the payments for the lease depicted in Example 8.4 were €4 000 in Year 1, €9 000 in Year 2, and €17 000 in Year 3, then, alongside the equipment asset, a lease asset would appear, measured respectively at €6 000 (€10 000 – €4 000) in Year 1, and €7 000 (€20 000 – €13 000) in Year 2.

Bear in mind that—even when the lessor accounts for an operating lease in the ways we have described in this section—the lessee still recognises a lease liability and a right-of-use asset as in Example 8.2.

> **MISCONCEPTION**
>
> An operating lease causes an asset to appear on the lessor's and the lessee's statements of financial position, which is nonsense.
>
> It is true that operating leases lead to the recognition of assets by both parties, but this is not nonsense. After all, a lease is recognised as an operating lease by the lessor because the lessor retains the risks and rewards of owning the physical asset. It would therefore be absurd for the lessor to account for it as if it had been sold. At the same time, the lessee is entitled to use the asset, and can be expected to use it beyond the next twelve months. That implies some measure of control, which is a good reason, along with the other reasons given in the previous misconception box, for the lessee to recognise as an asset the right to use it. Financial reporting ultimately strives to provide relevant information which most faithfully represents economic reality. In this situation, when the reality is ambiguous, it actually makes a lot of sense for both parties to recognise assets.

Air France-KLM's leases

2019 was Burberry's last year of applying the old accounting standard for leases (IAS 17). We shall therefore examine the financial statements of a different business, Air France-KLM, which elected to 'early adopt' IFRS 16 before 2020. In its consolidated balance sheet as at 31 December 2019, the business reported right-of-use assets of €5 175 million, and 'lease debt' of €4 120 million, split across the non-current and current liabilities sections. It is striking that the second largest asset class (after 'flight equipment') is made up of items the business does not in fact own! Similarly, its second largest liability is an obligation to pay for those same assets.

Note 20 reveals that more than half of the leased assets are aircraft, but the airline also leases maintenance equipment, real estate, and other assets. By far the largest movement in the right-of-use asset class is depreciation (which they call 'amortisation') of €1 358 million. Note 32 provides detail about the lease debt, showing a breakdown by major leased asset groups (again, aircraft leases top the list). In the case of the liability, the two biggest changes are increases due to 'new contract and renewals' of €589 million, and decreases due to 'reimbursements'—their word for lease payments—of €1 008 million.[2]

8.2 FOREIGN EXCHANGE

Any business which transacts, operates, or invests in a foreign country—if that country uses a different currency—needs to account for the effect of changes in foreign exchange rates. There are in fact two broad ways in which exchange rates can impact the reporting of international business activity:

- when a business transacts in a foreign currency (that is, buys or sells across currency borders);
- when a business runs an entire operation in a country that uses a different currency.

We will deal with each of these challenges—foreign transactions and **foreign operations**—in separate sections, but first we must introduce the notion of a **functional currency**.

8.2.1 Functional currency

A business's functional currency, also known as its measurement currency, is the currency—pounds, euros, dollars, yuan, rupees, and so on—which it must use to measure all the items in its financial statements. Typically, the functional currency is also the currency in which its financial statements are ultimately presented, though it may instead choose, before finalising the financial statements, to translate them from its functional currency to a different currency if, for example, it is listed on the stock exchange of a country that uses a different currency.

IAS 21, the accounting standard dealing with foreign exchange, defines a business's functional currency as 'the currency of the primary economic environment in which the entity operates'.[3] In many cases, identifying the functional currency requires no thought at all. For example, a Norwegian supermarket sets its selling prices in kroner, and the majority of its costs (inventory, labour, rent, and so on) are paid in kroner.

However, a business's functional currency is not always the currency of the country in which it is based. For example, shipping revenues are charged in US dollars, as are most shipping costs, like fuel, harbour fees, and the ships themselves. An Australian shipping company would thus usually have a functional currency of US dollars, despite being headquartered 'Down Under'.

> A business measures the items in its financial statements using its functional currency, which is the currency of the primary economic environment in which it operates.

8.2.2 **Reporting foreign transactions**

Suppose that on 1 December, a French business with a functional currency of euros purchases inventory on credit from a supplier in Sri Lanka. You know that on the date it obtains control of the inventory, it should recognise an inventory asset and an accounts payable liability to pay for it. However, the debt to the supplier is an amount of Sri Lankan rupees—Rs 120 000—and so the importer will have to translate this into its functional currency of euros in order to record the transaction.

An exchange rate on a particular day—as opposed to an average exchange rate across a period—is often referred to as a '**spot rate**'. If the spot rate on 1 December was €1 = Rs 160, the French business would record the asset and liability at an amount of €750 (Rs 120 000 ÷ Rs 160), as in Summary of Event 1.

SUMMARY OF EVENT 1 When the spot exchange rate is €1 = Rs 160, an importer whose functional currency is euros imports inventory for a purchase price of Rs 120 000.

Assets	−	Liabilities	=	Equity		Debit	Credit
+ £750						Inventory	
		+ £750					Accounts payable

When the time comes to pay the Sri Lankan supplier, the exchange rate will inevitably have changed. This introduces an accounting challenge: the amount of euros paid to settle the liability will be different from the amount at which it was recorded. And a similar challenge arises if financial statements need to be prepared between the date of acquisition and the date of settlement, for although the amount of rupees owed has not changed, the amount of euros owed will in all probability now be different from €750.

To resolve this challenge, accountants distinguish between 'monetary' and 'non-monetary' items. These terms are reasonably self-explanatory: in this case, the inventory asset is the non-monetary item, because it is a physical asset, and the accounts payable liability is the monetary item, because it represents an amount of money owed.

Monetary items are restated for changes in the exchange rate on the payment date, and also, where payment has not been made by the end of a financial period, at the reporting date. The differences that arise between the amount at which a monetary item is originally recorded and the amount to which it is restated are called **foreign exchange adjustments**, or foreign exchange differences, and are recognised in profit or loss in the year in which they arise.

Suppose that the French importer has a 31 December year-end, and on that date, the exchange rate is now €1 = Rs 200. The monetary item—the accounts payable—is thus restated to the €600 (Rs 120 000 ÷ Rs 200) owing on 31 December, resulting in a foreign exchange gain in profit or loss of €150 (€750 – €600) as in Summary of Event 2.

Gains and losses resulting from exchange differences on foreign transactions are reported in profit or loss.

SUMMARY OF EVENT 2 On its reporting date, when the spot exchange rate is €1 = Rs 200, the importer owes Rs 120 000 for inventory initially recorded at €750.

Assets	−	Liabilities	=	Equity
		− €150		
				+ €150 (income)

Debit	Credit
Accounts payable	
	Foreign exchange gain

When you think about it, it makes sense to report a gain, since the latest exchange rate indicates that the inventory will ultimately cost the importer less in euros than was expected at the time of purchase. Note, however, that the non-monetary item—the inventory asset—is not restated, and will simply be carried at its originally recorded cost of €750 (plus any other costs incurred to bring it to its location and condition, see section 6.5.1), until it is expensed as cost of sales.

Suppose now that in the following financial year the rupee strengthens a little against the euro, so that the exchange rate on 1 March, the date of settlement, is €1 = Rs 192. It thus turns out that in fact cash of €625 (Rs 120 000 ÷ Rs 192) is needed to settle the debt. This leads to a relatively small foreign exchange loss of €25 (€625 – €600) in profit or loss, as in Summary of Event 3.

SUMMARY OF EVENT 3 When the spot exchange rate is €1 = Rs 192, the importer settles the debt of Rs 120 000, last reported as €600.

Assets	−	Liabilities	=	Equity
− €625				
		− €600		
				− €25 (expense)

Debit	Credit
	Bank
Accounts payable	
Foreign exchange loss	

This is precisely the sort of loss that businesses often aim to avoid by using foreign currency derivatives such as the forward exchange contracts discussed in section 6.7.3. Now that you understand how the foreign exchange differences are accounted for, you may wish to turn back to that section and revisit the topic of hedge accounting. Doing so may help you to fully understand the overall effects of a hedged position on the financial statements.

8.2.3 Reporting foreign operations

Multinational corporations have business operations in other countries. These may include foreign branches not legally separate from the parent company, and also foreign-registered companies controlled by the group (see Chapter 9 to understand how different companies make up a group). If those countries use a different currency from the

Foreign operations are business units controlled by the main business, but operating in a different country to the one in which the main business is headquartered.

business's functional currency, the financial statements of those foreign operations need to be translated into the functional currency before they can be included in the financial statements of the business itself.

For example, Burberry would need to translate the results of its many non-UK operations into pounds sterling in order to prepare its financial statements for the global entity. You might think that this would be done simply by using the exchange rate at the financial year-end, but this is the procedure only for the business's assets and liabilities, which, after all, exist on the precise day of the year-end.

On the other hand, the income, expenses, and cash flows reported in the financial statements do not exist at the year-end; rather, they are movements that have occurred at some earlier point during the financial year. Thus, all income, expenses, and cash flows are translated at the rate on the transaction date (or, if this is impractical, at an average rate for the financial period). Because exchange rates vary during a year, this causes an exchange difference in the statement of financial position, as demonstrated by the following example.

Suppose that a business based in the UK has a foreign branch in the US whose first and only two transactions occur on 1 December: it buys inventory for $60 000 and sells it for $100 000. Neither the payable nor the receivable has been settled by the year-end of 31 December. The statements of comprehensive income and of financial position of the US branch would, of course, appear as in Example 8.5.

EXAMPLE 8.5

	US$
Statement of comprehensive income:	
Sales	100 000
Cost of sales	(60 000)
Profit for year	40 000
Statement of financial position:	
Asset: accounts receivable	100 000
Total assets	100 000
Equity: retained earnings	40 000
Liability: accounts payable	60 000
Total equity and liabilities	100 000

These dollar-denominated financial statements must be translated into the functional currency—pounds—so that they can be included in the global business's financial statements. Suppose that the relevant pound/dollar exchange rates are as follows:

Date	£1 =
1 December	$1.25
31 December	$1.20

Since the sales income was earned and the cost of sales expense incurred on 1 December, they are translated at the exchange rate on that date, resulting in figures of £80 000

($100 000 ÷ $1.25) and £48 000 ($60 000 ÷ $1.25), respectively. The profit in pounds on the transaction date was thus £32 000 (£80 000 – £48 000). **Retained earnings** on the statement of financial position, unaffected by any other transactions, will also be £32 000.

Now the receivable and payable, since they exist at the financial year-end, must be translated at the exchange rate on 31 December. So the asset is measured at £83 333 ($100 000 ÷ $1.20), and the liability at £50 000 ($60 000 ÷ $1.20). Can you see the challenge? Assets minus liabilities equals £33 333 (£83 333 – £50 000), and yet the only equity account—retained earnings—is measured at £32 000. If we left things as they are, A – L would not equal equity! The **accounting equation** would no longer hold and the '**balance sheet**' would not balance.

In this situation, accountants say that a **foreign currency translation difference** of £1 333 (£33 333 – £32 000) has arisen. As this is due to the strengthening of the dollar against the pound, it represents an economic gain for the UK-based business, and so it is reported as income in the statement of comprehensive income. However, as it is just an accident of translation, IAS 21 requires that it does not affect profit or loss, and is instead reported in OCI.

Like most items of OCI, gains and losses resulting from foreign currency translation differences are accumulated in a separate equity account on the statement of financial position, often called a 'foreign currency translation reserve (FCTR)'. By adding this £1 333 to equity, the accountants avoid breaking their cardinal rule and preserve the integrity of the accounting equation.

> Gains and losses resulting from exchange adjustments on translating foreign operations are reported as items of OCI and lead to an FCTR in equity.

Example 8.6 shows how the foreign operation's financial results would appear after being translated into pounds, so that they are ready to be added to the results of the global business.

EXAMPLE 8.6

	GBP
Statement of comprehensive income:	
Sales	80 000
Cost of sales	(48 000)
Profit for year	32 000
OCI: foreign currency translation differences	1 333
Total comprehensive income	33 333
Statement of financial position:	
Asset: accounts receivable	83 333
Total assets	83 333
Equity: retained earnings	32 000
Equity: foreign currency translation reserve (FCTR)	1 333
Liability: accounts payable	50 000
Total equity and liabilities	83 333

Had the exchange rate moved in the other direction—that is, if the pound strengthened against the dollar—the opposite effects would be reported. An expense would appear in OCI, showing how the foreign operation's results are worth less to the UK-based parent business by the end of the year. And a *negative* FCTR would appear in the statement of financial position to make sure that it balances.

You may have guessed correctly that businesses sometimes use hedges to shield themselves from potential losses caused by currency movements which diminish the value of their investments in foreign operations.

The UK business in our example might, for example, borrow $40 000 on 1 December. This liability would be an effective hedge against its net investment in the foreign operation because its value in pounds would be the exact inverse of the value of the equity generated by the US branch's profitable sale on that date. For example, by 31 December, the liability will change from being measured at £32 000 ($40 000 ÷ $1.25) to being measured at £33 333 ($40 000 ÷ $1.20). This movement of £1 333 offsets the £1 333 change in the value of the net investment in the operation, and—because it is a hedge—it is not reported as a foreign exchange adjustment in profit or loss. Instead, it is labelled a '**net investment hedge**' and appears in OCI, thus cancelling out the foreign currency translation difference reported there. Similarly, the effects of net investment hedges are accumulated separately in equity in a reserve often simply called a 'hedging reserve', or even within the FCTR itself.

In our example, the hedge turned out not to be necessary, as in fact the pound strengthened against the dollar, but in another period it may well provide valuable protection against a weakening of the pound.

Loans are not the only way to hedge against foreign exchange risks inherent in foreign operations. Another common tool is a forward exchange contract of the type described in section 6.7.3. No matter what means of hedging is used, the reporting principles described here still apply.

Only when the foreign operation is disposed of will the amount accumulated in the hedging reserve, along with the amount in the FCTR itself, be released to profit or loss.

> A hedge against potential losses caused by currency movements affecting an investment in a foreign operation results in net investment hedges in OCI, and a hedging reserve in equity.

8.2.4 Burberry's foreign exchange reporting

As a multinational business, Burberry has many foreign transactions. Although foreign exchange differences of the sort we discussed in section 8.2.2 do not appear on the face of the income statement, they certainly did affect the group. They are to be found in note 5, which shows how 2019 saw net gains of £4.5 million on the 'revaluation of monetary assets and liabilities'.

Turning to Burberry's translation of its foreign operations, you may have noticed that all of Burberry's items of OCI we have covered up to this point have been relatively small. However, its foreign currency translation differences have resulted in the one sizeable item of OCI. In this line-item, the statement of comprehensive income reports a gain of £14.6 million in 2019, by contrast with a loss of £50.2 million in 2018. Considering how many foreign operations Burberry has, it is unsurprising that differences in exchange rates can add up to such large movements. (Note 30 to the financial statements indicates all of the companies in the Burberry group, indicating a vast network of operations all over Europe, Asia, and North America.)

The FCTR column of the table in note 23 shows how its movements corresponded to the general trend of the British pound: relative to most currencies, it weakened during Burberry's 2018 year, amidst widespread uncertainty about how Brexit would be achieved, and then began a steady recovery from April 2018.

Note 26 on p 198 discloses that the 'Group uses forward foreign exchange contracts to hedge net assets of overseas subsidiaries', which explains the gain on net investment hedges of £1.6 million in OCI, and the hedging reserve of £5.4 million in the balance sheet. In most years, because the hedge is intended to cancel the effect of the item being hedged, you would expect the net investment hedges and the foreign currency translation differences to change in opposite directions, as they did in 2018. However, Burberry does not hedge all of its investments in foreign operations, and in such circumstances, you might from time to time find that the overall movements both turn out to be losses, or—as in 2019—gains.

Note 13 on intangible assets, note 14 on PPE, and note 21 on provisions all also disclose substantial effects caused by foreign exchange rate changes. This is because these notes provide reconciliations of the measurements of the items they describe: they show how the balances changed from the beginning to the end of the year. Of course, to the extent that these items belong to foreign operations, the balances at the beginning of a year are translated at a spot rate which is a year older than the rate used to translate the balances at the end of that year. Hence, some of the change in the balances is not caused by additions, derecognitions, or any other events affecting the assets or liabilities themselves, but instead is simply a function of exchange rate fluctuations.

8.3 DEFERRED TAX

Deferred tax is widely regarded as the most difficult concept to understand in accounting. This is largely because it is a notional concept created by the simple flourish of an accountant's pen.

In section 2.2.12, we observed how there are substantial differences between the principles used in determining accounting profit and the laws used to determine taxable income. Deferred tax arises because of these differences. In sections 8.3.1 and 8.3.2, we will therefore consider two such differences, so as to give you a sense of what the deferred tax figures in the financial statements represent.

> Deferred tax arises because of differences between the principles that determine accounting profit and the laws that determine taxable income.

8.3.1 Items measured at fair value

Virtually all countries charge tax on business income. In most countries, one form of these taxes is charged on the increase in the value of non-current assets. This is commonly called capital gains tax, or CGT, and it usually falls due only when the assets are sold. Depending on the jurisdiction, the tax is some percentage of the difference between the proceeds received from the sale of an asset and its original cost.

Suppose that in Year 1 a business in a country with a CGT rate of 20% acquires an equity investment (that is, the shares of another company) for €100 000. By the business's year-end, these shares have a market value of €160 000. You know from section 6.7.2 that shares are measured at fair value, and so the investment will be recognised in the statement of financial position at €160 000, and a gain of €60 000 (€100 000 – €60 000) will be reported in profit or loss in the statement of comprehensive income.

Yet these assets are measured at fair value—their exit price—so that they are represented at the amount that the business could get for them if it sold them. And if the business sold the shares for €160 000, CGT would be due on the €60 000 gain. So the business would not ultimately get €160 000, but rather €148 000 (€160 000 – 20% × €60 000). Therefore, if the business is going to measure the asset at the amount for which it could be sold, it stands to reason that the business ought also to recognise the liability for €12 000 (€60 000 × 20%) that would arise if it were indeed sold.

Accordingly, IAS 12, the accounting standard on tax, requires business in such circumstances to recognise a deferred tax liability. This is *not* a tax currently payable, since the CGT would only have to be paid if the shares are sold, but rather it is a *notional* tax reflecting the future tax consequences if the carrying amount of the asset were to be realised. Technically, then, the obligating event has not yet happened, and so the liability definition in the Conceptual Framework (see section 7.1.1) is not met. However, the Conceptual Framework itself admits that 'nothing in the Conceptual Framework overrides any standard', and so this is a rare occasion where a liability is recognised before the obligating event has occurred.[4]

> **MISCONCEPTION**
>
> The tax authority expects a business to pay the deferred tax that it reports on its statement of financial position.
>
> No. The deferred tax liability reports amounts that a business might never have to pay. In the example above, if the shares are never sold, the CGT will never be paid.

Consider now the statement of comprehensive income. When the shares were revalued to fair value, this caused a gain of €60 000 in profit or loss. But if the shares were sold for fair value, the net gain would be only €48 000 (€60 000 – €12 000). To reflect this, the business reports a notional 'deferred tax expense' of €12 000 in profit or loss to reduce the effect of the gain on profit or loss.

In the statement of comprehensive income, therefore, deferred tax generally achieves the principle of accrual accounting, ensuring that the tax consequences of items of income and expense are reported in the same period as the items of income and expense themselves.

Together, these two effects are entered into the accounting system as in Summary of Event 4.

8

Deferred tax ensures that the tax consequences of items of income and expense are reported in the same period as the items of income and expense themselves.

SUMMARY OF EVENT 4 Deferred tax effects of a fair value gain of €60 000 that would be taxed at 20% if realised.

Assets	–	Liabilities =	Equity		Debit	Credit
		+ €12 000				Deferred tax liability
			– €12 000 (expense)		Deferred tax expense	

Further increases in the share price would require similar deferred tax entries. Decreases in the share price would result in a **reversal** to bring the deferred tax liability down to the amount of tax that would be paid if the shares were sold at the lower price. Whenever in the future the shares are sold, the investment asset representing the shares will of course be derecognised, and any accumulated deferred tax effects relating to the shares will be fully reversed to remove all effects of the shares from the accounting system. Current tax payable will then be recognised and paid.

To keep the example simple, let's suppose that the shares are sold on the first day of Year 2 for their carrying amount of €160 000. The deferred tax entry passed in Year 1 is reversed, derecognising the liability, and causing deferred tax income that eliminates the effects of the tax actually paid on the now-realised gain of €60 000.

All of these effects are shown in Example 8.7 as follows. (The only figure that requires some calculation is the cash balance at the end of Year 2, which is equal to the proceeds on sale of €160 000, less the €100 000 spent in Year 1, less the tax arising on the sale.)

EXAMPLE 8.7

	Year 1 €	Year 2 €
Statement of comprehensive income:		
Fair value gain	60 000	–
Tax expense—current	–	(12 000)
Tax expense—deferred	(12 000)	12 000
Profit for year	48 000	–
Statement of financial position:		
Asset: cash	(100 000)	48 000
Asset: investment in shares	160 000	–
Total assets	60 000	48 000
Equity: retained earnings	48 000	48 000
Liability: deferred tax	12 000	–
Total equity and liabilities	60 000	48 000

Note how recognition of the deferred tax liability and expense in Year 1 reduces the reported profit for the year by the notional tax effects of the fair value adjustment; and their reversal in Year 2 prevents the actual tax charged for the year (called '**current tax**') from reducing Year 2 profits for the gain already recognised in Year 1.

The principles described in this section apply equally to any liability (say, a derivative) that is revalued downwards: deferred tax expense will reduce the fair value gain, and a deferred tax liability will appear in the statement of financial position. The principles also apply—but in the opposite direction—to fair value losses which result from liabilities being revalued upwards or assets being revalued downwards (provided there isn't an immediate tax deduction equivalent to the write-off). In these cases, instead of a deferred tax liability, a deferred tax *asset* is reported in the statement of financial position, along with deferred tax income in the statement of comprehensive income.

Deferred tax usually appears on the statement of financial position as a liability, but it can appear as an asset.

If the fair value adjustments are reported in OCI, like with PPE on the revaluation model (see section 6.2.1) or the business's publicly traded debt instruments revalued as a result of the business's own credit risk (see section 7.3.1), the deferred tax treatment is almost exactly the same, except that the expense or income will appear in the OCI section, and not in profit or loss. In other words, the deferred tax effect in the statement of comprehensive income is shown in the same section as the fair value adjustment.

8.3.2 Deferred income

Suppose that in Year 1, a business receives an advance payment of €150 from a customer for goods to be supplied in Year 2. We know from section 4.3.6 that this €150 will be recognised as a deferred income liability in Year 1's statement of financial position and will only be reported as revenue in Year 2's statement of comprehensive income, when it is earned. However, in some tax jurisdictions, advance receipts from customers are included in taxable income in the year in which they are received. Suppose this is the case here: the €150 is taxed on receipt, at, say, a rate of 20%, such that €30 (€150 × 20%) of tax has to be paid in Year 1.

For a moment, imagine that this is the business's only transaction, and ignore deferred tax. The resulting effects appear in Example 8.8.

EXAMPLE 8.8

	Year 1 €	Year 2 €
Statement of comprehensive income:		
Revenue	–	150
Tax expense—current	(30)	–
Profit/(loss) for year	(30)	150
Statement of financial position:		
Asset: cash [€150 receipt – €30 tax paid]	120	120
Total assets	120	120
Equity: retained earnings	(30)	120
Liability: deferred income	150	–
Total equity and liabilities	120	120

This reporting would be very misleading. Financial statements are meant to faithfully represent the economic reality of a business. Judged accordingly, there are two problems with the above financial statements. First, it is absurd that the business at the end of Year 1 should be reporting a loss in respect of a transaction that can only be described as a good thing! Second, paradoxically, the business's performance in Year 2 appears *too good*: profit of €150 seems to ignore the related tax charge.

You have probably already guessed the solution: just as the income was deferred, so should the tax be, as shown in Summary of Event 5.

SUMMARY OF EVENT 5 Deferred tax effects of an advance receipt of €150 from a customer, taxed at 20%.

In Year 1, the year that tax is charged yet income is not yet earned:

Assets	– Liabilities	= Equity		Debit	Credit
+ €30				Deferred tax asset	
		+ €30 (income)			Deferred tax income

In Year 2, the year that tax is not charged yet income is earned:

Assets	–	Liabilities	=	Equity		Debit	Credit
– €30							Deferred tax asset
				– €30 (expense)		Deferred tax expense	

The effect of these notional accounting adjustments on the financial statements is shown in Example 8.9, which represents the correct reporting for this transaction.

EXAMPLE 8.9

	Year 1 €	Year 2 €
Statement of comprehensive income:		
Revenue	–	150
Tax expense—current	(30)	–
Tax expense—deferred	30	(30)
Profit/(loss) for year	–	120
Statement of financial position:		
Asset: cash	120	120
Asset: deferred tax asset	30	–
Total assets	150	120
Equity: retained earnings	–	120
Liability: deferred income	150	–
Total equity and liabilities	150	120

This shows how, by accounting for deferred tax, the business reports a neutral overall effect on the statement of financial position in Year 1, when it has not yet earned any income. Also, it achieves the objective of accrual accounting by reporting both the income and the related tax expense in Year 2, when the goods or services are in fact provided.

8.3.3 Items whose accounting and tax treatments match up

Sections 8.3.1 and 8.3.2 described two relatively simple examples of items whose accounting and tax treatments differ. In practice, there are many more such items, and few of them are as simple as these two. For example, often the depreciation expense for an item of PPE is different from the annual tax deduction allowed for that item (often called a capital allowance). This can lead to substantial differences that must be recalculated each year for the entire useful life of the asset, in order to determine the correct deferred tax balance.

For many other items in a business's financial statements, there is simply no difference between the accounting principles used to prepare them and the laws for determining taxable income. Prominent examples usually include assets like land measured on the cost model, accounts receivable, and bank; and liabilities such as borrowings or accounts payable. No deferred tax arises on these items, as the following case demonstrates.

Suppose that a business owns a plot of land as an investment property. Like the shares in section 8.3.1, it has a cost of €100 000 but a market value of €160 000. However, unlike the shares, it is not revalued because the business has elected to measure it using the cost model (see section 6.3 for the subsequent measurement of investment properties). If it were sold for its carrying amount of €100 000, there would be no tax effect as there would be no capital gain. Thus, there is no need to make a deferred tax adjustment to the statement of financial position. Similarly, no deferred tax effect is required in the statement of comprehensive income, as no income or expense has so far arisen for deferred tax to offset.

Even though the investment property might be sold for €160 000, in which case CGT would fall due, there is no need to recognise deferred tax so long as the property is currently measured at its cost. Deferred tax does not arise in respect of *all* future taxes. It only arises if the accounting treatment of an item differs from its tax treatment.

> Deferred tax does not arise in respect of all future taxes. It only arises when the accounting treatment of an item is different from its tax treatment.

8.3.4 **Temporary and permanent differences**

However, not all differences between accounting and tax treatments give rise to deferred tax. It must also be true that these differences will ultimately *reverse* in future. That is, if the difference causes taxable income to be higher than profit before tax this year, deferred tax will only be recognised if, in future, taxable income will be *lower* than profit before tax by the same amount; and vice versa. Because they end up reversing, differences that lead to deferred tax are therefore called **temporary differences**.

There are instances where the accounting principles and tax law take divergent paths that never cross one another again. For example, if a regulator fines a business, the penalty will be accounted for as an expense of the business. However, it is clearly inappropriate for a business to earn a tax break for disregarding regulations, and so such penalties are *never* usually allowed to be deducted from taxable income.

This means that in a year where it receives a significant penalty, with all other things being equal, we would expect the business's taxable income to be above its profit before tax. However, in this case, there is no good reason to enter a deferred tax asset or income into the accounting system. This is because the difference will never reverse, because no tax deduction will ever be granted for the penalty. Unlike for the fair value gain on shares, the advance receipt from the customer, or the depreciation charge, there are no future tax effects to be taken into account now. So the penalty does not cause a temporary difference. Rather, it creates what is sometimes called a '**permanent difference**' between taxable income and profit before tax, which does not give rise to deferred tax.

> **8**
>
> Temporary differences between tax and accounting treatments are those which will ultimately reverse. They give rise to deferred tax.
>
> Permanent differences between tax and accounting treatments are those which will never reverse. They do not give rise to deferred tax.

8.3.5 **Tax losses**

You know that when a business earns a taxable profit, it must pay the required tax. However, you might be disappointed to learn that when a business makes a tax loss, the tax authority does not instead send money to the business! In fact, what usually happens is that the business is allowed to carry the loss forward to the next year, and to set this loss off against taxable income earned in that year.

For example, suppose that a business makes a tax loss of £100 000 in Year 1. Once this has been verified by the authority, it can be used to reduce tax payable in Year 2. Assuming a tax rate of 20%, and taxable income in Year 2 of £600 000, it would normally expect to pay tax of £120 000 (£600 000 × 20%) in Year 2. However, it can use its Year 1 tax loss to reduce the tax payable to £100 000 ((£600 000 − £100 000) × 20%). Tax of £20 000 will therefore be saved in Year 2. At the end of Year 1, this right to a future cash saving represents an asset, which accountants also label deferred tax.

At the end of Year 1, the business would thus report a deferred tax asset (debit) of £20 000 on the statement of financial position and a £20 000 deferred tax gain (credit) in profit or loss. The deferred tax asset will be derecognised in Year 2, increasing the total tax expense to the £120 000 appropriate to Year 2's income of £600 000. These effects on profit or loss can be seen, along with the deferred tax asset, in Example 8.10. We have assumed, for the sake of simplicity, that there are no other differences between tax and accounting treatments.

EXAMPLE 8.10

	Year 1 £	Year 2 £
Statement of comprehensive income:		
Profit/(loss) before tax	(100 000)	600 000
Tax expense—current	–	(100 000)
Tax expense—deferred	20 000	(20 000)
Profit/(loss) for year	(80 000)	480 000
Statement of financial position:		
Asset: deferred tax asset	20 000	–

If the business needs more than a year to become profitable enough to use the entire saving, then the deferred tax asset will be decreased, and the expense reported, more gradually, for as long as the tax loss offsets any taxable income.

However, a deferred tax asset for tax losses may only be recognised if it is probable that the business will have taxable income in the future, because, if not, the recognition criteria in section 6.1.2 are not satisfied. If it is unlikely that the business will make tax profits in the future, and therefore unlikely that the business will ever benefit from the current tax loss, the possible future tax saving is merely disclosed in the notes.

> If it is probable that tax losses will be used to offset future taxable income, they are recognised as deferred tax assets.

MISCONCEPTION

Because deferred tax is a notional accounting construct, the deferred tax amounts can be ignored by users of the financial statements.

Whilst one might be tempted to ignore deferred tax because it is conceptually challenging, one does so at one's peril. To fully appreciate the value of assets on the statement of financial position and the profit in the statement of comprehensive income, we need to consider their future tax consequences. For instance, in our first example of the shares, ignoring deferred tax would overstate the asset and the gain arising on its revaluation. Likewise, ignoring a deferred tax asset for tax losses would blind a user to something of real value, with the potential to increase future profits and reduce future cash outflows.

8.3.6 **Burberry's deferred tax**

Deferred tax is always shown as a non-current asset or non-current liability, even when the tax consequences are expected in the next financial year, and so it is easy to locate Burberry's 2019 deferred tax asset of £123.1 million and a deferred tax liability of £3.4 million. Note 10 reveals that deferred tax of £5.2 million was subtracted from current tax of £106.7 million, to determine the total tax expense charged to the 2019 income statement.

Between them, notes 10 and 15 provide a lot more information about how the deferred tax figures have arisen, including the following points of particular interest.

- The main reasons that deferred tax arose were: capital allowances; tax losses; and a difference between the ways inventory is treated for accounting and tax purposes. These effects were all recognised in profit or loss.
- There was a small (£0.2 million) deferred tax effect on OCI, arising on the valuation of share options (see section 10.3.4).
- The deferred tax balance for the year changed partly due to foreign exchange rate changes, in the same way as other asset and liabilities changed for this reason (see section 8.2.4).
- Deferred tax had to be recalculated as a result of tax rate changes that affected Burberry's foreign operations. This caused a slight reduction in 2019's tax expense, but in 2018 led to an additional £12.6 million of tax charged to the statement of comprehensive income. (This is shown halfway down p 184 of the 2019 annual report.)

CONCLUSION

In this chapter, we have dealt with some of the trickiest areas of accounting. Although we have examined these topics briefly, we have covered the basic concepts and introduced the most important jargon. We hope you consider this sufficient for a satisfactory understanding of these complex ideas.

SUMMARY OF KEY POINTS

- Unless the lease payments are of low value, or the lease term is less than twelve months, a lessee will account for a lease by recognising a right-of-use asset and a corresponding lease liability to pay for it.
- The lease liability is measured at the present value of the lease payments. In each reporting period, its carrying amount decreases by the difference between the actual lease payments and the interest charge representing the unwinding of the discount.
- The right-of-use asset also decreases during the lease period, by the amount of depreciation charged to it.

- This treatment prevents off-balance-sheet financing, allows for income to be contrasted with the assets which generate it, and generally enhances comparability between the financial statements of those businesses that lease assets and those that borrow to buy.
- Lessors distinguish between finance leases and operating leases. Finance leases are those where the substantial risks and rewards of ownership of the leased asset are transferred to the lessee; all other leases are operating leases.
- Lessors account for finance leases as if the leased asset has been sold on credit to the lessee: at the commencement of the lease, they recognise a profit or loss equal to the difference between the asset's carrying amount and the present value of the lease payments; and a receivable asset to which interest income is added over the lease period.
- Lessors account for operating leases by continuing to recognise the leased asset on their statements of financial position, depreciating them as usual, and simply reporting the lease payments received as income.
- A business measures the items in its financial statements using its functional currency, which is the currency of the primary economic environment in which it operates.
- When a business transacts in a foreign currency, if the exchange rate changes between the transaction and payment dates, a foreign currency adjustment arises, recognised as a gain or loss on the monetary item (such as the receivable or payable). Non-monetary items (such as inventory or PPE) are simply measured at the amount at which they were initially measured on the transaction date; that is, the spot rate on that date multiplied by the foreign currency amount.
- When a business includes an operation in a country that uses a different currency to the main business, the assets and liabilities of that operation are added to the financial statement of the main business using the foreign exchange rate at the year-end. Items of income or expense are translated at the foreign exchange rate on the transaction date (or an average rate for the period).
- This results in an imbalance on the statement of financial position, whereby A – L is not equal to E. Thus, a foreign currency translation reserve is recognised as an equity account to balance the equation. The movement in this foreign currency translation reserve is reported as a gain or loss in OCI, representing the main business's foreign exchange gain or loss because of the foreign operation.
- If a business hedges its exposure to currency risk due to a foreign operation, the gains or losses on translating the hedged position result in a net investment hedge recognised in OCI, which accumulates from year to year in a reserve in equity on the statement of financial position.
- Each year, most businesses experience differences between the tax and accounting treatments of some items. If these differences will reverse in future, they are called 'temporary differences', and they give rise to deferred tax.
- Deferred tax assets or liabilities represent the future tax effects of a business's assets and liabilities, only to the extent that their effects are accounted for in different periods for tax and accounting purposes.
- Deferred tax income or expense results in a business reporting the tax consequences of its items of income and expense in the same periods as the items themselves.
- Permanent differences are differences between tax and accounting treatments that will never reverse. They do not give rise to deferred tax.
- Tax losses give rise to deferred tax assets, so long as it is probable that the business will earn taxable income in the future against which to offset the losses.

8

CHAPTER QUESTIONS

The applied questions (marked 'AQ') and the discussion questions (marked 'DQ') relate to the financial statements of Daimler, contained in Appendix II. The suggested solutions to these questions, and also to the concept questions (marked 'CQ'), can be found in Appendix III.

Also, don't forget the **online resources** available at www.oup.com/he/winfield-graham-miller1e, which contain multiple-choice questions based on the material in this chapter, in addition to many other helpful resources, including two mini case studies, and accompanying questions and answers.

CONCEPT QUESTIONS

CQ 8.1   Briefly explain how leases affect a lessee's statement of financial position and statement of comprehensive income.

CQ 8.2   At what amount does the lessee initially measure the lease liability on its statement of financial position, and how does this liability change over the period of the lease?

CQ 8.3   Explain how gains and losses arise when a business transacts in a foreign currency, and identify the section of the statement of comprehensive income in which they are reported.

CQ 8.4   Explain how gains and losses arise when a business has a foreign operation, and identify the section of the statement of comprehensive income in which they are reported.

CQ 8.5   What is the essential reason that IFRS requires most businesses to account for deferred taxation?

APPLIED QUESTIONS

AQ 8.6   Daimler's statement of financial position reported an amount of €37 143 million for PPE as at 31 December 2019. To what extent does this amount include items of PPE leased by Daimler?

AQ 8.7   What were Daimler's amounts of depreciation and interest expense in 2019 in respect of its right-of-use assets?

AQ 8.8   What was the amount of the lease liability reported on Daimler's 2019 statement of financial position in respect of its right-of-use assets, and where on the statement was it reported?

AQ 8.9   What is Daimler's functional currency, and how does Daimler translate the assets and liabilities of its foreign companies into this functional currency?

AQ 8.10   In 2019, did Daimler report any gains or losses arising from translating its foreign companies into euros?

AQ 8.11   To what extent was the carrying amount of Daimler's PPE affected during 2019 by movements in the exchange rate between the euro and the currencies of the foreign operations in which some of its PPE is held?

AQ 8.12   Identify the deferred taxation assets and liabilities on Daimler's 2019 statement of financial position. Where could you discover more information about them?

AQ 8.13   Daimler's income tax for 2019 was reported at an amount of €1 121 million on its consolidated statement of income. How did deferred taxes affect this expense?

DISCUSSION QUESTIONS

DQ 8.14   On 1 January 2019, Daimler began accounting for most of its leases in term of the requirements of IFRS 16 (see the accounting policy note on p 230). Describe in broad terms the effects that the adoption of IFRS 16 had on the 2019 consolidated financial statements.

DQ 8.15   Is there any evidence to suggest that Daimler has not capitalised all of its leased assets? If so, what is this evidence?

DQ 8.16   What information contained in Daimler's 2019 financial statements would help users establish the extent to which Daimler employs derivative instruments such as forward exchange contracts to hedge against the risk of foreign currency losses?

DQ 8.17   On Daimler's 2019 consolidated statement of comprehensive income/loss is a positive amount of €475 million labelled 'Currency translation adjustments'. Why is this amount positive?

DQ 8.18   Using information contained in Daimler's 2019 financial statements, establish to what extent Daimler has unused tax credits arising from tax losses.

DQ 8.19   In its capacity as a lessor, Daimler has both finance and operating leases. Explain the difference between these two types of leases and indicate where in Daimler's financial statements you can find details of how Daimler accounts for them.

DQ 8.20   Table F.41 (p 264), labelled 'Receivables from financial services', includes an amount of €30 790 million in respect of 'Finance lease receivables'. What does this item represent and how has it been calculated?

DQ 8.21   Discuss how deferred tax has affected Daimler's OCI as reported on its consolidated statement of comprehensive income/loss.

INVESTIGATION QUESTIONS

IQ 8.22   Identify a listed retail company that is based in your country and obtain its financial statements. Establish the extent to which the assets reported on its statement of financial position are owned or leased.

IQ 8.23   Research how adoption of IFRS 16, the accounting standard on leases, affected the financial statements of retailers in your country that lease many of their retail outlets.

IQ 8.24   Identify a listed retail company that is based in your country and obtain its financial statements. Establish the extent to which foreign exchange movements have impacted the financial position and performance of this retailer.

REFERENCES

[1]   IASB 2016. *IASB Shines Light on Leases by Bringing Them onto the Balance Sheet*. IASB. 13 January. Available at: https://www.ifrs.org/news-and-events/2016/01/iasb-shines-light-on-leases-by-bringing-them-onto-the-balance-sheet.

[2]   Air France-KLM Group 2019. *Consolidated Financial Statements. January 1, 2019–December 31, 2019*. Available at: https://www.airfranceklm.com/sites/default/files/afklm_financial_statements_decembre_2019.pdf. The consolidated balance sheet appears on pp 6 and 7, while notes 20 and 32 are on pp 53 and 78, respectively.

[3]   IASB 2018. *IAS 21: The Effects of Changes in Foreign Exchange Rates*. Section 8.

[4]   IASB 2018. *Conceptual Framework for Financial Reporting*. SP1.2.

GROUP FINANCIAL STATEMENTS

Here are some of the things you will be able to do after reading this chapter:

- distinguish between companies and groups of companies, and explain how group financial statements report the activities of a single economic entity;
- identify subsidiaries, and outline the consolidation process to include their financial position and performance in the group financial statements;
- distinguish between wholly owned and partially owned subsidiaries, and describe the role of non-controlling interests in the consolidation of partially owned subsidiaries;
- provide examples of the sorts of business value from which goodwill arises, and explain the recognition and measurement principles that apply to goodwill;
- identify associates and joint ventures, and outline the equity accounting process to include their financial position and performance in the group financial statements.

Up until this point, we have been referring to each business we have discussed—real or imagined—as a single economic entity, regardless of its legal structure. We have been able to do this partly because of the **entity concept** we introduced in section 1.2.1: although sole traders and partnerships are not usually legal entities in their own right, the entity concept allows accountants to treat such a business as one economic entity by ignoring the personal transactions of the owners.

In this chapter, we confront a very different kind of complication in the legal structure of bigger businesses. Accountants get around this complication too, but understanding how they do so requires a bit more effort. Here's the complication: many businesses do not consist of just one incorporated entity; they actually consist of *many* such entities. Because companies can own shares in other companies, most medium and large businesses are in fact a conglomeration of companies, each with its own shares, and governed by its own board of directors. These conglomerations are called '**groups of companies**', or simply 'groups'.

Two companies belong to a group if one has purchased a significant proportion of the shares of the other. Depending on the degree of control or influence that comes with its shareholding, the investor company will regard the investee company as either a **subsidiary**, an **associate**, or a **joint venture** (terms which we will explain shortly).

Groups can be very complex, involving hundreds of companies, some of which, while being subsidiaries of one company in the group, have subsidiaries, associates, or joint ventures of their own, that therefore also form part of the group. Thus, there are groups within groups. It is even possible for a company to own shares in a company that is one of its own shareholders, a situation which is referred to as a 'crossholding'.

By listing the seventy-four companies in the group controlled by the company Burberry plc, note 30 to that business's 2019 financial statements reveals that it is in fact a group of seventy-five separate companies. However, the Burberry group does not contain the variety of subsidiaries, associates, and joint ventures that we need to discuss, so instead, in this chapter we shall refer regularly to the South Korean business, LG Electronics. Figure 9.1 illustrates the group's structure.

FIGURE 9.1 LG Electronics group structure on 31 December 2019 (group's shareholding in brackets)

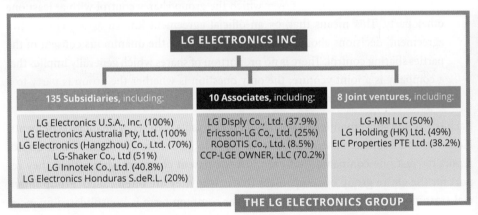

Source: LG Electronics 2019. *Separate Financial Statements, 31 December 2018 and 2017.* Available at: https://www.lg.com/global/pdf/ir_report/LGE_19%204Q_separate_f_signed.pdf.

The group consists of 154 companies from every habitable continent.[1] They are of four types, as follows:

- The **parent company**, LG Electronics Inc, sits atop the group. Every group has a single parent company, sometimes known as a holding company.

- The subsidiaries are businesses controlled by the parent company. 'Control' does not require the group to own 100% of a business, as you can see from the list of subsidiaries in Figure 9.1. In most cases, control is obtained by owning anything more than half of the voting power, which usually means more than half of a company's shares.

The company at the top of the corporate structure pyramid is referred to as the parent company or holding company.

9

Subsidiaries are businesses controlled by the parent company, usually because the group owns more than half of their shares.

Sometimes, it is even possible to control a company with less than that. For example, the notes to the financial statements explain that, despite only 40.8% of its shares being owned by the group, the subsidiary LG Innotek is controlled 'due to the size and dispersion of holdings of the other shareholders and their voting patterns at previous shareholder meetings'. Even more surprisingly, a shareholding of just 20% is sufficient to count LG Electronics Honduras as a subsidiary, because 'the Group has a right to appoint or dismiss the majority of its Board of Directors by virtue of an agreement with the other investors', implying that it has 'de facto control'.

Associates are businesses which the parent does not control, but over which it nevertheless can exert significant influence; usually due to a group shareholding of between 20% and 50%.

- Associates are businesses over which the parent can exert **significant influence**, which is 'the power to participate in the financial and operating decisions', without having actual control.[2] This usually implies that the group holds between 20% and 50% of the associate's shares, but again there are exceptions. For example, LG Electronics' note 14(b)(i) asserts that, despite owning only 8.5% of the shares in ROBOTIS, 'the group can exercise a significant influence in the Board of Directors', presumably by having the right to appoint a number of directors. Conversely, LG Electronics is able to exert significant influence only, not actual control, over CCP–LGE OWNER, despite holding more than 50% of its shares. This is because 'the Group does not have the right to control, by an agreement with shareholders'.

Joint ventures are businesses over which the group has joint control in terms of a joint control agreement.

- Joint ventures are businesses over which the group shares control with at least one other party. This means that, by an official agreement known as a 'joint control agreement', decisions about these businesses require the unanimous consent of the parties sharing control. There is no proportion of shares which generally implies that a company is a joint venture; the only question is whether the group is party to a joint control agreement over the businesses.

9

Each one of the abovementioned businesses prepares its own set of financial statements. However, the financial statements that we have looked at so far in this book do not report for just one company—not even just the parent company—but rather, they report for the entire group of companies. This is why they are often called '**group financial statements**' or 'group accounts'. (Another common term is 'consolidated financial statements'.)

Every group of companies—whether it is a parent and just one subsidiary, or a massive multinational of 154 companies like LG Electronics—produces group financial statements. Doing so is a complex process, and introduces some important features into the financial statements. In this chapter, we shall explain the fundamentals of the process, so that you can learn what these features mean.

9.1 WHY GROUP FINANCIAL STATEMENTS ARE PREPARED

Suppose that Company A has the following statement of financial position.

COMPANY STATEMENT OF FINANCIAL POSITION
of Company A, before acquisition of Company B

	€
Assets:	
Bank	20 000
Equity:	
Share capital	20 000

Company A then uses half of the money in its bank account to buy 100% of another business, Company B, from the former shareholders of Company B. The statement of financial position of Company B at the time that it is acquired by Company A is as follows.

COMPANY STATEMENT OF FINANCIAL POSITION
of Company B, at acquisition

	€
Assets:	
Land	100 000
Equity:	
Share capital	10 000
Liabilities:	
Borrowings	90 000
	100 000

As you might expect, the purchase consideration of €10 000 paid by Company A (the 'acquirer') to the former owners of Company B represents the net asset value of Company B (the 'acquiree'). In practice, though, it is common for an acquirer to pay more than the total equity on the statement of financial position of the acquiree. We shall deal with this scenario a little later.

MISCONCEPTION

A purchase of a company's shares is reported in that company's financial statements.

Usually, when a company's shares are bought, they are bought from the former shareholders, who receive cash from the buyer. This sort of trading of shares has no effect on the company's financial statements.

The company is only party to a purchase of shares if it is issuing them directly to shareholders. In this case, it receives the money, and reports a change to its bank asset and its equity structure in the financial statements (see section 10.3.1).

In the financial records of Company A, the purchase has decreased bank (credit) by €10 000, and added a new asset, the investment in Company B (debit). Immediately after the purchase, the statement of financial position of Company A would appear as follows.

9

COMPANY STATEMENT OF FINANCIAL POSITION
of Company A, at acquisition

	€
Assets:	
Investment	10 000
Bank	10 000
	20 000
Equity:	
Share capital	20 000

We now come to the root of why group accounting is necessary. The statement of financial position of Company A reveals assets of €20 000 represented by a bank asset of €10 000 and an investment of €10 000. But this investment asset hides the true nature of the assets and liabilities that Company A now controls. After all, if the land is productive, Company A benefits just as much as if it owned the land directly, and the borrowings impose just the same risks on Company A as if it owed the money itself.

Company A and Company B really form one business—one economic entity—with €10 000 in cash (owned by Company A), €100 000 of land (owned by Company B), and borrowings of €90 000 (owed by Company B). There is no substantive difference between this entity and a single company with the same assets and liabilities. Thus, for shareholders of Company A, a meaningful evaluation of their investment would require them to be able to understand the financial position and performance of this single economic entity.

Now, perhaps one way to do this would be for them to look at the two companies' sets of financial statements independently, but doing so would be quite demanding, and practically impossible if the group contained 154 companies, like the LG Electronics group!

Another problem with this approach is that there would not be enough information to identify and eliminate **intragroup transactions**, which are transactions between companies within the group. For example, suppose Company A sold goods to Company B for €6 000. If these goods had been purchased by Company A for €5 000, then Company A would have reported a profit of €1 000. However, if Company B had not itself sold the goods, from the perspective of the shareholders in Company A, no real economic activity has taken place: they are no better off, as no profit has been earned from the world outside of the group. It is as if one branch of LG Electronics sold goods to another branch: LG Electronics itself would not have made a sale, or any profit.

Group financial statements report the performance and position of the entire economic entity that we call the group, with the effects of intragroup transactions eliminated.

Fortunately, group financial statements solve both of these problems. These are a third set of financial statements, prepared in addition to the financial statements of Company A, reporting the results of Company A as a separate *legal* entity and of Company B, reporting the results of Company B as a separate *legal* entity. The group financial statements report the results of the entire group as one *economic* entity, with the effects of intragroup transactions removed.

Investors in Company A would only be presented with two of the abovementioned sets of financial statements: the group financial statements and Company A's own financial statements (referred to as the 'company' or 'separate' financial statements). They do not need to see Company B's financial statements (or indeed any other subsidiary's financial statements) as the key information is included in the group financial statements.

9

In Company A's own statement of financial position, its investment in the other group companies can be carried at either cost or fair value, or by another method called 'equity accounting', which we shall discuss later in this chapter. For the sake of the examples in this chapter, we assume that the parent measures its investment at cost in its own financial statements.

9.2 CONSOLIDATION OF SUBSIDIARIES

In section 6.1.1, we established that if a business controls an economic resource, then that resource is an asset of the business. Since a subsidiary is by definition controlled by the parent company, the parent also controls the assets of the subsidiary. Thus, to prepare group financial statements, the subsidiaries' assets are added to the assets of the parent. Not only that, but in fact the two companies' liabilities—income and expense—are also all added together, via a process called 'consolidation'.

Consolidation is the process by which subsidiaries are included in group financial statements.

9.2.1 Wholly owned subsidiaries

To demonstrate the process of consolidation, we'll begin with the simplest case: a **wholly owned subsidiary**, where 100% of the subsidiary's shares are owned by the group. We can thus return to our example of Companies A and B from section 9.1.

The group (or consolidated) statement of financial position is prepared by beginning with the parent company's statement of financial position, and then replacing the account representing the investment in the subsidiary (that is, Company A's investment asset of €10 000) with the subsidiary's assets (that is, Company B's land of €100 000) and liabilities (Company B's borrowings of €90 000). The share capital of the subsidiary is not added to the group statement, because it is an **intragroup item**: Company A owns Company B's shares. The only share capital reported for the group is the parent's share capital, as it represents the shares owned by the owners of the group.

9

GROUP STATEMENT OF FINANCIAL POSITION
of Company A and its subsidiary, at acquisition

	€
Assets:	
Land	100 000
Bank	10 000
	110 000
Equity:	
Share capital	20 000
Liabilities:	
Borrowings	90 000
	110 000

Any intragroup items beside the shareholding itself are also eliminated on consolidation. For example, if Company A had loaned money to Company B, then both Company

A's receivable asset and Company B's payable liability would be removed from the group statement of financial position.

To see how items of income and expense are consolidated, suppose that for the twelve months following the acquisition, the statements of comprehensive income of the parent company and its subsidiary are as follows.

COMPANY STATEMENTS OF COMPREHENSIVE INCOME
for Year 1

	Company A	Company B
	€	€
Sales	5 000	4 000
Cost of sales	(3 000)	(1 000)
Gross profit	2 000	3 000
Expenses	(1 000)	(500)
Profit	1 000	2 500
Other comprehensive income:		
Revaluation gain	–	300
Total comprehensive income	1 000	2 800

The assets, liabilities, income, and expenses of the parent and its subsidiaries are added together to create the group financial statements.

To prepare a group (or consolidated) statement of comprehensive income, the statements of comprehensive income of the parent and the subsidiary are added together, as follows.

GROUP STATEMENT OF COMPREHENSIVE INCOME
of Company A and its subsidiary, for Year 1

	€
Sales	9 000
Cost of sales	(4 000)
Gross profit	5 000
Expenses	(1 500)
Profit	3 500
Other comprehensive income:	
Revaluation gain	300
Total comprehensive income	3 800

All assets, liabilities, income, and expense that result from intragroup transactions are eliminated on consolidation.

In the same way that intragroup assets and liabilities are removed, so are intragroup items of income and expense. Had Company A sold goods to Company B for €600, earning a profit of €100, then all the effects of this transaction—including both the revenue and cost of sales (and thus also the profit)—would be eliminated on consolidation. Similarly, any dividends declared by the subsidiary and reported as income by the parent are eliminated on consolidation, as they are also an intragroup transaction.

To see how the first year's performance affects the group statement of financial position, suppose that the company statements of financial position of Companies A and B at the end of Year 1 are as follows.

COMPANY STATEMENTS OF FINANCIAL POSITION
at end of Year 1

	Company A	Company B
	€	€
Assets:		
Land	–	100 300
Investment	10 000	–
Bank	11 000	2 500
	21 000	102 800
Equity:		
Share capital	20 000	10 000
Retained earnings	1 000	2 500
Revaluation surplus	–	300
	21 000	12 800
Liabilities:		
Borrowings	–	90 000
	21 000	102 800

The group statement of financial position is again prepared by beginning with Company A's statement, and then replacing the investment asset with the assets and liabilities of Company B. The equity generated by Company B since the acquisition (represented by the retained earnings and revaluation surplus accounts) is also included.

GROUP STATEMENT OF FINANCIAL POSITION
of Company A and its subsidiary, at end of Year 1

	€
Assets:	
Land	100 300
Bank	13 500
	113 800
Equity:	
Share capital	20 000
Retained earnings	3 500
Revaluation surplus	300
	23 800
Liabilities:	
Borrowings	90 000
	113 800

9.2.2 Partially owned subsidiaries

We now turn to the case of a **partially owned subsidiary**, where the acquirer purchases less than 100% of the acquiree's shares, but nonetheless obtains control over it. For example, suppose that—instead of buying all of the shares for €10 000—Company A purchases 80% of the shares in Company B for €8 000, leaving it with cash of €12 000, as shown in the following company statements of financial position.

COMPANY STATEMENTS OF FINANCIAL POSITION
at acquisition

	Company A	Company B
	€	€
Assets:		
Land	–	100 000
Investment	8 000	–
Bank	12 000	–
	20 000	100 000
Equity:		
Share capital	20 000	10 000
Liabilities:		
Borrowings	–	90 000
	20 000	100 000

100% of a partially owned subsidiary's assets and liabilities are shown on the group statement of financial position.

The consolidation process is not what you might expect. Rather, it follows the exact same process as for wholly owned subsidiaries: begin with Company A's statement, remove the investment asset, and add 100% of Company B's assets and liabilities. In other words, the subsidiary's *entire* net asset value is added to the group statement, on the grounds that the parent controls it all, even though the proportion of benefits it will receive is limited to its shareholding.

This presents a mathematical challenge, however: an investment of €8 000 has been removed, but net assets of €10 000 have been added. The difference of €2 000 represents the portion of Company B's net assets which is attributable to its shareholders who do not have control: the shareholders outside of the group, who own just 20% of its shares. This figure is thus added to the equity section of the group statement of financial position, and labelled '**Non-controlling interests**' (**NCI**). This line-item may also be called 'Minority shareholders' interest' or 'Outside shareholders' interest'.

The proportion of net assets not owned by the group is shown in equity as 'non-controlling interests'.

GROUP STATEMENT OF FINANCIAL POSITION
of Company A and its subsidiary, at acquisition

	€
Assets:	
Land	100 000
Bank	12 000
	112 000
Equity:	
Share capital	20 000
Non-controlling interests	2 000
	22 000
Liabilities:	
Borrowings	90 000
	112 000

NCI represents the proportion of benefits generated by the subsidiary that will not flow to the parent. The larger the percentage of shares held by the group, the smaller the NCI figure on the group statement of financial position.

> **MISCONCEPTION**
>
> A business that owns 80% of a company should report only 80% of its assets and liabilities on the group statement of financial position.
>
> This is not an unreasonable suggestion, but it is not how a partially owned subsidiary is consolidated. Despite owning only 80% of the shares, the parent controls the entire subsidiary, and thus 100% of the net assets are reported on the consolidated statement of financial position. The fact that only 80% of the benefits will flow to the shareholders of the parent is acknowledged by showing in equity the non-controlling interests' share.

We turn now to the statement of comprehensive income. Suppose that the company statements of comprehensive income are again as follows, but this time Company A owns only 80% of Company B's shares.

COMPANY STATEMENTS OF COMPREHENSIVE INCOME
for Year 1

	Company A	Company B
	€	€
Sales	5 000	4 000
Cost of sales	(3 000)	(1 000)
Gross profit	2 000	3 000
Expenses	(1 000)	(500)
Profit	1 000	2 500
Other comprehensive income:		
Revaluation gain	–	300
Total comprehensive income	1 000	2 800

As with a wholly owned subsidiary, the group statement of comprehensive income will show 100% of the amounts reported in each line-item of the parent's and subsidiaries' statements of comprehensive income. In this case, group profit will thus be €3 500 and group **total comprehensive income** (TCI) will be €3 800.

However, 20% of Company B's profit and OCI is in fact attributable to NCI. The group statement of comprehensive income shows the split of both the group profit and the group TCI, dividing these figures into the portion attributable to owners of the parent (the shareholders of Company A), and the portion attributable to NCI (the other shareholders of Company B). In our example, the portion of group profit attributable to owners of the parent is calculated by adding Company A's profit of €1 000 to 80% of Company B's profit of €2 500, while the NCI figure is 20% of Company B's profit of €2 500. Similarly, the group TCI is split between €3 240 (€1 000 + 80% × €2 800) for the parent's owners, and €560 (20% × €2 800) for NCI.

The group statement of comprehensive income thus appears as follows:

GROUP STATEMENT OF COMPREHENSIVE INCOME
of Company A and its subsidiary, for Year 1

	€
Sales	9 000
Cost of sales	(4 000)
Gross profit	5 000
Expenses	(1 500)
Profit	3 500
Profit attributable to:	
Owners of the parent	3 000
Non-controlling interests	500
Other comprehensive income:	
Revaluation gain	300
Total comprehensive income	3 800
Total comprehensive income attributable to:	
Owners of the parent	3 240
Non-controlling interests	560

As time goes by, the NCI portion of equity in the group statement of financial position will grow beyond the €2 000 recognised on acquisition, indicating that shareholders outside the group are earning a share of post-acquisition TCI. For example, at the end of Year 1, the NCI figure on the statement of financial position will be €2 560 (€2 000 + €560).

9.2.3 Fair value adjustments

So far, we have assumed that the purchase consideration equals the acquirer's share of the acquiree's net asset value. For example, in section 9.2.1, Company A paid €10 000 for a 100% stake in a business with a net asset value of €10 000. In reality, however, the acquirer generally pays *more* than its share of the net asset value reported on the acquiree's statement of financial position.

One reason is that the acquiree's reported net asset value is almost certainly not based on the *fair value* of assets and liabilities. For example, many assets, like inventory and PPE on the cost model, are measured below fair value. Yet, when assets and liabilities are sold—even as part of a business acquisition—they ought to be sold for approximately what they are really worth, not for accounting valuations based on what the acquiree paid for them. Thus, the cost to the acquirer of these assets and liabilities is their fair value.

Suppose that Company A decides that Company B's borrowings are carried at their fair value of €90 000, but that the land is really worth €100 500. Company B uses the cost model to recognise land, which is why its statement of financial position understates its value, reporting it at only €100 000. Being prepared to pay for the value it is acquiring, Company A pays €10 500 (€100 500 − €90 000) for 100% of Company B. The following statements show how this price is accurately reported in the acquirer's financial statements, but the fair value of its land is not reported by the acquiree.

COMPANY STATEMENTS OF FINANCIAL POSITION
at acquisition

	Company A	Company B
	€	€
Assets:		
Land	–	100 000
Investment	10 500	–
Bank	9 500	–
	20 000	100 000
Equity:		
Share capital	20 000	10 000
Liabilities:		
Borrowings	–	90 000
	20 000	100 000

The consolidation exercise reports the acquiree's assets and liabilities at their fair values, which is, after all, their cost as far as the acquirer is concerned. This adjustment of land to its fair value is called a 'fair value adjustment' and leads to the following group statement of financial position at acquisition.

> The assets and liabilities of the subsidiary are measured in the group financial statements based on their fair values at acquisition.

GROUP STATEMENT OF FINANCIAL POSITION
of Company A and its subsidiary, at acquisition

	€
Assets:	
Land	100 500
Bank	9 500
	110 000
Equity:	
Share capital	20 000
Liabilities:	
Borrowings	90 000
	110 000

For the sake of simplicity, we have ignored the deferred tax implications of recognising a gain in the carrying amount of the land (see section 8.3 on deferred tax). If you care to think about this complexity, it is certainly within your grasp: the fair value adjustment to the carrying amount of land would likely lead to a temporary difference, requiring a deferred tax liability to be recognised in the group statement of financial position.

9.2.4 **Unrecognised assets and liabilities**

A second reason that the acquisition price will likely differ from the reported net asset value of the acquiree is that the acquiree may have assets and liabilities that are not recognised on its statement of financial position.

As explained in sections 6.1.2 and 7.1.4 respectively, some items can meet the asset or liability definition but nevertheless not satisfy the recognition criteria. This is the case with most internally generated intangibles, like brands and research (section 6.4.1) and with contingent liabilities (section 7.1.5). However, when an acquirer purchases a business that has such items, it will do its best to identify these items and adjust the purchase price accordingly.

We use the word 'identify' purposefully here, because these sorts of items fall into a category that IFRS 3, the standard on business combinations, describes as '**identifiable**'. By this, it mainly means that the items are 'capable of being separated and divided from the entity'.[3] In other words, they are, like most items, able to be identified, and even sold, separately from the business. Thus, a brand is identifiable, because a business could sell its brand, whereas a great team of well-trained staff is not identifiable, because they can't be divided from the business: the only way for someone to obtain the benefits of a business's staff cohort is to buy the business itself. (A few assets that cannot be separated from the business still count as identifiable according to IFRS 3, if they arise out of contractual or legal rights, such as a licence to operate in a specified area.)

Like with fair value adjustments, the parent company's perceptions of identifiable items are acknowledged when preparing group financial statements, even though they are missing from the subsidiary's own financial statements.

Suppose that Company A pays €10 600 to acquire Company B, leaving €9 400 in its bank account. The group accountants determine that Company B's statement of financial position misrepresents the value of the business not only because the fair value of the land is €100 500, but also because several items are not recognised: a brand with a fair value of €300; research findings with a fair value of €200; and a contingent liability with a fair value of €400. This fully explains the acquisition price of €10 600 (€100 500 + €300 + €200 − €90 000 − €400). The group statement of financial position thus appears as follows.

> Any identifiable assets and liabilities that have not been recognised by the subsidiary are recognised by the group and measured based on their fair values at acquisition.

9

GROUP STATEMENT OF FINANCIAL POSITION
of Company A and its subsidiary, at acquisition

	€
Assets:	
Land	100 500
Intangible—brand	300
Intangible—research	200
Bank	9 400
	110 400
Equity:	
Share capital	20 000
Liabilities:	
Borrowings	90 000
Contingent liability	400
	110 400

This undoubtedly paints a more faithful picture of the assets and liabilities within the group than a statement of financial position which ignores the two intangible assets and the contingent liability. And, although for its own financial reporting, Company B considers some of these items not to have met the recognition criteria, from a group perspective, they are part of the cost of acquisition and therefore should be reported on the group statement.

9.2.5 **LG Electronics' subsidiaries**

As required by law, LG Electronics published two sets of financial statements for 2019: the 'separate' financial statements, reporting the position and performance of the legal entity LG Electronics Inc;[4] and the consolidated financial statements, reporting the position and performance of the economic entity that consists of LG Electronics Inc, as well as the other 153 companies in the group.

The figures in the consolidated financial statements are appreciably larger than the figures in the same line-items in the company financials. On the statements of financial position, for example, the group's PPE is measured at ₩14 505 419 million ('fourteen-and-a-half trillion won'), compared to the company's PPE of only ₩7 331 504 million. This is because the asset on the company statement of financial position which represents its investment in subsidiaries has been replaced in the group statement with the actual assets (such as PPE, inventory, receivables, and so on) and liabilities of the subsidiary companies. (The investment in subsidiaries asset is not separately shown on the company statement of financial position, but it can be calculated using the information in note 13, which lists the carrying amount of all subsidiaries.)

Similarly, in the consolidated statements of profit or loss and comprehensive income, the income and expenses of the subsidiaries have been added to those of the parent company, such that the group's net sales figure is more than double that of the company. The group's subsidiaries in fact made a very real difference to the group's performance: in 2019, the company's loss of ₩196 118 million was converted on consolidation into a group profit of ₩179 948 million; and the difference was even larger in 2018!

As indicated in Figure 9.1 at the beginning of the chapter, the group contains several partially owned subsidiaries, and so it is no surprise that a portion of group equity reported on the consolidated statement of financial position—₩2 095 053 million out of total equity of ₩16 425 138 million—is held by non-controlling interests. These shareholders outside the group are also allocated their share of profit and total comprehensive income on the consolidated statements of profit or loss and comprehensive income.

In an accounting policy note titled 'Consolidation', the consolidated financial statements confirm that the subsidiaries' assets and liabilities have not simply been copied across from those companies' financial statements. Instead, the group has included all identifiable items, measuring them based on their fair values when the business was acquired. The note explains that 'identifiable assets acquired and liabilities and contingent liabilities assumed in a business combination are initially measured at their fair values on acquisition date'.[5]

9

9.3 GOODWILL

So far, we have discussed two reasons that an acquirer typically pays more for a business than the net asset value reported on its statement of financial position: the items on it are often not reported at fair value; and some identifiable items are not on it at all. Does this mean that an acquirer always pays an acquisition price equal to the fair value of 'identifiable net assets' (that is, the fair value of identifiable assets minus the fair value of identifiable liabilities)?

No, it doesn't. In fact, many acquisitions are priced even higher than that. This does not necessarily mean that they are overpriced, for an acquirer might reasonably be willing to pay extra just to gain control of the acquiree, or for the synergistic benefits arising from the integration of the acquiree into the group. Also, the whole business may simply be worth more than the sum of its parts, because of a blend of features that do not meet the definition of identifiable assets, like excellent management, well-trained staff, a fine reputation, loyal customers, and lucrative prospects.

All of these possibilities amount to a third kind of reason that the acquirer might consider the value of the business to be more than the reported equity of the acquiree. The name for this multifaceted source of additional value is 'goodwill'.

9.3.1 Recognition and initial measurement of goodwill

Of course, most business leaders would claim, probably correctly, that their businesses are worth more than the identifiable net asset value. However, they are prevented from recognising such 'internally generated' goodwill on their statements of financial position for the same reason that other internally generated intangible assets are not recognised: their value cannot be measured reliably (see section 6.4.1). Simply believing your business is worth more than the sum of its identifiable parts is not sufficient to justify recognition of an actual amount for this additional value.

However, when a business is acquired, the acquirer's share of the fair value of the identifiable net assets is determined using the procedures described in sections 9.1 and 9.2. This means that, by subtracting this from the purchase price, a precise measurement of the additional value in the business can be established. This 'purchased' goodwill *is* therefore recognised on the group statement of financial position, using this initial measurement.

Suppose that when Company A acquires Company B, the fair value of identifiable net assets is established to be €10 600, for the same reasons given in section 9.2.4. However, this time Company A pays €12 000 for the 100% stake in Company B, leaving only €8 000 in Company A's bank account. This implies that the acquirer has paid €1 400 (€12 000 – €10 600) for goodwill. It's important to see that goodwill is not calculated directly, by measuring the sorts of things that constitute it, like the value of gaining control, potential synergies, excellent management, well-trained staff, a good reputation, loyal customers, or great prospects. These things are not reliably measurable. Instead, goodwill is calculated simply as the difference between the purchase price and what *is* measurable; that is, the fair value of identifiable net assets.

Sidenote (left margin):

Three reasons the acquisition price is not usually the investee's reported net asset value: assets are not at fair value; some identifiable assets and liabilities are not recognised; and goodwill.

Goodwill represents all the reasons that the value of the business from the acquirer's perspective is higher than the fair value of identifiable net assets.

9

Goodwill is equal to the difference between the purchase consideration and the acquirer's share of the fair value of identifiable net assets.

This acquisition will thus be reported as follows.

GROUP STATEMENT OF FINANCIAL POSITION
of Company A and its subsidiary, at acquisition

	€
Assets:	
Land	100 500
Goodwill	1 400
Intangible—brand	300
Intangible—research	200
Bank	8 000
	110 400
Equity:	
Share capital	20 000
Liabilities:	
Borrowings	90 000
Contingent liability	400
	110 400

It is worth noting that goodwill can be recognised when a business of any form is acquired, including when the acquirer simply buys the net assets of an existing business directly, rather than taking control of them indirectly by buying a sufficient stake in the company which owns them. In this case, the acquired assets and liabilities, along with the goodwill, appear on the acquirer's company statement of financial position, and no consolidation is required.

9.3.2 Subsequent measurement of goodwill

After acquisition, the reporting of goodwill is quite straightforward: it is subject to an annual impairment test. In other words, the recoverable amount of the goodwill is calculated each year, and if the recoverable amount is considered to be lower than its carrying amount, then the goodwill is written down (credit) to its recoverable amount. This impairment is shown as an expense (debit) in profit or loss.

While goodwill must be written down where necessary, it is never revalued upwards. This even applies to reversals of goodwill impairments: unlike for most impaired assets, if goodwill is written down one year, its carrying amount cannot be increased if it is later thought to have increased in value.

> Goodwill is subject to an annual impairment test and written down, if necessary, through profit or loss.

MISCONCEPTION

Everyone agrees on the accounting treatment of goodwill.

No, there is a fair amount of controversy over how to account for goodwill. For example, the calculation of the recoverable amount of goodwill is notoriously complex, involving many difficult estimates about the future prospects of the acquired business.

If you do not fully accept the current treatment, you are not alone.

9

9.3.3 Bargain purchase (negative goodwill)

On rare occasions, the acquirer manages to buy a business for *less* than its share of the fair value of its identifiable net assets. After all, the price of any transaction is determined not purely by fundamentals (the intrinsic value of the resource for sale), but also by less quantitative economic forces. For example, if the acquiree's shares are listed, and share prices are currently depressed due to a bleak economic outlook, the acquirer may be able to buy a target company's shares for less than the fundamentals suggest they are really worth. Even in more optimistic times, a similar opportunity might present itself if, say, the shareholders of an unlisted company were eager to sell quickly, and thus willing to accept a discounted price.

When an acquirer pays less than the fair value of identifiable net assets, this negative goodwill is recognised as income on acquisition, and referred to as a bargain purchase gain.

Let us return to the example we used in section 9.3.1, but now suppose that Company B's shares have been inherited by the children of its recently deceased founder and chief executive officer (CEO). As the children are more interested in money than in business, they agree to sell their shares to Company A for a total of €9 600, leaving €10 400 in Company A's bank account.

The €1 000 difference between this purchase price and the fair value of the identifiable net assets of €10 600 is called a **bargain purchase gain**, or **negative goodwill**. It is regarded as a gift to Company A, and therefore €1 000 is recognised immediately on acquisition as income in the profit or loss section of the group statement of comprehensive income.

In the group statement of financial position, all identifiable assets, liabilities, and contingent liabilities are reported just as before. No goodwill is recognised, of course, and instead—consistent with its recognition as income—the bargain purchase gain increases retained earnings by €1 000, as follows.

9

GROUP STATEMENT OF FINANCIAL POSITION
of Company A and its subsidiary, at acquisition

	€
Assets:	
Land	100 500
Intangible—brand	300
Intangible—research	200
Bank	10 400
	111 400
Equity:	
Share capital	20 000
Retained earnings	1 000
Liabilities:	
Borrowings	90 000
Contingent liability	400
	111 400

9.3.4 **LG Electronics' goodwill**

Goodwill quite often appears on the statement of financial position as a line-item in itself; but it is not uncommon for it to be included in the intangible assets line-item. LG Electronics has taken the latter approach, for note 13 reveals that on 31 December 2019, goodwill was the largest component of intangible assets.

Goodwill that year increased due to business combinations by ₩1 853 million, and decreased somewhat due to impairments, and also sales of businesses whose acquisitions had caused goodwill to be recognised in previous years. However, it was in 2018 that goodwill changed much more significantly, thanks to the acquisition of a major subsidiary, ZKW Holding GmbH, an Austrian manufacturer of vehicle components.

The calculation of the goodwill arising on this acquisition is very helpfully detailed in note 39(c), which lists the acquiree's assets and liabilities, split into fourteen categories, culminating in a figure of ₩856 763 million for the fair value of total identifiable net assets. From this figure, non-controlling interests of ₩420 001 million are subtracted to determine that, of the ₩979 108 million paid to acquire the group's share of the business, ₩542 346 million was goodwill. A footnote explains that the group was willing to pay so much more than the fair value of identifiable net assets because it anticipated 'an increase in sales from integration of business'. In other words, the synergistic benefits of assimilating ZKW Holding into the LG Electronics group were considered worth this substantial premium, equivalent to more than €400 million on the date of sale.

It goes without saying that this is a lot to pay for the efficiencies to be gained by merging the operations of two business. Alert users of the financial statements would therefore use the information in this note, together with other, contextual factors, to form their own view as to whether the acquisition makes economic sense.

9.3.5 **More real-world examples of goodwill**

Goodwill can have dramatic effects on a business's financial statements. With the rise of global tech firms, this has never been so true. Two features of the tech industry mean that very large amounts of goodwill are increasingly appearing on business's statements of financial position. First, a large proportion of their value resides in ideas and future prospects that are not easily identifiable as assets in the strict accounting sense. Second, the recent history of the industry is that successful start-ups tend to be acquired for enormous sums by more established firms seeking dominance.

Take Facebook's 2014 acquisition of the messaging app business, Whatsapp Inc. At the time, Whatsapp had fifty-five employees.[6] Presumably they had some computers, furniture, and office equipment, but these do not even show up on Facebook's analysis of the assets it was acquiring because that analysis is rounded to millions of US dollars.[7] At the time, Whatsapp was earning neither profits nor cash: in fact, it was US$33 million in debt. Facebook did recognise some intangible assets on acquisition—'acquired users', 'trade names', and 'acquired technology', which it valued at a little shy of $2 billion. Yet the acquisition price was famously more than $17 billion! This meant that Facebook recognised goodwill from the acquisition of more than US$15 billion. In other words, about 10% of the purchase price was for identifiable intangible assets, and 90% was goodwill.

Facebook claimed that this goodwill—an amount larger than many countries' GDPs—was paid for 'expected synergies from future growth, from potential monetisation opportunities, from strategic advantages provided in the mobile ecosystem, and from expansion of our mobile messaging offerings'. This sort of claim is sometimes not enough to convince investors that the acquisition's price tag was worth it. While it is easily conceivable that an acquiree's tangible assets will yield future cash inflows, it is much harder to trust in the value of such abstract ideas. However, in Facebook's case, the market reacted positively: Facebook's share price rallied on the news.

Goodwill does not always have such positive effects on a business's financial statements, nor are the most significant effects confined to tech firms. In 2018, General Electric (GE), a massive US conglomerate whose assets are ordinarily much more physical, reported a goodwill impairment that was larger even than the price Facebook paid for Whatsapp. In 2015, when it purchased the French energy business, Alstom, it reported that the goodwill was worth US$17.3 billion. This resulted from a rather interesting calculation: in a sign that perhaps it should have known better, GE estimated its share of the fair value of Alstom's identifiable net assets to be *negative* US$7.2 billion, and yet it paid US$10.1 billion for the company.[8]

In 2018, when GE performed an impairment test, it determined that its original assessment of Alstom's future prospects, based largely on the performance of fossil fuels, had been far too optimistic, and in fact the goodwill was worthless. Including write-offs relating to other acquisitions, in 2018 GE wrote off over US$22 billion in goodwill, against revenues that were less than US$75 billion.[9] The loss for the year was approximately equal to the goodwill impairment, unsurprisingly coinciding with a severe drop in the GE share price.

9.4 EQUITY ACCOUNTING OF ASSOCIATES AND JOINT VENTURES

The process for including associates and joint ventures in group financial statements is called equity accounting.

We now come to the two other types of companies that a group may contain—associates and joint ventures—over which the parent respectively has significant influence or shares joint control. The process by which these companies are included in the group financial statements is known as '**equity accounting**' or the '**equity method**'.

Suppose that Company A acquires a 40% stake in Company B for €4 000, being 40% of the fair value of its net assets of €10 000. If Company A is able to exert significant influence over Company B after acquisition, then Company B would be an associate of Company A. Alternatively, if Company A enters into a joint control agreement with another shareholder of Company B, then Company B would be a joint venture of Company A (and also of the other party to the joint control agreement). Either way, Company A equity accounts Company B in its group financial statements (that is, the same set of financial statements in which any subsidiaries of Company A are consolidated).

For the purposes of this example, the statements of financial position of Companies A and B *before* the acquisition are as follows.

COMPANY STATEMENTS OF FINANCIAL POSITION
Before acquisition

	Company A	Company B
	€	€
Assets:		
Land	–	100 000
Bank	20 000	–
	20 000	100 000
Equity:		
Share capital	20 000	10 000
Liabilities:		
Borrowings	–	90 000
	20 000	100 000

9.4.1 **Principles of equity accounting**

Equity accounting an associate or joint venture is very different from consolidating a subsidiary: *none* of the specific assets and liabilities of the associate are included. The group statement of financial position merely reports an asset called 'investment in associate' or 'investment in joint venture', measured initially at the cost of the acquisition, as follows.

GROUP STATEMENT OF FINANCIAL POSITION
of Company A and its associate, at acquisition

	€
Assets:	
Investment in associate/joint venture	4 000
Bank	16 000
	20 000
Equity:	
Share capital	20 000

At this stage, the company statement of financial position of Company A and the group statement of financial position look exactly the same, with the investment in the associate or joint venture reported at an amount equal to its cost of €4 000. However, in most cases, this is only true at acquisition, because thereafter in the *group* statement the investment will be measured at the original cost *plus* the parent's share of post-acquisition TCI of the investee company, *minus* any of this TCI already received as dividends. (Recall that in Company A's own statement of financial position, its investment in group companies may remain at cost—as we are assuming in this chapter—or be carried at fair value, or be equity accounted. Only in the latter case would associates and joint ventures continue to be reported the same way in both sets of financial statements.)

Suppose that after a year of trading, Company B pays a dividend of €1 000, and so Company A receives €400 (40% × €1 000). According to the requirements of its accounting policy to carry the investment at cost in its own financial statements, this is the only form of income that Company A reports as earned from its investment in Company B. Thus, the statements of comprehensive income of Companies A and B for the first year after acquisition may appear as follows.

COMPANY STATEMENTS OF COMPREHENSIVE INCOME
for Year 1

	Company A €	Company B €
Sales	5 000	4 000
Cost of sales	(3 000)	(1 000)
Gross profit	2 000	3 000
Dividend income	400	–
Expenses	(1 000)	(500)
Profit	1 400	2 500
Other comprehensive income:		
Revaluation gain	–	300
Total comprehensive income	1 400	2 800

Note that Company B's TCI for the year is substantially more than the €1 000 of dividends it has declared. Ordinarily, when an investor owns a small proportion of a company's shares, it is prudent to do as Company A has done here, and recognise no more than the dividend income, despite the presence of undistributed earnings. After all, there is no way for an investor without influence to ensure that these are retained and available for distribution later.

However, in this case, Company A does have significant influence over its associate, or joint control over its joint venture, and so it can most likely prevent Company B from squandering the undistributed income. As Company B has in fact earned €2 800 during the year, €1 120 (€2 800 × 40%) is attributable to Company A. Following this logic, equity accounting involves replacing the dividend income from the investee company with the parent's share of its entire TCI. This is shown in two separate line-items in the group statement of comprehensive income: one to indicate the parent's share of profit or loss (40% × €2 500), and the other to represent the parent's share of **other comprehensive income** (OCI) (40% × €300), as follows.

In the statement of comprehensive income, equity accounting recognises in profit or loss the parent's share of profit in one line, and in OCI, the parent's share of OCI, if any.

GROUP STATEMENT OF COMPREHENSIVE INCOME

of Company A and its associate or joint venture, for Year 1

	€
Sales	5 000
Cost of sales	(3 000)
Gross profit	2 000
Expenses	(1 000)
Share of profit of associate or joint venture	1 000
Profit	2 000
Other comprehensive income:	
Share of OCI of associate or joint venture	120
Total comprehensive income	2 120

In the group statement of financial position at the end of Year 1, the investment asset now increases from the original cost of €4 000, by the €1 120 attributable to the group, less the €400 dividend that the parent has received, to determine the carrying amount of €4 720. The dividend received is also an asset of the group, but it is already reflected in the bank balance.

> In the statement of financial position, the investment in associate asset is measured at acquisition cost, plus the group's share of post-acquisition TCI, less dividends received by the group from the associate.

GROUP STATEMENT OF FINANCIAL POSITION

of Company A and its associate, at end of Year 1

	€
Assets:	
Investment in associate or joint venture	4 720
Bank	17 400
	22 120
Equity:	
Share capital	20 000
Retained earnings	2 000
Revaluation surplus	120
	22 120

Note that in the equity section of the statement of financial position, the parent's share of Company B's post-acquisition TCI is divided between retained earnings (representing its €1 000 share of profit) and the revaluation surplus (representing its €120 share of the revaluation gain).

Equity accounting continues in this way, each year reporting the group's share of the investee company's earnings in the statement of comprehensive income; and increasing the asset in the statement of financial position by this amount, minus any dividends received.

9.4.2 **LG Electronics' associates and joint ventures**

The accounting policy notes to the company financial statements of LG Electronics Inc explain that, as expected, 'associates and joint ventures are recorded at acquisition cost'.[10] By adding up the carrying amounts of the associates and joint ventures listed in note 13, we can work out that a total cost of ₩3 877 285 million is allocated to these companies in the 2019 separate statement of financial position.

However, on the face of the group's consolidated statement of financial position, the line-item 'investments in associates and joint ventures' reports a carrying amount of ₩4 544 521 million. The difference between these two figures indicates the group's share of post-acquisition earnings from these companies.

In the consolidated statement of profit or loss, the group's share of the profit or loss earned by associates and joint ventures is encapsulated in the line 'Loss from equity method valuation', indicating a loss for the year of ₩1 052 096 million. In the consolidated statement of comprehensive income, two lines refer to the equity accounted entities: 'Share of remeasurements of associates' (a gain of ₩32 457 million), and 'Share of OCI (excluding remeasurements) of associates and joint ventures' (a gain of ₩39 014 million).

Note 13 to the group financial statements presents a great deal of information about associates and joint ventures, which allows us to identify the effect that each associate and joint venture had on performance. In fact, the entire equity-accounted loss for 2019 is explained by the major associate LG Display Co, Ltd having a very bad year: LG Electronics' 37.9% share of its loss amounted to ₩1 081 220 million!

9.5 **THE GROUP STATEMENT OF CASH FLOWS**

The group statement of cash flows is blessedly straightforward. As explained in section 2.2.15, a statement of cash flows summarises the movements in the business's bank balance on the statement of financial position. And you now know that the bank asset on the group statement is composed of the parent company's bank balance plus 100% of the subsidiaries' bank balances. The associates' and joint ventures' cash balances are not included in the group bank balance because equity accounting simply includes the group's share of their cash as part of the single investment asset recognised for them.

Thus, a group statement of cash flows is constructed as follows:

- Each line-item reported on the group statement of cash flows is composed of the related cash flow for the parent company and the subsidiaries, even if they are partially owned. This involves a simple addition of the company statements of cash flows, with just one nuance: intragroup cash flows are eliminated.

- The cash flows generated by associates and joint ventures are not added to each line-item in this way. Rather, just the dividends they pay to the group appear in 'dividends received'.

- If the group prepares its operating activities section using the indirect method (see section 5.4.3), any profit from associates and joint ventures must be subtracted from operating profit in order to obtain cash generated from operations (CGFO), as these profits are not associated with group CGFO. Conversely, equity accounted losses are added on the indirect method, as can be seen in note 35 to LG Electronics' consolidated financial statements.

- As we described in section 5.5, any cash flows paid to acquire subsidiaries, associates, and joint ventures are disclosed as cash outflows in the investing activities section, and proceeds on any disposals are reported as cash inflows.

CONCLUSION

Group financial statements are very different from the financial statements of the parent company itself, partly because they are created by consolidating the parent's and subsidiaries' assets, liabilities, income, and expense; and partly because they contain features such as goodwill, attributions to NCI, and line-items resulting from the equity accounting of associates and joint ventures. This means two things: first, group financial statements are almost always more relevant and useful for assessing a business's financial position and performance than the company financial statements; and second, they are difficult, if not impossible, to understand without a basic grasp of the complex procedures used to prepare them.

We hope that in this chapter we have convinced you of the value of the information in group financial statements, and helped you to understand how they are put together, so that you are able in future to obtain maximum benefit from using them.

9

SUMMARY OF KEY POINTS

- A business is a single economic entity, but if it is sizeable, its legal structure usually consists of a group of multiple companies.
- A single parent company sits atop the group. The other companies in the group are subsidiaries (if they are controlled by the parent), associates (if the parent can exert significant influence over them), and/or joint ventures (if the group shares joint control over them).
- To report the financial position and performance of this single economic entity, a set of group financial statements is prepared and presented, in addition to the parent's own company financial statements.
- Compared to the company financial statements, the group financial statements facilitate a more meaningful evaluation of the parent company's shareholders' investment because they provide a consolidated report of the effects of the economic activities of the entire group.
- The effects of all intragroup items are eliminated when preparing group financial statements.

■ Subsidiaries (those businesses over which the parent has control) are consolidated. This involves reporting 100% of the assets and liabilities of the subsidiary in the group statement of financial position. If the subsidiary is partially owned, the portion of the net assets that are not owned by the parent is shown in equity as NCI.

■ Similarly, the group statement of comprehensive income reports 100% of each item of income and expense from the subsidiary's statement of comprehensive income, with both profit and TCI split between the amounts attributable to the parent and the amounts attributable to NCI.

■ There are three reasons that the acquisition price paid for an investee company is not usually the investee's net asset value: assets are not always measured at their fair values; some identifiable assets and liabilities may not be recognised; and goodwill.

■ In the group financial statements, the assets and liabilities of the subsidiary are initially measured in the group financial statements based on their fair values at acquisition.

■ Any identifiable assets and liabilities that have not been recognised by the subsidiary are recognised by the group and measured based on their fair values at acquisition.

■ Goodwill describes a range of reasons the business might be worth more to the acquirer than the fair value of its identifiable net assets, such as excellent management, a fine reputation, loyal customers, lucrative prospects, and synergistic benefits arising from integration into the group.

■ Goodwill is recognised as an asset on acquisition, measured as the difference between the purchase consideration and the acquirer's share of the fair value of the identifiable net assets.

■ Goodwill is not amortised, but is instead subject to annual impairment tests.

■ Associates and joint ventures are equity accounted in group financial statements, which involves recognising an asset 'investment in associate/joint venture' in the group statement of financial position, measured at the acquisition cost plus the parent's share of post-acquisition TCI, less any portion already received through dividends.

■ The profit or loss section of the group statement of comprehensive income shows the parent's share of associate's/joint ventures' profit or loss, whether paid as a dividend or not. If the investee has items of OCI, the parent's share of these amounts is reported separately in the OCI section.

■ Broadly speaking, the group statement of cash flows reports all the cash flows of the parent and the subsidiaries, whether partially or wholly owned, and only dividends received from associates and joint ventures.

CHAPTER QUESTIONS

The applied questions (marked 'AQ') and the discussion questions (marked 'DQ') relate to the financial statements of Daimler, contained in Appendix II. The suggested solutions to these questions, and also to the concept questions (marked 'CQ'), can be found in Appendix III.

Also, don't forget the **online resources** available at www.oup.com/he/winfield-graham-miller1e, which contain multiple-choice questions based on the material in this chapter, in addition to many other helpful resources, including two mini case studies, and accompanying questions and answers.

CONCEPT QUESTIONS

CQ 9.1   Briefly explain what is meant by the terms 'parent company', 'subsidiary', and 'associate'.

CQ 9.2   Describe the consolidation process for including a wholly owned subsidiary in group financial statements.

CQ 9.3   Describe the consolidation process for including a partially owned subsidiary in group financial statements.

CQ 9.4   What is goodwill, and how is it calculated?

CQ 9.5   What do the figures for 'investment in associates' and 'share of profit in associates' (which appear in some group financial statements) represent?

APPLIED QUESTIONS

AQ 9.6   Does the Daimler group include subsidiary, associate, and joint venture companies? Where in the notes to the financial statements could one find out more about group entities?

AQ 9.7   What portion of Daimler's 2019 net profit was attributable to the NCI in Daimler's many subsidiaries?

AQ 9.8   What portion of the net assets reported on Daimler's statement of financial position at 31 December 2019 was attributable to NCI?

AQ 9.9   Does Daimler's statement of financial position include any goodwill and, if so, what was the amount of goodwill reported by the group on 31 December 2019?

AQ 9.10   What was the carrying amount of Daimler's associates on 31 December 2019?

AQ 9.11   What was the total of the equity-accounted earnings that Daimler reported in 2019 in respect of its associates and joint ventures?

AQ 9.12   What was the amount of dividends that Daimler received from its associates during 2019?

AQ 9.13   What is the name of Daimler's largest associate? What percentage of this company's shares does Daimler own?

DISCUSSION QUESTIONS

DQ 9.14   If Daimler sold goods to any of its numerous subsidiary companies during 2019, would these sales be included in the revenue amount of €172 745 million reported on its consolidated statement of income? Explain your answer.

DQ 9.15   Indicate three items reported on the face of the 2019 consolidated financial statements which indicate that Daimler has partially owned subsidiary companies.

DQ 9.16   Daimler's consolidated statement of financial position reports an amount for PPE of €37 143 million. Is the PPE of Daimler's subsidiaries and associates included in this amount?

DQ 9.17   The goodwill included on Daimler's statement of financial position as at 31 December 2019 amounted to €1 217 million (see Table F.25 on p 255). When did this goodwill arise, and is it still carried at the amount at which it was initially measured?

DQ 9.18   Did Daimler acquire any businesses during 2019 that gave rise to goodwill? If so, how was the goodwill calculated?

9

DQ 9.19   Are the cash flows of Daimler's subsidiaries, associates, and joint ventures included in its consolidated statement of cash flows? If so, how are they included?

DQ 9.20   How does Daimler include the results of associates and joint ventures in the group financial statements if the associates' and joint ventures' financial statements are not available in time (because of different year-ends or delayed reporting)?

INVESTIGATION QUESTIONS

IQ 9.21   Identify a listed retail company that is based in your country and obtain its financial statements. Establish whether it has subsidiaries, associates, and/or joint ventures. If so, determine the manner in which the results of these companies have been included in the consolidated/group financial statements.

IQ 9.22   Identify a listed company in your country that has recently made a major acquisition of another company. Identify the purchase price, the fair value of the identifiable net assets acquired, and the goodwill (or possibly the bargain purchase) that arose on this acquisition.

IQ 9.23   In this chapter, you learnt that goodwill is subject to an annual impairment test, which may result in a write-down expense for goodwill in profit and loss. Investigate the reasons that two or three companies listed in your country have impaired goodwill in the past few years.

REFERENCES

1   See notes 1(a), 14(b)(i), and 14(b)(ii) for the full lists of the subsidiaries, associates, and joint ventures.
2   IASB 2018. *IAS 28: Investments in Associates and Joint Ventures*. Section 3.
3   IASB 2018. *IFRS 3: Business Combinations*. Appendix A.
4   LG Electronics 2019. *Separate Financial Statements, December 31, 2018 and 2017*. Available at: https://www.lg.com/global/pdf/ir_report/LGE_19%204Q_separate_f_signed.pdf.
5   LG Electronics 2019. *Consolidated Financial Statements, December 31, 2019 and 2018*, p 34.
6   NBC News 2014. 'WhatsApp's 55 Employees Are Rich. So Now What?' 21 February. Available at: https://www.nbcnews.com/tech/tech-news/whatsapps-55-employees-are-rich-so-now-what-n34851.
7   Facebook 2014. *Annual Report 2014*, p 69. Available at: https://s21.q4cdn.com/399680738/files/doc_financials/annual_reports/FB2014AR.pdf.
8   Financial Times 2018. 'GE's $23bn Writedown Is a Case of Goodwill Gone Bad'. 4 October. Available at: https://www.ft.com/content/9beb58f4-c756-11e8-ba8f-ee390057b8c9.
9   General Electric 2018. *2018 Annual Report*, p 94. Available at: https://www.ge.com/sites/default/files/GE_AR18.pdf.
10   LG Electronics 2019. *Separate Financial Statements, December 31, 2018 and 2017*, p 16.

EQUITY

- explain why a business's total equity is not a reliable valuation of the business, and why its financial reporting about equity nonetheless contains useful information;
- describe the function, layout, and logic of the statement of changes in equity;
- provide examples of the most common transactions between businesses and their owners, such as share issues, dividends, share buybacks, and the issue and exercise of share options, and describe how each is reported in the financial statements;
- identify the reserves on the statement of financial position and differentiate between distributable and non-distributable reserves;
- demonstrate how accounting policy changes and material errors lead to the restatement of equity balances in the statement of changes in equity.

This chapter builds on material covered in earlier chapters. If you don't feel comfortable with any of the following items, we recommend that you briefly go back now to the sections referenced.

CHAPTER 10

- The **accounting equation** (described in section 2.2.1) underpins the accounting system. One formulation is A = E + L, which shows how **assets** are funded by a combination of equity and debt.

- One way to understand '**equity**' is that it describes the business funding that can be attributed to the owners. It consists of two basic components: owners' contributions of **capital**; and the value that the business has created, but not yet paid out to the owners as a dividend (section 1.3.2 and 1.3.6 explain this in more detail).

- Equity can also be understood as the accounting value, or **book value**, of the owners' claim on the business. Another formulation of the accounting equation is A – L = E, demonstrating that the business's book value equals its **net asset value** (again, see section 2.2.1).

- This conception of equity is consistent with the formal International Financial Reporting Standards (IFRS) definition of the term: 'the residual interest in the assets of the entity after deducting all its **liabilities**'.[1]

- The **statement of financial position**, or **balance sheet**, reports a business's assets, liabilities, and equity, laid out according to the accounting equation (section 2.2.14 offers a basic example).

- The equity section of the statement of financial position contains various equity accounts which report, amongst other things, the accumulated effects of: **capital** contributions by owners; the business's **retained earnings**; each item of **other comprehensive income** (OCI) reported by the business; and the **non-controlling interests'** (NCI's) share of **partially owned subsidiaries** (section 4.8 lists all items of OCI, and section 9.2.2 explains NCI).

- **Income** is defined as an increase in equity that is not the result of a **capital contribution** by owners, and **expenses** are defined as decreases in equity that are not the result of distributions to owners (these definition are in section 2.1.2).

- All items of income and expense for a period, and only the items of income and expense, are reported on the **statement of comprehensive income**, using **accrual accounting** (described in section 2.2.8), in either the **profit or loss** or **OCI section** (section 4.1 describes the statement format, and section 4.2 offers an explanation of the OCI section).

By now, you will have realised that each of the five elements of accounting is intimately connected with the others. This is perhaps truest of equity. After all, it represents the difference between assets and liabilities, and, unless equity changes, no income or expense ever arises. Thus, in every chapter up to this point, equity has played a supporting role. Now, having thoroughly explored the other four elements, we place it front and centre, to see what the reporting of equity itself reveals about a business.

Unfortunately, it does *not* provide the comprehensive valuation of the business that we might hope for, but the information about equity does reveal important insights about a business's activities. In this chapter, you will learn how to read the one financial statement we have not yet covered—the statement of changes in equity—and see how it connects with the other financial statements. You will also become familiar with a wide range of transactions between businesses and their owners, and how they are reported. Finally, we will show you how changes in accounting policies and material errors affect the reporting of equity in particular, and also the financial statements more generally.

10.1 A POOR MEASURE OF BUSINESS VALUE

At first glance, many people would expect equity, or book value, to be a reliable estimate of what a business is worth. After all, according to A − L = E, it purports to represent the value of the business's assets minus the amounts owed against those assets. As we established in section 2.1.1, 'What you have, minus what you owe, is what you are worth.'

Yet in section 9.3 we revealed that there are three kinds of reasons that, when an acquirer purchases another business, the purchase price rarely equals the net asset value;

The book value, or total equity, of a business is widely regarded as a poor measure of a business's true worth.

in other words, the value of a business is almost never reliably represented by the total equity figure reported in its statement of financial position.

First, many assets are measured in the financial statements at amounts well below their true value to the business. Consider, for example, inventory or property, plant and equipment (PPE) measured using the cost model. The carrying amounts of these assets are based on the amounts that were paid for them, and yet the very reason they were acquired is that they will bring in benefits substantially in excess of their cost!

Second, there are many assets which are not recognised by the business because they fail the recognition criteria (see section 6.1.2). These include internally generated brands, trademarks, and intellectual property. As we observed in section 6.4.6, these are increasingly the most valuable assets of contemporary businesses, and yet, since they are not recognised in the financial statements, they are not included in its book value. Similarly, a business may have **contingent liabilities** (see section 7.1.5), also not recognised on the statement of financial position, which also cause a difference (in this case a negative one) between a business's true value and its book value.

Third, there is a whole range of other factors—collectively called **goodwill**—which potentially make a business worth more to the acquirer than the fair value of its identifiable net assets (see section 9.3). For example, a business's competent staff and management do not meet the asset definition we covered in section 6.1.1, even though they may add enormous value to the business. It is as if the accounting standard-setters have never heard the expression, 'Our people are our greatest asset', for they refuse to allow human resources onto the statement of financial position. Furthermore, financial accountants do not measure the value of a business's reputation, its loyal customers, or its future prospects. If, say, the business has won a big, lucrative contract starting next year, nothing to do with this contract would appear in the financial statements. Goodwill is not recognised to the extent that it has been internally generated. And, although it is recognised if it is purchased as part of a business acquisition, it is never revalued upwards after that. Similarly, commitments are not reported on the statement of financial position, even though the underlying future events might make a sizeable difference to the value of the business.

> **MISCONCEPTION**
>
> The net asset value of a business is a reliable measure of its value.
>
> Many business managers talk about net asset value this way, but in fact it usually amounts to an incomplete and inaccurate depiction of the business's worth. This is because it is calculated strictly by subtracting the recognised liabilities from the value of the recognised assets measured according to IFRS principles.
>
> In fact, the Conceptual Framework admits that 'financial statements are not designed to show an entity's value', explaining that equity therefore does not generally equal the market value of a company's shares, or the amount for which it could be sold in its entirety.[2] We will discuss effective ways to value a business in Chapter 12.

You might wonder: if equity does not provide a reliable valuation, then why pay it any attention at all? Well, there are at least two reasons. First, because of the principle of **prudence** that underlies the recognition and measurement of assets and liabilities, it will generally be the case that equity approximates a potentially informative *minimum value* of

10

the business. For instance, if a business reports positive equity (that is, a higher total assets figure than total liabilities), it is unlikely to go bust.

Second, and even more importantly, even if the informational value of an aggregate figure like 'total equity', 'total assets', and 'total liabilities' is not high, each individual item of information that makes up the total is potentially helpful in understanding the business.

For example, the equity accounts represent the different ways in which the owner's claim on the business has arisen: the share capital account was created when shareholders contributed cash to the company; the **retained earnings** account usually shows the amount of undistributed **profits**; the revaluation surplus indicates how much of the owners' claim is represented by increases in the **fair value** of PPE carried on the **revaluation model** (see section 6.2.1); and so on.

Like most accounts on the statement of financial position, the equity accounts tend to change from one year to the next. With assets and liabilities, the details explaining how the accounts change are reported in varying notes to the financial statements, but to show the changes in equity accounts, IFRS offers another whole financial statement: the statement of changes in equity.

> The primary significance of financial reporting about equity is in the details about business events affecting the value and ownership of the business.

10.2 THE STATEMENT OF CHANGES IN EQUITY

> The accounts in the equity section of the statement of financial position are represented by columns in the statement of changes in equity.

Together with the statement of financial position, statement of comprehensive income, and statement of cash flows, this statement completes the list of financial statements required by IFRS. Unlike the others, which simply report the amounts in the business's accounts, this statement seeks to show the *changes* in accounts, and so its layout is fundamentally different. Whereas the rows of other financial statements represent accounts, and the columns represent years (or some other financial period), it is the columns of the statement of changes in equity which contain the information for each account. Each row relates to an event which has caused one or more of these accounts to change.

To see this for yourself, take a look at the Burberry statement of changes in equity in Appendix I and compare it to the balances on each account in the equity section of the balance sheet. For example, halfway down the column for the share premium account, you will find the balance sheet's £214.6 million balance as at 31 March 2018, and at the bottom of the column is the £216.9 million as at 30 March 2019. In the same column, between these figures, a line-item on the statement of changes in equity reveals that it was the exercise of share options which caused the £2.3 million increase. Higher up the column, the same event in the previous financial year caused a £3.2 million increase.

The other columns represent other equity accounts listed on the balance sheet, and then, furthest to the right, there are two columns representing totals, separated by the NCI column. To the left of NCI is the total equity attributable only to shareholders of the parent company (Burberry has abbreviated this simply to 'Total'), and to its right is the 'Total equity', which includes the NCI.

Thus, the horizontal arrangement on the statement of changes in equity corresponds with the vertical arrangement in the equity section of the balance sheet. You will see this clearly if you cast your eye across the figures in the last line on the statement of changes in equity, and compare them to the 2019 balances on the equity accounts in the balance sheet. The only difference is caused by the column headed 'Other reserves', aggregating the information for three accounts shown separately on the balance sheet: the capital reserve, the hedging reserve, and the foreign currency translation reserve.

Let's now turn to the rows, which represent the year's events that affected equity. These are sorted into two groups:

- *the events that affect* **total comprehensive income** *(TCI)*, summarising the activity aimed at achieving the distinguishing business objective of creating business value;
- *the events which involve transactions with owners*, summarising the transfers of value between them and the business.

Thus, Burberry's profit for the 2019 year (an increase in the retained earnings column of £339.3 million) is shown contributing to the subtotal 'Total comprehensive income for the year', whereas Burberry's shareholders' exercising of their share options appears under the heading 'Transactions with owners'.

Profit is by far the largest, but not the only, contributor to TCI. In sections 6.7 and 8.2 we explained how and why Burberry's balance sheet reports a hedging reserve and a foreign currency translation reserve. These have been grouped on the statement of changes in equity into the 'Other reserves' column, along with the capital reserve, which we will discuss later. IFRS requires that the effects of items of OCI appear separately from the row for profit or loss. This could be done in a single row showing the total OCI £12.7 million being added in the 'Other reserves' column, with a more detailed breakdown in the notes. However, Burberry has chosen to put this detail on the face of the statement of changes in equity, presenting each item of OCI—**cash flow hedges**, **net investment hedges**, and **foreign currency translation differences**—in its own row, followed by a row for their tax effects.

In other businesses' statements of changes in equity, you might find the effects of some of the other items of OCI that were listed in section 4.8. For example, a business which measures its PPE using the revaluation model would report a line-item such as 'Revaluation gains/losses', alongside a movement in the column for the account usually called 'Revaluation surplus' (see section 6.2.1).

Thus, while each of the statement's columns represents an account in the statement of financial position, each of the rows reported in the section summarising TCI represents an item reported in the statement of comprehensive income. This means that the previous chapters of this book equip you to understand everything in the TCI section.

Figure 10.1 illustrates the connections between Burberry's statement of changes in equity and each of the other financial statements. As the statement of changes in equity is prepared using the principle of accrual accounting, rather than the cash basis, there is no explicit connection to the statement of cash flows.

Items on the statement of changes in equity are categorised into two broad groups: those relating to comprehensive income, and those reporting transactions with owners.

Coming from the statement of comprehensive income, profit or loss and items of OCI appear in the appropriate columns in the statement of changes in equity.

10

FIGURE 10.1 How Burberry's statement of changes in equity connects to other financial statements

Income statement

	Note	52 weeks to 30 March 2019 £m	Year to 31 March 2018 £m
Revenue	3	2,720.2	2,732.8
Cost of sales		(859.4)	(835.4)
Gross profit		1,860.8	1,897.4
Net operating expenses	4	(1,423.6)	(1,487.1)
Operating profit		437.2	410.3
Financing			
Finance income		8.7	7.8
Finance expense		(3.6)	(3.5)
Other financing charge		(1.7)	(2.0)
Net finance income	9	3.4	2.3
Profit before taxation	5	440.6	412.6
Taxation	10	(101.5)	(119.0)
Profit for the year		339.1	293.6
Attributable to:			
Owners of the Company		339.3	293.5
Non-controlling interest		(0.2)	0.1
Profit for the year		339.1	293.6
Earnings per share			
Basic	11	82.3p	68.9p
Diluted	11	81.7p	68.4p
Reconciliation of adjusted profit before taxation:		£m	£m
Profit before taxation		440.6	412.6
Adjusting items:			
Adjusting operating items	5	0.9	56.3
Adjusting financing items	5	1.7	2.0
Adjusted profit before taxation-non-GAAP measure		443.2	470.9
Adjusted earnings per share-non-GAAP measure			
Basic	11	82.7p	82.8p
Diluted	11	82.1p	82.1p
Dividends per share			
Interim	12	11.0p	11.0p
Proposed final (not recognised as a liability at 30 March/31 March)	12	31.5p	30.3p

Profit

Items of OCI

Statement of comprehensive income

	Note	52 weeks to 30 March 2019 £m	Year to 31 March 2018 £m
Profit for the year		339.1	296.6
Other comprehensive income:			
Cash flow hedges	23	(2.1)	(10.0)
Net investment hedges	23	1.6	2.3
Foreign currency translation differences		14.6	(50.2)
Tax on other comprehensive income:			
Cash flow hedges	10	0.4	1.9
Net investment hedges	10	(0.2)	(0.4)
Foreign currency translation differences	10	(1.3)	3.6
Other comprehensive income for the year, net of tax		13.0	(52.8)
Total comprehensive income for the year		352.1	240.8
Total comprehensive income attributable to:			
Owners of the Company		352.0	241.2
Non-controlling interest		0.1	(0.4)
		352.1	240.8

	Note
Balance as at 31 March 2017	
Profit for the year	
Other comprehensive income:	
Cash flow hedges	23
Net investment hedges	23
Foreign currency translation differences	23
Tax on other comprehensive income	23
Total comprehensive income for the year	
Transactions with owners:	
Employee share incentive schemes	
Value of share options granted	
Value of share options transferred to liabilities	
Tax on share options granted	
Exercise of share options	
Purchase of own shares	
Share buy-back	
Held by ESOP trusts	
Dividends paid in the year	
Balance as at 31 March 2018	
Adjustment on initial application of IFRS 9	
Adjusted balance as at 1 April 2018	
Profit for the year	
Other comprehensive income:	
Cash flow hedges	23
Net investment hedges	23
Foreign currency translation differnces	23
Tax on other comprehensive income	23
Total comprehensive income for the year	
Transactions with owners:	
Employee share incentive schemes	
Value of share options granted	
Value of share options transferred to liabilities	
Tax on share options granted	
Exercise of share options	
Purchase of own shares	
Share buy-back	
Held by ESOP trusts	
Dividends paid in the year	
Balance as at 30 March 2019	

10

Balance sheet

Equity accounts

	Ordinary share capital £m	Share premium account £m	Other reserves £m	Retained earnings £m	Total £m	Non-controlling interest £m	Total equity £m
	0.2	211.4	311.9	1,169.0	1,692.5	5.3	1,697.8
	–	–	–	293.5	293.5	0.1	293.6
	–	–	(10.0)	–	(10.0)	–	(10.0)
	–	–	2.3	–	2.3	–	2.3
	–	–	(49.7)	–	(49.7)	(0.5)	(50.2)
	–	–	5.1	–	5.1	–	5.1
			(52.3)	293.5	241.2	(0.4)	240.8
	–	–	–	17.1	17.1	–	17.1
	–	–	–	(0.4)	(0.4)	–	(0.4)
	–	–	–	(0.1)	(0.1)	–	(0.1)
	–	3.2	–	–	3.2	–	3.2
	–	–	–	(351.7)	(351.7)	–	(351.7)
	–	–	–	(11.9)	(11.9)	–	(11.9)
	–	–	–	(169.4)	(169.4)	–	(169.4)
	0.2	214.6	259.6	946.1	1,420.5	4.9	1,425.4
	–	–	–	(0.2)	(0.2)	–	(0.2)
	0.2	214.6	259.6	945.9	1,420.3	4.9	1,425.2
	–	–	–	339.3	339.3	(0.2)	339.1
	–	–	(2.1)	–	(2.1)	–	(2.1)
	–	–	1.6	–	1.6	–	1.6
	–	–	14.3	–	14.3	0.3	14.3
	–	–	(1.1)	–	(1.1)	–	(1.1)
	–	–	12.7	339.3	352.0	0.1	352.1
	–	–	–	157	157	–	157
	–	–	–	(2.5)	(2.5)	–	(2.5)
	–	–	–	1.8	1.8	–	1.8
	–	2.3	–	–	2.3	–	2.3
	–	–	–	(150.7)	(150.7)	–	(150.7)
	–	–	–	(12.8)	(12.8)	–	(12.8)
	–	–	–	(171.1)	(171.1)	–	(171.1)
	0.2	216.9	272.3	965.6	1,455.0	5.0	1,460.0

Attributable to owners of the Company

These transactions with owners don't match up explicitly with another financial statement

	Note	As at 30 March 2019 £m	As at 31 March 2018 £m
ASSETS			
Non-current assets			
Intangible assets	13	221.0	180.1
Property, plant and equipment	14	306.9	313.6
Investment properties		2.5	2.6
Deferred tax assets	15	123.1	115.5
Trade and other receivables	16	70.1	69.2
Derivative financial assets	18	–	0.3
		723.6	681.3
Current assets			
Inventories	17	465.1	411.8
Trade and other receivables	16	251.1	206.3
Derivative financial assets	18	3.0	1.6
Income tax receivables	19	14.9	6.7
Cash and cash equivalents		874.5	915.3
		1,608.6	1,541.7
Total assets		2,332.2	2,223.0
LIABILITIES			
Non-current liabilities			
Trade and other payables	20	(176.5)	(168.1)
Deferred tax liabilities	15	(3.4)	(4.2)
Derivative financial liabilities	18	(0.4)	(0.1)
Retirement benefit obligations		(1.4)	(0.9)
Provisions for other liabilities and charges	21	(50.7)	(71.4)
		(232.1)	(244.7)
Current liabilities			
Bank overdrafts	22	(37.2)	(23.2)
Derivative financial liabilities	18	(5.5)	(3.8)
Trade and other payables	20	(525.7)	(460.9)
Provisions for other liabilities and charges	21	(34.6)	(32.1)
Income tax liabilities		(37.1)	(32.9)
		(640.1)	(552.9)
Total liabilities		(872.2)	(797.6)
Net assets		1,460.0	1,425.4
EQUITY			
Capital and reserves attributable to owners of the Company			
Ordinary share capital	23	0.2	0.2
Share premium account		216.9	214.6
Capital reserve	23	41.1	41.1
Hedging reserve	23	3.5	3.8
Foreign currency translation reserve	23	227.7	214.7
Retained earnings		965.6	946.1
Equity attributable to owners of the Company		1,455.0	1,420.5
Non-controlling interest in equity		5.0	4.9
Total equity		1,460.0	1,425.4

10

10.3 TRANSACTIONS WITH OWNERS

The section of the statement of changes in equity which presents transactions with owners contains information about a whole variety of events that we still need to discuss. In this section, we shall describe the most common transactions between a business and its owners, and explain how they are (or, in some cases, are not) reported in the financial statements.

10.3.1 Share issues

The most basic transaction with the owner of a business is the transaction which almost always comes first, when a business begins: the owners' capital contribution, leading to the recognition of a **bank asset**, and an equity account called share capital (see section 2.2.1). Of course, capital contributions do not happen just once, but whenever the business judges that the best way to raise funding is directly from owners.

However, share capital might not be the only account used to report shareholders' contributions. Like many companies, Burberry reports a far larger amount in the **share premium** account.

The distinction between 'share capital' and 'share premium' is explained by the fact that, like in many legal jurisdictions, when companies are **incorporated** in the UK, they assign a **par value**, also known as 'nominal' or 'face' value, to their shares. Shares may initially be issued at their par value, but subsequent share issues are almost always priced at a higher amount than the par value. The share premium is the difference between the issue price and the par value. So, for example, if a business wishes to raise €50 million, it might issue 10 million shares at an issue price of €5.00 each. How this share issue would be entered into the accounting system would depend on the par value, as in the Summary of Event 1.

SUMMARY OF EVENT 1 Issue of 10 million shares for a share price of €5.00 each.

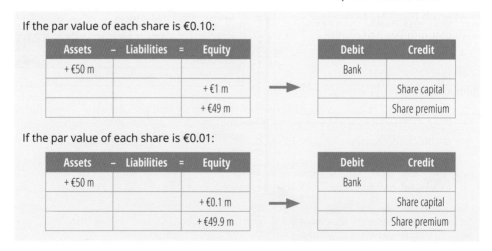

If the par value of each share is €0.10:

Assets	– Liabilities	=	Equity		Debit	Credit
+ €50 m					Bank	
			+ €1 m			Share capital
			+ €49 m			Share premium

If the par value of each share is €0.01:

Assets	– Liabilities	=	Equity		Debit	Credit
+ €50 m					Bank	
			+ €0.1 m			Share capital
			+ €49.9 m			Share premium

Although the share capital and share premium accounts appear separately in the financial statements, the difference is in fact arbitrary: the only information of significance is that the share capital and share premium together equal the €50 million of funding raised by the business.

Note 23 to the 2019 Burberry financial statements reveals that on 30 March 2019, approximately 411 million shares were in issue, and discloses the details of the business's share capital and share premium:

- share capital of £0.2 million (411 million × £0.0005 par value)
- share premium of £216.9 million. The share premium per share would have differed with the issue price each time shares were issued during the history of the company.

Not all legal jurisdictions require shares to have a par value, in which case all the capital raised in a share issue may be added to the share capital account.

You may wonder how financial statements are affected by the daily movements in the share price, as the company's shares are traded on the stock exchange. The answer is that there is no effect, because those 'buys' and 'sells' are between external investors: the company itself is not a party to the transaction. The financial statements report only the effects of transactions to which the business is a party. Of course, as the market price of the shares changes, this does indicate a difference in how much investors would be willing to pay were shares to be issued, but, until an issue actually occurs, the variations in the share price have no effect.

For most companies, share issues are very infrequent, with the directors preferring instead to obtain funding either by reinvesting profits or by taking on debt. For example, Burberry's only truly sizeable share issue occurred in 2002, when it listed on the London Stock Exchange. Prior to the listing, only 500 shares had been in issue, but a further 499 999 500 shares were issued on listing.[3]

10.3.2 **Share buybacks**

How was it that after listing in 2002, Burberry had 500 million shares in issue, and yet in 2019 that number had dropped to about 411 million? The explanation for the decrease is that in the intervening years the group reacquired some of its own shares, in what is called a **share buyback**. Indeed, in most jurisdictions, companies may legally buy back some of their shares. They do this for a variety of reasons, including:

- to transfer cash to shareholders without paying them a dividend (this might be more tax efficient, or simply avoid creating expectations of higher dividends in future years);
- in a private company, to buy out the shares of a shareholder who wishes to exit;
- in a listed company, to take advantage of an undervalued share price.

The last of these reasons requires an explanation. Suppose, for the sake of simplicity, that a company has 100 shares in issue, and that the directors believe the true value of the

---

The distinction between share capital and share premium is usually arbitrary, but their sum generally reports the amounts shareholders have paid for their shares.

Daily movements in the share price do not affect the financial statements.

10

In a share buyback, a company reacquires shares that it has previously issued.

company is €1 000. The market price ought to be €10 per share, but imagine that (perhaps because of a negative outlook about the overall economy) the share price is only €8. This presents an opportunity to take advantage of the undervalued share price through a buyback. Let's say that the company has cash available to buy up 20% of the shares at the current price, spending €160 (20 × €8). Once that is done, the true value of the company will be €840 (the original value of €1 000 minus the €160 cash spent). The correct value of the remaining shares has thus increased to €10.50 (€840 ÷ 80 shares). Now, when the market distortion corrects (that is, when the investors recognise that the business is worth more than €8), existing shareholders will be delighted to see the price of their shares move not to €10—the correct valuation before the buyback—but to the new correct valuation of €10.50.

> Share buybacks often seek to take advantage of an undervalued share price.

On paper, buybacks imply an historical gain or loss. After all, the shares were issued for one price, and now they are being bought back for what is almost certainly a different price. If the twenty reacquired shares in our example had originally been issued for €9 each, then by paying €8 to reacquire them, the company would in theory have gained €1 per share. Had they been issued for €2 each, the company would hypothetically have lost €6 per share. However, transactions with owners are explicitly excluded from the definitions of income and expense, and so these gains and losses are not recognised in profit or loss. Instead, IFRS requires that the effects of share buybacks are recognised directly in the equity accounts that appear on the statement of financial position. For example, the entire amount spent by Burberry to reacquire shares in 2019 was reported simply as a subtraction in retained earnings, as shown in Summary of Event 2.

SUMMARY OF EVENT 2 Burberry spent £150.7 million to buy back its own shares in 2019.

Assets	–	Liabilities	=	Equity		Debit	Credit
– £150.7 m							Bank
				– £150.7 m		Retained earnings	

However, this is not the only way that buybacks are reported: exactly which accounts are used to report this decrease in equity differs from one jurisdiction to another, and even from one company to another. These variations have no significant implications for the users of financial statements, who are mainly interested in the overall change in equity, not how it is split up between equity accounts, and so we won't go into them.

You may be wondering what happens to reacquired shares after the buyback. One option is that they are immediately cancelled, thus reducing the number of shares in issue. In some jurisdictions, this is the only option, but elsewhere the company is permitted not to cancel the shares, and to retain the option of selling them to future investors. When this happens, the reacquired shares are known as **treasury shares**.

> Treasury shares are the company's reacquired shares which have not been cancelled.

While they continue to be owned by the company itself, treasury shares typically lose their rights to vote and to receive dividends. However, technically treasury shares are still in issue, and so another term describes the issued shares held by the other shareholders:

they are called the **outstanding shares**. (In fact, one of the several complexities involved in the calculation of **earnings per share** (EPS) that we mentioned in section 4.9.2 is that it uses the number of outstanding shares, not issued shares.)

$$\text{Outstanding shares} = \text{Issued shares} - \text{Treasury shares}$$

Burberry has several Employee Share Option Plans (ESOPs), in terms of which employees can acquire shares in the company, and the group has set up trusts to hold the shares and supply them to employees when needed. In 2019, Burberry paid £12.8 million for shares to be 'held by ESOP trusts', reported on the statement of changes in equity in the same way as the shares reacquired directly by the company. From the group's perspective, they are treasury shares until they are acquired by the employees. In section 10.3.4, you will learn about how the employees' acquisition of these shares is reported.

10.3.3 Dividends

Dividends are the primary means by which a company rewards shareholders for holding its shares: a straightforward distribution of some of the value created by the business. (Of course, the other usual means by which shareholders can obtain cash from their investment is to sell them, but this—except in the rare case of a share buyback—is a transaction with another investor, not with the company itself.)

As explained in section 2.2.14, because dividends are not an expense of the business, they are not reported in the statement of comprehensive income, and instead appear as a direct deduction from retained earnings. As such, the total amount of dividends declared is to be found in the statement of changes in equity, in the retained earnings column. By looking at this column in Burberry's 2019 statement of changes in equity, we can see that a total of £171.1 million was declared as dividends.

Section 2.2.14 showed how on declaration date dividends are recognised as a liability called 'shareholders for dividend', to be settled with cash sometime later. If Burberry had declared but not paid a dividend by the year-end, the shareholders for dividend liability would have appeared in the statement of financial position, and the dividend figures in the statement of changes in equity and statement of cash flows would have differed. However, the £171.1 million was both declared *and* paid out, so the overall effect on the accounting system was the same as for Burberry's share buyback, as in Summary of Event 3.

SUMMARY OF EVENT 3 Burberry declared and paid out £171.1 million as dividends.

Assets	–	Liabilities	=	Equity		Debit	Credit
– £171.1 m							Bank
				– £171.1 m		Retained earnings	

In order to make sure that dividends reward shareholders in proportion to the number of shares they own, dividends are declared as an amount per share. The dividends per share

(DPS) information is also disclosed in the financial statements, often appearing at the bottom of the statement of changes in equity, but it may instead appear in the notes to the financial statements.

Burberry's DPS information is shown in two places. The DPS actually *paid* during the year (that is, the 2018 final dividends of 30.3 p, and the 2019 interim dividends of 11.0 p) is disclosed in note 12 to the financial statements. It is the latter two figures which together make up the total dividends paid of £171.1 million, shown in the statement of changes in equity.

As we noted in section 4.9, the group took the unusual decision to disclose certain DPS figures at the bottom its income statement. These are the figures for the interim dividends declared and paid halfway through 2019 (11.0 p), and the final dividends *proposed* for 2019 (31.5 p). On 30 March 2019, the status of the final dividend was merely 'proposed'— not 'declared' or 'paid'—because it was only approved by shareholders at the AGM in the following financial year. It was thus not accounted for in the 2019 financial statements, yet it is clearly based on 2019 profitability, and so Burberry has disclosed it, in accordance with the requirement of IAS 1, the standard on presentation of the financial statements.

10.3.4 **Share options**

A **share option** is a right, with no obligation, to buy or sell shares in a company at a certain price on a certain future date. Options are usually granted to directors and other employees to encourage them to work hard and create value for the business, thereby increasing the share price. For example, if its share price is currently trading at £10, then a company may grant employees options today (the 'grant date') to buy shares in three years' time (the 'exercise date') for £15 (the 'strike price'). If the employees are required to work for the business for a specified period of time in order to become entitled to their options, this is called the 'vesting period'.

The employees' incentive is to drive up the share price beyond £15. Suppose that the share price in three years' time is £20. They would then presumably pay £15 to buy shares (known as 'exercising their options'), and choose either to sell them immediately for an immediate cash profit or to hold the share in the hope that the share price continues to improve. In any event, they would have made a gain of £5 on exercising their options.

If, however, the share price on the exercise date is less than £15, the option holders would not exercise their options, since they have no obligation to do so. No money would be paid and no shares would be issued. So long as the trading price of the shares remains below the strike price, the options are described colloquially as 'out of the money' or 'underwater'.

On the grant date, even though they are out of the money, these options have value. This may at first seem counterintuitive: many people might be tempted to say that an underwater option has no value. If you are tempted to think this way, ask yourself: if it were your option, would you toss it in the bin? The answer is clearly no, as, although it may *appear* to be worth nothing now, it will definitely be worth holding onto in case the share price rises above £15 by the exercise date.

> A share option is a right, with no obligation, to buy or sell shares in a company at a certain price on a certain future date.

10

IFRS 2, the accounting standard that deals with share-based payments, refers to options granted in return for employees' services (and also for other services and goods) as 'equity-settled share-based payments'. The correct accounting treatment is to report the value of the options as an expense in profit or loss over the vesting period, and as an increase in the equity section of the statement of financial position.

Suppose that 10 000 options are granted to employees to take up shares (currently trading at £10) for £15 in three years' time. Suppose too that, using a complex method such as Black–Scholes or the binomial model, each of these options are valued at £2 each. Over the vesting period, the business should therefore report an expense (debit) of £20 000 (10 000 × £2) in profit or loss, and an increase of £20 000 in equity (credit) in the statement of financial position. To do this, companies either create a separate equity account called a **'share-based payments reserve'**, or they simply increase retained earnings, shown below in Summary of Event 4.

> The value of share options granted is reported over the vesting period as an expense in profit or loss, and as an increase in an equity account on the statement of financial position.

SUMMARY OF EVENT 4 A business grants 10 000 share options with a value of €20 each on the grant date.

Assets	–	Liabilities	=	Equity		Debit	Credit
				– €20 000 (expense)		Staff costs	
				+ €20 000			Retained earnings/share-based payments reserve

The key conceptual point to note is that this treatment means that there is no effect on the overall net asset value of the business, as the expense decreases profit and therefore retained earnings, which is then offset by the direct increase in equity. Nevertheless, the reporting of an expense means that profit, TCI, and EPS all decrease.

You'll be forgiven for questioning the sense of this accounting treatment. To see the logic behind the two effects, consider the two roles played by the recipients of the share options. On one hand, the options make them potential owners, and we know that transactions with owners are excluded from the definitions of income and expense. They therefore ought to be reported directly in equity (not in profit or loss, or OCI), similar to the accounting treatment of a share issue.

On the other hand, the recipients of the options are not just potential owners; they are also employees. They have only been granted these options because of *that* role: it is part of their remuneration package as employees. In effect, the value of the options is a cost of employment. Viewed from this perspective, like any other staff cost, it ought to result in an expense in profit or loss.

Note 27 to Burberry's financial statements explains that its executives and senior management, depending on their performance, are awarded options to buy shares for free, and that less senior employees are entitled to join a Savings-Related Share Options Scheme, and an All Employee Share Plan. The granting of share options by these Employee Share Option Plans (ESOPs) led to an expense in 2019 of £15.7 million,

10

representing the portion of their value on the grant date that had vested that year. This effect is matched by a line-item in the statement of changes in equity called 'Value of share options granted', which increased retained earnings, revealing that Burberry does not use a separate share-based payments reserve. A little lower down the statement, 'Tax on share options granted' of £1.8 million has been added back to retained earnings, consistent with the requirement that income tax effects are reported wherever the related item is reported.

You might be wondering what happens when share options are exercised. To return to our example, if the shares are eventually issued for £15, there is an increase (credit) of £150 000 (10 000 × £15) in the relevant capital account(s), and bank increases (debit) by £150 000. The business may also choose to transfer the amount that they previously recognised in equity to the relevant capital account(s) (credit), so that the entire value of the transaction is reported there. In other words, it could remove the £20 000 from the equity account in which it was previously reported and transfer it to capital, to report the entire value of the transaction there: £170 000, made up of £150 000 in cash and £20 000 in employees' services. Alternatively, the business can choose simply to leave the additional £20 000 where it was reported when the options were granted, as in Summary of Event 5.

SUMMARY OF EVENT 5 Option holders exercise 10 000 options with a strike price of €15 each.

Required entry to record the receipt of cash and the issue of shares (assuming a par value of €1 per share):

Assets	– Liabilities	=	Equity		Debit	Credit
+ €150 000					Bank	
			+ €10 000			Share capital
			+ €140 000			Share premium

Optional entry to move the entire value of the transaction to the capital accounts:

Assets	– Liabilities	=	Equity		Debit	Credit
			– €20 000		Retained earnings/ share-based payments reserve	
			+ €20 000			Share premium

Burberry's employees' exercising of their share options in 2019 was reported as an increase of £2.3 million in the share premium column of the statement of changes in equity. This was the amount they had to pay to exercise their options. Burberry has chosen not to transfer to share premium the amounts it had recognised in retained earnings when the options were granted.

10.3.5 **Other transactions with shareholders**

Three common transactions involving a company's shares which we haven't yet mentioned are:

- *Rights issues.* These are share issues only to existing shareholders, who can elect whether or not to buy the shares in some specified proportion to their current shareholding. Many do, as the price is usually below the market price when the rights offer is made. The financial reporting for rights issues is just the same as for any other share issue.

- *Bonus issues*, *capitalisation issues*, or *scrip dividends*. These are different names for the same event: zero-cost share issues to existing shareholders in lieu of cash dividends. As there is no cash flow to or from the company, its total value is unchanged, so in theory the market share price will just step down to adjust for the additional shares in issue. You may well therefore wonder what the purpose is, but nonetheless, companies unable or unwilling to pay cash to shareholders sometimes use bonus issues to give the impression of rewarding shareholders with the additional shares. The effect on the financial statements is for the retained earnings account to decrease (debit), like when dividends are actually paid, but for the capital account(s) to increase (credit), instead of cash.

- *Conversions of debt instruments.* 'Convertible bonds' and 'convertible debentures' are examples of debt instruments which are (or may become) convertible to shares. The terms governing the conversion will vary from one instrument to another, but when a conversion like this occurs, the financial reporting effect is a decrease of any amount previously accounted for by the company as a liability (debit) and an increase in the capital account(s).

This completes our discussion of the most common transactions between a business and its shareholders that have an effect on the financial statements. However, finance is a field of great variety and constant innovation, and so you may well spot a transaction in a business's statement of changes in equity that is different to those we have discussed. If so, we recommend that you read the related note to the financial statements, and then do an internet search to better understand the transaction.

10.3.6 **Share activity with no effect on the financial statements**

We have already observed that the sale of shares between investors external to the company will have no effect on the company's financial statements, as the company itself is not a party to the transaction. There are other events involving a company's shares which have no financial reporting effect. We think it will be valuable for you to know a little about the most common ones, so we will cover them briefly.

- *Delisting.* This describes the removal of a company's shares from the stock exchange on which they have been listed. It does not mean that the shares are cancelled, or that they can no longer be traded. Instead, it simply means that they cannot be traded with the ease they once were. There is no effect on the financial reporting of the business for much the same reason that there would be no effect were a business to remove an item of inventory from its online store and place it on a shelf in its shop.

- *Share splits*. If a company is very successful, its share price might get so high that smaller investors cannot afford to buy many of its shares. In such a case, the company might choose to split its shares, so that each share currently in issue is replaced with a greater number of shares. For example, in 2014, Apple Inc had a 7 : 1 share split, to drop its price from over $600 to under $100.[4] Unlike a bonus issue, a share split is not in lieu of cash dividends, and so there is no transfer from the retained earnings account. In a share split, if the shares had a par value before the split, then their par value is also divided according to the split. Thus, even the share capital and share premium accounts remain just the same as before the split.

- *Share consolidations*, or *reverse share splits*. These describe the much rarer opposite of the share split, in which existing shareholders' shares are replaced by fewer shares. For example, a shareholder who owned 400 shares before a 4 : 1 consolidation would own just 100 shares afterwards. The market share price should adjust proportionally, which explains the usual purpose of these events: to raise the price to meet either the stock exchange's regulations or investor's preferences. There is no financial reporting effect for the same reasons as for share splits.

> **MISCONCEPTION**
>
> A two-for-one share split will double the value of the company.
>
> Wrong. Whatever a company does with its shares, the value of the business will only increase if the transaction leads to the business obtaining something of value, usually cash. At best, a share split simply makes the company's shares more marketable. (See Chapter 12 for more on the value of a business.)

10.4 NON-DISTRIBUTABLE RESERVES

The term 'reserve', which is used in the equity section of many businesses' statements of financial position and in their statements of changes in equity, has the potential to be confusing. In a non-accounting sense, a reserve is usually a sum of money (or other resources) that has been set aside for some future purpose. However, accountants use the term to describe the equity accounts on the statement of financial position (or the columns in the statement of changes in equity) other than share capital.

Examples we have covered earlier in the book are the cash flow hedging reserve (section 6.7.3), foreign currency translation reserve (section 8.2.3), and share-based payments reserve (section 10.3.4). Note, however, that not all reserves are strictly labelled as such. For example, retained earnings is often the largest reserve on a business's statement of financial position, yet—although it is called by several other names, including 'accumulated profit' and 'retained profit'—its name rarely, if ever, includes the word 'reserve'.

You may come across the terms 'distributable reserve' and 'non-distributable reserve'. Retained earnings is a classic example of a distributable reserve because it is typically the reserve out of which distributions are made to owners. (In other words, dividends are subtracted from retained earnings.) On the other hand, non-distributable reserves contain those portions of the business's reserves which are not available for distribution, according to either company policy or regulatory requirements.

Some businesses report a reserve simply labelled 'Non-distributable reserve', whereas others give their non-distributable reserves more specific names, such as 'Net unrealised gains reserve' or 'Capital reserve'. Indeed, Burberry's 2019 balance sheet reported a capital reserve of £41.1 million. Note 23 explains that this reserve arose due to the 'statutory requirements of subsidiaries' (in other words, reserves in subsidiary companies which are not legally distributable) and the capital redemption reserve. The capital redemption reserve is a requirement of UK law, preventing the par value of shares reacquired via a buyback from being distributed as dividends to shareholders.

> Non-distributable reserves contain the portion of a business's reserves that may not be distributed to owners, to comply with either company policy or regulatory requirements.

10.5 RESTATEMENT OF EQUITY BALANCES

Sometimes, you will see the word 'restated' in the financial statements. This is either because the business has changed an accounting policy, or it has had to correct a material error.

10.5.1 Accounting policy changes

From time to time, businesses change their accounting policies. They do this either because a new accounting standard requires the change, or because the standards offer a choice of accounting policies and switching to a different policy would provide more useful information to users of the financial statements. Examples of accounting policy choices include choices between:

- the cost model and the revaluation model for PPE (section 6.2.2);
- the cost model and the fair value model for investment properties (section 6.3);
- cost formulas for inventory, like 'first-in, first-out' (FIFO) or weighted average cost (section 6.5.2).

The effects of changes in accounting policies on the reported figures can be dramatic. This can be somewhat disconcerting for first-time users of the financial statements, and quite disruptive for users who follow a business's financial reporting from year to year. We shall therefore now take you through a comprehensive example of an accounting policy change, so that you understand their effects precisely.

Suppose that a business decides that measuring its investment property at fair value would result in more relevant information than measuring it at cost, as it has been doing since

10

incorporation. As is typical, the fair value of the property has steadily risen, or 'appreciated', since the business acquired it ten years ago. At first glance, this may seem quite straightforward: at the end of the current year, the business would change the measurement model from cost to fair value, and recognise the resulting gain in profit or loss. However, consider the size of this effect: by now, the fair value of the property far exceeds the cost. Also, bear in mind that the cost model involves a depreciation charge, so the carrying amount on the cost model would be even lower than the cost. This year's profit would include a huge gain, the likes of which has never been reported in prior years, and is unlikely ever to be reported again.

This threatens at least two important characteristics that financial information should have if it is to be useful: faithful representation and comparability. By reporting the effects of many years as if they had happened in a single year, the current year's financial statements are not faithfully representative of the current year's events; nor are they comparable with past and future years. To eliminate these threats, accountants apply 'retrospective restatement', which means they adjust the financial results of previous years as if the new policy had always applied. Thus, only the current year's effects are reported in the current year, and there is a reliable basis for comparison with previous years.

Of course, accountants cannot travel back in time and change the content of the financial statements that were published in previous years. However, what they can do is change the prior year figures next to the current year's results published in this year's annual report.

To demonstrate, let us put some numbers to the scenario we have been imagining. Suppose that the business's sole investment property was acquired ten years ago at a cost of €110 000. Since then, it has been measured using the cost model, and depreciated by €5 000 per year. If the cost model were again applied in Year 10, the property would be reported at an amount of €60 000 (€110 000 − 10 × €5 000). However, the fair value of this property is now €200 000, and the business has decided that this is the more relevant measurement.

Now, the business's accountants cannot just recognise a €140 000 (€200 000 − €60 000) fair value gain in Year 10. Instead, they must prepare Year 10's financial statements, and, alongside them, Year 9 financial statements too, as if the new policy had always been in place. To do so, they must determine the fair value of the property at the end of Years 8 and 9. Suppose that these are €150 000 and €170 000, respectively.

To recap, all of the information relating to the investment property is as follows in Example 10.1.

EXAMPLE 10.1

	Year 8 €	Year 9 €	Year 10 €
Carrying amount on cost model (old policy)	70 000	65 000	60 000
Fair value (carrying amount on new policy)	150 000	170 000	200 000

Using this information, it is relatively easy to work out what information should appear in the statements of financial position and statements of comprehensive income in the Year 10 annual report. Alongside the carrying amount of €200 000 for Year 10, the statement of financial position should report a carrying amount of €170 000 for Year 9. And the

Accounting policy changes necessitate a process of retrospective restatement, in order to ensure faithful representation and comparability.

statement of comprehensive income should report a fair value gain in Year 10 of €30 000 (€200 000 – €170 000) and in Year 9 of €20 000 (€170 000 – €150 000). Example 10.2 shows how the investment property will be reported in these two financial statements.

EXAMPLE 10.2

Statement of financial position	Year 10	Year 9 (restated)
Investment property	€200 000	€170 000

Statement of comprehensive income	Year 10	Year 9 (restated)
Profit or loss section:		
Fair value gains on investment property	€30 000	€20 000

The statement of changes in equity in Year 10's annual report will report the fair value gains as changes in retained earnings for Years 9 and 10. So far so good, but there is still work to be done by the business's accountants: the opening balance of retained earnings will also need to be different on the new policy than was previously reported.

To determine the size of this effect, look again at Example 10.1, focusing on the difference between the carrying amounts in Year 8. Had the business applied the new policy in Year 8, the carrying amount of the investment property would have been higher by €80 000. This also means that profits over Years 1–8 would have been higher by €80 000 on the new policy. This is the sum of the €40 000 (€150 000 – €110 000) cumulative fair value gains that would have been recognised in profit or loss on the new policy, and the €40 000 (€5 000 × 8 years) total depreciation expense that was in fact expensed in profit or loss on the old policy. And this means that the opening balance of retained earnings in Year 9 would have been €80 000 higher.

Thus, Example 10.3 shows how the investment property would affect the statement of changes in equity presented in the Year 10 annual report. To set the record straight, IAS 8 requires that the Year 9 information begins with the retained earnings opening balance as it was previously reported, and then reveals to users the effect of the policy change adjustment. As we don't know what the totals would have been, given how they are influenced by so many different events, we have marked them with 'xxx'.

EXAMPLE 10.3

Statement of changes in equity	Retained earnings €
Year 9 opening balance, as previously reported	xxx
Effect of accounting policy change	+ 80 000
Year 9 restated opening balance	xxx
Profit for Year 9 [showing only the amount relating to the investment property]	20 000
Year 10 opening balance	xxx
Profit for Year 10 [showing only the amount relating to the investment property]	30 000
Year 10 closing balance	xxx

10

Note that, unlike the statement of changes in equity, the statements of financial position and comprehensive income do not show any differences caused by the restatement, and instead simply report the figures according to the new policy. On the face of these statements, the only acknowledgement that the prior year figures are different from those which were previously published is the word 'restated' added to the headings of those columns. The notes to the financial statements, however, do provide more detail, including the reason for the restatement, and the relevant amounts.

10.5.2 Material errors

There is only one other instance in which accountants restate previously reported balances: and that is when a material error is discovered in past financial statements. This must be corrected, and the process to do so is very similar to what we've described for changes in accounting policies, along with substantial note disclosure to explain the error.

It is worth observing that, as explained in section 6.2.2, changes in accounting estimates do not result in retrospective restatement. There are many instances when accountants are required to make estimates: the balance of trade receivables that will be uncollectible; the amount of inventory that will become obsolete; the fair values of various assets and liabilities; the assumptions underlying depreciation calculations; the cost of repairing goods sold under warranty; and so on and so forth.

You might imagine that, when a business discovers that it made these estimates incorrectly, these would be treated as errors. But consider how many estimates are made, and also the inevitable truth that by some degree these will be wrong most—if not all—of the time. It is impractical to retrospectively restate financial statements for faulty estimates: instead, the resulting adjustments are applied *prospectively*, which is to say that they do not affect financial statements for previous years. They are taken into account in the current year, and—to the extent that they affect coming years—in future years' financial statements too. IFRS requires information about substantial changes in estimates to be provided in the notes to the financial statements.

If you are wondering what distinguishes an error from an incorrect estimate, IAS 8 states that 'errors include the effects of mathematical mistakes, mistakes in applying accounting policies, oversights or misinterpretations of facts, and fraud'.[5] These errors are 'material' if they might have influenced the decision of a user of the financial statements. In many cases, the IAS 8 description of errors helps accountants distinguish neatly between corrections of errors and changes in estimates; in more ambiguous cases, they once again need to apply their judgement.

10.5.3 Burberry's restated equity

The reporting of errors by a listed company is very rare, and so it is no surprise that Burberry's 2019 financial statements contain no such disclosure. (For an example of a material error, see section 13.2.2, which describes how Tesco had to restate its 2014 financial statements because of 'upfronting'.) Burberry does, however, report an accounting

Only changes in accounting policies and material errors result in retrospective restatement of financial information.

10

policy change, as a result of the group's adoption in its 2019 financial year of IFRS 9, the accounting standard about financial instruments. Because of a special dispensation in that standard, this policy change has not quite been reported in the way described in section 10.5.1. While accounting policy changes usually ought to be applied to the prior year, IFRS 9 gave businesses permission to apply the standard only to the year in which they adopted it, and not to prior years.

Of course, the opening retained earnings balance for the 2019 year did have to be restated, and so the effect of the accounting policy change is shown not at the very top of that column in the statement of changes in equity, where you would expect, but halfway down, in the line 'adjustment on initial application of IFRS 9'. The effect is so small—a mere £200 000—that no one could reasonably be concerned about the problems of faithful representation and comparability which can arise without the usual retrospective restatement of the prior year.

CONCLUSION

Although total equity is a poor measure of a business's worth, the information about equity in the statement of financial position, and even more so in the statement of changes in equity, is useful in a variety of ways. As is so often the case in financial reporting, the devil is in the detail!

For one thing, the statement of changes in equity enables us to track the movement of items of profit or loss and OCI from the statement of comprehensive income to the statement of financial position. For another, it provides a detailed understanding of the effects of all of the business's transactions with owners during the financial year, including the value of share options issued this year. A detailed inspection of a business's equity also reveals which reserves are available for distribution to owners, and which are not. Finally, when businesses change their accounting policies, the statement of changes in equity shows how dramatic the effect of the new policy has been.

Thus, financial reporting about equity is not very different from financial reporting about assets, liabilities, income, and expense: each item of information is just one more piece in a gigantic puzzle. While some pieces may be bigger than others, you would not want to build a puzzle while missing even one piece! However, if you are now eager to begin to learn how to put it all together, and allow the bigger picture to emerge—to *use* the financial statements in order to produce an overall evaluation of the business—then you have come to precisely the right point in this book. Chapter 11, on financial analysis, and Chapter 12, on valuations, aim to do precisely that.

SUMMARY OF KEY POINTS

■ There are three reasons that equity is a poor measure of a business's value: assets are not at fair value; some identifiable assets and liabilities are not included in net asset value; and a range of other items of value—collectively known as goodwill—are also not generally included, such as the quality of staff, the business's reputation, and its future prospects.

■ The statement of changes in equity reports the movements in the accounts that appear in the equity section of the statement of financial position, represented in columns.

■ Each row on the statement of changes in equity represents a movement in an equity account, split into two sections: those which affect TCI (and which are also reported on the statement of comprehensive income); and those which result from transactions with owners.

■ Transactions with owners include share issues, share buybacks, dividends, share options, rights issues, bonus issues, and conversions of debt instruments. Each of these is reported directly in the relevant equity account on the statement of financial position. Notably, the granting of share options also causes an expense to be reported in profit or loss.

■ Some share activity has no effect on the financial statements, for example: trading of shares between investors external to the company; delisting; share splits; and share consolidations.

■ The term 'reserve' describes the equity accounts other than share capital. Some reserves are labelled 'Non-distributable', indicating that—either by law or company policy—amounts in them may not be distributed to owners.

■ When a business changes its accounting policy, relevant amounts in the financial statements for prior years are retrospectively restated to enhance comparability, and to ensure that the current year's reporting faithfully represents events. In the statement of changes in equity, the effect of the policy change on the prior year's opening equity balances is shown.

■ A material error in past financial statements also results in retrospective restatement, in addition to full disclosure of the details of the error. Errors are mistakes, misinterpretations, or misrepresentations, and should not be confused with incorrect accounting estimates.

■ Incorrect accounting estimates result in prospective adjustment. That is, they are taken into account in the current year, and—to any relevant extent—in future years' financial statements.

CHAPTER QUESTIONS

The applied questions (marked 'AQ') and the discussion questions (marked 'DQ') relate to the financial statements of Daimler, contained in Appendix II. The suggested solutions to these questions, and also to the concept questions (marked 'CQ'), can be found in Appendix III.

 Also, don't forget the **online resources** available at www.oup.com/he/winfield-graham-miller1e, which contain multiple-choice questions based on the material in this chapter, in addition to many other helpful resources, including two mini case studies, and accompanying questions and answers.

CONCEPT QUESTIONS

CQ 10.1   Briefly explain what is meant by the accounting term 'equity'.

CQ 10.2   Describe the reasons why a business's equity, despite being called the 'book value' or 'accounting value', is a poor measure of its true value.

CQ 10.3   Describe in general terms what the statement of changes in equity helps us to understand about the business.

CQ 10.4   Briefly describe the layout and logic of the statement of changes in equity.

CQ 10.5   Contrast the way in which changes in accounting policies and changes in accounting estimates are represented in the financial statements.

APPLIED QUESTIONS

AQ 10.6   What was Daimler's total equity on 31 December 2019? What portion of this equity was attributable to the shareholders of Daimler and what portion was attributable to NCI, the other shareholders of Daimler's subsidiaries who are outside the group?

AQ 10.7   What are the individual components of Daimler's equity on 31 December 2019, and how have these components been reported in Daimler's statement of changes in equity?

AQ 10.8   Why is there no share premium account reported in the equity section of Daimler's consolidated statement of financial position?

AQ 10.9   By referring to the statement of changes in equity, explain whether the Daimler group issued any shares to its shareholders during its 2019 financial year.

AQ 10.10   Did Daimler report a share-based payment expense during 2019? If so, how much was it?

AQ 10.11   By referring to Daimler's statement of changes in equity, explain the three major reasons for the movement in the retained earnings balance during the 2019 year.

AQ 10.12   What amount of dividends was paid in 2019 by Daimler's consolidated, partially owned subsidiaries to the NCI of these subsidiaries?

AQ 10.13   Identify the heading of the column in Daimler's statement of changes in equity that shows changes in Daimler's foreign currency translation reserve (FCTR), and describe what effect the translation of foreign operations had on the equity attributable to shareholders of Daimler in 2019.

DISCUSSION QUESTIONS

DQ 10.14   Note 20 (p 270) of the consolidated financial statements reports that Daimler had 1 070 million shares in issue on 31 December 2019, when the share price (available at https://www.daimler.com) was €49.37. Using these figures, calculate the market value of the group (known as market capitalisation) on 31 December 2019, and contrast this value with Daimler's book value on that date. (Hint: if you're stuck, have look at section 12.1.2.)

DQ 10.15   Can Daimler's Board of Management issue new shares?

DQ 10.16   Discuss whether there is any evidence that Daimler changed accounting policies during the 2019 financial year. If there is any such evidence, briefly outline the nature of the changes.

DQ 10.17   Discuss whether there is any evidence that Daimler executed any share buybacks during the 2019 financial year. If there is any such evidence, briefly describe what happened to the shares that were bought back.

DQ 10.18   Dividends totalling €3 477 million were reported in the retained earnings column of the 2019 statement of changes in equity. The same figure is reported as

10

'Dividends paid to shareholders of Daimler AG' in the investing activities section of the 2019 statement of cash flows. Explain whether this dividend is for the 2019 year.

DQ 10.19 If €963 million will be paid as a dividend for the year ended 31 December 2019, why is this amount not reported as a liability in Daimler's consolidated statement of financial position?

DQ 10.20 Why did Daimler reduce the dividend from €3.25 per share in 2018 to €0.90 per share in 2019 (see note 20, p 271)?

INVESTIGATION QUESTIONS

IQ 10.21 Download the financial statements of two businesses listed in your country which compete with one another in the same industry or sector. Compare and contrast the major items of equity shown on their respective statements of changes in equity.

IQ 10.22 Investigate how legal requirements relating to share issues within your jurisdiction have affected how share issues are reported on the face of the statement of financial position. Pay particular attention to the names of the capital account(s); whether shares have par values; and regulation relating to share buybacks.

IQ 10.23 Identify a company listed in your country whose financial statements were reportedly affected by a change in accounting policy. Download the business's financial statements and establish for yourself how significant the change was. Evaluate whether the accounting policy appeared to make the financial statements more relevant and more faithfully representative of economic reality.

REFERENCES

[1] IASB 2018. *Conceptual Framework for Financial Reporting.* Section 4.2.

[2] IASB 2018. *Conceptual Framework for Financial Reporting.* Section 6.88.

[3] Burberry Group, plc 2003. *Annual Report and Accounts 2002/03.* Available at: https://www.zonebourse.com/BURBERRY-GROUP-PLC-4003938/pdf/8226/Burberry.

[4] For an account of Apple's 2014 share split (called a 'stock split' in the US), and some investor reactions, see: https://money.cnn.com/2014/06/09/investing/apple-stock-split-reactions.

[5] IASB 2008. *IAS 8: Accounting Policies, Changes in Accounting Estimates and Errors.* Section 5.

FINANCIAL ANALYSIS

In Chapter 1, we identified the distinguishing objective of a business: to grow the own-ers' wealth by creating business value. We observed that in order to achieve this objec-tive, the management team needs to optimise the financing, investing, and operating activities of the business. In the chapters since, we have gradually revealed how the effects of all of these decisions are reported in the financial statements.

The aim of **financial analysis** is to examine the financial statements to see whether value has indeed been created, and, most importantly, to determine whether this will continue.

People who do financial analysis are not typically historians, interested in the past for its own sake. Instead, they study a business's past financial record in order to come to an opinion about its future. If the analyst is a manager in the business, for example, this opinion will then inform the decisions they will make to improve the business's future performance.

Many other analysts are external to the business. For example, an investor, or a fi-nancial analyst at an investment firm, analyses companies in order to decide whether to buy their shares, or to maintain their existing investments. Creditors of the business, such as major suppliers and banks, would use financial analysis to evaluate the busi-ness's **credit risk**. Similarly, prudent employees might analyse their employer's business

CHAPTER 11

The aim of financial analysis is to examine the financial statements to form an opinion about the value that it has created, and to determine its prospects for doing so in the future.

to determine their job stability; and unions might do the same in order to inform their negotiations with management.

Whilst the particular methods of financial analysis used by different analysts vary, the general approach is common to all. Broadly speaking, there are three stages, as follows:

1. learning about the business's operating context by reading the financial statements;
2. understanding the main story of the financial statements;
3. ratio analysis, to provide greater depth to the analysis.

The three stages of financial analysis are: reading the financial statements; understanding the story; and ratio analysis.

When they first learn about financial analysis, people often make the mistake of thinking of it as an exercise in pure maths. They jump straight to the calculation of ratios, without first engaging with every relevant piece of available information, to form a broad understanding of the business's context. Before even beginning the first step here, a good analyst therefore sets out to absorb the wealth of useful information reported in the **management commentary** sections of the annual report, other company releases, and the financial press.

A very important contextual consideration is the economic conditions that pertained during the year under analysis. For example, any analysis of financial years affected by Covid-19 should, of course, take the economic impact of the virus into account. It would not be appropriate to expect Burberry's 2020 year to keep pace with its 2019 year, given how significantly all bricks-and-mortar retailers were affected by lockdowns and other social distancing measures in 2020.

As the real-world financial statements included in this book cover periods before the Covid-19 crisis, you will not see its effects in them, but by the time you are reading this, financial statements that have been affected will be available. When looking at them, keep an eye out for the sorts of items that are likely to have arisen from the crisis: depressed revenues, asset impairments, revised judgements and estimates, and possibly onerous contracts.

This book has already taken you through the first stage of analysis. Not only have you learned how to read financial statements in general, but you have also had the opportunity to do this with two real-life businesses—Burberry and Daimler—acquiring knowledge of their broader context along the way. In this chapter, you will learn to perform the second and third stages of financial analysis. Again, we will use Burberry as the main in-chapter example, and at the end of the chapter you will have an opportunity to practise for yourself using Daimler.

11

11.1 KEY CONCEPTS IN ANALYSIS

First, we shall introduce two important concepts that underpin financial analysis.

11.1.1 Risk versus return

Of course, no one knows what will happen in the future. Financial analysis is an exercise in using information about events that have already happened to work out the best guess about events to come. But it is also important to establish how likely that guess is to be wrong. In other words, the uncertainty of the future requires an analyst to form an opinion not only about the likely performance of the business, but also about the risks which might threaten that performance.

In section 1.3.2, the example of Mr Cautious and Ms Risky demonstrated how increasing the level of debt in a business's capital structure improves the chance of generating higher returns, but also makes the business inherently riskier. This is but one of many cases where a decision that increases the probability of higher returns also exposes the business to a higher degree of risk.

From an investor's point of view, this alignment of expected return and risk makes perfect sense: the only justification for taking on higher risk is the potential for a higher return. The investor's maxim, 'High risk, high return' describes one kind of available **risk–return profile**, but a market also offers many 'low risk, low return' and 'medium risk, medium return' investment opportunities. The yield on government debt is lower than the rental rates on top-rated commercial property, which are lower than the expected return from the shares of a multinational company, which is lower than what an entrepreneur hopes to make from a start-up. This is precisely because each investment comes with an increasing degree of risk.

The aim of most investors is to find opportunities that have the right kind of risk–return profile, but where the risk is a little lower, and/or the expected return a little higher, than similar investments. When analysing a business, it is therefore imperative always to consider both expected return and risk.

> A business's risk-return profile is the combination of two things: the amount of value the business can be expected to create in future (the return); and the likelihood of that happening (the risk).

11.1.2 Benchmarks

Later in this chapter you will learn about the debt–equity ratio, which tells an analyst, well, what it sounds like: the ratio of a business's debt to its equity. Suppose that during your financial analysis of a business you calculate that it has a debt–equity ratio of 2.0. On the face of it, this means that the business employs twice as much debt funding as equity funding. But how should this fact influence your opinion about the business? Is this a 'good' capital structure? Is it risky? Or perhaps the better question is this one: is the business striking the right balance between leveraging returns for shareholders effectively, and exposing them to too much risk?

On its own, any figure that emerges from the financial statements is very difficult to judge. For example, just take Burberry's 2019 profit of £339.1 million. That certainly sounds like a lot of money to an individual, but, for a massive global retail corporation, does it indicate a disappointing performance, or an adequate one? Or was 2019 a fantastic year for Burberry?

We cannot answer any of these questions without drawing comparisons. Even seasoned analysts, who might *feel* they are able to make a judgement without doing so, are in fact relying on the bases for comparison they have built up through their experience.

When financial information is used for comparisons, it is called a '**benchmark**'. Three typical benchmarks are:

- prior year information about the business under analysis;
- comparable information about direct competitors;
- average information for the business's industry or sector.

As we demonstrate financial analysis in this chapter using Burberry's 2019 financial year as an example, we shall refer to two of these kinds of benchmarks: Burberry's prior year and the comparable year of its direct competitor, Prada, a group of companies headquartered in Italy. The similarity of these two businesses can be seen in Table 11.1.

TABLE 11.1 Key features of Burberry and Prada, indicating that Prada is a suitable benchmark for Burberry

	Burberry	Prada
Sector	Luxury apparel and accessories	Luxury apparel and accessories
Employees	More than 10 000	More than 13 000
Directly operated stores	431	634
Countries	33	70
Revenue	£2.7 billion	€3.1 billion
Year-end	End of March	31 December

Source: Burberry plc 2019. *2018/19 Annual Report.* Available at: https://www.burberryplc.com/content/dam/burberry/corporate/oar/documents/Burberry_201819-Annual-Report.pdf; Prada SpA 2018. *Annual Report 2018.* Available at: https://www.pradagroup.com/content/dam/pradagroup/documents/Shareholderinformation/2019/inglese/e-Annual%20Report%202018.pdf.

Of course, there are differences between these two groups—most of Prada's apparel is footwear; accessories constitute a much higher proportion of its products; and it has more employees and stores, operating in more countries—but no two businesses are exactly the same. There is certainly enough overlap in terms of brands and size that they compete closely in many markets, and so serve as good benchmarks for each other.

Prada is listed on the Hong Kong Stock Exchange, and hence reports according to the International Financial Reporting Standards (IFRS), so the financial statements of the two groups are comparable. Because Prada's year-end is 31 December, we shall contrast Burberry's 2019 financial statements (dated 30 March 2019) with Prada's 2018 financial statements, in the knowledge that these financial years are comparable, as they have nine months in common.

11.2 UNDERSTANDING THE MAIN STORY OF THE FINANCIAL STATEMENTS

11

At heart, financial statements tell a story about the business.

Once analysts have become familiar with the main content of the financial statements, as you have done for Burberry's 2019 year if you have worked through all or most of the preceding chapters, they move to the second stage. In aiming to provide decision-useful information, financial statements provide an enormous amount of valuable data, but at heart they tell a fairly simple story about the business. In the second stage, analysts must make sure that they understand this story.

11.2.1 **The plot summary**

There is, of course, a wide variety of ways to tell the stories of successful business, but essentially they all follow the same plot. Here is a summary of that plot:

1. The business uses its funding to invest in some assets.
2. The assets produce revenue.
3. From that revenue, the business earns profit.
4. The profit is converted into operating cash flows.
5. The operating cash flows combines with other cash flow activities in some way.
6. This combination of cash flows influences how the assets are funded.

Like a show with three characters, the story is told by the statement of financial position, income statement (or profit or loss section of the statement of comprehensive income), and statement of cash flows, all working together. Thus, in the second stage of analysis, to understand the story, we ask six questions of these three financial statements, as depicted in the next illustration you will encounter, Figure 11.1.

To demonstrate this second stage of analysis, we will now ask each of these questions of Burberry's 2019 financial year.

11.2.2 **What sorts of assets has the business invested in?**

The four biggest assets on Burberry's statement of financial position are typical of a retailer. **Property, plant & equipment (PPE)** provides the infrastructure it needs to be able to distribute and sell large stocks of **inventory**. Trade **receivables** are the result of selling much of that inventory on credit, which, together with the cash sales, brings in flows of **cash**.

Like any investment, each of these assets has its own risk–return profile. The one with the lowest risk and lowest expected return is trade receivables, which typically returns no more cash than its carrying amount, followed closely by cash, which—at least while it remains cash in a bank account—earns a very low interest rate. Inventory, especially high-priced luxury goods of the type marketed by Burberry, offers a much higher relative return (the difference between its cost and its selling price) for a higher risk (the risk that it goes unsold). The PPE has the potential to produce a high return in the form of the sales that it enables, and it also carries a higher risk that this return is lower than expected.

It is surprising that cash and cash equivalents is by far the largest asset. Of course, a retailer needs cash on hand in order to continually replenish inventory, pay bills, and provide change to customers, but in 2019, Burberry's cash reserves were worth more than double the next largest asset! Given that Burberry's shareholders have chosen to invest in equity, it is safe to say that they expect their investment to have a relatively high

The analyst identifies the largest assets, and investigates any that seem surprising.

11

FIGURE 11.1 Six key questions to ask of the financial statements in order to understand their main story

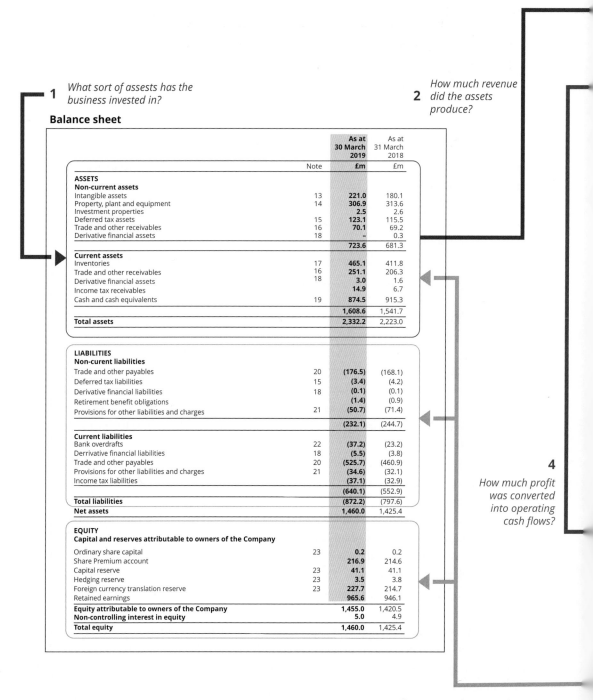

1 *What sort of assets has the business invested in?*

2 *How much revenue did the assets produce?*

Balance sheet

	Note	As at 30 March 2019 £m	As at 31 March 2018 £m
ASSETS			
Non-current assets			
Intangible assets	13	221.0	180.1
Property, plant and equipment	14	306.9	313.6
Investment properties		2.5	2.6
Deferred tax assets	15	123.1	115.5
Trade and other receivables	16	70.1	69.2
Derivative financial assets	18	–	0.3
		723.6	681.3
Current assets			
Inventories	17	465.1	411.8
Trade and other receivables	16	251.1	206.3
Derivative financial assets	18	3.0	1.6
Income tax receivables		14.9	6.7
Cash and cash equivalents	19	874.5	915.3
		1,608.6	1,541.7
Total assets		2,332.2	2,223.0
LIABILITIES			
Non-curent liabilities			
Trade and other payables	20	(176.5)	(168.1)
Deferred tax liabilities	15	(3.4)	(4.2)
Derivative financial liabilities	18	(0.1)	(0.1)
Retirement benefit obligations		(1.4)	(0.9)
Provisions for other liabilities and charges	21	(50.7)	(71.4)
		(232.1)	(244.7)
Current liabilities			
Bank overdrafts	22	(37.2)	(23.2)
Derrivative financial liabilities	18	(5.5)	(3.8)
Trade and other payables	20	(525.7)	(460.9)
Provisions for other liabilities and charges	21	(34.6)	(32.1)
Income tax liabilities		(37.1)	(32.9)
		(640.1)	(552.9)
Total liabilities		(872.2)	(797.6)
Net assets		1,460.0	1,425.4
EQUITY			
Capital and reserves attributable to owners of the Company			
Ordinary share capital	23	0.2	0.2
Share Premium account		216.9	214.6
Capital reserve	23	41.1	41.1
Hedging reserve	23	3.5	3.8
Foreign currency translation reserve	23	227.7	214.7
Retained earnings		965.6	946.1
Equity attributable to owners of the Company		1,455.0	1,420.5
Non-controlling interest in equity		5.0	4.9
Total equity		1,460.0	1,425.4

4 *How much profit was converted into operating cash flows?*

6 *How are the assets funded?*

Income statement

	Note	52 weeks to 30 March 2019 £m	Years to 31 March 2018 £m
Revenue	3	2,720.0	2,732.8
Cost of sales		(859.4)	(835.4)
Gross profit		1,860.8	1,897.4
Net operating expenses	4	(1,423.6)	(1,487.1)
Operating profit		437.2	410.3
Financing			
Finance income		8.7	7.8
Finance expense		(3.6)	(3.5)
Other financing charge		(1.7)	(2.0)
Net finance income	9	3.4	2.3
Profit before taxation	5	440.6	412.6
Taxation	10	(101.5)	(119.0)
Profit for the year		339.1	293.6
Attributable to:			
Owners of the Company		339.3	293.5
Non-controlling interest		(0.2)	0.1
Profit for the year		339.1	293.6
Earnings per share			
Basic	11	82.3p	68.9p
Diluted	11	81.7p	68.4p
Reconciliation of adjusted profit before taxation:		£m	£m
Profit before taxation		440.6	412.6
Adjusting items:			
Adjusting operating items:	5	0.9	56.3
Adjusting financing items:	5	1.7	2.0
Adjusted profit before taxation-non-GAAP measure		443.2	470.9
Adjusted earnings per share-non-GAAP measure			
Basic	11	82.7p	82.8p
Diluted	11	82.1p	82.1p
Dividends per share			
Interim	12	11.0p	11.0p
Proposed final (not recognised as a liability at 30 March/31 March)	12	31.5p	30.3p

How much profit was earned from the revenue? **3**

Statement of cash flows

	Note	52 weeks to 30 March 2019 £m	Years to 31 March 2018 £m
Cash flows from operating activities			
Operating profit		437.2	410.3
Depreciation	14	87.2	105.8
Amortisation	13	28.6	25.5
Net impairment of intangible assets	13	3.9	6.5
Net impairment of property, plant and equipment	14	7.9	10.7
Loss on disposal of property, plant and equipment and intangible assets		1.2	2.7
Gain on disposal of Beauty operations	6	(6.9)	(5.2)
Gain on derivative instruments		(2.4)	(3.5)
Charge in respect of employee share incentive schemes		15.7	17.1
Receipt from settlement of equity swap contracts		2.5	0.5
(Increase) / decrease in inventories		(59.3)	37.2
(Increase) / decrease in receivables		(54.6)	68.1
Increase in payables and provisions		54.9	115.5
Cash generated from operating activities		515.9	791.2
Interest received		8.1	7.2
Interest paid		(1.8)	(1.6)
Taxation paid		(110.8)	(118.4)
Net cash generated from operating activities		411.4	678.4
Cash flows from investing activities			
Purchase of property, plant and equipment		(62.6)	(57.5)
Purchase of intangible assets		(48.0)	(48.5)
Proceeds from disposal of Beauty operations, net of cash costs paid	6	0.6	61.1
Acquisition of subsidiary	28	(14.5)	–
Net cash outflow from investing activities		(124.5)	(44.9)
Cash flows from financing activities			
Dividends paid in the year	12	(171.1)	(169.4)
Payment to non-controlling interest	20	(11.1)	(3.0)
Issue of ordinary share capital		2.3	3.2
Purchase of own shares through share buy-back	23	(150.7)	(355.0)
Purchase of own shares by ESOP trusts		(12.8)	(11.9)
Net cash outflow from financing activities		(343.4)	(536.1)
Net (decrease) / increase in cash and cash equivalents		(56.5)	97.4
Effect of exchange rate changes		1.7	(14.5)
Cash and cash equivalents at beginning of year		892.1	809.2
Cash and cash equivalents at end of year		837.3	892.1

How did operating cash flows combine with other cash flow activities? **5**

11

risk–reward profile. Instead of holding more than a third of the asset base as cash and cash equivalents, many analysts might have thought that the business should really have been purchasing assets with more productive potential, or paying out the cash to shareholders through larger **dividends** or **share buybacks**. (See section 5.4.4 for a detailed discussion of how efficient **working capital** management generally involves keeping cash balances as low as possible.)

However, in the years leading up to 2019, stockpiling cash reserves was a trend among global businesses. The reasons include: to insure against a negative economic outlook; to have immediate access to funds with which to act quickly if a lucrative business acquisition opportunity emerges; and to avoid paying taxes when repatriating money earned by foreign subsidiaries.[1] The two most famous examples of this trend made news midway through 2019 when Alphabet Inc, the parent company of Google, overtook Apple Inc as the world's most cash-rich company: at the time, Alphabet had amassed $117 billion of cash reserves, compared to Apple's mere $102 billion![2]

Of course, with the benefit of hindsight, the strategy of building up cash reserves now seems to be prophetically wise in light of the Covid-19 pandemic that hit the world in 2020, putting intense strain on the cash flows of almost every business.

It is also important for an analyst to consider whether any significant assets might be missing from the statement. Recall that in section 6.4.6 we identified a weakness of financial reporting in the contemporary economy: many businesses' most valuable assets are intangible assets, which do not satisfy IFRS's criteria for recognition on the statement of financial position, and do not even appear in the notes. Most often, the problem is one of measurability, for there seems to be no reliable, objectively verifiable way to estimate the value of intangible assets such as internally generated brands. When it is impossible to reach consensus on even a rough estimate of what the brand is worth, then IFRS's **prudent** solution is not to mention it at all.

This, however, does not mean that analysts should also ignore the asset's existence. Instead, it is imperative that they do the research to work out what value they believe should be ascribed to the intangible assets of the business, and factor this into their analysis. For example, in section 6.4.5 we observed that Burberry's brand may well be worth more than the total of its recognised assets. A good analyst will therefore take account of this brand value, even while the financial statements themselves do not. The higher this value, the more significantly it will affect their opinion about the future potential of the business, but equally, the higher the risk associated with an incorrect estimate.

One source of information about missing assets is the **integrated report**, which recognises intellectual capital like brands as one of the six capitals in a business. We will discuss the integrated report in section 14.2.2.

Finally, an analyst should establish if any major business units were acquired or sold, which may of course have a significant impact on what sorts of assets the group has.

The analyst considers whether any significant assets might be missing from the statement of financial position.

11

The analyst establishes whether any major business units have been bought or sold, and any implications for the composition of assets.

As we discussed in section 5.5, Burberry made a relatively modest acquisition in 2019—the manufacturer of leather products called Burberry Manifattura—having made a much more significant disposal near the beginning of its 2018 year, when it sold its Beauty operation along with the related licensing rights to Coty for more than £60 million. That disposal virtually eliminated an entire product division of fragrance and beauty products. Although it had been Burberry's smallest product division, it was nevertheless sizeable enough for its absence to make a difference to any analysis of the business, as you will see as we progress through this chapter.

11.2.3 How much revenue did the assets produce?

Despite a modest growth in Burberry's asset base, the group's 2019 revenues of £2.7 billion were no higher than in 2018: in fact, as we established in section 4.3.8, they declined by 0.5%. Market conditions were not to blame: as Burberry's management admits, 'the luxury market grew by 5%' during the year.[3] Moreover, Prada managed to increase revenues by 14.6%, while its assets decreased slightly.

The real explanation for the flatlining of revenue is probably in the group's internal strategy. In its 2018/19 Annual Report, Burberry outlined the multiyear strategy that it embarked on that year, explaining that to begin with it would 'build the foundation', before launching the 'accelerate-and-grow' phase from the 2021 financial year onwards.[4] The fact that the group was in the first year of its foundation-building phase is probably the reason that assets increased without a commensurate growth in revenue. An analyst should remember to test this hypothesis when performing analysis in future years, to see if the 'foundation' really does indeed set the scene for expansion.

11.2.4 How much profit was earned from the revenue?

Strictly speaking, the accounting measure of whether the value of the business has increased is the difference between all items of income and expense; that is, total comprehensive income (TCI). However, analysts tend to overlook the entire OCI section, and focus instead on the profit figure in the income statement.

> **MISCONCEPTION**
>
> **Profit is a better measure of business performance than TCI.**
>
> While it is true that most analysts pay far more attention to profit than TCI, and prefer to use profit as the measure of overall performance in financial ratios, it is far from clear that they should. TCI is in fact—as the name suggests—the more 'comprehensive' measure of changes in business value.
>
> The statement of comprehensive income was introduced by the IASB in 2007,[5] and, although that may seem like long enough ago for analysts to warm to it, analysts have been slow to do so. Perhaps because of the specialised nature of items of OCI, the fact that they are generally **unrealised**, or their typically small size, analysts tend to ignore them. In this chapter, we have therefore not been revolutionary—or brave—enough to suggest that TCI should be used wherever profit has traditionally been used.

11

> However, in time, financial analysts may come to agree with the IASB, and give TCI its due. After all, in reality a revaluation gain on a property classified as PPE indicates no less value creation than the same gain on an investment property, despite the fact that one is reported in OCI and the other is in profit or loss.

Given its importance, assessing the profitability of a business is a multi-layered exercise (as several remaining sections of this chapter will show), but the first layer is a simple look at the profit for the year and how it has changed. In Burberry's case, £339.1 million of profit indicates that the Group was indeed profitable in 2019, and a quick calculation reveals that this was an increase of 15.5% on the previous year. By contrast, Prada's 'net income' for the comparable period of €208.2 million was less than its prior financial year.[6]

When considering the significance of year-on-year changes, an analyst must take into account the inflation rate (that is, the average change in the price of goods). Except in hyperinflationary environments, financial reporting makes no adjustment for the effects of inflation, and so any changes calculated using accounting figures are 'nominal', as opposed to 'real'. The average UK inflation rate for the year ended March 2019 was 1.8%, so the real improvement in Burberry's profit was still a very impressive 13.7% (15.5% – 1.8%).[7]

It is interesting that this substantial increase in Burberry's profits was earned from essentially the same amount of revenue. This is in direct contrast with Prada, which increased revenues substantially, but earned less profit. Ordinarily, one would expect improvements in revenues to translate into higher profits.

The common-sized income statement

An excellent way to investigate how a business earned profit from its revenue is to use a technique called common-sizing. Common-sizing can be used to spot important relationships on any financial statement. However, the financial statement that is by far most frequently common-sized is the income statement. It is effectively a reproduction of the income statement, except each item is expressed as a percentage of revenue. Burberry's common-sized income statement is shown in Example 11.1.

EXAMPLE 11.1

Burberry's common-sized group income statement			
	2019	2018	Difference (in % points)
Revenue	100.0	100.0	
Cost of sales	(31.6)	(30.6)	+ 1.0-
Gross profit	68.4	69.4	
Net operating expenses	(52.3)	(54.4)	– 2.1
Operating profit	16.1	15.0	
Net finance income	0.1	0.1	+ 0.0
Profit before taxation	16.2	15.1	
Taxation	(3.7)	(4.4)	– 0.7
Profit for the year	12.5	10.7	+ 1.8

Looking down each column in a common-sized financial statement reveals the relative size of each line-item. For example, we can see that almost a third of Burberry's revenue is absorbed by the cost of the inventory sold; and more than half by its net operating expenses; whereas, net finance income is negligible. In 2019, 12.5% of revenue was earned as profit.

In the last column, you can see at a glance how the relative size of each item has changed. For example, in 2019 Burberry spent 1% more of its revenue on its inventory than it did in 2018, but saved 2.1% by reducing its net operating costs. This, together with a substantial fall in the proportion of revenue paid away in tax, explains how in 2019 Burberry was able to keep 1.8% more of its revenue as profit than in 2018.

Alternative performance measures

Section 4.6 explained that many businesses disclose their own **alternative performance measures** (APMs), like earnings before interest, taxes, depreciation, and amortisation (EBITDA) and underlying profit, usually in an attempt to provide a superior indicator of future cash flows. Burberry's APM, 'Adjusted profit before taxation—non-GAAP measure', amounted to £443.2 million in 2019, only slightly different from the profit before tax calculated in terms of IFRS.

The difference was much more significant in 2018, when the APM was not only £58.3 million higher than the IFRS measure, but also £27.7 million higher than the 2019 APM. Notes 6 and 7 reveal that the biggest reason for the difference between profitability according to IFRS and the APM was restructuring costs of £54.5 million, which were removed from the APM calculation because 'they are considered material and one-off in nature'. By the company's own measure, Burberry's sustainable profits declined by 5.9% from £470.9 million in 2018 to £443.2 million in 2019. This, along with our observations of plateauing revenues, casts further doubt on the sustainability of the 15.5% increase in profit, and gives additional cause for further investigation.

The APM relies on internal knowledge of each item of income and expense. It is therefore impossible to calculate a comparable measure for competitors. The only meaningful benchmark is the business's historical APM.

11.2.5 How much profit was converted into operating cash flows?

We have given a lot of attention in earlier sections of this book to operating cash flows. For example, section 1.3.4 established that net operating cash inflows are the ultimate measure of value creation, and section 5.2 explained why this is: cash is real, unlike profit, which is a notional construct of the accounting equation. In section 5.3, we demonstrated how to measure a business's **quality of earnings**: the extent to which accrual-based profit figures are converted into equivalent cash figures in the statement of cash flows.

Essential to this part of financial analysis is a clear understanding of **working capital**. The analyst must establish whether inventory and receivables generate sufficient cash such that, when added to the cash on hand, the business can meet its short-term payment obligations. To help answer this question, the statement of cash flows prepared on the indirect method reveals the cash effects of the year's changes in working capital, described in detail in section 5.4.4.

In Burberry's case, as we observed in section 5.4.6, quality of earnings was very high: in both 2018 and 2019, **cash generated from operating activities** (CGFO) was substantially higher than operating profit as a result of non-cash items such as depreciation and, especially in 2018, efficient working capital movements. Overall, while the income statement reported a 2019 profit of £339.1 million, the statement of cash flows reported net CGFO of £411.4 million.

We shall not continue to revisit this material here, but—given how vital it is to effective financial analysis—we suggest that you go back and read the abovementioned sections again if you feel that you may need a reminder.

11.2.6 How did operating cash flow combine with other cash flow activities?

There are several different possibilities for how a business's operating, investing, and financing cash flows come together.

One element of the scenario hardly ever varies. Except in rare circumstances, such as the sale of an extremely valuable item of PPE, a business's investing activities require cash to fund the replacement and possible expansion of non-current assets. This is indicated by a negative net cash flow at the bottom of the investing activities section of the statement of cash flows. Indeed, Burberry's net investing cash flows were negative in both 2018 and 2019, despite proceeds of £61.1 million on the sale to Coty of the Beauty operation in 2018.

The variations generally arise with respect to the source of the money spent on these investing activities. Sometimes, the net operating cash flows are negative, and all of the funding must come from financing activities such as share issues or bank loans. Sometimes, investing activities are partly paid for out of operating cash flows, and partly out of financing cash flows. If sufficient, cash reserves accumulated in previous years may also be used. A better situation is one where operating cash flows are able to pay for investing activities on their own, without the need to raise new share capital or debt. And the ideal situation is one in which operating cash inflows are so high that they can pay for investing activities with money left over to be able to fund cash outflows to providers of funding, such as dividends, share buybacks, and loan repayments.

In both 2018 and 2019, Burberry was in this ideal situation. In 2019, for example, the £411.1 million generated from operating activities could cover the £124.5 million required for investing activities, and also most of the £343.4 million for financing activities (including ambitious share buybacks), leaving the group needing to draw on only £56.6 million of its large pile of surplus cash accumulated in previous years.

When analysing a business whose cash flows are not quite so strong as Burberry's, an important question to ask is whether the operating cash flow can cover interest payments and dividends. If it cannot, this is a potential problem, because it shows that in the current year the business was not sustainable. While it is acceptable to fund new investments by raising new funding, or eating into cash reserves, in ordinary circumstances an established business should be able to pay a return to its providers of funding.

11.2.7 How are the assets funded?

The last question brings us full circle back to the statement of financial position, where we find not only the assets acquired, but also the liabilities and equity used to fund them. We have already considered the assets; now let's ask some questions about the funding.

First, is the business **solvent**? That is, are total assets greater than total liabilities? If not, the carrying amounts of assets are insufficient to repay the debt funding of the business. It's not uncommon for this to happen in a business's early years, while assets are depreciating but the business is still developing sustainable revenue streams. But if an established business is insolvent, that may well be a signal of an impending bankruptcy, and a real cause for concern. There is no need for worry in Burberry's case, of course: assets of £2 332.2 million, compared with liabilities of £872.2 million, represent an emphatically solvent business.

The analyst establishes whether the business is solvent.

A second question to ask is: what sorts of liabilities does the business owe? Burberry's largest liability category is current trade and other payables. This is a relatively low-risk liability, because it is not interest-bearing, and a large retailer usually has a fair degree of control about when it should settle its obligation to suppliers.

There is substantially more risk in interest-bearing liabilities, which usually require not only regular payments of interest, but also repayment according to strict timelines, and sometimes include covenants that restrict the business's other financing activities. Burberry reports very few interest-bearing liabilities. This is confirmed by a quick glance at finance expense in the income statement: it is just £3.6 million, virtually unchanged from the previous year, and not much more than 1% of profit. Burberry is exposed to no real risk of being unable to make interest payments or repayments of long-term debts.

The analyst considers the size and nature of liabilities, paying especially close attention to interest-bearing liabilities.

Third, are there any undisclosed liabilities? To identify these, it is worth scanning the notes to the financial statements for contingent liabilities, which are liabilities that for some reason do not qualify for recognition. Burberry's note 31 declined to specify any, reassuring us that 'the Group does not currently expect the outcome of these contingent liabilities to have a material effect on the Group's financial condition'. It would be prudent to scan the financial press for any articles which might contradict this claim by exposing potentially costly litigation against the business, for example. Failing that, it is a reasonable assumption that a business like Burberry has no skeletons in its closet, since it does not operate in a highly regulated industry like food or health care, and is not routinely exposed to litigation by customers, like a tobacco company. For companies more exposed to the risk of litigation, for example, an analyst might expect something like the twenty-one pages of contingent liabilities disclosure prepared by British American Tobacco (see section 7.1.7).

11

The analyst considers whether any significant liabilities might be missing from the statement of financial position.

At the end of its 2019 year, many commentators might have said that Burberry was missing out on an opportunity to improve returns to shareholders via the judicious use of more debt (see section 11.3.5). However, in the light of the hardships brought on by the Covid-19 pandemic, it was better for Burberry not to be exposed to the risk that would accompany additional debt.

11.3 INTRODUCTION TO RATIO ANALYSIS

Financial ratios help us to see things that are not immediately obvious.

The second stage of analysis taught us how to understand the main story told by the business's financial statements, but there is so much more information to mine from the financial statements. We thus embark on the third stage, ratio analysis, which reveals important relationships that cannot be inferred just by looking at the financial statements.

Most discussions of financial ratios segregate them into the five main aspects of the business which they measure: **asset efficiency**, **profitability**, **leverage**, **liquidity**, and market performance. We will look at each of these areas, but let's first discuss a ratio that measures multiple aspects of business performance: return on equity (ROE).

Return on equity is widely regarded as the most important financial ratio.

Widely regarded as the most important ratio of all, ROE is considered by some to be a profitability ratio. This is not wrong if 'profitability' is taken to mean financial performance in the broadest sense. In this chapter, however, we use the term 'profitability' in a narrower sense to describe only the matter of whether and how profit is earned from revenue.

11.3.1 Return on equity

We noted earlier that Burberry's 2019 profit of £339.1 million was a substantial improvement on the previous year, but that doesn't mean it represents an objectively successful year of creating value. Perhaps 2018 profits were low, and made a mediocre 2019 result look much better than it truly was. How can we know how good a profit of £339.1 million really is?

To answer this question, suppose for a moment that next year you become the owner of a boutique clothing store on a high street in a small city in the UK. Would you be happy if, in its first year under your leadership, this single store made a profit of £339.1 million? Of course you would! You might well retire immediately, and live out the rest of your days trying nobly, but ultimately failing, to spend that single year of earnings.

On the other hand, suppose that the giant US e-tailer, Amazon, earned the equivalent of £339.1 million. This would be nothing short of disastrous for a company which in the year ended 31 December 2018 earned more than US$10 billion in profits.[8] Why is the same amount of profit a pipedream for one business, and a fireable offence for another? The answer is obvious, of course: it's because of the difference in the size of the businesses.

This means that if we want to judge profit in context, we need to judge it against the best measure we have of the business's size. That is, we need to judge it against equity, by calculating the ROE.

$$\text{Return on equity} = \frac{\text{Profit}}{\text{Average total equity}} \times 100$$

The idea of relating one figure to another is central to the usefulness of ratios. It is a common statement in business (as in life) that 'everything's relative': ratio analysis allows us to see the ways in which certain items of financial information relate to other items.

However, relating a figure from the statement of comprehensive income to a figure from the statement of financial position introduces a computational issue. Figures from the statement of comprehensive income, like profit, have arisen over the entire year. On the other hand, figures from the statement of financial position, like equity, are balances for an instant in time: the year-end date. As the carrying amounts of assets and liabilities change from day to day, equity also changes daily. In an ideal world, therefore, we would compare profits and equity each day, and add the results together to get a ROE for the year. However, this is neither possible nor necessary: instead, the formula requires us to compare profit for the whole year to the average equity.

> **MISCONCEPTION**
>
> **The ROE is the return for the business owners.**
>
> Not exactly. ROE is the return earned on the book value of the owners' claim on the business. The actual return to shareholders of a listed company can be calculated using a different ratio—total shareholder return—which will be presented in section 11.8.1.

For each ratio we cover in this chapter, we shall present the calculations for Burberry's 2019 year, as well as the two benchmarks, as follows. (The figures in Prada's financial statements are presented in thousands of euros. We recommend that you download the Prada *Annual Report 2018*, and locate these figures in it. We have left the figures as they appear in the report, with a 'k' to indicate thousands, rather than rounding them to millions, to help you locate them.)

> **Burberry's return on equity:**
> 2019: £339.1 m ÷ [(£1 425.2 m + £1 460.0 m) ÷ 2] × 100   **23.5%**
> *2018: £293.6 m ÷ [(£1 697.8 m + £1 425.4 m) ÷ 2] × 100   18.8%*
> *Prada: €208 182 k ÷ [(€2 866 171 k + €2 897 069 k) ÷ 2] × 100   7.2%*

These ROEs now give us ample evidence to claim that Burberry's 2019 year was successful, as it increased the value of equity by a higher proportion than in the previous year, and by much more than Prada did in the comparable year.

11

Note that ratios allow us to make comparisons between businesses of different sizes. It would not be fair to compare Burberry's profit of £339.1 million directly with Prada's profit of €208.2 million, precisely because the values of the two businesses are different. However, comparing returns on equity is fair, as the book values are explicitly taken into account by the ratio. For similar reasons, ratios also eliminate the need to translate results denominated in different currencies.

Bear in mind that most analysts are seeking to make a forecast about the business's future. So we must now ask: is Burberry's strong ROE sustainable? And what does it tell us about the risks to which the business is exposed? To find the answers, we must dig deeper and come to an understanding of *why* ROE changed in the way it did.

Many years ago, the US multinational Du Pont came up with an ingenious way (now known as '**Du Pont analysis**') to uncover the 'drivers of ROE' using three more financial ratios. Each ratio measures how the business performed in one of three key aspects of business performance.

11.3.2 The first driver of ROE: asset efficiency

The analysts at Du Pont reasoned that the first way for a business to achieve a good ROE is to use its assets as efficiently as possible to generate revenue. We can measure this aspect of performance—known as asset efficiency—with a ratio called 'total asset turnover' (TAT).

$$\text{Total asset turnover} = \frac{\text{Revenue}}{\text{Average total assets}}$$

TAT relates the business's revenue (or turnover) to the assets that were used to generate it. To understand why it measures asset efficiency, consider two businesses, one with a TAT of 2.00, and the other with a TAT of 1.50. Clearly, the business which generates €200 of revenue for every €100 invested in assets is able to use its assets more efficiently than the other, which generates only €150 of revenue for every €100 invested in assets. Burberry is less efficient than both of these hypothetical businesses, as the following calculations show.

Overall asset efficiency is measured by the total asset turnover (TAT) ratio.

11

Burberry's total asset turnover:

2019: £2 720.2 m ÷ [(£2 223.0 m + £2 332.2 m) ÷ 2]   **1.19 times**

2018: £2 732.8 m ÷ [(£2 413.4 m + £2 223.0 m) ÷ 2]   *1.18 times*

Prada: €3 142 148 k ÷ [(€4 739 375 k + €4 678 812 k) ÷ 2]   *0.67 times*

Calculating the ratios is not nearly as difficult as interpreting them, and so to help you learn how to do that, we have developed a methodology which we call **AMBER analysis**. This requires us to answers the five essential questions that any analyst should ask about any ratio, which are as follows.

- *Aspect*. What aspect of business performance is measured by this ratio?
- *Message*. What straightforward message about the business is delivered by this ratio?

- _Benchmark(s)_. In respect of this ratio, how does the business compare to the benchmark(s)?

- _Explanation_. What has caused the results for this ratio and for the benchmarks? Are they explained by information in the financial statements, or by the economic context? Does this ratio connect up with other elements of our analysis, like the story which emerged in the second stage of analysis, or aspects of the business measured by other ratios?

- _Risk_. What business risk(s) does this ratio tell us about?

Let's now perform an AMBER analysis of Burberry's TAT, as we will do for each ratio that we present in this chapter. (We have not yet performed an AMBER analysis of ROE because we will only know the 'E' and the 'R' when we reach section 11.3.5, which is where we will therefore present it.)

- _Aspect_. TAT is the overall measure of asset efficiency.

- _Message_. For every £100 that Burberry had invested in assets in 2019, it produced £119 of revenue.

- _Benchmark(s)_. Burberry became no more efficient, and no less efficient, between 2018 and 2019. However, there is a striking difference between Burberry's and Prada's TAT. This is no doubt a major reason for the superiority of Burberry's ROE: it has managed to generate far more revenue from its assets than Prada has.

- _Explanation_. Sometimes, the reason for a ratio not changing is that the components of the ratio are moving by the same amount—for example, TAT would stay the same if both assets and revenue increased by 10%—but in this case the explanation is that neither component has changed much. This is perhaps the best way to understand what has happened (or rather, _not_ happened) to TAT: if an established business chooses not to expand its asset base, it can hardly expect a surge in revenues. The reasons for the difference between Burberry's and Prada's asset efficiency will become clear when we analyse some more efficiency ratios in section 11.4.

- _Risk_. The vast difference with Prada's efficiency suggests that it is possible that Burberry's TAT is too high. This happens when the business underinvests in new assets, and uses its existing assets to the point of break-down. Analysts sometimes call this 'sweating the assets too hard'. The risk is that short-term improvements in efficiency are paid for later with diminished market share due to underinvestment, and higher costs due to maintenance and down-time. In this case, however, two facts redeem Burberry. First, the group has increased its asset base during the year; and second, the fact that this level of efficiency was also achieved in the prior year suggests that it is in fact sustainable.

11

> **MISCONCEPTION**
>
> A very small change in a ratio indicates a meaningful difference.
>
> If the change in Burberry's TAT from 1.18 to 1.19 tempted you to conclude that Burberry became a little more efficient, then you are not alone. However, this is a mistake that novice analysts often make: paying too much attention to very small differences

between ratios. The tiny change in Burberry's TAT is not a slight improvement, but rather it implies that there has been no discernible change in the business's overall asset efficiency.

Remember that the value of assets changes from day to day, there was one less day in Burberry's 2019 year than in its 2018 year, and that many items in the financial statements are estimated at amounts that are inevitably at least slightly wrong. For all these reasons, little discrepancies are essentially meaningless.

11.3.3 **The second driver of ROE: profitability**

Asset efficiency cannot be the only aspect of a business to get right in order to optimise overall performance. Imagine a business which generates €100 million of revenue from €1 million of assets, but then has expenses of €150 million. Notwithstanding that its TAT of 100.0 times puts both Burberry and Prada to shame, the business is losing €50 million a year!

Overall profitability is measured by the net margin (NM) ratio.

You can probably see what this imaginary business is getting wrong: it is failing to earn a good profit from each euro of revenue. This aspect of the business is called profitability, which involves getting the right mix between the cost and selling price of the business's products or services, and controlling other costs like salaries, rent, and so on. This is best measured by the financial ratio called 'net margin'.

$$\text{Net margin} = \frac{\text{Profit (after tax)}}{\text{Revenue}} \times 100$$

Burberry's net margin:

2019: £339.1 m ÷ £2 720.2 m × 100   **12.5%**

2018: £293.6 m ÷ £2 732.8 m × 100   10.7%

Prada: €208 182 k ÷ €3 142 148 k × 100   6.6%

- *Aspect.* Net margin is the overall measure of a business's profitability.
- *Message.* In 2019, for every £100 that Burberry earned in revenue, £87.50 was spent to cover costs, leaving £12.50 as profit.
- *Benchmark(s).* Burberry's net margin improved significantly between 2018 and 2019. Note that the difference appears small because the numbers are small, but 2019's figure represents a year-on-year improvement of 1.8 percentage points. Although this may not sound like a lot, it is a very substantial *relative* increase of 16.8% (1.8 ÷ 10.7 × 100). Moreover, Prada was much less profitable than Burberry, earning just €6.60 of profit from every €100 of revenue.
- *Explanation.* If you recognise Burberry's net margin, that's probably because it appeared in the common-sized income statement in section 11.2.4. That exercise has already explained Burberry's improvement in profitability: a substantial reduction in operating expenses, together with a smaller tax saving, was more than enough to counter the effects of increasing cost of sales.

We shall explore this explanation in more detail, and explain the favourable comparison to Prada, in section 11.5, which presents more profitability ratios.

- *Risk*. The comparison with Prada gives us an extra reason to think that perhaps Burberry's prices are too high. Should we therefore conclude that Burberry might be at risk of pricing itself out of the luxury goods market? Let's not be so hasty. When one considers that Burberry was by far the more efficient business, it is not at all clear that Burberry's pricing is having an adverse effect on revenue.

While Burberry's overall asset efficiency did not change between 2018 and 2019, its profitability did, thus driving some of the improvement in ROE.

11.3.4 The relationship between asset efficiency and profitability

Asset efficiency and profitability are interconnected. Pricing, for example, can affect both aspects of performance. On the whole, if a business increases prices, that may improve profitability (because the amount of profit earned from each €100 of revenue goes up) but reduce asset efficiency (because the decline in sales volumes may decrease revenue overall). Indeed, often in practice TAT and net margin move in opposite directions. It is sometimes useful, therefore, to calculate a new ratio which measures the combined effect of these two aspects of performance. This is return on assets (ROA), which measures how well the business has been able to use its assets to generate not revenue, but profits.

$$\text{Return on assets} = \frac{\text{Profit}}{\text{Average total assets}} \times 100$$

The fact that ROA is the result of the combined effects of asset efficiency and profitability can be seen in the following equation: a mathematical proof that the formula for ROA is equal to the product of the formula for TAT and the formula for the net margin.

The drivers of ROA are asset efficiency (measured by TAT) and profitability (measured by NM).

$$\text{ROA} = \frac{\text{Profit}}{\text{Average total assets}} \times 100 = \frac{\text{Revenue}}{\text{Average total assets}} \times \frac{\text{Profit}}{\text{Revenue}} \times 100$$

Given what we have already learned about Burberry and Prada's asset efficiency and margins, it should come as no surprise that Burberry's 2019 ROA was an improvement on 2018, and that it far exceeded Prada's. (The calculations below demonstrate two ways to work out ROA: first, using the ROA formula; and second, by multiplying TAT by net margin. Any small differences creep in only as a result of rounding.)

> **Burberry's return on assets**:
> 2019: £339.1 m ÷ [(£2 223.0 m + £2 332.2 m) ÷ 2] × 100 = 1.19 × 12.5%   **14.9%**
> *2018: £293.6 m ÷ [(£2 413.4 m + £2 223.0 m) ÷ 2] × 100 = 1.18 × 10.7%*   *12.7%*
> *Prada: €208 182 k ÷ [(€4 739 375 k + €4 678 812 k) ÷ 2] × 100 = 0.67 × 6.6%*   *4.4%*

11

- *Aspect*. ROA measures how effectively the business has been able to use its assets to generate profits.
- *Message*. From every £100 of assets that Burberry had during 2019, the company earned £14.90 for its shareholders.
- *Benchmark(s)*. In 2019, Burberry's ROA handily beat the prior year, and was more than three times better than Prada's.
- *Explanation*. ROA was up on 2018 because the business had managed to improve its profitability without sacrificing efficiency. It was much higher than its competitor's ROA as a result of both superior efficiency and profitability. For an explanation of each of these, refer back to the AMBER analyses of TAT and net margin.
- *Risk*. The ROA and its drivers contain no convincing signs that Burberry is exposed to any significant risk, for the reasons discussed in the AMBER analyses of TAT and net margin.

It may be tempting to think that ROA is in fact the most important measure of business performance. After all, doesn't ROA neatly summarise everything that a business aims to do: invest in assets, and make as much profit from them as possible? Well, if businesses were people, then perhaps ROA would indeed be all that they would care about. But, while many businesses are legal persons, they are not *people* like the owners (or, in the case of businesses owned by other businesses, like their owners' owners). Remember, the distinguishing objective of business is to create value for the *owners*. So the most important measure of business performance is not to increase profit relative to *assets*, but rather to increase profits relative to the owners' interest in the business, represented by *equity*. Which leads us back to what we have already stated: the most important measure of business performance is ROE.

11.3.5 The third driver of ROE: leverage

ROA captures the effects of the first two drivers of ROE: asset efficiency and profitability. The third driver makes the difference between ROA and ROE. You may be able to work out what it is, when you consider that the difference is in the **denominator**: ROE's is equity; ROA's is assets. And the difference between equity and assets, of course, is liabilities.

Thus, by using liabilities in its capital structure, a business can take a good ROA and make it an even better ROE. As you learned through the example of Mr Cautious and Ms Risky all the way back in section 1.3.2, this is known as **leverage** or **gearing**. Increasing the amount of debt can lever up the returns to owners, though not without also raising the business's risk profile.

One ratio used to measure leverage is the equity multiplier, also known as the financial leverage multiplier.

Leverage can be measured using the equity multiplier (EM).

$$\text{Equity multiplier} = \frac{\text{Average total assets}}{\text{Average total equity}}$$

At first sight, you may be surprised that this ratio measures the amount of debt in the business. After all, liabilities seem to be the one item missing from the formula. But remember that the **numerator**, being the business's assets, is also equal to equity plus liabilities. Given that the denominator is equity, movements in the equity multiplier are a precise function of changes in the amount of the business's liabilities. This can be shown with a simple example, supposing that a business's financial position is as follows.

Assets	–	Liabilities	=	Equity
€100		€20		€80

The equity multiplier is 1.25 (€100 ÷ €80). But what happens if the business takes on more debt by, say, acquiring additional assets worth €20, financed entirely by debt?

Assets	–	Liabilities	=	Equity
€120		€40		€80

Now the equity multiplier increases to 1.5 (€120 ÷ €80). So we can see that the higher the business's debt levels, or leverage, the higher the equity multiplier.

Burberry's equity multiplier:

2019: [(£2 223.0 m + £2 332.2 m) ÷ 2] ÷ [(£1 425.2 m + £1 460.1 m) ÷ 2]	**1.58 times**
2018: [(£2 413.4 m + £2 223.0 m) ÷ 2] ÷ [(£1 697.8 m + £1 425.4 m) ÷ 2]	*1.48 times*
Prada: [(€4 739 375 k + €4 678 812 k) ÷ 2] ÷ [(€2 866 171 k + €2 897 069) ÷ 2]	*1.63 times*

- *Aspect.* The equity multiplier measures leverage.

- *Message.* Assets are 1.58 times equity. More importantly, if we take Burberry's 2019 ROA of 14.9%, and multiply it by the equity multiplier of 1.58, we get the ROE of 23.5%. (The mathematical proof in section 11.3.6 will show why this is true.)

- *Benchmark(s).* By increasing its leverage between 2018 and 2019, Burberry improved the degree by which it geared up its ROA to produce a higher ROE. However, it did not do this quite as effectively as Prada, which took advantage of higher levels of debt in its capital structure to turn its ROA of 4.4% into a ROE of 7.1%.

- *Explanation.* The source of many businesses' leverage is bank loans and other interest-bearing borrowings, but a quick glance at Burberry's statement of financial position reveals no such line-items. Prada, on the other hand, has close to half a billion euros of 'long-term financial payables', which explains its larger multiplier. Burberry has made a business decision not to use any significant interest-bearing debt as it is in a cash-flush situation, and can use its existing cash resources to finance asset acquisitions. However, the business does have *some* liabilities, the largest of which is trade and other payables. In other words, Burberry is taking advantage of the credit granted by its suppliers to partially fund its operations, and has done this to a greater degree in 2019 than in 2018.

- *Risk.* If a business is efficient and profitable, the more debt that it takes on, the greater will be the multiplier, and hence the greater the ROE. However, if the business has assumed too much debt during an economic downturn (when profits fall, interest rates rise, and margins become negative), then the equity multiplier will work in the opposite direction and reduce ROE by a greater amount than it would have been reduced had there been little or no debt. This was demonstrated in Example 1.2 in section 1.3.2. The general rule is: the higher the equity multiplier, the more powerful the leverage, but the greater the risk. The *type* of debt also matters, of course. Overall, Burberry's exposure to debt-related risk is very low, for two reasons. First, the proportion of debt funding is relatively small; and second, virtually all of its debt is interest-free. As we mentioned at the end of section 11.2.7, this turned out to put Burberry in a stronger position when Covid-19 hit.

11.3.6 Du Pont analysis

Asset efficiency, profitability, and leverage can be mathematically proved to be the three drivers of ROE, as follows.

$$\text{ROE} = \frac{\text{Profit}}{\text{Average total equity}} \times 100$$

$$= \frac{\text{Revenue}}{\text{Average total assets}} \times \frac{\text{Profit}}{\text{Revenue}} \times 100 \times \frac{\text{Average total assets}}{\text{Average total equity}}$$

$$= \text{Total asset turnover} \times \text{Net margin} \times \text{Equity multiplier}$$

The three drivers of ROE are: asset efficiency (measured by TAT); profitability (measured by NM); and leverage (measured by EM).

Thus, the power of the Du Pont model is revealed: to improve overall business performance, managers can focus on three separate aspects, and, by improving one or more of these, while keeping the other(s) stable, they can be sure that ROE will increase.

From an external analyst's perspective, the Du Pont analysis is a powerful way to understand why ROE has changed, which is clearly vital for predicting future performance. To demonstrate, Example 11.2 shows the full Du Pont analysis for Burberry in 2019. (You may notice that the right-hand side of the 2018 equation actually comes to 18.7%; this is merely the result of a rounding error.)

EXAMPLE 11.2

	ROE (overall performance)		TAT (asset efficiency)		Net margin (profitability)		Equity multiplier (leverage)
2019	23.5%	=	1.19	×	12.5%	×	1.58
2018	18.8%	=	1.18	×	10.7%	×	1.48
Prada	7.1%	=	0.67	×	6.5%	×	1.63

At a glance, we can now see how Burberry improved its ROE in 2019, and so we are finally in a position to perform an AMBER analysis of Burberry's ROE, as follows.

- *Aspect*. ROE measures overall business performance.

- *Message*. For every £100 of equity in 2019, the business returned profits of £23.50.

- *Benchmark(s)*. Burberry's ROE improved significantly between 2018 and 2019, and outperformed Prada's by more than three times.

- *Explanation*. While using its assets no less efficiently to generate revenue, it increased the amount of profit earned from each pound of revenue, and at the same time leveraged these profits more effectively by increasing the debt funding. Its ROE far surpassed Prada's because it was substantially more efficient and profitable, despite somewhat lower leverage.

- *Risk*. Burberry seems to be subject to no obvious, major risks: it is not sweating assets too hard, scaring away customers with margins that are too high, or exposing itself to high risks of default on debt repayments. If it has access to lucrative new investment opportunities, it looks well positioned to take on a little more risk in the pursuit of even higher returns: it has the capacity to use its huge cash reserves and raise some debt to fund expansion.

Of course, no serious analyst would restrict themselves to calculating just the Du Pont ratios. For each aspect of business performance, there are many more ratios. In the same way that Du Pont allows an analyst to dig down into the three drivers of ROE, these other ratios can reveal why each driver of ROE has changed, and paint a much more detailed picture of the business. To demonstrate their usefulness, in the next few sections, we will discuss many of these additional ratios, each time using an AMBER analysis for Burberry. We have also included a few further ratios in the advanced material available with the **online resources**.

11.4 ANALYSING ASSET EFFICIENCY

While TAT measures overall asset efficiency, the various other efficiency or activity ratios measure the efficiency with which the business has employed specific asset categories.

11.4.1 Fixed asset turnover

$$\text{Fixed asset turnover} = \frac{\text{Revenue}}{\text{Average property, plant \& equipment}}$$

Burberry's fixed asset turnover:

2019: £2 720.2 m ÷ [(£313.6 m + £306.9 m) ÷ 2]	**8.77 times**	
2018: £2 732.8 m ÷ [(£399.6 m + £313.6 m) ÷ 2]	*7.66 times*	
Prada: €3 142 148 k ÷ [(€1 522 783 k + €1 577 352 k) ÷ 2]	*2.03 times*	

- *Aspect*. This ratio measures how efficiently PPE has been used to generate revenue. ('Fixed assets' is an old term still commonly used in business to describe the assets more frequently categorised as PPE on contemporary financial statements.)

- *Message*. In 2019, for every £100 of PPE in which Burberry had invested, the business generated revenue of £877.

- *Benchmark(s)*. Burberry's fixed asset turnover improved by 14.5% between 2018 and 2019. This reflects very positively on the business's asset efficiency, but even more remarkable is the fact that Burberry's utilisation of PPE appears to be over four times more efficient than that of Prada.

- *Explanation*. The improvement from 2018 to 2019 is the result of Burberry's reducing its investment in PPE whilst nonetheless maintaining stable revenues. The vast difference with Prada's fixed asset turnover is more difficult to explain. A possible explanation would be Burberry's having a much higher proportion of franchise stores, as these would earn revenue without adding to the carrying amount of PPE. However, this appears not to be the case: at their respective year-ends, Burberry had forty-four franchise stores, versus Prada's thirty-four.[9] In the absence of any other explanation, it seems that Burberry's operations simply require a much lower relative investment in PPE than Prada's operations require. This may be partly as a result of a strategy to spend more on intangible assets, and less on physical assets, for Burberry has recognised a need to prioritise 'investment in capabilities such as digital and brand experience over physical infrastructure'.[10] Prada, on the other hand, appears to have invested more in physical stores.

- *Risk*. High asset turnover ratios are efficient, but they may also signal a risk that the business is underinvesting in PPE. Generally speaking, businesses must continually maintain, update, and upgrade their infrastructure in order to remain competitive, and to avoid high maintenance and replacement costs later. To assess this risk, it is often helpful to compare depreciation (£87.2 million for Burberry in 2019) against PPE additions (£75.8 million). We did this in section 5.5, where we discussed how this would be a sign of potential underinvestment were it not for the abovementioned strategy to switch from investing in physical assets to intangible assets. It's worth noting that, of course, the strategy may be misjudged, and that choosing not to maintain its physical asset base may cost Burberry in the long term. This is a judgement that each analyst will need to make for themselves.

11.4.2 Days inventory on hand

$$\text{Days inventory on hand} = \frac{\text{Average inventory} \times 365}{\text{Cost of sales}}$$

Burberry's days inventory on hand:

2019: [(£411.8 m + £465.1 m) ÷ 2 × 365] ÷ £859.4 m	**186.2 days**	
2018: [(£505.3 m + £411.8 m) ÷ 2 × 365] ÷ £835.4 m	*200.3 days*	
Prada: [(€569 929 k + €631 791 k) ÷ 2 × 365] ÷ €879 554 k	*249.3 days*	

- *Aspect.* This ratio, also known as 'days inventory', 'days in inventory', and 'inventory period', measures how efficiently inventory has been managed.

- *Message.* On average, in 2019 it took Burberry 186.2 days to sell an item of inventory. After purchase, inventory sat in Burberry's warehouses and on its shelves for about half a year before it was sold!

- *Benchmark(s).* Unlike the ratios we have covered up to this point, decreases in this ratio represent an improvement, because quicker sales mean that money is available sooner to fund activities such as buying more inventory, or paying salaries, and so on. Similarly, the fact that the ratio is lower than Prada's indicates that Burberry has managed its inventory more efficiently than its competitor. However, it is important to note that many businesses make much more efficient use of inventory. For example, Amazon's days inventory in the comparable year was just 42.4 days, and the days inventory of most grocery retailers tends to be well below that, for obvious reasons.[11]

- *Explanation.* Luxury goods retailers such as Burberry and Prada tend to have much higher days inventory ratios than other sellers, because it is in the nature of luxury products that customers do not, and cannot afford to, buy them frequently. In some ways, having inventory sit on the shelf is an advantage, for it is a form of marketing for the business: people enter luxury goods stores, and buy an item there, partly because the inventory on display appeals to them. A major reason for Burberry's improvement since 2018 is a consequence of the group selling off a major operation that year—the Beauty operation sold to Coty we noted at the end of section 11.2.2—which reduced the group's inventory levels substantially. Also, some efficiencies may have been generated by the business's efforts to develop 'a more agile supply chain' in 2019.[12]

- *Risk.* While there may be some advantages in longer inventory days ratios for luxury goods retailers, they introduce some important risks: inefficient cash flow management (because money is tied up in inventory), increased holding costs (such as the required warehouse space and insurance costs), and potentially also an increased risk of out-of-date inventory. On the other hand, businesses should not seek to drive their inventory days ratios down too low: the inventory days figure is an average, so if it is very low, this means that some items are likely experiencing **stock-outs**, wasting opportunities to generate revenue. One way to drive days inventory very low without at the same time introducing stock-outs would be to build a 'just-in-time' system to bring in inventory only when it is needed, but that only comes with very high supply chain costs.

A frequently used alternative to the days inventory ratio is called 'inventory turnover'. Although it is expressed very differently from days inventory, it uses the same two inputs, and therefore contains the same informational value. We have included it in the advanced material available with the **online resources**.

11.4.3 Collection period

$$\text{Collection period} = \frac{\text{Average trade receivables} \times 365}{\text{Revenue}}$$

Burberry's collection period:

2019: [(£117.0 m + £119.7 m *from note 16 in 2019*) ÷ 2 × 365] ÷ £2 720.2 m	**15.9 days**	
2018: [(£191.8 m + £117.0 m from note 16 in 2018) ÷ 2 × 365] ÷ £2 732.8 m	*20.6 days*	
Prada: [(€289 973 k + €321 913 k from note 10) ÷ 2 × 365] ÷ €3 142 148 k	*35.5 days*	

- *Aspect.* The collection period, also called 'days sales outstanding', measures how efficiently trade receivables have been managed.
- *Message.* On average, in 2019 there were 15.9 days between Burberry's making sales and collecting the cash from customers. (A business like Burberry with a high proportion of cash sales has a low collection period. Naturally, if all sales were for cash, then the collection period would be zero days.)
- *Benchmark(s).* Like the decline in inventory, this decline also represents an improvement in efficiency because it indicates quicker cash inflows. Burberry is substantially more efficient than Prada, which took more than twice as long to collect its debts.
- *Explanation.* Again, the year-on-year decrease at Burberry is most likely explained by the sale of the Beauty operation, as the group no longer includes its debtors, which were part of the opening trade receivables balance included in the 2018 ratio calculation. The most likely explanation for the difference between Burberry and Prada is the simplest one: Prada allows more customers to buy on credit.
- *Risk.* Although insisting on cash-only sales or tighter terms for credit sales is more efficient, it risks losing revenues from customers who would be prepared to buy from the business if it offered more generous payment terms. Indeed, some retailers are prepared to tolerate collection periods of many months as a result of a deliberate strategy to drive high sales volumes.

This ratio is sometimes confused with the ratio called 'debtors' collection period', which measures the average time it takes to collect cash specifically from the customers who have purchased goods on credit (*not* from all customers, as with the collection period). The formula for debtors' collection period is almost the same as for collection period, except that the denominator of the ratio is *credit* sales. It is sometimes difficult to establish this figure, as it is not required to be disclosed in the financial statements.

The debtors' collection period is useful for determining how well receivables are managed by the business, whereas the collection period gives an indication of the overall efficiency of the business in collecting cash from all of its customers.

11

11.4.4 **Settlement period**

$$\text{Settlement period} = \frac{\text{Average trade payables} \times 365}{\text{Cost of sales}}$$

Burberry's settlement period:

2019: [(£153.2 m + £221.6 m *from note 20 in 2019*) ÷ 2 × 365] ÷ £859.4 m	**79.6 days**
2018: [(£172.3 m + £153.2 m *from note 20 in 2018*) ÷ 2 × 365] ÷ £835.4 m	*71.1 days*
Prada: [(€313 697 k + €315 211 k *from note 21*) ÷ 2 × 365] ÷ €879 554 k	*130.5 days*

- *Aspect.* The settlement period, also known as 'days payable outstanding', measures how efficiently trade payables have been managed.

- *Message.* On average, in 2019 it took Burberry 79.6 days to settle its trade payables.

- *Benchmark(s).* Burberry settled its debts to creditors an average of 8.5 days later in 2019 than in 2018. This is an improvement in efficiency—that is, better for operating cash flows—as the business had a longer period to use this money for its own purposes, before paying it over to creditors. However, this is one measure on which Burberry is less efficient than Prada, which takes an average of about four months to settle its debts to suppliers.

- *Explanation.* When trying to explain a movement in a ratio, it is often helpful to look at the components of the formula. In this case, the cost of sales figure changed very little, but there was a major increase of £68.4 million in trade payables during 2019, which is what caused the ratio to improve, more than compensating for the negative effect of selling the Beauty operation. There is a very short note in the strategic report section of the Burberry annual report which seems to offer the best explanation of this increase in trade payables: 'the timing of payments'.[13] It seems that Burberry has taken an active step to push out the settlement period by delaying payment to suppliers. Perhaps the management team was inspired to do this by their competitors: Prada, for example, seems to have negotiated substantially more favourable terms with its suppliers.

- *Risk.* Generally, trade payables is a form of interest-free financing, and so there are no interest-saving incentives to decrease settlement period. However, Prada does disclose that about €35 million of its trade payables balance is overdue,[14] which probably does come with an interest cost. The longer settlement period also potentially damages the business's relationship with suppliers, who might refuse to sell goods to the business if the business is taking unreasonably long to pay. Indeed, a very long settlement period is often an early signal that a business has a cash flow problem. Certainly, the €421 million of short-term financial payables and bank overdrafts in Prada's 2018 statement of financial position makes it clear that it had substantially less cash available to it than did Burberry.

11

11.4.5 **Operating cycle**

The operating cycle measures the overall efficiency of the business's management of working capital.

The operating cycle, also called the 'working capital cycle' or 'cash conversion cycle', puts together the three ratios we have just covered into a single, all-encompassing measure of the efficiency of working capital management. Before reading this section, it would be very helpful for you to review the part of section 5.4.4 entitled 'Working capital management', where the importance of effective working capital management was first explained.

$$\text{Operating cycle} = \text{Inventory days} + \text{Collection period} - \text{Settlement period}$$

Burberry's operating cycle:

2019: 186.2 + 15.9 – 79.6	**122.5 days**
2018: 200.3 + 20.6 – 71.1	*149.8 days*
Prada: 249.3 + 35.5 – 130.5	*154.3 days*

- *Aspect.* This ratio measures the overall efficiency of working capital management.

- *Message.* In 2019, Burberry's working capital tied up cash for an average of 122.5 days without earning a return. This is because, after buying the average item of inventory, the group waited 186.2 days to sell it, and a further 15.9 days to collect the cash from that sale, and yet paid the supplier of the inventory 79.6 days into this 202.1 day period. Thus, for each item of inventory that it bought and sold, the business had to wait an average of 122.5 days between the payment and receipt of cash.

- *Benchmark(s).* This was more efficient than its performance in 2018, as the business's resources were tied up without earning income for almost four weeks less. It was more efficient than Prada by a slightly larger margin.

- *Explanation.* To explain the operating cycle, we need to refer back to the explanations for its components. The reason for the improvement since the prior year was that the inventory days and collection period had both become shorter, while the settlement period had lengthened. Although two of these movements are best explained by the sale of the Beauty operation in 2018, the movement in the settlement period seems to be the result of a fundamental change in the management of the existing operations' working capital. By comparison with Prada, Burberry was less efficient in terms of the settlement period, but more than made up for this with a much shorter inventory days and collection period.

- *Risk.* Any discussion of risks associated with this ratio should refer back to the equivalent discussion about the ratio's three components. By aggregating these three, the analyst learns nothing new about the risks to which the business is exposed.

Burberry's operating cycle can be illustrated as follows in Figure 11.2.

FIGURE 11.2 Depiction of Burberry's operating cycle in 2019

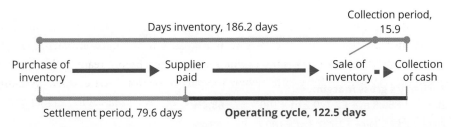

The ideal operating cycle is as low as possible. A few retailers in fact manage to achieve a negative operating cycle through relatively quick inventory turnovers, very low (or no) receivables, and a comparatively long settlement period. This means that for a number of days before they have to pay their suppliers, their customers' money can be used to generate further income for the business, for example by using the funds to finance the acquisition of other assets, or simply by earning interest. Tesco, the giant UK food retailer, achieves a negative operating cycle, which can be depicted for 2019 as follows in Figure 11.3.[15]

FIGURE 11.3 Depiction of Tesco's operating cycle in 2019

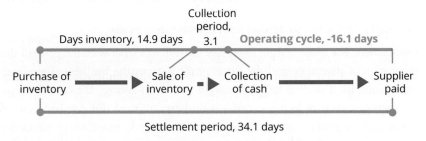

Tesco keeps its days inventory very short, partly out of necessity given that a large number of its products are perishable, and has an extremely short collection period because the vast bulk of its sales are for cash. The business prides itself on its relationships with suppliers, paying them relatively quickly, but even so, this settlement period of 34.1 days is 16.1 days longer than the 18.0 days between buying inventory and collecting the cash. Tesco's working capital generates cash so readily, in fact, that the business is able to run Tesco Bank, which by the end of its 2019 financial year had loans outstanding to customers and others of more than £12 billion!

11.5 ANALYSING PROFITABILITY

The profitability ratios focus on the statement of comprehensive income, mainly comparing its various subtotals to revenue. This means that, just like net margin (the overall measure of profitability), both of the additional ratios we discuss in this section appeared on the common-sized income statement we presented earlier in section 11.2.4.

11.5.1 **Gross margin**

$$\text{Gross margin} = \frac{\text{Gross profit}}{\text{Revenue}} \times 100$$

Burberry's gross margin:

2019: £1 860.8 m ÷ £2 720.2 m × 100	**68.4%**
2018: £1 897.4 m ÷ £2 732.8 m × 100	*69.4%*
Prada: €2 262 594 k ÷ €3 142 148 k × 100	*72.0%*

- *Aspect*. This ratio, also known as the 'gross profit percentage', measures the kind of profitability that is most fundamental to a manufacturer or retailer: the proportion of revenue that is left over after paying the direct costs of bringing inventory to its location and condition for sale.

- *Message*. For every £100 of revenue that Burberry generated in 2019, £31.60 was spent on the costs of inventory, leaving £68.40 as a contribution to other operating expenses, finance costs, tax, and profit.

- *Benchmark(s)*. On this measure, in 2019 Burberry was slightly less profitable than it had been in 2018, and somewhat less profitable than Prada.

- *Explanation*. The gross margin expresses the difference between the price of the average item of inventory and the gross profit it earns the business. Therefore, the explanation for a decline in gross margin is that on average the cost of inventory has increased relative to price. Perhaps Burberry allowed this gap between selling prices and inventory costs to shrink a little in order to maintain revenues during the foundation-building phase of their new corporate strategy that we mentioned in section 11.2.3. Burberry's gross margin is below Prada's because Prada marks up its inventory by slightly more than Burberry.

- *Risk*. Gross margin can be an indicator of two quite different kinds of risks. If it is very low, even if this drives large sales volumes, the profit earned from each sale may be insufficient to cover the other expenses of the business. If it is very high, the business may be making its products too expensive, and jeopardising its sales volumes. Neither risk seems to be high in Burberry's case: we know from our basic analysis that it is earning a good profit, and its revenues are not declining significantly. After all, in the luxury goods market, high gross margins are to be expected. (For example, compare Burberry's and Prada's gross margins to Amazon's, of 40.2%, and Tesco's of 6.5%.)

MISCONCEPTION

If revenues increase by 20%, then the gross margin should also increase by 20%.

No. The gross margin is gross profit expressed as a percentage of revenue, so the only way for it to increase is for gross profit to increase by a higher proportion than revenue. A business with growing revenues will earn more profit simply by keeping margins stable. A small increase in gross margin (or indeed any margin) is impressive.

> **MISCONCEPTION**
>
> If the gross margin declines, this is a bad sign.
>
> Whilst this is sometimes true, a lower gross margin is not always bad. Sometimes the gross margin declines but the absolute profit increases, and so the business is in fact better off. It can be a wise business strategy to reduce selling prices (that is, accept a lower gross margin) in order to increase market share. The increase in volumes may well compensate for the lower margin per item sold.

11.5.2 Operating margin

$$\text{Operating margin} = \frac{\text{Operating profit}}{\text{Revenue}} \times 100$$

Burberry's operating margin:

2019: £437.2 m ÷ £2 720.2 m × 100   **16.1%**

2018: £410.3 m ÷ £2 732.8 m × 100   *15.0%*

Prada: €323 846 k ÷ €3 142 148 k × 100   *10.3%*

- *Aspect.* This profitability ratio measures the proportion of revenue that is left over after paying for all operating costs.

- *Message.* For every £100 of revenue that Burberry generated in 2019, £83.90 was spent on the cost of sales and other operating expenses, leaving £16.10 as a contribution to financing expenses, taxation, and profit.

- *Benchmark(s).* On this measure, in 2019 Burberry was somewhat more profitable than it had been in 2018, and a good deal more profitable than Prada, retaining 56% more revenue as operating profit than the Italian retailer.

- *Explanation.* It is impressive that Burberry's operating margin improved despite a decline in the gross margin, as it means that there were substantial operating expense savings in 2019. The explanation for this is twofold. One is improved operational performance in 2019, in line with the business's strategy. For example, the group focused and streamlined its operations via Burberry Business Services, a shared service centre aimed at simplifying processes and cutting costs across the business.[16] The other explanation is the unusually high operating expenses in the prior year due to the restructuring costs of £54.5 million that we noted in the discussion of Burberry's APM in section 11.2.4. Although they lowered Burberry's operating margin in 2018, these restructuring costs may well have laid the foundation for the substantially lower operating costs in 2019 which enabled it to outperform Prada on this measure so dramatically.

- *Risk.* A declining operating margin is, of course, an indication that the business may run the risk of making losses in future, as it suggests that the market requires product prices to drop to the point that they may not even cover costs. A very high operating margin may indicate that the business is missing out on an opportunity

11

to earn higher profit overall by dropping its prices, expanding its market share, and benefiting from large increases in sales volumes. Neither of these risks seemed to apply to Burberry in 2019.

11.6 ANALYSING LEVERAGE

The equity multiplier is typically only used to measure leverage as part of a Du Pont analysis. More commonly, the proportion of debt funding is measured using the debt ratio or the debt–equity ratio. However, these two ratios provide no more or less information than the equity multiplier does, and so we will omit a discussion about benchmarks, explanations, and risks. The times interest earned, however, does provide an analyst with new information, and so we will discuss it in full.

11.6.1 Debt ratio and debt–equity ratio

$$\text{Debt ratio} = \frac{\text{Total liabilities}}{\text{Total assets}} \times 100$$

Burberry's debt ratio:

2019: £872.2 m ÷ £2 332.2 m × 100	**37.4%**
2018: £797.6 m ÷ £2 223.0 m × 100	*35.9%*
Prada: €1 781 743 k ÷ €4 678 812 k × 100	*38.1%*

$$\text{Debt - equity ratio} = \frac{\text{Total liabilities}}{\text{Total equity}}$$

Burberry's debt-equity ratio:

2019: £872.2 m ÷ £1 460.0 m	**0.60**
2018: £797.6 m ÷ £1 425.4 m	*0.56*
Prada: €1 781 743 k ÷ €2 897 069 k	*0.62*

- *Aspect.* Like the equity multiplier, these two ratios measure the amount of debt in the capital structure of the business.
- *Message.* The debt ratio indicates that at the 2019 year-end, 37.4% of Burberry's assets were funded by liabilities. The accounting equation means that the remaining 62.6% of assets were funded by equity. It is therefore no surprise that the debt–equity ratio reports that debt funding was 0.6 times equity funding.

For a discussion about benchmarks, explanations, and risks relating to leverage, refer to section 11.3.5 about the equity multiplier. To understand why these three measures of leverage—the equity multiplier, debt ratio, and debt–equity ratio—report precisely the same information, albeit expressed differently, consider again the example we used in the earlier section. Suppose that a business's financial position is as follows.

Assets	–	Liabilities	=	Equity
€100		€20		€80

In this example, the debt ratio is 20% (€20 ÷ €100 × 100), indicating that 20% of assets are funded by debt, and the other 80% by equity. Meanwhile, the debt–equity ratio is 0.25 times (€20 ÷ €80), which tells us that the debt-funding is one-quarter of the amount of equity-funding. The equity multiplier is 1.25 (€100 ÷ €80). If you think about it, given any one of these ratios, you could have worked out the other two without even looking at the numbers. For example, the equity multiplier is always equal to one plus the debt–equity ratio.

Now, if the business acquires additional assets worth €20, financed entirely by debt, the accounting equation changes as follows.

Assets	–	Liabilities	=	Equity
€120		€40		€80

The debt ratio increases to 33% (€40 ÷ €120 × 100), the debt–equity ratio becomes 0.5 times (€40 ÷ €80), and the new equity multiplier is 1.5 (€120 ÷ €80). Thus, the figures move in tandem, depending entirely on how much debt the business takes on.

> **MISCONCEPTION**
>
> **For each business, there is a perfect debt ratio.**
>
> No. There is no perfect debt (or indeed any other) ratio. Many factors influence how much debt funding is appropriate, and these factors may change from time to time.
>
> For example, if the business anticipates high profits when interest rates are low, the business could use more debt to take advantage of the positive effects of leverage. However, when interest rates rise, or when lower profits are expected, the same business should perhaps reduce debt levels to lower the risk of not being able to meet its interest payments.

11

To investigate a business's leverage further, analysts sometimes use a modified version of one of these leverage ratios. The most common variation substitutes only the interest-bearing debt for the liabilities, because non-interest-bearing debt is less risky and therefore less relevant when determining the business's exposure.

A second variation is to deduct cash and cash equivalents from the amount of debt (and, if it is the debt ratio being modified, also from assets). The reason is that the cash could, if necessary, reduce the debt and so the net figures are most indicative of the risk of the business being unable to repay the remaining liabilities. There would be no sense in an analyst attempting to calculate such a modified ratio for Burberry in 2019, however, because—powerfully demonstrating just how low the group's default risk is—the business's cash reserves are greater than its total liabilities!

11.6.2 Times interest earned

$$\text{Times interest earned} = \frac{\text{Profit before interest expense and tax expense}}{\text{Interest expense}}$$

Burberry's times interest earned:
2019: (£440.6 m + £0.6 m *from note 9 in 2019*) ÷ £0.6m	**735.3 times**
2018: *(£412.6 m + £1.3 m from note 9 in 2018) ÷ £1.3 m*	*318.4 times*
Prada: *(€302 538 k + €13 543 k from note 33) ÷ €13 543 k*	*23.3 times*

- *Aspect.* This leverage ratio, also called 'interest cover', contrasts the interest that the business was charged during the year with the profit that the business made before taking this interest into account.

- *Message.* In 2019, Burberry's profit before interest and tax expense was 735.3 times its interest expense. In other words, the business's operating profit covered its interest bill more than 700 times over. In effect, this means that the risk of Burberry being unable to meet its interest payments in the near future is vanishingly small.

- *Benchmark(s).* The group's exposure to risk was also tiny in 2018, though it was even smaller in 2019. Prada's times interest earned is much lower, indicating that technically it has a higher exposure to a risk of default. Nonetheless, it is also relatively safe: its profits could be slashed to a tiny fraction of current levels, and yet it would still be able to make its interest payments.

- *Explanation.* Burberry has virtually no interest-bearing borrowings, and Prada has very few.

- *Risk.* Thus, both Burberry and Prada have extremely low exposures to the risk of not being able to meet interest payments when they fall due.

Let us consider a business for whom the times interest earned ratio is more relevant: the US food producer, Campbell Soup Company (CSC). At its 2019 year-end, this business had a debt ratio of 91.5% ($12 036 m ÷ $13 148 m), which—for an established company—is an unusually high proportion of assets to be funded by liabilities. The majority of this debt was interest-bearing, which led to a times interest earned ratio of 2.8 times (($625 m + $356 m) ÷ $356 m).[17] This means that if profits had fallen the following year by 64% (1.8 ÷ 2.8 × 100), CSC would have been unable to honour its interest commitments. This represents a much less comfortable margin of safety than Burberry's and Prada's, and a much more significant risk that CSC might not be able to service its debt in the future.

However, bear in mind that debt has a multiplying effect on returns, so provided that CSC makes a profit which *does* cover its interest bill, its highly leveraged position is actually beneficial. This was the case in 2019: CSC earned $211 million in profit, which translated into a ROE of 17.0% ($211 m ÷ [($1 112 m + 1 373 m) ÷ 2]). Had the CSC had Burberry's debt ratio of 37.4%, rather than 91.5%, then its ROE would have been less than 3%!

If a business has comparatively high levels of interest-bearing debt and the interest arising on this debt is consuming a relatively large proportion of operating profit, analysts might well conclude that the business should be less aggressive, and take on less debt. Although this would reduce the extent to which healthy profits are leveraged upwards, it would also seriously reduce the likelihood of a poor operating profit (or loss) being leveraged downwards. Of course, other analysts with a higher appetite for risk might believe that the higher risk is worth the higher return.

11.7 ANALYSING LIQUIDITY

We now move to an aspect of the business which we have not yet addressed. Liquidity is not one of the drivers of ROE, but it is nonetheless an aspect of the business which can have an enormous effect on its performance. That is because illiquid businesses very quickly fail.

A liquid business is one which can settle its short-term payables when they fall due. These include amounts due to suppliers, employees, the tax authority, providers of short-term borrowings, long-term lenders whose interest is due, and so on. In other words, a liquid business can cover its current liabilities.

Of course, not all current liabilities are due immediately: indeed, by definition, some may only be payable eleven or even twelve months from the reporting date. Therefore to be liquid, a business does not have to maintain a bank balance equal to its current liabilities. Yet, except in the very beginning, a business is clearly not sustainable if it has to use sources such as long-term liabilities or equity to meet its short-term payment obligations. The money must either come from the bank asset, or from the other assets which will deliver cash sooner rather than later, such as trade receivables and inventory.

11.7.1 Current ratio

$$\text{Current ratio} = \frac{\text{Current assets}}{\text{Current liabilities}}$$

Burberry's current ratio:

2019: £1 608.6 m ÷ £640.1 m   **2.5 times**

2018: £1 541.7 m ÷ £552.9 m   2.8 times

Prada: €1 761 610 k ÷ €986 861 k   1.8 times

- *Aspect.* The current ratio provides the most straightforward evaluation of a business's liquidity, by measuring the extent to which its current assets cover its current liabilities.

- *Message.* In 2019, Burberry's current assets were 2.5 times its current liabilities. In other words, there was £250 of cash, receivables, and inventory that could potentially be used to pay for every £100 of current liabilities.

- *Benchmark(s).* Although Burberry's current ratio had declined slightly since 2018, the British group was significantly more liquid than Prada.

- *Explanation.* To really understand liquidity, it is important to check the mix of current assets. Burberry's huge cash balances make it extremely liquid. However, if, say, a large proportion of current assets had consisted of inventory with a slow turnover, the business may have liquidity concerns even despite a current ratio of 2.5.

- *Risk.* Burberry is not exposed to any serious liquidity risk.

Like all ratios, the 'correct' current ratio differs from industry to industry, and from business to business. For example, Tesco's 2019 current ratio was just 0.6, arising from current assets of £12.6 billion and current liabilities of £20.7 billion. Whereas for many businesses this would be untenable, at Tesco it was not a sign of a liquidity crisis. Recall from Figure 11.3 and the discussion towards the end of section 11.4.5 that Tesco's operating cycle generates cash from inventory and receivables in about half the time it requires to pay suppliers. Tesco even manages to pay its suppliers in less than thirty-five days, which gives it some wiggle room if in fact liquidity were to become an issue at any point: presumably the business could pay suppliers later.

In the same way that each business's peculiar circumstances should influence how we interpret liquidity ratios, they should also determine which liquidity ratio is most appropriate to use. As we shall see, for a business like Prada, the acid test ratio is a more appropriate measure of liquidity than the current ratio.

MISCONCEPTION

Each aspect of a business can be considered in isolation.

No. Each aspect of a business is connected to the other aspects. For example, a high current ratio implies large amounts of cash, receivables, and inventory. Yet excess current assets are inefficient. If a business reduces current assets in an effort to improve efficiency, then not only does it increase its exposure to liquidity risk, but less generous credit terms incentivise would-be customers to shop elsewhere, and low inventory

11

levels increase the risk of stock-outs and/or higher supply-chain costs. If, to prevent a liquidity crunch, the business tries to drive down current liabilities, this would reduce its potential to leverage returns to shareholders upwards.

Thus, you can see that liquidity, efficiency, profitability, and leverage are all inter-related. To a large extent, the art of business success is finding the right balance between all these different aspects. Whenever you are attempting to explain a ratio, it is therefore a good idea to think about how it connects with the rest of your analysis. It's also probably best to avoid being too dogmatic in your comments about a ratio, because—whether that ratio seems to you to be very good or bad—the underlying explanation may well have caused some other ratio to experience a quite different result.

11.7.2 **Acid test ratio**

$$\text{Acid test ratio} = \frac{\text{Current assets} - \text{Inventory}}{\text{Current liabilities}}$$

Burberry's acid test ratio:

2019: (£1 608.6 m – £465.1 m) ÷ £640.1 m	**1.8 times**	
2018: (£1 541.7 m – £411.8 m) ÷ £552.9 m	2.0 times	
Prada: (€1 761 610k – €631 791) ÷ €986 861 k	1.1 times	

- *Aspect*. The acid test ratio evaluates a business's liquidity by measuring the extent to which current assets other than inventory cover its current liabilities.

- *Message*. Burberry's remaining current assets (that is, cash and receivables) cover its current liabilities 1.8 times.

- *Benchmark(s)*. Like the current ratio, despite a slight year-on-year deterioration, this measure indicated that Burberry was a lot more liquid than Prada.

- *Explanation*. Inventory is the least liquid of the current assets, which is to say that it takes the longest to generate a cash flow. (Do not be fooled if the days inventory is shorter than the collection period. Inventory is still less liquid than trade receivables because *both* periods must pass before it generates cash.) We have already established that Burberry's high cash balance means that it has no liquidity issues, but Prada is a good example of a business for whom the acid test is useful. Given the days inventory of nearly 250 days, we know that inventory will not deliver cash until long after its biggest current liability, trade payables, is due. However, since the collection period shows that average receivables deliver cash within 35.5 days, the acid test ratio of greater than 1.0 indicates that receivables and cash together will be sufficient for Prada to meet its short-term commitments.

- *Risk*. Thus, both Burberry and Prada have low levels of liquidity risk.

11

11.8 **MARKET RATIOS**

All the ratios that we have calculated so far use figures drawn from the financial statements. In addition to these accounting numbers, if the business is a company listed on a stock exchange, there is another valuable piece of information, published daily, that can be used for analysis. This is the share price, a figure which represents the market consensus about the value of one of the company's shares.

The share price enables analysts to calculate another whole category of financial ratios, known as the market ratios. These combine certain figures from the financial statements with the share price to reveal valuable information of direct relevance to an investor.

The share price of most listed companies changes every day, but, as we are not able to give you the share price on the date you are reading these words, in this section we shall use the share prices at each company's year-end, which are as follows.

TABLE 11.2 Share price information for Burberry and Prada[18]

Burberry, 30 March 2019: 1954.5 p or £19.545
Burberry, 31 March 2018: 1696.0 p or £16.96
Burberry, 31 March 2017: 1740.0 p or £17.40
Prada, 31 December 2018: €2.87
Prada, 31 December 2017: €3.02

11.8.1 **Total shareholder return**

$$\text{Total shareholder return} = \frac{\text{Change in share price} + \text{dividends per share}}{\text{Share price at beginning of period}} \times 100$$

Burberry's total shareholder return:
2019: [(1 954.5 p − 1 696.0 p + 41.3 p) ÷ 1 696.0 p] × 100   **17.7%**
2018: [(1 696.0 p − 1 740.0 p + 39.4 p) ÷ 1 740.0 p] × 100   *−0.3%*
Prada: [(€2.87 − €3.02 + €0.06) ÷ €3.02] × 100   *−3.0%*

- *Aspect*. Total shareholder return (TSR), sometimes also called the 'return to shareholders', is a market ratio measuring the business's overall market performance as a function of the dividends paid and the change in the share price. (To calculate Burberry's dividends per share (DPS), we used the information about dividends paid during the financial year. That is, the sum of the interim DPS and the prior-year final DPS from note 12.)

- *Message*. Shareholders who owned Burberry shares throughout its 2019 financial year earned a return for the year of 17.7%.

- *Benchmark(s)*. This is way better than the TSR for the 2018 year, which was just less than zero. Prada's shareholders lost 3% on their investment. It is clear that Burberry's

2019 TSR was a success: not simply because of these favourable comparisons, but also because an annual return of 17% beats the vast majority of other investment opportunities. For example, the average return for companies listed on the London Stock Exchange in that period was less than 2%.[19]

- *Explanation.* Burberry's 2019 return was composed of 2.4% (41.3 p ÷ 1 696.0 p × 100) cash return in the form of dividends, and 15.3% (258.5 p ÷ 1 696.0 p × 100) notional return based on the increase in the share price of 258.5 p (1954.5 p − 1696.0 p). The slightly negative TSR in the 2018 year was the result of the DPS being just less than the year's drop in the share price. The difference was greater for Prada's shareholders.

- *Risk.* Investments in shares (referred to as 'equity investments' in the finance in-dustry) always come with relatively high risk. The average risk–return profiles of the typical alternative investment instruments—debt, property, and money market funds—are lower than for equities. This can be seen in the way that Burberry's TSR has varied from one year to the next. It is also the reason that financial advisers gen-erally recommend that investors diversify their equity investments by buying shares in several different companies, and plan to hold them for many years.

11.8.2 Price–earnings ratio

$$\text{Price-earnings ratio} = \frac{\text{Share price (on any given date)}}{\text{Most recent earnings per share}}$$

The price–earnings ratio (formally abbreviated as PER) is also called the 'price–earnings multiple', and often referred to simply as the business's 'PE'. It is the ratio most frequently used by analysts to evaluate the market's perception of the business. (It is common to talk about 'the market' as if it has a single mind and coordinated actions. In fact, the market is made up of a broad spectrum of different investors with differing levels of skills, knowl-edge, and experience. Nonetheless, for each investor, there is a common feature of all the other investors: they are all someone else! It is all those other investors whom each inves-tor refers to as 'the market'.)

One of the key inputs into the PE formula is earnings per share (EPS), which we dis-cussed in detail in section 4.9.1. The PE ratio is best understood by imagining two com-panies, A and B, with figures such as those in Example 11.3.

EXAMPLE 11.3

	Company A €	Company B €
Share price	100	200
Earnings per share	10	10
Price–earnings ratio	100 ÷ 10 = 10.0	200 ÷ 10 = 20.0

11

Both these companies have made EPS of €10, so one might expect an investor to be indifferent between holding a share in Company A or B. Yet, even though they have in the past year increased the value of the company per share by the same amount, the share price of Company B is twice that of Company A. In other words, as the PEs clearly show, while investors are willing to pay €10 for every €1 of Company A's current earnings, for Company B they are willing to pay €20 for €1 of its current earnings.

When this happens, the only reasonable explanations are:

(1) the market expects Company B to perform much better in the future than Company A; or

(2) the market perceives Company A to be riskier than Company B (one always pays less for something that is riskier; think about what you would pay for a car with no brakes); or

(3) both 1 and 2.

> The PE tells us about the market's perception of the future potential returns of the business and/or the perceived risk attached to the business.

Whichever explanation is correct, the message of the PE ratio is simple and clear: relative to its current earnings, the market perceives Company B to be the better investment.

In practice, there is some variation in the PE formula that analysts use. In the denominator, for example, different analysts use different EPS figures, such as those discussed in sections 4.9.4 and 4.9.5. Here, we have used the simplest of all: basic EPS. Whichever EPS figure is used, it stays the same throughout a given financial period, whereas the numerator changes from day to day as the share price changes. Daily PEs for all listed companies are therefore reported online and in the financial pages of most newspapers. We have calculated the following PEs on the companies' year-end dates.

Burberry's price–earnings ratio:

2019: 1 954.5 p ÷ 82.3 p   **23.7 times**

2018: 1 696.0 p ÷ 68.9 p   *24.6 time*

Prada: €2.87 ÷ €0.08   *35.9 times*

- *Aspect*. The PE ratio is a market ratio measuring 'market sentiment', the market's perception of the company.

- *Message*. At the end of its 2019 year, the market as a whole considered Burberry to be worth 23.7 times its 2019 earnings. Another way to express this is that investors were willing to pay £23.70 for £1 of the company's current earnings.

- *Benchmark(s)*. Relative to each year's earnings, the market was slightly less optimistic about Burberry than it had been a year ago. And, at their respective year-ends, the market had considerably higher expectations about Prada's ability to improve its earnings in future.

- *Explanation*. We know that in 2019 Burberry's profit turned out to be 15.5% higher than in 2018, partly due to one-off restructuring costs in 2018. A possible explanation for the dip in the PE is that the market correctly anticipated this, and doesn't expect quite the same rate of growth in 2020 and beyond. The most likely reason that Prada's PE is so much higher is that the market believes that Prada is a solid company whose earnings will bounce back from their underwhelming 2018 levels.

- *Risk*. It is difficult to separate out the market's expectations of future profitability from its perception of risk. It may be that the Italian group is perceived to be less risky, or perhaps the different PEs are entirely the result of divergent expectations of future profitability.

The PE tells us which company is perceived by the market to be the better company, relative to its current earnings. But this is not the same as asking which is in fact the better company. The market may, after all, be wrong. During the information technology (IT) boom of the 1990s, many IT companies were trading on PEs as high as 70, indicating that the prices being paid for shares in these companies were not based on current earnings at all, but rather on the widespread belief that these companies would have exceptional performance in the future. However, in most cases this was a severe misjudgement, and, as people realised that simply being in the IT sector was not enough to guarantee huge future profits, share prices plunged, and the 'dot com bubble' burst.

In early 2020, as we write these words, there are again several well-known examples of tech firms with dizzyingly high PEs, and some with massive market values that have never once made a profit. An increasing number of analysts believe that these companies will experience a similar crash.

On the other hand, there have been many companies which were undervalued by the market and thus ended up making a few skilled investors a lot of money when their performance exceeded everyone else's expectations.

Successful investors are able to use their own analyses to identify the true value of a company (see Chapter 12 on valuations); and use indicators like the PE to assess the market's perception of the company's value; and then take advantage of the opportunities presented by a difference between these two assessments.

The earnings yield is another common ratio, but it contains no more information than the PE ratio, as it is in fact the reciprocal of the PE, expressed as a percentage. For this reason, we have included it in the advanced material available with the **online resources**.

11.8.3 Dividend yield

$$\text{Dividend yield} = \frac{\text{Most recent dividends per share}}{\text{Share price (on any given date)}} \times 100$$

The dividend yield expresses DPS as a percentage return on the share price. It is essentially the cash portion of the TRS we analysed in section 11.8.1, updated for changes in the share price.

Burberry's dividend yield:

2019: (41.3 p ÷ 1 954.5 p) × 100   **2.1%**

2018: (39.4 p ÷ 1 696.0 p) × 100   *2.3%*

Prada: (€0.06 ÷ €2.87) × 100   *2.1%*

- *Aspect.* Dividend yield is a market ratio measuring the cash return on a company's shares.

- *Message.* If a shareholder paid for a share on the date of analysis, and if the past year's dividends were maintained into the future, they would make a cash return of 2.1%.

- *Benchmark(s).* This is a slight decline versus 2018, and an exact match with Prada. It compares favourably with the average interest received from a UK savings over that period, which was 1.4%.[20]

- *Explanation.* Companies know that some investors appreciate a cash return, and they are also aware that dropping their dividends per share payments tends to be interpreted by the market as a signal that the business is experiencing cash flow problems (see a full discussion of this in section 1.3.5). For both of these reasons, unless they really are in peril, or have some other very good reason for keeping the cash (like a major acquisition), they will inevitably pay out dividends which are in line with past policy and market norms. This is what Burberry and Prada have done. The only reason for Burberry's slight dip between 2018 and 2019 is the increase in the share price.

- *Risk.* The higher the dividend yield, the higher the risk that the current level of dividends cannot be maintained in future. To determine the sustainability of dividends, some analysts also concern themselves with the question of whether *profit* can cover dividends, which they measure with a ratio called 'dividend cover' (this is discussed in the advanced material for this available with the **online resources**). However, dividends are paid in cash, and so most good analysts prefer to use their analysis of cash flows to assess the business's ability to reward shareholders with dividends, as we did in section 5.6.

Dividends are perceived differently by different types of investors. Some investors have no interest in receiving dividends, but prefer to get their return on investment solely via the increase in share price. For these investors, dividend yield is largely irrelevant. Other investors are interested in receiving a cash return, and therefore rate businesses highly if they have strong dividend yields.

There is a danger of reading too much into the dividend yield. After all, although the two groups' dividend yields were the same, we know from the TRS analysis that it would have been substantially better to be a shareholder in Burberry than in Prada during the period under analysis, because the non-cash return (that is, the change in the share price) was very good in Burberry's case, but negative in Prada's case.

11.9 CHALLENGES IN FINANCIAL ANALYSIS

In this section, we briefly outline the most common challenges, limitations, and pitfalls that an analyst might encounter when doing financial analysis.

11.9.1 **Which ratios to use?**

A challenge when doing ratio analysis is deciding which ratio, from all of the available ratios, to use. In this chapter, we have introduced a handful of the most commonly used ratios, but one could calculate hundreds more ratios for each business.

Some of these are variations of existing ratios: for example, in a business with a large proportion of intellectual property, one might calculate an intangible asset turnover ratio akin to the fixed asset turnover ratio. Other ratios apply to specific industries. For example, a retailer may evaluate the efficiency of its sales force by calculating sales per full-time employee.

Conversely, some ratios are not applicable to certain businesses or industries. For example, there is no benefit in calculating an inventory turnover ratio for a bank, which has no inventory. (Instead, other ratios might be more appropriate in a banking environment, such as the ratio of interest received to interest paid.)

The answer to the question of which ratios to use comes with experience: the more analysis one does, the more familiar one will get with the appropriate ratios to use in a given situation. The ratios presented in this chapter form a good start, but we encourage you to expand your repertoire, so long as you don't allow yourself to get bogged down in unnecessary detail.

11.9.2 **The skewing effects of business expansion**

More often than not, asset turnover ratios decrease in a year of expansion. It is therefore advisable not to jump too quickly to conclusions about decreased efficiency, as they may simply be temporary. One frequent reason for the apparent decline is mathematical: by averaging asset balances in the denominators of these ratios, we implicitly assume that assets have been purchased evenly over the year. If, however, a large proportion of assets were acquired towards the end of the year, then the ratio would have been skewed downwards, because their effect on revenue in the numerator would be proportionally lower than their effect in the denominator. Equally, if the assets were mostly acquired early on in the year, the ratio would be skewed upwards.

The other reason is commercial: even if assets are in fact purchased evenly through the year, it is unreasonable to expect these new assets to generate revenues at the same rate as existing assets. For example, one should not expect new retail stores to generate sales in their first few months at the same rate as older stores with established customer bases.

Thus, if an expanding business appears to be suffering a decline in efficiency, don't panic! Rather, try to establish whether the new assets will generate sales at a more favourable rate in future years.

11.9.3 **Tweaking the numbers**

Some items on the financial statements are ambiguous. For example, a deferred tax liability is not necessarily wholly debt (see section 8.3 for an explanation of deferred tax). To the extent that it reflects increased taxes to be paid in the future, for example because

11

of an accelerated tax write-off of PPE, it is a true liability. However, to the extent that it represents tax that will never be paid, such as the notional tax on shares that will never be sold, it is not really a liability at all, and ought instead to be treated as equity.

Seasoned analysts who respect this ambiguity sometimes try to split the deferred tax figure into its debt and equity components, and use the revised figures to calculate their financial ratios. Others, who doubt their ability to split the figure accurately, instead revise the financial information for ratios by omitting deferred tax altogether.

We discussed in section 11.2.2 the way that intangible assets are not often recognised. Some analysts may choose to respond to this by adding their own estimates of the missing assets' value to the asset totals they insert into their ratio formulas. Similarly, it is important to adjust for differences in goodwill between businesses if, for example, the company being analysed has a large goodwill balance as a result of many business acquisitions, while its competitor used as a benchmark recognises no goodwill because it is all internally generated.

When performing an analysis that compares two businesses, a particular comparability challenge arises if they use different accounting policies and estimates. For example, in section 2.2.9 we observed how the depreciation charge can double, or halve, depending on the estimate of the asset's useful life, with potentially dramatic effects on both profit and assets. Ideally, an analyst would choose as a benchmark a competitor with similar accounting policies and estimates to the business they are analysing. Alternatively, the analyst may choose to adjust the accounting figures as far as possible to create the effect of similar policies and estimates.

Analysts tweak not only the data they input to the ratios, but also the ratio formulas themselves. Some analysts choose to average figures from the statement of financial position, as we did in this chapter, on the grounds that this reduces the impact of day-to-day variation; whereas others prefer to use year-end balances, in the belief that they convey the most recent information. In their formulas for days inventory, collection period, and settlement period, some analysts might use some lower constant in place of 365, on the grounds that the business's financial year has fewer than 365 working days. And so on.

Investment firms tend to develop their own in-house ways of calculating financial ratios, which they keep secret but tout to potential clients as their competitive advantage. Perhaps you too wish to tweak the formulas or their inputs as we have laid them out in this chapter—that is your right, and may be the key to your own investing success! What we have done is present the classic ways of calculating ratios, which have stood the test of time.

11.9.4 Inconsistent formulas

Of course, different formulas give different results. Once you have settled on a particular formula, it is therefore vital that you make sure the ratio is calculated using that formula exactly: for current and prior years, comparable businesses, and industry averages.

In particular, industry averages are usually produced by a third party. If you use industry averages as one of your benchmarks, you therefore must inform yourself as to the formulas that were used to calculate them, and use the same ones for your calculations about the business you are analysing. Apples must be compared with apples.

11.9.5 **Aggregated information**

The information contained in the financial statements of a business is really a collection (or aggregation) of the financial results of all the divisions and operations within the business. These various business segments may sell vastly different products or services, or operate in different countries, each with its own risk–return profile.

Suppose that a group contains a manufacturer of household furniture and a retailer of general merchandise. The risk–return profile of each segment is very distinct: manufacturing furniture would be subject to risks such as timber availability and price changes, as well as climatic effects on plantations owned; whilst general merchandise retail would be subject to cyclical demand risks, risks created by providing warranties, and the risk of extending credit to customers who are not creditworthy. An analysis of the group's aggregated financial information would help us understand the business as a whole, but a proper analysis would require a detailed understanding of the risk–return profile of each of the underlying businesses.

Thankfully, every company whose debt or equity is traded in a public market is required to prepare a segmental report. This is usually presented as a note to the financial statements that disaggregates key information by segment.

These segments may be distinguished according to products or services, along geographical lines, or on some other meaningful basis determined by the way in which financial information is reported internally to management. Roughly speaking, if a reporting line makes up 10% or more of the business, it should be included as a separate segment in the segmental report.

> The objective of segmental reporting is to disaggregate the results in order to display the different risk–return profiles of the various segments of the business.

Segmental reporting is necessary when analysing a diversified group of companies, but it is valuable even for a business such as Burberry, which is largely dedicated to one basic activity: retailing luxury goods. Indeed, Burberry's segmental report (note 3 to its 2019 financial statements) shows how the group distinguishes between its various segments in three different ways: its two 'channels to market' (retail/wholesale and licensing); its five product divisions (accessories, women's, men's, children's/other, and beauty); and its three destination regions (Asia Pacific; 'EMEIA': that is, Europe, Middle East, India, and Africa; and the Americas).

Just a short time spent reading through the segmental report reveals a lot about Burberry's various markets, such as that accessories contribute about 38% of its sales; apparel about 54%; and beauty now just 6% after the sale to Coty. Also, the group's biggest retail/wholesale geographical market is Asia Pacific (41%), followed by EMEIA (36%), and then the Americas (23%). Customers in the UK purchased £311.7 million of the £957.4 million of goods sold to the EMEIA region. Thus, segmental reporting can give an analyst a very quick and helpful sense of how and where a business makes its money.

11.9.6 **Contradictory results**

All too often, the results of various ratios give mixed signals. For example, in our analysis of Burberry in this chapter, we discovered that the business managed PPE, inventory, and trade receivables more efficiently between 2018 and 2019, and yet the overall measure of asset efficiency, TAT, revealed that the overall asset efficiency did not change. When this sort of contradiction emerges, it is important to double-check your results, and then search for an explanation. (In this case, the answer to the mystery lies in the effect that the sale of the Beauty operation had on the 2018 averages for PPE, inventory, and trade receivables.)

The legendarily successful investor Warren Buffet has claimed that 'if you can't understand a . . . managerial explanation, it's usually because the CEO doesn't want you to',[21] which no doubt often applies to the information in the financial statements themselves. A word of caution, though: listed companies are so large and complex that their financial statements will inevitably contain at least a few small mysteries that cannot be fully resolved by an external analyst. It is important not to overreact to these, and rather to recognise the point at which they become so significant that there is cause for genuine concern. (In Chapter 13, we shall share some renowned examples of financial statements where genuine concern was very much warranted.)

When confronted with contradictory results, we encourage you to be patient, to rise to the challenge, and to feel inspired by the fact that analysis is rather like detective work. Not every clue is obvious, nor will any single clue necessarily solve the mystery. Yet if you gather enough information to be able to see the significant patterns, you will undoubtedly unlock many valuable messages hidden just beneath the surface of the financial statements.

CONCLUSION

We have written this book for non-specialists so that they may be able to understand financial statements. This is not just an academic exercise; it has a practical purpose: we want you to be able to *use* financial statements to infer meaningful and valuable things about businesses. In short, we want you to develop the skills of financial analysis. In many ways, the entire book has been leading up to this point. The preceding chapters have taught you how to read the financial statements, and learn about the context in which the business finds itself—the first of the three stages of analysis—and now this chapter has exposed you to the second and third stages.

Exposure is, of course, just the beginning. You must now practise these skills. For example, you should take the chance to do that with Daimler, using the exercises at the end of the chapter. But don't let that be the end of your journey. Like any language, the language of accounting is mastered by continual reading and use. The trick to becoming really proficient is examining and analysing as many financial statements as you can.

So, after Daimler, choose an industry with which you are already somewhat familiar. Why not try analysing the business you work for, or a listed company in the industry you plan to work in? Or get yourself a copy of the most recent financial statements of a business you know by virtue of being a customer: somewhere you shop regularly.

If you feel that there is no business with which you are familiar and whose financial statements you can access, then perhaps just download the latest financial statements of Burberry, about which you have learned an enormous amount simply by reading this book. By the time you are reading these words, Burberry will have released new financial statements.

By making it this far, you have achieved a great deal. The remaining chapters will answer a few outstanding questions, and explore some new topics that you will hopefully find as fascinating as we do.

SUMMARY OF KEY POINTS

- Financial analysis aims to examine the financial statements to see whether value has indeed been created, and to determine whether it will continue to be created.

- It consists of three stages: reading the financial statements; understanding the main story of the financial statements; and ratio analysis.

- The amount of value the business can be expected to create in future is called 'expected return'; and the likelihood of that happening is referred to as 'risk'. An analyst must seek to understand not only the business's expected return, but also its risk.

- The risk–return profile of each investment opportunity differs, but it is generally true that higher expected returns come with higher levels of risk.

- Figures and financial ratios are difficult, if not impossible, to judge without some basis for comparison, called a benchmark. The three benchmarks typically used in financial analysis are: prior year information; competitor information; and average information for the industry or sector.

- To understand the main story of the financial statements, the six key questions to ask are: 'What sorts of assets has the business invested in?'; 'How much revenue did the assets produce?'; 'How much profit was earned from the revenue?'; 'How much profit was converted into operating cash flows?'; 'How did operating cash flows combine with other cash flow activities?'; and 'How are the assets funded?'

- Financial ratios enable an analyst to see the ways in which certain items of financial information relate to other items, delivering insights about five aspects of business performance that cannot be inferred simply from reading the financial statements.

- AMBER analysis provides an effective structure to the interpretation of each ratio. It stands for 'aspect', 'message', 'benchmark(s)', 'explanation', and 'risk'.

- ROE contrasts profit with equity. It is widely regarded as the most important financial ratio, as it measures overall business performance.

- Du Pont analysis enables a deeper understanding of ROE by calculating its three drivers: total asset turnover, net margin, and the equity multiplier. These ratios are each an overall measure of an important aspect of business performance: asset efficiency, profitability, and leverage.

- Within each of these three aspects of business performance, there are further ratios. Each ratio enables an analysis of specific features within that aspect. For example, the fixed asset turnover ratio measures the efficiency of PPE; gross margin measures the profitability of inventory; times interest earned measures the business's exposure to the risk of not being able to make interest payments.

- A particularly important set of asset efficiency ratios concerns working capital management: days inventory, collection period, settlement period, and operating cycle.

- A fourth aspect of business performance is liquidity. The liquidity ratios measure liquidity risk: the business's risk of not meeting short-term payment obligations.

- Efficiency, profitability, leverage, and liquidity are all interrelated. To a large extent, the art of business success is finding the right balance between all these different aspects.

- The fifth aspect is market performance. The market ratios combine information from the financial statements with the share price to deliver insights about listed companies.

- Financial analysis is a difficult exercise, filled with various challenges. To learn how to deal with these challenges, and to improve as an analyst, there is no substitute for practice.

11

CHAPTER QUESTIONS

The applied questions (marked 'AQ') and the discussion questions (marked 'DQ') relate to the financial statements of Daimler, contained in Appendix II. The suggested solutions to these questions, and also to the concept questions (marked 'CQ'), can be found in Appendix III.

Also, don't forget the **online resources** available at www.oup.com/he/winfield-graham-miller1e, which contain multiple-choice questions based on the material in this chapter. You will also find many other helpful resources, including two mini case studies with accompanying questions and answers, and advanced material applicable to financial analysis.

CONCEPT QUESTIONS

CQ 11.1 Briefly outline the three stages of financial analysis.

CQ 11.2 Name three typical benchmarks that can be used as a basis for comparison when performing financial analysis.

CQ 11.3 If a company is listed, ratio analysis is usually performed on five different aspects of the business. Identify and briefly explain these aspects.

CQ 11.4 What five questions should an analyst ask about a ratio when using an AMBER analysis?

CQ 11.5 List and briefly describe some of the challenges that an analyst may experience when performing ratio analysis.

APPLIED QUESTIONS

AQ 11.6 Using Daimler's consolidated statement of income, construct a common-sized group income statement for the 2019 and 2018 financial years. (Hint: if you wish to include an operating profit subtotal, it may be helpful to refer to 'Interest and similar expense' in Table F.16 on p 251 of the annual report.)

AQ 11.7 Calculate Daimler's return on equity for the 2019 and 2018 financial years, together with the ratios that measure the three drivers of this return on equity. Present all of these ratios in the format of a Du Pont analysis. Note: Daimler's equity and total assets at 31 December 2017 were €65 159 and €255 345, respectively.

AQ 11.8 In the table below, you have been provided with a number of efficiency, profitability, leverage, and liquidity ratios for Daimler's 2018 financial year. Calculate these same ratios for Daimler's 2019 financial year.

	2018
Fixed asset turnover (times)	5.7
Days inventory on hand (days)	75.0
Collection period (days)	26.8
Settlement period (days)	36.2
Operating cycle (days)	65.6
Gross margin (%)	19.8
Debt ratio (%)	76.5
Debt–equity ratio (%)	3.3

	2018
Times interest earned (times)	17.1
Current ratio (times)	1.2
Acid test ratio (times)	0.9

DISCUSSION QUESTIONS

DQ 11.9 Using the common-sized income statement that you constructed in AQ 11.6, make five meaningful observations about Daimler's income and expenses. Be sure to look for interesting relationships both vertically and horizontally.

DQ 11.10 Perform an AMBER analysis on each of the four 2019 ratios that you calculated in AQ 11.7 above, using as a benchmark the 2018 ratios that you calculated. For this exercise, imagine that you are performing the analysis soon after the year-end, before the extreme effects of the looming Covid-19 pandemic became relevant.

DQ 11.11 Perform an AMBER analysis on each of the 2019 ratios that you calculated in AQ 11.8 above, using as a benchmark the 2018 ratios that we provided. Again, imagine that you are performing the analysis in the early days of 2020, without the benefit of hindsight about the Covid-19 pandemic.

INVESTIGATION QUESTIONS

IQ 11.12 Identify a listed retail company that is based in your country and obtain its financial statements. Calculate its key asset efficiency, profitability, leverage, and liquidity ratios. Then perform an AMBER analysis on each of these ratios, using as a benchmark the ratios that have been presented for Burberry in this chapter.

IQ 11.13 For the listed retailer that you identified in IQ 11.12, obtain that retailer's price–earnings multiple and dividend yield from either the financial press or the internet. Perform an AMBER analysis on each of these ratios, using as a benchmark the ratios of its competitors.

REFERENCES

[1] Macmillan, I, Prakash, S, and Shoult, R 2014. 'The Cash Paradox: How Record Cash Reserves Are Influencing Corporate Behaviour'. *Deloitte Review*, Issue 15. 28 July. Available at: https://www2.deloitte.com/us/en/insights/deloitte-review/issue-15/excess-cash-growth-strategies.html.

[2] Waters, R 2019. 'Google Parent Alphabet Overtakes Apple to Become New King of Cash'. *Financial Times*. 31 July. Available at: https://www.ft.com/content/332dd974-b349-11e9-8cb2-799a3a8cf37b.

[3] From Burberry *2018/19 Annual Report*, p 18.

[4] From Burberry *2018/19 Annual Report*, p 22.

[5] IASB 2007. 'IASB Issues Revised Standard on the Presentation of Financial Statements'. Press Release. 6 September 2007. Available at: https://www.iasplus.com/en/binary/pressrel/0709ias1revpr.pdf.

[6] These figures, and all other financial information for Prada used in this chapter, come from the consolidated financial statements contained on pp 138–229 of the Prada *2018 Annual Report*. Available at: https://www.iasplus.com/en/binary/pressrel/0709ias1revpr.pdf.

11

7   Office for National Statistics 2019. *Consumer Price Inflation, UK: March 2019*. Statistical bulletin. 17 April. Available at: https://www.ons.gov.uk/economy/inflationandpriceindices/bulletins/consumerpriceinflation/march2019/pdf.

8   Amazon.com Inc 2019. *Amazon 2018 Annual Report*. Available at: https://s2.q4cdn.com/299287126/files/doc_financials/annual/2018-Annual-Report.pdf.

9   From Burberry *2018/19 Annual Report*, p 70 and Prada *2018 Annual Report*, p 63.

10 From *Burberry 2018/19 Annual Report*, p 19.

11 Ratios for Amazon.com Inc's 2018 year have been calculated from the figures disclosed in the *2018 Annual Report*. Available at: https://ir.aboutamazon.com/static-files/0f9e36b1-7e1e-4b52-be17-145dc9d8b5ec. The share price information used later in the chapter comes from Google.

12 From Burberry *2018/19 Annual Report*, p 38.

13 From Burberry *2018/19 Annual Report*, p 69.

14 From Prada *2018 Annual Report*, p 184.

15 Tesco plc 2019. *Annual Report and Financial Statements 2019*. Available at: https://www.tescoplc.com/media/476422/tesco_ara2019_full_report_web.pdf.

16 From Burberry *2018/19 Annual Report*, p 38.

17 Campbell Soup Company 2019. *2019 Annual Report*, pp 39 and 41. Available at: https://www.campbellsoupcompany.com/wp-content/uploads/sites/31/2019/10/Campbell-Soup-Company-2019-Annual-Report.pdf.

18 Share price information for Burberry was obtained from sharesmagazine.co.uk. Available at: https://www.sharesmagazine.co.uk/shares/share/BRBY/historic-prices. Share price information for Prada was obtained from Google, and exchange rate information was obtained from www.exchange-rates.org.

19 FTSE ALSI data obtained from the London Stock Exchange website. Available at: https://www.londonstockexchange.com/exchange/prices-and-markets/stocks/indices/summary/summary-indices-chart.html?index=ASX.

20 Deposit rate information was obtained from: http://www.swanlowpark.co.uk/savings-interest-annual.

21 Berkshire Hathaway Inc 2002. *Chairman's Letter, 2002*. Available at: https://www.berkshirehathaway.com/letters/2002pdf.pdf.

BUSINESS VALUATIONS

Here are some of the things you will be able to do after reading this chapter:

- distinguish between three different ways of thinking about a business's value, and describe why business valuations are performed;
- list and explain the steps involved in a valuation using a discounted cash flow model;
- demonstrate a dividend-based approach to cash flow valuation, using the Gordon growth model;
- describe the basic approach of multiples valuation methods, using market-to-book, price–earnings, and enterprise value multiples as examples;
- discuss the weaknesses of the two basic approaches to business valuations, and how their results are contrasted in practice in order to improve the accuracy of a valuation.

In Chapter 11, you learned that managers, investors, creditors, employees, and other stakeholders in a business regularly perform financial analyses of a business in order to form an opinion about its risk–return profile; that is, the amount of value the business can be expected to create in future, and also the likelihood of this expected return. In this chapter, you will learn how a few of these stakeholders sometimes take the additional step of performing a business valuation, which essentially involves calculating the business's value.

CHAPTER 12

12.1 THREE MEANINGS OF VALUE

First, we should consider what 'value' means. Generally speaking, the value of something is what it is worth, but this is not the only way that people talk about a business's value. Let us briefly unpack each of the three quite different ways in which the term is used.

12.1.1 **Book value**

Section 10.1 observed how the total equity of a business is often referred to as its '**book value**', which may give the impression that it represents a reliable estimate of what the business is worth. For example, one might think that on 30 March 2019 Burberry was really worth its total equity of £1 460.0 million.

However, the section also identified three kinds of reasons that the total equity figure reported on a business's statement of financial position almost certainly does *not* amount to an accurate valuation of a business's worth: assets are not at fair value; some identifiable assets and liabilities are not included in net asset value; and a range of other items of value—collectively known as goodwill—are also not generally included, such as the quality of staff, the business's reputation, and its future prospects.

The book value, or total equity, of a business is widely regarded as a poor measure of a business's true worth.

12.1.2 **Market value**

The shares of companies listed on a stock exchange are typically traded every day. The price of each trade is recorded and made public almost immediately. (For example, you can discover the price of the most recent trade of Burberry's shares by typing 'Burberry share price' into Google's search engine.) The share price can be used to calculate the **market capitalisation** (or 'market cap') of the business.

The market value of a listed business is its market capitalisation.

$$\text{Market capitalisation} = \text{Share price} \times \text{Number of outstanding shares}$$

For example, on 30 March 2019, Burberry had 411 456 001 shares **outstanding** and its share price on the London Stock Exchange was £1 954.5 p, thus giving the business a market capitalisation of £8 041.9 million. If you have understood the reasons that book value is not a good measure of a business's worth, it should not surprise you that the business's market value is much higher than its book value of £1 460.0 million: this is entirely typical.

Section 6.1.5 explained that accountants refer to the share price as the 'fair value' of a share, and section 6.7.2 described how the share price is therefore used to measure a business's investments in another company's shares. Many people agree with IFRS that there is no better measure of what a share is worth than the amount that someone else just chose to pay for it. It follows that if the value of a single share is the share price, then the value of all the shares—the entire business, in other words—is the market capitalisation. This is why the market cap is often described as the 'market value' of the business.

However, this is also not a reliable measure of a business's true worth, for at least three reasons. First, it is a theoretical figure: if someone were really to begin buying large volumes of shares, the forces of supply and demand would cause the share price to increase quickly. (In fact, to acquire all the shares in a listed company, acquirers do not simply buy up the shares on the exchange, but instead they typically make a single offer to all shareholders, at a premium to the current share price, following formal procedures which vary depending on the jurisdiction.)

Second, although investors do seek to establish a more reliable valuation of a company than book value (eg by thinking about what its assets are really worth, and taking into account the items not recognised on the statement of financial position), they may easily miscalculate its value. For an example, look no further than the massive overvaluations of technology shares in the dot com bubble described in section 11.8.2.

Third, share prices are influenced by factors which have little, if anything, to do with the company itself: changes in the attractiveness of other investment opportunities; flows of foreign capital in or out of the country; day-to-day national political dramas; and so on. If we were to accept that market value is an accurate measure of a business's worth, then we would also have to accept the absurd idea that the business is fundamentally worth more or less each day, in correspondence with share price fluctuations, despite the fact that most of the time nothing about the business itself changes significantly from one day to the next.

> The market value of a business is not a dependable measure of its true worth.

12.1.3 **Intrinsic value**

When people wish to distinguish what a business is actually worth from its book value or market value, they often use a term like 'true value' or 'real value'. The technical term is '**intrinsic value**', conveying how actual worth depends on the internal attributes of the business itself, and is unaffected by the wide variety of market effects that have nothing to do with the business.

The internal attributes that determine a business's intrinsic value are easily described: they are whatever will affect the business's ability to generate cash flows. After all, when a person acquires a business, in essence what they are buying is simply the right to the cash flows that the business will generate in the future. As we described in section 1.3.4, this is how a business creates value for its owners: by taking the cash it receives from providers of funding and using the value creation cycle to generate net operating cash inflows. Thus, the intrinsic value of the business is no more or less than the value of its future cash flows.

> The intrinsic value of the business is simply the value of its future cash flows.

Of course, a business's intrinsic value can never be known precisely, for the future is uncertain. Any attempt to find the intrinsic value—that is, to *value a business*—is therefore subject to the valuers' opinions, judgements, and estimates about the future. For this reason, they will often determine a range of potential intrinsic values, rather than a single figure.

In this chapter, we will mainly consider *how* to value a business, but for a moment, let's quickly establish the reasons *why* we would want to do so.

12

12.2 **WHY VALUE A BUSINESS?**

The most obvious time to perform a valuation is when deciding whether to buy or sell the business in its entirety. An acquirer wants to pay no more than what the business is worth, and a seller wants to receive no less than that figure. Each will therefore typically calculate an intrinsic value to determine the limits of an acceptable price.

Similarly, professional investors deciding whether to purchase, sell, or continue to hold a subset of the shares in a listed company will frequently value the business in order to determine the intrinsic value of each share. If they perceive the intrinsic value to be above the price, they typically purchase more shares, whereas if the price is higher than the intrinsic value, they usually sell the shares they hold.

Suppose that a listed company has 1 million outstanding shares, and an investor's valuation establishes that the company is worth €15 million. The intrinsic value is thus €15 per share. If the current share price is less than this intrinsic value—€12, say—then the share is 'undervalued', and the investor should purchase shares (assuming the absence of even better investment opportunities). On the other hand, if the share price is €20, the investor would judge the shares to be 'overvalued', and would not buy them. Indeed, it would probably be a good idea to sell any shares they hold.

> The primary reason to value a business is to determine how much to pay or accept for a sale of the business, or for some of its shares.

Sometimes a valuation is performed even though there is no intention to buy or sell part or all of the business. For example, if Business A owns shares in Business B, which is unlisted, Business A may need to value Business B in order to comply with the accounting requirements relating to investment assets that we covered in section 6.7.2.

From time to time, a business's management team may choose to value the business in order to be able to respond quickly to offers to purchase the business. Even if they do not intend to regularly conduct a complete valuation exercise, a business's managers must be alive to the principles and methods of valuing businesses. Since their responsibility is effectively to increase the intrinsic value of the business they run, it is essential that they know how that value may be determined.

As will become clear, valuation techniques often rely on reported profit figures. This explains why, in their attempt to satisfy their responsibility to maximise intrinsic value, a good management team motivates its entire organisation to focus on meeting profit targets.

MISCONCEPTION

The intrinsic value of a business can be determined with confidence.

No. The fact is that no investor has perfect foresight, and all veteran investors have made bad investments. There is no magic valuation technique which will reliably produce an accurate business valuation every time.

Instead, good analysts will always use several different techniques—including both the DCF and valuations multiples approaches that we shall describe in this chapter—to produce different valuations of the business. They will then compare and contrast these different valuations as objectively as possible, to arrive at their best estimate of intrinsic value.

12.3 DISCOUNTED CASH FLOWS

We have established that the intrinsic value of a business is the value of the cash flows it will generate in the future. Thanks to the concept of the **time value of money**, we also know that an amount of cash received in the future is worth less than the same amount of cash received today. Thus, to obtain the value of the business today, the future cash flows must be discounted to their present value. Thus, the most direct way to calculate a business's intrinsic value is the **discounted cash flow model** (or 'DCF').

In the next few sections, we shall describe each step of the methodology, and then, in section 12.3.5, we shall demonstrate a DCF valuation.

The DCF model values a business by determining the present value of its predicted future cash flows.

12.3.1 Free cash flows

The cash flows used as inputs in a DCF valuation are the yearly future cash flows available (or free) to be distributed to the providers of debt and equity funding. They are thus often referred to as 'free cash flows', resulting in an alternative name for the DCF model itself: the free cash flow model.

The free cash flows are usually calculated by starting with the latest financial statements, and using all other available information (including the conclusions of a comprehensive financial analysis), to forecast the future cash operating profit for each foreseeable future year. From these future operating profit figures, the following future outflows must be subtracted:

- the taxes to be paid on these operating profits;
- predicted capital expenditure to expand the business;
- anticipated increases in net working capital. (As explained in section 5.4.4, working capital requirements increase as revenues grow, and these changes in working capital lead to differences between the accrual-based profit figures and the actual cash flows.)

The result of this calculation is an estimate of free cash flow for as many years as can be estimated. The exact number of years will vary, but usually it would be between three and five.

12.3.2 Present value

The discount rate typically used in a DCF calculation is the company's 'weighted average cost of capital', or 'WACC'. In this sense, 'capital' refers to both sources of business funding: equity and debt. The cost of each source is the expected return that providers of each source of funding expect. For example, if shareholders expect a 10% return on their investment in the business, and lenders charge 5% interest on their loans to the business, the WACC is the average of 5% and 10%. This average is weighted by the relative volumes of equity and debt funding, so if 60% of the business is funded by equity and 40% by debt, the WACC would be 8% (60% × 10% + 40% × 5%).

The discount rate is used to calculate the present value of all the forecast future cash flows. This can be done manually using the complicated formulas you might have learned at school, or more easily with a financial calculator or spreadsheet.

12

The weighted average cost of capital, or WACC, estimates the average cost of a business's equity and debt, in proportion to the amount of each source of funding.

12.3.3 **Terminal value**

So far, the model tells us the present value of the cash flows for the years that the person doing the valuation can forecast with sufficient confidence. But the DCF must also value the cash flows beyond that period, into the far distant future. For example, if free cash flows for the next three years have been forecast and discounted to present value, then an estimated value still needs to be found for the less predictable free cash flows earned four years from now, and beyond. This is done by first deciding a growth rate by which cash flows can be assumed to grow beyond the third forecast year into the future. Then the valuer applies the formula for the present value of a perpetuity to an infinite stream of cash flows increasing at this growth rate. Again, a calculator or spreadsheet makes the calculation considerably easier.

This amount—the present value of the free cash flows beyond the period for which cash flows have been specifically forecast—is known as the 'terminal value'. Once it has been calculated, it is added to the present value of all the forecast future cash flows, to obtain the present value of all future cash flows expected to be generated by the business's operations.

12.3.4 **Adjustments**

A business may have some non-operating assets, for example cash balances larger than it requires for its operations, speculative financial investments, or a vacant plot of land being held purely as an investment. These have not yet been included in the valuation so far, as they do not result in operating cash flows. So one kind of adjustment required at this point is to add the market value of these sorts of items to the present value of future operating cash flows, to arrive at a valuation for the business as a whole.

However, the objective of a DCF exercise is usually to calculate the intrinsic value of *equity*, and so this leads to a second kind of adjustment: the market value of any debt is subtracted from the value of the whole business to obtain the value of the equity alone. To obtain the intrinsic value per share, the value of the equity can simply be divided by the number of outstanding shares.

The steps in a DCF model valuation are: (1) calculating the future free cash flows; (2) discounting these to present value; (3) calculating the terminal value; and (4) performing a few adjustments.

12.3.5 **DCF valuation example**

12

You have no doubt realised by now that a DCF valuation is a time-consuming and intricate exercise, involving a great deal of thinking to support the many different assumptions to be made. We shall therefore not attempt a valuation of a business as large and complex as Burberry here, for it would consume far too many pages. Instead, Example 12.1 contains a simplified worked example showing the basic steps of a DCF valuation for an imaginary business.

To make most sense of this example, we recommend that you go row by row, each time reading the related note before moving to the next row.

EXAMPLE 12.1

Example of a simple DCF valuation (in £ m, except for intrinsic value per share)	Note	Year 1	Year 2	Year 3
Revenue	1	1 000	1 020	1 050
Operating margin	2	10%	10%	10%
Operating profit (profit before interest and tax)	3	100	102	105
Non-cash items	4	15	16	17
Cash operating profit		115	118	122
Increase in net working capital	5	(12)	(15)	(10)
Tax paid	6	(17)	(17)	(18)
Capital expenditure	7	(5)	(8)	(6)
Free cash flows		81	78	88
Present value of free cash flows (discounted at WACC of 5%)	8	77.1	70.7	76.0
Present value of Years 1–3	9	223.8	–	–
Terminal value (present value of cash flows beyond Year 3)	10	2 584.6	–	–
Present value of future cash flows from operations		2 808.4	–	–
Market value of non-operating assets	11	50.0	–	–
Intrinsic value of the entire business		2 858.4	–	–
Market value of debt	12	(300.0)	–	–
Intrinsic value of equity		2 558.4	–	–
Intrinsic value per share	13	£25.584	–	–

Notes:

1. We estimate the revenue for as many years as we believe that we have enough information to do so. In this case, we feel capable of predicting revenue for the next three years.

2. We determine that it is reasonable to assume that operating margins will remain constant at 10%.

3. Revenue × operating margin = operating profit.

4. The effects of items which impact operating profit but do not affect operating cash flows—such as depreciation, impairment, fair value adjustments, and profits or losses on sale of non-current assets—are removed from operating profit to obtain cash flows. This is similar to the way these items are treated on the statement of cash flows on the indirect method (see section 5.4.3).

5. The effect of any anticipated increases (or decreases) in working capital (that is, inventory, accounts receivable, and accounts payable) is included in order to further adjust the accrual-based figures to cash-based figures (see section 5.4.4).

6. The expected amount of taxation to be paid is subtracted. Deferred tax is ignored, as it does not represent a cash flow.

7. The amount expected to be paid for capital expenditure required to expand and maintain operations is also subtracted.

8. This is the result of applying the present value formula, using the WACC we have assumed of 5%. For example, in Year 1 the calculation is: £81 m ÷ 1.05 = £77.1 m.

9. £77.1 m + £70.7 m + £76.0 m = £223.8 m.

10. The steps for calculating the terminal value are as follows: (a) assume cash flows beyond Year 3 grow at a constant rate (we have assumed 2%); (b) use the formula for the present value of a perpetuity to calculate the value of the terminal value in Year 3 [£88 m x 1.02 ÷ (5% – 2%) = £2 992.0 m]; (c) discount this Year 3 value to the present value at the beginning of Year 1 [£2 992.0 ÷ (1.05)³ = £2 584.6 m].

11. The value of non-operating assets (such as extra cash reserves and other non-operating investments) is added to the present value of future operating cash flows to obtain the value of the entire business.

12. To obtain the value of the business's equity only, the market value of its debt is removed.

13. Assuming the business is a company with 100 million shares outstanding, £2 558.4 m ÷ 100 m = £25.584.

12.3.6 **The main weakness of the DCF model**

The DCF model values the very essence of a business's intrinsic value—future cash flows—and is thus the most direct and conceptually sound way to value a business. For this reason, it is sometimes called a 'fundamental valuation'.

Note, though, the number of variables we had to estimate in order to come up with this valuation, including: rates of revenue growth; operating margin movements; figures for non-cash items; changes in inventory, receivables, and payables; payments for capital expenditure and tax; the market value of non-operating assets; and WACC (which can itself only be determined by estimating several more inputs). We also assumed that—beyond the foreseeable future—the business's fortunes would conform to a linear, constant pattern. A decent DCF valuation must therefore involve careful research to justify the variables used as inputs, and will include more granular calculations to reduce its reliance on any assumptions that appear to be simplistic.

However, in an uncertain business world, even an expert's best guess will be at least somewhat incorrect. Small variations in some inputs—such as WACC, the growth rate used to calculate the terminal value, and the predicted changes in revenue—can have very large effects on the model's output, meaning that these inputs do not have to be very wrong in order to make huge differences to the ultimate valuation. To deal with this weakness of DCF valuations, they are subjected to sensitivity analysis, in which the inputs are varied to test the size of the swing in the output. Although this doesn't make the model more accurate, it at least reveals the scale of the consequences of erroneous assumptions and estimates, and also helps the valuer determine a range of potential intrinsic values.

12.3.7 **Dividend-based cash flow valuation methods**

To value some businesses, many investors use a variation of the DCF approach, which focuses only on dividends. After all, dividends are often the only way that shareholders receive cash from an investment that they continue to hold. One of the most popular such methods is called the 'Gordon growth model', which assumes that dividends will grow at a constant rate, and then values these cash inflows in perpetuity, using the following formula.

$$\text{Intrinsic value} = \frac{\text{Dividend expected next year}}{\text{Required rate of return} - \text{dividend growth rate}}$$

Suppose that this year a business paid a dividend of £80 million, which is expected to grow in the future at a rate of 3% per year. This means that next year's dividend is expected to be £82.4 million (£80 m × 1.03). If equity investors require a rate of return of 8%, then the intrinsic value of the business according to the Gordon growth model formula is £1 648 million [£82.4 m ÷ (0.08 − 0.03)].

An advantage of dividend-based models is that they are much simpler than the full DCF model, and require far fewer estimates and assumptions.

However, they are generally based on an assumption that is unlikely to hold in reality: that dividends will continue to grow indefinitely at a constant rate. In practice, most businesses vary their dividend amounts according to market conditions and their own circumstances. Furthermore, even dividends that do remain fairly steady tend to be a varying fraction of a business's operating cash flows, and therefore are not a precise indicator of the value creation potential of the business.

Dividend-based cash flow methods are therefore best used to value a select group of businesses whose dividends are likely to grow constantly, and are closely linked to operating cash flows.

12.4 VALUATION MULTIPLES

Valuation methods which discount cash flows usually require a great deal of research and investigation. Also, although they aim directly at the essence of a business's intrinsic value, the inputs to these methods are based on assumptions and estimates, and so the output cannot amount to anything more precise than an estimate. In fact, because there are so many estimated inputs in a full DCF calculation, estimation errors could be compounded to produce an output that is very inaccurate. For all of these reasons, many people choose to value businesses with a less direct approach, using a valuation multiple.

Valuation methods that use multiples begin with a known figure about the business, usually taken from its financial statements, and then apply a multiple to this figure to estimate the business's intrinsic value. The multiple is generally developed from one of two data sources. When it is based on the multiples of comparable businesses, it is known as a 'comparable trading multiple'. When it is instead based on historical multiples in similar business acquisitions, it is often called a 'precedent transaction multiple'. Either way, the variable to be used in the valuation is usually adjusted for factors that are peculiar to the business being valued.

These methods are similar to how real estate agents might value a residential property. They start by measuring the area of the property. They then use their knowledge of the selling prices of other properties in the area (precedent transactions) to calculate a multiple: the price per square metre for the area. This multiple they then refine for the property being valued, based on how its features (like finishings, age, condition, and so on) make it different from the average property. Finally, they multiply the property's area by the refined multiple to arrive at a valuation for the property.

Suppose that we wish to value an unlisted business which, like Burberry, sells luxury apparel and accessories, but which operates in only one of Burberry's geographic segments, the United Kingdom. We have a copy of the company's financial statements, but we have access to much less information than the enormous volumes of statistics, articles, and announcements published about listed companies like Burberry. Perhaps the most significant piece of missing information is a share price (a market value), as this would be a helpful starting point for our valuation.

12

However, the vast amounts of information about Burberry are not entirely useless. As the two businesses are so similar, their financial statements will contain many similar sorts of items, and thus one could expect that, if the unlisted business were listed, its market value would correspond to elements of its financial statements in a way that is similar to the way that Burberry's market value corresponds to the same elements of *its* financial statements. We should therefore be able to use Burberry's multiples as comparable trading multiples for the unlisted business we wish to value.

We shall now do this to demonstrate three common multiples valuation methods. Bear in mind that an alternative would be to use average multiples across several comparable businesses, or to use multiples based on historical acquisitions of similar businesses.

12.4.1 Market-to-book ratio

One method used to estimate the business's value is based on a ratio called the 'market-to-book ratio'.

$$\text{Market-to-book ratio} = \frac{\text{Market capitalisation}}{\text{Total equity}}$$

We would begin valuing the unlisted business by first calculating this ratio for Burberry.

> **Burberry's market-to-book ratio:**
> 30 March 2019: £8 041.9 m ÷ £1 460.0 m = **5.5 times**

The market-to-book ratio of Burberry on 30 March 2019 indicates that the market value of Burberry was 5.5 times higher than the book value. Thus, the market considers Burberry to be worth approximately 5.5 times more than the equity reported on its balance sheet.

If we assume a similar ratio for the unlisted business, we can estimate what its market value would be if it were listed. For example, if its statement of financial position reports total equity of £600 million, a rough approximation of its potential market value would be £3 300 million (£600 m × 5.5).

However, the assumption that the ratio would be the same across both businesses is probably mistaken. On the face of it, the unlisted business is riskier than Burberry because being unlisted means it has less access to capital, and also its smaller area of operations means it is more vulnerable to the peculiar economic conditions of an isolated region. The greater risk translates into a higher expected return, which means investors would not be willing to pay as much for £1 of the unlisted business's equity as they would for £1 of Burberry's equity. The multiple applied to the unlisted business's equity should therefore probably be reduced to less than 5.5.

Financial analysis, using Burberry as a benchmark, would no doubt reveal further differences (both favourable and unfavourable) between the two businesses, leading to further refinements of the multiple. Of course, the more experience we have in making these refinements to the multiple, the more accurate they are likely to be.

Suppose that, after a comprehensive financial analysis, we judge that the unlisted business is fundamentally operationally strong, with effective management and good growth prospects. In this case, although we should reduce the multiple on account of the higher risk, we should limit the reduction to a relatively small amount. If, say, the refined multiple was 4.0, then our estimate of the unlisted business's value would change to £2 400 million (£600 m × 4.0).

The market-to-book ratio method involves multiplying the total equity of the business by a suitable market-to-book ratio.

12.4.2 **Price–earnings multiple**

Many valuation experts put much greater store in figures on the statement of comprehensive income than those on the statement of financial position. We know, for example, that Burberry's brand may well be its largest asset, and yet it does not appear on its balance sheet. On the other hand, every sale of Burberry's branded products is reported in the revenue figure on its income statement.

Furthermore, as we noted in section 5.2 when contrasting the informational value of cash flows versus accrual-based profit figures, there is a case to be made that the smoothing effects of accrual accounting make the current year's profit a better indicator of future cash flows—the ultimate source of intrinsic value—than any other figure in the financial statements, including those in the current year's statement of cash flows.

There are consequently a number of valuation multiples which, unlike the price-to-book ratio, are intended to be applied to profit-based figures, and which are commonly considered to be much more reliable indicators of business value. One of these is the price–earnings ratio (PE). In section 11.8.2, we established that Burberry's PE at 30 March 2019 was 23.75 times (1 954.5 p ÷ 82.3 p), indicating that on that date, investors in Burberry were prepared to pay £23.75 for each £1 of the current earnings. The basic formula we used to calculate these figures was as follows.

$$\text{PE ratio} = \frac{\text{Share price}}{\text{EPS}}$$

Changing the subject of the PE formula gives us a new equation, as follows.

$$\text{Share price} = \text{EPS} \times \text{PE ratio}$$

This formulation demonstrates how we can think of Burberry's share price of 1 954.5 p as its earnings per share of 82.3 pence multiplied by its PE of 23.75.

If we multiply both sides of the equation by the number of outstanding shares, the equation changes again.

$$\text{Share price} \times \text{Outstanding shares} = (\text{EPS} \times \text{Outstanding shares}) \times \text{PE ratio}$$
$$\text{Market value} = \text{Earnings} \times \text{PE ratio}$$

This equation shows that it is possible to calculate the market value of a listed company by multiplying its earnings by its PE ratio. For example, Burberry's market capitalisation of roughly £8 040 million is the product of its profit of £339.1 million and its PE of 23.75 (rounding errors explain why this is slightly off). This is the premise behind

12

another way of valuing an unlisted business, known as the 'price–earnings valuation method'.

Suppose that the unlisted business we are trying to value reports a profit of £110 million per year in its statement of comprehensive income. To value the business using the PE valuation method, all we need do is multiply this earnings figure by an appropriate PE ratio.

Because the business is unlisted, there is no PE ratio published for it, but we can estimate one using Burberry's PE of 23.75 as a starting point. Just as we did in section 12.4.1, we refine this multiple for differences between the unlisted business and Burberry. If, as before, we suppose that a detailed financial analysis of the unlisted business reveals that its prospects are fundamentally good despite the higher risks inherent in being unlisted and operating in a smaller segment, the appropriate multiple would again be lower—but not by a lot—than Burberry's.

If the appropriate PE multiple is, say, 17.0, then the PE valuation method would estimate the business's value at £1 870 million (£110 million × 17.0).

> The PE valuation method involves multiplying the earnings of the business by a PE ratio appropriate to the business.

12.4.3 Enterprise value multiple

A criticism of the PE valuation method is that, because it relies on the market value of equity—share prices—to determine value, it overlooks the role played by the other source of business funding—debt—in ways that can throw out the valuations it produces. One way to deal with this problem is instead to use a valuation multiple method that is indifferent to capital structure because it values the entire business, or 'enterprise'. The most popular such method is called the 'enterprise multiple valuation method'.

Enterprise value is the full value of the business's operations. As such, it includes the market value of both sources of funding (equity, represented by the market capitalisation plus any **non-controlling interests**, and the fair value of the business's debt), and excludes non-operating assets (which in practice are often simplified just to the business's cash holdings). For example, Burberry's and Prada's enterprise values would typically be calculated as follows in Example 12.2.

EXAMPLE 12.2

Enterprise valuation calculations	Burberry 30/3/19 £	Prada 31/12/18 €
Market capitalisation [for Burberry, see section 12.1.2; for Prada: €2.87 × 2 558.8 m]	8 041.9 m	7 343.8 m
Non-controlling interests [from balance sheets]	5.0 m	19.0 m
Fair value of liabilities [assumed to be equal to carrying amounts in balance sheets]	872.2 m	1 781.7 m
Cash holdings [from balance sheets]	– 874.2 m	– 599.8 m
Enterprise value	8 044.9 m	8 544.7 m

Note that, because Burberry's cash and cash equivalents are so near in size to its liabilities, its enterprise value happens to be very close to its market capitalisation, but this is unusual.

We have thus also calculated Prada's enterprise value to show you the more typical scenario, in which the enterprise value is substantially above the market value.

In section 4.6, we introduced the common proxy for sustainable operating cash flows known as 'EBITDA', which stands for 'earnings before interest, tax, depreciation and amortisation'. Burberry's EBITDA in 2019, calculated by adding back the depreciation and amortisation figures in note 5 from the operating profit in the income statement, was £553.0 million (£437.2 m + £87.2 m + £28.6 m).

The most frequently used enterprise value multiple is calculated by dividing enterprise value by EBITDA, as follows.

$$\text{Enterprise value multiple} = \frac{\text{Enterprise value}}{\text{EBITDA}}$$

According to this formula, Burberry's enterprise value multiple was 14.5 (£8 044.9 m ÷ £553.0 m), indicating that for every £1 of EBITDA, its providers of equity and debt were willing to fund a total of £14.50 of enterprise value. This multiple could then be refined in similar ways to the multiples we have already discussed, and applied to the EBITDA of our unlisted business, in order to deduce an enterprise value for that business. If the unlisted business reports EBITDA of £150 million, and we determine the appropriate multiple to be 11.0, then its enterprise value is £1 650 million (£150 m × 11.0). To obtain the value of equity, we could subtract the value of the business's debt (say, £300 million) from this figure, to obtain an equity valuation of €1 350 million.

> The enterprise value method involves multiplying the business's EBITDA by a suitable enterprise value multiple.

This method is often used to value a business for a takeover where the debt would need to be repaid, and is particularly suitable when the businesses being compared have different capital structures.

12.4.4 Main weakness of the valuation multiples approach

The key feature of the valuation multiples methods, in comparison with the much more sophisticated DCF, is their simplicity. In some ways, this is a virtue, but it is also a weakness. On each method, the valuation is the result of just two figures multiplied together, which means that unless each figure is almost perfect, the valuation may be very inaccurate. And the truth is that both figures can easily be wrong.

The multiple (which in each of our examples was market-to-book ratio, PE, and the enterprise value multiple) may be wrong because the business whose multiple is used as a starting point may in fact be a poor basis for comparison. It could also be wrong because there is a lot of guesswork involved in refining that initial multiple. The first of these issues may be somewhat countered by basing the multiple on a diversity of businesses in

12

the same industry; and the second issue can be mitigated by experience. But these are not complete solutions: it is entirely possible for a seasoned investment professional refining a multiple derived from a variety of comparable businesses to misjudge what multiple is appropriate.

The other figure, the amount extracted from the financial statements of the company being valued (in our examples, this was equity, profit, and EBITDA, respectively) may not be right for the valuation calculation. This is not to say that the financial statements contain an accounting irregularity (although they might, as Chapter 13 will discuss), but rather that the business's circumstances might cause the extracted figure to give a misleading valuation. For example, if the business has incurred a large loss on a discontinued operation, the profit figure and EBITDA may both substantially underestimate the value of the business going forward.

To lessen the impact of outdated events, some valuations are done by applying the multiples to estimates of future figures, a technique known as using 'forward ratios', as opposed to using historical, or 'trailing' ratios. Again, though, this is not a perfect solution, as anyone who has ever tried to predict the future will confirm.

Apart from their susceptibility to error, a second weakness of earnings multiple methods is that at best they approximate the business's potential market value, not its intrinsic value. After all, the multiples are ultimately based on the market capitalisations of comparable listed companies, or the price of some historical acquisition, and so underlying these methods is the assumption that some value in the market is a proxy for intrinsic value. For reasons we discussed in section 12.1.2, that assumption is frequently mistaken.

Ultimately, the valuation multiples methods are best used as ways to obtain a rough estimate of a business's value that can be used as a reality check on the output of the fundamental valuation produced by a DCF valuation. If they encounter differences between the valuations based on the different approaches, the person performing the valuation would inspect their DCF for assumptions or estimates that might be too optimistic or pessimistic, and consider revising the valuation so that it is more within range of the results of the multiples methods, though not necessarily equal to any of them. This will, on average, lead to a more plausible valuation.

CONCLUSION

This chapter has presented just the most common valuation methods in use for most kinds of business. There are countless variations on these approaches, some unique to individual investors who believe they have found the best valuation formula. There are also other approaches, many of which are used to value specific types of businesses, such as property businesses or investment businesses, based on the kinds of assets that they own.

The intrinsic value of a business is the value of its future cash flows, but estimating this figure is a tremendously difficult exercise. No single method can be relied on, partly because all methods depend on guesses and assumptions that are inevitably wrong. Good investors use their experience and a combination of valuation methods to estimate intrinsic values which are 'more right' than the rest of the market. After all, if you can determine that a share is undervalued, you can make money by buying it now and selling it when it rises after other investors reach the same realisation, even if your estimate of the amount of undervaluation was not entirely accurate.

SUMMARY OF KEY POINTS

- When people talk about a business's value, they are usually talking about its book value, its market value, or its intrinsic value.
- A business's book value is usually a poor measure of what a business is worth, for the three reasons described in the summary of Chapter 10.
- A listed company's market value is its market capitalisation, which is the result of multiplying its share price by the number of shares outstanding.
- Market value is also not a reliable measure of what a business is really worth, for three reasons: all of the shares cannot in practice be purchased for the current share price; even if investors do seek to value a share based on the fundamentals of the company, they may miscalculate its value; and share prices are usually influenced by a range of factors that have little or nothing to do with the fundamentals of the business.
- The intrinsic value of a business is what it is really worth. It is this figure which a business valuation seeks to identify.
- The primary reason to perform a business valuation is to determine how much to pay or accept for a sale of the business, or for some of its shares.
- A business valuation which uses the discounted cash flow model (DCF) is a fundamental valuation, in the sense that it aims to measure the intrinsic value directly, by calculating the present value of the future cash flows of the business.
- The steps typically involved in a DCF valuation are: calculate the free cash flows for the foreseeable future; discount them to present value using the weighted average cost of capital; add the present value of the estimated cash flows beyond the foreseeable future (the terminal amount); add the market value of non-operating assets; and subtract the market value of debt.
- The main weakness of a DCF is the number of assumptions and estimates that it requires, which, if wrong, can often cause large swings in the final valuation. It is thus important to perform a sensitivity analysis on the valuation; that is, to measure the size of the swings by varying the inputs.
- An example of a dividend-based cash flow valuation is the Gordon growth model, which requires just three inputs. However, this method is unlikely to produce an accurate valuation unless the business's dividends will grow constantly, and are closely linked to operating cash flows.
- The alternative approach to valuation does not try to measure intrinsic value directly, but instead applies a valuation multiple to some known figure drawn from the business's financial statements.
- The steps involved in a valuation multiples approach are: determine a measurable proxy of intrinsic value, such as market capitalisation, enterprise value, or the acquisition price of precedent transactions; decide what figure from the benchmark financial statements you wish to divide the proxy of intrinsic value by to obtain a valuation multiple; refine that multiple for the circumstances of the business you are valuing; multiply the refined multiple by the relevant figure from that business's financial statements.

12

- Examples of this approach use the following multiples: the market-to-book value ratio; the price–earnings multiple; and the enterprise value multiple.
- A virtue of the multiples valuation approach is its simplicity, but two weaknesses common to all of these methods are: because they ultimately rely on just two numbers multiplied together, errors in either number can make the valuation very inaccurate; and the multiples have to be based on some proxy of intrinsic value, which may itself be inaccurate.
- Because every method has weaknesses, a good business valuation employs multiple approaches and methods, and then contrasts the results of each of these to determine a plausible range for the final valuation.

CHAPTER QUESTIONS

Don't forget the **online resources** available at www.oup.com/he/winfield-graham-miller1e, which contain multiple-choice questions based on the material in this chapter, in addition to many other helpful resources.

CONCEPT QUESTIONS

CQ 12.1   Explain what the terms 'book value' and 'market value' mean when applied to a business. Briefly identify how these different valuations are calculated, and therefore what they are based on.

CQ 12.2   Identify and briefly explain the two main approaches used to value a business (that is, to estimate its intrinsic value).

CQ 12.3   Describe the four main steps of the DCF valuation model.

CQ 12.4   Briefly describe in words how the formula for the Gordon growth model values a business.

CQ 12.5   Briefly explain how to value an unlisted business using a price–earnings multiple valuation approach.

INVESTIGATION QUESTIONS

IQ 12.6   Identify three listed retail companies based in your country and obtain their financial statements. Calculate and then compare their market-to-book ratios. Can you explain the differences?

IQ 12.7   Compare and contrast the valuation methodologies most often used to value businesses in your country or region. (Hint: large accounting and law firms often publish valuation surveys that outline the methodologies they use.)

CREATIVE ACCOUNTING

Here are some of the things you will be able to do after reading this chapter:

- comfortably use terms like 'creative accounting', 'accounting irregularity', 'money laundering', 'Ponzi scheme', 'channel stuffing', 'upfronting', 'related parties', and others;
- describe four reasons that a business might prepare misleading accounting information;
- identify a wide variety of commonly perpetrated kinds of accounting irregularities, and describe well-known examples of each kind;
- list several types of countermeasure to reduce or expose accounting irregularities, and briefly discuss their key features and merits;
- discuss the degree to which accounting irregularities caused the 2007–8 global financial crisis.

In most walks of life, creativity is considered a good thing, but not in the accounting profession. **Creative accounting** describes the manipulation of a business's bookkeeping records and financial statements to achieve an ulterior motive. When financial accountants 'cook the books' in this way, they are acting unethically and usually also illegally; after all, their primary role is to faithfully and objectively present the financial effects of a business's activity.

Nevertheless, throughout recorded history a few accountants and business executives have purposefully misled the users of financial statements. When discovered, a media scandal, financial ruin, and even jail time typically follow.

In this chapter, we shall cover a broad variety of **accounting irregularities**, and recount some well-known cases. We shall also discuss what countermeasures are available to protect users of financial statements from the risk that they may become victims of accounting irregularities.

An accounting irregularity is an item incorrectly included in, or omitted from, the accounting records and financial statements, with the purpose of misleading others.

CHAPTER 13

13.1 REASONS TO PREPARE MISLEADING INFORMATION

There are four main reasons why someone might seek to make accounting information misleading: to facilitate the laundering of money; to attract cash into a Ponzi scheme; to cover up theft; and to obscure bad news. Let's take a closer look at each of these in turn.

13.1.1 Money laundering

Suppose, just for a moment, that you run an illegal drug business. Essentially, you buy drugs from manufacturers and distribute them to drug users. Your customers don't pay you directly into a bank account, because neither you nor they want an official record of a criminal transaction. If your business is successful, before long, you will have a lot of cash. You will need to deposit at least some of this cash into a bank account, both because having piles of cash makes you the target of other criminals, and also because some of the things you want to buy—houses, boats, diamond tiaras—cannot be bought for cash. However, if you simply put the money into your own bank account, when the bank reports these vast sums to the authorities, you will not be able to show that you earned it legally. The money is 'dirty', and so to spend it without being found out, you must clean, or launder, it.

One way to do this—to create the illusion that you acquired your ill-gotten gains legitimately—is to buy a non-criminal business, known as a 'front', and pretend that the illegal money was generated by the front. This involves accounting irregularities, because a record of legitimate income has to be fabricated. Whether the front is a restaurant, a dry cleaners, or any other business, a false record of customers and sales to them would need to be created to make the cash appear to have come from them.

> Dirty money can be laundered by passing it through a front: an apparently legitimate business whose cash inflows are faked.

There is an enormous amount of criminal activity in the world—the United Nations estimates that as much as $2 trillion[1] is laundered each year—but we presume (hopefully correctly!) that readers of this book are not involved in it. Also, we are writing primarily about financial statements that report the affairs of sizeable businesses with a broad ownership, unlike the sort of businesses used for money laundering. A reader of this book is thus unlikely to be involved with a front, so let's move on.

13.1.2 Attracting cash into a Ponzi scheme

The Ponzi scheme is named after Charles Ponzi, who in 1920 made $15 million in eight months by cheating unsuspecting Americans out of their savings.[2] It relies on creative accounting to maintain the fiction that new investors' money is being invested, when in fact it is being used for two quite different purposes: to provide a sham return to other investors; and to enrich the swindler.

The largest known Ponzi scheme was arranged by Bernie Madoff, an extremely well-connected and widely trusted New Yorker, who over a long career in finance nurtured a reputation as a genius investor. In 2009, at the age of seventy-one, Madoff received a prison sentence of 150 years[3] for cheating more than 4 800 victims out of an estimated $65 billion over at least two decades.[4]

Madoff's scheme worked as follows: he told investors that he could use their money to buy investments which would earn them consistent returns of 10–12%. He compiled investment reports listing the financial instruments in which their money had purportedly been invested, which had indeed earned the promised returns. However, these reports were just the product of creative accounting: in reality, the instruments were selected in retrospect, to achieve the illusion of the requisite growth. Madoff had not invested their money at all.

If you think about it, if he stole $40 for every $100 given to him, he would be able to create the impression of a 12% return for five years simply by paying the other $60 back to the investors, $12 at a time. Better still, many investors don't want to receive regular cash from their investments anyway (why wouldn't you want your savings to earn 12% for a little longer?), allowing Madoff to pretend to reinvest their money, while instead using it to pay returns to others. And, given the apparent miraculously consistent high performance of his fund, new investors were perpetually adding more money to it, which could be used to pay returns to earlier investors. It is this feature of a successful Ponzi scheme which means that it is sometimes also known as a 'pyramid scheme', and which explains how Madoff's swindle lasted as long as it did. In fact, it may well have lasted for Madoff's entire life were it not for the global financial crisis in 2007–8, which led to an unprecedented number of requests for distributions from the fund, to the extent that the cash float he had set aside was insufficient.

> Ponzi schemes can be sustained as long as the victims do not request that their faked returns are paid out, and/or new investors keep joining.

Ponzi schemes are so effective that they have been used countless times all over the world, and will no doubt continue to be used as long as there are people who don't mind making a profit at someone else's expense. You will most likely avoid being suckered if you maintain a firm belief in the old adage that if something appears too good to be true, it probably is.

13.1.3 Covering up theft

> The financial statements of listed businesses may contain accounting irregularities designed to conceal theft.

On the other hand, even if you remain realistic about the sorts of promises that a Ponzi schemer makes, it is quite possible that at some point you will consider investing in, or working for, a business whose financial statements contain accounting irregularities intended to cover up theft of the business's resources. One of the best known and most shocking examples of this occurred when, in 2002, L Dennis Kozlowski, the chief executive officer (CEO) of the US conglomerate Tyco International, was discovered to have stolen $600 million from the company.[5] He and his second-in-command had doctored the accounts to make the stolen money look like legitimate loans, salaries, and expenses. In three infamous examples, he spent $6 000 on a shower curtain, $15 000 on an umbrella stand, and $2 million on a birthday party in Sardinia for his wife, all covered up to look like genuine business expenditure.[6]

13

13.1.4 **Obscuring bad news**

Poor business performance reflects badly on the executives running the business, and thus threatens their appointments as well as their compensation, which is usually highly dependent on what is reported in the financial statements. They therefore have a strong incentive to hide negative financial information. This temptation has allegedly seduced the executives of a very long list of infamous businesses, including Enron, Toshiba, Lehman Brothers, Pescanova, Steinhoff, Carillion,[7] and many more, into cooking the books. Often, this involves inflating earnings, overstating assets, and sometimes also understating or even hiding risky liabilities, to make the business appear to be better off than it really is.

In section 7.2.2, we discussed one counterintuitive way, employed by Freddie Mac and other excessively **prudent** businesses, to hide bad news: first, hide some good news. By improperly creating a provision in years of higher-than-expected profitability, some businesses have artificially deferred some of their earnings, to be released in a future year when things may not go so well. However, most creative accountants are not so forward-thinking to engage in this kind of profit-smoothing, and instead simply resort to illicit financial engineering only when the bad news has already hit.

13.2 COMMON ACCOUNTING IRREGULARITIES

Given how many listed businesses' financial statements have included accounting irregularities intended either to cover up fraud or to hide bad news, there is a real risk that you might at some point become unwittingly involved with one of them. In this section, we will discuss some of the wide variety of ways in which the books are most often cooked. Then, before you are entirely overcome by pessimism, in section 13.3 we shall describe some countermeasures that might prevent, or at least allow us to identify, them.

13.2.1 **Falsifying income**

The simplest way to artificially inflate a business's performance is to pretend that it is making sales which do not in fact exist. Patisserie Valerie in the UK,[8] Alberta Motor Association in Canada,[9] Satyam Computer Services in India, Pescanova in Spain, and Tyco and Symbol Technologies in the US are just a small handful of the many businesses that have in recent years been caught inventing income that isn't really there.

For example, at Satyam Computer Services, an IT services company whose shares were traded on the New York Stock Exchange, over 6 000 fake invoices were allegedly created, and then false bank statements drawn up to create the illusion of these bogus bills being paid. By 2008, the business was reporting $1 billion in cash and other deposits that it simply didn't have.[10]

Similarly, a 2013 forensic audit of Pescanova, a large fishing company listed on the Madrid Stock Exchange, revealed that executives had been falsifying invoices for years. In an audacious twist on the typical scam, which simply inflates revenue without any increase in actual cash flow, the business convinced various banks to factor the receivables that these invoices purported to create. (Factoring involves a bank paying the business at a discounted rate for the right to collect its debts.) Needless to say, it was not long before the banks discovered that they had been sold a fiction.[11]

A subtler accounting trick was played by Tyco in its ADT securities services business, under the leadership of the fraudster mentioned in section 13.1.3, L Dennis Kozlowski. Home security systems are sold and installed by dealers whom ADT then pays a lump sum for the right to take over the contract with the customer. On payment, this amount is recognised by ADT as a contract asset. In accordance with the principles of accrual accounting, this asset is then expensed over time as ADT provides security services, and recognises the monthly payments from customers as income.

At the time of the Tyco scam, a typical dealer's fee was about $1 000, and the going monthly rate paid by homeowners was about $30 per month. Assuming that the expected life of the average contract is fifty months, implying a monthly expense of $20 ($1 000 ÷ 50), the correct accounting for a contract is shown in Summary of Event 1, delivering a $10 monthly profit over the life of the contract.

> 'Factoring' involves a bank paying the business at a discounted rate for the right to collect its debts. It is a common practice, and not irregular unless the receivables are fraudulent.

SUMMARY OF EVENT 1 Tyco pays $1 000 to dealer for right to take over home security service contract, expected to last for fifty months, during which the customer pays a contract fee of $30 per month.

On the date of payment:

Assets	− Liabilities	= Equity		Debit	Credit
− $1 000					Bank
+ $1 000				Contract asset	

For each month in the expected fifty months' contract period, the fee is received and the asset is amortised:

Assets	− Liabilities	= Equity		Debit	Credit
+ $30				Bank	
		+ $30 (income)			Revenue
− $20					Contract asset
		− $20 (expense)		Cost of sales	

However, Tyco's trick was to overpay the dealers by $200, and then demand reimbursement of the overpayment. In its books, it would recognise the cost of the contract asset at the $1 200 paid, and treat the $200 reimbursement as immediate income. What Tyco recorded is summarised in Summary of Event 2.

13

SUMMARY OF EVENT 2 Tyco pays $1 200 to the dealer and demands immediate reimbursement of $200.

On the date of payment:

Assets	−	Liabilities	=	Equity		Debit	Credit
− $1 200							Bank
+ $1 200						Contract asset	

On immediate reimbursement:

Assets	−	Liabilities	=	Equity		Debit	Credit
+ $200						Bank	
				+ $200 (income)			Revenue

For each month in the contract period, the larger contract asset leads to a slightly higher expense:

Assets	−	Liabilities	=	Equity		Debit	Credit
+ $30						Bank	
				+ $30 (income)			Revenue
− $24							Contract asset
				− $24 (expense)		Cost of sales	

At the end of the day, Tyco's cash balance didn't change, yet it now appeared to have a stronger statement of financial position (as a result of larger contract assets), and also higher profits in the statement of comprehensive income (as a result of the $200 immediate revenue on all new contracts easily outweighing the slightly higher monthly expense on existing contracts). The non-existent earnings boost amounted to almost $200 million between 1999 and 2001, before an investigation brought about by Kozlowski's other misdeeds exposed them.[12]

Our final example of falsifying income comes from Symbol Technologies, a US manufacturer of bar code scanners and related IT products, which between 1999 and 2002 engaged in a fraudulent scheme known as 'channel stuffing'. The name refers to the channel from supplier to customer, which in this case is stuffed by the supplier with far more products than the customer can possibly sell. As is usual in such a fraud, Symbol Technologies stuffed channels on the understanding that the customers would not have to pay unless and until they resold the product to an end-user. The product could be, and inevitably was, returned to Symbol at no cost. In some cases, customers were even paid just for placing the excessive orders.

As explained in section 4.3.1, revenue should be recognised when control over the goods has passed from supplier to customer, yet in this case the passing of control was not complete, for Symbol Technologies retained all relevant risks inherent in the goods, and indeed could be reasonably expected to reclaim possession of the goods before long. Had the business applied the accounting standards correctly, $200 million of revenues would not have been reported.[13]

'Channel stuffing' involves transferring more goods to customers than they can sell, allowing them to return the goods later. Although control has not truly passed, the supplier reports the revenue.

13

13.2.2 **Upfronting income**

Some accounting irregularities inflate income without the perpetrators' stooping to the level of deceit inherent in creating fictitious transactions. Instead, the income they recognise is genuine; it is just recognised earlier than is appropriate.

In section 4.3.1, you learned that revenue from services should be recognised once the service has been performed *and* the customer has acquired the benefits of the performance. This often means that income should be recognised evenly over the period of the contract, or sometimes only at the end of the contract. However, if a business were to account for this income more aggressively, by '**upfronting**' the income, it could increase its revenues in earlier periods.

'Upfronting' involves recognising revenue earlier than it should be recognised according to the accounting standards.

A prominent example is Tesco, the UK supermarket chain. In the retail sector, suppliers typically offer supermarket chains rebates that are conditional on achieving certain sales targets, and the supermarkets recognise these rebates as revenue. The key thing is that this 'commercial income' should only be recognised when it has been earned, which is when the sales targets have actually been met. However, in the first half of 2014 Tesco was too ambitious in recognising rebates from suppliers, and later reported a material error for that year (see section 10.5.2), restating its revenue for that period downwards by £250 million, and admitting that it had 'accelerated recognition of commercial income'.[14] In the ensuing scandal, the business was fined £129 million and its share price lost almost half of its value.[15]

13.2.3 **Incorrectly deferring expenses**

Of course, it is possible to give profits a boost by doing the inverse of pulling next year's income forward to this year: pushing this year's expenses back to a future year. As it happens, Toshiba provides a mirror image of the Tesco case. As a supplier, the Japanese conglomerate pays rebates to retailers, but in 2014, it was caught failing to recognise the cost of rebates that ought to have reduced profit that year. The business was instead planning to recognise them the following year.

This was not the only reduction in profit that Toshiba incorrectly deferred in 2014: the business even went to the extreme of asking the suppliers of advertising, logistics, and other services to delay sending their invoices until the following year. Although the services had indeed been received, the absence of these documents emboldened the business to report the expense after the fact, contrary to the demands of accrual accounting.

These and other related practices at Toshiba led the investigators to conclude that 'it can generally be understood by anyone without any accounting expertise that this sort of treatment is a diversion from appropriate accounting practice'.[16]

WorldCom was a US telecoms business that made headlines with one of the major accounting scandals at the start of the millennium. Instead of avoiding bills like Toshiba, WorldCom received and paid the bill for one of its major costs, called 'line costs', which were fees for using other telecoms firms' communications lines during the year. However,

13

it avoided recognising these payments correctly as expenses by instead capitalising them as intangible assets! That way, it managed also to inflate the business's asset value, while at the same time reducing the expense to a small trickle into the statement of comprehensive income over several years, as the bogus assets were amortised.[17]

13.2.4 Failing to impair assets when appropriate

Section 6.1.8 explained that if assets like property, plant and equipment (PPE) show signs of unexpected deterioration, they should be impaired to their recoverable amounts. Similarly, section 6.5 described how inventory at year-end must be written down to net realisable value if necessary. In section 8.3.5, we mentioned how deferred tax assets relating to tax losses carried forward ought only to be recognised if the business will likely have taxable income in the future. And in section 9.3.2, we observed that goodwill is subject to an annual impairment test.

From time to time, businesses flout one or more of these requirements, and fail to impair assets when they should. Indeed, another of the allegations against WorldCom in 2000 was that it purposefully manipulated its impairment of accounts receivable in order to artificially boost profitability. Section 6.6.3 described how accounts receivable should be impaired: an allowance for doubtful debts is used to reduce the carrying amount to what it really expects to receive from customers. The bigger the allowance, the smaller the reported receivables balance, and the larger the bad debts expense.

> If the figures are large enough, a small percentage manipulation of an accounting estimate can cause a swing big enough to alter an investment decision.

Without justification, WorldCom changed its allowance for doubtful debts from 16.9% of the amount owed at the end of one quarter, to 15.5% at the end of the next. Although this may not sound like a big difference, and was overlooked by many investors, the enormous size of its debtors book meant that profits for the quarter were $69 million higher than they would have been had the allowance been held steady.[18]

Around the same time, two competing US telecoms firms, Global Crossing and Qwest, collaborated with each other to pull off some extremely bold accounting chicanery that combined two tricks: avoiding impairing assets and also falsifying income. After laying large fibre-optic cable networks in a highly competitive market, these two businesses discovered that the price they could charge customers for use of the networks' capacity was much lower than they had hoped. But rather than impair the underperforming assets, they instead used them to make sales way above market value—with each other!

In terms of these 'capacity swaps', they sold the right to use their networks to the competitor, while in exchange purchasing the right to use the competitor's network. The *sale* created the appearance of healthy revenues from the very assets that they should have been impairing.[19] You may be wondering, though: didn't the *purchase* lead to an expense that would cancel out these revenues? No, because they took advantage of an accounting loophole that allowed them to capitalise the cost of the purchase, to be amortised over the period for which their right to use the other companies network lasted, which was often between fifteen and twenty-five years. Summary of Event 3 demonstrates this, using the figure of $100 000, which was the reported value of the two companies' capacity swaps in just six months of 2001.[20]

SUMMARY OF EVENT 3 Business swapped $100 million of network capacity with a competitor.

The capacity given to the competitor was recorded as follows:

Assets	−	Liabilities	=	Equity
+ $100 m				
				+ $100 m (income)

Debit	Credit
Accounts receivable	
	Revenue

The capacity acquired from the competitor was recorded as follows:

Assets	−	Liabilities	=	Equity
		+ $100 m		
+ $100 m				

Debit	Credit
	Accounts payable
Capacity asset	

Then the debts were offset (or cash was simply exchanged, to create the appearance of cash flows):

Assets	−	Liabilities	=	Equity
− $100 m				
		− $100 m		

Debit	Credit
	Accounts receivable
Accounts payable	

If you trace the result of these entries in the accounting system, you see that each business would report revenue, profit, and an asset of $100 million, with the amortisation expense related to the capacity asset only required to trickle slowly into the financial statements over the next twenty or so years! That is an incredible outcome for two businesses that should have been reporting large impairment losses, and no revenue, profit, or assets from transactions that would never even have happened were it not for the opportunity they presented to do some creative accounting!

13.2.5 Misclassifying liabilities

In section 7.1.6, we mentioned the case of the Australian real-estate investment trust, Centro Group, which misled investors by disclosing current liabilities as non-current, causing the repayment to appear less imminent and therefore the debt to appear less risky.

A similar case arose when the UK conglomerate Carillion went into liquidation amid concerns about several of its accounting practices. One of these was a misclassification of the liabilities it owed banks. These amounts started out being owed to Carillion's suppliers, but then the business entered into an arrangement known as 'reverse factoring'. Factoring was explained in section 13.2.1; *reverse* factoring involves the supplier being paid its debt quickly by a bank, minus a small discount, and the business (Carillion, in this case) repaying the bank over a longer term. This is not in itself an irregular practice: a business with short-term cash flow issues might enter into such an arrangement to make sure that its suppliers are paid timeously.

However, the problem arose when, in its 2016 statement of financial position, Carillion classified the resulting £498 million owed to banks not as bank loans, but rather as 'Other

13

It doesn't much matter what names a business gives the items in its financial statements; what does matter is how they are classified.

creditors', as if it was still owed to the suppliers. Analysts consider large bank borrowings, and substantial increases in them, to be important signs of potential cash flow problems, and thus the misclassification—which caused bank borrowings to be understated by more than 75%—hid the extent of the business's liquidity issues.[21]

13.2.6 Not consolidating controlled entities

Businesses sometimes set up separate legal entities—companies, trusts, and so on—to accomplish a narrow or well-defined objective. These legal entities are referred to as 'special purpose entities' (SPEs), 'special purpose vehicles' (SPVs), or 'structured entities'. In most cases, these SPEs are set up to accomplish valid business objectives. For example, many businesses set up trusts to facilitate the buying and selling of shares on behalf of employee share ownership plans (ESOPs), like Burberry has done (see section 10.3.4).

However, sometimes SPEs have been used purely for the sake of creative accounting. This was the case with Enron, once the seventh biggest company in the US, which was famously declared bankrupt in 2001. Enron set up a number of SPEs to which it sold assets at amounts greater than their book values, thus allowing the company to report a gain in profit or loss. These SPEs were not owned by Enron, but had been set up by various senior employees. They borrowed heavily from the banks, using Enron shares as collateral, thereby obtaining the cash necessary to finance the purchase of the over-priced assets. Figure 13.1 illustrates an example of how this scheme worked.

FIGURE 13.1 Illustration of Enron's use of SPEs

An SPE might borrow $10 million from a bank and use this to purchase an asset from Enron. If the carrying amount of the asset in Enron's statement of financial position had been $8 million, then Enron would show a profit on the sale of the asset of $2 million. All that the shareholders, banks, and other users would see in the financial statements would be the profit of $2 million. The liability of $10 million would be in the SPE, and obscured from their view. By all accounts, these transactions happened on a gigantic scale at Enron, such that the profits drove up the Enron share price, which in turn encouraged the banks to hand out more loans to the SPEs, given that they were secured against the shares.

However, because the SPEs were effectively controlled by Enron, International Financial Reporting Standards (IFRS) accounting requirements would have required that they be consolidated into the Enron group financial statements. Had this happened, the reality would have been plain to see, for—as explained in section 9.2.1—**intragroup transactions** would be eliminated. In preparing the group financial statements, the profit on sale of assets to the SPE would have been reversed, the assets would have been restated at cost, and a liability for the bank loans would have been reported on Enron's group statement of financial position.

> If an entity under the control of the group is not consolidated, the financial statements can be severely manipulated in multiple ways.

By not reporting these loans—the only real transactions with entities outside of the group—on its statement of financial position, Enron was engaging in a favourite trick of creative accountants everywhere known as '**off-balance-sheet financing**'. The advantage of keeping liabilities out of the financial statements is, of course, that the business appears less risky.

13.2.7 **A buffet of cooked books**

Of course, when accountants and business executives cross legal and ethical lines by preparing financial statements that violate accounting standards, they often do not stop at one kind of transgression. Many of the companies mentioned so far did not use just one book-cooking recipe, but instead served up an entire buffet! A fairly recent example was Steinhoff, an international retailer headquartered in South Africa, with a major presence in Europe. In just four days of trading in December 2017, Steinhoff's shares lost almost 90% of their value when credible allegations of major accounting fraud came to light.

In a report later released by the team of forensic accountants appointed to investigate what happened, it was revealed that a small group of people at the company, under the leadership of its CEO, Markus Jooste, were perpetrating many of the kinds of irregularities that we have already described in this chapter, and also one or two new ones. For example, Steinhoff had been:

- falsifying at least €6.5 billion 'fictitious or irregular transactions', mostly involving brands, intellectual property, and 'know-how';
- not consolidating entities that were in truth controlled by the group, to avoid having to eliminate the falsified sales that were in fact intragroup transactions;
- failing to impair goodwill. In some cases, this was achieved by cash 'contributions' paid by the parent company to loss-making subsidiaries. Although these cash flows were eliminated on consolidation, they nonetheless argued for maintaining the carrying amount of goodwill;
- reclassifying the receivables created by the falsified sales as assets about which fewer questions would be asked, like properties and trademarks (which then required more false income to be created in order to prevent these assets from appearing inefficient).[22]

13

13.3 **COUNTERMEASURES**

At this point, you may be at risk of losing faith in every accountant, if not in humanity as a whole. You may also be wondering if you should ever trust a set of financial statements. The good news is that things are not as bleak as section 13.2 might suggest. For every one of the businesses it mentions, there are hundreds of others whose financial statements are not suspect. Indeed, many of the countermeasures against accounting irregularities are strengthening over time.

In this section, we will discuss some of these countermeasures.

13.3.1 **Financial regulation**

The Enron catastrophe and accompanying scandals at the beginning of the millennium led the US to tighten financial regulation dramatically. Within a few years, about two dozen business leaders were serving prison sentences; more than $15 billion had been paid in fines, and as compensation to shareholders for their losses; and major regulatory legislation had been passed into law.

The most significant new legislation was the Sarbanes–Oxley Act of 2002, which established accounting and auditing oversight bodies, made executives personally responsible for the accuracy of their businesses' financial statements, and introduced several other effective measures against fraud and accounting irregularities. Although it was initially resisted by many in the business community, most aspects of the law have now become accepted as sensible, integral features of corporate culture across the world.[23] For example, it is now typical for any large business to have a whistle-blowing hotline, accessible via phone, email, or a website, to allow employees to anonymously report any concerns they have about the ethics or legality of its inner workings. This is no minor change, for the Association of Certified Fraud Examiners reports that a hotline is at least twice as effective in detecting fraud as any other mechanism.[24]

The US is far from the only country to tighten financial regulation in recent times. Many countries have introduced new legislation, or overhauled existing legislation, to reduce fraud and to improve the reliability of financial reporting.

Following the Sarbanes–Oxley Act in the US, most countries have significantly tightened financial regulation.

Corporate governance is the system by which organisations, including businesses, are directed and governed.

13.3.2 **Corporate governance codes**

At the same time that actual law to limit accounting irregularities has been strengthened, 'soft law' has also been developed. This generally consists of a national code of **corporate governance**, which sets out principles that aim to strengthen oversight of the key decisions made by a business's leaders. For example, corporate governance codes typically require a substantial number of independent or non-executive members of company boards. Since these members are not involved in the running of the company, and not remunerated based on its performance, they have no incentive to allow the financial statements to be

13

manipulated: instead, one of their primary roles is to interrogate the recommendations, and sometimes temper the impulses, of the executive management.

Although corporate governance codes are not typically enforced in the same way as actual law, most large businesses cannot ignore them: for example, the executive branch of the EU, the European Commission, requires all listed companies in the EU to produce an annual corporate governance report.[25] In other countries, stock exchanges themselves insist on such reports. Typically, these requirements include a 'comply-or-explain' approach. Sometimes alternatively described as 'apply or explain', this means that companies must either apply each encoded principle of good corporate governance or explain why they have not applied it. The intention is that, unlike the 'comply-or-else' approach taken by most regulators, this principles-based approach makes corporate governance more adaptable to the specific circumstances of each business, and encourages management to think proactively about best practice, rather than simply to think of corporate governance as a tick-box exercise.

Of course, given that corporate governance codes have been around for two decades or more, while accounting irregularities have continued to emerge, the efficacy of this approach is highly debatable.

13.3.3 Improvements in accounting standards

As explained in Chapter 3, IFRS is constantly evolving every year, as new standards are released and old standards are updated. All of this activity aims to achieve a variety of important objectives, not least making financial statements more relevant, comparable, understandable, and more faithfully representative of economic reality. Another goal underpins these objectives: to make it more difficult to mislead the users of financial statements.

We mentioned in section 13.2.4 that Global Crossing and Qwest were able to create their accounting fictions partly with the help of US GAAP at the time, which allowed the sale side of their capacity swaps to be treated as immediate revenue, but the purchase side to be capitalised.

Enron's treatment of SPEs did in fact breach the accounting standards, but some commentators point out that the perpetrators could have done something similar without breaking the rules. At the time, it was fairly easy to devise a scheme like the one illustrated in Figure 13.1 so that it was legitimate: to avoid consolidation, US regulations then required that just 3% of the equity of an SPE be funded by a source outside the group![26]

In terms of IFRS too, a form of off-balance-sheet financing was permissible in the past. The previous leasing standard allowed many businesses leasing PPE simply to expense the lease payments, instead of recognising a lease asset and a lease liability to pay for it, as IFRS 16 now requires. As explained in section 8.1.1, the new standard reduces the potential for misleading information because it means that a business which chooses to finance its productive capacity through long-term lease contracts now prepares a statement of financial position that looks much like another business which acquires similar assets using another form of debt financing, like bank loans.

> IFRS 16 is an example of a new accounting standard which has reduced the potential for misleading information to be presented in financial statements prepared according to IFRS.

13

A similar case can be made for the new accounting standard about revenue. One of the criticisms of the accounting policies of Carillion, the listed UK business mentioned in section 13.2.5, was that the revenue estimates made by management were far too optimistic. Had Carillion been required to report its revenue according to IFRS 15 (see section 4.3), rather than the standard which applied at the time, it would have had to report approximately £100 million less in retained earnings.[27]

Thus, improvements in accounting standards can play an effective role in preventing misrepresentations in the financial statements.

13.3.4 **Auditing**

Section 1.2.6 explained that the task of **auditors** is to ensure that the information in the financial statements is valid, accurate, and complete. Very large businesses usually employ internal auditors to monitor and maintain their systems of financial controls; and all listed companies and most other **public interest entities (PIEs)** also have external auditors. The rationale is that an external auditor is independent of the business, and therefore has no incentive to allow any accounting irregularities to creep into the business's financial statements.

However, in practice, this is simply not true: external auditors have historically developed long, friendly relationships with their clients; they have been permitted to earn a great deal of money through providing other services to their audit clients; and, perhaps most problematically, their audit fees are paid by the same clients about whom they are meant to report objectively. This quite plain conflict of interest has prompted some to invoke the American writer Upton Sinclair, who wrote: 'It is difficult to get a man to understand something, when his salary depends on his not understanding it.'[28]

Furthermore, although there are many small and some medium-sized audit firms, there are only four giants: the so-called 'Big Four', known most commonly as Deloitte, PWC, EY, and KPMG. The fact that there are so few firms with sufficient resources to audit multinational corporations leads to not infrequent accusations that they behave as an oligopoly, keeping fees high, while looking the other way when a client's financial statements contain a problem.[29]

Auditing standards have recently trended towards greater independence between audit firms and their clients.

Nonetheless, the oversight of auditors is improving, and auditors are increasingly held responsible for the roles they have played in recent accounting scandals. Auditors must register with a regulatory authority, and in most jurisdictions the authority holds auditors to standards based on those released by the International Federation of Accountants (IFAC). In recent years, the law, regulator's rules, and also these standards have generally demanded much greater levels of independence from auditors, for example by: constraining the number of years that a firm can audit a client before the appointment must be rotated to a different firm;[30] limiting the other services that can be provided to an audit client; and prohibiting an audit firm from continuing to audit a client if the firm's independence may be compromised by its dependence on the fee.[31]

13

> **MISCONCEPTION**
>
> When auditors approve the financial statements, they are stating that everything in them is correct.
>
> Although there are some differences between auditors' responsibilities in different juris-dictions, generally no audit opinion goes so far as to state that every item in the financial statements is correct. In the UK, for example, a clean audit report (technically known as an 'unmodified opinion') is issued when the auditor has concluded that the financial state-ments give a true and fair view of the business's affairs at year-end and its profit for the year, and that they comply in all material respects with the applicable reporting framework.

13.3.5 Accounting ethics

Because of their specialist knowledge and skills, a key element of the work performed by accountants and auditors is that they are *trusted* to prepare and review financial state-ments that faithfully reflect the activities of a business. After all, financial statements that cannot be believed are not just worthless; they in fact cause severe economic harm, as anyone who owned Steinhoff shares in December 2017 will no doubt confirm. The ero-sion of trust is bad for everyone, including and especially the accountants themselves, whose employment depends on being trusted. Thus, as one major accounting scandal has followed another over the past two decades, the accounting profession has recognised a pressing need to address its own ethics.

IFAC and its members—all the major accounting bodies from across the world—have worked hard to hold accountants responsible for observing high ethical standards. Most accounting organisations have adopted the International Code of Ethics for Professional Accountants, which lays out five fundamental principles—integrity; objectivity; profes-sional competence and due care; confidentiality; and professional behaviour—and pro-vides more than a hundred pages of guidance on how these apply to a wide range of work done by accountants and auditors. A major advance occurred in 2017, when provisions were added to the Code about 'non-compliance with laws and regulations', stipulating when it is in fact appropriate to break confidentiality, and a precise series of actions to take when an irregularity is suspected.[32]

The accounting profession itself is making a concerted effort to improve the ethical conduct of accountants and auditors.

Improvements in the Code have been accompanied by substantial education campaigns to teach accountants how to avoid and prevent ethical misconduct. Not only have ethics modules been added to the curriculum that students experience on the way to qualifying, but professional accountants in practice are also exposed to ethics training through con-tinuing professional development (CPD) programmes. As you might imagine, though, the extent to which people can be trained to be more ethical is a matter of heated debate.[33]

13.3.6 Thorough analysis of the financial statements

It would be reckless to presume that the responsibility for rooting out accounting irregu-larities can simply be left to regulators, standard-setters, auditors, and accountants. Users of financial statements ought to see themselves as responsible too. After all, investors have

13

often been duped into supporting a business when a thorough analysis of the information in the financial statements should have alerted them to problems.

For example, Carillion's financial reporting contained several signals of its impending downfall. With nothing more than the financial statements, a savvy user could have seen that: the gross margin was only 7%, which is low for a conglomerate with substantial interests in construction; the business owed its pension fund so much that it would take six years of current earnings to make good the deficit; goodwill in the statement of financial position was larger than total equity; and operating cash flows were much lower than operating profits.[34]

Elsewhere in this book—for example, in sections 5.3 and 11.2.4—we have emphasised that this last point about the **quality of earnings** is key to evaluating the future prospects of a business. In general, Chapter 11 demonstrated how the most insightful analyses scrutinise key relationships between different figures, often in different financial statements. When such scrutiny reveals a relationship that doesn't make sense, this is often a sign that the reporting on its surface is misleading.

Another example of this is the relationship between tax expense and profit before tax. For example, if a business operating in Europe reports a tax expense that is only 10% of its profit before tax, this would be well below the average tax rates where it operates. Of course, we should not expect tax expense to be exactly equal to the tax rate multiplied by the profit before tax (see sections 2.2.12 and 8.3.3), yet it is not unreasonable to anticipate that it would be in the ballpark.

If a mismatch like this occurs as a result of some deception by the business's management, it is generally the case that the tax charge is correct and the profits overstated. After all, the penalties for underpaying tax are typically more probable, well defined, and sizeable than the possible costs of overstating profit.

The lesson here is that accounting irregularities can often be identified by analysing key relationships. If a relationship is surprising, it is worth further investigation. If the explanation is found and makes sense, then the analyst can feel more confident in the reliability of the financial statements. Yet if a surprise cannot be explained, or if the explanation itself is concerning, then the analyst should consider this a serious red flag.

A thorough analysis also involves reading all the way to the end of the notes to the financial statements. For example, we observed in section 7.1.5 that this is usually where to find potentially crucial reporting about contingent liabilities. Another item that does not appear in the financial statements, and often only shows up in the last of the notes—despite being a vital indicator of future cash outflows—is the business's commitments (see section 7.1.2).

A similarly late appearance is made by an item that we have not yet discussed: related party disclosures. These are important to help users understand the extent to which businesses are entering into transactions with parties that are related to them, and perhaps more importantly, the terms and conditions of these transactions. For example, reading this note might be how an analyst could uncover an elaborate Enron-like scheme involving SPEs.

Sidebar notes (left margin):

Thorough analysis of a business's financial statements can expose problems that other analysts may not spot.

Low quality of earnings can indicate an accounting irregularity.

Tax expense that appears to be well below the statutory tax rate is another potential indicator of an accounting irregularity.

Important liabilities that have been omitted from the financial statements may be reported in the notes about contingent liabilities or commitments.

13

Related parties can be people or entities. People include significant shareholders, directors, managers with major responsibilities, and close family members of these people. Entities include companies in the same group and retirement funds for the business's employees.

Related party disclosure thus ensures that an investor in a business would know if the business's CEO had, say, directed the business to purchase goods from her husband's business at a price 50% above the normal price.

Such disclosure can also reveal more complex abuses of power. Suppose that Business A owns 100% of Business B, and 60% of Business C, and then uses its controlling position to instruct Business C to sell goods to Business B for $2 million below cost, as depicted in Figure 13.2.

Businesses must disclose their transactions with related parties, including the terms and conditions of these transactions.

FIGURE 13.2 A complex related party transaction

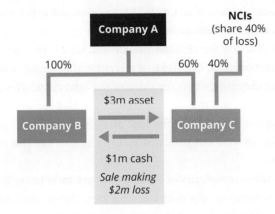

In the group financial statements, the intragroup transaction would be eliminated, but $800 000 ($2 m × 40%) would disappear from the non-controlling interest's (NCI's) share of profits, and instead be attributable to the parent. Fortunately, a careful reading of the related party transactions note would alert the NCIs to this kind of scheme.

Thus, whilst transactions with related parties are not always inappropriate, they are all disclosed so that analysts can be informed about them, and come to their own conclusions.

13.4 DID ACCOUNTING IRREGULARITIES CREATE THE GLOBAL FINANCIAL CRISIS?

Before concluding a chapter on accounting irregularities, it is appropriate to consider a question that has been asked in recent years about the global financial crisis (GFC) of 2007–8: were accounting irregularities to blame? Like the Covid-19 crisis, this was an extreme economic event, the effects of which are still felt around the world. Many informed observers claim that a Great Depression was only narrowly avoided. We ought to interrogate its causes.

Certainly, some accounting irregularities were involved. Early in the crisis, the investment bank Lehman Brothers collapsed, and its financial statements were indeed found to contain accounting irregularities, most notably due to a practice known inside the bank as 'Repo 105'. This involved large holdings of financial instruments that the bank had leveraged (bought on credit) being sold just before a reporting date in order to make the bank's leverage ratios appear less risky, only to be bought back again immediately after the reporting date.[35]

Yet accounting irregularities were not widely reported. Many other companies beside Lehman either went bankrupt, were bailed out by governments, or were acquired under duress, though no irregularities were discovered in their financial statements.

The fact is that a combination of factors led to the crisis, and experts place differing emphases on each factor. One was the excessive use of debt in the market: consumers became highly leveraged, as did commercial and investment banks. We have observed several times that debt can be beneficial, but also that it is risky. The downside of leverage became obvious to all during the crisis, when the value of the assets used as security against this debt declined considerably in value. In fact, some argue that the assets were never really worth enough to support the debt in the first place: that the banks gave mortgages to customers whose houses were not sufficient security against the risk of them defaulting on their repayments.

Another factor was the complexity of the financial products being traded. Using complicated financial arrangements, the debt was repackaged into derivative instruments and sold around the world. Inappropriately high credit ratings were given to these derivatives by ratings agencies, and thus investors relying on these ratings paid far too much for what were really very risky financial instruments.

When the market finally began to realise that these assets were overrated, prices nosedived, and the banks and other financial institutions were left holding assets whose fair values were quickly dwarfed by their liabilities, which remained the same. In much the same way as the homeowners did not have the cash to make their mortgage payments, the banks could not sell their financial assets for enough money to discharge their own debt obligations, and—almost overnight—gigantic firms went under. (Two of the most compelling accounts of the GFC are offered by the films *The Big Short* (2015) and *Margin Call* (2011). If you haven't seen them already, consider watching them for homework!)

As in any disaster scenario, there was much finger-pointing in many different directions. Some even blamed accounting itself, claiming that US and international financial reporting standards were responsible for the chaos in the market. A subsequent review by the International Accounting Standards Board (IASB) identified several issues which needed urgent attention. These included the need to simplify the standard that dealt with financial instruments, especially with respect to off-balance-sheet items, and the principles relating to asset impairments. The IASB made quick strides to produce new standards

Two powerful explanations for the GFC are overleveraged markets and the trading of complex derivatives whose risks were underestimated by ratings agencies.

13

addressing these issues. The hope is that, if similarly bad business decisions are again made by investment banks and others, their financial statements will inform users sufficiently and early enough that a crisis will be averted.

CONCLUSION

Human ingenuity is not always a force for good, and the field of financial reporting is no different. Creative accounting has been used to manipulate businesses' financial statements in myriad ways that mislead users into making decisions that are against their own interests but advantageous to the perpetrator. This is unethical, usually illegal, and—given the relatively advanced stage of development of IFRS accounting standards—almost always contrary to accounting standards.

Perhaps the real-world examples that we have included in this chapter have filled you with a sense of awe at the cunning of the tricksters, but we hope that your confidence has also been boosted in realising that—at this point in the book—you know enough to be able to understand how so many accounting scams have been pulled off. We likewise hope that you feel that you have an idea of what to look for to make sure that you do not become a victim yourself.

After all, regulations across the world are generally strengthening and constantly diminishing the likelihood of exposure of financial misdeeds, but at the same time, more accounting irregularities are inevitable. It is thus important for users of financial statements to take responsibility for interrogating the statements rigorously enough that they are not played for fools.

SUMMARY OF KEY POINTS

- 'Creative accounting' generally describes the ethical, and often illegal, practice of preparing financial reports which contain accounting irregularities.
- An accounting irregularity is an item incorrectly included in, or omitted from, the accounting records and financial statements, with the purpose of misleading others.
- Accounting irregularities are perpetrated for a variety of reasons, including to: launder money; attract cash into a Ponzi scheme; cover up theft; and obscure bad news.
- Common kinds of irregularities include: falsifying income; upfronting income; incorrectly deferring expenses; failing to impair assets when appropriate; misclassifying liabilities; and not consolidating controlled entities.
- Many businesses which resort to perpetrating an accounting irregularity do not stop at just one. Their financial statements often contain a wide variety of irregularities.
- Countermeasures against accounting irregularities include: financial regulation, corporate governance codes, improvements in accounting standards, auditing, and accounting ethics.
- Users of financial statements can also often identify suspect financial reporting for themselves, for example by: identifying low quality of earnings; interrogating seemingly low tax rates; investigating the notes for evidence of unrecognised liabilities; and carefully considering the reporting of related parties and related party transactions.

13

- Some commentators attributed the global financial crisis to widespread accounting irregularities. However, although some irregularities did contribute to the crisis, better candidates for broad explanations are overleveraged markets, and the trading of complex derivatives whose risks were underestimated by ratings agencies.
- Although accounting standards should not be held responsible for the crisis, the IASB did respond to the crisis, especially by tightening up IFRS 9 on financial instruments.

CHAPTER QUESTIONS

The suggested solutions to the concept questions (marked 'CQ') can be found in Appendix III. Also, don't forget the **online resources** available at www.oup.com/he/winfield-graham-miller1e, which contain multiple-choice questions based on the material in this chapter, in addition to many other helpful resources.

CONCEPT QUESTIONS

CQ 13.1 List the four main reasons that someone would seek to make accounting information misleading.

CQ 13.2 List six accounting irregularities that appear commonly in financial statements.

CQ 13.3 Briefly outline what you understand by the term 'upfronting income'.

CQ 13.4 Why does the misclassification of liabilities potentially mislead the users of financial statements?

CQ 13.5 Explain the importance of the 'related parties' note to the financial statements.

INVESTIGATION QUESTIONS

IQ 13.6 Identify a recent accounting irregularity that occurred in your country or region. (Hint: try googling 'accounting scandal'.) Establish the likely reason why it was perpetrated and the manner in which it was perpetrated.

IQ 13.7 Establish which types of businesses in your country are required to have their financial statements audited.

IQ 13.8 Identify the corporate governance codes used in your country or region. Establish to what extent the introduction of these codes has improved the efficacy of corporate governance.

REFERENCES

[1] United Nations Office on Drugs and Crime 2020. *Money-Laundering and Globalization*. United Nations official website. Available at: https://www.unodc.org/unodc/en/money-laundering/globalization.html.

[2] Darby, M 1998. 'In Ponzi We Trust'. Smithsonian Magazine. December issue. Available at: https://www.smithsonianmag.com/history/in-ponzi-we-trust-64016168.

[3] Henriques, D 2009. 'Madoff Is Sentenced to 150 Years for Ponzi Scheme'. *New York Times*. 29 June. Available at: https://www.nytimes.com/2009/06/30/business/30madoff.html.

4   McCool, G and Graybow, M 2009. 'Madoff Pleads Guilty, Is Jailed for $65 Billion Fraud'. *Reuters*. 13 March. Available at: https://www.reuters.com/article/us-madoff/madoff-pleads-guilty-is-jailed-for-65-billion-fraud-idUSTRE52A5JK20090313.

5   Sorkin, AR 2002. '2 Top Tyco Executives Charged with 600 Million Fraud Scheme'. *New York Times*. 13 September. Available at: https://www.nytimes.com/2002/09/13/business/2-top-tyco-executives-charged-with-600-million-fraud-scheme.html.

6   Bloomberg News 2009. 'S.E.C. Ends Case against 2 at Tyco'. *New York Times*. 14 July. Available at: https://www.nytimes.com/2009/07/15/business/15tyco.html.

7   Curry, R 2018. 'Carillion Finance Director Blew the Whistle on Irregular Accounting', Board Papers Show. *The Daily Telegraph*. 27 February. Available at: https://www.telegraph.co.uk/business/2018/02/27/carillion-finance-director-blew-whistle-irregular-accounting.

8   BBC 2019. 'Patisserie Valerie Says Accounting Scandal Worse than Thought'. 16 January. Available at: https://www.bbc.com/news/business-46897543.

9   CBC News 2018. 'Former Alberta Motor Association Executive Sentenced to 5 Years for Fraud'. 26 February. Available at: https://www.cbc.ca/news/canada/edmonton/alberta-motor-association-vice-president-fraud-1.4552905.

10 This is according to a complaint filed by the US Securities and Exchange Commission in the District Court of Columbia on 5 April 2011. Available at: https://www.sec.gov/divisions/enforce/claims/docs/satyam-complaint.pdf.

11 Moffett, M 2013. 'Chairman of Fishing Giant Pescanova Quits'. *The Wall Street Journal*. 17 July. Available at: https://www.wsj.com/articles/SB10001424127887324263404578612130976494140.

12 Sorkin, AR and Berenson, A 2002. 'Tyco Admits Using Accounting Tricks to Inflate Earnings'. *New York Times*. 31 December. Available at: https://www.nytimes.com/2002/12/31/business/corporate-conduct-overview-tyco-admits-using-accounting-tricks-inflate-earnings.html.

13 Lohr, S 2004. 'Ex-Executives at Symbol Are Indicted'. *New York Times*. 4 June. Available at: https://www.nytimes.com/2004/06/04/business/ex-executives-at-symbol-are-indicted.html.

14 Bergin, T 2014. 'Tesco-Style Accounting Risks Well Known in Retail Industry'. *Reuters*. 23 September. Available at: https://uk.reuters.com/article/uk-tescoaccounting/tesco-style-accounting-risks-well-known-in-retail-industry-idUKKCN0HI2DF20140923.

15 Cox, J 2017. 'Tesco Fined 129 Million by Serious Fraud Office for Overstating Profits'. *The Independent*. 28 March. Available at: https://www.independent.co.uk/news/business/news/tesco-fined-129-million-by-serious-fraud-office-overstating-profits-a7653166.html.

16 Independent Investigation Committee for Toshiba Corporation 2015. *Investigation Report*. 20 July, p 218. Available at: https://www.toshiba.co.jp/about/ir/en/news/20151208_2.pdf.

17 Drucker, J and Sender, H 2002. 'WorldCom Accounting Debacle Shows How Easy Fraud Can Be'. *Wall Street Journal*. 17 June. Available at: https://www.wsj.com/articles/SB102513134054041480.

18 Sender, H 2002. 'Accounting Issues at WorldCom Speak Volumes about Disclosures'. *Wall Street Journal*. 21 August. Available at: https://www.wsj.com/articles/SB102987635688318515.

19 Romero, S 2002. 'Internal Notes Questioned Qwest's Swaps'. *New York Times*. 25 September. Available at: https://www.nytimes.com/2002/09/25/business/internal-notes-questioned-qwest-s-swaps.html.

20 Romero, S 2002. 'Global Crossing under Scrutiny for Its Trading'. *New York Times*. 12 February. Available at: https://www.nytimes.com/2002/02/12/business/global-crossing-under-scrutiny-for-its-trading.html.

21 Trentmann, N 2018. 'Carillion Collapse Highlights Accounting Shortcomings—Moody's'. *Wall Street Journal*. 14 March. Available at: https://blogs.wsj.com/cfo/2018/03/14/carillion-collapse-highlights-accounting-shortcomings-moodys.

22 Steinhoff International Holdings NV 2019. *Overview of Forensic Investigation*. 15 March. Available at: http://www.steinhoffinternational.com/downloads/2019/overview-of-forensic-investigation.pdf.

23 Masters, B 2011. 'Enron's Fall Raised the Bar in Regulation'. *Financial Times*. 1 December. Available at: https://www.ft.com/content/9790ea78-1aa9-11e1-ae14-00144feabdc0.

24 Association of Certified Fraud Examiners (ACFE) 2014. *Report To the Nations on Occupational Fraud and Abuse*, p 4. Available at: https://www.acfe.com/rttn/docs/2014-report-to-nations.pdf.

25 International Finance Corporation 2015. *A Guide to Corporate Governance Practices in the European Union*. Available at: https://www.ifc.org/wps/wcm/connect/506d49a2-3763-4fe4-a783-5d58e37b8906/CG_Practices_in_EU_Guide.pdf?MOD=AJPERES&CVID=kNmxTtG.

13

[26] Newman, NF 2007. 'Enron and the Special Purpose Entities—Use or Abuse—the Real Problem—the Real Focus'. *Law and Business Review of the Americas*, Vol 13, No 1, Article 5, pp 97–137. Available at: https://scholar.smu.edu/cgi/viewcontent.cgi?article=1268&context=lbra.

[27] Higson, C 2018. *Two Lessons from the Failure of Carillion*. Think at London Business School. 6 February. Available at: https://www.london.edu/think/two-lessons-from-the-failure-of-carillion.

[28] Sinclair, U 1994. *I, Candidate for Governor: And How I Got Licked*. University of California Press.

[29] Brooks, R 2018. 'The Financial Scandal No One Is Talking About'. *The Guardian*. 29 May. Available at: https://www.theguardian.com/news/2018/may/29/the-financial-scandal-no-one-is-talking-about-big-four-accountancy-firms.

[30] Tysiac, K 2014. 'Mandatory Audit Firm Rotation Rules Published in EU'. *Journal of Accountancy*. 28 May. Available at: https://www.journalofaccountancy.com/news/2014/may/201410229.html.

[31] Cohn, M 2020. 'IESBA Proposes Major Revisions to Independence Standards for Auditors'. *Accounting Today*. 22 January. Available at: https://www.accountingtoday.com/news/iesba-proposes-major-revisions-to-independence-standards-for-auditors.

[32] International Federation of Accountants 2018. *Handbook of the International Code of Ethics for Professional Accountants*. Available at: https://www.ifac.org/system/files/publications/files/IESBA-Handbook-Code-of-Ethics-2018.pdf.

[33] Bampton, R and Maclagan, P 2005. 'Why Teach Ethics to Accounting Students? A Response to the Sceptics'. *Business Ethics: A European Review*, Vol 14, No. 3. July. Available at: https://doi.org/10.1111/j.1467-8608.2005.00410.x.

[34] Ryans, J and Tuna, I 2019. *Can Regulation Stop Financial Scandals?* Think at London Business School. 28 October. Available at: https://www.london.edu/think/can-regulation-stop-financial-scandals.

[35] De la Merced, MJ and Sorkin, AR 2010. 'Report Details How Lehman Hid Its Woes'. *New York Times*. 11 March. Available at: https://www.nytimes.com/2010/03/12/business/12lehman.html.

TRENDS IN CORPORATE REPORTING

Here are some of the things you will be able to do after reading this chapter:

- describe foreseeable continued developments in International Financing Reporting Standards (IFRS);
- discuss the potential effects that technologies such as XBRL and Blockchain could have on financial accounting;
- give a brief history and the current status of environmental, social, and governance reporting;
- discuss integrated thinking and the concept of the six capitals, and describe the purpose, layout, and content of integrated reports;
- explain the usual content, informational value, and bias of the management commentary section of a business's annual report.

If you have read all of the preceding chapters, you have already learned everything required to understand the hundreds of thousands of **financial statements** currently being published using **IFRS**. In this final chapter, to prepare you for future developments, we will briefly cover some emerging trends in financial reporting. To deepen your understanding of corporate reporting more generally, we will also introduce you to some of the other reports that businesses publish along with their financial statements.

The term 'corporate reporting' describes a variety of reports that a business might publish, including the financial statements, management commentary, and the environmental, social, and governance (ESG) and integrated reports.

14.1 DEVELOPMENTS IN FINANCIAL REPORTING

Some of the changes in financial reporting are being driven from within, by the **International Accounting Standards Board (IASB)**, while others are the result of external forces.

14.1.1 **Increasing use of fair value**

A general trend in the history of accounting standards is a move away from using an asset's cost, and towards using its **fair value**, as the basis for measuring it. At present (with a few exceptions, most notably for inventory), IFRS either requires assets to be measured using fair value or allows businesses the option to use fair value. For example, shares are required to be measured at fair value, and there are fair value options for the measurement of property, plant and equipment (PPE), investment properties, and intangibles. (Chapter 6 describes the measurement of assets in detail.)

Deciding which is the better measurement basis isn't as straightforward as you may think, as the following example will show. Suppose that, many years ago, a business purchased a small office block as an investment, spending €100 000. Now, after many years of property inflation, it rents the building out for an annual rental income of €60 000.

If the investment property is reported on the business's statement of financial position at cost, the annual yield appears to be 60% (€60 000 ÷ €100 000 × 100). This is a fantastic return, but completely misleading. If the building's fair value—what it could be sold for today—has increased to, say, €2 million, the return is in fact only 3% (€60 000 ÷ €2 m × 100).

Certainly, much more *relevant* information will result if the asset is reported on the statement of financial position at its fair value of €2 million. Management's decisions (eg about whether the business's resources might be more productively used elsewhere) would be better informed; and the quality of those decisions could be much more easily evaluated by users of the financial statements.

However, there are several concerns about the move towards reporting assets at fair value. First, market values vary—think, for example, of the share prices of companies held as investments—and this variation can cause much more earnings volatility, which elevates the business's **risk–return profile**, and can even tempt managers into resorting to **creative accounting** in order to smooth profits.

Second, there are concerns about the *reliability* of the fair value estimate. The fair value of some assets like shares can be measured relatively accurately, but not so for others, for example distinctive buildings in areas where too few buildings are sold to establish an average market value. Furthermore, measuring the fair values of many other types of assets—think of intangible assets like intellectual property—is close to impossible.

The unreliability of fair value estimates makes it easier for less scrupulous managers to choose fair values that suit them; and it also increases the likelihood that even well-meaning business leaders may inadvertently get the valuation very wrong.

Reducing this likelihood requires employing independent valuation consultants and paying for second or third opinions. This leads to a third concern about fair value measurement, which is that it adds a substantial expense that never used to apply to items simply measured using their cost.

For now, by stipulating a complicated variety of measurement principles, choices, and disclosure requirements, current accounting standards do their best to find a balance between the relevance of fair values and the concerns about them. However, this appears to be an area of financial reporting that is not entirely settled.

Measuring assets at fair value produces more relevant information.

A concern about using fair value is the potential for earnings volatility.

Another concern about fair value is the reliability of measurement.

A third concern about using fair value is that it can be expensive.

14

It may be that technological developments in the areas of Big Data and artificial intelligence will shift the debate about using fair values. For example, perhaps access to huge volumes of data, and the processing capability to interrogate them using machine-learning software, will make estimating the fair value of many more items much more reliable and less costly. If so, we could expect an increasing number of assets to appear in the financial statements at their fair values.

14.1.2 Development of new accounting standards

Since they began setting accounting standards in 2001, the members of the IASB have had their work cut out for them. Their initial mandate to harmonise diverse national accounting standards, as well as two major economic events (the major accounting scandals that hit world headlines as they were getting started, and the global financial crisis of 2007–8) required them to release and revise standards at a frenetic pace. They needed to respond rapidly to the demands of capital markets justifiably frustrated that financial statements were not as useful as they could be. The IASB now considers the major reforms to be complete, but it still has several important projects ahead of it.[1]

If you are interested to see what is in the pipeline, have a look at the IASB's work plan at https://www.ifrs.org/projects/work-plan, or just google 'IASB work plan'.

Perhaps the most significant of the IASB's current standard-setting projects is the Primary Financial Statements project, which aims to standardise the subtotals used in the profit or loss section of the statement of comprehensive income. 'Profit or loss' itself is currently the only subtotal that is defined by IFRS, and so each business chooses for itself what goes into other subtotals like operating profit or earnings before interest, taxes, depreciation, and amortisation (EBITDA). According to the chairman of the IASB, its:

> technical staff looked at 60 companies in different countries and industry sectors. About 70% of those companies used an Operating Profit subtotal, but there were no fewer than nine different versions of that subtotal . . . Some included investment incomes, others did not. Some included profits from joint ventures, others did not. And some excluded various items they consider non-operating or non-recurring. This is what financial reporting looks like in the absence of standards.[2]

The Primary Financial Statements project also aims to set constraints and principles for management to apply when reporting alternative performance measures (see section 4.6), labelling items of income or expense as 'unusual', and aggregating like items (such as 'operating costs') together. All of these planned initiatives should improve the comparability and reliability of the figures in different businesses' financial statements.

14.1.3 XBRL and iXBRL

If you have read this book as carefully as we are hoping, you have by now looked at several businesses' financial statements: certainly Burberry's and Daimler's, and perhaps also a few others that you have accessed yourself. It is impossible to do this without noticing

The IASB will be standardising the subtotals which appear in the profit or loss section of the statement of comprehensive income.

14

something rather disappointing: the differences between them extend far beyond what items are included in operating profit. Even if the two businesses are in the same industry in the same regions, the financial statements' layout and sequencing varies; they use assorted words to describe the same thing; and they provide varying amounts of detail about each item.

If you have gone one step further and attempted to do an analysis of a business, you have probably already discovered that it is easiest to calculate ratios by first entering the data into a computer (a spreadsheeting package works well). If so, you may have wondered whether you were wasting your time doing data entry that has clearly already been done in order to prepare the financial statements. If you have analysed more than one business, you would have wished not only that you could save yourself the time of data capture, but also that there wasn't such wide variation in different businesses' financial reporting conventions.

The good news is that there is in fact a system that grants both of these wishes. It is called eXtensible Business Reporting Language, or **XBRL**. With XBRL, a business tags each item in its financial statements with an appropriate code and other information, such as the reporting period. For example, Burberry's total PPE would be tagged as 'ifrs-full:PropertyPlantAndEquipment' to indicate that it is the PPE as measured according to the **full IFRS** standards. This creates a data set that can be digitally shared and manipulated by anyone with access. Most commonly, businesses then use a related piece of software called Inline XBRL, or iXBRL, to share machine-readable financial statements that are also designed for human viewing.

According to the non-profit XBRL consortium that oversees the use of XBRL and iXBRL, the technology enables 'people using the information to do so in the way that best suits their needs, including by using different languages, alternative currencies and in their preferred style'; and also allows them to be 'confident that the data provided to them conforms to a set of sophisticated pre-defined definitions'.[3]

Since XBRL was first developed just before the turn of the millennium, it has steadily been adopted around the world, and now over 100 regulators require businesses to report using iXBRL. These include Her Majesty's Revenue and Customs in the UK (since 2011), the Securities and Exchange Commission in the US (since 2018), and the European Securities and Markets Authority (since 2020).[4]

It is estimated that tens of millions of businesses use the technology, although in many cases they limit its use to their regulatory filings, rather than making their financial statements publicly available in iXBRL. It seems likely that, as users of the financial statements become more aware of its existence and advantages, businesses will be incentivised to make XBRL information more widely accessible.

14.1.4 **Blockchain**

The technology underlying Bitcoin and other cryptocurrencies is called blockchain. Its uses go well beyond enabling digital currencies, for it is essentially an accounting system concerned with the entry and retention of data. In this sense, blockchain is a ledger:

Margin note: Financial statements prepared using XBRL and iXBRL are machine-readable, and the items in them conform to a single set of definitions.

a store of information about items like assets and liabilities, and events like purchases and sales.

What makes blockchain special is that it is uniquely designed using cryptography and computer networks to ensure that it cannot be manipulated, providing certainty about the authenticity of the information it contains. For example, it is possible using blockchain to record the transfer of an asset in such a way that the information is fully verified and instantly publicly available. This is true of cash assets too, which means that a blockchain accounting system can eliminate the so-called 'double-spend' problem, preventing people from using one amount of money to make a second purchase before the processing of the first purchase is complete.

The recording of accounting information is called 'bookkeeping' because it originally involved the use of books with names like 'journals' and 'ledgers'. In the computer age, these paper-based records were digitised into accounting software packages. Blockchain may be the next step in this evolution, modifying or usurping the various available packages to reduce costly reconciliation and maintenance of the information.

For users of financial statements, the full range of advantages that blockchain may bring is not yet clear. To the extent that it lowers the cost of managing accounting information, investors should be happy. Likewise, users ought to welcome the reduction in instances of accounting irregularities that would be brought by certainty about the ownership of assets, and responsibility for liabilities. It is also possible that the technology could enable the inclusion of more useful information in the financial statements. For example, by dramatically increasing the breadth of publicly available data, blockchain may facilitate the measurement of items that are currently considered too difficult or unreliable to measure using fair value.[5]

> Blockchain allows for instant updating of financial information that is verified with absolute certainty.

MISCONCEPTION

The development of technologies such as artificial intelligence, machine learning, blockchain, and XBRL will render the accountant, or the analyst, obsolete.

Whilst these new developments will certainly improve the efficiency and accuracy of the bookkeeping process, businesses will still need individuals to apply the complex judgements and opinions that are required in terms of IFRS.

Similarly, while analysis may be improved by the assistance of technology, it will be a long time before machines will be able to interpret financial statements with the acumen and instincts of a good analyst.

14.2 OTHER CORPORATE REPORTS

Most businesses produce several different corporate reports to meet the various information needs of all their stakeholders. Often, one or more of these is bundled together with the financial statements into a single yearly communication, most commonly known as a business's annual report.

14

The precise history of these other corporate reports varies from one stock exchange, country, and region to the next. Generally, however, businesses have been publishing financial statements in some form for hundreds of years. In the 1970s, the first additional corporate report to emerge was the **management commentary** that now almost always accompanies the release of a set of financial statements. By 2000, a lot of businesses had also begun reporting about governance, remuneration, sustainability and other ethical issues. Most recently, many businesses have been producing an integrated report, emphasising strategy and value creation.

As explained in section 3.2, IFRS exists to standardise financial reporting, and has been adopted widely across the globe. However, the same level of standardisation does not exist for the other corporate reports. While this section will describe some international organisations that offer guidance, their requirements are looser than the demands of IFRS. Also, much additional corporate reporting is simply volunteered by businesses, often without applying a codified approach. Perhaps in time more comprehensive, stricter standards will emerge.

We shall now briefly outline the three additional corporate reports most frequently used around the world.

> Other forms of corporate reporting are either not standardised, or not standardised as strictly as financial reporting.

14.2.1 Environmental, social, and governance reporting

As public pressure for businesses to operate in a more sustainable and ethical way have intensified, so too has the demand for them to produce reports about how they are doing this. In its earlier days, this form of reporting was known as 'triple bottom line' accounting, because it required a business to measure and report not only its financial performance, but also its social and environment performance. Thus, for some time, it was common to find annual reports combining information about the 'three Ps': profit, people, and planet. Over time, however, the idea to include financial information along with the news about a business's other effects on the world went out of favour, perhaps because financial statements were always prepared separately anyway.

Today, the term '**environmental, social and governance (ESG) reporting**' describes the ways that a business communicates its performance in realms other than the financial. The information about these realms may be presented in one report, perhaps called an 'ESG report'; or it may be split up, for example by publishing a 'sustainability report' about the business's interaction with people and the environment, and then reporting governance information in a stand-alone report, or in its own section of the annual report.

> ESG reporting aims to communicate to all of a business's stakeholders about its important non-financial aspects.

Governance reporting, especially because it contains information about executive remuneration, is often highly regulated, with the requirements differing from one country and stock exchange to another.

The most widely accepted standards for sustainability reporting are the Global Reporting Initiative's (GRI) Sustainability Reporting Standards, which guide organisations in identifying and reporting on key sustainability issues. As each organisation's issues are unique to it, no two sustainability reports look the same.

An easily accessible example of ESG reporting is the sustainability report of the UK energy company SSE, easily accessed by googling 'SSE sustainability report'. It includes sections on sustainability strategy, climate change, affordable and clean energy, its transmission network and development of renewable energy, how economic value is shared, how the company provides a decent place to work, safety and health, environment, business culture, human rights, and modern slavery. The report includes metrics about SSE's performance with respect to a wide range of environmental, economic, social, and gender pay issues.[6]

14.2.2 Integrated reporting

ESG reporting has spawned another variety of corporate reporting, whose origins are often traced to 2004, when HRH The Prince of Wales, a keen champion of the environment, established the Accounting for Sustainability Project (A4S). This brought together executives, investors, standard-setters, accounting bodies, and representatives from the United Nations in an attempt to fundamentally shift businesses' approach to sustainability issues. Their deliberations revealed an absence of business thinking which integrates financial and non-financial issues. The separation of financial and ESG reporting was one symptom of this absence.

As business leaders began to accept the importance of 'integrated thinking', the need arose for a corporate report to communicate their businesses' performance in this new light. Thus, the International Integrated Reporting Committee (IIRC) was established in 2010, and produced the International Integrated Reporting Framework in 2013. This Framework provides guidance about to how to prepare an **integrated report**, defined as 'a concise communication about how an organisation's strategy, governance, performance and prospects, in the context of its external environment, lead to the creation of value in the short, medium and long term'.[7]

> The integrated report aims to communicate the results of a business's integrated thinking about financial and non-financial matters to providers of funding.

Although there is naturally some overlap between integrated reporting and ESG reporting, they are written for different audiences. While sustainability reporting is aimed at a broad variety of stakeholders with widely differing needs, the integrated report is currently aimed at providers of financial capital. (Talks are under way, however, to expand the integrated report's audience to include providers of other forms of capital.)

This new form of corporate reporting therefore has the potential to be a very useful tool for an analyst; an important supplement to the 'main story of the financial statements' covered in section 11.2.

MISCONCEPTION

Integrated reports are basically interchangeable with sustainability or ESG reports.

No, these two kind of reports have different purposes. Sustainability and ESG reports communicate non-financial information, whereas the integrated report communicates the results of the business's integrated thinking (that is, its value creation strategy), which combines financial and non-financial considerations. Also, for the time being at least, the two forms of reporting are aimed at quite different audiences.

14

Listed companies in Brazil and South Africa are required to produce integrated reports, and many businesses in Japan, the Netherlands, Germany, France, the UK, Italy, South Korea, Sri Lanka, India, and the US are doing so voluntarily.

Many more businesses now include many of the concepts and principles of the IIRC's Framework within their annual reports, without explicitly using the label 'integrated report'. In some jurisdictions, this is the result of regulatory requirements. For example, the UK Companies Act requires every company above a certain size to include within its annual report a 'strategic report' that contains many of the elements of an integrated report.

The six capitals

A fundamental concept of the IIRC's Framework is that integrated thinking requires attention to six kinds of resources and relationships, which it calls 'capitals'. These are:

- financial capital (the available financial resources);
- manufactured capital (physical objects, such as equipment and inventory);
- intellectual capital (knowledge-based intangibles, such as intellectual property and systems);
- human capital (staff competency, capability, and motivation);
- social and relationship capital (relationships with stakeholders such as customers, suppliers, and communities);
- natural capital (all renewable and non-renewable environmental resources which the business relies on, such as air, water, and land).

The integrated report contains information about six capitals: financial; manufactured; intellectual; human; social and relationship; and natural.

The idea is that businesses must use all of these six capitals to create value in the short, medium, and long term for themselves and others, including the providers of capital.

Now, the financial statements do contain some information about the first two capitals in this list, but the integrated report goes further, for example identifying the pool of funds that will be required to create value over time and the location of retail property and productivity of machinery.

As we have observed in sections 6.4.6 and 11.2.2, while some intellectual capital may be reported in the statement of financial position as intangible assets, financial reporting tends to omit many intangible assets like brands, systems, expertise, and so on. The integrated report, however, does contain much-needed reporting about these other intellectual resources, including an explanation of how they will be used to create value.

The other three capitals are not reported at all in the financial statements, and so the integrated report is a valuable resource to gain an understanding about these aspects of the business.

Content and layout of an integrated report

The IIRC's Framework does not set standards for integrated reporting in the same way that IFRS stipulates how financial reporting should be done. Rather, each organisation is encouraged to tell its value creation story in its own unique way.

TABLE 14.1 the IIRC's Integrated Reporting Framework's principles for layout and content elements

Guiding principles for layout	Content elements
• Maintain a strategic focus	• The internal and external environment
• Present a holistic picture of the organisation	• Governance structures
• Include insights into the needs and interests of various stakeholder groups	• Business model
	• Risks and opportunities
• Include only items material to the value creation story	• Strategy and resource allocation
• Be concise, reliable, and consistent	• Performance
	• Outlook
	• Basis of presentation

To assist businesses in working out how to do this, the Framework lists some guiding principles for the content and layout of an integrated report, along with eight content elements that each integrated report should contain. These are shown in Table 14.1 above.

Businesses are further encouraged to include both financial and non-financial targets measuring the achievement of strategy objectives, as well as comparisons with previous targets.

MISCONCEPTION

Business valuations can afford to ignore the integrated report, since most valuation models (including the DCF and multiples approaches) use exclusively inputs drawn from the financial statements.

Whilst inputs to most valuation models are indeed financial in nature, the additional information in an integrated report is likely to be very helpful. For example, estimates of the future cash flows in the DCF model require some knowledge of the brands and human resources that the business has at its disposal.

Similarly, when using a valuation multiple method, the process of refining the benchmark multiple will be enhanced by knowing every relevant fact about the business's operations, potential risks, and returns.

Some of this information is available in an integrated report, but not in a set of financial statements.

14.2.3 Management commentary

In most annual reports, the financial statements are preceded by what is known as the management commentary section. As its name implies, this section gives the management team an opportunity to comment about key aspects of the business's performance in the past year, and its prospects in the foreseeable future. Typically, management makes the most of this opportunity. For example, the first 100 or so pages of Burberry's 2019 annual report was management commentary.

Historically, management commentaries include descriptions of items like the following: the nature of the business; management's objectives and strategies; the most significant resources, risks and relationships; the results of operations and prospects; and also critical performance measures and indicators.[8] However, the precise contents vary from business to business, as they are entirely up to the discretion of management.

Management commentaries were the subject of a 2010 IASB 'practice statement': a non-binding collection of advice about the sort of commentary that might best accompany a set of financial statements prepared according to IFRS. This is currently being revised by the IASB, with the updated version still expected to be non-binding. It is expected to encourage management to prepare commentary which covers more of the sorts of information that currently appears in ESG and integrated reports. According to the chairman of the IASB:

> We want companies to report on what is strategically important to them, including how remuneration policies align with their long-term objectives. There will be more focus on intangibles that underpin companies' long-term success. And of course, companies would be expected to tell how sustainability issues, including climate change, may impact their business if that impact is material.[9]

Regardless of whether management commentary is prepared in accordance with the older or newer practice statement, it certainly contributes important background and explanatory information. And some of its content may be audited, for example to verify figures, comply with regulatory requirements, or to assess the reasonableness of management's interpretation of financial information. At the same time, however, management commentaries ought to be viewed with a healthy dose of scepticism, as not all elements are audited, and they do not have to conform to a rigorous set of standards. This means that they may well have been contrived to show management in a good light by overstating the importance of positive results, omitting or playing down potentially negative information, or both.

> The contents of the management commentary section of the annual report are entirely at management's discretion, although the IASB offers some advice in a practice statement.

CONCLUSION

Corporate reporting is a dynamic field. New forms of corporate reporting have been developed to provide valuable information about the ESG and strategic aspects of a business's activity. Meanwhile, the rapid evolution of IFRS standards over the past two decades has dramatically improved the usefulness of the financial statements, with more advances still ahead of us.

From the perspective of a user of the financial statements, this is welcome progress. The new corporate reports offer, at minimum, helpful context to better understand a business's financial information, if not a whole new dimension for evaluating its current performance and future prospects. These additional tools mean that a person able to interpret IFRS-based financial statements truly does hold the key to understanding any business.

For an illustration of corporate reporting in the real-world, visit the **online resources** (www.oup.com/he/winfield-graham-miller1e).

SUMMARY OF KEY POINTS

- The use of fair value to measure assets has been on the increase. Fair value measurement results in more relevant reporting, but there are concerns: it can increase earnings volatility; it can lead to less reliable reporting; and it can be costly. We may see the use of fair value increase as technology lessens some of these concerns.
- The new accounting standards that are in development by the IASB can be viewed online on its work plan page. The most significant of these is currently the Primary Financial Statements Project, which will standardise the subtotals used in the profit or loss section of the statement of comprehensive income.
- Financial statements prepared using XBRL and iXBRL are machine-readable, and the items in them conform to a single set of definitions. This is potentially very useful, as it allows for easy presentation in whatever languages, currency, or style a user prefers; increases confidence in what reported figures represent; and speeds manipulation and comparison of financial data.
- Blockchain is essentially a ledger that allows for instant updating of financial information that is verified with absolute certainty. It has potential as an accounting platform, for example by lowering the cost of managing financial information; reducing accounting irregularities; and improving measurability.
- ESG reporting aims to communicate to all of a business's stakeholders about its important non-financial aspects. It is not closely regulated or standardised. Some businesses release a sustainability report, or a governance report, or both, and some simply include reporting about ESG matters in their annual reports.
- Integrated reporting is a fairly recent development, which seeks to communicate the results of an organisation's integrated thinking about six capitals—financial; manufactured; intellectual; human; social and relationship; and natural—and how the business uses them to create value over the short, medium, and long term.
- The International Integrated Reporting Committee (IIRC) has released a framework that sets out the fundamental concepts, layout, and content elements of an integrated report, which is required to be produced by listed companies in a few countries, and which is increasingly being produced voluntarily by businesses around the world.
- The management commentary section of an annual report is compiled and produced at the discretion of a business's management team. An IASB practice statement recommends some guidelines for management commentaries, and some aspects may be audited. However, although it often contains valuable explanatory information, it should be regarded with scepticism because it is likely to have been contrived to show management in the best possible light.

CHAPTER QUESTIONS

The suggested solutions to the concept questions (marked 'CQ') can be found in Appendix III. Also, don't forget the **online resources** available at www.oup.com/he/winfield-graham-miller1e, which contain multiple-choice questions based on the material in this chapter, in addition to many other helpful resources.

14

CONCEPT QUESTIONS

CQ 14.1 Explain the trade-off between using fair value or cost as the basis for measuring assets to be reported in the statement of financial position.

CQ 14.2 Briefly outline the aims of the IASB's Primary Financial Statements project.

CQ 14.3 Explain what 'XBRL' refers to, and identify two of its advantages.

CQ 14.4 What is the key difference between an ESG report and an integrated report?

CQ 14.5 Broadly speaking, what sort of information is communicated in the management commentary section of an annual report?

INVESTIGATION QUESTIONS

IQ 14.6 Inspect the IASB's workplan (available at https://www.ifrs.org/projects/work-plan). To what extent do you think that the IASB's current initiatives will improve the degree to which financial statements will provide users with relevant information that faithfully represents economic reality?

IQ 14.7 Select a relatively new technology such as blockchain, XBRL, artificial intelligence, or another of your choosing. Investigate the extent to which companies in your country are currently using this technology, and its effects on the local accounting profession in general, and financial statements in particular.

IQ 14.8 Investigate the corporate reporting requirements that apply to companies listed on the stock exchange nearest to you. (Hint: these requirements may be mandated by legislation or by the stock exchange itself.)

REFERENCES

[1] Hoogervorst, H 2019. Strengthening the Relevance of Financial Reporting. IFRS Foundation Conference. 20 June. Available at: https://www.ifrs.org/news-and-events/2019/06/strengthening-the-relevance-of-financial-reporting.

[2] ibid.

[3] Xbrl.org 2020. *An Introduction to XBRL: The Basics of XBRL for Business and Accounting Professionals.* Available at: https://www.xbrl.org/the-standard/what/an-introduction-to-xbrl.

[4] Cohn, M 2017. 'XBRL Makes Progress Globally'. *Accounting Today.* 28 July. Available at: https://www.accountingtoday.com/news/xbrl-makes-progress-globally.

[5] Institute of Chartered Accountants of England and Wales (ICAEW) 2020. *Blockchain and the Future of Accountancy.* Available at: https://www.icaew.com/technical/technology/blockchain/blockchain-articles/blockchain-and-the-accounting-perspective.

[6] SSE plc 2019. *Sustainability Report 2019.* Available at: https://sse.com/media/623847/SSE-Sustainability-report-2019-FINAL-spreads.pdf.

[7] International Integrated Reporting Committee 2013. *International Integrated Reporting Framework*, p 7. Available at: https://integratedreporting.org/wp-content/uploads/2015/03/13-12-08-THE-INTERNATIONAL-IR-FRAMEWORK-2-1.pdf.

[8] IASB 2010. *Practice Statement 1: Management Commentary.*

[9] Hoogervorst, H 2019. Strengthening the Relevance of Financial Reporting. IFRS Foundation Conference. 20 June. Available at: https://www.ifrs.org/news-and-events/2019/06/strengthening-the-relevance-of-financial-reporting.

APPENDIX I
BURBERRY 2019 FINANCIAL STATEMENTS

Burberry Group plc is one of the world's largest luxury fashion businesses, with more than 400 retail locations operated in over 30 countries by as many as 10 000 employees. It is headquartered in London, and its shares are listed on the London Stock Exchange.

This appendix contains Burberry's group financial statements for the year ended 30 March 2019, which are referred to throughout this book. We recommend that you look at the relevant parts whenever Burberry is mentioned in the text, as it is vital to see the real-world application of what you are learning.

The notes to accompany the financial statements are not included here; however, we often refer to these notes, and so it is likewise important for you to be able to look at them from time to time. Please therefore download the 2018/19 Annual Report, available at https://www .burberryplc.com/content/dam/burberry/corporate/oar/documents/Burberry_201819-Annual-Report.pdf, or simply type 'Burberry annual report 2019' into your web browser. The financial statements presented here are from pp 160–4 and the notes begin on p 165 of the report.

GROUP INCOME STATEMENT

	Note	52 weeks to 30 March 2019 £m	Year to 31 March 2018 £m
Revenue	3	2,720.2	2,732.8
Cost of sales		(859.4)	(835.4)
Gross profit		1,860.8	1,897.4
Net operating expenses	4	(1,423.6)	(1,487.1)
Operating profit		437.2	410.3
Financing			
Finance income		8.7	7.8
Finance expense		(3.6)	(3.5)
Other financing charge		(1.7)	(2.0)
Net finance income	9	3.4	2.3
Profit before taxation	5	440.6	412.6
Taxation	10	(101.5)	(119.0)
Profit for the year		339.1	293.6
Attributable to:			
Owners of the Company		339.3	293.5
Non-controlling interest		(0.2)	0.1
Profit for the year		339.1	293.6

(Continued)

GROUP INCOME STATEMENT (*CONTINUED*)

	Note	52 weeks to 30 March 2019 £m	Year to 31 March 2018 £m
Earnings per share			
Basic	11	**82.3p**	68.9p
Diluted	11	**81.7p**	68.4p
Reconciliation of adjusted profit before taxation:			
Profit before taxation		**440.6**	412.6
Adjusting items:			
Adjusting operating items	5	**0.9**	56.3
Adjusting financing items	5	**1.7**	2.0
Adjusted profit before taxation – non-GAAP measure		**443.2**	470.9
Adjusted earnings per share – non-GAAP measure			
Basic	11	**82.7p**	82.8p
Diluted	11	**82.1p**	82.1p
Dividends per share			
Interim	12	**11.0p**	11.0p
Proposed final (not recognised as a liability at 30 March/31 March)	12	**31.5p**	30.3p

GROUP STATEMENT OF COMPREHENSIVE INCOME

	Note	52 weeks to 30 March 2019 £m	Year to 31 March 2018 £m
Profit for the year		**339.1**	293.6
Other comprehensive income:			
Cash flow hedges	23	**(2.1)**	(10.0)
Net investment hedges	23	**1.6**	2.3
Foreign currency translation differences		**14.6**	(50.2)
Tax on other comprehensive income:			
Cash flow hedges	10	**0.4**	1.9
Net investment hedges	10	**(0.2)**	(0.4)
Foreign currency translation differences	10	**(1.3)**	3.6
Other comprehensive income for the year, net of tax		**13.0**	(52.8)
Total comprehensive income for the year		**352.1**	240.8
Total comprehensive income attributable to:			
Owners of the Company		**352.0**	241.2
Non-controlling interest		**0.1**	(0.4)
		352.1	240.8

GROUP BALANCE SHEET

	Note	As at 30 March 2019 £m	As at 31 March 2018 £m
ASSETS			
Non-current assets			
Intangible assets	13	**221.0**	180.1
Property, plant and equipment	14	**306.9**	313.6
Investment properties		**2.5**	2.6
Deferred tax assets	15	**123.1**	115.5
Trade and other receivables	16	**70.1**	69.2
Derivative financial assets	18	**–**	0.3
		723.6	681.3
Current assets			
Inventories	17	**465.1**	411.8
Trade and other receivables	16	**251.1**	206.3
Derivative financial assets	18	**3.0**	1.6
Income tax receivables		**14.9**	6.7
Cash and cash equivalents	19	**874.5**	915.3
		1,608.6	1,541.7
Total assets		**2,332.2**	2,223.0
LIABILITIES			
Non-current liabilities			
Trade and other payables	20	**(176.5)**	(168.1)
Deferred tax liabilities	15	**(3.4)**	(4.2)
Derivative financial liabilities	18	**(0.1)**	(0.1)
Retirement benefit obligations		**(1.4)**	(0.9)
Provisions for other liabilities and charges	21	**(50.7)**	(71.4)
		(232.1)	(244.7)
Current liabilities			
Bank overdrafts	22	**(37.2)**	(23.2)
Derivative financial liabilities	18	**(5.5)**	(3.8)
Trade and other payables	20	**(525.7)**	(460.9)
Provisions for other liabilities and charges	21	**(34.6)**	(32.1)
Income tax liabilities		**(37.1)**	(32.9)
		(640.1)	(552.9)
Total liabilities		**(872.2)**	(797.6)
Net assets		**1,460.0**	1,425.4

(*Continued*)

GROUP BALANCE SHEET (*CONTINUED*)

	Note	As at 30 March 2019 £m	As at 31 March 2018 £m
EQUITY			
Capital and reserves attributable to owners of the Company			
Ordinary share capital	23	**0.2**	0.2
Share premium account		**216.9**	214.6
Capital reserve	23	**41.1**	41.1
Hedging reserve	23	**3.5**	3.8
Foreign currency translation reserve	23	**227.7**	214.7
Retained earnings		**965.6**	946.1
Equity attributable to owners of the Company		**1,455.0**	1,420.5
Non-controlling interest in equity		**5.0**	4.9
Total equity		**1,460.0**	1,425.4

GROUP STATEMENT OF CHANGES IN EQUITY

	Note	Attributable to owners of the Company					Non-controlling interest £m	Total equity £m
		Ordinary share capital £m	Share premium account £m	Other reserves £m	Retained earnings £m	Total £m		
Balance as at 31 March 2017		0.2	211.4	311.9	1,169.0	1,692.5	5.3	1,697.8
Profit for the year		–	–	–	293.5	293.5	0.1	293.6
Other comprehensive income:								
Cash flow hedges	23	–	–	(10.0)	–	(10.0)	–	(10.0)
Net investment hedges	23	–	–	2.3	–	2.3	–	2.3
Foreign currency translation differences	23	–	–	(49.7)	–	(49.7)	(0.5)	(50.2)
Tax on other comprehensive income	23	–	–	5.1	–	5.1	–	5.1
Total comprehensive income for the year		–	–	(52.3)	293.5	241.2	(0.4)	240.8
Transactions with owners:								
Employee share incentive schemes								
Value of share options granted		–	–	–	17.1	17.1	–	17.1
Value of share options transferred to liabilities		–	–	–	(0.4)	(0.4)	–	(0.4)
Tax on share options granted		–	–	–	(0.1)	(0.1)	–	(0.1)
Exercise of share options		–	3.2	–	–	3.2	–	3.2

(*Continued*)

GROUP STATEMENT OF CHANGES IN EQUITY (*CONTINUED*)

	Note	Ordinary share capital £m	Share premium account £m	Other reserves £m	Retained earnings £m	Total £m	Non-controlling interest £m	Total equity £m
Purchase of own shares								
Share buy-back		–	–	–	(351.7)	(351.7)	–	(351.7)
Held by ESOP trusts		–	–	–	(11.9)	(11.9)	–	(11.9)
Dividends paid in the year		–	–	–	(169.4)	(169.4)	–	(169.4)
Balance as at 31 March 2018		**0.2**	**214.6**	**259.6**	**946.1**	**1,420.5**	**4.9**	**1,425.4**
Adjustment on initial application of IFRS 9		–	–	–	(0.2)	(0.2)	–	(0.2)
Adjusted balance as at 1 April 2018		**0.2**	**214.6**	**259.6**	**945.9**	**1,420.3**	**4.9**	**1,425.2**
Profit for the year		–	–	–	339.3	339.3	(0.2)	339.1
Other comprehensive income:								
Cash flow hedges	23	–	–	(2.1)	–	(2.1)	–	(2.1)
Net investment hedges	23	–	–	1.6	–	1.6	–	1.6
Foreign currency translation differences	23	–	–	14.3	–	14.3	0.3	14.6
Tax on other comprehensive income	23	–	–	(1.1)	–	(1.1)	–	(1.1)
Total comprehensive income for the year		–	–	12.7	339.3	352.0	0.1	352.1
Transactions with owners: Employee share incentive schemes								
Value of share options granted		–	–	–	15.7	15.7	–	15.7
Value of share options transferred to liabilities		–	–	–	(2.5)	(2.5)	–	(2.5)
Tax on share options granted		–	–	–	1.8	1.8	–	1.8
Exercise of share options		–	2.3	–	–	2.3	–	2.3
Purchase of own shares								
Share buy-back		–	–	–	(150.7)	(150.7)	–	(150.7)
Held by ESOP trusts		–	–	–	(12.8)	(12.8)	–	(12.8)
Dividends paid in the year		–	–	–	(171.1)	(171.1)	–	(171.1)
Balance as at 30 March 2019		**0.2**	**216.9**	**272.3**	**965.6**	**1,455.0**	**5.0**	**1,460.0**

GROUP STATEMENT OF CASH FLOWS

	Note	52 weeks to 30 March 2019 £m	Year to 31 March 2018 £m
Cash flows from operating activities			
Operating profit		437.2	410.3
Depreciation	14	87.2	105.8
Amortisation	13	28.6	25.5
Net impairment of intangible assets	13	3.9	6.5
Net impairment of property, plant and equipment	14	7.9	10.7
Loss on disposal of property, plant and equipment and intangible assets		1.2	2.7
Gain on disposal of Beauty operations	6	(6.9)	(5.2)
Gain on derivative instruments		(2.4)	(3.5)
Charge in respect of employee share incentive schemes		15.7	17.1
Receipt from settlement of equity swap contracts		2.5	0.5
(Increase) / decrease in inventories		(59.3)	37.2
(Increase) / decrease in receivables		(54.6)	68.1
Increase in payables and provisions		54.9	115.5
Cash generated from operating activities		515.9	791.2
Interest received		8.1	7.2
Interest paid		(1.8)	(1.6)
Taxation paid		(110.8)	(118.4)
Net cash generated from operating activities		411.4	678.4
Cash flows from investing activities			
Purchase of property, plant and equipment		(62.6)	(57.5)
Purchase of intangible assets		(48.0)	(48.5)
Proceeds from disposal of Beauty operations, net of cash costs paid	6	0.6	61.1
Acquisition of subsidiary	28	(14.5)	–
Net cash outflow from investing activities		(124.5)	(44.9)
Cash flows from financing activities			
Dividends paid in the year	12	(171.1)	(169.4)
Payment to non-controlling interest	20	(11.1)	(3.0)
Issue of ordinary share capital		2.3	3.2
Purchase of own shares through share buy-back	23	(150.7)	(355.0)
Purchase of own shares by ESOP trusts		(12.8)	(11.9)
Net cash outflow from financing activities		(343.4)	(536.1)
Net (decrease) / increase in cash and cash equivalents		(56.5)	97.4
Effect of exchange rate changes		1.7	(14.5)
Cash and cash equivalents at beginning of year		892.1	809.2
Cash and cash equivalents at end of year		837.3	892.1

(Continued)

GROUP STATEMENT OF CASH FLOWS (*CONTINUED*)

	Note	As at 30 March 2019 £m	As at 31 March 2018 £m
Cash and cash equivalents as per the Balance Sheet	19	**874.5**	915.3
Bank overdrafts	22	**(37.2)**	(23.2)
Net cash		**837.3**	892.1

APPENDIX II
DAIMLER 2019 FINANCIAL STATEMENTS

Daimler AG is one of the world's largest vehicle manufacturing businesses, best known for its Mercedes-Benz brand. Headquartered in Stuttgart, Germany, it employs almost 300 000 people across more than 160 countries. Its shares are listed on the Frankfurt Stock Exchange.

This appendix contains Daimler's consolidated financial statements for the year ended 31 December 2019, which are referred to in the questions at the end of most chapters of this book. You will need to look at the relevant parts whenever a question asks you about Daimler.

The notes to the financial statements are not included here. However, you will need to refer to them too. Please therefore download the 2019 Annual Report, available at https://www.daimler.com/documents/investors/reports/annual-report/daimler/daimler-ir-annual-report-2019-incl-combined-management-report-daimler-ag.pdf, or simply type 'Daimler annual report 2019' into your web browser. The financial statements presented here are copied from pp 224–9 and the notes begin on p 230 of the report.

CONSOLIDATED STATEMENT OF INCOME

F.01

In millions of euros	Note	2019	2018
Revenue	4	**172,745**	167,362
Cost of sales	5	**-143,580**	-134,295
Gross profit		**29,165**	33,067
Selling expenses	5	**-12,801**	-13,067
General administrative expenses	5	**-4,050**	-4,036
Research and non-capitalized development costs	5	**-6,586**	-6,581
Other operating income	6	**2,837**	2,330
Other operating expense	6	**-4,469**	-1,462
Profit on equity-method investments, net	13	**479**	656
Other financial income/expense, net	7	**-262**	210
Interest income	8	**397**	271
Interest expense	8	**-880**	-793
Profit before income taxes		**3,830**	10,595
Income taxes	9	**-1,121**	-3,013
Net profit		**2,709**	7,582
thereof profit attributable to non-controlling interests		**332**	333
thereof profit attributable to shareholders of Daimler AG		**2,377**	7,249

(Continued)

CONSOLIDATED STATEMENT OF INCOME (*CONTINUED*)

	Note	2019	2018
Earnings per share (in euros)			
for profit attributable to shareholders of Daimler AG	**36**		
Basic		**2.22**	6.78
Diluted		**2.22**	6.78

CONSOLIDATED STATEMENT OF COMPREHENSIVE INCOME/LOSS

F.02

	Daimler Group 2019	Shareholders of Daimler AG 2019	Non-controlling interests 2019	Daimler Group 2018	Shareholders of Daimler AG 2018	Non-controlling interests 2018
In millions of euros						
Net profit	**2,709**	**2,377**	**332**	7,582	7,249	333
Currency translation adjustments	**475**	**458**	**17**	234	214	20
Debt instruments						
Unrealized gains/losses (pre-tax)	**6**	**6**	**–**	-29	-29	–
Taxes on unrealized gains/losses and on reclassifications	**-1**	**-1**	**–**	9	9	–
Debt instruments (after tax)	**5**	**5**	**–**	-20	-20	–
Derivative financial instruments						
Unrealized gains/losses (pre-tax)	**-1,616**	**-1,615**	**-1**	-1,080	-1,081	1
Reclassifications to profit and loss (pre-tax)	**979**	**978**	**1**	-722	-722	–
Taxes on unrealized gains/losses and on reclassifications	**186**	**186**	**–**	537	537	–
Derivative financial instruments (after tax)	**-451**	**-451**	**–**	-1,265	-1,266 1	1
Equity-method investments						
Unrealized gains/losses (pre-tax)	**-26**	**-26**	**–**	-3	-3	–
Taxes on unrealized gains/losses and on reclassifications	**–**	**–**	**–**	-1	-1	–
Equity-method investments (after tax)	**-26**	**-26**	**–**	-4	-4	–
Items that may be reclassified to profit/loss	**3**	**-14**	**17**	-1,055	-1,076	21

(*Continued*)

CONSOLIDATED STATEMENT OF COMPREHENSIVE INCOME/LOSS (*CONTINUED*)

	Daimler Group 2019	Shareholders of Daimler AG 2019	Non-controlling interests 2019	Daimler Group 2018	Shareholders of Daimler AG 2018	Non-controlling interests 2018
Actuarial gains/losses on equity-method investments (pre-tax)	-1	-1	–	-1	-1	–
Actuarial gains/losses on equity-method investments (after tax)	-1	-1	–	-1	-1	–
Actuarial gains/losses from pensions and similar obligations (pre-tax)	-2,403	-2,403	–	-1,627	-1,625	-2
Taxes on actuarial gains/losses from pensions and similar obligations	232	232	–	171	171	–
Actuarial gains/losses from pensions and similar obligations (after tax)	-2,171	-2,171	–	-1,456	-1,454	-2
Equity instruments						
Unrealized gains/losses (pre-tax)	7	6	1	-16	-15	-1
Taxes on unrealized gains/losses and on reclassifications	4	4	–	12	12	–
Equity instruments (after tax)	11	10	1	-4	-3	-1
Items that will not be reclassified to profit/loss	-2,161	-2,162	1	-1,461	-1,458	-3
Other comprehensive income/loss, net of taxes	-2,158	-2,176	18	-2,516	-2,534	18
Total comprehensive income	551	201	350	5,066	4,715	351

CONSOLIDATED STATEMENT OF FINANCIAL POSITION

F.03

		At December 31,	
	Note	2019	2018
In millions of euros			
Assets			
Intangible assets	10	15,978	14,801
Property, plant and equipment	11	37,143	30,948
Equipment on operating leases	12	51,482	49,476
Equity-method investments	13	5,949	4,860
Receivables from financial services	14	52,880	51,300
Marketable debt securities and similar investments	15	770	722
Other financial assets	16	3,347	2,763
Deferred tax assets	9	5,803	4,021
Other assets	17	1,286	1,115
Total non-current assets		174,638	160,006

(*Continued*)

CONSOLIDATED STATEMENT OF FINANCIAL POSITION (*CONTINUED*)

	Note	2019	2018
Inventories	18	29,757	29,489
Trade receivables	19	12,332	12,586
Receivables from financial services	14	50,781	45,440
Cash and cash equivalents		18,883	15,853
Marketable debt securities and similar investments	15	7,885	8,855
Other financial assets	16	2,736	2,970
Other assets	17	5,426	5,889
Assets held for sale		–	531
Total current assets		**127,800**	121,613
Total assets		**302,438**	281,619
Equity and liabilities			
Share capital		3,070	3,070
Capital reserves		11,552	11,710
Retained earnings		46,329	49,490
Other reserves		393	397
Equity attributable to shareholders of Daimler AG		**61,344**	64,667
Non-controlling interests		1,497	1,386
Total equity	20	**62,841**	66,053
Provisions for pensions and similar obligations	22	9,728	7,393
Provisions for other risks	23	10,597	7,734
Financing liabilities	24	99,179	88,662
Other financial liabilities	25	2,112	2,375
Deferred tax liabilities	9	3,935	3,762
Deferred income	26	1,598	1,612
Contract and refund liabilities	27	6,060	5,438
Other liabilities	28	586	638
Total non-current liabilities		**133,795**	117,614
Trade payables		12,707	14,185
Provisions for other risks	23	10,327	7,828
Financing liabilities	24	62,601	56,240
Other financial liabilities	25	7,752	7,657
Deferred income	26	1,624	1,580
Contract and refund liabilities	27	7,571	7,081
Other liabilities	28	3,220	3,169
Liabilities held for sale		–	212
Total current liabilities		**105,802**	97,952
Total equity and liabilities		**302,438**	281,619

CONSOLIDATED STATEMENT OF CHANGES IN EQUITY

F.05

In millions of euros	Share capital	Capital reserves	Retained earnings	Currency translation	Equity instruments/debt instruments
Balance at January 1, 2018	3,070	11,742	47,555	258	38
Net profit	–	–	7,249	–	–
Other comprehensive income/loss before taxes	–	–	-1,626	214	-44
Deferred taxes on other comprehensive income	–	–	171	–	21
Total comprehensive income/loss	–	–	5,794	214	-23
Dividends	–	–	-3,905	–	–
Capital increase/Issue of new shares	–	–	–	–	–
Acquisition of treasury shares	–	–	–	–	–
Issue and disposal of treasury shares	–	–	–	–	–
Changes in ownership interests in subsidiaries	–	-32	–	–	–
Other	–	–	46	–	–
Balance at December 31, 2018	3,070	11,710	49,490	472	15
Balance at January 1, 2019	**3,070**	**11,710**	**49,490**	**472**	**15**
Net profit	–	–	**2,377**	–	–
Other comprehensive income/loss before taxes	–	–	**-2,404**	**458**	**12**
Deferred taxes on other comprehensive income	–	–	**232**	–	**3**
Total comprehensive income/loss	–	–	**205**	**458**	**15**
Dividends	–	–	**-3,477**	–	–
Changes in the consolidated group	–	–	**-14**	–	–
Capital increase/Issue of new shares	–	–	–	–	–
Acquisition of treasury shares	–	–	–	–	–
Issue and disposal of treasury shares	–	–	–	–	–
Changes in ownership interests in subsidiaries	–	**-158**	–	–	–
Other	–	–	**125**	–	–
Balance at December 31, 2019	**3,070**	**11,552**	**46,329**	**930**	**30**

Derivative financial instruments	Other reserves — Items that may be reclassified in profit/loss — Share of investments accounted for using the equity method	Treasury share	Equity attributable to share-holders of Daimler AG	Non-controlling interests	Total equity	In millions of euros
1,171	9	–	63,843	1,282	65,125	**Balance at January 1, 2018**
–	–	–	7,249	333	7,582	Net profit
-1,803	-3	–	-3,262	18	-3,244	Other comprehensive income/loss before taxes
537	-1	–	728	–	728	Deferred taxes on other comprehensive income
-1,266	-4	–	4,715	351	5,066	Total comprehensive income/loss
–	–	–	-3,905	-315	-4,220	Dividends
–	–	–	–	80	80	Capital increase/Issue of new shares
–	–	-50	-50	–	-50	Acquisition of treasury shares
–	–	50	50	–	50	Issue and disposal of treasury shares
–	–	–	-32	-13	-45	Changes in ownership interests in subsidiaries
–	–	–	46	1	47	Other
-95	5	–	64,667	1,386	66,053	**Balance at December 31, 2018**
-95	**5**	**–**	**64,667**	**1,386**	**66,053**	**Balance at January 1, 2019**
–	–	–	2,377	332	2,709	Net profit
-637	-26	–	-2,597	18	-2,579	Other comprehensive income/loss before taxes
186	–	–	421	–	421	Deferred taxes on other comprehensive income
-451	-26	–	201	350	551	Total comprehensive income/loss
–	–	–	-3,477	-288	-3,765	Dividends
–	–	–	-14	5	-9	Changes in the consolidated group
–	–	–	–	54	54	Capital increase/Issue of new shares
–	–	-42	-42	–	-42	Acquisition of treasury shares
–	–	42	42	–	42	Issue and disposal of treasury shares
–	–	–	-158	-16	-174	Changes in ownership interests in subsidiaries
–	–	–	125	6	131	Other
-546	**-21**	**–**	**61,344**	**1,497**	**62,841**	**Balance at December 31, 2019**

CONSOLIDATED STATEMENT OF CASH FLOWS

F.04

	2019	2018
In millions of euros		
Profit before income taxes	3,830	10,595
Depreciation and amortization/impairments	7,751	6,305
Other non-cash expense and income	24	-872
Gains ( )/losses (+) on disposals of assets	-761	-178
Change in operating assets and liabilities		
Inventories	99	-3,850
Trade receivables	-346	-884
Trade payables	-1,625	1,694
Receivables from financial services	-4,664	-10,257
Vehicles on operating leases	-1,156	-1,609
Other operating assets and liabilities	5,641	877
Dividends received from equity-method investments	1,202	1,380
Income taxes paid	-2,107	-2,858
Cash provided by operating activities	7,888	343
Additions to property, plant and equipment	-7,199	-7,534
Additions to intangible assets	-3,636	-3,167
Proceeds from disposals of property, plant and equipment and intangible assets	429	644
Investments in shareholdings	-1,619	-780
Proceeds from disposals of shareholdings	394	363
Acquisition of marketable debt securities and similar investments	-5,960	-5,739
Proceeds from sales of marketable debt securities and similar investments	7,014	6,210
Other	-30	82
Cash used for investing activities	-10,607	-9,921
Change in short-term financing liabilities	840	2,637
Additions to long-term financing liabilities	63,607	71,137
Repayment of long-term financing liabilities	-55,043	-56,318
Dividend paid to shareholders of Daimler AG	-3,477	-3,905
Dividends paid to non-controlling interests	-263	-315
Proceeds from the issue of share capital	85	118
Acquisition of treasury shares	-42	-50
Acquisition of non-controlling interests in subsidiaries	-79	-78
Cash provided by financing activities	5,628	13,226
Effect of foreign exchange rate changes on cash and cash equivalents	121	133
Net increase in cash and cash equivalents	3,030	3,781
Cash and cash equivalents at beginning of period	15,853	12,072
Cash and cash equivalents at end of period	18,883	15,853

APPENDIX III
SOLUTIONS TO CHAPTER QUESTIONS

This appendix contains suggested solutions to all of the questions asked at the end of each chapter, except for the investigation questions (IQs), for which suggested solutions are not appropriate. Note that any page references mentioned in these solutions refer to the Daimler 2019 Annual Report, available for download at https://www.daimler.com/documents/investors/reports/annual-report/daimler/daimler-ir-annual-report-2019-incl-combined-management-report-daimler-ag.pdf, or simply by typing 'Daimler annual report 2019' into a web browser.

SOLUTIONS | **CHAPTER 1**

CQ 1.1   The purpose of management accounting is to package the financial information of the business into reports that are tailored to the specific and unique internal decision-making needs of the business's management; for example, to decide which of two products the business should manufacture. These reports are often detailed and will vary from business to business. Financial accounting, on the other hand, results in financial reports that are highly standardised and which are aimed at users who are external to the business (that is, existing and potential investors, lenders, and other creditors).

CQ 1.2   The two usual benefits of being incorporated are limited liability (which protects the shareholders against being held liable for the debts of the business) and perpetual succession (that is, the ability for the business's accounting to continue irrespective of changes in ownership). Other benefits may include: tax savings (depending on where the business is located); the avoidance of owners having to take on management responsibility (because the business can transact in its own capacity); and the ease of transferring portions of business ownership.

CQ 1.3   A company's being 'listed' simply means that its shares are traded on a stock exchange.

CQ 1.4   To leverage a business's capital structure means to add a substantial proportion of debt funding. The purpose is usually to increase returns to owners. It will achieve this purpose if the cost of borrowing money (that is, the interest rate on the debt) is lower than the rate of return on the business's investments (or, speaking more generally, if the business earns healthy profits).

CQ 1.5   Viewed from the perspective of the providers of funding, the four phases in the value creation cycle are: financing activities, investing activities, operating activities, and the dividend decision.

CQ 1.6   The statement of financial position (or balance sheet) gives a snapshot of what assets have been purchased and how they have been financed. The statement of comprehensive income gives one view of the business's financial performance, focusing on the revenue, expenses, and profit of the business during the reporting period. The statement of cash flows shows another view of the financial performance of the business; that is, the cash inflows and outflows during the reporting period. The statement of changes in equity shows the movements during the year for the various categories of equity reported on the business's statement of financial position.

CHAPTER 2

SOLUTIONS

CQ 2.1 The five accounting elements are: assets, liabilities, equity, income, and expenses. Assets are items that are controlled by the business. Liabilities are amounts that are owed by the business. Equity is the total of the funding attributable to owners, or alternatively the accounting value of the owners' claim on the business (calculated by subtracting liabilities from assets). Items of income are increases in the equity of the business which do not result from contributions by owners. Expenses are decreases in equity which are not caused by distributions to owners.

CQ 2.2 In the formulation A = E + L, equity is one of the two sources of funding which have been used to acquire the business's assets. It is the source which is attributable to the business's owners. In this sense, equity consists of two distinct components: first, the amounts contributed by the owners; and second, the retained earnings of the business (that is, the value created by the business which has not (yet) been distributed to owners).

In the formulation A − L = E, equity reflects the accounting value of the owners' claim on a business, also known as the 'book value' of the business. The equation reveals that it is calculated by subtracting the business's liabilities from its assets. Equity is a notional concept insofar as it does not really exist, but is rather the result of accountants' calculations.

CQ 2.3 'Accrual accounting' refers to a fundamental concept of accounting convention which requires the effects of transactions to be reported in the period in which the transactions occur, irrespective of when the related cash flow occurs. An example of this is when a sale is made on credit: the sale is reported in the statement of comprehensive income as soon as the sale has occurred, which may be well before any cash is collected.

CQ 2.4 Yes, all items of income and expense that are reported in the statement of comprehensive income also affect equity on the statement of financial position, in a variety of individual line-items. For example, the income and expenses that appear in the profit-or-less section of the statement of comprehensive income affect the line-item 'retained earnings', whilst the gain resulting from a revaluation of land affects the line-item 'revaluation surplus'.

CQ 2.5 Both statements report the financial performance of the business during the reporting period, but from different perspectives. The statement of cash flows simply shows the cash that has flowed into or out of the business's bank account. The statement of comprehensive income is more complex because it applies the concept of accrual accounting. This results in items of income and expense being reported when the economic event occurs (eg when the sale takes place), irrespective of whether cash has flowed into or out of the business.

SOLUTIONS | **CHAPTER 3**

CQ 3.1 'GAAP' is an acronym for 'generally accepted accounting practice' and can describe any commonly used set of rules or guidelines used to prepare financial statements. 'IFRS' stands for 'International Financial Reporting Standards', and is one such set of GAAP standards. Developed by the International Accounting Standards Board (IASB), it has become the set of standards most commonly used around the world, except in the US. The GAAP standards used in the US are known as 'FASBs', and are named after the standard-setting body which develops them, the Financial Accounting Standards Board.

CQ 3.2 IFRS takes a principles-based approach to financial reporting, whilst the FASBs take a more rules-based approach. In other words, the requirements of IFRS are broader and more conceptual than the requirements of the FASBs, which are much more detailed, with fewer options and less room for financial accountants to exercise discretion.

CQ 3.3 Neither. Non-US companies who have a listing in the US are not required to report in terms of US GAAP and, since 2007, are not even required to provide a reconciliation between amounts they report in terms of IFRS and the amounts that would be reported in terms of US GAAP.

CQ 3.4 The IASB's objective is to develop a single set of high-quality, understandable, enforceable, and globally accepted financial reporting standards based on clearly articulated principles.

CQ 3.5 IFRS is often criticised for being too complicated; for including inconsistencies in its treatment of similar items; and for allowing too many options in the way that items may be measured.

SOLUTIONS | **CHAPTER 4**

CQ 4.1 The one-statement format contains two discrete sections, usually presented on a single page. The first is called the 'profit-or-loss' section, and the second is called the 'other-comprehensive-income' section. This statement is additive, insofar as the profit-or-loss section flows into the other-comprehensive-income section. The last line is the total comprehensive income for the period.

   The two-statement format first presents an income statement containing items of profit or loss culminating in a profit (or if negative, a loss) figure. In a separate statement, called the 'statement of comprehensive income', usually presented on a separate page, the starting point is the profit (or loss) figure brought forward from the income statement, to which is added the items of other comprehensive income, culminating in total comprehensive income for the period.

CQ 4.2 'Income' is a term that collectively refers to all the items that increase the equity of the business other than those resulting from contributions by the owners. 'Revenue' is a subset of income and relates only to those items of income that arise in the ordinary course of business. For example, a gain on the sale of an item of equipment is income, but it is not revenue.

CQ 4.3   The €5 million would be reported as income, for it has had the effect of increasing the equity of the business (by increasing the left side of A − L = E) without being a contribution by the owners. However, this income would be reported as other comprehensive income, and would not be added to profit.

CQ 4.4   The tax payable by a business is based on the jurisdiction's specific rules and regulations for determining taxable income, and is not based on accounting profit calculated in accordance with IFRS.

CQ 4.5   Earnings per share is basically calculated by dividing the profit for the year by the average number of shares in issue during that year. For shareholders, this is an important measure of performance, as it shows how much of the profit is attributable to each share, thereby helping them to make better performance comparisons over time and between different businesses.

AQ 4.6   As Daimler has a 31 December year-end, its 2019 consolidated statement of income would report the effects of events that took place between 1 January 2019 and 31 December 2019.

AQ 4.7   Daimler has used the two-statement format. Its first statement is named the 'consolidated statement of income' and this reflects all the items of income and expense other than items of other comprehensive income. This first statement concludes with a net profit figure. The second statement, named the 'consolidated statement of comprehensive income/loss', commences with the net profit brought forward from the consolidated statement of income. To this is added a variety of items of other comprehensive income in order to determine total comprehensive income.

AQ 4.8   As Daimler complies with IFRS (see the note on p 230 of its consolidated financial statements), and therefore applies the principles of accrual accounting to determine income, we can safely assume that this revenue figure would include both sales made for cash and on credit. Furthermore, there are definitely credit sales within the group, as a trade receivables asset is recognised on the statement of financial position. In addition to this, a careful reading of the accounting policy note on revenue recognition on p 234 indicates that revenue includes credit sales.

AQ 4.9   Daimler's other operating income includes costs recharged to third parties, government grants, rental income, and a variety of other amounts. A breakdown is shown in note 6 (on p 251).

AQ 4.10   Cost of sales reflects the total cost of the inventory that has been consumed during the year. This comprises the costs of purchase, costs of conversion, and all other costs of bringing the items to their location and condition for sale. Table F.11 on p 250 gives a detailed breakdown of this amount. On the other hand, the selling expenses reflect the cost of making the sales, rather than the products. These are mainly marketing costs. An explanation of this amount is given in note 5 on p 250.

AQ 4.11   If the basic earnings per share figure is the same as the diluted earnings per share figure, this indicates that, at present, there are no outstanding share options or similar arrangements which create a risk of a potential dilution to the value of the existing shareholders' shares in future.

AQ 4.12   Daimler's net profit of €2 709 million minus its other comprehensive loss of €2 158 million equals its total comprehensive income of €551 million.

DQ 4.13   Daimler increased its revenue from €167 362 million in 2018 to €172 745 million in 2019. This represents an increase of 3.2%, which is a reasonably healthy increase in revenue during what can be considered to be fairly difficult economic times.

DQ 4.14   In note 4 to the consolidated financial statements, Daimler disaggregates its revenue into: (a) types of services and products (eg Mercedes-Benz cars, Daimler buses, etc); and (b) geographic region in which the goods are sold (eg Europe, Asia, etc).

DQ 4.15   This would have had no effect on the cost of sales amount in the statement of income. Cost of sales reports the cost of the goods *that have been sold* and not the costs of goods purchased. This large purchase of inventory towards the year-end would instead be reported as an increase in the inventories asset reported on the statement of financial position.

DQ 4.16   The interest expense on the statement of income is €880 million. Profits would therefore have been reduced by this amount, which is approximately 19% of the profit before interest expense (calculated as €880 million divided by the sum of €880 million and €3 830 million). Finance costs therefore had a significant, but relatively modest, effect on Daimler's profits during 2019.

DQ 4.17   Daimler's net profit declined significantly between 2018 and 2019, from €7 582 million to €2 709 million. This was caused in part by extremely difficult trading conditions during the year and by the costs of the ongoing government and legal proceedings related to diesel vehicles. Information about this is available in note 6 on p 251, in the section about other operating expenses.

DQ 4.18   The decrease in gross profit means that Daimler's costs of sales increased by substantially more than revenue (in fact, it declined by 6.9%). This could be as a result of increased unit production costs not being passed on to the customer in the selling price, or the discounting of selling prices, for example.

DQ 4.19   The three major items contributing to other comprehensive income/loss were a foreign currency translation gain of €475 million, a loss on derivative financial instruments of €451 million, and an actuarial loss from pensions and similar obligations of €2 171. (These items are dealt with in more detail in Chapters 6–8.) None of these items are indicative of Daimler's ability to manufacture, distribute, or sell motor vehicles, and so the net profit amount is a more meaningful measure of Daimler's core business performance.

DQ 4.20   Yes, there is evidence of multiple performance obligations with respect to Daimler's sales. Note 4 on p 249 (dealing with revenue) clearly states that some of the items that are sold contain '. . . performance obligations that are unsatisfied (or partially unsatisfied) . . .' and that these unsatisfied performance conditions are '. . . derived from long-term service and maintenance contracts and extended warranties'. So, in addition to the sale of vehicles, Daimler is also responsible for servicing, maintenance, and warranty claims.

Daimler therefore recognises the revenue arising from each of these items separately. In terms of timing, the portion of revenue that relates to the sale of the car will be recognised on the date of sale (that is, when control of the car passes to the customer), and the portions relating to the servicing, maintenance, and warranties will be deferred at the time of sale and recognised when the business has provided the service and the customer has acquired the benefits. Note 4 shows the amount of revenue that was deferred at 31 December 2019: €8 701 million.

CHAPTER 5

SOLUTIONS

CQ 5.1   Within the operating activities section, we find the cash inflows and outflows that relate to the principal revenue-producing activities of the business, including cash receipts from customers, cash payments to suppliers and employees, tax payments, and sometimes interest receipts and interest and dividend payments. (Businesses have a choice where these last three items are presented.) Within the investing activities section, we find cash flows relating to the acquisition and sale of non-current assets and/or entire business units, and sometimes interest received. Within the financing section, we find cash inflows from the issue of shares and raising of loans, and the cash outflows relating to the repayment of loans and/or share buybacks. Dividends paid and interest paid are sometimes also included here.

CQ 5.2   Both of these statements are important, but in different ways. We use the statement of comprehensive income to understand the business's activities based on accrual accounting, which is arguably better for predicting long-term operating cash flows. The statement of cash flows helps us to understand the cash inflows and outflows produced this year by the business's activities, which indicates the short-term sustainability of the business, and can also be used as a check on the authenticity of the figures in the statement of comprehensive income.

CQ 5.3   The direct method arrives at the cash generated from operations figure by deducting the cash paid to suppliers and employees from the amount of cash received from customers. The indirect method, on the other hand, calculates the cash generated from operations amount *indirectly* by starting with the operating profit figure and reversing the effects of every difference between operating profit and cash generated from operations. It is important to note that both methods arrive at the same figure for cash generated from operations.

CQ 5.4   The four main components of working capital are inventories, accounts receivable, accounts payable, and cash. On a cash flow statement which uses the indirect method, the movements (that is, the increases or decreases from the beginning of the year to the end of the year) in inventories, accounts receivable, and accounts payable are key to explaining the difference between profit and cash generated from operations in that year.

CQ 5.5   At the bottom of a statement of cash flows, the net cash flows for the year from operating, investing, and financing activities, together with the effect of any necessary currency adjustments, are added to the opening cash balance reported in the statement of financial position at the beginning of the year. The result is equal to the closing cash balance reported in the statement of financial position at the end of the year.

AQ 5.6   The cash inflows from operating activities of €7 888 million, together with the cash inflows from financing activities of €5 628 million, less the cash outflows from investing activities of €10 607 million, plus the foreign currency effect of €121 million, resulted in a net increase in cash equivalents of €3 030 million (€7 888 million + €5 628 million – €10 607 million + €121 million).

AQ 5.7   The amount of tax reported on the 2019 statement of income reflects the tax expense in respect of the 2019 financial year's taxable income. The income taxes figure on the 2019 statement of cash flows reflects the amount of tax that was actually paid to the tax authorities during 2019. Some reasons that these figures could be different include: Daimler could have overpaid tax, which is usually due before the taxable income figure is known; the amount paid may include tax payments for 2018, or indeed any other previous year; the expense figure may include a large 'deferred tax' effect. (In actual fact, the last of these seems to be the major reason for the difference. We shall cover deferred tax in section 8.3.)

AQ 5.8   As Daimler presents its statement of cash flows using the indirect method, it needs to adjust the profit before income taxes (the starting point in the calculation) for any amounts included in that profit figure that are not associated with operating cash flows. Neither depreciation, amortisation, nor impairment, which have been deducted in the calculation of the profit amount, are associated with operating cash flows. They therefore all need to be added back to arrive at the cash flow figure.

AQ 5.9   This movement in inventories of €99 million in 2019 represents a decrease in inventories during the year. This is apparent from the fact that it has been added in the indirect method statement of cash flows. Decreases in inventories mean that the business has been expensing more items than it has purchased, causing cash generated from operations to be higher than operating profit (or profit before income taxes in Daimler's case). This is why decreases in inventories are added on the indirect method.

AQ 5.10   This movement in trade payables of €1 625 in 2019 represents a decrease in trade payables during the year. This is apparent from the fact that it has been subtracted in the indirect method statement of cash flows. Decreases in trade payables mean that the business has been paying for more items than it has been expensing, causing cash generated from operations to be lower than operating profit (or profit before income taxes in Daimler's case). This is why decreases in trade payables are subtracted on the indirect method.

AQ 5.11   Daimler could have chosen to present dividends paid in the operating activities section of its statement of cash flows.

AQ 5.12   This amount is an adjustment that needs to be made when a business has cash holdings that are in currencies other than those which the business uses to report. As Daimler reports in euros, any cash holdings in currencies other than euros would need to be translated into euros, and the changes in exchange rates result in an increased or decreased euro amount of cash held, without there being any actual flow of cash. This line-item is therefore required in order for the net cash flow for the year to reconcile with the opening and closing cash balances.

AQ 5.13   The amount of €18 833 reflected as cash and cash equivalents at the end of the 2019 statement of cash flows are reported as cash and cash equivalents in the current assets section of the 2019 statement of financial position.

DQ 5.14   Daimler presents its statement of cash flows using the indirect method. A direct statement of cash flows would start with the line item 'cash received from customers', and Daimler's statement clearly does not. Instead, an indirect statement of cash flows starts with a profit figure taken from the statement of comprehensive income and then makes adjustments to this figure to arrive at an operating cash flow figure, as is the case here.

DQ 5.15 There were four items of working capital that had a negative effect on cash flows (trade receivables, trade payables, receivables from financial services, and vehicles on operating leases), totalling €7 791 million. The decrease in inventories and an item labelled 'Other operating assets and liabilities' had a combined positive effect on cash flows of €5 740 million. The net result is therefore a negative cash effect of €2 051 million (€7 791 million – €5 740 million).

DQ 5.16 This increase in operating cash flow in 2019 was mainly as a result of (a) inventories declining during 2019 (€99 million) compared to a huge increase in 2018 (€3 850 million); (b) a significantly smaller increase in receivables from financial services in 2019 (€4 664 million), compared to 2018 (€10 257 million); and (c) the large 2019 decrease in the working capital item 'Other operating assets and liabilities' of €5 641 million.

DQ 5.17 During 2019, Daimler acquired property, plant and equipment at a cash cost of €7 199 million, and paid €3 636 million for intangible assets.

DQ 5.18 It appears that Daimler raised a loan (which they call 'long-term financing liabilities') of €63 607 million and repaid another loan of €55 043 million, causing a net increase in long-term borrowings of €8 564 million. The only other significant financing activity was the payment of a dividend to shareholders of €3 477 million. There do not appear to be any significant share issues or buybacks.

DQ 5.19 In 2019, Daimler generated a net cash inflow from operations of €7 888 million, which is a significantly larger amount than its net profit of €2 709 million. Although a major explanation for this difference was depreciation and amortisation/impairments of €7 751 million, it is not especially surprising that an auto manufacturer would have large accounting adjustments like these. Other major explanations for the difference are therefore potentially more interesting: the decline in receivables from financial services (€4 664 million) and the increase in the working capital item 'Other operating assets and liabilities' (€5 641 million).

DQ 5.20 Table F.69 on p 282 shows that the major component of the item 'Other operating assets and liabilities' is an increase in provisions totalling €5 217 million. Note 29 on the same page informs us that increased provisions relate to 'ongoing governmental and legal proceedings and measures taken with regard to Mercedes-Benz diesel vehicles in several regions, as well as an updated assessment for an expanded recall of vehicles with Takata airbags'. Provisions are dealt with in section 7.3 in the chapter on liabilities. For now, it is sufficient to appreciate that Daimler has taken the €5 217 million as an expense (debit) in the calculation of profit, but has not yet paid over this amount, and so it has been recognised as a liability (credit). As such, the increase in this amount needs to be added back to profit in order to calculate operating cash flows, in much the same way as increases in accounts payable.

DQ 5.21 Note 29 on p 282 tells us that €64 million of the cash and cash equivalents amount is restricted as a result of being in subsidiary companies which are located in countries where exchange controls apply. Therefore, this amount can be spent only in those specific countries and is not available to be used more generally by Daimler.

CQ 6.1   A business's expenditure results in a decrease (credit) in the bank account. This may be capitalised (that is, recognised as an asset (debit) in the statement of financial position) if it meets the asset definition and the recognition criteria. Alternatively, if the asset definition and recognition criteria are not met, then the expenditure will be reported as an expense (debit) in the statement of comprehensive income.

CQ 6.2   Yes. There is no requirement in the asset definition (or recognition criteria) that an asset is legally owned by the business. The key part of the asset definition is that the business has control of the asset, which can be achieved without ownership, as is the case when an asset is leased.

CQ 6.3   The economic benefits associated with a current asset are expected to be realised within twelve months of the reporting date, whereas the benefits associated with a non-current asset are expected to be realised over a period that extends beyond twelve months from the reporting date.

CQ 6.4   'Subsequent costs' refer to any additional expenditure on an asset after its acquisition. These costs will be either capitalised by being added to the asset's carrying amount, or expensed in the statement of comprehensive income. 'Subsequent measurement' refers to the method by which the carrying amount of an asset is measured in subsequent reporting periods. A variety of subsequent measurement models is used, including historic cost, fair value, and others. All assets require subsequent measurement, but subsequent costs only arise when there is expenditure on an asset after its acquisition.

CQ 6.5   Impairment is a three-step process. First, each asset is reviewed for signs of impairment. If there are no signs of impairment, no further action is required. Second, if there are signs of impairment, then a 'recoverable amount' is calculated, which is the higher of the asset's value in use and its fair value less costs to sell. Third, if the recoverable amount is lower than the current carrying amount of the asset, then its carrying amount is decreased by the difference between the carrying amount and the recoverable amount.

AQ 6.6   At 31 December 2019, the book value of Daimler's assets, as shown on its statement of financial position, was €302 438 million. This comprises current assets of €127 800 million and non-current assets of €174 638 million.

AQ 6.7   Property, plant and equipment (PPE) could have increased as a result of acquisitions of other businesses or purchases by Daimler itself. (We cannot include revaluations in this list, as the accounting policy notes imply that Daimler does not use the revaluation model for PPE.) Decreases in PPE could be a result of disposals, depreciation, or impairment. There is, however, no need to speculate on these movements, as table F.27 (on p 256) provides all the details about these movements.

AQ 6.8   Table F.27 (on p 256) reports that the 2019 depreciation expense relating to PPE (excluding right-of-use assets) was €4 692 million.

AQ 6.9   Table F.25 (on p 265) reports that the 2019 amortisation expense relating to intangible assets was €2 397 million. Table F.26 (on the same page) shows that most of this expense (€2 258 million) was included in the cost of sales line-item on the consolidated statement of income.

AQ 6.10 During the course of Daimler's business activities, it spends money on research and development activities. The accounting standards require all costs in the research phase to be expensed in the statement of comprehensive income. However, costs incurred in the development phase, which begins once it becomes clear that continued work will probably result in future economic benefits, are capitalised. Thus, the figure of €12 525 million represents development expenditure that is likely to realise at least this amount of future economic benefits.

AQ 6.11 Table F.48 (on p 268) shows us that inventories comprise: €3 321 million of raw materials and manufacturing supplies; €4 290 million of work-in-progress; €21 922 million of finished goods, parts, and products for resale; and finally €224 million of advance payments to suppliers. The advance payments will be reclassified as raw materials when delivery takes place. The raw materials and work-in-progress amounts will be added to the finished goods amount once these items are complete. And finally, when the finished goods are sold, all of these amounts will ultimately be removed from inventory (credit) and reported as cost of sales (debit) on the consolidated statement of income.

AQ 6.12 No, the trade receivables amount on the statement of financial position does not include amounts that are not expected to be collected. Rather, it is reported net of the allowance for doubtful debts, which is the business's estimate of the amount it will not collect. Thus, the value of the receivables that Daimler has estimated it will not collect is the €243 million reported in Table F.49 (on p 268) as the allowance for doubtful debts. This has been subtracted from gross receivables of €12 575 million, resulting in the carrying amount of €12 332 million.

AQ 6.13 Note 40 (on p 314) reports three significant events after the reporting period (that is, events that occurred after the end of the reporting period, but before the finalisation of the financial statements). They are: agreements in respect of voluntary employee retrenchments; the establishment of a joint venture; and the sale of shares in a company that Daimler owns. These are all 'non-adjusting' events, as they did not provide evidence of conditions that existed at the year-end. They are thus merely disclosed in the notes, rather than causing adjustments to the figures in the financial statements themselves.

DQ 6.14 Nowhere. The value of a business's staff is not reported on its statement of financial position, because human capital does not meet the definition of an asset as staff are not 'controlled' by their employer.

DQ 6.15 The Mercedes-Benz brand has always been part of the Daimler organisation, which was formed in 1926, when the company that first made the Mercedes-Benz vehicles merged with another automaker. Accountants describe brands that have not been purchased as 'internally generated', and do not recognise them on the statement of financial position, as there is a high level of measurement uncertainty about them. (The only brands that would be recognised on the statement of financial position would be those brands that Daimler has acquired over the years. Such brands are measured at the acquisition cost, and not at their fair value.)

DQ 6.16 There would be a number of assets on the statement of financial position that are measured below their fair value. For example, the fair value of brands that Daimler acquired in the past may now be well above their acquisition cost. Also, as Daimler uses the cost model to value PPE, there might be assets within this category which have appreciated in value over the years and which are now worth much more than their depreciated cost. Also, of course, the fair value of Daimler's inventory will, on the whole, be above its cost.

DQ 6.17 The category 'technical equipment and machinery' would include items like computer hardware, whose useful life may be only five years, given the rapid pace of technological change. On the other hand, this category would also include large machines used in the production process, which could have a useful life of twenty-five years, given that they would not become outdated or worn out in a shorter period of time.

DQ 6.18 Determining which assets have the greatest potential to generate future cash flows is subjective. However, assets such as cash and cash equivalents are generally agreed to be low risk, as there is virtual certainty that they will hold their value. Similarly, land and buildings are also considered to be assets that will maintain their value (unless, for instance, they are in a jurisdiction where there is risk of expropriation). On the other hand, assets such as intangible assets are considered to be riskier. For example, future cash flows from brands might decline significantly with changes in customer tastes or if the brand suffers reputational damage.

DQ 6.19 First, no revaluation gains or losses are reported in the 'Other comprehensive income' (OCI) section of the consolidated statement of comprehensive income/ loss. Second, there is no 'revaluations' line-item in the detailed PPE reconciliation in Table F.27 on p 256. (A third indication that the revaluation model is not used is the absence of a revaluation surplus equity account in the statement of changes in equity. You will learn about this in section 10.2.)

DQ 6.20 If Daimler had chosen to use the revaluation model for PPE, it is likely that the depreciation charge would be higher, and consequently a lower net profit would be reported on the consolidated statement of income. Furthermore, a revaluation gain would be reported in the OCI section of the consolidated statement of comprehensive income/loss, increasing both OCI and 'Total comprehensive income' (TCI). The consolidated statement of financial position would report a higher carrying amount for PPE and total assets, as well as an increase in 'other reserves', and consequently higher total equity. There would be no effect on the consolidated statement of cash flows.

DQ 6.21 Daimler's financial accountants would need to exercise judgement and opinion in determining both the estimated useful life and residual value of items of PPE. Both estimates affect the depreciation charge, and hence the carrying amount of PPE. In addition to this, judgement will be exercised when reviewing items of PPE for signs of impairment. If it is judged that signs of impairment do exist, then further judgement and opinion is required to determine the recoverable amount (because this involves estimating fair value, costs to sell, and value in use), thus also affecting the carrying amount of PPE.

SOLUTIONS | CHAPTER 7

CQ 7.1 Liabilities are a good indication of the future cash outflows of the business. Understanding these is a vital component of establishing the business's future prospects.

CQ 7.2 The three key elements of the liability definition are: the business must have an obligation; the obligation must be to transfer an economic resource in the future; and the key event giving rise to the obligation must have happened, making the obligation 'present'.

CQ 7.3   If the future expenditure does not meet the definition of a liability, it is known as a commitment, which may be disclosed in the notes to the financial statements.

CQ 7.4   If a liability does not satisfy the recognition criteria, it is called a contingent liability, and it is disclosed in the notes to the financial statements (unless the probability of an outflow to settle the liability is remote).

CQ 7.5   A provision is a liability where there is some uncertainty about the amount to be settled, or the timing of the settlement, or both the amount and the timing.

CQ 7.6   A provision is measured at the best estimate of the amount required to settle the provision, or to be paid to a third party to assume the obligation; and discounted to present value when the time value of money is material.

AQ 7.7   Daimler reported total liabilities of €239 597 million, split between non-current liabilities of €133 795 million and current liabilities of €105 802 million.

AQ 7.8   Table F.62 (on p 279) shows us that 'Provisions for other risks' consists of: product warranties (that is, the expected costs of future legal and contractual warranty claims, as well as expected costs for goodwill concessions and recall campaigns); personnel and social costs (that is, the expected costs of employee anniversary bonuses, profit-sharing arrangements, management bonuses, and early retirement and partial retirement plans); as well as a category classified as 'Other', which includes a variety of other expected costs.

AQ 7.9   The provision for product warranties was subject to various movements during the 2019 year, both up and down. There was an increase of €5 215 million due to the additional obligation arising from sales during that year, an increase of €45 million representing the unwinding of the discount (called 'compounding' by Daimler), and an increase of €38 million relating to currency translation (which we cover in sections 8.2.3 and 8.2.4). The provision decreased as a result of a utilisation of €3 423 million, representing portions of the opening balance which were settled during the year, and a reversal of €210 million, representing provisions no longer required. The net effect of all these movements was the €1 665 million increase in the provision.

AQ 7.10 The other effects of the movements in the product warranties provision were:
  * additions (credit): an expense (debit) in profit and loss, most likely cost of sales;
  * unwinding of discount, called 'compounding' by Daimler (credit): interest expense or finance costs in profit and loss (debit);
  * utilisations (debit): bank or inventory (credit);
  * reversals (debit): income in profit and loss to offset the expense(s) that had previously been charged (credit);
  * currency translation and other changes: these result from the inclusion of the results of Daimler's foreign operations (see sections 8.2.3 and 8.2.4).

AQ 7.11 Page 246 includes a detailed explanation of how Daimler estimates its product warranty provision. The estimate is based on 'historical warranty claim experience' and assumptions of 'future warranty claims and goodwill, as well as possible recall campaigns for each model series', based on the 'experience of the frequency and extent of vehicle faults in the past'. Furthermore, these 'estimates also include assumptions on the amounts of potential repair costs per vehicle and the possible effect of time or mileage limits'.

AQ 7.12 Daimler's income tax liability is €1 710 million and is reported in the current and non-current line-items labelled 'Other liabilities' (see Table F.68 on p 281). €1 128 million of the total tax liability is included in the current portion of 'Other liabilities', whilst €582 million is included in the non-current portion.

AQ 7.13   Notes and bonds reported as liabilities are interest-bearing borrowings, where Daimler has given a written promise to pay known amounts, on specific dates, to the holders of the bonds or notes. Bonds usually involve a longer credit period than notes.

DQ 7.14   Yes. Since many users of financial statements seek to establish the timing of future cash flows, any incorrect classification of liabilities between current and non-current will distort the user's view of the risk of these cash flows. Current liabilities are generally more risky, as the cash outflows to settle them will happen sooner. [Note: there is no indication that current and non-current liabilities were in fact misclassified in Daimler's financial statements.]

DQ 7.15   Most liabilities involve some estimation as to the amount or timing of the associated future cash outflows. The item on this statement of financial position where both the timing and amount of the future cash flow is reasonably certain is the item 'Trade payables'. Daimler would buy a certain amount of goods or services from its suppliers, for which invoices would specify the exact amounts to be paid and the date by which they should be paid.

DQ 7.16   Yes, Daimler has a number of contingent liabilities, which are liabilities that do not satisfy the criteria for recognition as liabilities. Information about them is disclosed in notes 30 and 31 (on pp 283–6).

DQ 7.17   Daimler reported a provision for pensions and similar obligations of €9 728 million on its statement of financial position. This represents the liability that Daimler has in terms of its various defined benefit pension plans (that is, where Daimler has guaranteed its employees a pension of a certain amount) and similar obligations. Note 22 (commencing on p 273) provides the detail about how this amount was determined. Although this is a considerable amount in euros, it is only 3.2% of Daimler's total assets (€9 728 million ÷ €302 438 million × 100).

DQ 7.18   Yes, Daimler has a financial liability that is measured at fair value through profit or loss. Note 25 (on p 280) tells us that 'financial liabilities measured at fair value through profit and loss relate exclusively to derivative financial instruments which are not used in hedge accounting'.

DQ 7.19   Daimler has recognised a provision of €4 902 million with respect to 'litigation risks and legal proceedings' within the 'provision for other risks' line-item on the consolidated statement of financial position (see Table F.62 on p 279). This amount would comprise the portion of the legal claims against Daimler that satisfy the criteria for recognition of a liability. The portion of the legal claims against Daimler that do not satisfy the recognition criteria is detailed in note 30 on pp 283–6.

DQ 7.20   No. Daimler did declare dividends for the second half of its 2019 year. The reason that the liability was not recognised on 31 December 2019 was that the dividend had not yet been declared by then, and so there was no obligation at that point. (Daimler's 2019 Annual Report explained on p 49 that a dividend of €0.90 per share for the 2019 financial year would be recommended at the Annual Shareholders' meeting on 1 April 2020.)

DQ 7.21   The most obvious current liability that will not be settled with cash is the 'deferred income' of €1 624 million. Daimler will settle this amount by providing customers with the products and/or services for which they have paid in advance.

CHAPTER 8

SOLUTIONS

CQ 8.1   A right-of-use asset and a lease liability are reported on the statement of financial position. The statement of comprehensive income reports depreciation expense in respect of the right-to-use asset and interest expense in respect of the lease liability.

CQ 8.2   The lease liability is initially measured at the present value of the future lease payments, calculated using an appropriate discount rate. In each period, this lease liability is increased by the notional interest charge and reduced by the amount of the lease payment. By the end of the lease period, the carrying amount of the lease liability will have reduced to zero.

CQ 8.3   The business uses exchange rates to convert foreign currencies into its functional currency. Because the exchange rate can change between the dates on which the related events are accounted for (eg between purchase and settlement), these changes lead to gains or losses being reported in profit or loss.

CQ 8.4   If the results of the foreign operation are denominated in a foreign currency, they need to be translated into the functional currency of the main business in order to be included in the financial statements. Because the exchange rate used for translating events during the year (such as a sale) is usually different from the rate used to translate balances at the end of the year (such as accounts receivable), these changes lead to gains or losses being reported in OCI.

CQ 8.5   Deferred tax essentially arises because there are differences between the IFRS principles used to determine accounting profit and the income tax laws that are used to determine the taxable income of a business.

AQ 8.6   Note 11 (p 256 and p 257) tells us that the PPE amount reported on the statement of financial position includes items with a carrying amount of €4 234 million (see Table F.28) that are leased by Daimler (in other words, right-of-use assets).

AQ 8.7   On Table F.29 (p 257), Daimler reports that the depreciation expense related to right-of-use assets was €678 million in 2019. Table F.30, on the same page, reveals that the interest charge related to these right-of-use assets was €98 million.

AQ 8.8   Table F.63 (p 279) reports that lease liabilities at 31 December 2019 were €4 240 million. This is split between the current and non-current line-items labelled 'financing liabilities' on the statement of financial position.

AQ 8.9   Daimler's functional currency is the euro. The foreign currency translation note on p 233 explains that 'assets and liabilities of foreign companies for which the functional currency is not the euro are translated into euros using period end exchange rates', as we would expect.

AQ 8.10   Yes, Daimler's consolidated statement of comprehensive income/loss reports a gain called 'currency translation adjustment' of €475 million. This represents the gain that Daimler incurred in 2019 when translating its foreign companies into euros.

AQ 8.11   Table F.27 (p 256) shows the year-on-year movement in the PPE balance, including amounts (labelled as 'other charges') of €153 million and €45 million, decreasing the costs and accumulated depreciation/impairment balances respectively, causing a net decrease of €108 million. The footnote to this item tells us that this amount is 'primarily charges from currency translation'. This amount therefore primarily reflects the effect of movements in the exchange rate between the euro and the currencies of the foreign operations in which some of its PPE is held.

AQ 8.12 Daimler reports deferred tax assets of €5 803 million and deferred tax liabilities of €3 935 million on its 2019 statement of financial position. Note 9 to the consolidated financial statements provides extensive detail about these assets and liabilities.

AQ 8.13 Table F.18 (p 252) gives a breakdown of the income tax expense, revealing that deferred taxes reduced the total income tax expense by €1 261 million (€1 127 million + €134 million).

DQ 8.14 Prior to the adoption of IFRS 16, many leased items did not give rise to assets and liabilities on the statement of financial position and the lease payments were simply expensed in the consolidated statement of income. On adoption of IFRS 16, virtually all leased assets were recognised as right-of-use assets, along with a corresponding lease liability, on the statement of financial position. This would increase total assets and liabilities. In the statement of income, the lease payments previously reported as expenses would have been replaced by amortisation and interest expenses.

DQ 8.15 Yes. On p 230, we are told that Daimler has elected (in accordance with IFRS 16) not to 'recognise a right-of-use asset and a lease liability' for 'leases with a lease term of 12 months or less (short-term leases) and for leases for which the underlying asset is of low value'. In addition to this, Table F.30 (p 257) includes an amount of €82 million, labelled as 'expenses from short-term leases' and an amount of €16 million labelled as 'expenses from leases of low value assets'. These expenses would not appear had Daimler capitalised all of its leased assets.

DQ 8.16 On p 243, Daimler explains that it uses derivative financial instruments to hedge currency risks. Extensive detail on how Daimler manages its foreign currency risks is provided from p 297 onwards, in the section that deals with the management of various financial risks.

DQ 8.17 The positive amount of €475 million reported in 2019 is a gain that would have arisen from a weakening of the euro against the non-euro currencies in which Daimler's foreign companies operate. A weakening of the euro has the effect of net assets denominated in other currencies being worth more in euro terms than they were at the beginning of 2019.

DQ 8.18 In Table F.22 (p 253), Daimler reveals that it had tax loss carryforwards and unused tax credits of €3 110 million on 31 December 2019.

DQ 8.19 A finance lease is one in which the risks and rewards associated with the leased asset have been transferred from the lessor to the lessee. On the other hand, an operating lease is one where the risks and rewards associated with the leased asset remain with the lessor. On p 238, Daimler sets out the details of how it accounts for both finance and operating leases.

DQ 8.20 Daimler has classified some of its lease agreements with lessees as finance leases. For these finance leases, the physical leased asset is derecognised as if it has been sold to the lessee, and instead finance lease receivables are recognised, representing the present value of future lease payments.

DQ 8.21 For each item of income and expense reported on Daimler's consolidated statement of comprehensive income/loss, the corresponding tax effect is shown. For example, a tax expense of €1 million is reported as the tax relating to the unrealised gains of €6 million on debt instruments. (As all these items of OCI appear to relate to unrealised gains and losses, it is reasonable to assume that the tax effects of these gains and losses are deferred tax and not current tax. Also, Table F.23 (p 254), which provides a reconciliation of the deferred tax balance, shows us that this assumption is correct, as the three items totalling €421 million (€3 million + €186 million + €232 million) in this reconciliation are equal to the total of the tax amounts (−€1 million + €186 million + €232 million + €4 million) appearing in OCI.)

CHAPTER 9

SOLUTIONS

CQ 9.1   The parent (or holding) company is at the top of the corporate structure pyramid, and effectively controls, or exerts significant influence over, all of the other companies in the group. A subsidiary is a company controlled by the parent company, usually because the parent company (or another company controlled by the parent) owns more than 50% of its shares. An associate is a company over which the parent company has significant influence, usually because the parent company (or a company controlled by the parent) owns between 20% and 50% of the shares.

CQ 9.2   First, all transactions between the subsidiary company and other companies in the group (known as intragroup transactions) are eliminated. Thereafter, on a line-by-line basis, the subsidiary's assets and liabilities are added to the assets and liabilities of the parent company; and each item of income or expense in the subsidiary is combined with the same items in the parent company. Similarly, the cash flows of the parent company and the subsidiary company are combined.

CQ 9.3   The same process described in CQ 9.2 is followed. The difference is that the statement of comprehensive income splits the group's profit and total comprehensive income (TCI) between the amounts attributable to owners of the parent and the amounts attributable to non-controlling interests (NCI). Similarly, the statement of financial position shows the group's equity split between the amount attributable to owners of the parent and the amount attributable to NCI.

CQ 9.4   Goodwill describes a range of reasons the business might be worth more to the acquirer than the fair value of its identifiable net assets, such as excellent management, a fine reputation, loyal customers, lucrative prospects, and synergistic benefits arising from integration into the group. It is recognised as an asset on acquisition, measured as the difference between the purchase consideration and the acquirer's share of the fair value of the identifiable net assets.

CQ 9.5   The 'investment in associates' figure represents the amount that was originally paid for any associates, plus the group's share of the post-acquisition TCI of associates, less any dividends that have been paid by associates to the group. The 'share of profit in associates' figure represents the group's share of the associates' profit or loss for the year.

AQ 9.6   Yes. The details of Daimler's subsidiaries, associates, and joint ventures are summarised in Table F.09 on p 247 of the consolidated financial statements. This table shows that Daimler had 537 subsidiaries, associates, and joint ventures at 31 December 2019, and also provides a breakdown between the various types of group entities. Furthermore, a detailed listing of these entities is presented in Table F.98, commencing on p 315.

AQ 9.7   The portion of the net profit that is attributable to NCI in 2019 was €332 million. This amount is reflected towards the bottom of Daimler's consolidated statement of income.

AQ 9.8   The portion of the net assets attributable to NCI was €1 497 million, shown immediately before the subtotal 'Total equity'.

AQ 9.9   Daimler's statement of financial position includes goodwill in the line-item 'Intangible assets'. Table F.25 (p 255) identifies an amount of €1 217 million on 31 December 2019.

AQ 9.10 Daimler's statement of financial position includes its associates within the line-item 'equity-method investments'. Table F.35 (p 259) reveals that associates were included in this figure at a carrying amount of €4 349 million on 31 December 2019.

AQ 9.11 The total equity accounted earnings that Daimler reported in 2019 was €479 million (labelled as 'profit/loss on equity investments, net' on its consolidated statement of income). Table F.35 (p 259) shows the breakdown of this amount split between associated companies and joint ventures.

AQ 9.12 Table F.36 (p 259) shows us that the dividends paid to Daimler by its associates during 2019 totalled €1 034 million (which consisted of €1 024 million from BBAC and €10 million from BAIC Motor).

AQ 9.13 Table F.36 (p 259) lists Daimler's largest associate as BBAC (which we are told on p 326 is the Beijing Benz Automotive Co Ltd) and that Daimler has a 49% equity interest in BBAC.

DQ 9.14 No. All intragroup transactions between Daimler and its subsidiary companies would be eliminated on consolidation, and would therefore not appear in the revenue amount presented on the consolidated statement of income. This is confirmed by the accounting policy note entitled 'Principles of consolidation' on p 232.

DQ 9.15 When a company consolidates partially owned subsidiaries, there will be references to NCI in profit and loss, OCI, and the statement of financial position. All three of these references are evident in Daimler's consolidated financial statements. The consolidated statement of income includes the line-item 'Thereof profit attributable to non-controlling interest'; the consolidated statement of comprehensive income/loss has a column for NCI; and the statement of financial position includes the line-item 'Non-controlling interests'.

DQ 9.16 No. While 100% of the PPE of the many subsidiaries that Daimler has consolidated is included in the group's PPE line-item, none of the PPE of the associates is included. This is because the associates have been equity accounted, not consolidated.

DQ 9.17 This goodwill arose when Daimler purchased businesses. Table F.25 (p 255) shows that it is not still carried at its initial measurement: the amount of €1 217 million consists of goodwill acquired of €1 493 million, less accumulated impairments of €276 million.

DQ 9.18 Table F.25 on p 255 states that goodwill increased by €117 million in 2019 as a result of business combinations (that is, acquisitions of businesses). It would have been calculated as the difference between the purchase considerations and Daimler's share of the fair value of the acquirees' identifiable net assets. The notes to the statement of cash flows (in this case, note 29 on p 282) would normally show us the details of this calculation. However, as this amount of €117 million is small relative to Daimler's operations, the group has chosen not to disclose the detail behind the calculation.

DQ 9.19 Each line of cash flows reported on Daimler's consolidated statement of cash flows will include the parent company's cash flows and 100% of the (consolidated) subsidiaries' cash flows, even if they are partially owned. Because they are equity accounted, the only cash flows relating to associates and joint ventures are the dividends received from them by the group.

DQ 9.20 The accounting policy note on p 232 states that 'the group's proportionate share of operations are included in Daimler's consolidated financial statements with a one to three-month time lag'. The note also states that 'significant events or transactions are accounted for without a time lag'. An example of this can be seen in Table F.36 on p 259, where we are told that the associate BAIC Motor 'is included in Daimler's consolidated financial statements with a three-month time lag'. This presumably means that BAIC Motor has a 31 October year-end.

CHAPTER 10

SOLUTIONS

CQ 10.1 Equity is defined in IFRS as 'the residual interest in the assets of the entity after deducting all its liabilities'. Because of this, the term is often used interchangeably with the term 'net assets' or 'net asset value'. It is also often described as the 'book value' or 'accounting value' of the business. Another way to think about equity is that it represents the business funding attributable to owners.

CQ 10.2 There are three broad reasons why the true value of a business is almost always different (usually higher) than its equity. Remember, equity is calculated by subtracting total liabilities, as measured by IFRS, from total assets, as measured by IFRS. Thus, the first reason is that several assets are almost certainly not measured at fair value (such as inventory and land measured on the cost model). The second is that some identifiable assets and liabilities are not recognised according to IFRS (such as internally generated brands). The third is that there is a range of other items of value—collectively known as goodwill—that are also not generally recognised by IFRS (such as the quality of staff, the business's reputation, and its future prospects).

CQ 10.3 The statement of changes in equity reports how each equity account reported on the statement of financial position has changed since the start of the reporting period, together with the comparative changes for the previous year.

CQ 10.4 The statement of changes in equity has columns for the equity accounts on the statement of financial position (though some may be aggregated into a single column) and rows to explain each movement in these accounts since the beginning of the reporting period. These movements are sorted into two groups. The first group contains those movements which affect TCI (further split into those that affect profit or loss and those that affect OCI). The second group contains those movements that involve transactions with owners, such as share issues or dividends.

CQ 10.5 When an accounting policy changes, there is usually a *retrospective* adjustment, which requires prior year comparative amounts, and the prior year opening balance on retained earnings, to be restated as if the new policy had always applied. Information is disclosed to enable the users of the financial statements to understand the effects of the change in policy. In contrast, when an accounting estimate changes, the adjustment is *prospective*: it is made in the current year, and in future years that may be affected by the change. Again, information is disclosed to enable the users to understand the effects of the change in estimate.

AQ 10.6   Daimler's statement of financial position and statement of changes in equity both show that its equity on 31 December 2019 totalled €62 841 million. This was split as follows: €61 344 million was attributable to Daimler's shareholders; and €1 497 million was attributable to NCI.

AQ 10.7   The components of Daimler's equity are listed on the statement of financial position as share capital, capital reserves, retained earnings, and other reserves. On the statement of changes in equity, the movements in share capital, capital reserves, and retained earnings are each shown in a separate column. The other reserves are, however, disaggregated into their various components: currency translation; equity/debt instruments; derivative financial instruments; and the portion of these three reserves that arise within equity accounted investments.

AQ 10.8   Note 20 (p 270) tells us that Daimler's share capital comprises shares of no par value. Where shares have no par value, the full amount of any capital raised in a share issue is included within one account, which in this case is called, as usual, 'share capital'.

AQ 10.9   Share issues would normally result in an increase in share capital. There is no evidence of this in the statement of changes of equity, and therefore it is safe to assume that no shares were issued during the year. This is confirmed by an explicit statement in note 20 (p 270): 'there has been no change in the number of shares outstanding/issued'. (Don't be fooled by the row labelled 'Capital increase/issue of new shares': as it affects only the NCI column, it must refer only to shares issued to NCI.)

AQ 10.10   Note 21 (p 271) shows us that Daimler expensed €71 million in respect of share-based payments during 2019.

AQ 10.11   The movement in the retained earnings balance was caused mainly by the net profit of €2 377 million, the total OCI movement net of tax of €2 172 million (€2 404 million – €232 million), and the dividends of €3 477 million.

AQ 10.12   The NCI column of the consolidated statement of changes in equity shows dividends of €288 million paid to NCI.

AQ 10.13   The column showing changes in Daimler's foreign currency translation reserve (FCTR) is headed 'Currency translation'. It reports that in 2019 equity increased by €458 million as a result of translating foreign operations.

DQ 10.14   Daimler's market capitalisation on 31 December 2019 was €52 826 million (€49.37 × 1 070 million shares in issue). This is slightly lower than its book value on the same date of €61 344 million (that is, the equity attributable to shareholders of Daimler). This is a somewhat unusual situation: more often, market capitalisation is substantially *higher* than book value.

DQ 10.15   Yes. Generally speaking, the management of a company can only issue new shares with the shareholders' approval. In this case, note 20 (p 270) explains that Daimler's shareholders have already 'authorized the Board of Management, with the consent of the Supervisory Board, to increase the share capital of Daimler AG . . . by a total amount of €1.0 billion' through the issue of new shares.

DQ 10.16   A change in accounting policy usually results in a retrospective adjustment, as described in CQ 10.5. However, no restatements appear in Daimler's statement of changes in equity, suggesting that perhaps no accounting policies were changed. Nonetheless, a note on p 230 indicates that on 1 January 2019 Daimler adopted IFRS 16, the new accounting standard on leases, which changed the way it accounts for many of its operating leases (see details on pp 230 and 231). The reason this didn't show up in the statement of changes in equity was that IFRS 16 allowed businesses to apply the standard only to the year in which they adopted it, and not to prior years.

DQ 10.17 The statement of changes in equity includes a column labelled 'Treasury shares' containing a negative amount of €42 million in a row labelled 'Acquisition of treasury shares'. This implies that shares to this value were bought back during the 2019 year. In the same column, a positive amount of €42 million cancels the effect of the acquisition, in a row labelled 'Issue and disposal of treasury shares'. The note dealing with the employee share purchase plan (p 270) explains that in fact the shares were reissued to employees.

DQ 10.18 The €3 477 million dividend reported in the 2019 statement of changes in equity and in the 2019 statement of cash flows is the 2018 dividend (declared early in 2019). Note 20 (p 271) states that the dividend for the year ended 31 December 2019 is €963 million. As this amount would be paid out in 2020, it appears in neither the 2019 statement of cash flows nor the 2019 statement of changes in equity.

DQ 10.19 Although it was in respect of the 2019 financial performance, the dividend of €963 million had not yet been declared by 31 December 2019. According to note 20 (p 271), it would only be proposed at the Annual Shareholder's Meeting in 2020. Thus, on 31 December 2019, Daimler had no obligation to pay the dividend, which therefore did not meet the definition of a liability.

DQ 10.20 On p 75 of Daimler's 2019 annual report, management reported that Daimler's dividend policy is to distribute 40% of the net profit attributable to Daimler shareholders, subject to considerations relating to free cash flows (which usually means operating cash flows minus capital expenditures). Thus, this 72% decline in dividends was a direct consequence of the 69% decline in net profit attributable to shareholders of Daimler (€2 377 million in 2019 versus €7 582 million in 2018).

CHAPTER 11

SOLUTIONS

CQ 11.1 The three stages of financial analysis are as follows: first, read the financial statements; then obtain an understanding of the main story presented by the financial statements; and third, perform ratio analysis to identify important relationships between different items of information.

CQ 11.2 The three typical benchmarks are: prior year information about the business under analysis; comparable information about direct competitors; and comparable industry or sector averages.

CQ 11.3 The first aspect is asset efficiency, the extent to which various assets have generated returns. The second is profitability, which measures how successfully revenue has been converted into profit. The third aspect is leverage, the degree to which debt is employed within the capital structure to leverage returns to shareholders. Fourth is liquidity, which shows the likelihood that the business will be able to settle its current liabilities as they fall due. The last aspect utilises the share price, along with other financial information, to assess performance from the market's perspective.

CQ 11.4 The five questions in an AMBER analysis are: 'What aspect of the business is measured by this ratio?'; 'What simple message about the business is inherent in the ratio?'; 'In respect of the ratio, how does the business compare to benchmarks?'; 'How can the business's ratio result be explained?'; and 'What does the ratio tell us about the risks to which the business is exposed?'

CQ 11.5 There are a number of challenges when performing a financial analysis, including the following:

- It is sometimes difficult to know which ratios to calculate, from the plethora of all available ratios.
- Some ratios can be skewed during periods of expansion and may not provide a realistic reflection of the underlying economic performance.
- Two businesses being compared may use different accounting policies and estimates, which requires adjustments in order to perform a like-for-like comparison.
- Industry or sector average ratios may be calculated using different formulas to the one preferred by the analyst.
- Financial statements always contain aggregated information, so it can sometimes be difficult to access the detailed information required for a detailed, consistent analysis.
- Sometimes, the results of different ratios can appear contradictory.

AQ 11.6

DAIMLER'S COMMON-SIZED GROUP INCOME STATEMENT

	2019	2018	Difference (in % points)
Revenue	100.0	100.0	
Cost of sales	(83.1)	(80.2)	+2.9
Gross profit	16.9	19.8	
Net operating expenses	(14.3)	(13.1)	+1.2
Operating profit	2.6	6.7	
Interest and similar expense	(0.4)	(0.4)	+0.0
Profit before income taxes	2.2	6.3	
Income taxes	(0.6)	(1.8)	−1.2
Net profit	1.6	4.5	−2.9

Note: there are several different ways to construct a common-sized income statement. For example, you may have chosen to include more rows, like Daimler's statement of income. Here, we have used as few rows as is reasonable. We obtained the 'interest and similar expense' figures from Table F.16 (€683 million in 2019; €660 million in 2018), and then simply calculated the operating profit (€4 513 million in 2019; €11 255 million in 2018) by adding these figures to each year's 'profit before income taxes'. We then found the aggregate 'net operating expenses' (€24 652 million in 2019; €21 812 million in 2018) by subtracting operating profit from the gross profit.

AQ 11.7

Daimler's return on equity:

2019: €2 709 m ÷ [(€66 053 m + €62 841 m) ÷ 2] × 100 = **4.2%**

2018: €7 582 m ÷ [(€65 159 m + €66 053 m) ÷ 2] × 100 = 11.6%

Daimler's total asset turnover:

2019: €172 745 m ÷ [(€281 619 m + €302 438 m) ÷ 2] = **0.59 times**

2018: €167 362 m ÷ [(€255 345 m + €281 619 m) ÷ 2] = 0.62 times

Daimler's net margin:

2019: €2 709 m ÷ €172 745 m × 100 = **1.6%**

2018: €7 582 m ÷ €167 362 m × 100 = 4.5%

Daimler's equity multiplier:

2019: [(€281 619 m + €302 438 m) ÷ 2] ÷ [(€66 053 m + €62 841 m) ÷ 2] = **4.53 times**

2018: [(€255 345 m + €281 619 m) ÷ 2] ÷ [(€65 159 m + €66 053 m) ÷ 2] = 4.09 times

Daimler's Du Pont analysis:

	ROE (overall performance)		TAT (asset efficiency)		Net margin (profitability)		Equity multiplier (leverage)
2019	4.2%*	=	0.59	×	1.6%	×	4.53
2018	*11.6%**	*=*	*0.62*	*×*	*4.5%*	*×*	*4.09*

* Slight differences due to rounding.

AQ 11.8

		2019	2018
Fixed asset turnover (times)	€172 745 m ÷ [(€30 948 m + €37 143 m) ÷ 2]	5.1	5.7
Days inventory on hand (days)	[(€29 489 m + €29 757 m) ÷ 2 × 365] ÷ €143 580 m	75.3	75.0
Collection period (days)	[(€12 586 m + €12 332 m) ÷ 2 × 365] ÷ €172 745 m	26.3	26.8
Settlement period (days)	[(€14 185 m + €12 707 m) ÷ 2 × 365] ÷ €143 580 m	34.2	36.2
Operating cycle (days)	75.3 days + 26.3 days − 34.2 days	67.4	65.6
Gross margin (%)	€29 165 m ÷ €172 450 m × 100	16.9	19.8
Debt ratio (%)	(€133 795 m + €105 802 m) ÷ €302 438 m × 100	79.2	76.5
Debt–equity (times)	(€133 795 m + €105 802 m) ÷ €62 841 m	3.8	3.3
Times interest earned (times)	(€3 830 m + €683 m) ÷ €683 m (Table F.16, p 251)	6.6	17.1
Current ratio (times)	€127 800 m ÷ €105 802 m	1.2	1.2
Acid test ratio (times)	(€127 800 m − €29 757 m) ÷ €105 802 m	0.9	0.9

DQ 11.9

1. Daimler's costs of inventory relative to its revenue were 2.9% higher in 2019 than in 2018.
2. During 2019, operating costs increased by 1.2% relative to revenue.
3. Finance costs remained stable relative to revenue.
4. The proportion of revenue paid away in tax declined by 1.2% relative to revenue.
5. The four items listed above culminated in Daimler earning 2.9% less of its revenue as profit.

Total asset turnover (TAT)

- *Aspect*. TAT is the overall measure of asset efficiency.
- *Message*. For every €100 that Daimler had invested in assets in 2019, it produced €59 of revenue.
- *Benchmark(s)*. Daimler became slightly less efficient at using its assets to generate revenue in 2019 compared to 2018.
- *Explanation*. Daimler's revenue increased by only 3.2%, whilst its net assets increased by 10.3%. Daimler's low revenue growth was a consequence of the world's low economic growth rate of 2.5% in 2019 (p 65), which was compounded by the contraction of the global car market by approximately 5% during the year (p 66). The 10.3% increase in Daimler's total assets was as a result of higher financial service assets, cash and cash equivalents, and the inclusion of right-of-use assets due to the adoption of IFRS 16, and the consequent capitalisation of many leases (p 86).
- *Risk*. Will Daimler be able to use its asset base to generate increased revenues in the future? With the events unfolding in 2020, this seems unlikely. However, the relatively large cash and cash equivalents balance at 31 December 2019 should stand Daimler in good stead as it enters 2020.

Net margin

- *Aspect*. Net margin is a key measure of a business's profitability.
- *Message*. In 2019, for every €100 that Daimler earned in revenue, €98.4 was spent to cover costs, leaving €1.60 as profit.
- *Benchmark(s)*. Daimler's net margin declined significantly between 2018 and 2019, from 4.5% to 1.6%.
- *Explanation*. Daimler's decline in profitability was caused by both a decline in gross margin and a significant increase in other operating costs. The decline in gross margin is discussed in DQ 11.11. The main reason for the increase in operating costs are the inclusion in 2019 of expenses of €4 200 million relating to the ongoing government and legal proceedings involving Mercedes-Benz's alleged manipulation of diesel emission tests (p 45), an expanded recall of vehicles, and expenses arising from a planned change in Daimler's product portfolio (p 71). This last item presumably relates to Daimler's intention to ramp up production of electric vehicles (p 95).
- *Risk*. If there are further declines in revenue, or more costs related to legal proceedings, Daimler may make a loss in future years.

Equity multiplier

- *Aspect*. The equity multiplier measures leverage.
- *Message*. Assets are 4.53 times equity.
- *Benchmark(s)*. By increasing its leverage between 2018 and 2019, Daimler managed to somewhat compensate for its declines in efficiency and profitability.
- *Explanation*. Daimler's liabilities increased during 2019, mainly as a result of increased financing liabilities (resulting from lease liabilities on right-of-use assets now having to be recognised on the statement of financial position) and increased provisions resulting from the ongoing government and legal

proceedings. The main source of Daimler's leverage is financing liabilities of €161 780 million (p 279), most of which appear to be interest-bearing borrowings.

- *Risk*. Daimler appears to have significant and increased amounts of debt in 2019. If efficiency and profits continue to fall, the increasing debt levels could put the business at risk of not being able to make loan repayments, or service interest costs, when they fall due.

Return on equity (ROE)

- *Aspect*. ROE measures overall business performance.
- *Message*. For every €100 of equity in 2019, the business returned profits of €4.20.
- *Benchmark(s)*. Daimler's ROE declined significantly between 2018 and 2019 from 11.6% to 4.2%.
- *Explanation*. Daimler's declining efficiency and profitability was only partially offset by slightly increased leverage. This low ROE is a direct consequence of what Daimler refers to as 'a challenging year' (p 26), which damaged the business's net margin in particular.
- *Risk*. Daimler is exposed to declining efficiency and profitability with increased leverage. Should there be further declines in efficiency and profitability, resulting in a negative return on assets, then the leverage multiplier will work in the opposite direction and leverage up the losses, resulting in a larger negative return on ROE.

DQ 11.11

Fixed asset turnover

- *Aspect*. This ratio measures how efficiently PPE has been used to generate revenue.
- *Message*. In 2019, for every €100 of PPE in which Daimler had invested, the business generated revenue of €510.
- *Benchmark(s)*. Daimler's fixed-asset turnover declined by 10.5% between 2018 and 2019.
- *Explanation*. This decline is partially due to right-of-use assets now being included in PPE, in terms of the new accounting treatment of leases (note 11, p 256). Excluding right-of-use assets, PPE increased by 6.3% [(€32 909 – €30 948) ÷ €30 948]. This increase is still higher than the 3.2% increase in revenue, showing that Daimler was not yet able to use its increased PPE base to achieve a similar increase in revenue.
- *Risk*. Revenues continue to decline, and PPE is not 'sweated' to the same extent as in previous years.

Days inventory on hand

- *Aspect*. This ratio measures how efficiently inventory has been managed.
- *Message*. On average in 2019, it took Daimler 75.3 days to sell an item of inventory.
- *Benchmark(s)*. There was no change to the amount of time Daimler kept inventory on hand in 2019 when compared to 2018.
- *Explanation*. The days inventory of a manufacturer includes the time it takes to turn raw materials into finished goods, so one would expect that a sizeable portion of Daimler's days inventory would be time that Daimler's vehicles spend in

production. The fact that overall inventory days has not changed during a slowing down of sales is evidence of good management of inventory levels.

- *Risk*. If sales continue to decline, Daimler may be stuck with inventories which cannot be sold.

Collection period

- *Aspect*. The collection period measures how efficiently trade receivables have been managed.
- *Message*. On average in 2019, there were 26.3 days between Daimler's sales and the collection of cash from customers.
- *Benchmark(s)*. Like inventory days, there was no significant change to the amount of time Daimler took to collect cash from its customers.
- *Explanation*. To think how Daimler's vehicles are sold all over the world, it is quite remarkable that the business manages to collect cash from its sales within less than a month on average, which can only be explained by vigilant management of its debtors. This is particularly impressive during a period where Daimler's customers might be experiencing financial difficulty themselves, and might be struggling to pay Daimler the amounts they owe.
- *Risk*. If the global economy continues to contract, Daimler may experience a lengthening of its collection period, with a corresponding decline in operating cash flows.

Settlement period

- *Aspect*. The settlement period measures how efficiently trade payables have been managed.
- *Message*. On average in 2019, it took Daimler 34.2 days to settle its trade payables.
- *Benchmark(s)*. Daimler settled its debts to creditors an average of 2.0 days earlier in 2019 than in 2018. This is a slight decline in efficiency, as the business had a shorter period to use this money for its own purposes, before paying it over to creditors.
- *Explanation*. Trade payables on the statement of financial position declined from €14 185 million in 2018 to €12 707 million in 2019. This 10.4% decline in trade payables, together with an increase in cost of sales, is the cause of the slight decline in the settlement period.
- *Risk*. A declining settlement period will have the effect of reducing operating cash flows.

Operating cycle

- *Aspect*. This ratio measures the overall efficiency of working capital management.
- *Message*. In 2019, Daimler's working capital tied up cash for an average of 67.4 days without earning a return. This is because, after buying the average item of inventory, the group took 75.3 days to sell the finished goods, and a further 26.3 days to collect the cash from the sale, meaning that in all it took 101.6 days to receive payment; whereas the supplier was paid within 34.2 days. Thus, for each item of inventory that it bought and sold, the business had to wait an average of 67.4 days between the payment and receipt of cash.

- *Benchmark(s)*. This is very slightly less efficient than its performance in 2018, as the business's working capital was tied up for 1.8 more days in 2019.
- *Explanation*. The main driver of this minor increase in the operating cycle is the 2.0-day decrease in the settlement period. Notwithstanding the slight increase in the operating cycle, Daimler has managed its working capital well during what are evidently difficult economic times in the automotive industry.
- *Risk*. This slight increase in Daimler's operating cycle is no cause for concern.

Gross margin

- *Aspect*. This ratio measures the kind of profitability that is most fundamental to a manufacturer such as Daimler: the proportion of revenue that is left over after paying the direct costs of bringing inventory to its location and condition for sale.
- *Message*. For every €100 of revenue that Daimler generated in 2019, €83.10 was spent on the costs of inventory, leaving €16.90 as a contribution to other operating expenses, finance costs, tax, and profit.
- *Benchmark(s)*. On this measure, in 2019 Daimler was less profitable than it had been in 2018.
- *Explanation*. The declining gross margin is a direct consequence of revenue increasing by only 3.2%, whilst cost of sales increased by 6.9%. A note on p 74 tells us that cost of sales in 2019 included expenses related to the ongoing governmental and legal proceedings in connection with Mercedes-Benz diesel vehicles and expenses in connection with a recall of some vehicles. Similar costs were presumably not incurred to the same extent in 2018. A declining gross margin indicates that Daimler is unable to pass on costs to its customers. In this case, it seems that costs of legal proceedings and product recalls are generally not the kind of cost that can be passed on to customers.
- *Risk*. The 14.6% decline in gross margin represents a sizeable risk of future losses for a manufacturer. After all, if too much of the revenue goes towards the cost of manufacture, there may not be enough left over to cover all of its other costs.

Debt ratio and debt–equity ratio

- *Aspect.* Like the equity multiplier, these two ratios measure the amount of debt in the capital structure of the business.
- *Message*. The debt ratio indicates that at the 2019 year-end, 79.2% of Daimler's assets were funded by liabilities (the remaining 20.8% of assets were funded by equity). It is therefore no surprise that the debt–equity ratio reports that debt funding was 3.8 times equity funding.
- *Benchmark, explanation, and risk*. This is covered in the equity multiplier discussion in DQ 11.10.

Times interest earned

- *Aspect*. Also a leverage ratio, times interest earned measures the specific risk of interest-bearing risk being so high that it becomes difficult to service the interest payments due.
- *Message*. In 2019, Daimler's profit before interest and tax expense was 6.6 times its interest expense. In other words, the business's operating profit covered its interest bill about 6.6 times over.

- *Benchmark(s)*. The group's exposure to risk has increased since 2018, as evidenced by the decline in interest cover from a far safer 17.1 times. Although a times interest earned of 6.6 times might appear to carry a relatively small risk of Daimler being unable to meet its interest payments, this trend is concerning. If it were to drop by as much again in the following year, Daimler may well have issues with servicing its debt in future.
- *Explanation*. The cause of this decline in the interest cover is mainly the 59.9% decline in profit before interest and tax from €11 255 million (€10 595 m + €660 m) in 2018 to €4 513 million (€3 830 m + €683 m) in 2019.
- *Risk*. Daimler has fairly significant interest-bearing borrowings and, should there be an economic downturn causing further declines in profitability and operating cash flows, Daimler may struggle to meet its interest payment commitments.

Current ratio

- *Aspect*. The current ratio evaluates a business's liquidity by measuring the extent to which its current assets cover its current liabilities.
- *Message*. In 2019, Daimler's current assets were 1.2 times its current liabilities. In other words, there was €120 of cash, receivables, and inventory that could potentially be used to pay for every €100 of current liabilities.
- *Benchmark(s)*. Daimler's current ratio was the same in 2019 as in the previous year, implying that—at least by this measure of liquidity risk—it is no better or worse off.
- *Explanation*. Although this ratio at first may seem to be low, it is instructive that it was no higher in 2018, when Daimler had a comparably good year. This suggests that Daimler can manage its liquidity despite a current ratio of 1.2, perhaps because it has quite large cash balances and sound operating cash flows.
- *Risk*. The current ratio does not provide strong evidence that Daimler is exposed to any serious liquidity risk.

Acid test ratio

- *Aspect*. The acid test ratio evaluates a business's liquidity by measuring the extent to which current assets other than inventory cover its current liabilities.
- *Message*. Daimler's remaining current assets (that is, cash and receivables) cover its current liabilities 0.9 times.
- *Benchmark(s)*. Like the current ratio, Daimler's acid test ratio was the same in 2019 as in the previous year, so this measure of liquidity risk has also held stable.
- *Explanation*. The acid test ratio may be more indicative of Daimler's liquidity risk than the current ratio, as we know from the working capital ratios that inventory takes an average about seventy-five days to sell, whereas trade payables is settled within little more than a month. However, this ratio has also been stable, and Daimler's cash balances and operating cash flows once again mitigate any apparent liquidity risk. Also, the most sizeable current asset after inventory is 'receivables from financial services', which most likely provides a fairly reliable monthly cash inflow.
- *Risk*. Daimler's exposure to liquidity risk is low. This finding is confirmed by our earlier analysis of the settlement period: businesses with liquidity problems are not usually able to keep their settlement period so low, nor can they allow it to decrease, as Daimler has done.

CHAPTER 12 | **SOLUTIONS**

CQ 12.1   The book value of a business is the total equity reported on its statement of financial position, calculated by subtracting the value of reported liabilities from the value of reported assets. The market value is the business's market capitalisation, calculated by multiplying the current share price by the number of shares outstanding. Thus, the book value is based on the recognition and measurement principles in IFRS, whereas the market value is based on investors' beliefs about the business.

CQ 12.2   One approach is the discounted cash flow (DCF) approach, which values a business by finding the present value of estimated future cash flows. The second is the valuation multiples approach, which values the business by finding the product of a known figure about a business (such as earnings) and a multiple based on a comparable business or precedent (such as a price–earnings (PE) ratio), refined for the particular circumstances of the business being valued.

CQ 12.3   First, the foreseeable free cash flows (that is, free cash flows for the next few years) are forecast. This is done by estimating cash operating profit based on estimates of revenue, operating margins, non-cash items, working capital movements, tax payments, and capital expenditure. Second, the present value of these forecast future free cash flows is calculated, often using the business's weighted average cost of capital as the discount rate. Third, the terminal value—the present value of the best estimate of free cash flows beyond the foreseeable future—is calculated and added to the present value of the free cash flows forecast for the foreseeable future. Fourth, some adjustments are made to arrive at the intrinsic value of the business. For example, the value of non-operating assets is added and the value of debt is subtracted.

CQ 12.4   The Gordon growth valuation model involves dividing the following year's expected dividend by the difference between the investor's required rate of return and the expected dividend growth rate.

CQ 12.5   A PE valuation multiplies the business's profit by a PE ratio that is appropriate to that business. This PE ratio is determined by the PEs of comparable businesses or the PEs implicit in historical acquisitions of similar business, and then refining these based on observable risk–return differences in the business being valued.

CHAPTER 13 | **SOLUTIONS**

CQ 13.1   The four main reasons to prepare misleading information are to: facilitate money laundering; attract cash into a Ponzi scheme; cover up theft; and obscure bad news.

CQ 13.2   The most common accounting irregularities are: falsifying income; upfronting income; incorrectly deferring expenses; failing to impair assets when appropriate; misclassifying liabilities; and not consolidating entities that the business controls.

CQ 13.3   Upfronting income is the practice of recognising income in the statement of comprehensive income earlier than appropriate. This results in an overstatement of the current year's profit.

CQ 13.4 Misclassifying some of the business's liabilities can cause them to be appear less risky than they really are. For example, non-current liabilities are perceived as less risky than current liabilities; accounts payable is perceived as less risky than bank loans.

CQ 13.5 Related party disclosures are important because they help users understand whether a business has entered into transactions with parties that are related to it, and if so, the terms and conditions of these transactions. Although they may be legitimate, such transactions are not at arm's length, and thus users ought to know to treat such transactions with some scepticism.

SOLUTIONS   CHAPTER 14

CQ 14.1 Measuring an asset using fair value often results in an amount that is more relevant for decision making, especially when the asset is worth much more than its cost. However, using fair value has the following potential downsides: it may increase earnings volatility, which alters perceptions of the business's risk–return profile, and may even incentivise accounting irregularities; it is less reliable than using cost as the measurement basis, because it requires assumptions and/or estimates; and it can lead to significant additional expenses for the business.

CQ 14.2 The main aim of the Primary Financial Statements project is to standardise the subtotals, such as operating profit and earnings before interest, taxes, depreciation, and amortisation (EBITDA), used in the profit-and-loss section of the statement of comprehensive income. The project also aims to set constraints and principles for alternative performance measures, labelling items of income or expense as unusual, and aggregating like items together.

CQ 14.3 XBRL stands for 'eXtensible Business Reporting Language'. It is a system that uses digital tags to identify each piece of financial data within the financial statements, making them machine-readable. The advantages of the data set created by XBRL include that it conforms to a single set of definitions and that it can be digitally shared and manipulated.

CQ 14.4 An environment, social, and governance (ESG) report communicates non-financial information, whereas an integrated report communicates information about the business's financial and non-financial activities in combination. Also, an ESG report is aimed at a wide variety of stakeholders, whereas an integrated report is aimed at providers of financial capital (although this may change in future).

CQ 14.5 The management commentary section of the annual report usually includes key aspects of the business's performance in the past year, as well as information about its prospects in the foreseeable future. In addition, it may also include other background and explanatory information about the business, such as: the nature of the business; management's objectives and strategies; the most significant resources, risks, and relationships; and also critical performance measures and indicators.

GLOSSARY

Many of the following denotations use language based on, or extracted directly from, the relevant document issued by the International Accounting Standards Board (IASB). The citations are contained earlier in the book, usually where the term is first mentioned.

Accounting The discipline of recording and reporting financial information about an entity.

Accounting equation A fundamental concept in financial accounting, defining the relationship between assets (A), liabilities (L), and equity (E). It is expressed in a variety of formulations, two of which are: A = E + L and A − L = E.

Accounting irregularity An item incorrectly included in, or omitted from, the accounting records and financial statements, with the purpose of misleading users.

Accounting policies The specific principles, bases, conventions, rules, and practices applied by a business in preparing and presenting financial statements.

Accounting standards Documents that lay out principles or rules which businesses must use to prepare their financial statements.

Accrual accounting The accounting basis on which the effects of transactions and other events are recognised and reported when the transactions occur, and not necessarily when cash is received or paid. In terms of International Finance Reporting Standards (IFRS), accrual accounting is used in preparing the statement of comprehensive income, the statement of financial position, and the statement of changes in equity.

Accrual adjustment An entry into the accounting system on the reporting date to ensure that the financial statements report events according to accrual accounting, rather than simply reporting the cash flows that were recorded during the reporting period.

Accrued expense A liability to pay for an expense that has been incurred, because the associated economic benefits have been consumed, but that has not yet been paid for.

Activity ratio An alternative term for a financial ratio that measures asset efficiency.

Allowance for doubtful debts An estimate of the amount by which the business's current debtors are expected to default; subtracted from the total amount owed by debtors in order to determine the carrying amount of a receivable asset. It is sometimes referred to (imprecisely) as a 'provision for doubtful debts'.

Alternative performance measures (APMs) Measures of performance that businesses choose to disclose in addition to the measures prescribed by the accounting standards. Some are used regularly and are well recognised, such as earnings before interest, taxes, depreciation, and amortisation (EBITDA), whereas others are unique to the business that chooses to use them.

AMBER analysis A technique for organising one's interpretations of a financial ratio into the following categories: aspect, message, benchmark, explanation, and risk. The technique is unique to this book.

Amortisation The systematic allocation of the depreciable amount of an intangible asset over its useful life.

Amortised cost A measurement method used for some financial assets and financial liabilities, whereby the amount used for initial measurement is subsequently adjusted for interest earned or incurred, and payments received or made.

Annual report A yearly communication published by a business which contains the financial statements for the past financial year and other information, including the management commentary.

Asset A present economic resource controlled by the business as a result of past events.

Asset efficiency The extent to which assets generate revenue and/or cash.

Asset manager An investment firm or individual that invests money on their clients' behalf.

Associate A business over which an investor (eg a parent company) has significant influence.

Audit The process by which an auditor verifies the validity, accuracy, and completeness of a business's financial statements, via a thorough investigation of its accounting system and records.

Bad debts expense An expense representing the amount by which a business's current debtors have defaulted or are expected to default.

Balance sheet Another name for the statement of financial position.

Bank In addition to sometimes referring to the financial institution that, for example, provides loans to businesses, this term is also customarily used as the name of the account used to represent a business's holdings of cash and cash equivalents.

Bargain purchase gain The amount by which the acquirer's share of the fair value of its identifiable net assets exceeds the purchase price of the business; sometimes called 'negative goodwill'.

Basic earnings per share A company's profit for the reporting period divided by the weighted average number of shares outstanding during the period.

Benchmark A basis for comparison used when performing **financial analysis**. Appropriate benchmarks include: prior year information about the business; comparable information about direct competitors; or average information for the business's industry or sector.

Board (of directors) The team of most senior people appointed to manage and/or oversee the affairs of a **company**.

Bond A long-term, interest-bearing **financial instrument** issued by a government, business, or other organisation, in order to raise debt funding.

Bookkeeping The recording function of accounting; distinct from the reporting function.

Book value The value of an item (or the entire business) according to the financial statements.

Capital This term has several different meanings in business, but in this book, it usually refers to the contributions made by a business's owners in exchange for their ownership stake.

Capital expenditure Money spent on assets. The term is most often used to describe expenditure on large, productive assets that expand the operating capacity of a business. Examples include factories, industrial equipment, software systems, and new retail locations.

Capital structure The mix of **debt** and **equity** used to fund a business.

Capitalisation The process of recognising expenditure as an asset, or part of the measurement of an asset.

Carrying amount The amount at which an item is measured in the accounting records.

Cash Cash on hand and demand deposits.

Cash basis (of accounting) The accounting basis on which only the cash effects of transactions are recognised and reported. It is the alternative accounting basis to **accrual accounting**. In terms of IFRS, the cash basis is only used in preparing the **statement of cash flows**.

Cash equivalents Short-term, highly liquid investments that are readily convertible to known amounts of cash and subject to an insignificant risk of changes in value.

Cash flows Inflows and outflows of **cash** and **cash equivalents**.

Cash flow hedge When a business hedges to reduce the potential risk of variability of cash flows related to an asset, liability, or some other sort of exposure.

Cash generated from operations The amount of cash generated (or utilised) by a business's **operating activities** in a reporting period; effectively the difference between cash received from customers and cash paid to suppliers and employees; an important line-item on the statement of cash flows.

Class (of assets) A group of assets of a similar nature used for similar purposes in a business's operations.

Commitment Future expenditure to which the business is committed, despite no liability having been recognised to pay for it yet (because the **obligating event** has not yet occurred).

Company A business that has been registered as such with the legal authorities. It is legally separate from its owners, and can therefore own assets, owe debts, sue, and be sued, all in its own name.

Company financial statements See **separate financial statements**.

Conceptual Framework (for Financial Reporting) A document set by the **IASB** which forms the cornerstone of **IFRS**. It deals with a host of foundational issues, which impact all IFRS **accounting standards**, including the definitions of, and broad **recognition** and **measurement** principles for, all the **elements** of accounting.

Consolidated financial statements See **group financial statements**.

Consolidation The accounting method used to include the results of subsidiaries in the group financial statements.

Constructive obligation An obligation that does not arise out of statute or **contract**, but rather out of an announcement, past practice, or published policy which has created a valid expectation that a business will transfer economic resources in future. It may meet the liability definition.

Contingent asset A possible asset whose existence is uncertain.

Contingent liability A liability which does not meet the **recognition criteria**.

Contract An agreement between two or more parties that has clear economic consequences for the parties; usually enforceable by law. Contracts may take a variety of forms and need not be in writing.

Control (of an economic resource) The right to direct the use of the economic resource.

Corporate governance The system by which organisations, including businesses, are directed and governed.

Cost The amount of cash or cash equivalents paid, or the **fair value** of the other consideration given, to acquire an asset at the time of its acquisition or construction. It includes other necessary amounts paid in order to get the asset into its location and condition for it to start being used.

Cost model A method of accounting for an asset whereby the asset is recognised at cost, and subsequently **depreciated**, if appropriate, based on this cost, and impaired where necessary.

Cost of sales An expense representing the cost of all **inventory** consumed during the reporting period, mostly through sale but also through loss, theft, waste, damage, obsolescence, and so on.

Creative accounting The manipulation of a business's **bookkeeping** records and financial statements to achieve an ulterior motive. It is also known as 'cooking the books'.

Credit One effect of an entry into a double-entry accounting system. Credits decrease asset accounts, and increase equity and liability accounts. Because an item of **income** is an increase in equity, it is recorded with a credit.

Credit risk See **default risk**.

Credit sale, or sale on credit A sale for which the seller allows the buyer to pay later, after control of the goods or services has transferred.

Creditor A person or entity that the business owes. The liability to pay suppliers is itself sometimes referred to as 'creditors', though the term 'accounts payable' or 'trade payables' is used more often in the financial statements.

Current asset Cash, items purchased for trading, and those whose benefits are usually expected to be obtained by the business's operating activities within twelve months of the reporting date. The classic examples are inventory, receivables, and cash and cash equivalents.

Current liabilities Liabilities that are expected to be settled within twelve months of the reporting date.

Current tax The amount of **income tax payable** (or recoverable) in respect of the taxable income (or tax loss) for a period; as opposed to deferred tax, which is a notional amount.

Debenture An interest-bearing financial instrument issued by a business, usually to the public, in order to raise debt funding.

Debit One effect of an entry into a double-entry accounting system. Debits increase asset accounts, and decrease equity and liability accounts. Because an item of expense is a decrease in equity, it is recorded with a debit.

Debt Amounts the business owes to others; see **liability**.

Debtor A person or entity that owes the business. The asset representing the amount owed by a business's customers is itself sometimes referred to as 'debtors', though the term 'accounts receivable' or 'trade receivables' is used more often in the financial statements.

Defaulting A debtor failing to pay the amount they owe.

Default risk The risk of a debtor **defaulting**.

Deferred income A liability representing a payment received in advance for goods or services yet to be provided by a business.

Deferred tax asset An amount of income tax recoverable in future periods in respect of **temporary differences**; or in respect of unused tax losses/credits.

Deferred tax liability An amount of income tax payable in future periods in respect of temporary differences.

Denominator In a formula involving one variable or expression above the line divided by another below it, the denominator is the variable or expression that is below the line.

Depreciable amount The cost of an asset (or other amount substituted for cost, in the case of revalued assets), less its **residual value**.

Depreciated cost The cost of a tangible asset, minus any accumulated depreciation charged to it.

Depreciation The expensing of the depreciable amount of a tangible asset over its useful life.

Derecognition The removal of an asset or liability from the accounting records and any subsequent financial statements.

This usually occurs because the business disposes of or fully consumes the asset, or settles the liability.

Derivative, or derivative financial instrument A complex financial contract to be settled at a future date, whose value is derived from something else, which is sometimes called 'the underlying', such as an interest rate, financial instrument price, commodity price, foreign exchange rate, index of prices or rates, credit rating, or credit index.

Diluted earnings per share An **earnings per share** figure that has been adjusted for the effects of all dilutive potential issues of shares (eg **share options** to be exercised in the future).

Dilution In this book, this term refers to a reduction in the value of an existing **shareholder's** shares due to an issue of new shares. Dilutions do not occur with every issue of new shares.

Direct method A method of reporting **cash generated from operations** on the statement of cash flows; typically discloses cash received from customers and cash paid to suppliers and employees.

Director In this book, this term refers to one of the most senior people appointed to manage and/or oversee the affairs of a **company**.

Discontinued operation A major business unit that the business as a whole has disposed of, or is going to dispose of in the near future.

Discount rate The percentage used to perform a **present value** calculation.

Discounted cash flow (DCF) model A method of business valuation that estimates its **intrinsic value** by calculating the present value of predicted future cash flows.

Dividend A distribution of value to shareholders, in proportion to their shareholdings.

Du Pont analysis A financial analysis technique in which the return on equity ratio is expressed as a function of further ratios (in this book, we have used three: total asset turnover, net margin, and the equity multiplier) to give an analyst insight into the main drivers of overall business performance.

Earnings Another word for **profit**.

Earnings per share, or EPS A measure of how much profit is attributable to each of a company's shares in a given reporting period. Includes 'basic' and 'diluted' varieties.

EBITDA Earnings before interest, tax, **depreciation**, and **amortisation**; often considered to be a proxy for cash **operating profit**.

Economic resource A right that has the potential to produce economic benefits. Economic resources include rights to: use a physical object; use intellectual property; and receive cash, goods, services, or other economic resources.

Element (of accounting) An asset, liability, or item of equity, income, or expense.

Employee benefits Compensation given to employees, which may include their standard pay, retirement benefits, child care, leave, and so on. It is treated as staff costs expense when the related work is performed by the employee.

Entity concept The accounting principle that requires even unincorporated businesses to be accounted for as if they are separate entities from their owners, so that the business's financial statements are unaffected by the owners' non-business transactions.

Environmental, social, and governance (ESG) reporting Communication to all of a business's **stakeholders** about its performance in non-financial respects. This information may be presented in one report, perhaps called an 'ESG report', or may be split up. Some or all of a business's ESG reporting may be in the **annual report**.

Equity The residual interest in the assets of the business after deducting all its liabilities; also, the amount of business funding attributable to owners.

Equity accounting, or the equity method A method of accounting used to include the results of **associates** and **joint ventures** in the group financial statements. It may also be used to represent the results of subsidiaries, associates, and joint ventures in the **parent company's** separate financial statements.

Equity instrument A contract that confers the right to share in the equity of a business, such as a company's share.

Event after the reporting period An event, favourable or unfavourable, that occurs between the reporting date and the date on which the financial statements are authorised for issue. Two types of events can be identified:

(a) those that provide evidence of conditions that existed at the reporting date ('adjusting events after the reporting period'); and

(b) those that are indicative of conditions that arose after the reporting date ('non-adjusting events after the reporting period').

Expenditure Spending; treated as an asset or an expense, depending on the circumstances.

Expense A decrease in the business's equity not caused by a distribution to owners.

Face (of a financial statement) An item is described as appearing on the face of a financial statement if it is readily visible on the statement itself, instead of being a constituent of some aggregated figure on the statement, or only disclosed in the **notes**.

Fair value The price that would be received to sell an asset, or paid to transfer a liability, in an orderly transaction between market participants at the measurement date.

Fair value model An option for the **subsequent measurement** of an asset or liability whereby the item is carried at an estimate of **fair value**, with **gains** or losses reported in **profit or loss** or other comprehensive income (depending on the item).

Finance lease A **lease** that transfers to the **lessee** the risks and rewards of owning the asset, regardless of whether legal title is transferred.

Financial accounting One of the two sub-disciplines of accounting; distinct from **management accounting**, it generates reports that are intended primarily for the purposes of informing the decisions made by people external to the business, particularly existing and potential investors, lenders, and other creditors.

Financial Accounting Standards Board The national standard-setting body in the US; sets accounting standards known as 'FASBs'.

Financial analysis The examination of a business's financial statements, in the context of other information about it, to form an opinion about the value that it has created, and to determine its prospects for creating value in the future.

Financial analyst A person, usually employed by an investment firm, who performs financial analysis for a living.

Financial asset An asset that is: cash; an **equity instrument** (such as a share) of another entity; a contractual right to receive cash or another financial asset (such as accounts receivable); a contractual right to exchange financial assets or financial liabilities with another entity under conditions that are potentially favourable to the business (such as **derivatives** with a positive value); or one of a few varieties of even more complex financial contracts.

Financial instrument A contract which gives rise to a financial asset for one party, and either a financial liability or an equity instrument for another party. For example, when a business issues shares, the shareholder has a financial asset and the business has issued an equity instrument.

Financial liability A contractual obligation to deliver cash or another financial asset to another entity (such as accounts payable), or to exchange financial assets or financial liabilities with another entity under conditions that are potentially unfavourable to the business (such as derivatives with a negative value); or one of a few varieties of even more complex financial contracts.

Financial reporting Essentially the same as financial accounting, although financial reporting refers exclusively to the reporting function, whereas financial accounting may in some contexts also refer to the recording function.

Financial reporting standards See **accounting standards**.

Financial statements The output of the financial accounting system; a set of standardised reports conveying detailed information about an entity's financial position and performance. They comprise the **statement of financial position**, the **statement of comprehensive income** (which may or may not include the **income statement**, or **statement of profit or loss**), the **statement of changes in equity**, and the **statement of cash flows**. (Sometimes, the term also refers to the notes to the financial statements.)

Financial year The twelve-month period for which a business prepares its financial statements to comply with regulatory reporting requirements. In many **jurisdictions**, this does not necessarily correspond with the calendar year, and may end in any month. Some businesses' financial years are not exactly equal to a year, and are instead a period of fifty-two or fifty-three weeks.

Financing activities A business's activities that result in changes to the size and composition of its **capital** and borrowings.

Fixed assets A term used in practice to describe items of **property, plant and equipment (PPE)**; it is no longer used much in financial statements.

Foreign currency translation difference A gain or loss resulting from the currency effects of translating **foreign operations**; reported in **other comprehensive income (OCI)**.

Foreign exchange adjustment A gain or loss resulting from the currency effects of foreign transactions; reported in profit or loss.

Foreign operation Business units controlled by the main business, but operating in a different country to the one in which the main business is headquartered.

Forward exchange contract A derivative financial instrument in terms of which the parties contract to buy and sell a certain amount of foreign currency at a stipulated exchange rate on a specified future date.

Full IFRS The complete set of IFRS accounting standards, distinct from the single standard **IFRS for small and medium-sized enterprises (SMEs)**.

Functional currency The currency of the primary economic environment in which the business operates.

Gain An alternative term to describe an item of income; mainly used to describe either an increase in an asset's **fair value**, or the sale of an asset for more than its carrying amount.

Gearing See '**leverage**'.

Generally accepted accounting practice (GAAP) A set of accounting standards, comprising comprehensive principles, rules, conventions, and other guidance about how to prepare financial statements. Technically, IFRS is a form of GAAP, although in practice the term usually refers to the standards released by the relevant national standard-setting body, as distinct from IFRS.

Goodwill The amount by which the purchase price of a business exceeds the acquirer's share of the **fair value** of its **identifiable net assets**; represents a range of reasons that a business might be worth more than the fair value of its identifiable net assets, such as excellent management, a fine reputation, loyal customers, lucrative prospects, and synergistic benefits that would arise if the business were acquired by another business.

Gordon growth model A method of business valuation that estimates its **intrinsic value** by calculating the present value of predicted **dividend** distributions.

Government grant Money received from the government that obliges the business to comply with whatever conditions are specified by the grant; recognised as a liability until the conditions are met.

Gross profit The difference between **cost of sales** and **revenue** from sale of goods and services.

Group (of companies) According to IFRS, a group consists of a **parent company** and its **subsidiaries**. Less formally, a group also includes any **associates** and **joint ventures**, although their results are included in **group financial statements** using a different method to that used for subsidiaries.

Group financial statements The financial statements of a **group of companies**, presenting the group as a single economic entity.

Hedge (a transaction) To enter into another transaction that will reduce the risk associated with the hedged transaction.

Identifiable (assets) Assets are identifiable if it is possible to separate them from the business itself, or if the assets relate to contractual or legal rights, even if these can't be separated from the business itself (such as a licence to operate in a specified area). Assets that are not identifiable constitute **goodwill**.

IFRS for SMEs A standard issued by the **IASB** for use by small and medium-sized entities. Essentially a simplification of **full IFRS**.

Immaterial Not **material**.

Impairment The process by which an asset's **carrying amount** is reduced to its **recoverable amount**, on the grounds that its current carrying amount is greater than the maximum amount of economic benefits that the business expects to recover from using or selling it.

Income An increase in the business's equity not caused by a contribution by owners.

Income statement An alternative name for the **profit or loss section** of the statement of comprehensive income. On the two-statement format of the statement of comprehensive income, the income statement is presented as a separate statement, and the **OCI section** and tabulation of total comprehensive income is presented on the other statement.

Income tax The tax charged on a business's (or person's) income, determined using rules stipulated by the tax authorities; a sizeable expense for most businesses.

Incorporation (of a business) To register a business with the legal authorities as an entity separate from its owners.

Indirect method A method of reporting **cash generated from operations** on the statement of cash flows by adjusting operating profit (or loss) for the differences between it and cash generated from operations.

Initial measurement The process of determining the amount at which an asset or liability is first recognised by the business; or that amount.

Intangible asset An identifiable, non-monetary asset without physical substance.

Integrated report A yearly report, mandatory in a handful of countries, but increasingly volunteered by many large companies and other organisations around the world, which aims to give a more holistic view of how value is created by a business, making use of the concepts of 'integrated thinking', and 'six capitals'.

Interim dividend A dividend declared and paid during the financial year, usually based on the business's performance during the first six months of the year.

Interim financial statements Financial statements prepared for a **reporting period** of less than a financial year. (If the period is not specified, it is usually the first half of a financial year.)

International Accounting Standards Board (or IASB) The international body that sets **IFRS**. Normally comprises fourteen members, representing every habitable continent, selected and overseen by an independent, not-for-profit, private-sector organisation working in the public interest, known as the IFRS Foundation.

International Financial Reporting Standards (or IFRS) The accounting standards set by the IASB. Over 140 of the world's accounting **jurisdictions** require that IFRS is used by all **public interest entities (PIEs)** in countries which designate PIEs, and by all listed companies in other countries.

Intragroup items or transactions An item relating to, or a transaction with, another business in the same **group**. The items, and any other effects of the transactions, are eliminated in the **group financial statements**.

Intrinsic value (of a business) The true worth of a business, as opposed to its **book value** and market value. For the majority of businesses, this cannot be known precisely, but only estimated.

Inventories Assets that are:

(a) held for sale in the ordinary course of business;

(b) in the process of production for such sale; or

(c) in the form of materials or supplies to be consumed in the production process or in the rendering of services.

Outside of the US, also known as '**stock**'.

Investing activities The acquisition and disposal of assets (in particular, **non-current assets** and short-term investments).

Investment property Property (that is, land, a building, part of a building, or both land and a building) held to earn rentals, or for capital appreciation, or both, rather than for use or sale in the ordinary course of business.

Joint venture A business over which two or more parties have joint control, which is the contractually agreed sharing of control.

Jurisdiction In this book, the term refers to a national or regional territory to which a single set of accounting regulation and related business legislation applies.

Lease An agreement whereby the **lessor** conveys to the **lessee** the right to control the use of an identified asset for a period of time, in exchange for a consideration.

Lessee The party to a lease contract who uses the leased asset but does not own it.

Lessor The party to a lease contract who owns the leased asset but does not use it.

Leverage The phenomenon by which additional debt in a business's **capital structure** has a multiplying effect on returns to the owners, positive or negative. Sometimes in practice the term simply means **debt**. Also known as '**gearing**'.

Liability A present obligation of the business to transfer an economic resource as a result of past events.

Limited liability A legal protection enjoyed by **shareholders** in most **companies**, preventing creditors from suing shareholders for debts owed by the company; in effect, this means that shareholders can lose no more than they paid to acquire the shares.

Liquidity The amount of cash available to a business; or the ease with which an asset can be converted into cash.

Liquidity risk The risk that a business runs out of cash because the cash generated by **current assets** is insufficient to cover its short-term payment obligations represented by **current liabilities**.

Listing The act of a company making its shares available to trade on a **stock exchange**.

Loss Either:

(a) *The opposite of profit:* a negative difference between income and expenses, excluding items of **OCI**; or

(b) *The opposite of gain:* an alternative term to describe an item of expense; mainly used to describe either a decrease in an asset's **fair value** or the sale of an asset for less than its carrying amount.

Management accounting One of the two sub-disciplines of accounting; distinct from **financial accounting**, it generates reports that are intended specifically for the purposes of informing management's decisions.

Management commentary The section of an **annual report**, usually preceding the financial statements, that is compiled and produced at the discretion of a business's management team. Includes, for example, information about: the nature of the business; management's objectives and strategies; significant resources, risks, and relationships; discussion of prospects in the foreseeable future, and also critical performance measures and indicators.

Mark to market The **revaluation** to **fair value** (the market price) of **financial assets** or **financial liabilities**.

Market capitalisation The product of a listed company's share price and the number of **outstanding shares**; widely regarded as the market value of the company.

Material (information) Information is material if omitting it or misstating it could influence the decisions that the users of the financial statements make on the basis of those financial statements.

Measurement The process of determining the amounts at which the **elements** of the financial statements are to be reported.

Minority interest See **non-controlling interest**.

Monetary items Units of currency held; and assets to be received, and liabilities to be paid, in a fixed and determinable amount of currency.

Net asset value, or net assets Technically, this means 'total assets minus total liabilities'. In practice, it often refers to the amount of a business's equity, which is equal to net asset value.

Net income An alternative expression for profit.

Net investment hedge When a business **hedges** against potential losses caused by currency movements affecting its net investment in **foreign operations**; results in a **gain** or **loss** in **OCI**.

Net realisable value The estimated selling price of **inventory** in the ordinary course of business less the estimated costs of completion and the estimated costs necessary to make the sale; in other words, the net amount that the business expects to realise from the sale of inventory.

Non-controlling interests Equity in a **subsidiary** not attributable, directly or indirectly, to the parent company; applies to the portion of a **partially owned subsidiary's** shares not owned by the group. It is also known as '**minority interest**' and '**outside shareholders' interest**'.

Non-current asset An asset that does not meet the definition of a **current asset**.

Notes to the financial statements Further financial disclosure that accompanies the **financial statements** themselves. Notes provide narrative descriptions of **accounting policies**, items, and events, detailed quantitative information about the composition of many items in the financial statements, and also information about items that do not qualify for recognition in those statements.

Numerator In a formula involving one variable or expression above the line divided by another below it, the numerator is the variable or expression that is above the line.

Obligating event The key event that gives rise to a business having a liability.

OCI section The section of the statement of comprehensive income that contains the items of **OCI**.

Off-balance-sheet financing The misleading accounting practice of not recognising a business's liabilities on its statement of financial position; largely prohibited by IFRS.

Onerous contract A non-cancellable contract whose future costs will outweigh the benefits; the difference between these costs and benefits is recognised as a liability immediately.

Operating activities The ways in which a business uses its assets to generate revenue, profit, and cash flows.

Operating expense Any expense incurred through a business's operating activities, except for cost of sales. It is distinct from finance expenses such as interest.

Operating lease A lease that is not a **finance lease**.

Operating profit Profit before taking into account interest and tax expense. It is usually calculated as revenue, minus cost of sales, minus **operating expenses**, plus any other items of non-interest income.

Other comprehensive income (OCI) Items of income and expense that are not recognised in profit or loss as required or permitted by IFRS, but which rather appear in the OCI section of the statement of comprehensive income.

Outside shareholders' interest See **non-controlling interest**.

Outstanding shares The number of shares a company has in issue, minus the number it is holding as **treasury shares**.

Parent company A company that controls one or more other businesses.

Partially owned subsidiary A **subsidiary** in which the **parent company** does not hold all of the shares.

Partnership An unincorporated business with more than one owner, who are called partners.

Payable A generic term for a liability that represents an amount of cash owed by the business.

Performance obligation Any promise in a contract with a customer to transfer a product and/or service.

Permanent difference A difference between the tax authority's rules for calculating taxable income and the IFRS principles used to determine profit before tax that will not reverse in future; does not lead to the recognition of deferred tax.

Present value A current estimate of the discounted value of a future cash flow, using an appropriate **discount rate** that takes the **time value of money** into account.

Private company A company whose shares are subject to trading restrictions.

Profit The positive difference between income and expenses, excluding items of **OCI**.

Profitability In this book, we use this term in a narrow sense, to describe the matter of whether and how profit is earned from revenue. It can also refer to financial performance more broadly.

Profit or loss section, or just 'profit or loss' The section of the statement of comprehensive income that contains all the items of income and expense except for items of **OCI**; ends with the profit or loss for the period.

Property, plant and equipment (PPE) Tangible items that:

(a) are held for use in the production or supply of goods or services, for rental to others, or for administrative purposes; and

(b) are expected to be used during more than one period.

Provision A liability of uncertain timing and/or amount.

Prudence The exercise of caution when making judgements under conditions of uncertainty, seeking to ensure that assets and income are not overstated, and that liabilities and expenses are not understated.

Public company A **company** whose shares are not subject to trading restrictions.

Public interest entity (PIE) A business or other organisation that has a high level of public accountability and transparency demanded of it. PIEs generally include all listed companies and other very large businesses. The precise definition of a PIE varies between **jurisdictions**.

Quality of earnings A measure of the extent to which a business's **profits** are converted into operating cash inflows.

Quality of revenue A measure of the extent to which a business's **revenue** is converted into cash received from customers.

Receivable An asset representing an amount of cash owed to the business.

Recognition The process of including an item in the statement of financial position or statement of comprehensive income.

Recognition criteria The requirements that an asset or liability must meet in order to be recognised. These are that its recognition should provide relevant and faithfully representative information. In practice, this means that there should not be: uncertainty about the item's existence; a low probability of a flow of economic benefits associated with the item; or a high level of measurement uncertainty.

Recoverable amount The maximum amount of economic benefits that a business expects to earn from an asset; measured at the higher of the asset's **fair value** less costs to sell and its **value in use**.

Related party People or entities with a close relationship to the business. People include significant **shareholders**,

directors, managers with major responsibilities, and close family members of these people. Entities include companies in the same group and retirement funds for the business's employees. Transactions with related parties must be disclosed in the notes.

Reporting date The last day of a **reporting period**.

Reporting period The period of time for which a set of financial statements reports. The effects of transactions that occur in the reporting period, and only their effects, are reported in the statement of comprehensive income, statement of cash flows, and the statement of changes in equity.

Residual value (of an asset) The estimated amount that the business would currently obtain from disposal of an asset, after deducting the estimated costs of disposal, if the asset were already of the age and in the condition expected at the end of its useful life.

Retained earnings An account representing the accumulated value created by the business that has not been distributed to owners; in simplest terms, equal to all the profit the business has ever earned, minus all the dividends it has ever distributed.

Revaluation Remeasurement of an asset or liability (often to **fair value**).

Revaluation model An option for the **subsequent measurement** of an item of PPE or intangible asset whereby the item is remeasured to an estimate of **fair value**, with **gains** or **losses** reported in **OCI**.

Revenue Income arising in the course of a business's ordinary activities.

Reversal An entry into the accounting system which reverses an earlier entry by debiting what was previously credited, and crediting what was previously debited.

Right-of-use asset An asset recognised by a **lessee** representing the value of its right to use the leased asset.

Risk–return profile A business's **risk–return profile** is the combination of the amount of value that it can be expected to create in future (the return) and the likelihood of that happening (the risk).

Sales, or sales income Revenue; or income from the sale of goods and the rendering of services.

Separate financial statements The financial statements of a **parent company** which treat the parent company as an economic entity separate from the **group**. **Subsidiaries** are not **consolidated**, and **associates** and **joint ventures** are not typically **equity accounted**.

Share-based payments A form of payment (often in respect of employment, but also for other services and goods) in the form of the company's shares, or based on the value of the company's shares; for example, share options granted to directors.

Share buyback A company's reacquisition of its own shares.

Shareholder The owner of a company's shares; thus, the closest thing there is to an owner of the company.

Share option A right, with no obligation, to buy or sell shares in a company at a certain price on or after a certain future date.

Significant influence The power to participate in the financial and operating policy decisions of a business, but not control over those policies; may be gained by share ownership, statute, or agreement.

Sole trader, or sole proprietor An unincorporated business, with just one owner.

Solvent The financial position of a business whose total assets are greater than total liabilities.

Spot rate An exchange rate for immediate delivery of a foreign currency, commodity, or **financial instrument**.

Stakeholder Anyone with a stake, or interest, in the business, or who is affected meaningfully by it.

Statement of cash flows The financial statement that reports all of a business's cash inflows and outflows for the reporting period.

Statement of changes in equity The financial statement that reports the movements in each of the business's equity accounts during the reporting period.

Statement of comprehensive income The financial statement that reports all of a business's items of income and expense for the reporting period. It is often presented as two statements.

Statement of financial position The financial statement that reports the business's assets, liabilities, and equity at the end of the reporting period.

Statement of profit or loss An alternative name for the **profit or loss section** of the statement of comprehensive income. On the two-statement format of the statement of comprehensive income, the statement of profit or loss is presented as a separate statement, and the **OCI section** and tabulation of total comprehensive income is presented on the other statement.

Statement of profit or loss and other comprehensive income An alternative name for the **statement of comprehensive income**.

Stock Outside of the US, an alternative term for **inventory**; in the US, the usual term for a company's shares.

Stock exchange A marketplace for company shares and other **financial instruments**. Shares do not have to be traded on a stock exchange, but when a company lists its shares on an exchange, it gets immediate access to a large network of potential investors.

Stock-out Depletion of a product line; running out of **inventory**.

Straight-line method A **depreciation** method that aims to charge an equal amount of depreciation for each year of an asset's useful life. It is distinct from the diminishing balance and units of production methods.

Subsequent costs Expenditure incurred on an asset after it has been recognised. It is only **capitalised** if it meets certain conditions.

Subsequent measurement The process of determining the carrying amount of an asset or liability on any statement of financial position prepared after it is first recognised, and before it is **derecognised**.

Subsidiary A business that is controlled by another business, known as the **parent company**.

Temporary difference A difference of timing between the tax authority's rules for calculating taxable income and the IFRS principles used to determine profit before tax that will reverse in future; leads to the recognition of deferred tax.

Time value of money A fundamental principle of finance which states that an amount of money in the future has less value than the same amount of money today.

Total comprehensive income (TCI) The change in equity during a period resulting from transactions and other events, other than those changes resulting from transactions with owners in their capacity as owners; calculated as the sum of profit or loss and total **OCI**.

Treasury shares A company's own shares that have been reacquired by the company, and not cancelled.

Turnover Revenue; or income from the sale of goods and the rendering of services.

Underlying profit A common **APM** which attempts to report the profit relating only to items that are likely to recur in future.

Unrealised income Income that has been earned but not yet received in cash. For example, until the cash has been collected from the customer, a **credit sale** represents **unrealised income**.

Unwinding the discount The process of gradually adding interest to the **carrying amount** of an item, after it is initially measured at its present value.

Upfronting An **accounting irregularity** involving recognising revenue earlier than it should be recognised according to the **accounting standards**, in order to appear more profitable.

Useful life Either:

(a) the period over which an asset is expected to be available for use by the business; or

(b) the number of production or similar units that the business expects to obtain from the asset.

Valuation multiples approach An approach to business valuation which approximates **intrinsic value** by applying a multiple (based on comparable businesses or precedent business acquisitions) to some known figure drawn from the business's financial statements.

Value creation cycle The cycle whereby a business creates value through its financing, investing, and operating activities, and then makes a decision about distributing (some of) this value to the business's owners.

Value in use The present value of estimated future cash flows expected to arise from the continuing use of an asset and from its disposal at the end of its useful life.

Wholly owned subsidiary A **subsidiary** in which the **parent company** holds all of the shares.

Working capital The combination of a business's **current assets** and **current liabilities**, viewed as working together so that short-term cash inflows cover required short-term cash outflows.

Write-down An **impairment** of an asset (to **net realisable value** in the case of **inventory**, or to **recoverable amount** in the case of most other assets).

XBRL A system that makes financial statements machine-readable, allowing for easy digital manipulation and ensuring that the items in them conform to consistent definitions.

INDEX

Note: Tables and figures are indicated by an italic *t* and *f* following the page number.